The Evolution of Human Sociality

The Evolution of Human Sociality

A Darwinian Conflict Perspective

Stephen K. Sanderson

ROWMAN & LITTLEFIELD PUBLISHERS, INC.
Lanham • Boulder • New York • Oxford

ROWMAN & LITTLEFIELD PUBLISHERS, INC.

Published in the United States of America
by Rowman & Littlefield Publishers, Inc.
4720 Boston Way, Lanham, Maryland 20706
www.rowmanlittlefield.com

12 Hid's Copse Road, Cumor Hill, Oxford OX2 9JJ, England

British Library Cataloging in Publication Information Available

Library of Congress Cataloging-in-Publication Data

Sanderson, Stephen K.
    The evolution of human sociality: a Darwinian conflict perspective / Stephen K. Sanderson.
      p. cm.
    Includes bibliographical references and index.
    ISBN 0-8476-9534-4 (alk. paper) — ISBN 0-8476-9535-2 (pbk.: alk. paper)
      1. Human evolution. 2. Social evolution. 3. Darwinism. I. Title.

GN281 .S254 2001
303.4—dc21

00-068849

Printed in the United States of America

∞™ The paper used in this publication meets the minimum requirements of American
National Standard for Information Sciences—Permanence of Paper for Printed Library
Materials, ANSI/NISO Z39.48-1992.

Nature has planted in our minds an insatiable longing to see the truth.

—Cicero

Knowledge is what we get when an observer, preferably a scientifically trained observer, provides us with a copy of reality that we can all recognize.

—Christopher Lasch

Do not become archivists of facts. Try to penetrate the secret of their occurrence, persistently search for the laws which govern them.

—Ivan Pavlov

Contents

Part V: Darwinian Conflict Theory: The Weight of the Evidence

Preface

The Evolution of Human Sociality is an attempt at a broad theoretical synthesis within the field of sociology and its closely allied sister discipline of anthropology. It is a labor of love that has resulted from nearly a quarter century of sustained thought. I explicate and critique all of the major theoretical approaches and try to draw what I consider the most useful elements of the best of these into a synthesized theory that I call *Darwinian conflict theory.* This theory, more properly called a theoretical perspective or strategy, in the most general sense is a synthesis of the tradition of economic and ecological materialism and conflict theory stemming from Marx and the tradition of biological materialism deriving from Darwin. I originally called this theory *synthetic materialism* (see Sanderson, 1998a, 1998b, 1999:403-8), but I have gradually come to feel that the name is too bland and uninformative. But everyone knows who Darwin was and why he is important, and conflict theory is a term that resonates well with sociologists and is immediately recognizable to them. And, in a sense, the new name is more accurate since Darwinian and neo-Darwinian evolutionary biology and sociobiology—the theoretical foundation of the book—represent a type of conflict theory in which people are competing in a vast game of survival, resource acquisition, and reproduction.

Approximately the first half of the book is taken up with critiques of existing theoretical approaches. More than anything else, I am concerned with the "logic of explanation" of each major approach. I am concerned, for example, with prototypical Marxist and functionalist modes of explanation, not with such things as the myriad characteristics of the functionalist school launched by Talcott Parsons or whether Marxists have started incorporating Weberian ideas into their theories. Another way of putting it is to say that I am concerned with the basic type of explanatory logic that each strategy carries, its most characteristic mode of explaining the social world. My discussion of each theoretical strategy is therefore quite deliberately highly restricted. This then leads to the full elaboration, in formal propositional form, of the synthetic theory.

The second half of the book lays out in as much detail as space allows the large amount of evidence, both qualitative and quantitative, that I claim supports Darwinian conflict theory. To a large extent this is the most important part of the book in terms of getting readers to be open to my approach. The substantive areas concerning which the evidence is drawn are those that have been of crucial concern to both sociology and anthropology for much of their existence. A significant omission is the topic of ethnicity. I leave this topic aside here because of space limitations and also because the topic is so important, so vast, and so emotionally charged that I feel it deserves a book of its own.

I am grateful to Donald Brown, Andre Gunder Frank, Art Alderson, Jerome Barkow, Alexandra Maryanski, Joseph Lopreato, Penny Anthon Green, Herbert Hunter, Alex Heckert, and Ray Scupin for their comments on early versions of the main ideas behind this book as they existed in various conference papers. Pierre van den Berghe and Bruce Lerro read the entire manuscript in its penultimate form and I am most grateful to them for having done so. Timothy Crippen read one of the early conference papers, the chapter on sociobiology, and all of the evidence chapters and made many useful comments that I have been able to incorporate into the final revisions.

I want to single out Pierre van den Berghe for special mention. He has influenced my thinking in this book more than any other single individual. When his book *Man in Society: A Biosocial View* first appeared in 1975, I was immediately taken by it and used it for several years as a text in my introductory course. Later he returned the favor by using various editions of my *Macrosociology: An Introduction to Human Societies* in his course on comparative societies until his retirement a few years ago. Pierre and I began an intellectual correspondence in the late 1970s that has continued down to this day, a correspondence that has been a source of great satisfaction for me. For many years he argued that most of my thinking was highly compatible with sociobiology and urged me to "take the plunge" and incorporate sociobiological ideas more fully. Eventually the lightbulb went on and I did, as this book testifies. Pierre has the crucial traits a good sociologist should have: irreverence, iconoclasm, wit, a resistance to intellectual fads, a methodological eclecticism, a willingness to put together the best of the best theoretical schools, and a penchant for the truth rather than the popularity of one's ideas. Had Pierre not existed, this book would not exist, at least not in its current form. I would therefore have had to invent him or not write the book. Pierre also suggested the book's title, which I gladly accepted over my two original titles in the interest of reaching the broadest possible audience.

Randall Collins, another sociologist for whom I have great admiration, does not like the theoretical synthesis this book creates even though I have tried to convince him that it is highly compatible with his own version of conflict theory and, in fact, serves as the necessary grounding for that theory. Randy even went so far as to urge me not to write the book, saying that there would be hostility to it from mainstream sociologists. It is the first time he has not been complimentary of one of my books. For better or worse, I have not heeded his advice. He is undoubtedly right: Many sociologists will reject the main arguments of this book. However, many of the leading ideas in modern thought were initially rejected, even in markedly hostile form, when they were first proposed. One thinks, for example, of Galileo or Darwin. I am not so presumptuous as to put myself in the company of these great men; I am simply saying that I believe that the most controversial ideas of this book will eventually lose their controversial status and become widely accepted throughout the social sciences. Indeed, the trend is already apparent, if not in my own discipline of sociology.

For a quarter of a century I have taught undergraduate and graduate courses in sociological theory at Indiana University of Pennsylvania. This has provided me with an enormous amount of intellectual stimulation and allowed me the opportunity to think through many of the ideas developed in this book much more thoroughly than would otherwise have been possible. I am extremely grateful to all of the students in these classes for having made all of this possible, especially to those who really challenged me to articulate and justify my arguments. I am also grateful to Indiana University of Pennsylvania for granting me a sabbatical leave during the fall semester of 1999 so I could finish the book's penultimate draft.

I am very pleased that my editor at Rowman & Littlefield, Dean Birkenkamp, agreed to publish this book and demonstrated such enthusiasm for it. Dean is easily the nicest editor in publishing and one of the best. I hope the book can live up to his expectations. Finally, I wish to thank my graduate assistant, Mary Reilly, for her extremely careful checking of the bibliography, which permitted me to correct several errors and provide missing references.

When I was about eleven or twelve years old I discovered biology and it was love at first sight. By the end of high school I somehow got diverted into psychology, and then in my first year of college into sociology. I was better at biology than at any other subject I ever studied, and perhaps should have stayed in it. But I have no regrets, because I have found the study of society fascinating. I have, in a sense, now come full circle, reuniting sociology with my first great love. It makes me very happy to be able to contribute to the unification of the biological and social sciences.

Most of the epigrams used throughout this book have been drawn from Thiessen (1998). Portions of chapter 10 were published in Stephen K. Sanderson and Joshua Dubrow, "Fertility decline in the modern world and in the original demographic transition: Testing three theories with cross-national data," *Population and Environment* 21:511-37, 2000. Portions of chapter 13 were published in Stephen K. Sanderson, "Explaining monogamy and polygyny in human societies: Comment on Kanazawa and Still," *Social Forces* September 2001. Portions of chapter 16 will be published in Stephen K. Sanderson, "Political evolution and war: A Darwinian conflict perspective." In Vincent S.E. Falger and John Vasquez (eds.), *Evolutionary International Relations: A Biopolitical Perspective* (Westport, CT: Greenwood Press, forthcoming 2001).

Introduction

Sociology as a whole, and sociological theory in particular, have become extremely fragmented in the past thirty years (Sanderson and Ellis, 1992; Lord and Sanderson, 1999[1]), and many sociologists believe that sociology is in a state of severe crisis (e.g., Horowitz, 1993; Lopreato and Crippen, 1999).[2] Eclecticism is the dominant outlook among sociologists in general and a common view among theorists. There is little consensus among sociologists or sociological theorists on a dominant theoretical perspective, with a wide range of perspectives being endorsed. Eclecticism is an understandable response to such fragmentation, but it is hardly a satisfactory stance; it is more a capitulation to the confusion resulting from fragmentation than anything else (Sanderson, 1987). One way of dealing with the eclecticism resulting from the lack of a dominant paradigm is theoretical synthesis—the merging of several perspectives into a new paradigm sharing elements of its ancestor paradigms but yet itself novel. This book sets forth a new perspective known as *Darwinian conflict theory*. Darwinian conflict theory takes elements from nearly all of the major sociological perspectives, but mostly from Marxian and Weberian conflict theory, rational choice theory, cultural materialism, and sociobiology. At its core, it represents a marriage between sociological conflict theory and Darwinian evolutionism. Certainly Darwinian conflict theory does not explain everything or solve all of sociology's theoretical problems. I claim only that it provides a way of bringing much of sociological theory together, and that in doing so it explains more social phenomena more parsimoniously than any other existing paradigm.

We need to start by asking what we mean by a theory. I distinguish between a *theory* and a *theoretical strategy*. A theory is *a statement or set of statements designed to explain any particular phenomenon or category of related phenomena*. The key words here are "particular" and "explain." Something has been explained when the basic causal forces giving rise to it have been identified. This can get complicated in the sense that there can be causal forces behind causal forces behind causal forces, etc., and so it is useful to distinguish between *proximate* and *ultimate* causation. Proximate causes are the immediate and direct causes of something, whereas ultimate causes lie deeper and are themselves the basis for the proximate causes. Whether we wish to stop an explanation by simply

1

identifying the proximate causes, or whether we want to go on to identify ultimate causes, depends on a lot of things, and varies from situation to situation. Usually theorists stop when they feel "intellectually satisfied," i.e., when they feel that they have understood something adequately and thus have no need to go any further.

Many social scientists consider prediction to be an important component of a successful theory. Prediction can be thought of in two different senses: (1) saying what the future will be like, or (2) making judgments about what empirical facts should be found to support a particular theory. The latter is much more important than the former, which is fortunate because social scientists, sociologists in particular, are notoriously deficient in the former. Basically, it is only prediction in the second sense that is relevant to testing theories. Some of our best theories cannot predict future events. Darwinian evolutionary theory, for example, is helpless to predict the future course of biological evolution even though it is one of the most powerful theories ever developed in any scientific field. Thus, prediction of the future should not be a criterion used to evaluate the worth of a theory.

As for "particular," this means that theories are specific and focus on one phenomenon or a small number of related phenomena. For example, we may wish to know why poverty continues to exist in affluent societies, why the Hindus sanctify the cow and taboo the eating of its flesh, why the kinds of religious movements known as revitalization movements exist, or why male monopolization of political leadership seems to be a cultural universal. To offer explanations of these particular social phenomena is to develop theories.

In sociology there are literally hundreds or thousands of theories, but most of these tend to fall into one or another theoretical strategy, by which I mean *a large body of interrelated theories, all of which share the same underlying concepts, assumptions, and principles*. What I am calling a theoretical strategy is essentially the same as what Harris (1979) calls a *research strategy*, and is similar to what philosophers of science have called *paradigms* (Kuhn, 1970), *research programs* (Lakatos, 1970), or *research traditions* (Laudan, 1977). In contrast to theories, theoretical strategies are very abstract and general. They focus not on one thing, or even a few related things, but on the whole universe of social phenomena. How many theoretical strategies there are in sociology depends on exactly how one wants to divide things up. My view is that sociology contains at a minimum five basic strategies based on their *logic of explanation*, or the basic way in which they try to explain the features of the social world: functionalism, conflict theory, social constructionism, exchange/rational choice theory, and sociobiology. The last of these has had little influence in sociology, but it is growing in importance and is making a great deal of headway among psychologists and anthropologists and thus should not be ignored. It is possible to subdivide some of these strategies, so that under conflict theory we have a divergence between Marxian and Weberian theories and under social constructionism we have symbolic interactionism and ethnomethodology. If we make these distinctions, that gives us seven strategies instead of five. I would also like to include in this list a theoretical strategy that is not well known to many sociologists. This is cultural materialism, which was developed in anthropology in the 1960s largely under the influence of Marvin Harris and his colleagues and students. Although it did not originate in sociology, it is an extremely important mode of social analysis that relates closely to Marxian conflict theory. This gives us a total of eight basic strategies, or six for those who might not wish to subdivide.

To understand theories and theoretical strategies properly we need to recall the distinction between the *explanandum* and the *explanans*. The explanandum is the *phenomenon being explained*, whereas the explanans is the *phenomenon doing the explaining*. Theories and theoretical strategies are identified *according to their explanans*, not their explananda. Thus, conflict theory is called such because it seeks to explain the structure of society as resulting from the conflicts between individuals and groups in the pursuit of their goals. It is not called conflict theory because it studies social conflict, and in fact it studies and seeks to explain many other social phenomena. This will be stating the obvious to some, but I make the point nonetheless because there is a tendency for sociologists to confuse the explanans with the explanandum in categorizing theories. For example, Lewis Coser's *The Functions of Social Conflict* (1956) is often identified as an example of conflict theory. In fact, the explanandum of this theory is social conflict, but its explanans is functionalist in nature; therefore, it is a functionalist theory. And Claude Lévi-Strauss's (1969a) work on marital exchange has been treated as an example of exchange theory (Ekeh, 1974), when in fact social exchange is the explanandum and Lévi-Strauss's explanans is derived from both functionalism and French structuralism.

The relationship between theories and theoretical strategies is one in which strategies guide the development of theories. It is theories that we are really after, because it is these that explain the specific social phenomena we want to have explained, but the most efficient ways to develop these theories is by the systematic employment of theoretical strategies as guides. No one understood this better than one of the greatest scientific theorists of all time, Albert Einstein: "As Einstein himself always emphasized, if we are bereft of general principles to guide us in our search for new theories we simply cannot hope to stumble upon good new theories" (Maxwell, 1974:284). Indeed, without general principles to guide us, the development of new theories would be nothing but a process of stumbling, hardly the royal road to truth.[3]

How can we decide whether any given theory or theoretical strategy is a good or useful one? I propose the following five criteria:

1. *Logical coherence.* Theories and theoretical strategies must hold together logically if they are to have any value. The various propositions that constitute a theory or theoretical strategy must be logically consistent and noncontradictory. They must also be clearly formulated so that their logic is understood and so that they can be tested empirically. These, of course, are absolutely minimum requirements for any theory or theoretical strategy.

2. *Empirical success.* This is the most important criterion for the evaluation of a theory or theoretical strategy. I adhere to a kind of "soft" or "sophisticated" falsificationism (Lakatos, 1970) which holds that the best theories are those that have been subjected to the largest number of and the most rigorous efforts at falsification and have survived those efforts reasonably well. The best theories are also those that are capable of making the best empirical predictions. It is not realistic to assume that most social scientists (or even natural scientists for that matter) are likely to be dispassionate about their own theories and thus likely to submit them

to rigorous falsifying efforts. However, science is a collective endeavor and theories are tested by social scientists other than their creators; these social scientists can be much more dispassionate.

3. *Parsimony.* Parsimony means simplicity, two senses of which must be distinguished, *simplicity as economy* and *simplicity as unification.* Simplicity as economy means that we wish to cut away all excess theoretical baggage and make use of the fewest concepts, principles, and assumptions, and that we want these concepts, principles, and assumptions to explain as many phenomena as possible. Perhaps the most famous advocate of this idea was the medieval thinker Occam, and his idea has since been known as "Occam's razor." Simplicity as unification expresses the idea that we want our explanations to show how the phenomena we study are integrated into a coherent whole. Simplicity in both senses has long been a major goal of theory development in the natural sciences, and it should be one in the social sciences as well. Einstein spent most of his later years searching for a unified field theory of physics, and a "theory of everything" is a major goal of physics and cosmology today (Barrow, 1991; Weinberg, 1993). Einstein understood the concept of parsimony better than anyone else ever has. He had a habit of shaving with ordinary hand soap rather than shaving lather. When questioned about this practice he is alleged to have said, "Two soaps? Why use two when one is enough?" He also refused to wear socks, arguing that they were needless. The philosopher of science Nicholas Maxwell (1974:265–66) explains further:

> That science persistently seeks simplicity, unity, coherence, order, lawfulness, harmony, beauty, explanatoriness or intelligibility in *some* sense of these terms can hardly be doubted by anyone. . . . Even the most casual glance at the history of physics, let us say, reveals the enormous importance that notions such as these have played in influencing the direction of research, and in influencing evaluations of contributions to knowledge. For example, the hope that nature may ultimately turn out to be simple, coherent, unified, or intelligible can be seen to lie behind the seventeenth century idea that all natural phenomena arise as a consequence of the arrangements and motions of a few different sorts of elementary corpuscles, interacting only by contact; the same hope lies behind the Faraday-Einstein idea that everything is made up of one unified field; and it lies behind Wheeler's idea . . . that there is in the end only curved empty space with changing topological features.
>
> Some of the greatest contributions to science are precisely contributions which "unify" apparently diverse phenomena. . . ; there is, for example, Newton's unification of the motion of terrestrial and astronomical bodies by means of his laws of motion and law of gravitation; Maxwell's unification of electricity, magnetism, and optics (further unified by the special theory of relativity); Einstein's unification of gravitation and geometry. Again, there is the discovery of the relatively few chemical elements, from which all the millions of diverse chemical compounds can be built up; there is Mendeleev's discovery of a pattern in the properties of the elements; and the twentieth century discovery that all matter is built up of just three types of particles—electrons, protons, and neutrons. There is the tremendous unification achieved by quantum theory—a few relatively simple physical postulates sufficing in principle to predict and explain all the vast diversity of physical and chemical properties of ordinary matter. And there is the discovery that all natural

phenomena can be understood in terms of just four (or even possibly only three) kinds of forces or interactions.

4. *Explanatory power relative to other theories.* No theory or theoretical strategy can be evaluated in a vacuum, but only in the context of other theories and strategies (Lakatos, 1970; Laudan, 1977). The key question becomes, "What is the competition like?" A theory whose competitors are judged worthless will still be considered valuable, even if it is not received enthusiastically and its empirical success is poor, because it is better than no theory at all. It can always be used as a basis for developing a better theory.

5. *Productivity.* Productivity, or what might be called *fruitfulness* (Kincaid, 1996), is the capacity to generate new insights and research over a length of time. Many (indeed, most) theoretical strategies exhaust themselves over time. Their capacity for generating new insights that can be explored empirically dries up; they then give way to new approaches with better potential.

It is of the utmost importance to make clear that the above criteria are, especially in sociology, to a considerable extent an idealization. If scientists were other than the human beings they are, this is how theory formulation and testing would proceed. But, because they are human, other factors enter in, such as *political ideology* or deeply ingrained *conceptual views* (Laudan, 1977). In sociology theory preference and choice are greatly affected by one's political views, which in turn are strongly affected by one's position in society. In research I have done on American sociologists in general (Sanderson and Ellis, 1992) and sociological theorists in particular (Lord and Sanderson, 1999), I have found that political ideology is far and away the most important determinant of a sociologist's theoretical choices.

Conceptual views are more subtle in their effects but nonetheless extremely important. These are broad worldviews of one type or another that are characteristic of a particular society or culture in a given historical period (Laudan, 1977). An excellent example of the operation of a conceptual view is the fate of Darwin's theory of evolution from about 1860 to 1940. His idea that evolution had occurred was widely accepted by scientists, but his proposed explanation for the evolutionary process—*natural selection*—was greatly resisted because it massively contradicted the deeply ingrained *concept of design* (Bowler, 1983, 1988). Laudan tells us more (1977:63):

> In our own time . . . there are several instances where seemingly serious arguments have been lodged against a scientific theory because of moral or ethical worldview difficulties. In the Soviet Union, the Lysenko affair is a case in point. Because evolutionary biology, with its denial of the transmission of acquired characteristics, ran counter to the Marxist view that man's very nature could be changed by his environment, there were strong reservations voiced against Darwinism and Mendelism and much support was given to a scientific research effort like Lysenko's which sought to find scientific evidence for the Marxist philosophy of man. In the West, similar constraints have recently confronted researchers and theorists examining the possibility of racial differences. It has been suggested that any scientific theory which would argue for differences of ability or intelligence between the various races

must necessarily be unsound, because such a doctrine runs counter to our egalitarian social and political framework.

So there is a range of extrascientific reasons that often draw scientists to, or make them antagonistic to, a particular theory or strategic approach. But on the whole the history of science, or at least natural science, shows that the procedures of science tend to win out in the long run. After all, the theory of natural selection was finally accepted when other questions were answered and when additional lines of evidence had been accumulated (provided mostly by the new science of population genetics). Scientific theories may be socially influenced, but their ultimate acceptance or rejection is based on criteria that are internal rather than external to science.

Today sociological theory has become a major area of specialization within sociology. Among the many specialized sections of the American Sociological Association there is a healthy and vigorous (in terms of numbers) theory section. What do sociological theorists do? For the most part, it seems that they do "general theory." This is theorizing on a grand scale about social life in general, and such theorizing usually has a strong philosophical basis and, most often, little contact with empirical reality. This can be seen simply by looking at the articles published in the leading theory journal, *Sociological Theory*, in recent years. As Janet Saltzman Chafetz (1993:1) has said, most of what is called sociological theory today falls under one or another of five basic types of intellectual activity:

> 1) the Talmudic exegesis of classics by long dead scholars and their minor revisions to fit more contemporary concerns (e.g., what did Marx, Weber, Parsons, etc., "really mean"? or how can their ideas be stretched to relate to each other or something else?); 2) the paraphrasing ("showing the relevance") of contemporary, mostly European, inevitably pretentious, often incomprehensible and typically "anti-positivistic" metatheories (e.g., Postmodernism, Poststructuralism, Semiotics, Hermeneutics, Discourse, and Critical Theory); 3) abstract epistemological and ontological navel-gazing (e.g., the relationship between agency/micro and structure/macro, theory as discourse, text as reality, all the "how to theorize about" papers); 4) conceptual development and (sometimes) application; and, closely related to this, 5) substantive, explanatory theory.

It is more than clear that Chafetz has very little use for the first three of these endeavors and strongly recommends that sociological theory should be developed in terms of the fifth mode.

Chafetz also argues that much very good theory is produced by sociologists who do not think of themselves as theorists or affiliate in any way with the theory organs of the discipline. I not only agree but would go further and suggest that *most of the very best theory is produced by sociologists (or anthropologists) who are not doing "general theory" in any way*. I have in mind people like Theda Skocpol (1979), Immanuel Wallerstein (1974a, 1974b, 1980, 1989), or Pierre van den Berghe (1978, 1979, 1981a). All of these scholars develop theory in the context of addressing one or more important substantive problems, and Skocpol is well known for her hostility to what she calls "the dead hand of metatheory." The one example of an important social theorist who is an exception to the above is Randall Collins (1975, 1979, 1986b, 1998), but he is the exception that proves the rule in that he is constantly engaged with important substantive issues. He is that rare individual who can move back and forth with ease between highly abstract theoretical principles and specific theories devoted to answering particular substantive questions. Chafetz goes on to suggest that sociologists should first and foremost be raising important questions about the empirical social world: Every sociologist should be a theorist, and no sociologist should be a theory specialist.

A similar view was taken two decades earlier by Irving Zeitlin (1973) in a major critique of sociological theory as it looked at that time. By way of harsh criticism of the extremely general and highly abstract theorizing of Talcott Parsons, Zeitlin claimed that the difficulty with Parsons's whole approach (1973:23–24) was that it was

> the wrong way to approach the task of constructing scientific theory. If one is genuinely interested in empirical social systems, one ought to have questions about their workings that one would like to answer. To do this, one does not begin with "society" in the abstract but with a specific society (or several of them) and with an interesting problem. Take these arbitrary examples: How did the slave system of the antebellum South compare and contrast with the slave systems of Greece and Rome? What were the causes of the Russian Revolution and why did that social convulsion occur there and not elsewhere? Why have some societies achieved considerable economic development while others have remained relatively "backward"? Or, finally, why was "modernization" achieved in the context of liberal-democratic institutions in some cases (England, the United States, France) and in the context of authoritarian, fascist, or totalitarian regimes in others (Germany, Japan, Russia)?

I am in very strong agreement with all of the points made by Chafetz and Zeitlin. Since Zeitlin wrote, things have actually gotten worse, because general theory today seems to be hermetically sealed off from the rest of sociology. General theorists spend more and more of their time reading the works of philosophers and, in many cases, literary critics, and I seriously doubt whether many nontheorist sociologists pay much attention at all to general theorists. Most nontheorist sociologists get their theory, to the extent that they have any, from within their substantive research areas, and what passes for theory there is usually at the other extreme from general theory: small-scale hypotheses or theoretical fragments that connect little if at all with the bigger theoretical paradigms or strategies. Nearly half a century ago Robert Merton (1957) urged a closer relationship between theory and empirical research. He was absolutely right to do so, in my view, and for awhile it looked as if sociologists were heeding his advice. But all that started to change in the 1970s, and theory and empirical research are in many ways farther apart today than they have ever been.

There is no better illustration of this trend toward the increasing bifurcation of theory and empirical research than the work of Jeffrey Alexander (1987, 1988). Not only does Alexander urge sociologists to theorize without reference to any particular empirical issue at all, but he even goes so far as to suggest that testing theories with empirical data is neither particularly necessary nor especially desirable. He argues that explanation and prediction should not be the only goals of social science and recommends as a key theoretical practice what he calls *discourse*, by which he means "modes of argument that are more consistently generalized and speculative than normal scientific discussion"

(1988:80). "Discourse," he says, "focuses on the process of reasoning rather than the results of immediate experience, and it becomes significant where there is no plain and evident truth. Discourse seeks persuasion through argument rather than prediction. Its persuasiveness is based on such qualities as logical coherence, expansiveness of scope, interpretive insight, value relevance, rhetorical force, beauty, and texture of argument" (1988:80). Alexander also holds that one of the most important tools of the sociological theorist is the use of *presuppositions*. These are highly general assumptions that sociologists make about the basic nature of social reality; sociologists' most important presuppositions have to do, Alexander avers, with their notions of the nature of social action and social order. The contrast between individualism and collectivism, for example, is basic to theorizing about social action and how it is produced. Good theorizing, Alexander claims, can only be done if it is guided by presuppositions, and presuppositions must play a crucial role in the evaluation of theories. As an example, Alexander notes that one of the most attractive dimensions of individualistic theories is that they attempt to preserve individual freedom.

In my view, Alexander's way of doing social theory is nothing short of an intellectual disaster.[4] Were we to follow his exhortations, sociology would be set back a good century or more and would have no way of moving forward or progressing. What we need, instead, is not more bifurcation between theory and empirical research but a vigorous reuniting of the two. That is one of the major goals of this book, which proceeds approximately as follows. In part I, I discuss theoretical strategies that I believe have not worked and cannot work, and by work I mean being able to explain a sizable chunk of the empirical world. These failed strategies are functionalism, social constructionism, structuralism, poststructuralism and postmodernism, and eclecticism. In part II, I discuss two theoretical strategies that I believe have led to many important insights but that still are inadequate in a number of ways: Marxian and Weberian conflict theory. I then turn in part III to the theoretical strategies I believe have worked best: rational choice theory, cultural materialism, and sociobiology.

These last three strategies, however, are incomplete in and of themselves and have been much too isolated from one another. They can and should be brought together in a synthesis, which I present in part IV under the name, as already indicated, of Darwinian conflict theory. Part V of the book is devoted to an extensive presentation of the large body of empirical evidence that I believe is highly consistent with and supportive of Darwinian conflict theory. Chapter 10 looks at reproductive behavior, chapter 11 examines human sexuality, chapter 12 explores sex and gender, and family, kinship, and marriage are the subject of chapter 13. Three more chapters complete the book. Chapter 14 looks at economic behavior and economic systems, chapter 15 at social hierarchies, and chapter 16 at politics and war. In all of these chapters I set forth a wide body of evidence drawn from many human societies throughout history and all over the globe. Many of the data come from anthropology, and some come from the work of historians. Naturally there is a great deal of sociological research discussed as well. Much of the evidence is drawn from the work of others, but I have generated a good deal of it myself by way of analyses of two large cross-cultural data banks, the *Ethnographic Atlas* (Murdock, 1967) and the Standard Cross-Cultural Sample (SCCS) (Murdock and

White, 1969). The former consists of data on 1,267 societies of every known type, whereas the latter is a sample of the former consisting of 186 societies highly representative of all of the world's major and minor regions. I have also put together my own cross-national data bank of contemporary nation-states and used it as the basis for several sets of quantitative analysis.

Let me stress once again that I do not claim that Darwinian conflict theory explains everything—what theoretical strategy could?—only that it explains a great deal more than its closest competitors. There are undoubtedly important areas of sociological inquiry that it does not specifically address (such as the study of large-scale organizations), but even then I think the available research will not contradict it.

NOTES

1. These articles are surveys of sociologists' theoretical preferences in the early to mid-1990s. The Sanderson and Ellis article is based on a national random sample of American sociologists. The Lord and Sanderson article is based on responses from about half of the members of the American Sociological Association's Theory Section, and therefore represents social theorists (mostly in North America, but there were also responses from theorists in other parts of the world, primarily South America and Europe). Both articles give an impression of extreme fragmentation in sociology and sociological theory and provide a picture of the "lay of the land" in terms of the degree of acceptance of a wide range of theoretical perspectives.

2. In an extremely insightful article that identifies the many things that are wrong with contemporary sociology, Jonathan Turner (1996) claims that sociology was never a unified or well-integrated discipline. It has always been divided into factions with very different visions of what sociology should be. I strongly agree with Turner, but there was a time when there was at least a modicum of *theoretical* unity and agreement within sociology. This was during the period of functionalist dominance between approximately the mid-1940s and the mid-1960s.

3. An excellent discussion of the role of theoretical strategies in theory generation is provided by Harris (1979:5–28), although Harris prefers the term research strategies.

4. A further indication of the problems with Alexander's conception of sociological theory is that at the annual meetings of the ASA in 1990 he said, in response to a question from the audience (believe it or not), "What difference does it make why a particular sociocultural system is organized as it is?" For an excellent critique of Alexander, see Rule (1997:98–119).

PART I

Sociological Explanations
That Do Not Work

1

Functionalist Explanations

BASIC PRINCIPLES

Functionalism is a term that has been widely used in the social sciences, sociology and anthropology in particular, to identify a variety of related lines of thought. For my purposes, a crucial distinction must be made between *functionalism as a theoretical school* and a *functionalist mode of social explanation*. The former incorporates the latter, but the latter can stand on its own and can be (and sometimes is) associated with other theoretical schools. Functionalism as a theoretical school began in anthropology in the early part of this century with the works of such prominent figures as Bronislaw Malinowski (1927, 1944) and A.R. Radcliffe-Brown (1948, 1952). These thinkers sought to identify the parts of society, show how they were interrelated, and demonstrate their function or functions for the maintenance of society. Both Radcliffe-Brown and Malinowski, especially the former, were greatly influenced by Emile Durkheim, whose ideas also had a major influence on sociological functionalism. Functionalism came into sociology partly by way of importation from anthropology and, more substantially, through the work of Talcott Parsons and his students and disciples. In *The Social System* (1951), Parsons generated a functionalist model of societies as social systems. He was preoccupied (virtually to the point of obsession) with the "problem of order," which had so exercised Durkheim, and his sociological theory is overwhelmingly devoted to dealing with this problem. Like Durkheim, Parsons strongly rejected nineteenth-century utilitarian thinking. Society could not be composed simply of individuals pursuing their own self-interests, for such a thing would not be stable. People require restraints in the form of values and norms, to which they commit themselves, in order for a stable social order to emerge and persist.

The functionalist school as a whole generally adhered to the following set of basic propositions, although not every functionalist would necessarily agree with every single proposition:

1. *The System Principle.* Societies are complex systems of interrelated and interdependent parts, each of which significantly influences the others.

13

2. *The Vital Function Principle.* Each part of a society exists because it has a vital function to perform, or essential role to play, in maintaining the existence or well-being of the society as a whole.

3. *The Principle of Functionalist Explanation.* The existence of any part of a society is explained when its function(s) for the society is (are) identified.

4. *The Consensus Principle.* All societies have mechanisms that integrate them, or that allow them to hold together; one of the most important of these mechanisms is the commitment of a society's members to a common set of beliefs and values.

5. *The Equilibrium Principle.* Societies tend toward a state of equilibrium or home-ostasis, and disturbances in any part of a society tend to bring about adjustments elsewhere in the society in order to restore the equilibrium.

6. *The Principle of Progressive Change.* Social change is an uncommon occurrence in society—stability is the norm—but when it does occur it generally leads to ben-eficial consequences for the society as a whole, improving somehow its overall functional efficiency.

It has been said many times but perhaps bears repeating that the functionalists' image of society is that of an *organism*. Indeed, forerunners of functionalism in the nineteenth century, such as Herbert Spencer, often described society *as* an organism. Just as organisms were complex systems of interdependent parts, so were societies. And just as the parts of an organism performed some essential function for the organism's well-being, so the parts of society performed important functions for their well-being.

The functionalist explanatory logic of greatest interest here is contained in the second and third principles above. Functionalist explanations are those that *explain some social phenomenon as existing and taking the form it does because it contributes to the overall well-being of the larger society or some subsystem of it.* Functionalist explanations in sociology are the equivalent of what evolutionary biologists call *group selection.*

In the late 1940s Parsons's student, Robert Merton, tinkered with the functionalist mode of explanation in order to make it more useful and empirically accurate. In his famous essay "Manifest and Latent Functions," published in his book *Social Theory and Social Structure* (1957), Merton argued that functionalism had taken on some unnecessary baggage and had become too rigid. It needed to be reformulated in some respects and made more flexible. Merton was officially reacting against some of Radcliffe-Brown's and Malinowski's ideas, but he must have had Parsons in mind too. Merton argued for the importance of at least four basic distinctions that had not been a part of functionalist thinking. First, a distinction had to be drawn between *manifest* and *latent* functions. Manifest functions were those that were both intended and recognized by society, whereas latent functions were those that were unintended and that generally went unrecognized. For example, a manifest function of the educational system is the transmission of knowledge, but a latent function is that it delays the entry of millions of college students into the job market. Merton spent a lot of time analyzing latent functions, which he sometimes referred to as *unintended consequences.* The unintended consequences of social action were to him a major part of social life. In addition, Merton argued that it cannot be assumed that all of a society's parts contribute in a positive way to its survival and well-being. Some of the parts may be *dysfunctional*, i.e., impede the efficient functioning of society. Therefore, Merton said, we must always be on the outlook for *dysfunctions* as well as *functions*. Merton also said that it is not always the whole society that is the reference point for functions and dysfunctions. A social structure may be functional for some segments of society and at the same time dysfunctional for other segments. We must always take into consideration whether something contributes (or subtracts) from the whole or simply one or more of the parts. Finally, Merton asserted that we cannot assume that just because a part fulfills a function that it is the only part that can do so. We must recognize that there are *functional equivalents* or *substitutes*. This means that not every part of a society is vital to that society (or its parts).[1]

CRITICAL ASSESSMENT

Merton's distinctions and clarifications were valuable at the time and made functionalism into a considerably more useful approach. However, Merton failed to do what was really needed, which was to break free from a functionalist mode of analysis altogether. As Randall Collins has said in perhaps the most insightful comment ever made on Mertonian functionalism, "Merton rose to prominence in the dark ages of American sociology, the cold war years of the 1940s and 1950s. He helped guide sociology across those mindless and repressive years, *even as he helped perpetuate the darkness*" (1977:154; emphasis added).

As all sociologists today know, in the 1960s functionalism came under heavy attack and by the mid-1970s had declined markedly in influence. The work of Parsons became the target of severe criticism, but functionalist work in general fell into disrepute. The leading criticisms were basically as follows (Dahrendorf, 1958; P. Cohen, 1968; Zeitlin, 1973; Giddens, 1981):

1. Functionalism tended to overemphasize the degree to which societies are harmonious, stable, and well-integrated systems. Some people, radicals in particular, called functionalism the "sunshine view" of society. Parsons, in particular, was obsessed with the "problem of order," and he gave too much attention to norms and values as determinants of that order.

2. Because of its overemphasis on harmony and stability, functionalism tended to neglect or play down the degree to which social conflict is a basic feature of social life.

3. With its exaggeration of harmony and underemphasis of conflict, it was charged that functionalism encouraged, at least implicitly, a conservative view of social life. That is, it tended to say that those aspects of society that do exist *must exist* because they make an important contribution to societal functioning. It was not necessarily charged that the functionalists were politically conservative, only that their perspective had conservative implications.

4. Functionalism generally limited itself to the study of a society at a single point in time (the present), and thus represented a markedly ahistorical approach.

5. Since functionalism tended to ignore the historical dimension of social life, it had great difficulty accounting for social change.

6. Functionalism presented a teleological and reified view of society by treating it as an organism, or at least like an organism. Functionalism treated societies as if they had "minds" or "consciousness" in the same sense that individuals do. Societies were said to adapt, to make decisions, and so on, but it is only individuals, many critics charged, who have these characteristics and can do these things. It is only individuals who have needs, adapt, make decisions, etc. In the words of Anthony Giddens (1981:17), "functionalist authors have been unable to see human beings as reasoning agents."

I essentially agree with all of these criticisms, but it is the last one that most concerns me. Basically, as Jonathan Turner and Alexandra Maryanski (1979) have argued, functionalism as an explanatory theory is dead (or at least should be dead). Not only does its teleological structure and its reification of society render it invalid on logical grounds, but functionalist theories can easily be shown to be inaccurate on empirical grounds. This can be demonstrated by way of a critical analysis of some well-known functionalist arguments.

SOME FUNCTIONALIST EXPLANATIONS AND THEIR PROBLEMS

Functionalism and Social Stratification

Over half a century ago Kingsley Davis and Wilbert Moore (1945) presented a functionalist analysis of stratification that was one of the earliest functionalist theories in sociology; it has become perhaps the single best-known functionalist theory of all time. Davis and Moore argued that stratification—by which they meant inequalities in the distribution of material and symbolic rewards—was a societal universal, and that it was so because it was necessary to the survival, or at least the smooth and efficient functioning, of any society. A crucial task faced by every society was that of motivating a sufficient number of its members to fill its most functionally important roles, and it accomplished this task by establishing greater rewards for those who would undertake the sacrifices necessary to perform these roles. Stratification thus evolved because it provided benefits for society as a whole, and no society could function effectively (or perhaps even survive at all) without it. As Davis and Moore put it, stratification is an unconsciously evolved mechanism whereby societies motivate enough of their members to fill their most functionally important social positions.

This theory has been one of the most frequently and extensively criticized theories in all of sociology. The most basic objections, and my responses to them, can be summarized below (Tumin, 1953; Huaco, 1963; Wrong, 1959, 1976, 1997):

1. The concept of "functional importance" that is critical to Davis and Moore's argument is both subjective and circular. Davis and Moore seem to identify a position as functionally important simply because it is highly rewarded, and then leap from there to the conclusion that it must be highly rewarded because it is

important to society. (*Response*: There is no certainty that this is what Davis and Moore have done, but there is strong suspicion on my part that they have.)

2. Davis and Moore's assumption that stratification systems help to promote the most efficient use of a society's talents is questionable. In fact, the more highly stratified a society is the less it can discover just how much talent it has because social rewards will be determined mostly by social inheritance rather than ability. (*Response*: This criticism has considerable force.)

3. Economic and symbolic rewards are not the only ways in which societies can motivate their members. They could be motivated by such incentives as "social duty" or "joy in work." (*Response*: While this may technically be true, this criticism has little force because the struggle for wealth, status, and power does seem to be a primary human motivation that usually overrides other motivations.)

4. Davis and Moore's theory is more an attempt to justify or legitimize stratification than to explain it. (*Response*: This criticism is badly misplaced and there is little evidence to suggest that Davis and Moore were ideologically rather than scientifically motivated. In fact, the sociologists who make this criticism may well be the ones with the ideological motives.)

5. The theory assumes a level of equal opportunity in society that is more an ideal than a reality. (*Response*: This criticism has considerable force, although it is probably overstated.)

6. Davis and Moore are unable to explain the full range or extent of inequality in any society. (*Response*: This is quite true, but Davis and Moore explicitly disclaim any attempt to explain why a given society has the type and degree of stratification that it does. Nevertheless, a good theory of stratification should do that, and Davis and Moore's does not.)

7. Davis and Moore ignore the dysfunctional consequences of stratification, such as the harm to self-image that befalls the members of subordinate classes and statuses. (*Response*: This criticism may be unfair because Davis and Moore do seem to show an awareness of the dysfunctions of stratification. They do not argue that stratification is functionally beneficial all of the time or in every way.)

8. The theory ignores the existence of roles that are very highly rewarded but that cannot logically be considered of any particular functional importance, such as professional athletes and entertainers. (*Response*: This criticism is unfair. Davis and Moore explictly point this out and say that it is an anomaly for their theory.)

The most important criticism I would personally make, however, is not listed here. This is the point, captured perfectly in Davis and Moore's claim that stratification is an *unconsciously evolved mechanism*, that Davis and Moore give us a reified theory of stratification. Like their teacher Talcott Parsons, Davis and Moore lost sight of the fact that it is individuals acting in society that create social structures, and that "society" itself does not exist as an entity in and of itself and therefore cannot act in the ways that individuals do. As Anthony Giddens (1981) would put it, the functionalists treat societies—and such of their features as stratification—as entities that operate "behind the backs" of individuals and without their knowledge or understanding. They have no theory of individual action or individual needs and aims, but it is only such action that is responsible for the creation of society.

Despite these objections, there is one point that can be made in Davis and Moore's favor. This concerns their argument that it is not only the level of functional importance of a social position that determines its rank. Its rank may also be determined by the degree of scarcity of individuals available to fill the position. The more scarce individuals are, the greater the rewards of the position they would fill. This argument is undoubtedly correct and of considerable importance to explaining stratification, but there is no need to link it to functionalism. Indeed, it makes more sense within the frameworks of the most important alternatives to a functionalist theory of stratification, which are Marxian and Weberian conflict theories and sociobiology. In later chapters we will discuss these theories and show how they can be united in a nonreified conception of stratification that is much more powerful than the functionalist theory.

Functionalism and Poverty (or, the Poverty of Functionalism)

Herbert Gans (1972) has used the Mertonian brand of functionalism in order to shed light on the persistence of poverty in American society. Gans tries to show that poverty persists because, despite being dysfunctional for the poor, it performs a variety of functions for the nonpoor. Since the nonpoor benefit from poverty, they have no incentive to eliminate it and thus it continues to exist. Gans identifies fifteen positive functions of poverty for the nonpoor, virtually all of which are latent functions. These include such things as making sure that "dirty work" gets done and that the nonpoor do not have to do it; creating certain types of jobs, such as those in the areas of social work and penology; helping merchants to sell goods that might otherwise go to waste, such as day-old bread, secondhand clothes, deteriorating automobiles, and decaying buildings; identifying and punishing a class of social deviants, which helps to uphold the legitimacy of dominant norms; and guaranteeing the higher social status of the nonpoor. Gans concludes that poverty can only be eliminated when the functions of poverty for the nonpoor disappear and are replaced by dysfunctions. Once the nonpoor lose more than they gain from the existence of a class of poor people, they will be motivated to end it.

Gans's analysis has a superficial plausibility, but on closer inspection it can be seen to be seriously wanting. For one thing, the fifteen positive functions Gans lists are for the most part merely asserted, never demonstrated in any kind of convincing way at all (Roach and Roach, 1973). Moreover, virtually all of these functions are latent functions, another name for which is simply unanticipated consequences. What good does it do simply to enumerate such consequences when what we really need is a genuine causal theory? And that is what Gans's analysis lacks. Nowhere in his article do we find him saying anything about the causes or origins of poverty. He simply assumes that, given the existence of poverty (however it may have originated), it has certain consequences that may lead to its perpetuation. Gans's analysis is a very good example, perhaps the best example we have, of the serious limitations of the Mertonian brand of functionalism. This is why Collins can claim with great justification that, although Merton helped to lead sociology through its dark ages, he also helped preserve the darkness.

Functionalism and Educational Expansion

One of the most striking facts about the modern world is the creation and expansion of mass education. Throughout the industrialized world, systems of public education were created in the nineteenth century and these systems have undergone enormous expansion in the twentieth century. Primary and secondary education are virtually universal in modern industrial societies, and, although it still has a long way to go, higher education seems to be headed in that direction. How to explain these developments? The functionalist argument (Clark, 1962; Trow, 1966) relates educational expansion to technological and occupational change. As modern societies have industrialized and urbanized, the occupational structure has shifted markedly. There has been a marked decline of jobs requiring little skill and a concomitant increase in jobs requiring more knowledge and skill. There has been, in other words, occupational upgrading, and this upgrading has required longer periods of training for the individuals who will perform this more highly skilled work. Where will they get this training? From the educational system, the functionalists answer, and thus educational systems have had to expand in proportion to technological change and occupational upgrading. Educational expansion is thus a response to changing societal needs.

There are several problems with this interpretation. Randall Collins (1979) notes that students learn few job-related skills in schools, and that schools (at least private high schools and most institutions of higher education) spend much more time transmitting and reinforcing a status culture than doing anything else. Krishan Kumar (1978) has shown that, regardless of whether or not schools once taught practical job-related skills, they seem to be doing an ever poorer job of it, as indicated by the marked decline of literacy and numeracy skills in Britain (and other industrial societies). In recent decades British employment agencies have made widespread complaints concerning the literacy skills of high school graduates, and universities have complained of the large number of students who are entering them without the elementary skills needed for success in their course work. Indeed, the same complaints have been made by American universities and employment agencies, and are beginning to be heard by the same institutions in other European countries, including Germany, which once had the most demanding educational system in the world. A good case could be made that American college graduates now know less (perhaps much less) than high school graduates did thirty or forty years ago. If increased schooling has come about because of the need for increasingly knowledgeable workers, then the system is failing miserably. But a good case can be made that, in fact, workers learn their job-relevant skills not in the formal educational system but rather in the very process of doing their jobs.

One of the linchpins of the functionalist theory of education is the assumption of a close relationship between greater education and increased worker productivity, but this assumption is dubious (Collins, 1979; Berg, 1971). One series of studies shows that there is no necessary relation between educational attainment and worker productivity (Berg, 1971). Ivar Berg (1971) has shown that in some cases worker performance and educational achievement are actually inversely related. Collins (1979) estimates that the functionalist theory explains perhaps 15 percent at best of the variance in educational expansion. Alternative theories are available from both the Marxian and Weberian conflict traditions, and we shall look at these in later chapters.

Functionalism and Social Evolution

One of the most persistent criticisms made of Talcott Parsons's functionalist model of society was that it assumed that societies are equilibrium-seeking systems, and as a result had no acceptable way of explaining social change. Apparently stung by this criticism, Parsons went on to write a pair of books (Parsons, 1966, 1971) in which he developed not only a theory of change, but one of the most elaborate and comprehensive theories of social change ever developed.

Parsons's theory is explicitly a theory of long-term social evolution. The key to social evolution for Parsons is increasing social differentiation, or the process by which societies produce more specialized structures that come to be related to each other in more complex ways. As social differentiation proceeds, it leads to what Parsons calls *adaptive upgrading*. Societies increase their *adaptive capacity*, or their overall ability to adjust to their environments and function efficiently. Critical to Parsons's theory is his concept of an *evolutionary universal*, which is a structural innovation that improves a society's level of functioning and also serves as a prerequisite to any future evolutionary advances. Parsons identifies six evolutionary universals. At an early stage of social evolution we find *social stratification* and *cultural legitimation*. Stratification allows a society to overcome the limitations of ascription by providing inducements for some individuals to become leaders, and cultural legitimation allows a society to develop a sense of identity and distinguish itself from other societies. At a later stage of social evolution *administrative bureaucracy* and *money and markets* are critical evolutionary universals. The former permits the institutionalization of authority, whereas the latter allows for a much more efficient acquisition and deployment of resources; both markedly increase societal efficiency. At the highest stage of social evolution we find two more evolutionary universals. *Generalized universalistic norms* are abstract legal rules that encompass an entire society, as exemplified by the Roman legal system and English common law; for Parsons, these were critical for the development of modernity. The *democratic association* involves elective office, the franchise, and collective decision-making. Its significance is that it roots the exercise of power in a broad social consensus.

Parsons marks off three major stages of social evolution that correspond to these six evolutionary universals. *Primitive societies* are highly undifferentiated and are based overwhelmingly on kinship ties. The emergence of stratification marks the transition from the most primitive of societies to a more advanced primitive type. *Intermediate societies* emerge next and contain two subtypes, *archaic societies* and *historic empires*. Archaic societies, such as ancient Egypt and Mesopotamia, created literate priesthoods that provided their respective societies with high levels of cultural legitimation, and religious and political roles became strongly differentiated. Parsons identifies the most important historic empires as ancient China, India, Islamic civilization, and Rome. They were characterized by major philosophical breakthroughs. In China this involved the creation of a governing class (the mandarins) whose status came to be defined in cultural terms. In India, a much more consistent religio-philosophical system was produced, and Islamic civilization created the solidary community of the faithful known as the *Umma*. The greatest philosophical breakthrough was achieved by Rome with its highly universalistic system of law. *Modern societies* represent the highest stage of social evolution. The earliest of these were the northwest European societies of Holland, France, and England, the last of which developed the most highly differentiated social institutions yet seen in the world. Critical to the development of modern societies were the Industrial Revolution and the democratic revolution. The Industrial Revolution created massive differentiation within the economy, and the democratic revolution brought into being a value system based on equality of opportunity, a vital mechanism of social integration for the new type of society that was being born. To this point in history, it is the United States that has carried modernity the farthest, and it represents, in Parsons's famous phrase, the "new lead society of contemporary modernity."

Parsons's theory is an impressive intellectual achievement; if only it were true, or even approximately true. My most fundamental criticisms of it can be summarized basically as follows:

1. The concept of differentiation is highly problematic, especially as a single overriding dimension of evolutionary change. There is little doubt that much of long-term social evolution can be described as a process of differentiation, but at the same time a great deal of this change has little if anything to do with the emergence of higher levels of specialization and integration. As Charles Tilly (1984) has pointed out, such major social processes as the diffusion of the world religions and the concentration of capital have little to do with differentiation, and *de*differentiation has been an important process throughout long-term evolution. Tilly points to such phenomena as the combination of small sovereignties into large national states, linguistic standardization, and the emergence of mass consumption in the twentieth century as good examples of the latter process. Like Tilly, Anthony Smith (1973) cautions that we should not elevate any tendency toward increasing differentiation into some sort of master principle of social evolution. The matter becomes even worse when, as Parsons does, the concept of differentiation is used not only to describe but to attempt to *explain* the long process of social evolution.

2. Parsons's concepts of adaptation and adaptive capacity are severely flawed. Parsons uses these concepts in his quintessentially functionalist manner, i.e., as characteristics and products of social systems. But, as pointed out earlier, social systems do not have "needs" or "imperatives," only individuals do, and it is only they that can adapt to anything. Moreover, in addition to giving us this highly reified notion of adaptation, Parsons compounds the problem by claiming that adaptation is somehow a process that improves throughout social evolution, i.e., that societies become adaptively upgraded and thus improve the efficiency of their functioning. This is very dubious at both the societal and the individual level. As Joseph Tainter (1988) has shown convincingly, throughout much of human history as societies have achieved higher levels of complexity they have displayed a remarkable tendency to become highly dysfunctional and to collapse; in Parsonian language, this is adaptive *down*grading. And at the individual level much the same thing is true: Throughout most of preindustrial social evolution, most individuals have become worse off rather than better off as societies have undergone dramatic changes (Harris, 1977; Sanderson, 1995b, 1999: chapter 8).

3. Parsons's evolutionary theory not only reifies society, but reifies history as well. In fact, his whole theory is a strongly Hegelianized, teleological theory of historical change. Although Parsons sees himself as largely indebted to Weber, there are surprisingly similar parallels between the historical theories of Parsons and Hegel. Just as Hegel thought that the historical process had an endpoint (Freedom, or complete human self-knowledge), so did Parsons (a society represented by generalized universalistic norms and the democratic association). Both Parsons and Hegel thought that at each major stage of historical development there was a single society that was ahead of all of the others. In ancient times this society was Rome, whereas in modern times it was Germany for Hegel and the United States—the "new lead society of contemporary modernity"—for Parsons. In addition, Parsons and Hegel were both theoretical idealists in the extreme. For Hegel, history was the unfolding of the Absolute Idea, and societies rested on a foundation of art, religion, and philosophy. For Parsons, the most important accomplishments in social evolution occur within the realm of ideas. The historic empires, for example, are marked by their so-called philosophical breakthroughs. A final similarity between Parsons and Hegel concerns their essential failure to give any role to individuals as agents of change. For both thinkers, individuals are simply pawns in a great historical process, which for Hegel was the "cunning of reason" and for Parsons the master process of social differentiation.

It is important to point out that this critique of Parsonian evolutionism does not imply a dismissal of evolutionary theories in general, only of this particular functionalist theory of social evolution. There are a number of theories of social evolution that are almost entirely free of the problems associated with Parsonian functionalism (see Sanderson, 1990, 1995b, 1999).

A SAVING GRACE

Although functionalism as a theoretical strategy does not work, there is something that can be salvaged. As Turner and Maryanski (1979) suggest, functionalism still retains an intuitive appeal for many sociologists in that it asks what the various features of society "do for" individuals and society. They suggest using this intuitive appeal as a methodological device to orient an analysis that can be carried out in terms of other perspectives. I agree, but would abandon the notion of what social structures do for *society* and ask instead what they do for the *individuals* that make up society. We are left with what I call *functional analysis*, which is similar in some respects to Merton's notion of the same name. Functional analysis assumes that many of the features of social life arise because they are adaptive, i.e., because they "do something" for individuals. This notion takes us completely away from functionalist notions of societal needs, system survival, equilibrium, and the like, and focuses instead on individuals and their needs and aims. Functional analysis as I conceive of it is already part of such perspectives as rational choice theory, some versions of social evolutionism, and anthropological cultural materialism. Indeed, it was used by Karl Marx when, for example, he described religion as the "opium of the people," as well as when he called the state the "executive committee of the ruling class." To take a more contemporary example, Lewis Coser (1964) has carried out a functional analysis of the role of eunuchs in agrarian societies of the past. In many of these societies, eunuchs were often employed to guard the harems of political rulers and to perform a variety of additional political functions. Since eunuchs were incapable of inseminating women, they were ideal for guarding wives whose offspring should, in the ruler's mind, only be those of the ruler himself. Moreover, eunuchs typically lost contact with their families of origin and as a result could be uniquely beneficial as servants to rulers.[2]

Despite my endorsement of functional analysis, I stress that it can be used only as a starting point and that it must be supplemented (and often is supplemented) with additional theoretical arguments. It is an orientational strategy that cannot stand alone. Functional analysis is often employed by Marxian and Weberian conflict theorists, by cultural materialists, and by rational choice theorists. Functional analysis by itself usually cannot identify causes, but when it is linked to a particular theoretical strategy it is in a position to do so.

NOTES

1. In this discussion I have deliberately left aside the recent school of sociological thought led by Jeffrey Alexander that has come to be known as neofunctionalism. Neofunctionalism makes little actual use of the functionalist mode of explanation as such, and concentrates instead on resurrecting, and to some extent revising, certain ideas of Talcott Parsons. There is great concern with norms and values and with the allegedly crucial role of ideas. Neofunctionalism would be more accurately called "neo-Parsonianism." Some of the leading contributors to neo-Parsonianism are Alexander (1984, 1985, 1987), Alexander and Colomy (1990), Holton and Turner (1986), Robertson and Turner (1991), and Sciulli and Gerstein (1985). For a sympathetic critical assessment of Alexander's neo-Parsonianism see Collins (1985a), and for an unsympathetic assessment see Sica (1983).

2. Marvin Harris's (1968, 1974, 1979) cultural materialism has often engaged in both functionalist explanation and functional analysis, with the latter tending to displace the former around the middle of Harris's career. Kincaid (1996:104) provides a laundry list of what he calls functionalist explanations, but it is clear that some of these only go as far as functional analysis. His examples of functional analysis include "educational systems exist in order to promote capitalist interests"; "welfare exists in order to promote labor discipline"; and "Inuit hunting group size exists in order to promote survival."

My distinction between functionalism and functional analysis has been anticipated by both Albert Szymanski (1971) and George Homans (1983), who both distinguish between individualistic and societal functionalism. They associate individualistic functionalism with Malinowski and (somewhat erroneously) with Merton and societal functionalism with Radcliffe-Brown and Parsons. Homans notes that the concept of function as used by individualistic functionalism can easily be translated into the concept of reward as used by his own exchange theory. However, my notion of functional analysis still differs in two important respects from Merton's: Merton talks not only (or even primarily) of individuals, but largely of social systems and subsystems, and he seems to limit himself to identifying consequences, whereas I am interested in identifying actual causes.

2

Social Constructionist Explanations

BASIC PRINCIPLES

Social constructionism is a name given in recent years to a family of theories that emphasize the "social construction of reality." Social constructionists tend to be idealists in the sense that they emphasize the powers of the human mind as the determining forces in the organization of society. It is these mental powers that crucially separate humans from other animals and that give human society its distinctive qualities. To say that social reality is constructed means a number of things: that society is created or made by humans through an active process of discussion, negotiation, and agreement; that the social constructions that people may arrive at are potentially extremely wide ranging because they are not constrained in any major way by external conditions; and that people have enormous freedom in the process of social construction. Social constructionist theories thus tend to be idealist, subjectivist, and highly voluntaristic when compared to other sociological theories. In sociology the two major schools of social constructionist thought are symbolic interactionism and ethnomethodology. However, it is possible to identify the work of some sociologists and other social scientists as constructionist in nature even though it does not fall in any obvious way into either of these formally identified schools. Jeffrey Weeks's book *Sexuality* (1986), for example, falls into this category. Weeks is a historian rather than a sociologist and there are many other examples of nonsociologists who engage in constructionist theorizing. Social constructionism is thus much broader than the two major sociological perspectives. Its boundaries now extend throughout the humanities and social sciences, and it has become very influential within the last decade or two.

The origins of symbolic interactionism are to be found in early American sociology, especially in the work of William Isaac Thomas, George Herbert Mead, and Charles Horton Cooley. Early American sociology, of course, was heavily centered on the University of Chicago and the "Chicago school." Thomas is famous for his "Thomas theorem" (which Merton, 1957, later renamed the "self-fulfilling prophecy"), which states that "what men define as real becomes real in its consequences." This idea is extremely notable for its emphasis on people's subjective definitions and how these definitions lead

24

to a particular social reality. Mead focused very heavily on the development of the self under the impact of people's internalization of social definitions. Cooley was also concerned with the development of the self, and formulated what he called the "looking-glass self": people's self-concepts are built up out of their perceptions of other people's perceptions of them.

The leading symbolic interactionist in modern sociology has been Herbert Blumer, and it was he who coined the term symbolic interactionism in 1937. Blumer was a student of Mead at Chicago and considered his own symbolic interactionism largely a formalization of Mead's thought. Blumer's leading ideas were brought together in his book *Symbolic Interactionism: Perspective and Method* (1969), a collection of previously published essays. Blumer set forth three basic principles as the essential claims of symbolic interactionism: human beings act toward things on the basis of the meanings that the things have for them; the meaning attributed to these things emerges from the social interaction that individuals have with their fellows; and these meanings are modified through an interpretive process used by individuals in dealing with the things they encounter. The key idea is obviously that of *meaning*. Things, including individuals and social situations, do not have meaning in and of themselves. Their meanings are not intrinsic, but come from a process of attribution or construction performed by creatures with the capacity for symbolization and symbolic communication. "Human activity," Blumer (1969:16) says, "consists of meeting a flow of situations in which [humans] have to act and . . . their action is built on the basis of what they note, how they assess and interpret what they note, and what kind of projected lines of action they map out." Moreover, social life is a process of constant flux: "New situations are constantly arising within the scope of group life that are problematic and for which existing rules are inadequate. . . . Such areas of unprescribed conduct are just as natural, indigenous, and recurrent in human group life as are those areas covered by pre-established and faithfully followed prescriptions of joint action" (1969:18).

Symbolic interactionism is not a completely unitary approach, and disagreement on various matters exists among the theorists of this school. At the highly voluntaristic end we can place Blumer himself, for whom the attribution of meaning seems to be little constrained (or not constrained at all) by external social forces. At the other end are symbolic interactionists like Sheldon Stryker (1980), who want to give more attention to these "external" forces. However, to me these different modes of symbolic interactionist theory are simply variations on a theme. Although less voluntaristic, the basic principles of Stryker's symbolic interactionism differ little from Blumer's. In brief summary, Stryker's principles are (1980:53–55):

1. Human behavior depends on a named world, and these names carry meanings that emerge from social interaction.
2. Among the named terms emerging from social interaction are symbols that designate social positions, and these positions carry the shared behavioral expectations that are conventionally called roles.
3. Persons who interact name one another and in doing so invoke expectations for each other's behavior.
4. Persons name themselves as well, and thus create a self.

5. In social interaction people define social situations and use their definitions to organize their own behavior.
6. However, social behavior is not determined by these definitions even though early definitions may constrain the possibility of alternative definitions emerging. Behavior is the product of a process of role-making, which is initiated by the expectations that emerge from the process of social definition.
7. The extent to which roles are "made" rather than simply "played" depends on the larger social structures within which people interact.
8. Because roles are made rather than played, changes can occur in the nature of social definitions, and these changes can lead to changes in larger social structures.

Except for principles 6 and 7, and the second half of principle 8, Stryker's principles do not differ significantly from Blumer's. I applaud Stryker's modifications of Blumer that put large-scale "external" structures into the picture, but the question is, Are most symbolic interactionists more on Blumer's side or on Stryker's? My impression is that more, perhaps many more, are closer to Blumer. Few symbolic interactionists give much emphasis, if any, to the constraints on social definitions or meaning attributions, and even Stryker himself fails to do so in a truly systematic way. As Gallant and Kleinman (1983) have pointed out, symbolic interactionism is inherently indeterministic, and its representatives share a strong opposition to deterministic sociologies. Gary Alan Fine (1993) claims that some of the leading ideas of symbolic interactionism have become incorporated into mainstream sociology, and thus that symbolic interactionism is no longer the theoretical "outsider" it once was. I suspect, however, that this is only true of Stryker's brand of symbolic interactionism.[1]

The other major branch of social constructionism in sociology, ethnomethodology, is the brainchild of the sociologist Harold Garfinkel (1967), a former student of Talcott Parsons. Garfinkel was very taken with Parsons's concept of social order, which, of course, was Parsons's overwhelming concern and for him the central problem of sociology. Garfinkel, however, thought that Parsons's approach to the problem of order was fundamentally wrong. According to Garfinkel, social order is not some sort of objective thing that is "out there" in the world, as Parsons would have it. Society is not some sort of objective system with "laws" of functioning. Rather, social order is something overwhelmingly subjective, and thus Garfinkel preferred to talk about a sense of social order. Social order lies in people's definitions of reality and the agreements they make with one another to support and perpetuate these definitions. Garfinkel coined an extremely interesting phrase, that of "cultural dopes." He thought that this is how Parsons conceived of the relationship between individuals and society. Social actors for Parsons were cultural dopes in the sense that they are seen as more or less passively absorbing external social influences. They internalize the norms and values of "society" and act in accordance with them. Garfinkel objected strongly to this conceptualization, arguing that individuals are not passive absorbers but active creators who construct and define their world. Individuals do not simply soak up external influences, but actively resist, define, and create.

Garfinkel went on to suggest that social order and thus society are extremely fragile things. People construct social reality and come to see it as normal and natural, or as perhaps the only way things can be. Society comes to be viewed by its participants as an external force that imposes itself on each individual by necessity. Individuals construct society through their mental definitions, but after doing so they somehow seem to lose sight of this fact and just take society for granted. However, Garfinkel suggested that despite this "normalization" of society, people still retain a vague sense of the fragility and vulnerability of it all. As a result, they develop strong psychological protections against any challenge to the most elementary of social constructions. To test this idea, Garfinkel designed the famous experiments that he called "breaching experiments." The idea was to have a confederate of an experimenter violate an extremely basic social norm and then observe the reaction of others. For example, a confederate may respond to the question, "How are you?" by answering "How am I in regard to what: my finances, my health, my . . . ?" Normally the reaction to such a response is either embarrassment, anger, or some combination of the two. Or a confederate might take a teddy bear into a bar, order drinks for it, and watch the reaction of the bartender. Garfinkel also asked some of his students to go home for Thanksgiving break and act like boarders in their own homes. They would ask permission to use the bathroom, or they might call their parents "Mr." and "Mrs." Garfinkel interpreted such severe reactions to these breaches of elementary norms as being the result of the profound sense of uneasiness that people feel about the solidity of social life. People somehow sense that society is a terribly fragile thing and can come tumbling down at any moment. This Garfinkel interprets as evidence for his major claim that social reality is just a mentally constructed reality, that there is nothing natural, lawlike, or objective about it, and that social change is primarily a matter of changing our social agreements.

It is interesting that ethnomethodologists are often political radicals, and a good many of them are, politically speaking, Marxists. Why should this be? The reason may be that ethnomethodology is attractive to such people because it has a simple agenda for dramatic social change: get people to alter their social definitions by showing them that their existing definitions are somehow flawed. Rebuild the world through cognitive change. In his discussion of the works of social phenomenologists, close cousins of ethnomethodologists, Marvin Harris says the following (1979:324–25):

> Phenomenological relativism satisfies many of its enthusiasts primarily because they regard it as a radicalizing and liberating point of view. During the 1960s the California phenomenologists even thought of themselves as members of a sociological "underground." . . . They saw phenomenology as a radical movement because it challenges positivism's claim to "God's truth." Phenomenology reduces the stance of the establishment's scientific "absolutist" objectivity to a mere arbitrary subjective experience among other arbitrary subjective experiences. . . . Hence phenomenology appeals to many anthropologists who are dissatisfied with the status quo, and who identify with the aspirations of oppressed minorities, the young, and the third world. The phenomenological stance represents for them a means of attacking the inequities of corporate industrialism and the technocratic establishment.

In comparing symbolic interactionism and ethnomethodology, some sociologists have stressed their similarities (e.g., Denzin, 1969; Rock, 1979; Petras and Meltzer, 1973; cf. Gallant and Kleinman, 1983), whereas others have stressed their differences (e.g., Zimmerman and Wieder, 1970; Perinbanayagam, 1974, 1975; cf. Gallant and Kleinman,

1983). Norman Denzin (1969) stresses that the fundamental similarity shared by the perspectives is the emphasis on the social construction of meaning, and Gallant and Kleinman (1983) emphasize that both approaches share an opposition to highly deterministic theories. Gallant and Kleinman also point to what they see as a number of basic differences: interactionists seek to interpret social action, whereas ethnomethodologists treat the process of interpretation as a subject for investigation; unlike interactionists, ethnomethodologists are not interested in describing situations or in setting forth propositions that apply to particular places under certain conditions, but rather attempt to find universal characteristics of individuals' constructing or accounting practices; and interactionists, when discussing possible constraints, are referring to social structure, whereas constraints for ethnomethodologists are interpretive rules. This last difference, to the extent that it is correct, would imply that ethnomethodology is more idealist and more theoretically radical than symbolic interactionism. One might also add that the symbolic interactionists have been much concerned with the self and its formation, whereas this concern has been absent in ethnomethodology. No doubt other differences could be listed as well. Despite these differences, for my purposes in this book I stress the similarities between these approaches, the most important of which is that social life is a construction based on the attribution of meaning to things, persons, and situations. The interactionists and the ethnomethodologists themselves can engage in all the theoretical hairsplitting that they wish, but to a theoretical outsider like myself these differences mean little.

Symbolic interactionism and ethnomethodology are usually thought of as distinctively microlevel approaches. Randall Collins (1988, 1994), for example, refers to both perspectives as "microinteractionist" sociologies. However, in recent years some symbolic interactionists have protested against this claim and have argued that symbolic interactionist theorists can do (and have actually done) macrolevel work. Blumer did write an entire book on the process of industrialization that was published after his death (Blumer, 1990). Stanford Lyman (1984) notes that Blumer studied race relations at the macro level. He argues that for Blumer "race relations could be studied by carefully charting the movement of the 'color line' in various institutional sectors and settings; and that racial conflict and accomodation [*sic*] belonged to an historically informed political and industrial sociology and not to psychology or psycho-analysis" (1984:111). Race relations for Blumer, Lyman (1984:117) notes, "partake first and foremost of a social construction of an invidious reality, a classifying process wherein peoples are categorized as belonging to hierarchically perceived racial groups." David Maines (1988) complains, almost bitterly, that Blumer's work has been misrepresented as exclusively microlevel not only by macrolevel theorists, but by the symbolic interactionists themselves. He notes that Blumer did important work in the areas of race relations, industrialization, industrial organization, and corporate organization. Lyman and Maines do help to set the record straight, but the fact remains that the vast majority of symbolic interactionist work has been at the micro level. Collins's characterization of this approach as a microinteractionist sociology is thus largely, if not totally, appropriate.

As for ethnomethodology, Richard Hilbert (1990, 1992) claims that it utterly transcends the micro-macro distinction. Social life is a continuous stream of reality construction in which "the same social practices generative of the so-called macrostructures are likewise and in identical fashion generative of microstructure and processes as well" (1990:795). This point is quite different from the arguments of Lyman and Maines that symbolic interactionism can be either micro or macro. Hilbert is telling us that ethnomethodology is *neither* micro nor macro. In a sense, from this point of view there is no real difference between the micro and the macro. As Hilbert (1990:805) puts it, "there is no distinction for ethnomethodologists to make between microstructure and macrostructure as they are simultaneously generated." In a very fundamental sense I think Hilbert is correct, and I would generalize his point to say that far too much has been made by sociologists of the micromacro distinction. The macro is just the micro on a larger scale of time, space, and number (Collins, 1981, 1988). However, at the same time it is impossible to deny that most of the time the ethnomethodologists' *subject matter*, if not their theoretical principles, is distinctively micro (actually what Collins calls "ultramicro"). We see this, for example, in the enormous amount of attention they have given to conversation analysis. One looks in vain for an analysis of anything even remotely approaching the sorts of phenomena, such as long-term social change, that are of greatest concern to macrosociologists.[2]

CRITICAL ASSESSMENT

Social constructionism has been severely criticized by many sociologists. Below I enumerate and discuss the most important of the criticisms that have been made (Stryker, 1980; Reynolds, 1993; Collins, 1988; J. Alexander, 1987).

1. *Social constructionism is too voluntaristic.* As discussed earlier, Blumer's symbolic interactionism is especially vulnerable to this criticism, although to a large extent it can be extended to most interactionists. Blumer seemed to assume that there were no constraints whatsoever acting on the process by which individuals construct social meanings (Collins, 1988, 1994). He and other symbolic interactionists have even gone as far as opposing the very practice that is so basic to mainstream sociology, viz., the identification of social factors or forces that impinge on behavior. To do this would apparently be too deterministic. Blumer seemed to think that society amounted to nothing but a plurality of selves in interaction, and that people could make society into anything they wanted (Zeitlin, 1973). Jeffrey Alexander (1987:218) puts it perfectly: "Symbolic interactionism . . . gives the actor complete sovereignty. It is a lot like good old American ideology. The actor is protean, the completely undetermined determiner, the mysterious, romantic, spontaneous creator of everything in the world." Alexander goes on to say that Blumer fervently embraced the randomness of social behavior and reveled in the unpredictability implied by his theoretical outlook. More recently, Manis and Meltzer (1994) have celebrated the role of chance in social life, although the phenomena they mention—e.g., the feminist revolution and the collapse of Communism—were anything but chancelike.

2. *Social construction is too microlevel, generally ignoring large-scale social structures, or at least treating them as nothing more than a framework within which meaning is attributed.* The protestations of Lyman, Maines, and Hilbert

notwithstanding, this criticism is generally well founded. Many sociologists would claim, and I would be one of them, that the most important large-scale structures are those of power and social class. To ignore these, as social constructionists generally do, invites sociological disaster.

3. *Social constructionism suffers from a strong idealist bias.* The tradition of German idealism lies behind much social constructionist thought. Blumer has declared that the "traditional position of idealism is that the 'world of reality' exists only in human experience and that it appears only in the form in which human beings 'see' the world. I think that this position is incontestable. It is impossible to cite a single instance of a characterization of the 'world of reality' that is not cast in the form of human imagery."

4. *Social constructionism is overly cognitive.* The processes whereby reality is socially constructed are limited to processes of thinking, and the important role of emotions and their biopsychological foundations is ignored. It has been said that Blumer "insists on individuals without organic drives" (Zeitlin, 1973:216).

5. *Social constructionist arguments tend to be ahistorical.* Although social constructionists focus on social process, emphasizing reality construction as a continuous flow of events in which meanings are constructed, deconstructed, and reconstructed, this is theorized in a purely abstract way and concrete historical phenomena are omitted from the picture. This is the dynamic version of the static claim that social constructionists ignore large-scale social structures. Alexander (1987:221) notes that, in a discussion of worker-management relations, Blumer "challenges the perspective which tries to place [these] relations in a historical perspective emphasizing the long-range trends of social development. While acknowledging that such constraints exist, he suggests that their effect on action is severely limited."

6. *Much of social constructionism, ethnomethodology in particular, engages in analyses that are trivial or banal.* Many ethnomethodologists have been preoccupied with the ultradetailed analysis of conversations (e.g., Schegloff, 1979). Others have examined how individuals "do walking" (Ryave and Schenkein, 1974), or how individuals know when to laugh in a social situation (Jefferson, 1979). Ethnomethodologists claim that valuable insights can be gleaned from such studies and applied to the understanding of more important phenomena. But I fail to see how this is the case. My impression is that ethnomethodologists have completely failed to deliver on this promise. Concerning Garfinkel's breaching experiments, Irving Zeitlin (1973:184) has said that the "value of these experiments for both the subject and the experimenter is . . . highly questionable. . . . And indeed nowhere are we told explicitly what Everyman or the social scientist might learn from these experiments, or what Garfinkel and his associates in fact concluded from them. Could this be because the conclusions tend to confirm what everyone knows?"

7. *Social constructionism suffers from serious epistemological and methodological problems.* It is often argued that this perspective has done little to produce testable scientific propositions, favoring instead intuitive understanding, and in some

cases rejecting empirical analysis altogether. For example, Blumer (1969: 30) has stated that one should "be very wary of the widespread reliance in social and psychological sciences on the testing of the hypothesis as the means of determining the empirical validity of theoretical schemes and models." This is not necessarily indicative of a throughly antiscientific outlook, but it certainly opposes the most important (and, I would add, most successful) way in which science has been practiced.

Despite these strong objections, I do not mean to be totally dismissive of social constructionism. I can readily agree that a great deal of social reality is constructed by individuals. This must obviously be the case inasmuch as social and cultural patterns differ so widely from place to place and time to time. Indeed, social constructionism makes an extremely important contribution, and provides a very useful antidote to functionalist reifications, by treating individuals as something very different from Parsonian "cultural dopes." For social constructionism, individuals do not passively absorb social and cultural influences, but are active agents in the creation of society. But the problem is that most versions of social constructionism give far too much freedom to individuals to do their constructing. Social constructionists seldom give us any criteria at all for understanding why you get some constructions in some times and places but very different constructions in other times and places, or why and how constructions change over time. In fact, social constructionists do not seem to think that it is important or even relevant to ask about the constraints that operate on constructions, because, as noted above, they assume that *there are no constraints* on people's constructions. In this sense, social life is essentially arbitrary. It can be anything people want it to be at any time and in any place.

Take some simple examples. The Hindus of India over a millennium ago arrived at the social construction, maintained still today, which defined the cow as a sacred animal that should not be eaten or harmed in any way. No other religion or society has embraced such socially constructed beliefs. And among the Jews for some three millennia, and the Moslems for nearly a millennium and a half, the pig has been socially constructed as a dirty and despicable animal that should be shunned as a food source. No other religions in the world have such a belief and practice, and indeed throughout the world the pig is one of the most common sources of animal protein. These religious beliefs and practices must be social constructions, but we cannot leave it at that. We need to inquire into the total range of conditions—social, cultural, economic, political, etc.—that have constrained the food habits of Hindus, Jews, and Moslems in the ways that they have. This social constructionism rarely does, and this is the main reason why it is an inadequate form of social theory.

Marx put matters well in a formulation that has been little improved on in a century and a half. "Men make their own history," he said, "but they do not make it just as they please; they do not make it under circumstances chosen by themselves, but under circumstances directly encountered, given, and transmitted from the past. The tradition of all the dead generations weighs like a nightmare on the brain of the living" (Marx, 1963[1852]:15).

SOME SUBSTANTIVE THEORIES

The serious problems with social constructionist explanations can best be shown by look-ing at some substantive theories. I concentrate on the application of social constructionist arguments to four major substantive areas of sociological concern: social deviance, human sexuality, science, and long-term social change.

Labeling Deviant Behavior

One of the most prominent symbolic interactionists of the second half of the twentieth century is Howard Becker. Becker's early work was much concerned with social de-viance, a major area for the application of symbolic interactionist ideas since their in-ception. Becker (1963) wrote a famous essay, "On Becoming a Marijuana User," which illustrates social constructionist ideas almost perfectly. He argued that the experience of marijuana use is quintessentially a social one. Whatever the physiological effects of the drug, people can only learn to judge smoking it as pleasurable if they smoke it as part of a group whose social definition of marijuana smoking stresses its pleasurable effects. Becker noted in this essay that the usual effect of marijuana on people who smoke it for the first time is very unpleasant. They are able to shift this experience toward the pleas-urable end of the spectrum only by absorbing their group's positive definition of the sit-uation. One wonders with respect to this argument about the role of the active chemi-cal ingredients in marijuana smoke. Have they no role in the emotional experience of marijuana smoking? Becker never tells us.

Becker (1963) is also the originator of the so-called labeling theory of deviance, one of the most influential theories in this area of sociology in the 1960s and 1970s. Label-ing theory emphasizes that deviance is not some sort of objective phenomenon, but rather a matter of social definition. Deviance involves breaking norms, which are de-fined by the group, and thus deviance is basically a matter of what people say it is. Peo-ple thus create deviance by establishing the norms whose violation constitutes deviance. Becker distinguished between primary and secondary deviance. Primary deviance is nor-mative violation that remains essentially private. A man embezzles money from the bank at which he works and no one is the wiser. Secondary deviance, on the other hand, is deviance that has come into the light of society's judgment. The man's embezzlement is discovered and there is a strong reaction against him. He is condemned by the com-munity, prosecuted, and labeled, and as a result acquires a deviant self-identity.

There is nothing wrong with this distinction per se; the problem results from what Becker does with it. In his *Outsiders: Studies in the Sociology of Deviance* (Becker, 1963), he announces that he will concentrate on secondary deviance and return before the end of the book to discuss primary deviance. Except he never does. The reason, I strongly suspect, is because labeling theory has precious little, if anything, to say about primary deviance. One of the most crucial things we want to know about deviant behavior is why it occurs in the first place. Becker insists that deviance is not an intrinsic property of a social act, but rather a matter of how society reacts to and judges that act. This is of course undeniable, but at the same time it is relatively banal. No intelligent or sane person would dispute the fact that social norms differ from society to society and from time to time, and that what is considered acceptable in some places and times is regarded as unacceptable in other places and at other times. Even Sociology 101 is not needed in order to understand that. However, whatever the social norms of any society, only some persons violate them, usually only a small minority. Certain crimes in modern industrial societies, for example, are concentrated among these societies' more economically marginal members, and yet only some of these economically marginal individuals commit these crimes. We want to know why, but can labeling theory tell us? Moreover, certain types of crimes are committed primarily by certain types of individuals. The best predictors of violent crimes such as murder and rape are age and sex (Daly and Wilson, 1988; Kanazawa and Still, 2000). These crimes are committed overwhelmingly by young men in all known societies, and are negatively judged and harshly punished in all of them. It is doubtful that labeling theory can explain these facts because its whole logic is rooted in the relativity of social constructions rather than the universal dimensions of human behavior.

Labeling theory's assumption that the labeling process is to a large extent arbitrary is poorly supported by empirical evidence. As Ronald Akers (1997) points out, society does not label individuals in a vacuum; for the most part, the police do not arrest until they have probable cause and courts do not apply criminal labels until it has been determined that illegal acts have in fact been committed. This means that deviant behavior must occur prior to any labeling process and must constitute the basis for that process. A deviant label appears to be more a result than a cause of any given individual's actual deviant conduct. Labeling theory also seems to overstress the degree to which individuals will accept and internalize the labels applied to them. People, even powerless people, generally resist deviant labels, fighting back against being labeled by others (Akers, 1997). And there is little empirical evidence to show that the labeling process is likely to create further deviance, one of the major claims of labeling theory. Ronald Akers (1997:106–7) has made the case as follows:

> Among those with the same level of primary deviance, the ones who escape detection and labeling are just as likely as those who are caught to repeat offenses and develop deviant careers. . . . the probability that offenders will desist is as high as, or higher than, the probability that they will persist in their deviant activities following official labeling.
>
> When prior offenses, personal propensities, social characteristics, and other nonlabeling correlates of deviant behavior are held constant, official stigmatizing labels make little difference in either the continuation or cessation of deviant behavior, self-concept, or a deviant career.

The Social Construction of Human Sexuality

Within the past twenty years there has been a flurry of work on human sexual behavior from a social constructionist standpoint, most of it sparked by the thinking of the French philosopher Michel Foucault (1978). One of the foremost advocates of this view of human sexuality is the British historian Jeffrey Weeks (1986). Sexuality, Weeks holds, is not biologically given but is produced by society through complex webs of social interaction and social definition. Thinking along the lines of Becker, he says that "each culture labels different practices as appropriate or inappropriate, moral or immoral, healthy or perverted" (1986:26). This is indeed true, but Weeks has a much more radical argument to make. Sexual orientation and behavior themselves are social rather than biological products. Heterosexuality, homosexuality, bisexuality, and presumably such extreme forms of sexual behavior as necrophilia or coprophilia, are socially rather than biologically determined. Human biology is not irrelevant, Weeks tells us, but its role is primarily that of providing potentialities and setting certain limits. Weeks is obviously not unaware of the fact that men have penises and women vaginas, but the most important thing is the *social meanings* that individuals in different times and places give to these sex organs. The organs in and of themselves do little.

A potentially embarrassing fact for Weeks's argument is that, with the possible exception of the Etoro of New Guinea (Harris, 1981; Herdt, 1984), heterosexuality is overwhelmingly the most common form of sexual activity in all known societies. Although homosexuality as a sexual preference is found in most societies, it usually does not pertain to more than a very small segment of the population. In modern industrial societies, for example, probably no more than 2 to 4 percent of the population prefers homosexuality to heterosexuality. This would seem to suggest that sexual orientation is rooted in our biological nature. But Weeks has an alternative. The distribution of sexual orientations in a society is a matter of power, he suggests, by which he presumably means that heterosexuals have had the power to define heterosexuality as right and normal and homosexuality as deviant. Does this mean that most people are heterosexual because they are simply conforming to social norms rather than expressing biological urges? Weeks does not say so explicitly, but Adrienne Rich (1980) does. For Rich, heterosexuality is essentially a political institution, and to express this notion she has coined the term *compulsory heterosexuality*. Heterosexuality is imposed by the powerful on the less powerful or powerless. Speaking in particular of female sexuality, Rich (1980:648) says that "for women heterosexuality may not be a 'preference' at all but something that has had to be imposed, managed, organized, propangandized, and maintained by force." Here again we see the politicized nature of many social constructionist arguments.

This has to be about the most extreme form of special pleading I have ever encountered. It is also an argument that would seem to fly enormously in the face of the facts, and to be completely illogical. Are we to believe that precisely the same kind of social construction, rooted in power and manipulation, is found in virtually every known society? How could it be that in countless societies separated by enormous distances of space and time that the vast majority of people construct heterosexuality as the most natural form of sexual behavior and behave accordingly? Rich suggests that this is rooted in male domination: Men wish to use women for their own sexual pleasures. But, if so, this implies that most men themselves are already heterosexuals, and thus begs the very question that Rich is attempting to answer. Even more problematic is the whole question of male and female anatomy. From the perspective of Darwinian evolutionary biology, one of the best empirically supported theories of all time, anatomical structures arise because they are adaptive for survival and reproductive success. Males have penises, women vaginas, and the one seems to fit into the other in a very smooth way. Surely, then, these structures must have evolved together, and as a result the brain must have evolved to give men and women the necessary drives to want to put them together. And think of the evolutionary results of human sexual orientation being primarily learned rather than innate. Imagine a species with complete indifference as to how it should behave sexually. What would happen to it? The only conceivable answer is that it would have no adaptive potential whatsoever because it would quickly be driven to extinction by other species that would outreproduce it. It is thus impossible to imagine a sexually indifferent species, because such a species could not exist more than a short time, and humans, as we know, have been around for several million years.

Moreover, there are a number of striking similarities in nonheterosexual behavior throughout the world (Weinrich, 1992). Homosexuals in widely divergent societies and cultures usually have a great deal of gender-reversed behavior, and this behavior is usually evident very early in life. Many societies have been found to have a sexual and gender role known among North American Indian groups as a *berdache*. This is a man who refuses male roles, dresses up in women's clothing, and enacts female roles; such a man is usually homosexual. In many societies there has been a form of substitutional (nonpreferential) homosexuality practiced by some men, and these men show a strong preference for young boys rather than older men. One of the most damaging facts for the social constructionist perspective is that homosexuals appear in most societies at about the same rate regardless of whether the society is accepting of homosexuality or hostile to it. If homosexuality is a socially constructed choice, why would some individuals make such a choice in a society that is intensely homophobic? It simply defies all logic.

To give the social constructionists their due, there is no doubt that social definitions of appropriate and inappropriate sexual behavior do differ widely throughout societal time and space (Ford and Beach, 1951; Broude and Greene, 1976). Some societies, such as India, have been extremely sex-positive and permissive, whereas others, especially Western societies after the rise of Christianity, have been highly sex-negative and restrictive (Bullough, 1976). But, as we have seen, there are definite limits, and even with respect to the variations it is by no means a certainty that different sexual attitudes and practices are arbitrary, uncaused constructions. That is a matter for empirical investigation.

Is Science a Social Construct?

In Britain in the late 1970s and early 1980s a number of sociologists began to engage in the study of science as a social product or social creation. At least two self-conscious schools crystalized, the "strong programme" and the "relativist programme" (Barnes, 1976; Bloor, 1976, 1981; H.M. Collins, 1981; Pinch, 1986; Knorr-Cetina and Mulkay, 1983). For the most part the sociologists engaged in this kind of work were borrowing from ethnomethodology. They held that traditional views of science as a highly empirical and objective phenomenon were seriously wrong. Science is a social construction, and the content of scientific ideas is determined not by empirical evidence but rather by social negotiation and the attempts to build consensus among networks of scientists. The power, resources, and interests of different scientists determine their bargaining strength and the way in which the social processes of negotiation will go, and thus the ideas that reign in any scientific field or subfield at any given time tend to be the socially constructed ideas of its most powerful members.

One of the primary objectives of these sociologists of science was, in good ethnomethodological fashion, to determine how scientists arrived at their constructions. A good deal of time was spent observing scientists actually at work in their laboratories. Numerous studies were carried out based on interviews of scientists as diverse as physicists and parapsychologists, who were asked how they went about reaching theoretical consensus (H.M. Collins, 1981; Collins and Pinch, 1982; Pickering, 1981; Latour and Woolgar, 1979). Harry Collins documents a number of instances in which advocates of one position attempted to bolster their own claims and discredit the findings of representatives of other positions on grounds that had little or nothing to do with the empirical evidence. Moreover, Collins has shown that the power and prestige of scientists are often important in determining the acceptability of their views.

On the whole, these arguments are not very convincing. There is little doubt that scientists, like other social actors, are influenced by considerations of power and prestige. After all, science, like other social instititutions, is a social process, and individual scientists like all social actors are motivated to satisfy their own interests. But the fact that social and political factors enter into the process whereby scientists deliberate about theories scarcely compels the radical conclusion that these factors are the only ones relevant to the outcome. Indeed, as the philosopher and historian of science Larry Laudan has pointed out, the most fundamental interest that scientists have is a *cognitive* one: They have an overriding interest in producing good theories. Although data are frequently ambiguous, and although scientific controversies often develop over their interpretation, the fact remains that scientists often reach very high levels of theoretical consensus and are able to settle controversies in ways that are unimaginable to nonscientists. This suggests that the natural world—the empirical evidence—does indeed act as a very powerful constraint on the beliefs of scientists. The philosopher of science Harold Kincaid (1996:38–39) puts it extremely well:

> Surely science is a social process and scientific belief does have social causes. Yet that fact does not *entail* that evidence, reasons, scientific method, and rationality do not ground science, for several reasons. For at least one sense of scientific rationality, the causal origin of a belief is irrelevant. . . . Even if scientists have their beliefs for social reasons, those beliefs might nonetheless have good evidence. For example, if I have a dream that causes me to believe arithmetic is incomplete, that does not preclude there being a proof for the claim as well. Or, racism and political agendas may explain why IQ studies are interpreted as they are, yet we can still ask whether those interpretations are valid. Beliefs can be caused and still be reasonable. . . .
>
> . . . Prestige and pecuniary gain may motivate scientists. Yet if the scientific community rewards the search for evidence and good theories with such commodities, then beliefs about evidence and so on can still drive scientific practice. Science will not be a mere social process. . . .
>
> . . . Suppose that in disputes over evidence we find that the most powerful scientists always win. It might nonetheless still be the case that those in power are generally *right*—that the social hierarchy on the whole plays a positive epistemic role. . . . So if scientific beliefs are produced by a social process, we can still ask how well that process promotes truth.

Beginning with Karl Marx, a number of scholars have argued that Darwin developed his theory of natural selection at least in part because of the brutal, dog-eat-dog industrializing capitalist society in which he lived. But even if true, this fact means little, because in the intervening century and a half overwhelming empirical evidence has led most biologists to the view that Darwin's theory is for the most part correct. Moreover, many sociologists have argued (e.g., Huaco, 1986) that conflict theory replaced functionalism in the sociology of the 1960s because of the tumultuous changes that were occurring in American society at the time. This is undoubtedly an important point, but we can still evaluate the merits of functionalism and conflict theory on purely empirical grounds.

But there is a more serious problem. The British sociologists of science and their epigones apparently have failed to see the profound irony and self-contradiction in their work. Here are sociologists who think of themselves, it seems, as scientists, but who are nevertheless committed to the claim that science cannot lay claim to objective truth. Here are people who are using science to make the claim that scientific ideas are social constructions rather than objective realities. Apparently it has not occurred to these sociologists to ask whether or not these ideas apply to themselves, and, if so, whether or not the ideas might be completely self-refuting (Laudan, 1982; Kincaid, 1996; Rule, 1997).[3] Indeed, social constructionist work on science has become even more cognitively radical rather than less (Mulkay, 1985; Gilbert and Mulkay, 1985; Woolgar, 1988; Latour, 1987).[4]

If one wants a sociological model of science, I would suggest that they look to the work of the historian of science David Hull (1988). Hull argues that science is indeed a social process, but it is the very nature of this process that has allowed it to be uniquely cumulative and progressive. Hull's view of science is essentially Darwinian. Science is an extremely competitive activity in which it is not nearly enough merely to be correct. One must vigorously promote one's own views, and survival in science generally goes to those who can stand the heat of conflict and competition with other scientists. Scientists, of course, do more than just compete. They often cooperate with each other by collaborating and by citing and discussing each other's work, but it is competition and conflict that are critical to scientific advance because only they give science a self-correcting mechanism. Aggressive and highly biased scientists are confronted by other equally aggressive and equally biased scientists, but whose biases are often profoundly different. As Hull (1988:321) has remarked, "The self-correction so important in science does not depend on scientists presenting totally unbiased results but on other scientists, with different biases, checking them." As a result, prolonged battles ensue in which better concepts and theories gradually win out over poorer ones.

Constructing Large-scale, Long-term Social Change

David Maines (1988) and Stanford Lyman (1984) have told us that symbolic interactionism has clear relevance for macrosociological theorizing and that it is wrong to label it as a strictly microlevel theory. Although they greatly overstate their case, they do have a legitimate point. Two of the best-known macrosociological applications of symbolic interactionism are found in the work of Herbert Blumer (1990) and Carl Couch

(1990), and these works are about as macrosociological as one can get. Blumer has attempted an interactionist understanding of industrialization in the modern world. Sociologists have, from virtually the very beginning of the discipline, been keen to separate the industrial from the preindustrial world and to identify the most important changes in social order that have occurred in the wake of industrialization. Blumer, it seems, objects to this whole line of inquiry, and repeatedly claims that industrialization in itself has not led to the many changes sociologists have associated with it. Industrialization, he says, has not been the causal force that has been claimed for it. Moreover, industrialization has been associated with many different lines of social development rather than with just one. He tells us that "a careful evaluation of the evidence forces one to the conclusion that industrialization is essentially neutral and indifferent to the character of the social happenings that follow in its wake. While industrialization clearly lays the groundwork for extensive social change, it does not determine or explain the particular social changes that take place" (Blumer, 1990:58). There is great variation, he says, in the social composition of owner, managerial, and worker groups, and there are many different forms of social relations that are associated with industrialization. What accounts for these divergent outcomes? Why, the process of social construction, itself an indeterminate force. We are repeatedly told that we must study how people enmeshed in social groups interpret the meaning of what is happening around them. For example, "Of much more importance than the makeup of the situations introduced by the industrializing process is *the way in which the situations are interpreted and defined* by the people who have to act in them. The definition and not the situation is crucial" (1990:121; emphasis added).

Blumer is right to an extent. Industrialization has not been associated with completely uniform outcomes in the organization of social life in all societies. For example, the Scandinavian countries and the Netherlands have much larger and more comprehensive welfare states than England and the United States, and the United States has remained a much more religious society than most other industrial societies. And often industrialization has been mistakenly identified as a cause of certain changes when in fact something else, related to industrialization, has been responsible. Nevertheless, industrialization has been associated with much greater uniformity in social life than Blumer is willing to acknowledge. Industrial societies differ in many crucial respects from large-scale agrarian societies (their immediate predecessors), and compared to agrarian societies modern industrial societies are remarkably alike. For example, they have very similar class structures and family arrangements; they all have systems of mass education, and even though these differ in some important respects, nothing even remotely like them was found in the preindustrial world; and without exception, they all have a parliamentary democratic mode of government, a type of government virtually never found in any preindustrial society (with ancient Greece and Rome being the only exceptions, and even then only partially) and absent from the majority of the less industrialized world. It would appear as though people in industrial societies have been responding in very similar ways to—making very similar social constructions about, if you like—the industrialization process. But not only does Blumer not wish to generalize, he does not wish to find any determinate forces lurking about anywhere. The process of social construction is an essentially arbitrary and indeterminate one with respect to the meaning of industrialization just as it is with respect to other social phenomena.

Lyman and Maines boast of Blumer's macrosociological applications of symbolic interactionism but, to be candid, I have difficulty seeing why. Blumer's theoretical insights into macrolevel phenomena are even thinner than his very limited insights at the micro level. But Carl Couch, in his *Constructing Civilizations* (1990), takes symbolic interactionism to a new nadir. Couch covers a much longer period of historical time than Blumer, for he wishes to understand social evolution over the past 10,000 years, and especially the rise of civilization beginning around 5,000 years ago. Couch talks just like Blumer. Even though social evolutionists have focused considerable attention on the evolution of technology and its determinate effects on the evolution of social life, Couch informs us that he will ignore this. Tools have no meaning in and of themselves; their significance has to be socially defined. Even though he is very interested in the rise of civilization, Couch informs us that he will not define it or even attempt to list its traits, for such an exercise is of dubious merit. Apparently you don't have to know what it is you are talking about in order to talk about it. Or, alternatively, Couch knows a civilization when he sees one even though he cannot (or will not) share that information with others.

The basic theoretical argument that can be found in Couch's book is the incessantly repeated refrain that social life is a human construct. The book is largely a descriptive account, drawn from anthropologists, archaeologists, and historians, of the main lines of social evolution. Couch depends on the arguments and data of social evolutionists, and he frankly admits that the rise of civilization was an evolutionary phenomenon. My view exactly (Sanderson, 1990, 1995b, 1999), but one not exactly compatible with social constructionism. For the most part this book could have been written in essentially the same way without using any theoretical perspective at all. Couch gets a fair amount of the story of long-term social evolution right, but many important pieces of the story are missing and Couch is often badly out of date and out of touch with the most important literature, which is not surprising for someone using a theoretical perspective that is totally unsuited to the study of social evolution. Perhaps these things are best left to specialists.

There is an extremely large literature on social evolution (much of it reviewed in Harris, 1968, and Sanderson, 1990, 1995b, 1999), and one of the most striking features of this literature is that it demonstrates the existence of remarkably parallel lines of social transformation all over the world over the past 10,000 years. If social evolution is a social construction, then humans everywhere have been arriving at markedly similar constructions. This can only suggest that these constructions have been subjected to markedly similar constraints. Social evolutionists have written hundreds of thousands if not millions of pages in their attempts to identify these constraints, but they are obviously of no interest to Couch.

NOTES

1. For a discussion of the work of several of the most important symbolic interactionists, see Stryker (1980:chapter 4). Important symbolic interactionists not discussed by Stryker are

Norman Denzin (1969, 1987, 1989), Howard Becker (1963, 1982), and Anselm Strauss (1959, 1975; Glaser and Strauss, 1965). Gary Alan Fine (1990) tries to show how broad the symbolic interactionist umbrella is and how open it is to merging with other theoretical perspectives. Jeffrey Alexander (1987:chapter 13), in a useful discussion, has distinguished four strands of symbolic interactionism. One of these is associated with the work of Erving Goffman. Although most sociologists have treated Goffman as a symbolic interactionist, this position has been strongly challenged by Randall Collins (1981, 1988, 1994). Collins sees Goffman as following more in the tradition of Durkheim and his emphasis on social rituals. I suspect Collins may be right, but I take no strong position on this matter. Probably the reason why Goffman is treated as a symbolic interactionist is not his way of explaining or thinking about the social world, but rather what he has studied: microlevel interaction. Still, Goffman's works sound a lot like the symbolic interactionists' works in their focus on what might be called the "inner world" of human groups and the details of ordinary life and face-to-face interaction.

There is yet another way of interpreting Goffman, and this is as a sociobiologist. Let me try to defend this heresy. Goffman was influenced by some of the work in human ethology that was carried out in the 1950s and 1960s, making use of such important ethological concepts as dominance and releasing stimuli, which he borrowed from Konrad Lorenz (Salter, 1995). Jerome Barkow (1989:74) comments that in Goffman's classic *The Presentation of Self in Everyday Life* (1959) there "is an image of human behaviour and motivation entirely consistent with sociobiological expectation. Here is the individual enormously concerned with how others view him/her, utterly preoccupied with self and with staging dress and appurtenances so as always to appear in the best possible light (to fall into Goffman's dramaturgical metaphor). Far more than does any sociobiologist, Goffman accentuates the negative." In Goffman's work we find people very concerned with their status relative to others, attempting to inflate their own status in other's eyes while at the same time deflating the status of these others in their own eyes. This preoccupation with status and social rank is one of the most fundamental themes in all of sociobiology.

I have long thought that the main reason for Collins's admiration of Goffman and his liberal use of Goffman's ideas is because Goffman gives us a microlevel conflict theory that fits hand in glove with Collins's own macrolevel conflict theory. However, both conflict theories mesh very well with the most basic claims of sociobiology, as I will try to show in a later chapter.

2. An excellent explication of Garfinkel's ethnomethodology has been written by Heritage (1984). Attewell (1974) provides a useful analysis and critique of the first main wave of ethnomethodology after Garfinkel. A highly accessible account of the development of ethnomethodology, some of its most important applications, and a defense of it against criticisms can be found in Sharrock and Anderson (1986). Richard Hilbert (1992) tries to show that the major concerns of ethnomethodology were already present in the classical sociology of Durkheim and Weber.

3. An extremely clever critique of the social constructionist view of science has been written by Randall Collins (1992). This critique shows vividly how the constructionist view of science is self-undermining, and Collins's arguments can be extended to social constructionism in general.

4. Ultimately, the social constructionist view of science converged with postmodernism. I discuss postmodernist views of science in chapter 3.

3

Structuralist, Poststructuralist, and Postmodernist Explanations

STRUCTURALIST EXPLANATIONS

Basic Principles

The school of social thought known as structuralism arose early in the twentieth century among linguistic theorists and was first incorporated into the social sciences by the French anthropologist Claude Lévi-Strauss. Lévi-Strauss's first major book was *Les Structures Élémentaires de la Parenté*, published in 1949 (and translated into English in 1969 under the title *The Elementary Structures of Kinship*—Lévi-Strauss, 1969a).[1] This was a long and dense book that strongly revealed the influence of Durkheim. In this work Lévi-Strauss described a variety of patterns of marital exchange in which kinship groups exchanged marriage partners in structured ways. He explained these exchanges in a double way, both functionally by means of how marital exchanges led to higher levels of social integration, and structurally by means of cognitive oppositions people carried around in their minds. I shall defer further analysis of Lévi-Strauss's theory until chapter 13, when the whole issue of marital exchange in human societies is discussed.

Lévi-Straussian structuralism is rooted in the idea that society is a kind of language or "text," and as such has to be read or decoded. It is a kind of "code" that has to be cracked. This code or text is a "totality" that has its own underlying logic, and it must be understood as a logically organized whole. Lévi-Strauss holds that the structure of society is underlain by a series of *binary oppositions,* or pairs of sharply contrasting ideas, and he argues that there is a fundamental tendency for the human mind to think in terms of these oppositions. Such oppositions are almost limitless, and include such obvious ones as up:down, right:left, inside:outside, earth:sky, male:female, ours:theirs, and so on. For Lévi-Strauss, the anthropologist's job in analyzing any culture is to figure out the basic binary oppositions that underlie that culture and serve as the basis for it. Since societies are integrated wholes or unities, the binary oppositions underlying any society must be systematically linked, and one of the tasks of the anthropologist is to ascertain what these links are.

41

What determines the particular binary oppositions that are of greatest significance in any society? It is hard to avoid the conclusion that this is an entirely arbitrary process. C.R. Badcock (1975:64), however, warns us against this conclusion, saying that "binary opposition is not totally arbitrary. It is not the gratuitous creation of the mind because the mind, being natural, obeys laws similar to those which determine the overall shape of things in general." Nevertheless, one looks in vain in the writings of Lévi-Strauss or of any other structuralist for even the slightest hint at the natural laws that might determine how the mind works in any particular time or place.

Critical Assessment

What can be made of structuralist theorizing? I suggest the following difficulties:[2]

1. Structuralism seems to give some sort of magical quality to the number 2, arguing that humans have a fundamental tendency to think in terms of pairs of opposites. Actually, there may be a lot to this. Consider, for example, such oppositions in sociology as functionalism:conflict theory, biological:cultural, structure:agency, and determinism:voluntarism. However, there is nothing sacred about the number 2 in human thought. Hegel thought that humans had a tendency to think in terms of three ideas: thesis, antithesis, and synthesis. Parsons formulated a three-way distinction among culture, social system, and personality, and we also have Wallerstein's famous distinction among core, periphery, and semiperiphery. Thus, even though binary thinking may be a major part of human thinking, nonbinary forms of thought must certainly be given their due.

2. Even if we grant that thinking in terms of pairs is the most fundamental pattern in human thought, there is still the problem of demonstrating that this tendency is the actual basis for culture and social organization, i.e., that it is of causal significance. The structuralists do not really offer any evidence to show that this is the case. And not only is structuralism difficult to verify, it is also difficult to falsify, for any reasonably intelligent and imaginative person can always think of a range of binary oppositions that might be posited to underlie some social or cultural pattern. If it can be shown that the argument for one particular binary opposition is false, another one can always be constructed. Indeed, binary oppositions can seemingly be constructed ad infinitum and ad nauseam. The structuralists, Lévi-Strauss in particular, seem to have deliberately placed themselves beyond the bounds of science, and in fact seem to reject science on epistemological grounds.

3. Structuralism has shown itself to be concerned with an extremely narrow range of social reality, mostly myth and other symbolic systems. It has had almost no concern at all with most of the major issues taken up by many of the greatest social scientists from the middle of the nineteenth century until the present. Stanley Diamond (1974:299), for example, points out that Lévi-Strauss's work has avoided "all mention of social processes such as exploitation, alienation, the extreme division of labor, modern war, [and] the character of the state, as sub-

jects worthy of complete attention." Like virtually all French social theory, the preoccupation of Lévi-Strauss and other structuralists has been overwhelmingly with the cognitive and the symbolic.

4. Perhaps most seriously, structuralism gives us an even more reified picture of social reality than functionalism. The origins of functionalism and structuralism are largely the same, as both spring from the classic work of Durkheim (Harris, 1968; Maryanski and Turner, 1991). Individuals are just as absent in structuralism as they are in functionalism. Structuralists might protest that it is individuals who formulate mental codes, but they certainly do not do so as genuine human agents. For Lévi-Strauss, it is not particular minds that create binary oppositions, but rather the universal human mind as an abstraction, and individuals seem to be prisoners of this abstraction. The mind has a logic of its own, and individuals are only the bearers of this logic. As Anthony Giddens (1987) has pointed out, in structuralism (as well as in its successor, poststructuralism, as we shall see) we have a form of social theory that involves "history without a subject." In Giddens's (1987:87–88) words, "Lévi-Strauss observes in a celebrated statement that he claims to show 'not how men think in myths, but how myths operate in men's minds without their being aware of the fact'; . . . There is no 'I think' in this characterization of the human mind. The unconscious categories of mind are the constitutive backdrop against which sentiments of selfhood exist. Consciousness is made possible by structures of mind not immediately available to it." Indeed, Ino Rossi (1974) does not call his edited book on structuralism *The Unconscious in Culture* for nothing.

Many more criticisms could be added to these. For example, Lévi-Strauss frequently compares himself to Marx, actually arguing that what he and Marx were doing was quite similar. Marx's significance, according to Lévi-Strauss, lay in recognizing and attempting to understand the existence of a deep structure that lay below the surface structure of social reality. This can only be regarded as an extremely peculiar interpretation of Marx, to say the least. Lévi-Strauss also argues that, like Marx, he himself is concerned with the impact of technoeconomic structures on other features of social life. Here we have a claim for structuralism that simply lacks all credibility. If there is anything that does not figure in structuralist explanations, it is the causal role of technology and economics.

Some Substantive Theories

The best way of evaluating structuralism, or any other theoretical strategy, is to examine the degree of success of its applications to actual social phenomena. How well do structuralist explanations actually work in explaining concrete social reality? Marvin Harris (1968, 1979) argues that they do not work at all and provides a lengthy discussion of several examples. Here I focus on three dismal structuralist failures, but many more could be added.

One of the more fascinating of Lévi-Strauss's structuralist explanations is his discussion of cannibalism. Lévi-Strauss makes a distinction between two kinds of cannibalism, exocannibalism and endocannibalism, and argues that each should be associated with a distinctive pattern of cooking. Exocannibalism occurs when people eat members outside of their own group (kinship group or tribe), whereas endocannibalism involves the eating of the members of one's own group. Lévi-Strauss creates the following linked oppositions: exocannibalism:endocannibalism::nature:culture::roasted:boiled. According to these linkages, exocannibals should roast human flesh, whereas endocannibals should boil it. Why? Because roasting involves cooking meat directly over a flame, whereas boiling involves some sort of pot, and since a pot is a cultural invention boiling has to be like culture, and roasting is like nature because it involves direct contact between meat and fire. Since culture is superior to nature, boiling is therefore superior to roasting. There is actually another hidden binary opposition in here, them:us; this gives us the linkage them:us::exocannibalism:endocannibalism. "Us" is superior to "them," and therefore endocannibalism will be superior to exocannibalism; therefore, endocannibals should be boilers and exocannibals roasters. It is all a matter of the underlying unity of the various binary oppositions, which form an irreducible whole.

These assertions were tested many years ago by Paul Shankman (1969), who used evidence drawn from some sixty cannibalistic societies. Shankman found no support at all for Lévi-Strauss's assertions. Of the exocannibalistic societies, only ten roasted and fifteen boiled, and of the endocannibalistic societies nine roasted and only two boiled. These data not only disconfirm Lévi-Strauss's argument, but are actually the reverse of that argument (quite strongly so in the case of the endocannibals). Moreover, there were several other forms of preparing human flesh that were never considered by Lévi-Strauss, in particular baking and smoking. Eight of the exocannibalistic societies prepared human flesh exclusively by baking, as did two of the endocannibalistic societies. Another eight of Shankman's societies used more than one method of cooking, with yet another eight consuming the flesh raw at least some of the time. These results compel Shankman to conclude that (1969:65) "ideas that have great appeal may, in fact, provide little intellectual nourishment. Therefore, as appetizing as may be the theoretical morsels offered by Lévi-Strauss, let us examine them carefully, lest by consuming them whole we become victims of our own gluttony." Thus, as a scientific theory of cannibalism, Lévi-Strauss's is a total failure.

The sociologist Orlando Patterson (1982) has developed a structuralist explanation of another exotic cultural practice, the use of eunuchs as political officials in agrarian societies. These castrated men were often employed in agrarian civilizations in a variety of administrative tasks, some even becoming important military leaders. Eunuchs were found in Hellenistic Greece, the Roman Empire, China, Persia, Turkey, Byzantium, and Ethiopia, indeed in the majority of preindustrial states (Balch, 1986). Patterson reviews some earlier explanations of the use of eunuchs, but finds them all wanting, or at least incomplete. He notes that eunuchs were invariably held in low esteem: As a result of their castration they became incontinent and thus often urinated on themselves (which prompted the Chinese expression "stinky as a eunuch" as a popular term of abuse), and almost everywhere they were associated with obscenity and dirt. There is thus an extreme paradox: "How could persons who were considered such foul, miserable specimens have been allowed to associate with monarchs who were not just absolute but in many cases considered semidivine, heaven's proxies on earth?" (Patterson, 1982:321–22). The solution to this paradox, Patterson claims, is that it is the product of the binary oppositions holy:profane, immortal:mortal, and pure:filthy. The very greatness and divinity of absolute rulers called forth, in good Hegelian dialectical fashion, its opposite, and this opposite was that of the eunuch. The one required the other.

There is in fact a much simpler explanation of the widespread use of eunuchs in agrarian civilizations, one that is far preferable to the virtually unverifiable and unfalsifiable one proposed by Patterson. Lewis Coser (1964) and Stephen Balch (1986) note that eunuchs were often used by rulers to guard their harems. Were they castrated, then, to eliminate sexual relations between themselves and their master's many wives and concubines? Patterson argues that this was the least important reason why agrarian rulers employed eunuchs because eunuchs were still capable of gratifying the sexual desires of women. Yes, but they could not have intercourse with, and, most importantly, could not *impregnate* women, and thus were in no position to cuckold rulers. Both Coser and Balch point out that the use of eunuchs was far more extensive than as harem guards; indeed, in some societies that had eunuchs, such as Byzantium, harems did not exist. Coser and Balch claim that eunuchs came to be extremely useful to agrarian rulers because they could be counted on to be loyal. They could not have families of their own and were usually completely separated from their own families of orientation, never to return to them. This meant that they would not develop interests that would compete with those of rulers, and this made them ideal for certain roles. Balch puts it well (1986:277–78):

> Generally speaking, eunuchs were most liable to be employed in those positions having intimate access to the physical person of the ruler, posts in which the ruler had to have the utmost confidence in the loyalty of his servant. Thus in Byzantium, Turkey, and China, eunuchs managed the inner palace services (which encompassed such sensitive operations as the preparation of the sovereign's meals), acted as royal bodyguards and messenger corps, and kept custody of the ruler's personal possessions. Even supervision of the harem entailed more than the guardianship of female virtue; it also frequently involved the oversight and tutelage of the younger royal princes.
>
> In an era where the phrase "back-stairs intrigue" could usually be understood quite literally, household management and political responsibility were inseparable. Within this realm the eunuch had unsurpassed advantages.

Patterson is not unaware of these sorts of arguments, and even grants them a certain credence. But they do not constitute a sufficient explanation, he says, or even the most important part of the explanation. It is hard to see why he would claim this. Why would someone reject an explanation rooted in the hardheaded realities of human interests in favor of an explanation that in all likelihood can be neither verified nor falsified and that requires some gigantic leaps of faith? Is it because French intellectuals and their epigones think they appear smarter and more distinct from the educated layperson if they make an argument that is not only counterintuitive but that flies directly in the face of common sense? One senses that this is often the motivation for structuralist arguments and their enthusiastic acceptance by some.

The final structuralist theory to be looked at is one developed by Louis Dumont (1980) with respect to the Hindu caste system. It is Dumont's view that this system, whatever else it may be, is primarily a state of mind. The caste system, he says, "is above all a system of ideas and values, a formal, comprehensible, rational system in the intellectual sense of the term" (1980:35). Dumont does not wish to deny that caste is also a stratified system of power and wealth, but for him this is clearly a very secondary part of the system. What intellectual principles, then, does caste represent? For Dumont there is one primary principle, which is the binary opposition between the pure and the impure. Caste as a hierarchical system only makes sense in terms of this fundamental cognitive contrast, for the pure is superior to the impure. However, Dumont warns that he is not saying that the opposition between the pure and the impure is the actual *cause* of the caste system, or that he is even talking about causation. The opposition between the pure and the impure is not the cause of the various caste distinctions, but is merely their *form*. It is not at all clear what this is supposed to mean, but then again this is not the first time that we have seen the structuralists separate themselves from the epistemology of science in formulating and attempting to win acceptance of their ideas.

One is particularly struck by Dumont's statement that "it is not impossible, although it is hardly conceivable at present, that in the future the politico-economic aspects will be shown to be in reality the fundamental ones, and the ideology secondary. Only we are not there yet" (1980:39). I would suggest, as does Joan Mencher (1974, 1980), that in fact we are there. Although the caste system has traditionally been viewed as being based on a high level of harmony and social legitimation, Mencher sees it as being much like any other stratified system. She focuses in particular on the relations between the highest caste, the Brahmins, and the lowest caste, the Harijans or "untouchables." Harijans suffer not only from a stigmatized identity, Mencher claims, but are highly cognizant of this fact. Moreover, they are generally poorer than all other castes and possess the least amount of land for cultivation. She notes that in a sample of five villages in Chingleput district studied in 1967, 85 percent of the untouchables owned less than one acre of land; in another sample of eight villages surveyed in 1971, 94 percent of the untouchables owned one acre of land or less; and in the village in Kerala state where Mencher did fieldwork in 1971, no untouchable family owned more than one acre of land. Mencher points out that Harijans suffer from economic exploitation by wealthy landowners and that they are clearly aware of this fact. She says that (1980:291) "fear of oppression and the use of brute force has dominated people's minds and hearts much more than appears in traditional pictures of Indian village life." "If this is true now," she says, "one can easily imagine the situation of untouchables in the past, in a village dominated by one or two wealthy families."

The Indian caste system is unique in a number of ways and no one has yet been able to understand why this particular type of stratification system, with its unusually elaborate rules of etiquette and its thousands of subcastes, arose. This problem has seemingly baffled the best minds. However, in its broadest sense caste is much like any other system of stratification. Those at the top control resources and enjoy much more power, privilege, and prestige than those at the bottom. One does not need structuralism to explain this fact, nor does structuralism help us in doing so. Later we will see what sociological theories can help us understand the emergence and elaboration of systems of social stratification.

POSTSTRUCTURALIST AND POSTMODERNIST EXPLANATIONS

Basic Principles

Structuralism was the rage in France mostly during the 1950s and 1960s. In the 1970s and 1980s it came to be replaced by what was initially called *poststructuralism,* which literally means, of course, "after structuralism." Like structuralism, poststructuralism is a French product, although it has come to be disseminated much more widely than structuralism ever was. The leading French poststructuralists are Michel Foucault (1973a, 1973b, 1976, 1978, 1979), Jean-François Lyotard (1985), and Jacques Derrida (1978). All are philosophers rather than sociologists, although Derrida is also regarded as a literary critic. Their influence has been enormous, both in Europe and in North America. They have had an immense impact on the field of literary criticism, and a considerable one on the social sciences (anthropology seemingly most of all).

What is the difference between poststructuralism and what has been called *postmodernism?* It seems to be essentially this: Poststructuralism is a phenomenon confined to the intellectual world, whether philosophy, literary criticism, or the social sciences; postmodernism, on the other hand, is a wider cultural movement that includes poststructuralism as one part of it. Postmodernism involves art, architecture, and other aspects of symbolic and ideational culture (Harvey, 1989). In most of the recent critical literature by philosophers and social scientists on these movements, postmodernism seems to have become the term of choice and is basically used synonomously with poststructuralism (the label "POMO" has become a fashionable shorthand). Therefore, I shall use this term as well, although it must be understood that I am discussing only the intellectual side of this whole movement, especially as it has affected the social sciences. Postmodernism's most basic notions are essentially as follows (Denzin, 1986; Collins, 1988; Kellner, 1990; Seidman, 1991, 1992; Seidman and Wagner, 1992; Rosenau, 1992a, 1992b; Kuznar, 1997; Harris, 1995, 1999):[3]

1. *Society as a text.* Postmodernism continues the structuralist theme of society as a text that has to be "read" and "decoded," but it pushes this theme in a much more cognitively radical and relativist direction. Derrida was primarily interested in literary criticism and his influence has been greatest in this field. He argued that no literary text can be read in any sort of "objective" way. No reading is definitive or final, indeed, no reading can necessarily be said to be any better than any other. The most that can be done is to *deconstruct* a text—break it down and expose all of its features, especially its hidden assumptions and biases. When applied to the world of social theories, Derrida's notion forces on us a radical historical relativism. We cannot get beyond the notion of a theory of the social world as simply one view among many others. We cannot say whether one theory is right, or even necessarily better than another. Since there is no real way of evaluating or comparing theories in any objective sense, there is thus no way of deciding the "truth value" of any perspective. Lyotard continues this line of thinking by claiming that all thought is centered in different

"language games," and these language games are radically incommensurable. However, according to the postmodernists this should not be a cause for worry. Indeed, we should revel in this intellectual diversity and celebrate it.

2. *A refusal to privilege science epistemologically.* The extreme cognitive radicalism and relativism of postmodernism are extended to the epistemological distinction between science and other forms of knowing. Postmodernism argues that science is just one way of knowing among others and that it does not deserve the privileged position it has been given in Western thought. Science is only another form of talk or "discourse," and it has to be deconstructed like any other discourse. In fact, many postmodernists go even further and attack science as an oppressive feature of modern Western civilization that we should either get rid of or humanize. Science is often attacked for being highly patriarchal, for example, and it is often suggested that getting more women involved in science would humanize it and thus improve it (Harding, 1986; Keller, 1985). In the words of Steven Seidman (1992:54), "Science appears more and more to be a discursive and institutional strategy to impose and maintain a hierarchical order. The claim to epistemic privilege seems to be a tactic to exclude, silence, or otherwise disempower socially threatening or marginal groups." This idea was stated some two decades earlier by the best-known postmodernist of them all, Michel Foucault. In the tradition of Nietzsche, Foucault saw the will to knowledge as the will to power, and science was thus inextricably implicated in the desire of some to control the behavior of others.

3. *The rejection of metanarratives.* Inasmuch as postmodernism rejects the deeply imbedded idea that there can be such a thing as objective knowledge or "truth," it has been extremely critical of what it calls *grand narratives* or *metanarratives,* which are comprehensive theoretical systems that aim toward full-blown explanations of society as a whole. In sociology this would include such approaches as historical materialism, functionalism, or social evolutionism. These comprehensive systems of thought are seen as looking for something that is unattainable. The most we can ever hope for is "local knowledge," or extremely limited forms of knowledge of specific social phenomena that occur within very small periods of time. Moreover, even such local knowledge is still imbued with the social, historical, and cultural situation of the knower. All theories of the social world arise from and reflect the social and cultural contexts of the formulators of those theories, and thus there can be no such thing as objective or value-free knowledge. It follows that men will produce different theories than women, whites different theories than blacks, working-class people different theories than middle-class or upper-class people, gays and lesbians different theories than heterosexuals, Europeans different theories than Asians or Africans, and so on. Every theory bears unmistakably the stamp of the sociocultural position of its creator. All knowledge is knowledge from a particular perspective.

4. *Social constructionism as the preferred explanatory mode.* Although the postmodernists are extreme cognitive radicals and relativists, and as such are very skeptical about any truth claims, when they do offer actual explanations of social phenomena these are most commonly social constructionist in nature. In fact, many postmodernists embrace a form of social constructionism so extreme that

it might even make symbolic interactionists and ethnomethodologists wince. We will see clear evidence of this below.

5. *A political position that identifies with the oppressed against the oppressor and that calls for the radical reorganization of society.* Postmodernists have been strong advocates of the "multiculturalism" that has been sweeping across the land in recent years. This position is a form of cultural relativism that asks us to "celebrate" (a favorite word of postmodernists) cultural differences. All cultures are seen as having equal value and should be recognized as such. Most postmodernists seem to find social and cultural oppression everywhere and advocate radical steps to eliminate it. There is the patriarchal oppression of women by men, the racist oppression of blacks by whites, the sexual oppression of gays and lesbians by heterosexuals, and so on. Many postmodernists seem to regard the most fundamental and pervasive form of human oppression in all of human history as the oppression by Europeans (especially male Europeans) and their descendants of nearly all of the rest of the world. These postmodernists strongly repudiate this "Eurocentrism." A Eurocentric perspective is one that argues, or at least implies, the superiority of Western civilization over all others. For many postmodernists, the world economic, political, and cultural domination of the Western world over the past several hundred years has been the basis for Eurocentrism in social theory. Virtually all traditional Western thinking is now under attack by these postmodernists for this Eurocentrism, which is seen as being so subtle that it penetrates the thinking of most intellectuals without their even realizing it. Postmodernism therefore calls for a radical overhaul of Western thought, the center point of which is a massive revision of university curricula so as to acknowledge the pernicious things that Europeans have done in the world and to provide space for previously "silenced voices."

Critical Assessment

In response to these arguments, I submit the following criticisms (Rosenau, 1992a, 1992b; Kellner, 1990; Best and Kellner, 1991; Ritzer, 1997; Harris, 1995, 1999):

1. The postmodernist attack on science as a Eurocentric product of an evil West that has created a new form of oppression is completely wrongheaded in several respects. Postmodernist views of science are for the most part simply more cognitively and politically extreme versions of the social constructionist arguments discussed in the last chapter, and so all of the criticisms of social constructionism and science apply a fortiori to postmodernism and science. Science fully deserves its privileged epistemological position because its intellectual success has been vastly superior to that of any other epistemology.[4] Moreover, science has proved its epistemological superiority by its enormous capacity for technological application. The technological advances of recent centuries, and especially of the twentieth century, would have been absolutely impossible without science. As David Deutsch (1997:324) remarks, "We can fly, whereas for most of human history

people could only dream of this. . . . The reason why we can fly is that we understand 'what is really out there' well enough to build flying machines. The reason why the ancients could not is that their understanding was objectively inferior to ours." And if push came to shove I suspect that most postmodernists would acknowledge this. We could, for example, ask postmodernists if they visit the doctor or dentist, have their children vaccinated, or use a modern personal computer. I have little doubt that the answer will almost invariably be yes. Moreover, the hostility shown to science by many postmodernists on the grounds that it has done more harm than good is hardly supportable (Rosenau, 1992b). Postmodernists often associate science with capitalist exploitation, military body counts, racism, sexism, and Stalinism and Nazism (Harris, 1995). But it is not science that is responsible for these things, even if science may have been the basis for the technology that made some of these things possible (Harris, 1995). All of these things must be laid at the feet of politics, not science. Furthermore, modern science and technology have raised the standard of living enormously for the average person in modern industrial societies, and people now live much longer and much healthier lives than was the case only a century ago. This is not to say, of course, that the impact of science has been completely positive, but simply that on balance the effects of science have been far more beneficial than harmful.

2. Quite apart from its views on science, I would also severely challenge the extreme relativism of postmodernism. The analogy with language—that scientific theories are only incommensurable language games—is utterly false. Different human languages are not incommensurable at all. While human languages may not be 100 percent translatable into one another, their levels of intertranslatability are extremely high, probably on the order of 99 percent. Social theories are also highly intertranslatable and can be compared and evaluated. Furthermore, it is wrong to argue that historical and social context overwhelmingly determine the formulation and acceptance or rejection of social theories. Historical and social context do play a role, but that role is much less than what postmodernists imagine. For example, in two recent surveys of the theoretical thinking of sociologists and social theorists (Sanderson and Ellis, 1992; Lord and Sanderson, 1999) I have found that gender bears far less relationship to theory choice than postmodernism claims.

3. Although postmodernists portray themselves as extremely flexible thinkers who allow for all possibilities, I would like to suggest that they are in one very fundamental sense among the most rigid and dogmatic of thinkers. They seem to be implying that if an interpretation cannot be conclusively shown to be true—and with considerable justification they claim that no interpretation can—then the only alternative is complete uncertainty and undecidability. Apparently the postmodernists have not heard of probabilism, the view which asserts that, even though it may not be possible to claim certainty for a view, it is still possible to say that some views are much more likely to be correct than others because the weight of evidence is on their side. There are many examples of views that are obviously better than others. Copernican astronomy was better (more accurate) than Ptolemaian, Einstein's theory of gravitation was an improvement on Newton's, and Darwin's theory

No they're not
No they say
here is "perfect"

of evolution was better than Lamarck's (Weinberg, 1993). And what of objectivity? Even if complete objectivity in social analysis may be impossible, it is still possible to use objectivity <u>as an ideal</u> that can be approached. Some thinkers can be more objective than others. Postmodernists seem to be saying that if something is not perfectly knowable then it is not knowable at all, or that if someone is not perfectly objective they are not capable of objectivity at all. What kind of rigid either/or thinking is that? Their relative intolerance of political views other than their own is also clear evidence of rigid and dogmatic thinking, and it is no accident that post-modernists and their sympathizers are greatly overrepresented among leaders of the "political correctness" movement on American university campuses today.

4. To expand on this very last point, the postmodernists seem to politicize everything and find oppression everywhere (Himmelfarb, 1994; Gross and Levitt, 1994; R. Lee, 1992). To read the postmodernists, one would think that oppression in all of its varieties was invented in Europe in the sixteenth century. Dead white European males are blamed for everything. With the rise of Europe to economic and po-litical supremacy in the world after about AD 1500, there emerged slavery, colo-nialism, racism, and sexism, after which followed such forms of oppression as those based on sexual orientation. Never mind that colonialism precedes European ad-vance by several millennia, that slavery has been found all over the world for thou-sands of years (including in the very societies that contributed Africans to the Eu-ropean slave trade), or that sexism is an extremely common human institution. The root of all of these forms of oppression from the postmodernist perspective seems to be capitalism. Despite not being Marxists theoretically, many postmodernists sound like Marxists politically. But the postmodernists both exaggerate the extent of oppression and err by placing the blame on capitalism, as we will see in chapter 4. And what of the postmodernists themselves? Are they to be regarded as free of political and moral blame, as they appear to be suggesting? It seems not. As Marvin Harris (1995) and Anthony Giddens (1982) have pointed out, the inspiration for Foucault was none other than Friedrich Nietzsche and his "will to power," a con-cept that inspired the Nazis. Harris also notes that Jacques Derrida was a student of Paul de Man, who broadcast Nazi propaganda on Belgian radio during World War II, and that Derrida also championed the cause of another Nazi supporter, Martin Heidegger. As for Foucault himself, he apparently continued to frequent the San Francisco bathhouses in the early 1980s after he knew he had AIDS (Miller, 1992; Harris, 1995). Foucault has also urged us to "sing the praise of murderers." Harris concludes that in view of all these circumstances, "history provides little justifica-tion for postmodernists to claim the moral high ground for themselves" (1995:73).

They don't want the Moral High Ground

5. I save the most devastating criticism for last: the fatal flaw of radical self-contradiction. Postmodernists claim that there is no such thing as objective truth and that all grand narratives are unworkable and should be aban-doned. But what is postmodernism itself? Is it not a perspective that claims validity for itself as a worldview? Is it not, in fact, a rather grand system based on some extremely large and sweeping claims, actually a kind of grand narrative of its own? It is difficult to resist these conclusions, which, if valid,

Hypocracy is Ok for Postmodernists. You can only judge a theory within its own context.

[handwritten: O = 1]

[handwritten marginalia: And also Every reason]

lead to automatic self-destruction. Postmodernism is a (presumably objectively valid) perspective which claims that there is no such thing as an objectively valid perspective. If it is true that there are no objectively valid perspectives, then postmodernism certainly cannot be one, and thus there is no reason whatsoever for anyone to take it at all seriously. Pauline Rosenau (1992b:90) puts it perfectly (cf. Kellner, 1990; Harris, 1995, 1999):

> The post-modern view—there is no truth, and all is construction—is itself the ultimate contradiction. By making this statement post-modernists assume a position of privilege. They assert as true their own view that "there is no truth." In so doing they affirm the possibility of truth itself. Few post-modernists escape this dilemma, but those who try . . . relativize everything, including their own statements. They say even their own views are not privileged. They warn their readers that the views they express are only their own and not superior to the opinions of others. But even this relativist position, once stated positively, implicitly assumes truth. It assumes truth in the statement that what they are saying is not more veracious than any other position. There is simply no logical escape from this contradiction except to remain silent.

[handwritten: Systems try not using logic. Kant's Rhetoric]

As noted earlier, postmodernism's contribution to social theory is largely negative in the sense that it focuses on what we cannot and should not do rather than what we can and should do. Nevertheless, the postmodernists do theorize and offer explanations of various social phenomena. When they do, they most often engage in social constructionist arguments, but these arguments are usually extreme even by the standards of symbolic interactionists, ethnomethodologists, and other social constructionists. Let us look at some examples of extreme constructionist reasoning in the work of postmodernists.

Crime as a Social Construct: Constitutive Criminology

In chapter 2 we examined the deficiencies of the labeling theory of deviant behavior. This theory lives on in a much more extreme form that is identified by its advocates, Stuart Henry and Dragan Milovanovic (1991), as *constitutive criminology*. According to Henry and Milovanovic, constitutive criminology is a synthetic approach that draws on left realism, socialist feminism, poststructuralism, critical legal theory, the intellectual history of constitutive thinking, and discourse analysis. They specifically acknowledge indebtedness to the sociologists Bourdieu and Giddens, the ethnomethodological work of Knorr-Cetina and Cicourel, and the postmodernists Baudrillard, Deleuze and Guattari, Derrida, Foucault, and Lacan. The main arguments of constitutive criminology are:

- Crime and human subjects are codetermined through crime control ideology and its capacity to reproduce and transform.
- Discursive practices are the context for the structuring of crime and its institutions of control.
- Symbolic violence is the hidden ideological dimension of legal domination.
- Crime control agencies make use of sense data to construct meaning and sustain crime control institutions as relatively autonomous structures.

It is not completely clear what all of this means, but Henry and Milovanovic apparently intend to say that crime does not exist in and of itself as an objective reality, but rather is "created" by the powers of social control institutions in conjuction with individual agents (i.e., it is "coproduced"). In Henry and Milovanovic's own words (1991:307–8):

> Our position calls for an abandoning of the futile search for the causes of crime because that simply elaborates the distinctions that maintain crime as a separate reality while failing to address how it is that crime is constituted as a part of society. We are concerned, instead, with the ways in which human agents actively coproduce that which they take to be crime. As a signifier, this perspective directs attention to the way that crime is constituted as an expansive and permeating mode of discourse, a continuously growing script—a text, narrative—whose writers are human agents.

The authors appear to be saying that crime only exists because we talk about it, and thus the "solution" to the "problem" of crime is simply to deconstruct or deconstitute it. We should stop talking about it, dramatizing it, and recording it. We should withdraw energy from it and deny its existence as an independent phenomenon. To do this is to challenge the structures of domination that constitute crime.

It is hard to know whether Henry and Milovanovic are serious or are putting us on. Do they really believe that crime has no objective existence and that it would disappear if we, ordinary citizens and control agencies alike, stopped talking about it or recording it? And doesn't talking about it and recording it imply that there is an "it" to be recorded. They say that crime exists because "agents act out criminal patterns," because some individuals "seek to control criminal behavior," and when social scientists "research, philosophize about, and explain crime." But again, all this seems to imply the realist and objectivist ontology that Henry and Milovanovic are at such pains to deny. Henry and Milovanovic themselves are certainly continuing to "philosophize about" crime. Ronald Akers (1997) notes that the authors seem to be recommending the complete abandonment of criminology since they not only fail to offer a testable theory of crime but reject the notion that such an entity could ever exist. Constitutive criminology perpetuates the problems of Becker's labeling theory discussed earlier and then some. Henry and Milovanovic subtitle their article "The Maturation of Critical Theory." If this is a mature critical theory, I think I prefer a more immature one, or perhaps a mature theory of a noncritical variety.

[handwritten marginalia: More laws Make More criminals]

Constructing and Deconstructing (but Not Reconstructing) the Past

Postmodernism has had a major impact in anthropology, including in its subfield of archaeology. Postmodernist archaeology is more specifically known as *postprocessual* archaeology, and is represented by such archaeologists as Ian Hodder (1990, 1991) and Michael Shanks and Christopher Tilley (1987a, 1987b). The fundamental argument of postprocessualism is the cognitively radical claim that there is no objective past; there is the past (or pasts) only as it is (they are) constructed by active human subjects. This claim is linked to a radical antiscience stance and to a radical political position. Archaeology as it has been practiced in recent years, especially the so-called *processual* archaeology of the 1960s and 1970s, has been dominated by a misguided search for laws and has been the basis for the oppression of subordinated and marginalized groups. Hodder distinguishes between "established" and "alternative" ideologies and characterizes them as follows (1991:166):

> By "established" I mean the archaeology written by Western, upper middle-class, and largely Anglo-Saxon males. The three "alternative" perspectives I wish to identify as having an emergent impact on the largely non-critical establishment position, are indigenous archaeologies, feminist archaeology, and working-class and other perspectives within the contemporary West. In all these instances, two points can be made: first, the past is subjectively constructed in the present, and secondly, the subjective past is involved in power strategies today.

As Richard Watson (1990) has pointed out, Shanks and Tilley argue that all theories are incorrigibly tainted by the political interests of the theorists, that an objective understanding of the past is impossible, that humans act intentionally and freely, and that social life in both the present and the past is a conceptual and linguistic production. They follow the perspective of idealist antiscience that leads from Heidegger to Derrida. The past is constructed rather than discovered, and there are at best only local and politically motivated conceptions of truth and falsehood. In Shanks and Tilley's (1987b) own words, "Anything 'discovered' about the past is not a passive reflection of what the 'facts' may or may not tell us. Archaeological texts which re-present the past have an expressive, rhetorical and persuasive purpose. They are not, and cannot be, neutral expositions of facticity of the past" (1987b:205; cited in Watson, 1990). Shanks and Tilley are also resolutely anticapitalist and see traditional archaeology as supporting capitalism. They tell us that it "is quite evident that the past may be used for expressing a wide variety of supportive ideas and values for capitalist society, naturalized and legitimized through an emphasis on tradition and long-term time scales: myths of genius; individuality; patriarchy; humanity's essential economic nature; the universality and inevitability of technological development as progressive; the naturalness of social stability as opposed to contradiction; the inferiority or superiority of certain forms of social organization, etc." (1987b:205; cited in Watson, 1990).

Persuasive critiques of postprocessualism have been written by Earle and Preucel (1987), Harris (1991), and Watson (1990). Watson accuses Shanks and Tilley of deliberate misinterpretation, inconsistent and fallacious arguments, rhetorical tricks, and overall intellectual dishonesty. These criticisms apparently do not bother them, Watson notes, because for Shanks and Tilley notions of intellectual honesty and dishonesty are illegitimate "totalizing categorical schemes." Watson also points out that Shanks and Tilley's own arguments—and, I would add, all social constructionist and postmodernist arguments—are ultimately self-defeating. If the past does not objectively exist and is just a social construction, then Shanks and Tilley's own archaeology must be just another social construction with no objective validity and thus no reason for anyone to take it seriously. In discussing Hodder's work, Harris (1995) notes that Hodder in recent years seems to be retracting some of his more extreme views, admitting, for example, the necessity of a "guarded objectivity." According to Harris (1995:65–66), "Hodder makes this slippery concession . . . for a most practical reason. He has come to realize that he has to have some means of preventing archaeology from being taken over by 'creationists, looters, metal detector users, and other fringe archaeologists.' . . . If truth and knowledge are contingent and multiple, he might end up undermining the subordinate groups that he wants to help and lose his job to boot. After all, if fiction is the outcome of science, why shouldn't creationists, looters, and metal detector users be put in control of Cambridge's Archaeology Department?"

Watson comes to the conclusion that, if we pay attention to what they do rather than what they say, Shanks and Tilley are actually doing science themselves, however covertly. They are, for example, stating lawlike generalizations about how material goods are spatially related to grave sites. And, indeed, to practice archaeology scientifically makes the greatest of sense. Since the 1960s there has been a revolution in archaeology in which an enormous amount of information has become available about cultures from all over the world over the past 10,000 to 12,000 years. This information has been extremely useful in telling us that societies have evolved along parallel lines in many parts of the world throughout this long period of time. This is especially so in regard to the Neolithic Revolution that began approximately 10,000 years ago, as well as with respect to the rise of the state beginning some 5,000 years ago (Harris, 1968, 1979; Sanderson, 1999). Lawlike generalizations can be and have been made about the processes involved. If the past is a construction, then it has been a remarkably uniform one throughout world history and prehistory, which can only mean that social constructions are not arbitrary but occur within the context of definite constraints.

A Queer Kind of Sociology

The most recent strand of thought to emerge from postmodernism is what is known by the unseemly name of *queer theory*. Its praises have been sung by, inter alia, Arlene Stein and Ken Plummer (1994) and Steven Seidman (1996). Stein and Plummer note that queer theory began as an academic movement located in the most elite American universities in the late 1980s. These authors delineate four basic "hallmarks" of queer theory (1994:181–82):

> 1) a conceptualization of sexuality which sees sexual power embodied in different levels of social life, expressed discursively and enforced through boundaries and binary divides; 2) the problematization of sexual and gender categories, and of identities in general. Identities are always on uncertain ground, entailing displacements of identification and knowing; 3) a rejection of civil rights strategies in favor of a politics of carnival, transgression, and parody which leads to deconstruction, decentering, revisionist readings, and an antiassimilationist politics; 4) a willingness to interrogate areas which normally would not be seen as the terrain of sexuality, and to conduct "queer" readings of ostensibly heterosexual or nonsexualized texts.

The thick jargon (highly characteristic of postmodernism in general) makes it difficult to know exactly what this is supposed to mean, but the queer theorists seem to be saying something like the following: sexual identities and orientations are, like all identities and orientations, socially constructed and not given in the nature of things; social life is permeated, far more than has been realized, by sexual categories and meanings;

heterosexuals have dominated intellectual, social, and political life heretofore and thus "heterosexism" has shaped thought and institutions; intellectual, social, and political life need to be reinterpreted ("deconstructed," "reread") from the perspective of gays and lesbians; queer theory as an intellectual movement is driven by the political aim of restructuring society along "queer" lines.

Queer theorists apparently wish to go much further than earlier gay and lesbian identity movements. Politically, they want to "normalize homosexuality by making heterosexuality deviant" (Stein and Plummer, 1994:183). The problem with this argument is that, as noted in our discussion of social construction and human sexuality in chapter 2, in every known society (with one or two possible exceptions) heterosexuality is overwhelmingly the most common form of sexual behavior that people are engaged in. The queer theorists interpret sexual orientation as a pure social construction, which is not only improbable but impossible. No sexually reproducing species could have evolved whose sexual orientation was left to some sort of learning process, because such a species, even in the minimal form of only an individual organism or two, would be rapidly driven to extinction by heterosexually imprinted competitors. In chapter 11, I shall review some of the rapidly mounting evidence which suggests that sexual orientation is deeply wired into the human brain. Presumably the queer theorists would scoff at such evidence—sexual "essentialism" they would call it—but from a political standpoint they should embrace it. It is the best news gays and lesbians have probably ever had, because it challenges the notion that homosexuality is some sort of perverse choice made by willful social deviants. It is a major step toward eliminating the stigmatization of homosexuality.

In the intellectual world, queer theorists like Stein and Plummer hope to see queer theory transform sociology. They look forward to a rereading of major sociological works from a queer perspective. "What happens to Giddens's structuration theory," they ask, "if hetero/homo issues are brought into the foreground? How might *Street Corner Society* or *Learning to Labor* look if homo/hetero issues were placed at center stage? How would the work of a Smelser, a Habermas, or an Alexander look if they lost their heterosexual and heterosexist assumptions and placed 'queer' concerns in their frame of analysis" (1994:185). Stein and Plummer want to reread the sociological classics from a queer standpoint. And the point they say, quoting Michael Warner (1991:18), is "to make theory queer, and not just to have a theory about queers." I find this more than just slightly unsettling. None of the sociologists that Stein and Plummer refer to—Giddens, Whyte, Willis, Smelser, Habermas, or Alexander—has any particular concern for sexuality, and in this light it is extremely difficult to see how any of their works could possibly be called "heterosexist." Stein and Plummer would probably reply that the heterosexism is subtle, unconscious, and detectable only by a queer theorist. The problem I have with all this business is that it represents not only the forceful injection of politics into theory, but the making of theory into the slave of politics. Queer theory is also confrontational and highly polarizing with its absurd statement that it is heterosexuality that must be deemed deviant. It has become unfashionable to say so in an increasingly politicized discipline such as sociology, but politics is usually the kiss of death for theory (R. Collins, 1975; Horowitz, 1993), and queer theory, as well as its more general postmodern parent, are dripping with ideology from every conceptual pore. That alone should be serious cause for concern among social theorists who still adhere to the notion that theory is about explaining the social world.

A NOTE ON ECLECTICISM

Despite my rejection of postmodernism, it might be argued that the more moderate doctrine of eclecticism could still be embraced by sociologists as a general orienting perspective. How does eclecticism differ from postmodernism? Eclecticism is the open advocacy of the use of multiple theoretical perspectives in explaining social phenomena. Eclectics assume that all theoretical strategies have at least some usefulness and that none should be used exclusively. Postmodernism, by contrast, assumes a kind of radical skepticism regarding all theories, and on principle rejects the notion that *any* general perspective or grand narrative can be made to work. Eclectics do not object to general theoretical perspectives, grand narratives included. They simply object to the use of any general perspective to the exclusion of others.[5]

Some years ago I wrote a strong critique of eclecticism in sociology (Sanderson, 1987) that paralleled a critique of eclecticism in anthropology written somewhat earlier by Marvin Harris (1979:chapter 10). (Readers are encouraged to consult these discussions in order to get the full force of the objections, but a brief summary can be given here.) I have found eclecticism to be an extremely common outlook among sociologists. In a study using a representative national sample of American sociologists (Sanderson and Ellis, 1992), it was found that some 60 percent of sociologists endorsed eclecticism to one extent or another. In a more recent study of sociological theorists in Western societies (Lord and Sanderson, 1999), eclecticism was less common but still subscribed to by a healthy minority of respondents. One of the most common arguments in favor of eclecticism is that the only alternative to it is some type of dogmatism; in this view, eclectics are open-minded and noneclectics are closed-minded thinkers who refuse to consider any position but their own. This argument, though, turns out to be a red herring, and a particularly egregious one at that. Dogmatism is a matter of the style or structure of thinking, not its content. While those who advocate a single perspective may sometimes be dogmatic in their thinking, many others are not. It is not a question of whether one advocates a single perspective or not, but rather of the willingness of any perspective's advocate to show enough flexibility to consider the merits of other perspectives and to give up his or her own perspective if the evidence mounting against it becomes compelling. Indeed, eclectics themselves are sometimes quite dogmatic in their embracement and defense of eclecticism.

Another common argument made by eclectics is that it is only by the use of this kind of outlook that any degree of completeness can be given to sociological explanations. The assumption is that all perspectives are partial, and thus many must be used in conjunction if we are to be able to explain a large amount of social reality. There are at least two serious problems with this argument. The first is that it assumes in advance that any given perspective is necessarily partial. Although this is often true, theoretical strategies differ in just how partial they are, and it is still possible to argue in principle that there is (or at least can be) such a thing as a complete theoretical perspective. To know whether any particular theory gives only a partial understanding, or to know just how large or how small this partial understanding is, is a question that is best settled empirically. The matter should not be foreclosed on a priori grounds. A second problem is that the completeness of explanation is only one goal of science, and not the most important goal at that. Two goals that are more important than completeness are consistency and coherence. Another extremely important goal is parsimony. Sacrificing these goals in favor of completeness amounts to a serious misplacement of scientific priorities.

I argue against eclecticism on three major grounds. First, eclecticism forces us to sacrifice the aim of logical consistency in theorizing. As I noted in this book's introduction, this criterion of theoretical adequacy is the most basic, since if this goal is not met none of the others can be. It is almost always the case that at least some of the theoretical strategies that eclectics are drawing on have fundamentally opposing grounding assumptions and theoretical concepts and principles. Think, for example, of the simultaneous use of such radically different approaches as functionalism and Marxism, ethnomethodology and sociobiology, or, in anthropology, cultural materialism and French structuralism. The problems of consistency are bad enough when only two such perspectives are being used at a time, but imagine the level of confusion that is being generated if more than two are being drawn upon. Eclecticism, in other words, unavoidably leads to incoherent explanations.

A second major difficulty with eclecticism is that it violates the time-honored scientific aim of parsimony or simplicity. In the introduction I distinguished two senses of simplicity, which I called simplicity as economy and simplicity as unification. Simplicity as economy involves seeking those theories that require the fewest concepts and principles. Eclecticism directly undermines this scientific aim because, by drawing on different theoretical traditions, it expands rather than contracts the number of concepts and principles to be relied on. Simplicity as unification is the aim of developing theoretical strategies that demonstrate an underlying interconnectedness, unity, or coherence to the phenomena being explained. Developing theoretical strategies that meet the criterion of simplicity as unification means developing strategies that link the explanation to A to that of B, of B to that of C, and so on, rather than relying on separate explanations for each phenomenon to be explained. Eclecticism profoundly undermines the achievement of simplicity as unification because it treats the world not as simple and unified but as complex and disjointed. Eclectics may believe in an intelligibility to the world, but if so it is an intelligibility that is extraordinarily complex and diverse, one that has nothing in common with intelligibility as conceived by scientists like Darwin and Einstein.

Finally, the strategy of theory testing advocated by philosophers of science like Imre Lakatos (1970) and Larry Laudan (1977), that of comparative theory assessment, becomes impossible within the framework of eclecticism. Where eclecticism prevails, comparative theory evaluation cannot occur because the eclectic has already decided in advance that all theories are partially valid interpretations that should be used jointly rather than scrutinized for their relative merits. Comparative theory assessment means following an empirical strategy of "let the best theory win," but eclectics have already decided that there is no such thing as a "best theory." If one is not looking for such a thing, it is not likely to be found.

What, then, are the alternatives? In my view, there are three. The first and undoubtedly most common is the open-minded commitment to one basic theoretical strategy with the objective being to push it as far as it can possibly go. This is without doubt the most common approach of those sociologists who have commanded the most attention. Not only was it the practice of virtually all of the great classical sociologists, but it is clearly the aim of the greatest ones today. One thinks of Immanuel Wallerstein and world-system theory, Randall Collins and neo-Weberian theory, Pierre van den Berghe and sociobiology, Michael Hechter and rational choice theory, Marvin Harris and cultural materialism, and so on. We cannot see what a theoretical strategy can do until we test its limits. If it turns out to be less than a complete strategy, which it almost certainly will, then there are other options.

One of these options is what Laudan (1977) calls the simultaneous acceptance and pursuit of theoretical strategies. Acceptance of a theoretical strategy means taking it as being true, or at least a close approximation to the truth. However, one can pursue a strategy without making a commitment to its truth value. Pursuing a strategy means employing it as a guide to research on the grounds that it *might* be true. Simultaneous acceptance of one strategy while pursuing one or more others is not eclecticism, because the scientist is accepting only one theoretical strategy at a time. This orientation, however, can only be of provisional use; at some point, a decision has to be made either to give up on the pursued strategy or to accept it and reject the previously accepted strategy. Or, one can accept both strategies but try to blend them into some sort of synthesis. It is this option that I think is the best alternative to eclecticism. Synthesis differs in a crucial way from eclecticism. The latter is a mere mechanical juxtaposition of theoretical strategies, using one at one time and others at other times, or using several at one time to explain different dimensions of a phenomenon. Synthesis, however, means taking elements from several strategies and combining them in a novel way into a new strategy that is separate and distinct from its parents. Marx did this with British political economy, Hegelian philosophy, and French socialism. Harris did it with historical materialism, cultural ecology, and social evolutionism. And, as we shall see, I will be trying to do it with several theoretical approaches.[6]

NOTES

1. In addition to *The Elementary Structures of Kinship,* Lévi-Strauss's most important works are *Structural Anthropology* (1963), *The Savage Mind* (1966), *The Raw and The Cooked* (1969b), *From Honey to Ashes* (1973a), *Tristes Tropiques* (1973b), and *The View from Afar* (1985). Good explications of Lévi-Straussian structuralism are found in Rossi (1974), Badcock (1975), Kurzweil (1980), and Harris (1968, 1979). See also Maryanski and Turner (1991) and Collins (1988).

2. From the point of view of sociology or anthropology, some of the best critiques ever written of Lévi-Strauss are those of Marvin Harris (1968, 1979). See also Badcock (1975), Giddens (1987), Kurzweil (1980), and Collins (1988). Good critiques of Lévi-Straussian myth analysis are found in Harris (1979) and Thomas, Kronenfeld, and Kronenfeld (1976).

3.   See also Best and Kellner (1991), Dickens and Fontana (1994), Hollinger (1994), and Ritzer (1997). The Fall 1991 issue of *Sociological Theory* contains several articles advocating (as well as criticizing) postmodernism. The collection by Seidman and Wagner (1992) is excellent for explication, advocacy, and critique. David Harvey (1989) does an excellent job of describing post-modernism as an intellectual and artistic movement and "postmodernity" as a social and cultural condition of the late twentieth century.

4.   Excellent discussions providing sharp critiques of postmodern views of science can be found in Gross and Levitt (1994) and Sokal and Bricmont (1998). Sokal, who is a physicist, made a name for himself by writing a phony article intended as a postmodern critique of modern physics and submitting it to a postmodernist journal. When the journal published this con-trivance, thinking it a serious work, a minor scandal ensued, leading many to reiterate what they had thought all along: The postmodernists could not tell the difference between fact and fiction and did not particularly care if there was one. The article is reprinted in Sokal and Bricmont's book and the background to the article is discussed.

Sokal and Bricmont (1998:197–205) try to account for the extraordinary popularity post-modernism has enjoyed. They offer three reasons, the most important of which, in my view, is the political discouragement and disillusionment of segments of the political left. The authors also (1998:205–9) identify what they regard as the three most serious negative consequences of post-modernism: a wasting of time and energy in the social sciences, a cultural confusion favoring ob-scurantism, and a weakening of the political left. Sokal and Bricmont point out that the ludicrous ideas of the postmodern left tend to make the entire left, including its reasonable political ideas, look ridiculous.

5.   Eclecticism should be carefully distinguished from what might be called theoretical *plu-ralism*, which is the establishment and maintenance of an intellectual atmosphere in which scien-tists have full freedom to pursue their own ideas unhindered by scientific or political orthodox-ies. Despite rejecting eclecticism, I advocate pluralism to the strongest degree possible; science would be dead without it.

6.   It might be wondered why sociologists are so strongly inclined toward eclecticism. I see two reasons. For one thing, sociology has always had a very strong attraction for people who tend to see the world in relativistic ways, and relativism easily slides into eclecticism (indeed, the two are overlapping and highly similar). Eclecticism is also likely to be extremely common during pe-riods when there is a great deal of theoretical fragmentation, and this has been the case in sociol-ogy for over thirty years. When there are a large number of opposing and often hostile theoreti-cal camps, eclecticism is the path of least resistance taken by many sociologists in what they can only regard as very confusing times.

PART II

Sociological Explanations
That Work Better

4

Marxian Conflict Explanations

BASIC PRINCIPLES OF SOCIOLOGICAL CONFLICT THEORY

Since the 1960s sociologists have spoken of something they have called *conflict theory*, which for many replaced functionalism during the 1960s and 1970s. Initially the term seemed to be merely a more politically neutral one to identify a Marxian perspective, but for some sociologists conflict theory is broader than Marxism. The most prominent sociologist in this regard is Randall Collins. For him, the conflict perspective includes not only Marx and the Marxists, but also Weber and a number of other social theorists extending back to earlier times. Collins has laid out his version of conflict theory most thoroughly in his book *Conflict Sociology* (1975) and in an excellent article entitled "Reassessments of Sociological History: The Empirical Validity of the Conflict Tradition" (Collins, 1974). Collins describes the essence of conflict theory in the following way (1974:148):

> The basic stance of conflict theory was taken by Machiavelli. Its fundamental element is a capacity for naturalistic realism, for sustained periods of intellectual detachment from the rhetoric of popular controversy. Men follow their own interests; success breeds honor; power breeds ambition; morality is based on violence, but works best by deception, especially through the deliberate staging of dramatic gestures; mass support is useful in the struggle of elites, and can be manipulated by show, especially of the externals of religion. This line of analysis was advanced by Marx's sociology, which specifies the conditions shaping interests and conflicts, describes the resources that enable particular interests to dominate, and generalizes about the relationship between the ideological surface of public consciousness and the real events below. Parallel developments were made by the realism of modern historiography, by the German theorists of *Realpolitik* and of the conquest theory of the state. A sophisticated synthesis of these lines of thought with elements of Marxian sociology was accomplished by Max Weber, and applied to more limited topics of modern politics by Robert Michels and his successors.

I have tried to formalize conflict theory by reducing it to the following set of formal propositions:

1. Social life is primarily an arena of conflict or struggle between and among opposing individuals and groups. [Contrast this conception of social life with the functionalist notion that society is an organism whose parts work together for the good of the whole.]
2. Economic resources and social power are the primary things over which individuals and groups compete and struggle. [The Marxian brand will emphasize the former, whereas the Weberian brand tends to emphasize the latter: power struggles in their various forms.]
3. The typical outcome of these struggles is the division of societies into dominant and subordinate groups; this is the reality of social domination.
4. The basic social patterns of a society are heavily determined by the social influence of dominant groups. [This says that dominant groups have a much greater capacity to influence the structure of society than do other groups, and that they try to do so in order to realize their various interests. This is probably the most important of all the propositions listed here.]
5. Social conflict and struggle both within and between societies constitute powerful forces for social change.
6. Since conflict and struggle are basic features of social life, social change is both common and frequent. [Contrast this proposition with the functionalist notion that societies are equilibrium-seeking systems.]

It is important to have a clear understanding of the meaning of the term "conflict." It is often assumed that it always involves some sort of overt hostility, such as war, revolution, race riots, and the like. These are indeed important forms of conflict, but conflict theorists use the term much more broadly. The essential meaning of conflict here is *opposition of interests*. Individuals and groups are engaged in conflict whenever they are struggling for competing ends so that the gains of one party create losses for another party (or other parties). For example, in Marxian conflict theory, the capitalist class seeks profit, which it can only earn by the exploitation of the working class. It is also important to recognize that conflict theory does not focus simply on conflict. It is interested in explaining all aspects of social life, harmony as well as conflict, cooperation as well as competition. In conflict theory, conflict as a result of clashing interests is the explanans, and its explananda are wide ranging and diverse. I make this simple point because some sociologists have taken works like Lewis Coser's *The Functions of Social Conflict* (1956) to be exercises in conflict theory, when in fact this work focuses on conflict as an instrument of group integration. It is therefore an exercise in functionalism rather than conflict theory.

Let us now turn to the first strand of sociological conflict theory, Marxian conflict theory.

MARX AND CLASSICAL MARXISM

In his writings Marx developed both a general theory and a more specific theory. His general theory, developed in collaboration with his lifelong friend Friedrich Engels, has come to be known as *historical materialism*. (Marx and Engels called it originally "The Materialist Conception of History.") It was considered to be a general theory of human society and historical change. The specific theory, by contrast, applied only to the latest stage of historical development, capitalist society. My understanding of the essentials of Marx's general theory is fairly traditional. Marx and Engels divided all societies into two major components, *base* and *superstructure*. The base was the underlying economic foundation of all societies and the part on which the other parts of society rested and depended. The base consisted of forces and relations of production. The *forces of production* were those things vital to the process of economic production, including the natural environment and all of its features, but especially the level of technological development that a society had achieved. The *relations of production* were the social relationships formed by individuals as they entered into the process of economic production. These relations were fundamentally relations of *ownership* of the productive forces. Marx acknowledged that in the earliest and simplest societies the productive forces were generally communally owned, i.e., there was no private property or private ownership. But in later societies private ownership developed when a segment of the population claimed control over the productive resources and the right to use those resources as they pleased. The relations of production, when they were private, gave rise to *social classes*, and thus the class structure of a society was rooted in these relations. The forces and relations of production taken together yielded a *mode of production*, which was the economic base of society. The second major component of every society, the superstructure, consisted of everything not in the base, especially politics, law, consciousness, family, and religion. Marx especially emphasized politics and consciousness, and often referred to the superstructure as the "political and ideological superstructure."

What was the relationship between base and superstructure? For Marx and Engels, the base largely determined the superstructure, and therefore the particular characteristics of the superstructure were shaped by the particular features of the base. As the base went, so went the superstructure. The base-superstructure relationship also applied to historical change. The base would change first, and as it changed so the superstructure would be transformed. Superstructures and bases had to be compatible, so changes in one necessitated changes in the other. At one time much ink was spilled over the specific extent to which the base determined the superstructure, with some neo-Marxists in the 1970s and 1980s claiming that Marx saw the relationship between base and superstructure as more or less reciprocal. I do not think Marx ever intended any such thing. Marx acknowledged that there was no one-to-one relationship between base and superstructure, and that in some circumstances aspects of the superstructure could determine aspects of the base, but the main flow of causation was from base to superstructure.

As is well known, Marx joined this materialist understanding of society with Hegel's dialectic, a process in which change occurs as the result of internal contradictions. In

Hegel's case, these contradictions occurred within the realm of the human mind. Marx rejected Hegel's idealism but retained the dialectic as "the rational kernel within the mystical shell." Marx converted Hegel's dialectical idealism into dialectical *materialism.* The contradictions were not in the thought processes of humans, but in their modes of production. Contradictions tore modes of production apart, and changes in these modes of production necessitated changes in the superstructure. In this way societies evolved throughout history. Marx identified four major historical stages that societies have gone through, and one yet to come.

1. *Primitive Communism:* This was characteristic of early societies that lived by hunting and gathering, by the herding of animals, or by agriculture; these societies were technologically very primitive but communal rather than private relations of production prevailed.
2. *Slavery:* Slavery, sometimes called the ancient mode of production, was characteristic especially of such societies as ancient Greece and Rome. Technology was much more advanced, which was a genuine form of progress for Marx, but private relations in the form of masters and slaves had replaced communal relations. Society was now class divided.
3. *Feudalism:* This mode of production was characteristic of Europe from the fall of Rome until the early modern period, thus lasting for nearly 1,000 years. Class relations were based on feudal landlords and serfs; this class division replaced master-slave relations.
4. *Capitalism:* Capitalism began in a rudimentary way in the sixteenth century and began to take its classic form in the eighteenth century. Feudal relations of landlord and serf were replaced by relations between capitalists and workers. Society became urbanized and industrialized. Capitalists (the bourgeoisie) were the owners of the forces of production in the form of capital (technology, machines, buildings, money, etc.) and they subordinated a working class (proletariat) that owned nothing but their own labor power (their capacity to work), and therefore the workers had to sell this labor power to capitalists in the form of a wage in order to live.
5. *Socialism:* Socialism involved the overthrow of capitalist private property and the collectivization of ownership of the means of production. When socialism emerged triumphant, the old capitalist class structure would be destroyed and a new "socialist man" would replace the greedy and selfish members of capitalist society.

Marx assumed that this evolutionary process produced human progress and would culminate in a type of society, socialist society, without fundamental contradictions. Humans would gain true freedom here, which for Marx consisted of the equal opportunity of every person to realize his or her potential as a member of the human species. Marx thought that capitalism produced more freedom than previous societies, but that it was still limited to a small segment of the population. Socialism would produce true freedom for everyone.[1]

Now what of Marx's specific theory, his theory of capitalist society? Marx saw capitalism as an economic system with three essential characteristics: (1) private ownership of the means of production, which was devoted to (2) the production of goods for sale in a market with the aim being to realize the maximum profit and accumulate profit over time, and in which (3) an entire class of the population is paid wages in return for the work its members perform. The driving engine of capitalism, for Marx, was the *accumulation process*. Capitalists are driven by the desire to make the maximum profit, but also by the desire to reinvest a portion of that profit so as to expand the scale of their operations and accumulate capital over time.

By way of his famous theory of surplus value, Marx concluded that there is an inherent antagonism, an inevitable class struggle, between capitalists and workers. Capitalists can only achieve their economic objective, maximum capital accumulation, through exploitation, and yet at the same time workers are doing all they can to resist this exploitation. The more one group benefits, the more the other loses out. The inherent class antagonism of capitalism, for Marx and later Marxists, is at the very core of capitalist society, and plays a major role in shaping the features of that society.

NEO-MARXISM

Although Marxian theory was moribund among Western sociologists throughout much of the twentieth century, it came to be revived in Western Europe and North America in the 1960s and 1970s. A variety of different versions were created, some of which were quite critical of other versions. [2] Neo-Marxists assume, as did Marx, that it is the *class struggle* of capitalist society that is the key to understanding it. The class struggle is the root cause of all other forms of struggle or conflict within capitalism. As in any society, in capitalist society the superstructure rests on the base and is determined by it. The function of the superstructure is to stabilize the base by supporting the dominant class (i.e., ruling class) in its economic aims. The superstructure therefore must be compatible with the base. Marxism assumes that the design of the superstructure is influenced disproportionately by the dominant class. The most important parts of the superstructure are politics and ideology. Thus, the dominant class wants a political system and a broad set of social beliefs and values that aids it in achieving its economic objectives.

The key point is that Marxists see the nature of capitalist society as being shaped by the needs and demands of the capitalist class. They generally dislike capitalism (often intensely so) and blame what they regard as its many failures and problems on the capitalist class's pursuit of profit. This is perhaps the most prominent theme in Marxist sociological writing. This theme is directly associated with another prominent theme, viz., that the solution to the problems of capitalism are to be found in getting rid of capitalism and replacing it by socialism.

Some scholars, Marxists and non-Marxists alike, have asserted that Marxism is actually a form of functionalist social theory. By this it is meant that Marxism makes use of the Principle of Functionalist Explanation that is at the heart of the Parsons-Merton functionalist school, but that also may be found outside this school. Harris (1968), a non-Marxist, has referred to Marx as a "diachronic causal functionalist," and Albert Szymanski (1971:38), a prominent Marxist, claims that "Marx analyzed the major institutions of capitalist society in terms of the contributions they make to the social system of capitalism. He traced all major aspects of society to their relationship to profit maximization. Religion is interpreted as the opium of the people; the state as the managing committee of the bourgeoisie; the family as a replica in miniature of the greater society, etc." Szymanski goes on to say that contemporary Marxism is also functionalist, referring to Baran and Sweezy's *Monopoly Capital* (1966) as a thoroughly functionalist work. However, I beg to differ. Marx was not, and contemporary Marxists are not (with perhaps the partial exception of structural Marxists in the tradition of Althusser, which includes Szymanski himself—see note 2), using the Principle of Functionalist Explanation, appearances notwithstanding. Despite terminology to the contrary, Marxists are not looking at the effects of something on the capitalist *system*, but rather at their impact on the capitalist *class*. The Principle of Functionalist Explanation assumes that a social phenomenon is explained when its role in maintaining the larger society is identified. This is not what Marxists are doing. They are employing what I earlier termed functional analysis, which means explaining, within an overall conflict perspective, how a social phenomenon benefits particular individuals (alone or in the aggregate).

We are now in a position to state the central notions of Marxian theory, ideas that all or virtually all Marxists share. To my mind, they are:

1. *Materialism:* Nearly all Marxists see themselves as materialists, but there are some significant variations. In the 1970s and 1980s the idea became popular that Marx was not an "economic determinist," and that he gave a great deal of freedom of the superstructure to influence the base. Some so-called Marxists argued that Marx saw a two-way rather than a one-way relationship between base and superstructure. A few even gave up materialism for idealism, while still thinking of themselves as Marxists. I myself, however, regard Marx as a strong materialist (even an "economic determinist," if you like), and regard abandonment of this doctrine in favor of a two-way concept or any form of idealism as eviscerating the theoretical core of Marxism and thus killing it.

2. *Dialectics:* Nearly all scholars calling themselves Marxists accept this, and many Marxists seem to see it as an almost sacred concept.

3. *Class struggle:* All Marxists accept this as an essential tool for analyzing modern capitalist societies, and all class-divided precapitalist societies.

4. *The "evils of capitalism":* Virtually all Marxists, if not all, blame the capitalist class and its profit motive for all or at least most of the problems and difficulties of modern capitalist society.

5. *The superiority of socialism:* Virtually all Marxists agree that socialism—not necessarily any actually existing socialism, but at least some future form of socialism—will overcome most of the limitations of capitalism.

6. *The doctrine of the unity of theory and practice:* Virtually all Marxists regard intellectual life and political life as inseparable, and believe that political practice is absolutely essential. "Ideas for the sake of ideas" is thus unacceptable. Moreover, for most Marxists practice is to guide theory rather than the other way around.

CRITICAL ASSESSMENT

Before considering and evaluating a number of specific neo-Marxian theories, let us see what can be made of Marxism and neo-Marxism as a whole.

1. Because of its insistence that theory must be devoted to and informed by politics, it takes on a serious political bias. Let's face it: Marxists see what they want to see, and their intellectual conclusions are tremendously guided by this political bias. My view is an old-fashioned one: Social scientists should try to be as "objective" and "value-neutral" as possible, and politics should be informed by theory, not the other way around.

2. Marxism goes much too far in laying the blame for the many problems of modern capitalist society on the capitalist class and its incessant search for profits. Certainly some of the problems of modern society have their roots in the capitalistic profit motive, but the Marxists greatly overdo it in their emphasis on class domination. Capitalism certainly has some things to answer for, but it has also had some notable successes too, and Marxists are inclined to sweep these under the rug. Anthony Giddens (1981) mentions two in particular: creating a very high level of general affluence, and the establishment of liberal democracy. These themselves have their limitations, but their positive side cannot be overlooked. (In my *Social Transformations* [Sanderson, 1999:chapter 9] I give a fairly detailed balance sheet of what I regard as the positive and negative features of capitalism.)

3. Then there is the horrendous failure of Marx's predictions. Workers have not become more impoverished, but quite the contrary. The working class within capitalism is not revolutionary at all. Socialism has never emerged in the most advanced capitalist societies, but, on the contrary, in the most backward agrarian regions of the world, and it was the peasantry rather than the proletariat that was the revolutionary class. And since the late 1980s we are living in a world that is experiencing the "transition from socialism back to capitalism," the very opposite of what Marx predicted.

4. Marxists have a very strong tendency to romanticize the working class—seeing in it everything that is good and liberating—and socialism as an economic system. But actually existing forms of socialist society have been for the most part a disaster (Kornai, 1992; Courteois et al., 1999), and these forms give little reason for optimism about any future form of socialism. Indeed, looking at what is happening in Russia and Eastern Europe, China, Cuba, etc. today, what rational and objective person could any longer be a Marxist in a political sense? Even in the Third World, socialist societies have shown little developmental potential, and less-developed capitalist societies such as Taiwan and South Korea have performed much better. Capitalism has shown much more resilience than Marx ever anticipated, and it has solved many of its earlier problems. It has far more life in it than Marx ever imagined.

5. One of the things that has gotten Marxism into one difficulty after another is its unrealistic conception of human nature (Boshu, 1994). Despite its conflict

orientation, it assumes that conflict is socially created rather than natural. Humans are nonegoistic beings who are simply shaped by the demands of their society. What we need is a conflict theory that abandons this nonegoistic assumption in favor of one emphasizing that all humans everywhere naturally pursue their self-interests. We can get there partially with Weber, and cultural materialism and sociobiology, especially the latter, will take us further in this egoistic direction. The Marxist-oriented philosopher Peter Singer (1999:32) stresses the need for Marxists to shed their antipathy toward Darwin—their irrational fear of biology—and unite Marxism with Darwinism: "It is time to recognise that the way in which the mode of production influences our ideas, our politics, and our consciousness is through the specific features of our biological inheritance."

6. The Marxian theory of history, as an evolutionary scheme, is very seriously, if not fatally, flawed. Its stages of evolutionary development are seriously misidentified, and it greatly oversimplifies history by seeing it as the outcome of a dialectic of class struggle. Important factors, such as population growth and environmental depletion, are ignored as causal agents in historical change. One can find a much more adequate account of social evolution in the work of such modern anthropologists as Marvin Harris (1977), and my own *Social Transformations* (Sanderson, 1995b, 1999) attempts to formulate a general theory of social evolution that incorporates some of the insights of Marxian thinking but that is generally non-Marxian.

7. Anthony Giddens (1981) points out that there are three major forms of social conflict that are analyzed poorly by Marxism: *conflict between states, ethnic conflict,* and *conflict between the sexes.* Marx had an incredibly naïve, almost childlike, view of the state as simply (or at least largely) the agent of the dominant class. To a substantial extent it is, but it is much more than that. The state did not wither away under socialism, but in fact was strengthened. And Marx did not give any serious consideration to the international military role of states in the world order. With respect to ethnicity, ethnic conflict emerged far earlier than capitalism and is rampant all over the world, including in actually existing socialist societies. Although ethnic conflict may be significantly exacerbated by economic forces, there is more to it than that. And one of the modern expressions of ethnicity, nationalism, was never appreciated by Marx. With respect to gender conflict, male domination is far older than capitalism, and many social scientists regard it as a true human universal. Marxist theories of gender are some of the worst theories ever developed, what with their simplistic notion that the exploitation of women is rooted in class exploitation. In fact, women have fared far better under capitalism than under most types of precapitalist society.[3]

And yet it would be a grave mistake to be dismissive of Marxian theory, its serious deficiencies notwithstanding. Marxism has achieved a number of extremely important insights. Its materialist and conflict orientation is clearly moving us in the right direction. Class domination is a reality in modern capitalism, and in many precapitalist societies, and states are very significantly controlled by capitalists. Neo-Marxian theories such as Wallerstein's world-system theory give much insight into the inequalities of the world economic order, despite its limitations. And much of Marxism's theoretical foundation is in general right—the material base does largely shape the rest of society. Marxism's materialist orientation needs to be revised and built upon—I shall argue later that Marvin Harris's cultural materialism has proved to be a very useful way of accomplishing this—but it has pointed us in the right direction. And it is no doubt the case that capital accumulation is the driving engine of capitalist development and thus of the overall historical trajectory of modern capitalist society, indeed of the modern world as a whole.

Marxism also helps us to see that capitalism does contain contradictions that impede its functioning. Although capitalism has, at least partially, overcome these contradictions, Marxism shows us that the ultimate contradiction may prove too much. This is the ecological contradiction—capitalism's horrendous impact on the environment and its massive depletion of resources—which has already brought us near the brink of economic and ecological collapse (Meadows, Meadows, and Randers, 1992; Sanderson, 1999).

SOME SUBSTANTIVE THEORIES AND THEIR PROBLEMS

Marxism and American Education

In their celebrated book *Schooling in Capitalist America* (1976), the economists Samuel Bowles and Herbert Gintis developed a Marxian theory of the American educational system and its growth and expansion since the middle of the nineteenth century. Their starting point is a critique of the American educational system, which is informed by their notion of what an ideal educational system should be like. A proper educational system, they say, is one that promotes in students the development of all of their potentials and abilities. It would foster creativity, originality, and independent thought. But the American educational system falls far short of this ideal. It promotes conformity to dominant norms and values and indoctrinates rather than truly educates. Through this system, students are indoctrinated into celebration of the capitalist system and its associated institutions as the best of all systems.

Why does education in America take this form? The answer, according to Bowles and Gintis, is that it has never been an autonomous or independent institution. It has been hemmed in in its development from the very beginning by the surrounding capitalist system and the needs and aims of the capitalist class. It has been bent to the service of profit maximization and capital accumulation rather than to the intellectual needs of students. The most crucial part of Bowles and Gintis's analysis is what they call the *correspondence principle*. This principle asserts that the social relations of the educational world will mirror or reflect the social relations of the economy and the workplace. Just as the workplace is hierarchical or stratified, so is the educational system. The various levels of the total educational system function to prepare students for the roles they will eventually play within the capitalist workplace. At the bottom of the workplace hierarchy are jobs that stress rule-following and order-taking, with few opportunities being available for the exercise of independent thought. Within the educational system, students who do not get beyond the level of high school or, at best, community college, are fed into the workplace at this low level. The social atmosphere of the high schools and community colleges therefore is highly authoritarian in order to prepare their graduates for their workplace roles. At the middle level of the workplace hierarchy, dependability and commitment to the organization are stressed, and there is greater opportunity for the exercise of independent thought and decision-making. Most four-year public colleges and universities are feeding their graduates into this level of the workplace hierarchy. They are therefore less authoritarian than high schools and community colleges, and they give students more opportunity for the exercise of critical thought and intellectual independence. At the top level of the workplace hierarchy are jobs that require a great deal of independence and creativity. The educational level that corresponds to this workplace level consists of the elite private liberal arts colleges and the elite private (and some public) universities. These institutions are feeding their graduates into the workplace at this highest level, and therefore they must place great emphasis on intellectual independence, self-reliance, and creativity in their students.

Bowles and Gintis also take a historical perspective on the American educational system, looking at how it originated and expanded over time. They note that public primary education got its start in the 1840s under the influence of educational leaders like Horace Mann. This educational thrust corresponded closely to the American industrial revolution, and the two were not related by accident. As America industrialized, there was a critical need for capitalists to socialize the emerging working class in order to make it less recalcitrant and accept its role within the larger economic order. Bowles and Gintis pay particular attention to the composition of school boards in Massachusetts and claim that capitalists were overrepresented on these boards because they wanted to take a direct role in shaping educational life. They go on to trace out other major changes within American education, such as the expansion of the public high school in the late nineteenth century and the expansion of higher education shortly after the middle of the twentieth century. These changes, too, were said to be related to major transformations within the capitalist system.

Does this theory work? No, I believe it does not. At least five major criticisms can be launched against it:

1. Bowles and Gintis make the common Marxist mistake of blaming capitalism (and capitalists) per se for whatever they do not like about a society that happens to be capitalist, in this case the way the educational system is structured. It is simply a terrible oversimplification to blame the faults of the educational system on capitalists' desire for profit maximization. Mass culture and American anti-intellectualism may be bigger factors in explaining the boredom and dissatisfaction of students, both today and in earlier periods.

2. A closely related theme is Bowles and Gintis's claim that schools are hierarchical because the capitalist workplace is hierarchical. In actuality, it is probably far more accurate to say that hierarchies will develop in any organization beyond a certain size (Michels's iron law of oligarchy) (Murphy, 1988).

3. Bowles and Gintis seem to assume that education is something that schools have imposed on the working class against their wishes, but a great deal of evidence suggests that workers have vigorously sought education (Collins, 1979).

4. The causal link between the development of the educational system and indus-trialization seems highly problematic, because a very different situation has been found in other industrial societies. In England, for example, mass education began at least a century after the onset of industrialization, and in Germany mass education began long before industrialization. In Japan and in a number of Western European countries there was not the fit between the timing of the emergence of mass education and the timing of industrialization suggested by Bowles and Gintis for the United States (Boli, Ramirez, and Meyer, 1985). Moreover, Bowles and Gintis see the emergence of mass education as a predom-inantly urban phenomenon, but considerable evidence suggests that it began first in rural areas (Meyer, Tyack, Nagel, and Gordon, 1979).

5. The authors suggest that the long-run solution to the problems associated with the American educational system is the replacement of capitalism by socialism. Here again we see another of the classic arguments of Marxists, and in this case (as in so many others) it proves false. It is doubtful that a truly nonindoctrinative educational system is possible, but even if it were, the actually existing socialist so-cieties have been well known for their extremely indoctrinative systems. By com-parison with socialist educational systems, those in capitalist societies are remark-able for their high levels of openness and tolerance of critical thought.

In sum, it seems to me that Bowles and Gintis's treatment of education is sympto-matic of several of the most serious difficulties of Marxian sociological theory.[4]

Marxism and Racial Antagonism

Racial antagonism is a complex phenomenon consisting of any or all of the following mental or behavioral patterns: prejudice, racism, discrimination or exclusion, segrega-tion, and stratification. The two societies that have exhibited such phenomena to the greatest degree have clearly been South Africa and the United States. What has been called the *orthodox Marxist theory* of racial antagonism assumes that such antagonism is derived from the class struggle between capitalists and workers (Cox, 1948; Szymanski, 1976; Reich, 1977). If there are racial subpopulations within the working class, capital-ists can seize on this fact by attempting to divide the working class along racial lines. They can promote racial antagonism as a "divide and conquer" strategy that is designed to weaken the working class organizationally and thus cheapen its labor.

This interpretation of racial antagonism seems to me much too simplistic; moreover, it tends toward a kind of conspiracy theory: Evil men in high places plot behind closed doors to oppress and exploit a large segment of the population. Unfortunately, the ten-dency toward conspiratorial arguments is another weakness that is often found within Marxian theories. Fortunately, there is an alternative within the Marxian tradition. This is Edna Bonacich's (1972, 1979) *split labor market theory,* which might be called the "un-orthodox" Marxian theory because it deviates in a crucial way from a major Marxian as-sumption and it introduces the assumptions of rational choice theory into the argu-ment. Bonacich's theory assumes that racial antagonism is the result of the clashing interests of three social groups: capitalists, higher-paid labor, and cheaper labor. Higher-paid and cheaper labor are two segments of the working class that are often found in capitalist societies. Higher-paid labor, which Bonacich also refers to as an "aristocracy of labor," is a segment of the working class that is relatively privileged compared to other segments of the class. Cheaper labor is at the opposite extreme. It is a segment of the working class with a very low standard of living compared to other workers.

If the working class is divided along these lines then a *split labor market* is said to exist. It provides a prime condition for the formation of racial antagonism if higher-paid and cheaper labor are, for various historical reasons (such as a legacy of slavery), also differentiated along racial lines. The economic interests of capitalists are, other things equal, to employ the cheapest labor they can find. The interests of higher-paid labor involve maintaining their privileged position in the labor market, whereas the interests of cheaper labor involve doing whatever they can to improve their low position. In a sense, higher-paid labor has nothing to gain but everything to lose, whereas cheaper labor has nothing to lose and everything to gain. Conditions may arise such that capitalists who are employing higher-paid labor discover a pool of cheaper labor and wish to employ them in place of higher-paid labor. The interests of higher-paid labor are now directly threatened, and, given that higher-paid and cheaper labor are racially differentiated, higher-paid labor may use racially oriented strategies to prevent cheaper labor from competing with them. Bonacich identifies two possible strategies. One, an exclusion movement, involves pressing governments to restrict the immigration of cheaper labor, to keep them from moving into the country where higher-paid labor is located in order to prevent them from competing with higher-paid labor. This strategy will only work, however, if cheaper labor resides in a foreign country or territory. When this is not the case, higher-paid labor must resort to using a caste system, which means setting up a system of racial exclusion whereby cheaper labor is not permitted, by law or by custom, to compete for the jobs of higher-paid labor.

Ndabezitha and Sanderson (1988) used this theory to try to understand the formation of apartheid in South Africa. South Africa began its industrialization process in 1886 with the discovery of gold, and the gold mines fell under the ownership of English capitalists. High skill levels were needed to mine gold, and workers with these skills had to be brought in from the British Isles and Australia. They were lured to South Africa with the promise of high wages, and they became highly paid labor. Many of the white Afrikaner farmers in South Africa, who were descendants of the original Dutch settlers, got drawn into mine work around the turn of the century and came to constitute a group of semiskilled medium-paid workers. The mine owners also drew African tribesmen into mine work through a variety of coercive methods. These workers were highly unskilled and were paid extremely low wages, earning only about one-twelfth of the wage level of skilled workers. There thus was formed in South Africa around the turn of the twentieth century a complex split labor market, and the splits in the labor market corresponded closely to racial differences.

Around 1900 the invention of the jackhammer made it possible for unskilled African workers to do the work that the highly skilled workers had been doing, and as a result the mine owners desperately wanted to put African workers to work at the jobs controlled by both highly skilled English workers and medium-skilled Afrikaner workers. What resulted from all this was an explosive situation of racial and labor conflict as white workers vigorously sought a job color bar that would prevent Africans from taking over their jobs, and as the mine owners tried everything they could to employ African workers in the positions occupied by whites. By 1924 the open conflict was resolved in favor of the white workers. A government was elected that began the early establishment of a job color bar in the gold mining industry that would later (in 1948) come to be expanded into the official policy known as apartheid.

This interpretation of racial antagonism seems to me highly preferable to the orthodox Marxian theory. Orthodox Marxists have resisted the split labor market theory in part because it violates their deeply rooted belief that the working class can never be a reactionary force. But it seems to me that Bonacich's introduction of rational choice assumptions makes the theory far more realistic. People everywhere are following their own interests, and they will do what they can to protect those interests when they are threatened. If Marxism is to have much of a future, it must become much more open to these "bourgeois" theories. (See Sanderson, 1995a:351–52, for an application of split labor market theory to the outbreak of racial antagonism in post–World War II Britain; Boswell, 1986, applies the theory to the consequences of Chinese immigration to the United States in the second half of the nineteenth century.)

Although I see the split labor market theory in much more favorable terms than the orthodox Marxian theory, the former is itself limited in its explanatory power. Ethnic (if not racial) antagonism is virtually a human universal (van den Berghe, 1981a; Reynolds, Falger, and Vine, 1986), and thus exists under a wide range of conditions in which no split labor market is present. We thus encounter once again the limitations of a Marxian perspective. Split labor markets may intensify ethnic or racial antagonism, but they seemingly cannot account for it in the first place.

World-System Theory

Immanuel Wallerstein (1974a, 1974b, 1979, 1980, 1989), the originator of *world-system theory*, has joined Marx, the Annales historian Fernand Braudel, and the dependency theory of Andre Gunder Frank into a theoretical synthesis whose goal is to understand the historical development of capitalism over the past 500 years and its future possibilities. To understand Wallerstein's thinking it is important to consider his assessment of what went wrong with Marx's predictions. As we have seen, and as is widely known, these predictions have been greatly falsified by history. Wallerstein argues that Marx's predictions went awry for two reasons. First, his timing was too early. Marx anticipated the coming socialist revolution within his own lifetime, possibly, or at least not long after. Wallerstein believes that Marx will turn out to be right in the end, but with the proviso that the coming socialist revolution will occur much later, about a century or so from the present time. Marx made this mistake, Wallerstein argues, because he had the wrong unit of analysis. Marx was thinking of capitalism as confined to nation-states rather than as a much larger system that encompassed many societies, or what Wallerstein has come to call a *world-system*. Capitalist development occurs within this system as a whole, not within individual nation-states or societies, and it will take a good deal more time before world capitalism is ripe for a socialist transition.

What, then, is a world-system? It is any comparatively large social system with a complex division of labor, and it includes multiple societies and cultures. Wallerstein sees two basic kinds of world-systems, *world-empires* and *world-economies.* World-empires, such as the Roman Empire or many Chinese or Indian dynasties, are world-systems that are politically and militarily centralized or unified. World-economies, on the other hand, are world-systems lacking political and military centralization. The only long-lasting world-economy in world history, according to Wallerstein, has been the *capitalist world-economy,* which began in the sixteenth century and is still in existence today. What is the structure of this world-economy? According to Wallerstein, it consists of three dynamically interacting components: the *core,* the *periphery,* and the *semiperiphery.* The core consists of the most economically and technologically advanced societies. The richest capitalists reside and operate here, exploiting wage workers within the core and, even more so, other kinds of workers in the semiperiphery and periphery. The periphery consists of the most economically backward and underdeveloped societies that are heavily exploited by the core. Historically, peripheral societies and regions have concentrated on raw materials production for export using some sort of forced labor. The semiperiphery is an in-between zone that is both exploiter and exploited. It ordinarily contains a mixture of core-like and periphery-like economic activities.

Wallerstein argues that the capitalist world-economy has passed through several stages from the sixteenth century to the present time. It has been an expanding system, which means that it has been spreading to cover more and more of the globe, and an evolving system, or one in which capitalist methods of production have been applied with ever greater intensity wherever capitalism has gone.

I have found world-system theory to be tremendously useful in understanding many features of the evolution of the modern world over the past 500 years. It identifies some of the most crucial features of social evolution over this period of time, and it helps to make sense of the current world economic and political setup. World-system theory has been both fervently embraced and severely criticized. In my *Social Transformations* (Sanderson, 1995b, 1999:231–42) I have summarized and evaluated the most basic criticisms. These are that world-system theory is excessively holistic, seeing everything within the system as being determined by the system as a whole; that it is economically reductionist, seeing politics as just the expression of economics; that as an abstract model it has committed many serious errors of historical accuracy; that it has been unable to corroborate its notion of unequal exchange between core and periphery; that it has erroneously insisted that the periphery is essential for the development of the core; that the concept of semiperiphery is highly ambiguous and of limited use; that it engages in functionalist and teleological reasoning; that it has often erroneously seen the periphery becoming absolutely immiserized over time; and that it has been un-Marxist in being "circulationist" rather than "productionist" (Brenner's, 1977, famous "neo-Smithian Marxism"). Some of these criticisms land telling blows, I think, but others are not especially damaging. (Because of space limitations I leave readers to their own resources in studying and evaluating these criticisms, as they may wish.[5])

However, I would like to add one additional criticism that was alluded to but not really developed in *Social Transformations.* World-system theory stresses the exploitation of the semiperiphery and periphery by the core. There is much that is sensible in this, and it would be irresponsible to deny that an enormous amount of capitalist exploitation has gone on throughout the world over the past 500 years, much of it quite brutal. And yet a somewhat broader perspective is needed. Quite apart from any exploitation of the periphery and semiperiphery by the core, the core countries will generally continue to maintain their advantage because they "got there first" and because their control of world markets makes it difficult for peripheral and semiperipheral countries to make a great deal of headway. Putting it another way, I think it is something of a distortion to take a highly "systemic" approach and say that the periphery exists in order to enrich the core, or that a capitalist world-system "requires" a core-periphery hierarchy. This is just too functionalist. What I am suggesting is that we need a more "ecological" model of world capitalism than that offered by world-system theory. Randall Collins has developed this idea more fully. In a letter to me (Nov. 1, 1996) he says the following:

> You place stress on the world system itself, after it evolves, as the unit of evolution. This is a useful viewpoint, but it can be taken further. I think that perhaps the most important thing we learn from biological evolution is that speciation occurs by adaptation in niches, which are comprised by the evolution of surrounding species. Species provide niches for one another. Interestingly, one can see this in the social realm: all kinds of different social organizations provide niches [within] which yet other social organizations can emerge. So although world systems can be units of evolution, their parts are evolving too as they provide niches for one another. Cores emerge by finding niches comprised by peripheries; semiperipheries emerge when they find niches no one else is filling. This is consonant with the line of theorizing about capitalism which comes from Harrison White, and which resonates well with Schumpeter's view of entrepreneurship. That is, capitalist firms prosper to the extent that they find niches, avoiding competition with other firms that would bring down profit; capitalism in this view is so to speak evolution at the organizational (and product) level speeded up by competition to find noncompetitive niches; since after a while these niches disappear, entrepreneurs "evolve" further by innovating to find yet newer niches.
>
> This is a respect in which the White/Schumpeter model may help bail out world system theory from a difficulty: the problem of the necessity of the periphery for core development, with its accompanying concept of exploitation through unequal exchange. The theoretical problem is to explain the empirical pattern; why does the core continue to get relatively richer at the "expense" (statistically speaking) of the periphery, even though absolute development often takes place, and there is no clear mechanism for the inevitable transfer of wealth from one to the other? The White/Schumpeter model implies that capitalist core is financial, the entrepreneurs who put together new combinations of land, labor, capital, etc. in order to create the latest specialized niche; here profit can be made because of the "natural monopoly" that exists during the initial period of the innovation, with its absence of competitors. The process is always ongoing; competitors eventually come in, driving down profits; the core can stay ahead to the extent that it moves ahead to creating the next specialized niches, abandoning the older niches to the competitors. The periphery is structurally caught in a system in which there is always a niche-protected center and a market-exposed periphery; this actually occurs within societies as well as among them, but it is most pronounced at long distances from the core, where it is most difficult to be "in the action" that creates the cutting edge, where the profits are made. World system theorists haven't seen this because they still are Marxist to the degree of wanting to put production and exploitation in the center, not finance; but it is these financial networks of investors

who drive technological innovation, along with production and marketing strategies, whatever it takes to create a noncompetitive niche on the frontier.

I do not necessarily endorse all of the points made by Collins, but his general emphasis
on ecological competition over exploitation seems to me a very useful corrective to an
excessively exploitation-centered model of modern capitalism. Collins also helps give us
a more positive (or at least less negative) view of capitalism.

As a final remark on world-system theory, and one closely tied to what I have said
above, I would say that what is also missing is an appropriate set of microfoundations.
Not only does world-system theory distort by analyzing the operation of all of the parts
from the level of the system as a whole, but it has an inadequate theory of individual action. Just as Marx said that human nature is nothing but the totality of social relations,
so goes world-system theory. Human actors have no motives outside of the logic of the
system that they are caught up in. And yet much of the inner core (no pun intended)
of world-system theory cries out for not only a self-interested actor, but for the very type
of self-interested actor being advocated by Darwinian conflict theory. To me, world-system theory makes no sense at all without precisely the type of human actor I will be arguing for in these pages. But perhaps Wallerstein has smuggled that actor in through the
back door. Consider, for example, his explanation, in the first volume of *The Modern
World-System* (Wallerstein, 1974a), of the collapse of the feudal system. This occurred,
Wallerstein argues, because of a crisis within the old feudal economy. Landlords were
suffering from a severe deterioration in their revenues and so turned to capitalistic methods to stem the tide. Former landlords became capitalist farmers. Wallerstein seems to
be conceding that actors within the feudal system were driven by the rational calculation of gain, a point that seems exactly right to me. But if feudal actors acted out of rational self-interest, what is to stop us from arguing that actors in all modes of production throughout history and prehistory have been so motivated, and by virtue of their
innate tendencies? Nothing as far as I can tell. Most world-system theorists (and many
other types of social scientists as well) apparently believe that the notion of the rational
self-interested actor is just a cultural construct inextricably tied to bourgeois ideology.
The evidence, though, strongly suggests otherwise, as we will see in later chapters.

ADDENDUM

The efforts of Erik Olin Wright (1979, 1985, 1997) to develop a Marxian conceptualization of class are extremely noteworthy. He has pushed Marxian analysis in this area
about as far as anyone could, but he has constantly run up against the limits of Marxism.
He has undertaken at least one major overhaul of his formulations, and in his formulation that I regard as the best (Wright, 1985) it is clear that what he has produced is in
many ways as Weberian as it is Marxist. I am reminded of Frank Parkin's (1979:25) pithy
aphorism: "Inside every neo-Marxist there seems to be a Weberian struggling to get out."

I think that some of the most wrongheaded applications of Marxian theory have been
to the whole problem of gender. What we usually see here is a kind of extreme tunnel
vision in which patriarchy is laid almost entirely at the feet of capitalism. Most Marx-

ian sociologists studying gender fail to see that gender inequality is a phenomenon that bursts the boundaries of capitalism, indeed is a true human universal. (For a discussion of some representative Marxian analyses of patriarchy and capitalism, including her own Marxian theory, see Vogel, 1983.)

NOTES

1. Space limitations preclude a discussion of the complexity of Marx's dialectical and evolutionary theory of historical change. In recent years the most famous exegesis of historical materialism is that of G.A. Cohen (1978), who argued that Marx was a technological determinist who had a functionalist conceptualization of the relationship between the forces and relations of production. In this interpretation, the relations of production in any historical epoch are as they are because they are the relations that are optimal for the advance of the productive forces. This interpretation has been widely criticized and accepted by only a few. One of the best critiques is that of Richard Miller (1984). In my *Social Evolutionism* (Sanderson, 1990) I lay out Cohen's basic arguments and Miller's criticisms of them (and I agree with Miller's objections). For a view more sympathetic to Cohen, see Elster (1985). Other valuable contributions to this general issue are van Parijs (1993), Cohen (1984), and Wright, Levine, and Sober (1992)

2. Contemporary Marxist theory is extraordinarily diversified, and so much so that Immanuel Wallerstein barely exaggerates when he says that we live in "the era of a thousand Marxisms." Perhaps the three most important versions of neo-Marxian theory since the 1960s are structural Marxism, analytic or rational choice Marxism, and world-system theory. Structural Marxism fused basic Marxian principles with Lévi-Straussian structuralism, primarily under the direction of the French philosopher Louis Althusser (1969, 1971; Althusser and Balibar, 1970). What was created was an extremely rigid form of Marxism in which the capitalist system had its own logic utterly apart from acting individuals. Structural Marxism collapsed and was more or less abandoned after a relatively short life. In sociology some of the most important structural Marxists have been Nicos Poulantzas (1974, 1975) and Barry Hindess and Paul Hirst (1975). Two of the most prominent structural Marxists within anthropology have been Maurice Godelier (1975, 1977, 1978) and Jonathan Friedman (1974). For good critiques of structural Marxism, Althusser in particular, see Thompson (1978) and Benton (1984). See also Applebaum (1979) and Burris (1979). Harris (1979) provides an excellent critique of anthropological structural Marxism. For applications of structural Marxism to a specific substantive issue, the origins of apartheid in South Africa, see Johnstone (1976), Davies (1979), and Burawoy (1981); for critiques of these applications, see Bonacich (1981) and Ndabezitha and Sanderson (1988).

Analytic Marxism is sometimes called rational choice Marxism, but it may be more appropriate to view the latter as a subtype of the former (Carver and Thomas, 1995). Rational choice Marxism represents an attempt to insert the principles of rational choice theory, especially methodological individualism, into Marxism. In my view it is one of the most promising of the current Marxisms. It is highly active and growing. For discussions and criticisms of this approach see Carling (1986), Levine, Sober, and Wright (1987), Weldes (1989), Kieve (1986), Elster (1985), and Mayer (1994). A special issue of the journal *Theory and Society* (vol. 11, no. 4, 1982) is devoted to both advocacy and critique of rational choice Marxism.

To show how diverse contemporary Marxism can be, some Marxists have actually produced an idealist version of Marxism, what might be called "cultural Marxism." I have in mind E.P. Thompson and Eugene Genovese. See the former's *The Making of the English Working Class*

(1963), and the latter's "Materialism and Idealism in the History of Negro Slavery in the Americas" (1968).

World-system theory is discussed in the text.

3. A very useful and extremely sensible critique of Marxian theory has been written by Harris (1979:141–64).

4. It is interesting to note that Bowles and Gintis have given up most if not all of their theory. Indeed, they have abandoned Marxism in general. Gintis has become some sort of evolutionary game theorist and an active member of the Human Behavior and Evolution Society, an organization whose ideas are rooted in Darwinism and sociobiology.

5. The best book-length summaries of world-system theory are Chase-Dunn (1998) and Shannon (1996). See also Sanderson (1999:181–243).

5

Weberian Conflict Explanations

INTERPRETING WEBER

Just as in the case of Marx, there has been a great deal of discussion for many years concerning how to interpret the thought of Max Weber. The various interpretations that have been made of Weber's thought have been summarized by Jeffrey Alexander (1983). Weber has been seen as an idealist (Parsons, 1937; Kolko, 1959), as a voluntaristic antisystems theorist (Martindale, 1960; Bendix, 1961, 1971), as a bourgeois apologist (Marcuse, 1968), as a synthesizer of the materialist and idealist traditions (Bendix, 1961), as offering a developmental theory of history based on the concept of rationalization (Schluchter, 1981), as a bourgeois Marx (Salomon, 1920) or some other type of Marxist (Schumpeter, 1947; Lichtheim, 1972; Wiener, 1982), and as a type of conflict theorist (Gerth and Mills, 1946; Rex, 1961; Dahrendorf, 1959; Lockwood, 1956; Parkin, 1982; Collins, 1974, 1975, 1986a, 1986b). Alexander himself sees Weber as a theorist of the multidimensionality of social life but argues that throughout his career Weber moved progressively away from a normative (idealist) perspective and increasingly toward an instrumental (materialist) one. Collins (1986a) also sees Weber as multidimensional, but he chooses to emphasize the conflict dimension.

The most influential interpretation of Weber in American sociology, what we might call the "standard interpretation," was offered by the first American sociologist to discover Weber and argue for his importance, Talcott Parsons. Parsons's interpretation held sway for neary half a century. Parsons received his Ph.D. degree at the University of Heidelberg in 1927, just seven years after Weber died. There he met Alfred Weber, Max Weber's brother, and came to learn about Max's work. He ultimately translated much of it, beginning with Weber's classic *The Protestant Ethic and the Spirit of Capitalism*. Parsons was insistent upon seeing Weber as an anti-Marxist, and it is indeed significant that Parsons himself was vigorously anti-Marxist. Parsons emphasized those aspects of Weber's work in which Weber examined the impact of ideas on social life, including economic life, and thus Parsons seemed to view Weber's work as an idealist alternative to Marxian materialism. Parsons's Weber was a very "benign" Weber who, Parsons thought, was converging with Durkheim, Pareto, and Alfred Marshall on a "theory of action" (Parsons, 1937).

Although some had done so already, in the 1970s a number of sociologists (e.g., Cohen, Hazelrigg, and Pope, 1975) began to rethink the traditional interpretation of Weber. They alleged that Parsons's Weber was one-sided and incomplete, and in some respects downright wrong. This new thinking tended toward seeing Weber as offering a kind of conflict theory that was similar to Marxian theory in certain ways, but yet also crucially distinctive. Cohen, Hazelrigg, and Pope (1975) focused in particular on Parsons's translation of the German word *Herrschaft*. Parsons had translated this as "authority," which implied legitimation, but Cohen, Hazelrigg, and Pope translated it as "domination." For these authors, this gave Weber's thought a conflict dimension that was completely overlooked by Parsons. The conflict interpretation of Weber has been most thoroughly developed by Randall Collins. In his book *Max Weber: A Skeleton Key* (1986a), he argues that Weber was a very complex thinker whose thought tended in various directions. Collins claims that there is really more than one Weber, and that no singular interpretation is true to the facts. Collins believes, nevertheless, that Weber tended more toward a conflict perspective as he got older, and thus that the mature Weber was for the most part a conflict theorist. Collins also argues that for him (Collins) Weber's conflict theory is the most interesting part of his work and the most useful on which to build.[1]

Collins makes much of the fact that Max Weber's father (Max Weber Sr.) was a politician and the younger Weber came to be highly familiar with politics at an early age. He saw the maneuvering and posturing that goes on in political life, and the degree to which politics is a matter of hardheaded realities (what the Germans call *Realpolitik*). This gave him a perspective on political and social life that might be called *cynical realism:* social life as made up of individuals maneuvering for power and control over situations and over each other. This perspective was a key part of Weber's overall sociological perspective.

I wish to follow Collins's argument that Weber's conflict theory is the most important and fruitful part of his complex and variegated work. According to Collins, Weber used and built on many Marxian fundamentals, such as the importance of material conditions, the influence of interests on ideology, and the existence and importance of class struggle. But Weber went further. He paid attention to many dimensions of conflict either underemphasized or ignored altogether by Marx: bureaucratic organizations as sources of multifaceted power struggles, the organization of the means of violence, the so-called means of emotional production, the role of status groups and parties in the stratification system, the relatively autonomous role of states, geopolitics and the international system of states, and, in general, the multidimensionality and pervasiveness of conflicting interests. Collins elaborates (1974:171–72):

> Weber is best known for a series of contributions that apparently break the Marxian mold. These include the importance of status groups—the dimension of stratification into communities distinguished by life style and ranked by prestige, communities which are built up and over and above class lines, and sometimes cutting across them; the importance of religion in setting personal attitudes and social change; the importance of legitimacy as the basis of stable political order. These are indeed important and original contributions by Weber; but they remain within the conflict tradition, and supplement rather than negate

the model of conflict over material goals and through material resources. To make this clear, I have reformulated the underlying principle under the term, *the control of the means of emotional production:* i.e., the conditions in the material world whereby individuals are influenced to experience emotions, especially social solidarity, fear, awe, or a sense of purpose. The implication is that these are resources to be used in conflicts (for the goals of power and wealth as well as for emotional gratification), and that the control of these means is itself affected by the distribution of resources resulting from other forms of conflict.

That is, Weber made a discovery analogous to those of Durkheim and Freud (and above all Nietzsche, on which he drew), when he recognized that people have emotional desires and susceptibilities, and that these are crucial for their social lives. Weber saw that particular conditions excite emotional dynamics; above all, conditions of conflict, deprivation, and threat on the one hand, and, on the other, ceremonies and displays which arouse emotions and resolve them into feelings of solidarity and awe. Manipulation of the settings of such face-to-face encounters is the basis of religion. Weber does not reduce religion to economic interests, although he shows that social classes have their typical religious propensities; rather, it is to be understood as a distinctive area of emotional gratification, and the product of a distinctive group, the priests. With his sense of the internal conflicts of organizations, Weber recognizes religious developments as proceeding from the interests of religious elites themselves in struggling for dominance both vis-à-vis each other (in which the outcomes are influenced by the material conditions of church organization, analogous to the principles of political struggle), and in relation to the public and to the state, which makes use of religion in its own struggles.

The distinctiveness of Weberian conflict theory can be seen in more detail by way of a point-by-point comparison of Weber and Marx, and thus of contemporary Weberians and contemporary Marxists.

WEBER AND MARX, WEBERIANS AND MARXISTS

The fundamental differences between Marxian and Weberian conflict theory can be summarized in terms of the following ten points:[2]

1. *Methodological individualism vs. holism:* Nearly everyone agrees that Weber was a methodological individualist, and most would agree that Marx was a holist. Consider, for example, the following passages from the work of each. In the first volume of *Economy and Society* (1978[1923]:14) Weber says that "for sociological purposes there is no such thing as a collective personality which 'acts.' When reference is made in a sociological context to a state, a nation, a corporation, a family, or an army corps, or to similar collectivities, what is meant is, on the contrary, *only* a certain kind of development of actual or possible social actions of individual persons." This is an obvious warning that sociological concepts should not be reified. By contrast, in the first volume of *Capital* (1967[1867]:10), Marx takes a classically holist view: "I paint the capitalist and the landlord in no sense *couleur de rose.* But here individuals are dealt with only in so far as they are the personifications of economic categories, embodiments of particular class-relations and class-interests. My standpoint, from which the

evolution of the economic formation of society is viewed as a process of natural history, can less than any other make the individual responsible for relations whose creature he socially remains, however much he may subjectively raise himself above them." I think it is fair to say that most contemporary Weberians and most contemporary Marxists are true to these methodological dicta.

2. *The nature of social stratification:* As suggested by Val Burris (1987), Marxians and Weberians differ in at least four basic ways with respect to the stratified structures of society: (a) Marx (and Marxists) hold a unidimensional view of stratification whereby class is the central phenomenon, whereas Weber (and Weberians) hold a multidimensional view in which two other dimensions of stratification, status groups and parties, are regarded as just as important as, and sometimes more important than, class; (b) Marxists conceptualize class as an objective structure of social relations; Weberians, on the other hand, conceptualize it from the perspective of individual social action; (c) for Marxists, class relations and class conflict are all about exploitation, and political and ideological domination are largely mechanisms for achieving exploitation; however, for Weberians domination is regarded as an end in itself quite apart from the aim of exploitation; (d) for Marxists, classes emerge from relations of production, but for Weberians classes emerge primarily from market relations. Some of these themes are explored in more detail below.

3. *Class struggle and other forms of struggle:* Just as class is the central sociological variable for Marxism, the Marxian position holds that class struggle is the most fundamental form of struggle and that it underlies all other forms of struggle (Burris, 1987; Wenger, 1987). This position has been called, mostly by critics of Marxism, "class reductionism." Thus, in feudal societies, for example, the class struggle between landlords and peasants underlay struggles that went on in the areas of the state, religion, etc. In capitalist societies, it is the class struggle between capitalists and workers that forms the foundation for the existence of other forms of struggle, such as political, racial, religious, or ideological struggle. Weberians argue that Marxian class reductionism is an overstatement and oversimplification. They claim that class struggle, while an important form of struggle in many societies, is not necessarily the most important form of struggle, nor is it necessarily the foundation for other forms of struggle. For contemporary Weberian conflict theorists, struggles in the areas of politics, ethnicity, or religion are just as important as, and in some instances more important than, class struggles, and these other forms of struggle have to be explained in their own right, not just by relating them to class struggle (Parkin, 1979). Nonclass forms of struggle have a high degree of autonomy from class struggle.

4. *The inevitability of conflict, domination, and inequality:* Despite their hostility to capitalism, Marxists are highly optimistic—even today after the upheavals in Eastern Europe in 1989 and the Soviet Union in 1991—that socialism is capable of eliminating the capitalist class struggle and ending fundamental social inequalities. There is nothing inevitable about class antagonisms and the other forms of antagonism that flow from it. The Weberians, by contrast, are much more pessimistic, arguing that social conflict is an inevitable and thus permanent feature of human

societies. Try as you might, you cannot get rid of basic social conflict. If you rid society of one type, others will remain and might even intensify (I. Cohen, 1985). Weber is famous for his argument against the Marxists that socialism would intensify the power of the state rather than lead to its withering away, and thus would increase the conflict between the state and the citizenry. Here is the way that Weber phrases his argument (1978[1923]:38–39): "The struggle, often latent, which takes place between human individuals or social types, for advantages and for survival, . . . will be called 'selection.' . . . It is only in the sense of 'selection' that it seems, according to our experience, that conflict is empirically inevitable, and it is furthermore only in the sense of *biological* selection that it is inevitable in principle. Selection is inevitable because apparently no way can be worked out of eliminating it completely. Even the most strictly pacific order can eliminate means of conflict and the objects of and impulses to conflict only partially. Other modes of conflict would come to the fore, possibly in processes of open competition. But even on the utopian assumption that all competition were completely eliminated, conditions would still lead to a latent process of selection, biological or social, which would favor the types best adapted to the conditions, whether their relevant qualities were mainly determined by heredity or environment."

5. *The nature and role of the state:* Marx himself, and the majority of Marxists, have by and large viewed the state in largely class reductionist terms, i.e., as the political agent of the ruling class (although in recent decades this position has been modified considerably by some Marxists, especially by Poulantzas and other structural Marxists, so that the state has more autonomy). Weberians think that the state is usually tied to the ruling class to some extent, but that any sort of class reductionism is a great oversimplification. Weberians hold that the state is a force in its own right, and that the personnel of the state have their own interests (Collins, 1975; Skocpol, 1979; Parkin, 1979). These interests are not reducible to the interests of the dominant class, and may often conflict with those interests. For Weberians, the state is another conflict group, another group seeking domination. Weberians also give special emphasis to the international role of states, especially their military roles (Collins, 1975, 1986b; Skocpol, 1979). States not only seek domination of their own subject populations, but carry out incessant diplomatic and military relations with other states and often seek to dominate them as well. For Weberians, the international states system and geopolitics are due major consideration.

6. *The role of ideas in history:* Marx argued that history was guided by a dialectical process in which changes in the forces and relations of production were fundamental and led to changes in the superstructure, including consciousness or ideas. Weber thought that the Marxian model in this regard was only partially correct. Marxian materialism, he said, was only a half-truth. Ideas, Weber argued, could be and often were causal forces in their own right. Weber did not claim that the proper corrective to the one-sidedness of Marxian materialism was an equally one-sided idealism, but rather that one should be open to both points of view. In fact, Weber argued for a much more multidimensional view of causation than Marx, arguing that ideas, economics, politics, etc., could all

mutually determine a given social outcome. The idea of multidimensionality was a critical one for Weber (J. Alexander, 1983).

7. *Bureaucracies and organizational power struggles:* Marx paid virtually no attention at all to large-scale bureaucratic organizations in their own right, but for Weber this was a major concern. Weber saw bureaucratic structures, rather than the class relations of capitalism, as the basis for the emergence of rigid, cold, impersonal relations, the famous "iron cage." Moreover, contemporary Weberians have spent a great deal of time analyzing the organizational dynamics of this form of social organization (e.g., Collins, 1975:chapter 6), something Marxists certainly have not done.

8. *The master trend of modern history:* Marx saw the master trend of modern history, of course, as the progression from capitalism to socialism. Even though things have not developed in the way that Marx predicted, such recent Marxists as Immanuel Wallerstein still think that Marx was right in a general sense, and that world socialism will still follow world capitalism (it will just take longer and will occur at a world level rather than at the level of the nation-state). Weberians see it differently. Weber himself thought that the emergence of socialism was a real possibility, but that the real master trend of modern history was the rationalization of the social world, especially as this was embodied in the bureaucratic form of organization and in modern science and technology. The world will be increasingly governed by impersonal rules and procedures, and by the desire for the calculability and predictability of results. For Weber and for many neo-Weberians, this is an inexorable trend.

9. *The causes of alienation:* Marx thought that the root cause of the alienation of workers was the capitalist organization of production, which was rooted in private relations of production and the aim of capitalist accumulation. Weber, on the other hand, argued that the alienation and deprivation of the working class was rooted in bureaucracy rather than private property. As Wolfgang Mommsen (1985:242) points out, "Weber was convinced that neither private appropriation nor the uneven distribution of property can be regarded as essential causes of the alienation and deprivation of the working classes. The elimination of private control over the means of production leaves the fundamental problem untouched, namely, the superiority of those in the dominant economic positions who exercise control over the masses of workers. It is the problem of control, not the formal disposition of property, which is crucial. Therefore, Weber saw the roots of alienation, not in property relations, but in omnipotent structures of bureaucratic domination, which modern industrial capitalism produced in ever-increasing numbers."

10. *Capitalism vs. socialism:* Closely related to this point is the whole issue of capitalism vs. socialism as desirable economic systems. Marx, of course, was intensely hostile to capitalism and thought that its eradication would greatly ease the plight of workers. Weber, by contrast, was much more pessimistic about the possibilities inherent in socialism. As Mommsen (1985:254) has noted, "Weber did not hide the defects of capitalism, yet he was unable to imagine any workable alternative. . . . Despite all of capitalism's shortcomings, he preferred it to every conceivable form

of socialist economy. He was convinced that socialists, insofar as they wished to be serious about realizing their moral principles, would either have to accept considerable regression in both technology and civilization or else be compelled to create gigantic bureaucracies in the face of which the people, including the workers, would be unable to accomplish anything. Compared to any form of socialism, capitalism appeared to offer far better conditions for the survival of free societies in the age of bureaucracy."

CRITICAL ASSESSMENT

I assess these ten points essentially as follows:[3]

1. The methodological individualism of Weberian theory is an excellent antidote to the reifications of functionalism and, to some extent, Marxism.
2. Concerning the nature of stratification, I side with the Weberians regarding the multidimensionality of stratification and class as a structure of individual action. With regard to the relationship between exploitation and political and ideological domination I think that each side is partially right: Political and ideological domination are often means to secure exploitation and to rationalize it, but they can often be sought in their own right. Concerning whether classes arise from production or the market, again I think that each side is partially right.
3. I take a halfway position regarding the Marxian and Weberian views of class struggle and its relation to other forms of struggle. I would argue that often other forms of struggle are rooted in class struggle, but perhaps just as often these other forms of struggle have their own logic quite apart from class struggle. Class struggle is more important than the Weberians claim, but less important than the Marxists claim. The whole issue has to be treated as an empirical question and examined on a case-by-case basis.
4. The cynical, hardheaded realism of Weberian conflict theory is an extremely positive attribute. This is where Weberian theory has it all over Marxism. For Weberians, society is fundamentally a struggle for power that is inevitable and unending. Weberianism has a much more realistic view of the nature of the state, of the permanence of conflict and inequality, and thus of the deeper motives that impel human behavior. However, Weberians seem to stop short on this whole matter. The issue I am speaking of is the fundamental question of human nature. Did Weber have a theory of human nature, if only implicitly? Walter Wallace (1990:209) asserts that he did, noting that "although he does not say it in so many words, Weber quite unmistakably regards personal self-interest as innate and universal among humans. . . . personal self-interest is already fixed by genetic inheritance in all human individuals and needs no further fixing there by external imposition. Weber also regards personal self-interest as motivationally prior to 'ideas'—i.e., learned values such as 'duty, honor, the pursuit of beauty, a religious call,' etc." The best support I know of for Wallace's claim are Weber's words

quoted in the fourth point in the preceding list. Here Weber speaks in an almost Darwinian way. Be that as it may, it must be pointed out that the contemporary Weberian Randall Collins explicitly disavows the need for any theory of human nature. In a short essay (R. Collins, 1983) he strongly repudiates sociobiology, even going as far as to claim (quite erroneously) that contemporary developments in biology undermine sociobiological principles. Moreover, he has said the following (Collins, 1975:59; emphasis added): "For conflict theory, the basic insight is that human beings are sociable but highly conflict prone animals. Why is there conflict? Above all else, there is conflict because violent coercion is always a potential resource, and it is a zero-sum sort. *This does not imply anything about the inherence of drives to dominate.*" But why not such drives? If conflict is ubiquitous, it would seem obvious that this must have something to do with the kind of animal humans are. Collins only refuses to take that step because he has been inoculated against any sort of biological argument during his training and tenure as a sociologist and conditioned to accepted Durkheim's dictum—Durkheim is also a great thinker for Collins—that social facts can only be explained in terms of other social facts. The profound irony is that Collins's own theory is for the most part highly consistent with, and subsumable within, sociobiological principles. Collins does not seem to realize that his version of Weberian conflict theory, as it now stands, is profoundly incomplete and lacks "first principles." If humans are conflict prone, it is essential to explain why. Otherwise, one's theoretical perspective is oddly suspended in mid-air without anything to ground it.

5. Concerning the nature and role of the state, I also take a position halfway between the Weberians and the Marxists. There is considerable evidence showing that, in both capitalist and precapitalist societies, the dominant economic class exerts a great deal of influence on the actions of the state. On the other hand, the Weberians are right when they emphasize that the state is often autonomous and its interests often conflict with those of the dominant economic class. As in the case of the relation between class struggle and other forms of struggle, the Marxian view goes a little too far in one direction and the Weberian view a little too far in the other. Or at least that is how I read the evidence.

6. I disagree with the Weberian compromise on the materialism/idealism debate. The whole point of this book is to propose and defend a vigorous materialism. Ideas may sometimes be important, but I think they pale in significance in comparison with material forces. I do not accept, for example, Weber's argument about the role of the Protestant ethic in the rise of capitalism, nor do I agree with his more general sociological argument about the relationship between types of religious orientation and economic systems. Just as strong a case can be made for the reverse argument—that it was the rise of capitalism that was responsible for the spread of Protestantism throughout the Western world, if not for the origins of Protestant ideas themselves. (I provide a critique of the Protestant ethic thesis in Sanderson, 1999:159–62.) Collins has vigorously defended the Protestant ethic thesis, and has tried to extend the logic of this sort of argument by claiming that Buddhist monasteries in Japan during the early centuries of the second

millennium AD contributed in a very significant way to the development of Japanese capitalism (Collins, 1997). Collins claims that the significance of the monasteries is that they were centers of vigorous economic activity and that they helped provide the discipline needed for a healthy capitalist economy. But Collins fails to provide any argument or evidence to show how the economic activity of the monasteries got beyond itself and came to be transferred to the larger society. I have always been puzzled by claims for the impact of religious ideas on economic behavior, which seem to me intuitively implausible. Frankly, I am at a loss to understand why they have been proposed at all.

7. I am in strong agreement with the Weberian emphasis on bureaucracies and the need to understand their organizational dynamics. This is clearly something that is a serious lacuna for Marxism.

8. Marxism has failed terribly in its prediction of the collapse of capitalism and the transition to a socialist society. In the twentieth century state socialism has emerged in various parts of the world, but mostly in very underdeveloped societies, not, as Marx predicted, in the most advanced capitalist societies. Moreover, since 1989 we have been witnessing the reverse trend: the transition back to capitalism from socialism. In view of these failures, and of organizational and technological changes in the last century, Weber's argument that increasing rationalization is the main trend of modern history seems much more plausible.

9. On the causes of alienation, I think the evidence will strongly support the Weberian argument that alienation is rooted in bureaucracy and rationalization rather than private relations of production (cf. Blauner, 1964; for a different view, see Braverman, 1974, although, ironically, Braverman's work can be reinterpreted along Weberian lines).

10. Capitalism has a lot to answer for, but socialism so far has been an overwhelming failure (Kornai, 1992; Courtois et al., 1999), and on most criteria of human well-being one would choose capitalism comes out the winner. The Weberian view that we should stick with capitalism and try to improve it seems the clear victor on this count at this point in history.

SOME SUBSTANTIVE APPLICATIONS

State-Centered Theories of Revolution

As already noted, the classical Marxian theory of revolution has failed miserably. The reason for this failure seems to be that Marx completely overlooked one major arena of social life—the political realm—in his overwhelming focus on the economy and class relations. As Theda Skocpol (1979) has pointed out, a consideration of socioeconomic and class relations is crucial to an adequate theory of revolution, but by itself it is insufficient. Serious attention must also be given to the organization of political life, especially to such things as the political resources peasants may be able to draw upon to press their cause, as well as to the degree to which states may or may not be able to quell peasant revolutionary activity. Explanations of revolutions must focus on both the economic and the political.

Chapter 5

Since the late 1970s there has been not only increasing recognition of the importance of a range of political factors in revolutionary change, but the explicit formulation of theories that make such factors central. Not all of these theories are explicitly Weberian, but they are highly consistent with the spirit of Weber. As Collins (1993) has suggested, they are all *state-centered* theories. Charles Tilly (1978) was one of the first to formulate an explicitly political theory of revolutions, his so-called *resource mobilization theory*. According to this theory, collective action (a term Tilly prefers to revolution, and which includes political conflicts other than revolutions) is the result of a combination of several factors. Collective action is most likely when populations share common *interests*, are well *organized*, control important *resources*, have sufficient *power*, are not *repressed* by governments or other groups, and have the *opportunity* to act. Tilly points out that there are two types of governmental actions that tend to enhance the commitment of a population to revolutionary claims. The first of these involves the sudden failure on the part of the government to meet obligations that a population regards as well established and essential to its own well-being, e.g., the provision of employment, welfare services, protection, or access to justice. The second type of action is when a government rapidly or unexpectedly increases its extraction of resources from the population, such as increased taxation, the commandeering of land or crops, or labor conscription for public works projects.

Also critical to the formation of revolutionary situations is an inability or an unwillingness of a government to engage in the repression of the actions of contending groups. A government may simply lack the necessary coercive power to overcome contenders, and for a number of reasons: the government may have suffered a depletion of its military resources, the contending group may over time have acquired powerful military resources, or the contending group may implant itself in a rough and unknown terrain or adopt military tactics that are unfamiliar and thus difficult to combat. On some occasions governments may have sufficient coercive means to put down contenders but may be unwilling for one reason or another to use them. For example, the use of coercive resources against contenders may be extremely unpopular among other segments of the population and may therefore run the risk of alienating these groups. This discussion applies only to revolutionary *situations*, i.e., revolutionary activity undertaken by a significant segment of a society's population. For revolutionary situations to be *successful*—the vast majority are not—revolutionary coalitions must be established between the revolutionary contenders and members of the polity, and this coalition must control substantial military force.

Several scholars have built on the foundations established by Tilly. Theda Skocpol (1979, 1994) has developed a theory of the Great Revolutions, viz., France in 1789, Russia in 1917, and China from 1911 to 1949. Skocpol argues that any good theory of social revolutions must strictly follow three guidelines: it must be a nonvoluntarist, structural theory; it must focus closely on the international context in which societies and governments are situated; and it must treat the state as an actor that is substantially independent of the needs and goals of the economically dominant class. Skocpol's theory is that the Great Revolutions resulted from a combination of two critical circumstances: a massive crisis within the governments of France, Russia, and China, and widespread rebellion by subordinate classes, the peasantry in particular. State crises were the result of both severe international political and military pressures and economic deprivations that led to widespread dissatisfaction within the population. Governments could not implement reforms necessary to deal with the military threats they encountered. War in particular, she claims, was the key factor in state crises. But this is only half of the story. The other key factor in successful revolution was widespread peasant revolt. Skocpol argues that these successful revolutions could not have occurred had such revolt not been coupled with political crises.

At the time that Skocpol was writing (the late 1970s), her work was the best sociological work on revolutions ever produced. However, some extremely important state-centered theories of revolution have been developed since then, one of which was produced by Skocpol's own student, Jack Goldstone (1991). Goldstone accepts Skocpol's overall argument about the importance of state crises and popular uprisings, but his emphasis is different. He claims that war has not been the main cause of state crises, and that in focusing on peasant revolt Skocpol ignores urban disorder. Goldstone analyzes what he calls *state breakdowns,* which are governmental crises so severe that they cripple the capacity of a government to govern. Only some state breakdowns become actual revolutions. Goldstone argues that state breakdowns in both historical Europe and Asia were cyclical in nature and occurred in two major waves peaking in the mid-seventeenth and mid-nineteenth centuries. Between these two waves were periods of relative political stability. It is Goldstone's view that state breakdowns were precipitated primarily by the negative effects of population growth. This gives his theory a dimension that is absent in the other state-centered theories. Population grew, Goldstone claims, primarily during periods when mortality was low, and mortality was low when the incidence of contagious disease was low. When population grew, a series of negative consequences ensued. Because a larger population meant increased demand, prices increased, and this generally led to an increase in taxation. However, states had difficulty raising taxes to the extent necessary to make them fiscally stable, and a state fiscal crisis was normally the result. This crisis became even worse if there were increased military demands on the state purse. Population growth also had a negative effect on social and economic elites because it increased the number of competitors for elite positions. As more people competed for the same number of elite positions, more would have their aims frustrated, and thus dissatisfaction among these segments of society increased. Population growth also led to declining wages. Lower wages, in conjunction with higher prices, increased the level of both rural and urban misery and led to wage protests and food riots. When all of these circumstances were combined, the result was a state breakdown.

Another major state-centered theory of revolution has been produced by Timothy Wickham-Crowley (1992), whose focus is on revolutions in Latin America in the twentieth century. Latin American revolutionary efforts have generally been led by guerrilla movements. Guerrilla movements have generally not been led by the largest and most oppressed social class, the peasantry, but by well-educated members of the middle class. However, to be successful, guerrillas have needed the support of the peasantry. They have also needed military strength, which varied a great deal from one guerrilla movement to another. But even these two factors in combination were not enough, Wickham-Crowley claims. Another factor was crucial: the extent of a state's vulnerability to revolutionary movements. Wickham-Crowley shows that successful revolutions in Latin America have only occurred twice, in Cuba in 1959 and Nicaragua in 1979. Wickham-Crowley points to several common features of Cuban and Nicaraguan society that made them extremely vulnerable to successful revolutionary movements. In both instances, there were weak upper and middle classes that had little influence on the state, weak political parties, a nonprofessional army, and, most importantly, what Wickham-Crowley calls a *neopatrimonial state,* or *mafiacracy.* This is a type of state in which an extremely corrupt ruler makes the state into his own personal property, personally controls the military, suppresses political parties, and dispenses rewards and favors in a highly personalized manner. In a mafiacracy, the ruler is a savage dictator who controls the whole society and bends the state to his own personal ambitions and fancies. Wickham-Crowley argues that this type of regime is uniquely vulnerable to guerrilla movements because the ruler eventually alienates all of the major groups in the society, which in turn makes a broad revolutionary coalition possible.

Despite their differences, what all of these theories have in common is an emphasis on state vulnerability combined with the dissatisfaction of one or more major social groups as necessary factors in any successful revolution. This represents a great advance over the dead hand of Marxism as a theory of revolution. As Collins (1993) suggests, the theories all represent a kind of "political materialism," although it is clear that they include economic as well as political factors (and demographic ones in the case of Goldstone). Concerning the specific theories of Skocpol and Goldstone, Collins argues that they need not necessarily be seen as opposing and irreconcilable (1993:121):

> The point is not that we have two rival theories of revolution. Rather, there exists a core model of state breakdown—fiscal/administrative strain, elite conflict, popular revolt—plus a number of pathways towards crisis conditions in these factors. Population growth sometimes can play a very large role in building up crisis; at other times geopolitical conditions can have overwhelming effects. In many cases, population and geopolitics interact. This is especially likely to be the case in premodern states, where the state budget is overwhelmingly military and where population is so vulnerable to shifts in mortality from disease, while the economy is not very flexible in absorbing population growth.

Frank Parkin and Social Closure

In his book *Marxism and Class Theory: A Bourgeois Critique* (1979), the British sociologist Frank Parkin presents a neo-Weberian view of social domination and subordination in modern societies. Parkin argues that the Marxian view of domination as primarily class domination rooted in the ownership of capital is too narrow and limiting. Class domination surely exists, he says, but only alongside other forms of domination that are important in their own right. Parkin develops and elaborates a concept that can be found in rudimentary form in Weber: *social closure.* Social closure represents attempts on the part of individuals to form themselves into groups that monopolize certain resources, such monopolization being devoted to achieving and maintaining a privileged social position, or to cutting into the privileged position of other groups.

Parkin distinguishes three forms of closure: *exclusionary, usurpationary,* and *dual* closure. Exclusionary closure is exercised by dominant groups, or by groups seeking to become dominant. Their monopolization of resources gives them access to privilege and prestige and allows them to maintain their dominant position. Exclusionary closure is exercised by capitalists over workers, men over women, whites over blacks (in, for example,

South Africa and the United States), Protestants over Catholics (in Northern Ireland), or college graduates over high-school graduates. Usurpationary closure is exercised by subordinate groups who are seeking equality with dominant groups, or at least trying to reduce those groups' level of domination. It is a strategy designed to improve the group's level of privilege and prestige. Usurpationary closure is occurring when workers organize unions and go out on strike, when feminists protest against male privilege and domination, when blacks in the United States formed a civil rights movement, when South African blacks overthrew apartheid, when the Irish Republican Army bombs offices in England, or when an increasing number of high-school graduates seek entry into colleges and universities. Dual closure occurs when a social group engages simultaneously in both forms of closure. For example, if workers organize a labor union but try to prevent blacks from joining their union, then dual closure is at work.

The great advantage of Parkin's conceptualization is that it allows us to see that there are bases for domination other than class, and these bases may be to a large extent independent of class domination. Moreover, class domination can be reconceptualized as simply one of the various forms of exclusionary closure: It is a form of exclusionary closure based on ownership of the forces of production. Parkin's formulation also allows us to explain more successfully types of domination that Marxism does not explain very well, such as domination based on gender or on race and ethnicity. We can also use it to explain such things as the high incomes of physicians—the argument would be that they monopolize a valued skill that can command high fees in a market economy when the supply of doctors is limited (Collins, 1979)—or the existence of a stratification system in the old Soviet Union, a society without private ownership of the means of production.

Unfortunately, despite its cogency, Parkin ends up pushing his Weberian argument too far. For example, he says that (1979:38) "improbable as it may seem, Marxist class theory has also been pressed into service in the analysis of *apartheid.* To seek to impose class categories upon such a palpably racial system would seem to be somewhat akin to adopting a Parsonian integrationist model in the analysis of, say, modern Lebanon." Also speaking of South Africa, he says that it "is not a group's position in the division of labour or the productive process that determines its class location but the character of its primary mode of social closure. *White industrial workers in South Africa must be regarded as part of the dominant class by virtue of the fact that exclusion is their chief mode of operation and the source of their privileges*" (1979:94; emphasis added). In terms of the first statement, my response is that it depends on the type of Marxist class theory being used. As noted in chapter 4, Siyabonga Ndabezitha and I (Ndabezitha and Sanderson, 1988) analyzed the formation of apartheid in South Africa by looking at it through the lens of Edna Bonacich's (1972, 1981) split labor market theory of ethnic and racial antagonism, a theory that is Marxist but in a very unorthodox way. We found that the exclusion of black workers by white workers was clearly a fundamental part of the capitalist-worker relationship and could only be understood in terms of it. White workers were excluding black workers because of the tremendous economic threat that black workers posed to them, a threat only made possible by capitalists' desire to replace white higher-paid workers with cheaper black workers. Thus the racial system in South Africa has been inextricably intertwined with the class structure. While the dominant mode of exclusion in

South Africa is (or was) the *apartheid* system in the sense that it was the most publicly obvious and pervasive feature of social relations, that system in an explanatory sense was not an autonomous mode of exclusion but rather one rooted in the historical class relations of South African society. With respect to Parkin's second statement, I would say that it makes no sense at all to refer to white workers as part of a dominant *class,* but rather as part of a dominant *race.* The two are, as stated above, inextricably intertwined, but on an analytical level they are separate modes of exclusion.

Another dubious aspect of Parkin's analysis is his claim that in modern capitalist societies academic and professional qualifications are a form of exclusionary closure on a par with the private ownership of property (Murphy, 1988). As Raymond Murphy (1988:66–67) has said, "This conception obscures the vastly different power and advantages accruing to credentials and to property and the unequal importance of the two as rules of exclusion under capitalism." Murphy goes on to point out that in all capitalist societies private ownership of the means of production is the primary form of closure, a view with which I have no difficulty agreeing.[4]

Randall Collins and Educational Expansion

In his book *The Credential Society* (1979), Randall Collins has developed a powerful neo-Weberian theory of educational expansion. Collins's focus is on American society, but his findings are generalizable to some extent to other industrial societies. As Collins notes, in industrial societies, and American society in particular, there has been a huge growth of educational enrollments since the latter part of the nineteenth century. In the United States, public primary education began to develop in the 1840s, but secondary education lagged far behind. Even as late as 1870 only about 2 percent of the age-eligible population was enrolled in a secondary school. In the last decades of the nineteenth century public secondary education began to expand and by 1930 nearly half of fourteen-to-seventeen-year-olds were enrolled in a public secondary school; this more than doubled to nearly 93 percent by 1970 (it is only slightly higher today, apparently having gone about as far as it can). Enrollments in higher education were also extremely low in 1870 and did not begin to expand significantly until after the turn of the century. By 1950 nearly 30 percent of eighteen-to-twenty-one-year-olds were attending a higher educational institution. This rose to nearly 53 percent by 1970 and today is approximately 65 percent. Similar rates of expansion have occurred in other industrial societies, although enrollments in secondary and higher education have generally been lower. Collins attempts to explain why such educational expansion has occurred and why the United States has been the world leader in the size of enrollments, especially at the level of higher education.

Collins rejects both the Marxian theory of Bowles and Gintis and the functionalist theory as adequate explanations. He proposes instead an argument that relies on Weber's concept of status group and on Weber's notion of educational attainment as providing a valued credential. Collins suggests that the ethnic heterogeneity of the United States is what accounts for its high degree of educational expansion. Between 1880 and 1920, as everyone knows, there was a huge flood of European immigrants, especially from Eastern and Southern Europe, into the United States. This prompted a desire on the part of the dominant ethnic group, white Anglo-Saxon Protestants, to assimilate and Americanize the immigrants as much as possible. Primary education and, to some extent, secondary education, expanded to achieve this objective. However, once various ethnic groups were drawn into the educational system, they began to see that it had value for them quite apart from whatever may have been originally intended. They began to see that educational credentials—a diploma or degree, or at least so many years of schooling—had value in the labor market. Status groups in the form of ethnic groups began to push for more education because of its economic value, but a major unintended consequence was the inflation of educational credentials: Once more individuals attained credentials, they declined in value, i.e., they could not "purchase" the same type of job that they had before, largely because employers began to use credentials as a screening device for cutting the number of job applicants down to a manageable size. Under these circumstances, people had two possible responses. They could lower their job aspirations and settle for a job they had enough education to qualify for, or they could intensify their efforts and achieve a higher level of credentials. Most people chose the second route, which continued to fan the fire of credential inflation even more.

I agree with the credential inflation part of Collins's argument, but the ethnic heterogeneity part of the argument is not supported by the evidence. Collins argues that ethnic heterogeneity contributed to massive educational expansion in the United States because ethnic groups, as status groups, were locked into economic competition. More generally, he has argued that the societies with the largest educational systems are usually the most ethnically complex, citing the old Soviet Union, with its nearly one-hundred ethnic groups, as another example. To test this argument, I looked at the correlation between educational enrollments and ethnic heterogeneity using a large sample of contemporary nation-states. For the year 1990, ethnic heterogeneity correlated $-.447$ (Pearson r) with primary enrollments, $-.471$ with secondary enrollments, and $-.356$ with enrollments in higher education. Contrary to Collins, ethnic heterogeneity *inhibits* rather than promotes the expansion of educational enrollments.

In conclusion, Collins's theory of educational expansion has a serious flaw, but this flaw is far from fatal. The credential inflation part of the argument is the more important part, and this part can stand. It is then possible to argue that educational credentials expand by virtue of their own inherent logic as determined by levels of supply and demand, and by the extent to which the educational system becomes a major avenue for economic success in any given society (as it clearly has in American society).

NOTES

1. For an excellent discussion of how Parsons greatly overemphasized Weber's idealism and neglected his substantial materialism, see Bryan S. Turner (1981).

2. For an excellent overview of the various positions that have been taken regarding the compatibility or incompatibility of the ideas of Weber and Marx, see Schroeter (1985). Antonio and Glassman (1985) and Wiley (1987) contain many useful essays on the Marx-Weber connection.

3. See also Sanderson, "The Neo-Weberian Revolution: A Theoretical Balance Sheet" (1988).

4. See Murphy (1988, esp. pp. 64–82), for an only partially successful attempt to improve on Parkin's closure theory.

PART III

Sociological Explanations
That Work Best

6

Exchange and Rational Choice
Explanations

It is the individual only who is timeless. Societies, cultures, and civilizations—past and present—are often incomprehensible to outsiders, but the individual's hungers, anxieties, dreams, and preoccupations have remained unchanged throughout the millennia.

—*Eric Hoffer*

All disinterested kindness is inexplicable.   —*Arthur M. Schlesinger, Jr.*

HOMANS AND EXCHANGE THEORY

The ideas in the closely related theories known as exchange and rational choice theory stem from the nineteenth-century philosophy of utilitarianism. The utilitarians saw humans as cost-benefit calculators who chose courses of action that served their interests and avoided those lines of action that would be costly, i.e., that were detrimental to their interests. It was the aggregate behavior of individuals that constituted society. Durkheim was the first major sociologist to react strongly against this strain of thought. Durkheim insisted that societies were not simply collections of rationally calculating individuals. Society was a total set of social facts, a set of beliefs, values, and social norms. Individual conduct was not motivated by rational self-interest, but rather by the commitment of individuals to the norms and values of the group or society into which they had been socialized. And, for Durkheim, these norms and values had a nonrational foundation. Talcott Parsons continued this line of thinking and integrated it into his functionalist perspective. For the most part, the Durkheim-Parsons line of thought has become standard sociology, and most sociologists accept something more or less like this. Social structures come first and individuals are socialized into them. Beliefs, values, norms, and roles shape individual behavior. Society is not simply an aggregation of individuals, but a "total social fact" that individuals merely represent and carry along.

Exchange and rational choice theory are intended to be a strong antidote to this standard sociological model. Exchange theory emerged in the late 1950s and early 1960s,

99

its most prominent advocates being George Caspar Homans (1958, 1961, 1962, 1964, 1983, 1984) Peter Blau (1964), and John Thibaut and Harold Kelley (1959). Homans's work is clearly the exemplar of this brand of social theory in sociology. Homans agreed with Durkheim and Parsons that society was an "emergent" phenomenon, something more than just an aggregate of individuals. There really were social norms, roles, and institutions. However, Homans insisted that these phenomena could only be explained by reference to individual persons. Homans thought the basic principles of sociology had already been discovered by behavioral psychology and elementary economics. People seek rewards and avoid costs and follow the lines of action that bring the most rewards for the fewest costs. Homans set forth several formal theoretical propositions in which he elaborated on this basic notion. In simplest form these were:

1. Behavior that has been emitted in the past is more likely to be emitted in the present and future.
2. The more often a person's acitivity is rewarding to the behavior of another person, the more often that other person will emit the behavior.
3. The more valuable another person's behavior is to a person, the more often he will seek to act so as to elicit this rewarding behavior.
4. People experience satiation. Thus, the more frequently a person has been the object of a rewarding behavior performed by another person, the less valuable any additional unit of that behavior becomes.
5. People seek distributive justice, i.e., a level of rewards proportional to their input, or what they feel they deserve. When distributive justice fails to be realized, the more likely a person is to display anger.

Homans applied these basic principles to the behavior of individuals in a wide range of small-scale social groups, but he also understood them to be relevant to understanding the institutions of a society. Social institutions were the aggregate result of individuals making choices that were directed toward obtaining rewards and avoiding costs. Thus, Homans's exchange theory was neither strictly a microlevel nor a macrolevel theory. Homans was especially insistent that sociologists could not offer meaningful explanations so long as they explained human behavior as being what it was "because of the culture." Such sociologists—clearly the majority—Homans referred to as "culture vultures." The culture vultures begged the question, Homans insisted, as to why the culture was organized the way it was. We can give a *proximate* explanation of a person's behavior by saying it is a response to the culture of his or her society, but for an *ultimate* explanation—any truly meaningful explanation—we have to find out why this cultural pattern rather than some other pattern arose in the first place. For example, we can say that modern orthodox Jews and Moslems do not eat pork because this food taboo is a part of their religious traditions, but the really interesting question is why this taboo is found only in Judaism and Islam when pigs are raised and eaten all over the world. And Homans's argument, of course, is that such cultural norms arise because they are rewarding for people caught up in a particular situation.

I agree with Homans that a proper theory of human society must be rooted in the notion that individuals create society through elaborate networks of exchange, networks in which people are seeking to maximize rewards and minimize costs. I agree, at least in principle, with his attempted rehabilitation of the concept of *economic man*. It is the proper starting point for a general theory of human society. Nonetheless, Homans's work is replete with serious difficulties. Most obviously, his theory is highly simplistic; it contains only the bare bones of what a good theory must have. It is a skeleton with little or no meat on its bones. For example, although the concept of rewards is critical to Homans's theory, he fails to tell us nearly enough about the many kinds of rewards individuals seek and how these might be arranged in a hierarchy from most to least important. As Lopreato and Crippen (1999) have pointed out, Homans was a "giant with feeble shoulders," and his theory provided a very limited part of a much bigger story.

A second criticism relates to why Homans's perspective is called exchange theory. This is not a name chosen by Homans, and he in fact objects to it, but the name has stuck because Homans sees individuals exchanging rewards with each other while trying to minimize costs. Moreover, Homans has assumed that if individuals continue in their relationship they must find the relationship mutually satisfying. This assumption is, however, highly problematic, for it ignores the degree to which many social relationships are constrained by power and may be coercive and exploitative (Zeitlin, 1973; Collins, 1988). Human societies throughout history have been filled with a wide variety of coercive relationships: landlords and serfs, masters and slaves, capitalists and workers, men and women, Afrikaners and black Africans, and many more. Many relationships continue only by dint of the power of those who have it. And even if individuals have the ability to escape one coercive relationship, there may be few or no other options, or the cost of escaping the relationship may be too high. For example, it has become well known that many women in modern societies stay in violent and abusive relationships with their husbands because they fear that the costs of leaving would be too high (what would happen to the children, and so on). A theory that ignores the major role of coercion and exploitation in human relationships leaves a great deal to be desired.[1]

Homans also biased his theory much too far in the direction of behavioristic psychology, especially Skinner's operant conditioning. (In his autobiography [Homans, 1984], Homans describes in some detail his close relationship with B.F. Skinner.) He has focused heavily on the way in which behavior in the present has been shaped by the past (cf. Ekeh, 1974). What consequence has this had? Lopreato and Crippen (1999:29–30) explain:

> The fundamental flaw in Homans' Skinnerianism—and in exchange theory in general—was the perpetuation of Locke's *tabula rasa* assumption, namely the failure to understand that human beings cannot be conditioned to act outside of the potentials developed during the evolutionary history of our species. No doubt we behave as we do as a result of experience. The role of learning—or socialization, as sociologists prefer to say—cannot be denied. Without socialization we would not become human. But experience does not shape the development of behavior without guidance from innate predispositions. Thus we learn some things a great deal more easily than others, some more efficiently at certain stages of development than at others, and some not at all. Behaviorist theory focuses at best on the *how* of learned behavior—on the techniques of learning; it neglects the *why*, the *when*, and much of the *what*. . . . Accordingly, the real error does not lie in the sociologist's emphasis on socialization. The focus is justified. The problem lies in the failure to recognize that learning

is an evolved adaptation—that learning is "biased" in view of our species evolutionary history.

Lopreato and Crippen point out that one of Homans's central propositions is that individuals have a tendency to value rewards. Yet Homans simply takes this proposition as a given and makes no effort to explain why humans (or, indeed, any other organism) should value rewards. There is nothing in Homans's theory that tells us why individuals should make such a judgment, and an adequate theory of society must do so.

FROM EXCHANGE TO RATIONAL CHOICE

Modern rational choice theory is an outgrowth and extension of exchange theory. It has been developed most extensively by James Coleman (1990) and Michael Hechter (1983a, 1983b; Friedman and Hechter, 1988, 1990; Hechter, Opp, and Wippler, 1990; Hechter and Kanazawa, 1997), and their students and colleagues. Rational choice theory is grounded in the same fundamental principle—people orient their behavior towards maximizing rewards and minimizing costs and the institutions of society are the aggregate result of individual choices—but is considerably more sophisticated and nuanced. Rational choice theorists have constructed more elaborate and interesting models than Homans and other exchange theorists in order to explain many aspects of social behavior. An excellent summary of rational choice theory's basic principles is contained in an article by Debra Friedman and Michael Hechter (1988) (cf. Smelser, 1992):

1. Social behavior is the result of *actors* who are acting *purposively* or *intentionally* in accordance with a *hierarchy of preferences.* Actors are striving to realize these preferences with a minimum of cost. Actors are *rational calculators* of benefits and costs.

2. The rational calculations made by actors are subject to at least two kinds of *constraints.* The first type of constraint is a scarcity of resources. Individuals confront *opportunity costs,* or costs associated with foregoing certain courses of action. They also confront *institutional constraints,* which act as positive or negative sanctions on the net benefit of any given course of action.

3. Actors are in possession of a certain amount of *information* regarding what choices will best realize their preferences. Early rational choice theory tended to assume that actors had complete information, but more recent models assume that the amount of information individuals possess varies strikingly according to time and place.

4. Rational choice models use an *aggregation mechanism* to show how a given *social outcome* is achieved. With respect to such phenomena as voting behavior or economic markets, the aggregation outcome is simply the addition of individual choices. However, for most social phenomena the identification of an aggregation mechanism is considerably more difficult.

Misconceptions concerning rational choice theory abound, and so a number of clarifications are needed. It must be stressed that the conception of rationality that rational choice theory operates with is *each individual's own subjective sense* of what is in his or her self-interest. No assumption is being made that the individual's perception of his or her situation is correct, and, indeed, in many cases it will not be. The point is that individuals act rationally within the framework of *their own understanding* of their situation in life and what lines of action will be most rewarding and least costly. In many cases individuals do not possess sufficient information in order to make the choice that will realize their preference, and this is explicitly recognized by current versions of rational choice theory. A related point is that individuals make rational choices concerning the *means* they use to achieve their goals, not with respect to the *goals* themselves. It has been said, for example, that the fact that many people smoke, when smoking is obviously unhealthy, falsifies rational choice theory. But rational choice theory makes no assumptions about the rationality of individuals' goals.

It should also be mentioned that what is rational at the level of individual self-interest may not be collectively rational. Indeed, the aggregate effect of individually rational decisions frequently is a kind of social irrationality. For example, as noted in the previous discussion of neo-Weberian conflict theory, Randall Collins argues that in American society the individual pursuit of schooling is rational for persons who are seeking economic and status rewards, but the aggregate effect of many persons behaving in this way is to inflate educational credentials and cheapen degrees, thus requiring people to spend ever longer periods of time in school. (This example shows that rational choice theory and conflict theory, especially Weberian conflict theory, often converge, the obvious link being that human behavior is driven by individuals following their own interests; cf. Kiser and Hechter, 1998:797–98.) Moreover, individuals are not necessarily "maximizers." They may simply be doing what the economic theorist Herbert Simon (1976) long ago called "satisficing." That is, individuals are often content with what they deem to be a satisfactory rather than a maximum level of rewards. This is especially likely to be true in complex situations where it is difficult if not impossible to know how a maximum result could be achieved.

Both Durkheim and Parsons insisted that the utilitarians were wrong in their conception of society as an expression of individual self-interest because, they claimed, no society could be sustained on such a basis. Everyone expressing their self-interest would lead to the use of force, fraud, anarchy, and, in general, the Hobbesian "war of all against all." Therefore, selfish behavior had to be restrained by norms and values. But it is extremely important to point out that rational choice theory is not claiming that everyone *behaves* selfishly, only that their actions are *motivated* by the pursuit of self-interest. Indeed, individual self-interest expresses itself just as much in various forms of social cooperation as in conflict and competition (see chapter 14).

A common criticism of rational choice theory, as of exchange theory before it, is that it is reductionist in its exclusive focus on individuals. However, this is clearly not the case (Homans, 1984; Kincaid, 1996; Hechter, 1983a; Coleman, 1990). As Hechter (1983a:8) has argued, the methodological individualism of rational choice theory "represents a structural rather than atomistic kind of individualism. . . . In such an approach the structure first determines, to a greater or lesser extent, the constraints under which individuals act. While these constraints define the limits of the individual's possible action, they are insufficient to determine his or her behavior. In no way does this imply that individual attributes should be given greater weight than structural constraints; it merely asserts that social phenomena cannot be understood without taking the intentions and consequences of individual action into account." Homans tells us more about how social constraints work: "Both the individualist and the structural type of empirical propositions require psychological propositions for their explanation, for structures do not act on individuals automatically. They do so because *they establish some of the contingencies under which persons act:* their stimuli, rewards, and punishments; and the explanation why and how these contingencies affect behavior requires psychological general propositions" (1984:342; emphasis added).

Perhaps the biggest misconception concerning rational choice theory is that it is culturally biased. It is frequently claimed that rational choice theory takes modern capitalist society, with its norms and values of material acquisitiveness, norms and values that are culturally and historically unique, and projects them backward in time and across all social space to treat them as universal features of human nature (Zeitlin, 1973; Sahlins, 1976a; and many others). It then mistakenly derives capitalism itself from human nature. Rational choice theory may apply to modern capitalist society (which has enshrined the rational pursuit of self-interest), the story goes, but it certainly does not apply to precapitalist societies. This viewpoint, I shall argue, is mistaken, and badly so, but I shall leave it aside until the empirical chapters of this book, especially chapter 14. There I shall present a great deal of evidence to show that humans are rational calculators in all societies and at all times, even though their calculations often produce very different results in different times and places.

Finally, it is a mistake to suppose, as many sociologists do, that rational choice theory is a strictly microlevel theory. It clearly has a great deal of relevance for macrosocial phenomena, and a great deal of macrosociological research has been guided by rational choice assumptions (summarized in Friedman and Hechter, 1988; Hechter, 1983b; and Hechter and Kanazawa, 1997). Rational choice theory transcends the micro-macro divide and shows how the micro and macro levels are linked.

SOME EXEMPLARS

Friedman and Hechter (1988) and Hechter and Kanazawa (1997) have discussed studies of a wide range of social phenomena using a rational choice perspective. Space limitations permit only a brief summary of some of these studies. The economist Gary Becker (1991) has pioneered numerous studies of family organization using a rational choice perspective. South and Lloyd (1995) have shown that divorce rates are sensitive to the degree of availability of marital partners. The risk of marital dissolution is increased when there is an increase in the number of potential spouses in local marriage markets. A rational choice perspective has been applied with considerable success to crime. A well-known criminological theory, deterrence theory (Gibbs, 1975), represents an application of the rational choice perspective. Cornish and Clarke (1986) show that criminal behavior can be explained in terms of calculations of potential rewards and punishments and potential criminals' estimations of the probability of detection. Ethnographic studies carried out by Williams (1989), Jankowski (1991), and MacLeod (1995) show that teenagers from low-income neighborhoods decide to pursue criminal actions because they can make more money that way than from legitimate alternatives. Pezzin (1995) has shown that whether or not individuals adopt criminal careers, and how long these careers last, is a function of economic incentives and opportunity costs. In the arena of politics, William Brustein (1996) has tried to explain the popularity of the Nazi party in Germany in terms of economic incentives. Brustein claims that the Nazis were popular because they put into effect policies that appealed to the economic interests of a large and diverse segment of the German electorate. Edgar Kiser has studied various aspects of premodern political systems from a rational choice perspective. Kiser (1987) shows that monarchs in early modern Europe had more autonomy when they possessed independent resources and faced relatively weak monitoring. Kiser, Drass, and Brustein (1995) have shown that the frequency of early modern European warfare was a function of the degree of ruler autonomy. Rulers wanted war more than their subjects did, and the more autonomous rulers were, the more warfare they conducted. Kiser and Tong (1992) have looked at corruption in the state fiscal bureaucracies of late imperial China. They have shown that the nature and degree of corruption depended on the structural and institutional constraints imposed on rulers and state officials. The lower the level of monitoring and sanctioning of officials by rulers, the greater the degree of corruption. More interestingly, "rulers will weigh the costs of corruption and the costs of control, and will invest in control only when it provides a net benefit. . . . Rulers want to minimize total agency costs, which include both the costs of control and the costs due to lack of control (corruption). This implies that the greater the costs of control, the higher the level of corruption" (Kiser and Tong, 1992:303).

Within the past decade or so there has been vigorous application of rational choice theory to the analysis of religion (Stark, 1994 [and studies summarized there], 1996; Stark and Bainbridge, 1987). Rodney Stark and William Sims Bainbridge (1987) have presented a comprehensive theory of religion grounded in rational choice assumptions. Religion is rewarding because it acts to compensate in supernatural terms for desired secular rewards that are unavailable for one reason or another. Since scarce secular rewards are usually monopolized by the rich and powerful, religious compensators are of greatest relevance to the poor and powerless. For Stark and Bainbridge, religious organizations "are social enterprises whose primary purpose is to create, maintain, and exchange supernaturally based general compensators" (1987:42). In a recent book, Stark (1996) has used rational choice theory to understand the rapid spread of Christianity in the first three centuries AD. Assuming that there were 1,000 Christians in the year AD 40, Stark estimates that the number grew to nearly 34,000,000 by AD 350. What kind of compensation was Christianity offering that had such widespread popular appeal? Stark emphasizes mostly compensation for urban misery and disease. Cities were squalid, crime and social disorder were widespread, and there were many intense ethnic hostilities. Moreover, epidemic diseases were a constant fact of life, and Stark argues that the explanatory systems of antiquity, paganism and the Hellenistic philosophies, were much less able than Christianity to explain why people were living in such misery and to offer them comfort. When epidemics struck, it seems that Christians were more able than others to cope, and more of them actually survived. Stark's explanation of the success of Christianity closely resembles Marx's famous notion of religion as an "opium of the people"—an explanation that is actually a type of rational choice argument—except that Stark focuses on urban misery and disease rather than economic exploitation and political oppression.[2]

One of the most interesting applications of rational choice theory has been to human sexuality. In his book *Sex and Reason,* Richard Posner (1992:116) argues that "the balance of private costs and private benefits determines the relative frequency of different sexual practices." Using rational choice theory Posner is able to explain a remarkably wide range of sexual practices, among them the following:

1. Masturbation occurs more frequently among middle-class than among lower-class youths because middle-class youths begin to have intercourse at a later age.
2. Petting to orgasm and early marriage are found more frequently in highly religious societies because these societies discourage premarital intercourse.
3. The more intolerant a society is of male homosexuality, the greater the proportion of homosexuals who marry. This is because intolerance of homosexuality makes it more costly, and the more costly it is the more homosexuals will try to conceal it by marrying.
4. The lowest quality of sexual services among prostitutes is provided by streetwalkers and the highest quality by call girls. This is because the search costs—a major type of cost influencing the frequency of a sexual practice—with respect to streetwalkers are low whereas the search costs for call girls are much higher.
5. Bestiality is more common in rural than in urban areas because the search costs for animals are much lower in rural areas.
6. Urban areas will contain a higher percentage of homosexuals than rural areas because the search costs for homosexual mates are lower in the former.
7. In societies in which there is a high ratio of men to available women, opportunistic homosexuality and prostitution will be more frequent than in societies with an approximately equal ratio of men to available women.
8. As women have more alternative job opportunities in a society, prostitution will be less frequent.

CRITICAL ASSESSMENT

Rational choice theory has a great deal to offer, but it also has some significant limitations. My overall evaluation can be summarized basically as follows.[3] The basic foundational assumption of rational choice theory is correct. Individuals do act fundamentally in their own interests and the aggregation and multiplication of these interests is what underlies the basic institutions of society. Moreover, the institutions that people create serve as constraints within which further cost-benefit calculations occur. Rational choice theory, when appropriately complemented by other theories (more accurately, *synthesized with* other theories), is a good starting point for sociological analysis.

On the more critical side, it has to be acknowledged that rational choice theory has an overly cognitive conception of human action. This highly cognitive conception leads rational choice theory to overemphasize the role of conscious intentionality in human action, and to ignore or at least downplay the important role of emotions (Steklis and Walter, 1991; Scheff, 1992; Kanazawa, 2001; but see Lawler and Thye, 1999). Many of the reasons why humans act as they do are either unknown to them or poorly understood by them, and this limits the explanatory capacity of rational choice theory. Despite its virtues, rational choice theory is an incomplete mode of social analysis (Rule, 1997; Kanazawa, 2001).

But the most critical deficiency of rational choice theory is the problem of *preferences,* a deficiency that is freely acknowledged by rational choice theorists themselves (Kanazawa, 2001; Friedman and Hechter, 1988; Hechter, 1992, 1994). There are many goals and aims that people have that guide their self-interested behavior. People may seek rewards in the areas of wealth, prestige, love, sex, leisure time, religious salvation, and so on, and rational choice theory is able to tell us little or nothing concerning which preferences may be most important to individuals in particular times and places. For example, we have learned in recent years that hunter-gatherers do not tend to work very hard or long and that they are highly desirous of leisure time, yet in modern industrial societies people seem to be working harder and harder all the time in order to achieve economic success and personal fulfillment. Under what conditions do you get the one preference, and under what conditions do you get the other? So far rational choice theory has been silent on questions like these, probably because it is not really equipped to answer them. To do so we will have to invoke other theoretical approaches. But more on that in a moment.

Hechter (1992, 1994) is one of the few rational choice theorists who has devoted much effort to understanding where preferences or values come from. He calls attention to the so-called *typical value assumption* of rational choice theory, which holds that actors are motivated to attain such instrumental goods as wealth, power, and prestige, goods that can be exchanged for other goods that are valued in and of themselves. This assumption is highly realistic, in my view, but it is unfortunately a theoretically ungrounded assumption. No reason is given as to *why* people should value these things. Hechter then goes on to propose the idea of a *hierarchy of nested values* (1994:326–27):

> At the most fundamental level, biological determinants produce values that are common to or, perhaps, constitutive of all human beings. This source of values produces no variation to be explained. Ecological determinants of values indirectly influence the establishment of a set of social institutions that, in turn, highlight certain values at the expense of others. The Nuer offer a good example. Given the nature of the environment that the Nuer occupied, pastoralism was the most viable mode of production. To the degree that the social institutions of all pastoral societies take the same form, the members of such societies will have a set of common values—in addition to those that they share as members of the same species.
>
> Next come institutional determinants. To the degree that environmental conditions allow for the establishment of different kinds of social institutions, we would expect to find

members of these respective societies to have systematically different values. Clearly there is a great scope for institutional differentiation within the same ecological parameters. Advanced technology certainly loosens the coupling between social institutions and the environment. Hence, in advanced societies, we would expect that more variation in values would be due to social institutions than to ecological variables per se.

The penultimate cause of variation in personal values lies in idiosyncrasies of personal biography, some of which can be explained by individual patterns of group affiliation. Membership in each group may foster particular values. For example, we might expect to see (with a positive probability) certain kinds of common values held by Catholics as against Protestants, by members of the chamber of commerce as against union members and by sociologists as against economists.

There is much in this statement that is sensible, and it is certainly an improvement on rational choice theory's usual silence. Unfortunately, Hechter's formulation does not take us much beyond traditional sociology and anthropology, nor does he explain why it is that biology and ecology should be determinants of values.

The idea that human nature may provide a source of values and preferences is intriguing. This notion was hinted at by Homans as early as 1961 (1961:381, 383; see also Homans, 1984:159, 329), and in their pathbreaking article Friedman and Hechter (1988) suggest that biological drives may be a source of preferences (cf. Hirschleifer, 1977; Smith and Winterhalder, 1992a). Unfortunately, Homans and Friedman and Hechter merely state the idea without ever developing it in any way. The rational choice theorist who has done the most to link preferences to human biology is Satoshi Kanazawa (2001), who explicitly claims that sociobiology—or, as he prefers to call it, evolutionary psychology—provides rational choice theory with its missing preferences. This has long been my view as well. Linking rational choice theory with sociobiology not only provides the missing preferences, thus giving rational choice theory the necessary grounding in first principles that it has so far lacked (i.e., why people should be rational choosers); it also shows why emotions are important and why people have the emotions that they do (i.e., they have those that evolved by natural selection because they were adaptive), and it explains why people should seek wealth, power, and prestige (i.e., these are critical to achieving reproductive success). As Smith and Winterhalder have put it, the "sociobiological view of human decision-making offers a special refinement of the concept of self-interest" (1992a:48), and rationality itself is an evolved adaptation.

My grand conclusion is that rational choice theory, when linked with sociobiology, is the proper starting point for a unified theory of human society. Marvin Harris's cultural materialism (discussed in the next chapter), and both Marxian and Weberian conflict theory are also helpful in understanding human preferences, but, as I shall argue in chapter 9, the preferences stated by these theories cannot be understood except in light of sociobiology.

NOTES

1. Homans did sometimes acknowledge power differences (e.g., 1984:340), but these differences were never made an important part of his overall theorizing. Peter Blau (1964) explicitly

incorporated power and exploitation into his exchange theory, but in doing so he moved too far away from exchange theory itself.

2.   For a critical evaluation of rational choice theories of religion, see Young (1997).

3.   The April 1992 issue of *Theory and Society* contains four critiques of rational choice theory as set forth in James Coleman's *Foundations of Social Theory* (1990), along with a reply by Coleman. However, it seems to me that none of the critics has a very good grasp of that which they are criticizing. The Fall 1991 issue of *Sociological Theory* also contains several articles on rational choice theory. Denzin (1990) and Smelser (1992) are additional critiques of rational choice theory by well-known sociologists. The essay by Denzin is essentially a diatribe rather than a reasoned critique. Replies to his essay have been written by Hechter (1990) and Abell (1990).

7

Cultural Materialist Explanations

BASIC PRINCIPLES

Cultural materialism is a major theoretical strategy within anthropology that was developed in the 1960s and 1970s primarily by Marvin Harris.[1] The influence of this perspective among sociologists has been largely limited to those who have a comparative focus and who are highly conversant with anthropology. Most other sociologists would not have encountered it. However, there is no need to apologize for incorporating anthropological theory into social theory, broadly conceived. Much anthropological theory is just as relevant to explaining the basic features of social life as is theory generated by people identifying themselves professionally as sociologists.

Cultural materialism is a synthesis of three older theoretical approaches. First, Harris has drawn extensively on Marxian historical materialism, and so cultural materialism continues in the materialist theoretical tradition laid down by Marx and Engels in the nineteenth century. But it carries into this tradition the mode of anthropological theory called cultural ecology. Cultural ecology examines the impact of the physical environment and demography on cultural patterns. Harris has also been significantly influenced by the tradition of evolutionary thinking in anthropology from the nineteenth-century evolutionists down to such modern evolutionists as Leslie White, and as a result cultural materialism has a strong evolutionary component. Cultural patterns are seen as evolutionary phenomena, i.e., as the adaptive results of people responding to their needs in various times and places.

A crucial part of Harris's analysis is his formulation of what he calls the *universal pattern,* or the basic components that all societies have (Harris, 1979). Societies are trichotomized into an infrastructure, a structure, and a superstructure. The *infrastructure* consists principally of technology, ecosystems, demography, and technoenvironmental relationships. It can be subdivided into a *mode of production* and a *mode of reproduction.* The mode of production consists of those things that go into the process of producing the means of human survival, and includes subsistence technology and the basic features of the natural environment. The mode of reproduction consists of those things relating

110

to the production of human life itself. It includes demographic behavior (rates of population growth, population density, age and sex ratios, etc.) and the technology of birth and population control. The *structure* consists of political economy and domestic economy. Political economy involves stratification systems, forms of political organization, and war. Domestic economy includes patterns of marriage, family life, kinship, gender roles, and age roles. The *superstructure* is composed of such things as ideology, art, music, literature, rituals, sports and games, and science.

To complete Harris's conception of the universal pattern, we must take into account two additional distinctions that he regards as extremely important, one between "emics" and "etics," and another one between "mental" and "behavioral." Emics has to do with studying a culture by penetrating into the hearts and minds of the natives and feeling and seeing things from their point of view. Etics involves studying another culture by formulating methods that do not rely on "the native's point of view." The mental-behavioral distinction is one between what people think and what they actually do, between things that go on in the mind and actual behavioral patterns that people display. Harris combines these distinctions into his infrastructure-structure-superstructure distinction such that each major societal component has both an "etic-behavioral" and an "emic-mental" subcomponent. We thus end up with approximately the following:

- **Infrastructure:** *Etic-behavioral mode of production*—technology of subsistence, technoenvironmental relationships, ecosystems, work patterns. *Etic-behavioral mode of reproduction*—demography, mating patterns, fertility and mortality, nurturance of infants, medical control of demographic patterns, contraception, abortion, infanticide. *Emic-mental component*—ethnobotany, ethnozoology, subsistence lore, magic, religion, taboos.
- **Structure:** *Etic-behavioral domestic economy*—family structure, domestic division of labor, domestic socialization, age and sex roles, domestic discipline and hierarchies. *Etic-behavioral political economy*—political organization, taxation, tribute, political socialization, social classes and castes, police/military control, war. *Emic-mental component*—kinship, political ideology, ethnic and national ideologies, magic, religion, taboos.
- **Superstructure:** *Etic-behavioral superstructure*—art, music, dance, literature, rituals, sports, games, science. *Emic-mental component*—symbols, myths, aesthetic standards and philosophies, epistemologies, ideologies, magic, religion, taboos.

Having done all this, Harris then simplifies this scheme somewhat by lumping all of the mental and emic components together and referring to them as a whole as the *mental and emic superstructure*, which consists of the "conscious and unconscious cognitive goals, categories, rules, plans, values, philosophies, and beliefs about behavior elicited from the participants or inferred by the observer" (Harris, 1979:54). This yields a final universal pattern with four components: the etic-behavioral infrastructure, the etic-behavioral structure, the etic-behavioral superstructure, and the mental-emic superstructure.

As a materialist, Harris argues that *the flow of causation in social life is primarily from the etic-behavioral infrastructure to the etic-behavioral structure, and then from the*

etic-behavioral structure to the behavioral and mental-emic superstructures, or, more simply, *from infrastructure to structure and from structure to superstructure.* Harris insists,
however, that the relationships among these parts are probabilistic, so that "in general"
or "most of the time" this is the way things work. This means that there is some al-
lowance for feedback from superstructure to structure to infrastructure. But not only
does the infrastructure largely determine the structure and superstructure in a synchronic sense; from a diachronic perspective changes tend to occur first within infrastructures and these changes generate reverberating changes in structures and superstructures. The great theoretical principle that is operative here Harris calls the *principle
of infrastructural determinism.*

Why this causal priority of the infrastructure? Harris's answer is much the same as
Marx's. When Engels eulogized Marx at his funeral, he said that just as Darwin had discovered the law of evolution in nature, so had Marx discovered the law of evolution in
social life and history. This law was that mankind had first of all to deal with the problems of food, shelter, and clothing before it could go on to produce such things as politics and consciousness. For Marx the underlying economic base was logically prior because it dealt with the most fundamental dimensions of human survival and well-being.
Harris has provided, in principle, exactly the same defense of his version of materialism.
The infrastructure is primary because it consists of the means whereby humans produce
the basic conditions of human existence and reproduce human life itself. Structures and
superstructures are therefore adaptations to the infrastructural conditions that societies
lay down first.

Harris is frequently read as a functionalist (Friedman, 1974; Godelier, 1977). In *The
Rise of Anthropological Theory* (1968) he actually described Marxian theory approvingly
as a kind of "diachronic causal functionalism," and his early writings have a decidedly
functionalist cast. Functionalist analyses are rife in *Cows, Pigs, Wars, and Witches* (1974).
For example, his analysis of the Northwest Coast potlatch is clearly an ecological-func-
tionalist one in which the function of the potlatch was to redistribute food and wealth
from one region to another. Moreover, he has conceptualized war as having the societal
function of creating a more favorable balance between people and resources, especially
game animals (Harris, 1974, 1977; Divale and Harris, 1976). Perhaps his most blatant
use of functionalist reasoning is his heavy reliance (in *Cows, Pigs, Wars, and Witches*) on
Roy Rappaport's famous book *Pigs for the Ancestors* (1967), an ultrafunctionalist analysis if there ever was one. However, by the time of *Cannibals and Kings* (1977) Harris had
clearly begun to move away from functionalist arguments and largely replaced them
with rational choice assumptions. *Cultural Materialism* (1979) is quite explicit about
Harris's rational choice and individualist assumptions. What this means is that Harris
has shifted his thinking from explaining cultural patterns in terms of their adaptive
value for society to explaining them largely in terms of their adaptive value for individuals. As Harris (1979:60–61) has put it,

> the selection processes responsible for the divergent and convergent evolutionary trajecto-
> ries of sociocultural systems operate mainly on the individual level; individuals follow one
> rather than another course of action, and as a result the aggregate pattern changes. But I

don't mean to dismiss the possibility that many sociocultural traits are selected for by the differential survival of whole sociocultural systems—that is, by group selection. . . .

. . . Cultural evolution, like biological evolution, has (up to now at least) taken place through opportunistic changes that increase benefits and lower costs to individuals. Just as a species does not "struggle to survive" as a collective entity, but survives or not as a consequence of the adaptive changes of individual organisms, so too do sociocultural systems survive or not as a consequence of the adaptive changes in the thought and activities of individual men and women who respond opportunistically to cost-benefit options. If the sociocultural system survives as a result of patterns of thought and behavior selected for on the individual level, it is not because the group as such was successful but because some or all of the individuals in it were successful.

In my view, Harris's shift toward a more methodologically individualist conception of the unit of adaptation is the right move. The only problem is that his shift is incomplete, because he still assumes that group selection is operating in some instances (see also Harris, 1999:49–56). As I shall argue in chapter 9, there really is no such thing as group selection, and the belief that there is is a major impediment to the further advance of theory in the social sciences (cf. O'Meara, 1997).

What are the major similarities and differences between cultural materialism and Marxian historical materialism? The one major similarity, which is overwhelmingly important, is that they are both materialist approaches. The leading differences, also quite important, are basically as follows:

1. Harris has expanded the Marxian base-superstructure distinction into a three-way distinction.

2. Harris has broadened the notion of infrastructure to include ecosystems and demography, a major move. Marx sometimes referred to the natural environment as part of the productive forces, but it played little role in his analyses. For Harris it is of dramatic importance. Moreover, Marx was actively hostile to the idea that population growth was a major determinant of social organization or historical change. He strongly attacked Thomas Robert Malthus, who contended that the major cause of human misery was overpopulation. In introducing the demographic variable as a key causal variable, Harris has departed markedly from Marxism.

3. Harris has shifted the Marxian relations of production from infrastructure to structure, and thereby has made them dependent on technological, ecological, and demographic forces. Or at least this is formally what he has done, for in actuality he sometimes treats the relations of production as if they are still part of the infrastructure. One must pay attention not only to the formalities of Harris's classification scheme, but to his actual analyses. When Harris is analyzing preindustrial and precapitalist societies, he does tend to treat the relations of production (under the broad heading of "economy") as dependent on the infrastructure. However, when he analyzes modern capitalist societies he tends to treat the relations of production as of major causal significance and thus as part of the infrastructure.

4. Harris has emphatically rejected the dialectical component of historical materialism. In *The Rise of Anthropological Theory* (1968) and *Cultural Materialism*

(1979), Harris denounces the dialectic as mystical nonsense. It cannot be scientifically operationalized, he says, and thus is of no use as part of a theory of society. He refers to it as "the Hegelian monkey" on Marx and Engels's back. Harris says that it is always possible to identify a range of so-called contradictions in social life, but that the concept of dialectics gives us no way to determine what the most important contradictions are. We need to be able to answer the question, Harris says, "Will the real contradictions please stand up?"

5. Harris has added the "emic-etic" distinction to his materialist formulations (the "mental-behavioral" distinction was already implicitly there in Marx) and combined it with his infrastructure-structure-superstructure distinction.

CRITICAL ASSESSMENT

Cultural materialism has long been a very controversial approach. The reaction to Harris has often been highly polarized: His disciples and fellow travelers have defended him vigrously, whereas his opponents have often been out for blood. He has been criticized by the Marxists on the one hand as engaging in a revision of Marxism, which to many Marxists is simply not acceptable, and by the cultural idealists for what they see as an omission of the vital causal role of symbols and ideas (e.g., Genovese, 1968). Even some materialists have been critical of him for being too much of a materialist, in their eyes a "vulgar materialist" who crudely reduces the explanation of everything to material conditions (Friedman, 1974; Godelier, 1977). However, Harris has answered this charge, quite successfully I think, on many occasions (cf. Harris, 1987a). As noted above, his principle of infrastructural determinism is probabilistic, thus allowing the superstructure some causal role in the organization of social life.

My own view is that cultural materialism is one of the most sensible and useful theoretical approaches we have in the social sciences. Indeed, my book *Social Transformations* (1995b, 1999) develops a comprehensive materialist theory of social evolution that is largely an extension and formalization of cultural materialism. Nonetheless, there are some difficulties with cultural materialism that cannot escape notice. These involve the awkward problem of where to place "relations of production" or "economy" within the universal pattern and causal framework, the mixing of the emic-etic and mental-behavioral distinctions with the infrastructure-structure-superstructure distinction, and the highly negative stance toward sociobiology. Let me take up each of these problems in turn.

As noted above, Harris contends that one of the things that sharply distinguishes cultural materialism from Marxist or neo-Marxist historical materialism involves the location of the "relations of production" or "economy." Harris claims to have removed this component of social life from the infrastructure, where Marxism places it, and transferred it to the structure under the heading of "political economy." Harris argues that this change is crucial, for only by such a move can we hope to understand the forces that determine "economy," and why and how it changes. However, if one looks at the whole of Harris's work, one notices that "economy" often seems to end up back in the infrastructure, as when Harris refers to the "demo-techno-econo-environmental infrastructure."

One might claim that he is being inconsistent, sometimes treating "economy" as structure and sometimes treating it as infrastructure. This is what I thought for a long time. I held that Harris was being inconsistent in the application of his universal pattern, but that in this particular case the inconsistency was a good thing. I held that Harris actually had adopted an informal and unacknowledged rule of thumb whereby he kept "economy" in the structure when he was analyzing preindustrial and precapitalist societies, but shifted it to the infrastructure when he was analyzing social patterns within modern capitalist societies. This seemed sensible enough, for ecological and demographic factors do seem to have their greatest causal significance in preindustrial societies (although economic forces can be of enormous significance there too), whereas they take a back seat to economics in the modern capitalist world. I myself have struggled with this problem and tried to produce a clean and consistent classification system and have not succeeded as I had hoped. I concluded that it couldn't be done, or at least that I didn't know how to do it, or at the very least that if it could be done it might not be worth the time. We simply have to be satisfied with a little messiness in our models in order to make them work. We should treat our models as general guides rather than as rigid constructs that tie us down, which is what Harris seemingly had done in a very intelligent way.

A different interpretation of what Harris has done has been set forth by Brian Ferguson (1995b). Ferguson claims that Harris is being consistent but that he distinguishes two types of economy, "infrastructural economics" and "structural economics." Infrastructural economics for the most part seems to be technological applications to economy, whereas structural economics involves economic ownership, distribution, and exchange. In Ferguson's words (1995b:35), infrastructural economics involves "the way in which a given technology is applied to a specific environment to produce the energy on which social life depends," whereas structural economics consists of "division of labor, exchange and distribution of products and services, control over labor, and ownership or differential access to technology and natural resources." This does appear to be what Harris has done, for as he tells us (1979:64–65):

> I have therefore removed certain key aspects of what many Marxists mean by "relations of production" from infrastructure to structure and superstructure. The classic Marxist concept of "ownership of the means of production," for example, denotes differential access to the technology employed in subsistence production and hence is an organizational feature of structure rather than a part of infrastructure. . . .
>
> Similarly, I view patterns of exchange—e.g., reciprocity, redistribution, trade, markets, employment, money transactions—not as infrastructure but partly as etic structural components—aspects of domestic and political economy—and partly as emic and mental superstructural components.

And in his latest statement on the subject, Harris puts the matter this way (1999:142):

> Ambiguities about the meaning of economics need to be resolved. Economics appears as a component of both the infrastructural and structural subsystems. In the infrastructure, economics denotes the predominant production practices, such as foraging, irrigation agriculture, or industrial factory production—the mode of subsistence, in other words. In the structure, economics denotes the manner in which economic effort is organized. The latter

corresponds to the Marxist notion of the social relations of production—relations governed by such institutions as private or communal property and wages or other forms of compensation and exchange. Industrial factories, for example, are an infrastructural feature, while the organization of the factory—whether by workers' committees or by elite managers—is a structural feature.

But if Harris has done all of these things, the only part of "economy" that is left in infrastructure would appear to be mainly what he designates by other terms, such as technology ("forces of production"), modes of subsistence, and technoenvironmental relationships.

Ferguson seems to be right in terms of what Harris has formally done, but I cannot get rid of my original feeling that Harris is still being somewhat inconsistent. Consider his book *America Now* (1981). In this book Harris's entire focus is on American society and the fundamental changes it has undergone since the end of World War II. What seems to be doing most of the explanatory work there is the capitalist system and its changes. Why, for example, did women leave home and move into the labor force? It was because the service and information sector of the economy was expanding and women were in great demand by capitalists to fill the rapidly increasing number of jobs in this economic sector. Moreover, inflation was lowering the family's standard of living and as a result women were eager to seek work to keep that living standard as high as possible. Consider also Harris's (1992) analysis of the collapse of Communism in the Soviet Union. Here great emphasis is placed on the worsening economic problems the Soviet Union was experiencing since the 1970s. If economics is this important, then why is it not retained (formally) within the infrastructure, that part of the society with the greatest causal significance? Or is Harris just using good judgment in silently slipping economics back there in his mind? It seems to me a serious mistake to put so much of economics in the structure, because then we lose most of the explanatory power of capitalism, which Harris obviously wants to retain. And it is even worse to have "technology" in the infrastructure at the same time, because then we have our causation backwards, i.e., in capitalist societies the production relations (structure for Harris) would be determining part of the infrastructure.

Part of the difficulty here may simply be what Harris is thinking of when he uses terms like "economy" or "capitalism." For example, he says that "cultural materialism cannot be reconciled with classical Marxist interpretations of the inner dynamics of capitalism precisely because Marx accorded the essentially emic mental categories of capital and profits a predominant role in the further evolution of modern industrial society, whereas from the cultural materialist perspective the key to the future of capitalism lies in the conjunction of its etic behavioral components and especially in the feedback between political economy and the infrastructure" (Harris, 1979:65). But capital and profits are not emic and mental components at all; they are the most crucial behavioral characteristics of the capitalist system! The search for profits and the ceaseless accumulation of capital are the driving engine of capitalism, the entire logic of the system. It was the search for profits that was driving capitalists after World War II to seek out women in larger numbers to work in the expanding service and information sector of the economy. Capitalism as an economic system, then, can only be regarded as a vital part of the infrastructure of modern industrial societies.

In the end, then, my solution to the dilemma of where to place "economy" is to keep it together as a coherent whole (not to do so is to invite serious trouble, as we have seen), and to place it in infrastructure even though I recognize with Harris that in preindustrial societies "economy" is often shaped by other aspects of the infrastructure. Economy is just too basic and important to remove from infrastructure. We seem to have little choice, as I suggested earlier, but to learn to live with a somewhat messy model.

A second serious problem with cultural materialism as formulated by Harris involves his mixing of the emic-etic and mental-behavioral distinctions with the division of societies into infrastructural, structural, and superstructural components. I strongly agree with Harris about the importance of the emic-etic and mental-behavioral distinctions, but I do not think the former should be, or even logically can be, integrated with the infrastructure-structure-superstructure distinction. It has seemed to me that early on (e.g., Harris, 1968) Harris stressed that emic-etic was an epistemological distinction that had methodological relevance, not something that was part of the content of social life. I therefore took emics and etics to be epistemological concepts and nothing more. Even in later work Harris stresses the epistemological character of these concepts. In *Cultural Materialism* (1979) Harris entitles the chapter in which these concepts are discussed "The Epistemology of Cultural Materialism" and defines them in the following way (1979:32): "Emic operations have as their hallmark the elevation of the native informant to the status of the ultimate judge of the adequacy of the observer's descriptions and analyses. The test of the adequacy of emic analyses is their ability to generate statements the native accepts as real, meaningful, or appropriate." By contrast, "Etic operations have as their hallmark the elevation of observers to the status of ultimate judges of the categories and concepts used in descriptions and analyses. The test of the adequacy of etic accounts is simply their ability to generate scientifically productive theories about the causes of sociocultural differences and similarities. Rather than employ concepts that are necessarily real, meaningful, and appropriate from the native point of view, the observer is free to use alien categories and rules derived from the data language of science." From this it appears that Harris conceives of the emic-etic distinction as an epistemological one that has crucial methodological implications. Anthropological researchers can collect data by trying to get inside the heads of the natives and seeing their world as they conceptualize it (emics), or they can use categories that they have formulated as social scientists that do not depend on any agreement by the natives that these categories are meaningful (etics).

James Lett (1990) holds, as I do, that the concepts of emics and etics are epistemological categories, not ontological ones, but somehow Harris has ended up making them into ontological categories nonetheless (but while still treating them as if they were epistemological categories). Thus, by 1979 with the publication of *Cultural Materialism,* they become parts of sociocultural systems along with a more explicit distinction between mental and behavioral, which Harris admits he had formerly conflated with emic-etic. Whereas Harris had earlier (e.g., Harris, 1976) equated emic with mental and etic with behavioral, by 1979 he had come to recognize that mental life can be approached both emically and etically, as can actual behavior. Suffice it to say that the emic-etic distinction has always been a slippery one that has confused many social scientists, including Harris himself. To some extent, this confusion has actually gotten worse over time. Thus in a book devoted entirely to this issue (Headland, Pike, and Harris, 1990), we find Harris (1990) claiming that the emic-etic distinction has little to do with the insider-outsider or native-observer distinction, when in fact it appears that those distinctions are extremely close in meaning to the emic-etic distinction, if not exactly the same thing: Emic operations are those relying on the use of insiders or natives, whereas etic operations are those based on categories formulated by outside observers. (Moreover, the subtitle of the aforementioned book is *The Insider/Outsider Debate!*) This comes as quite a shock when in fact Harris's 1979 definitions of emics and etics (cited above) seem to indicate that they are precisely a matter of the insider's versus the outsider's point of view.

After careful study of Harris's and others' pronouncements on this matter, I have reluctantly come to the conclusion that Harris's emic-etic distinction is so complicated, so riddled with qualifications, and thus so confusing, that perhaps the best course of action is simply to drop it, at least for theoretical purposes (it might be retained as a methodological device). Not much is lost, and a great deal of clarity is gained, and besides it has been pointed out that Harris constantly violates his own pronouncements anyway—to wit, constantly producing emic explanations while claiming to generate etic ones (Oakes, 1981). Moreover, consider the fact that Harris admits that before 1979 he equated emic with mental and etic with behavioral, but that this apparently had no effect on his research conclusions! Again, this suggests that dropping the emic-etic distinction will result in no real loss and a significant gain in the clarity of what one is doing. As for how this bears on the infrastructure-structure-superstructure distinction, it could be reformulated in the following way:

- *Infrastructure:* Those natural phenomena and social forms vital to economic production and biological reproduction, and especially including the technology of subsistence, technoenvironmental relationships, ecosystems, labor patterns, "economy," knowledge and ideas bearing upon the subsistence quest and economic production, and demographic patterns (e.g., birth and death rates, age and sex composition of the population, technology of contraception and population regulation).
- *Structure:* Organized patterns of social behavior common to the members of a society, excluding those relating directly to production and reproduction, and especially including family and kinship patterns, gender and gender roles, political organization and war, social stratification, educational systems, and organized patterns of sport, games, and leisure.
- *Superstructure:* Beliefs, ideas, norms, values, and symbols shared by the members of a society, and especially including religion, taboos, mythology, art, music, literature, and science. The superstructure contrasts with the structure in that the structure is behavioral, the superstructure mental.

This seems to me a much cleaner and clearer way of identifying the universal pattern, which I shall incorporate later into my theoretical synthesis.

My final criticism of Harris involves his stance on sociobiology. Harris has been a resolute critic of this approach, although it must be acknowledged that his criticisms have been made largely from a conceptual and scientific standpoint and he has seldom descended to the level of most of the other critics by attacking sociobiology on political grounds. Harris's criticisms of sociobiology are some of the most intelligent that have been made. Nevertheless, I believe these criticisms to be misplaced and, actually, completely unnecessary. Shortly I shall argue that cultural materialism needs to be pushed in the direction of sociobiology and, in fact, that cultural materialist principles only make sense in light of sociobiological principles. Cultural materialism and sociobiology are natural friends, not enemies, and can easily be synthesized to produce a more general and powerful theoretical approach of exactly the type that Harris so clearly favors. In a recent article, Harris (1994) has argued that cultural materialism is alive and well and will not go away until something better comes along. I shall be arguing that something better has now come along, although that something includes a great deal of cultural materialism itself.

NOTE

1. Harris's most important publications are *The Rise of Anthropological Theory* (1968), *Cows, Pigs, Wars, and Witches: The Riddles of Culture* (1974), *Cannibals and Kings: The Origins of Cultures* (1977), *Cultural Materialism: The Struggle for a Science of Culture* (1979), *America Now: The Anthropology of a Changing Culture* (1981), *Good to Eat: Riddles of Food and Culture* (1985), *Death, Sex, and Fertility: Population Regulation in Preindustrial and Developing Societies* (Harris and Ross, 1987), and *Theories of Culture in Postmodern Times* (1999).

8

Sociobiological Explanations

It is universally acknowledged that there is a great uniformity among the actions of men, in all nations and ages, and that human nature remains the same in its principles and operations. The same motives always produce the same actions; the same events follow from the same causes.

—*David Hume*

The *tabula* of human nature was never *rasa* and now it is being read.

—*William D. Hamilton*

Theories that go counter to the facts of human nature are foredoomed.

—*Edith Hamilton*

All great truths begin as blasphemies.   —*George Bernard Shaw*

BASIC PRINCIPLES

Sociobiology may be said to have officially begun in 1975 with the publication of Edward O. Wilson's *Sociobiology: The New Synthesis*.[1] Wilson, a zoologist, defined sociobiology as "the study of the biological basis for social behavior in all animals." The vast majority of his book was taken up with a discussion of animals other than humans, and only the final chapter was devoted to humans. Here Wilson speculated about the biological foundations of human behavior. Sociobiology is to a considerable degree a reaction against what later came to be called the Standard Social Science Model (SSSM). The SSSM includes a wide variety of theoretical perspectives, but the basic assumption is that human social organization has little or nothing to do with human biology. The behavior of humans everywhere is largely determined by social and cultural influences external to individuals and their genetics. In its most extreme form, the SSSM holds that the mind is a tabula rasa on which society and culture write their script. Sociobiologists hold that

120

this view, which has been the dominant view among all social scientists for most of the twentieth century, is wrong, or at least a gross exaggeration and oversimplification.

Some social scientists were beginning to take the biological foundations of human behavior seriously before Wilson wrote his famous book. In 1971 Lionel Tiger and Robin Fox, two anthropologists, wrote *The Imperial Animal*, and in 1975 Pierre van den Berghe, a well-known sociologist, wrote *Man in Society: A Biosocial View.* These were what might be termed "protosociobiological" works. Tiger and Fox argued that humans come equipped with a *biogrammar*, or a basic set of biological templates that predispose their behavior along certain lines. Van den Berghe made the same point, referring to the human biological predispositions as *Anlagen*. The lists of predispositions offered by these authors overlap extensively, and they can be combined into one list as follows:

1. *Aggression:* Humans are by nature rather aggressive organisms, which means that they are prone to use violence, or the threat of violence, as a means of settling disputes and attaining desired ends.
2. *Hierarchy:* Humans are prone to organize themselves in rank-ordered systems, or systems in which the competition for status is of paramount importance.
3. *Male domination:* There is a strong tendency for males of the species to exert authority over females and to predominate in higher-status positions.
4. *Mother-infant bonding:* Women are biologically specialized for parenting to a degree that is significantly greater than men's tendency toward parental care.
5. *Territoriality:* Human individuals tend to be territorial creatures in the sense that they define and defend regional spaces all the way from small personal spaces to huge national states.
6. *Incest avoidance:* The general avoidance of incest among humans, widely considered to be a human universal, is rooted in a biological tendency that exists because of incest's harmful biological consequences.

It is critical to note that these social scientists stress that these are biological *predispositions* or *tendencies,* not rigid instincts, and as such interact in important ways with the social, cultural, and physical environment to produce the actual behavior that is observed in human societies. Social organization and behavior are always *biosocial* in the sense that they result from the complex interaction of the biological and the sociocultural. For example, despite a human tendency toward aggression, we see that, although some societies display very high levels of aggressive behavior, others display much lower levels of such behavior. The assumption is that some sociocultural conditions (such as resource competition) trigger high levels of aggression, whereas other sociocultural conditions (such as resource abundance) elicit only low levels of aggression. Similarly, despite a human tendency toward hierarchy, we see that some societies (such as most hunter-gatherers) have only minimal hierarchies, whereas others (such as agrarian and industrial societies) have much more elaborate hierarchies. Think of it this way: The sociocultural and physical environments are like the volume control knob on a radio; they can turn predispositions to higher levels or they can tone them down. In a few instances they might be able to turn these predispositions off; despite natural human sex drives, for example, there have been many priesthoods whose members have taken vows of celibacy. However, the predispositions tend to express themselves to at least some extent in all environments.

The sociobiology proper that was born in 1975 was rooted in an explicit theory known as the *theory of inclusive fitness* or *kin selection,* which is a specific dimension of neo-Darwinian evolutionary biology. As is well known, the central concept in Darwin's theory was that of *natural selection.* Darwin argued that in every population in every generation more offspring are produced than available resources can sustain. There thus results a *struggle for survival* among organisms, and it is the fittest organisms that have the best chance of surviving. Organisms are fit to the extent that they have the anatomical, physiological, and behavioral traits better suited, or better adapted, to coping with the conditions of a particular environment. Moreover, those organisms whose traits reveal relative adaptive advantage leave more offspring and thus also enjoy greater reproductive success. In Darwinian and neo-Darwinian terms, they have greater "fitness."

Darwin assumed that the organism was the unit of selection and that the traits of every organism evolved in accord with selfish reproductive interests. The assumption of selfishness was the only assumption that made sense, because organisms are competing in a game of survival and reproduction. However, Darwin also knew that organisms also behaved altruistically, often making sacrifices (including giving up their own lives), for the benefit of conspecifics. We know, and Darwin did also, that this kind of behavior is highly characteristic of the social insects, who have soldier castes biologically specialized for defending the hive at the cost of their own lives. At higher phylogenetic levels, we find a wide variety of altruistic behaviors. This fact of altruism seemed to be in contradiction to what Darwin was saying, and constituted a conundrum that took many years to solve. An elegant solution to the puzzle of the evolution of self-sacrifice was proposed in 1964 by the geneticist William Hamilton, considered by some the greatest theoretical biologist since Darwin. Hamilton argued that what created the puzzle was the assumption that it was the organism that was the unit of fitness. Hamilton argued that it was actually the *gene* that was the unit of fitness and that natural selection operates so as to preserve or eliminate genes rather than entire organisms. Hamilton claimed that there was a form of fitness called *inclusive fitness.* An organism's fitness is not simply a matter of its own survival, but involves the total number of its genes that are represented in the gene pool of its species. Organisms are more fit than others when they have a larger representation of their genes in the gene pool.

Inclusive fitness is sometimes called *kin selection* because it assumes that organisms tend to favor kin, and favor close kin more than distant kin, because they share genes in common with kin and an increasing number of genes in common as kinship becomes closer. Parents and their offspring share one-half of their genes, as do, on average, full siblings. Grandparents and grandchildren share one-quarter of their genes, and first cousins share, on average, one-eighth. Hamilton argued that organisms behaved so as to promote their inclusive fitness, and this could sometimes lead the organism to give up its own life. For example, if a mother bird warns three of her chicks that a predator is approaching them and in so doing diverts the predator's attention to her and causes him to eat her, she nevertheless saves three half-units of her genes, for a total of one-and-a-half units. Since she is dead, we have to subtract one unit of her genes (those inside her own body), but this leaves her with a net gain of one-half unit. The conclusion is that by warning her offspring she actually benefitted genetically despite causing her own death because she optimized the number of copies of her genes that she left in the gene pool. This leads to the further observation that what is altruism on the surface level (the level of actual behavior) is actually selfishness—genetic selfishness—at a deeper level (the level of the adaptive mechanisms that are triggering the behavior).

How does all this apply to human behavior? The basic argument is that *many features of human behavior and social organization result from efforts made by individuals to maximize their inclusive fitness.* No assumption is being made that humans have any conscious understanding that they are motivated in such a way; they are simply acting, to a large degree unconsciously, in accordance with evolved brain modules that arose during the course of hominid evolution. Let's look at the implications of this argument. The most fundamental implication is that men and women will have different ways of promoting their inclusive fitness, and thus different *reproductive strategies.* Males can maximize their inclusive fitness by inseminating as many females as possible, and thus we should expect men to have difficulty confining themselves to monogamous relationships. Instead, they should greatly desire a wide variety of sexual partners. Females, on the other hand, can have only a limited number of offspring in a lifetime, and it does not matter whether these offspring are produced by one man or several. Their inclusive fitness can best be served by choosing good mates, i.e., mates who will stick around and provide for the offspring. Philandering can actually reduce a woman's reproductive fitness in that it can reduce a man's commitment to her.[2]

But there is more to the story. If a man provides for offspring, he wants to be sure that these offspring are his. Aside from prereproductive death, the worst possible outcome with respect to a man's reproductive interests would be for him to provide for another man's offspring, thinking they are his own, and thus promote that man's inclusive fitness at the cost of his. Therefore, men should behave in ways so as to maximize their confidence that the offspring they are rearing are their own. Men attempt to maximize their confidence of paternity primarily through one or another type of mate guarding behavior, such as sequestering women (done throughout the Islamic world and in many other places and times) or fitting them with chastity belts when the men are away, and mate guarding behavior is driven by the evolved adaptation of male sexual jealousy. (These mate guarding behaviors are known as *anticuckoldry strategies;* a cuckolded man is one who has been deceived by his mate into believing that the offspring he is providing for are his own.)

An important qualification to the above is essential. It seems clear that in some societies individuals engage in behaviors that do not appear to promote their inclusive fitness. For this reason Joseph Lopreato (1989) has formulated what he calls the *modified maximization principle.* This principle holds that (1989:129) "organisms are predisposed to behave so as to maximize their inclusive fitness, but this predisposition is conditioned by the quest for creature comforts, by self-deception, and by autonomization of phenotype from genotype." As Timothy Crippen (1994:315) has stated, this principle "suggests that human behavior maximizes fitness unless its reproductive consequences are subverted by the desire to accumulate resources that engender pleasure, by self-denying or ascetic tendencies often stimulated by sacred beliefs and practices, and/or by motivations that once produced fitness maximizing behaviors (e.g., motivations underlying sexual activity), but that now are harnessed in the service of non-maximizing behaviors (e.g., sexual activity between individuals using some method of contraception)." This means that proximate constraints may subvert the tendency to maximize fitness. Crippen goes on to say that "for individuals living in demographically immense, class-divided, and technologically advanced societies, the proximate motives connected with the pursuit of pleasure and the aversion to pain may be harnessed in the service of behaviors that have little, and perhaps even negative, influence on an individual's inclusive fitness" (1994:318).

It is often assumed, especially by its critics, that sociobiology assumes some sort of *genetic determinism*, or direct one-to-one correspondence between genes and behavior. In fact, nothing could be further from the truth. Sociobiologists have always stressed the complex interaction between the biogram and the various and sundry features of the natural and social environment. Social behavior is always a *biosocial* phenomenon. Much of what is in the human biogram is *facultative* in nature, and humans are by far the most facultative of species (R. Alexander, 1990; Sober and Wilson, 1998). Facultative traits are those whose expression depends upon the organism's ability to carefully assess the environment and then respond with the appropriate adaptive behavior. These traits involve conditional strategies that give behavior considerable flexibility (R. Alexander, 1990). Richard Alexander (1990) nominates polyandry as a good example of a facultative trait. There are certainly no "genes for polyandry," but there are genes involved in building brains that direct individuals to assess their environment in such a way that they may adopt polyandrous marriage when it is the best way of promoting one's inclusive fitness. Likewise, there are certainly no "genes for cross-cousin marriage," but there are genes that lead to cross-cousin marriage's being adaptive under certain types of environmental conditions. Reproductive behavior also appears to be highly facultative, with individuals seemingly adjusting their fertility levels to the extent to which offspring are likely to survive. Where infant and child mortality are high, fertility levels tend to be high in order to produce a certain number of surviving offspring, but when the survival prospects of children are good the same number of surviving children can be produced by a lower level of overall fertility (Carey and Lopreato, 1995). Sexual maturation also appears to be facultatively controlled. It has been discovered that in economically marginal and stressful environments girls reach puberty earlier, and thus start reproduction earlier, presumably as an inclusive fitness promoting strategy (Chisholm, 1999). One final example of a facultative trait involves parental investment in offspring. Throughout the world's societies parental investment in sons usually exceeds parental investment in daughters, generally because sons have greater potential reproductive success. However, in a number of societies, or segments of societies, parents can promote their reproductive success better by investing more in daughters (Dickemann, 1979a; Cronk, 1989, 1991, 1999). Among the Mukogodo of Kenya, for example, daughters are shown clear favoritism, and the reason appears to be because girls have much better marital prospects than boys. Girls are usually able to marry, often having a good chance of obtaining high-status men from neighboring societies as husbands. Boys, on the other hand, frequently have a great deal of difficulty accumulating enough livestock to provide the bridewealth payments necessary to secure a wife. They may marry late in life, or never (Cronk, 1989, 1991, 1999).

What kind of evidence would support the basic predictions of sociobiology? One kind would be evidence showing that male sexual possession of females and males' desires for sexual variety are extremely common, if not universal, behaviors. Donald Symons's book *The Evolution of Human Sexuality* (1979), a sociobiological classic, presents a wealth of such evidence. We should also find evidence all over the world that "blood is thicker than water," i.e., that everywhere kin are favored over nonkin, and this is what we do find. Donald Brown (1991) argues persuasively that if a pattern of human behavior can be shown to be a true human universal or near-universal—found in all or virtually all societies—then there is a strong presumption that it rests on a solid biological foundation. (This should not be taken to imply that sociobiology is only relevant to explaining universals or near-universals. As the discussion of facultative traits showed, sociobiology is also extremely relevant to explaining a wide range of cultural variations. However, universals or near-universals are especially good evidence that a cultural trait is biologically rooted.) Below is a list of human universals or near-universals, not placed in any particular order of importance or meant to be exhaustive (Brown, 1991; Pinker, 1994):

1. Gossip, lying, misleading, verbal humor, humorous insults, poetic and rhetorical speech forms, storytelling, metaphor.
2. Binary distinctions.
3. Coy flirtations with the eyes; masking, modifying, and mimicking facial expressions; displays of affection.
4. Nonlinguistic vocal communication such as cries and squeals.
5. Adornment of bodies and arrangement of hair.
6. Drugs, both medicinal and recreational.
7. Male monopolization of political leadership, high-status positions, and warfare.
8. Great interest in the topic of sex; standards of sexual attractiveness.
9. Male sexual jealousy.
10. Sex as a service provided by women to men.
11. Husbands usually older than wives.
12. Men more aroused by visual sexual stimuli than women.
13. More aggression and violence by men.
14. Incest avoidance.
15. Language.
16. Abstract thinking.
17. Family, marriage, and kinship systems; families built around a mother and children, usually the biological mother and one or more men.
18. Kin terminologies; distinguishing of close kin from distant kin; favoring of close kin.
19. Facial expressions relating to happiness, sadness, anger, fear, surprise, disgust, and contempt.
20. Toolmaking and technology.
21. Making or using fire.

22. Group living and sociability.
23. Groups defined by locality or territory.
24. Socialization practices; children copying their elders.
25. Prestige seeking and allocation.
26. A division of labor based minimally on age and sex.
27. Conceptions of gender and gender roles.
28. Social cooperation.
29. Female monopolization of child care.
30. Political organization and leadership.
31. Social norms and values, and punishment for violations; sense of right and wrong; etiquette.
32. Standards of sexual modesty, sex generally in private, fondness for sweets, food taboos, discreetness in elimination of bodily wastes.
33. Ingroup-outgroup antagonisms.
34. Religion.
35. Worldviews.
36. Rituals.
37. Concepts of property.
38. Music and dance.
39. Art.
40. Symbolism.
41. Ethnocentrism.
42. Modes of economic production, distribution, and exchange.
43. Birth control and population regulation.

Alice Rossi (1984) argues that a pattern of social behavior can be suspected of having a biological basis if two or more of the following criteria are met:

1. There are consistent correlations between a behavior and a physiological sex attribute (body structure, sex chromosome type, hormonal type).
2. The pattern is found in infants and young children prior to the occurrence of major socialization influences, or the pattern emerges with the onset of puberty.
3. The pattern is stable across cultures.
4. Similar behavior patterns are found across species, especially the higher primates.

As we shall see in the chapters ahead, there are many patterns of human social behavior that meet at least two of these criteria and a fair number that meet all four.

TWO CONTROVERSIES

The Level of Selection

Our discussion thus far has clearly implied that sociobiology views the unit of selection as most commonly the genes contained within organisms (while not discounting evolution at the level of the individual organism itself). And, indeed, this is so. Darwin himself saw selection occurring at the level of the organism, which was why altruistic behavior puzzled him. In the early 1960s V.C. Wynne-Edwards (1962) set forth an argument for selection occurring at a higher level, or for *group selection*. Wynne-Edwards argued that organisms and species have the traits they do because these traits have evolved to benefit entire populations. For example, he explained the roosting behavior of birds as a behavior that allows a bird population to assess its population density and adjust it accordingly so that the entire population benefits. Although Wynne-Edwards is commonly cited as the chief proponent of group selection at this time, a number of evolutionary biologists in fact accepted it, at least as one possible mode of selection (Segerstråle, 2000).

However, just four years later the evolutionary biologist George Williams published a famous book, *Adaptation and Natural Selection* (1966), in which he claimed that adaptation should never be explained at a level higher than truly necessary and that most selection occurred at the level of the gene or the individual. He did not rule out the possibility of group selection, but thought it extremely rare. Williams's argument was echoed a decade later by Richard Dawkins, whose equally famous book *The Selfish Gene* (1976) helped to launch sociobiology. Dawkins argued that selection occurred basically at the level of the gene, and that organisms were largely vehicles for getting genes passed from one generation to the next: An organism is just a gene's way of making another gene.

The ideas of Williams and Dawkins have become widely accepted throughout evolutionary biology and sociobiology and are essentially the received wisdom. But the idea of group selection has not gone away. It has been pushed most vigorously by David Sloan Wilson and Elliott Sober (1994; Sober and Wilson, 1998). Wilson and Sober argue that selection is a complex multilevel phenomenon, but it is clearly evolution at the level of the group as a whole that interests them most. Much of human social life, they claim, can only be explained as the result of processes of between-group selection. They note, for example, that in tribal societies there is often relentless competition between lineages, which "compete against each other as corporate units, much as we expect individuals to compete when they are allowed to act as free agents" (Sober and Wilson, 1998:174). In discussing social norms, they hold that "most traditional human societies appear designed to suppress within-group processes that are dysfunctional for the group, and as a result natural selection has operated and adaptations have accumulated at the group level. Human social groups often function as adaptive units and are perceived as such by indigenous people and the ethnographers who study them" (Sober and Wilson, 1998:192). Sober and Wilson also refer to Raymond Kelly's (1985) work on the interaction between the Nuer and the Dinka, African pastoral societies. Conflict between these societies was gradually resolved in favor of the political supremacy of the Nuer, and for Sober and Wilson this could only have been because of between-group selection. The Nuer were adaptively superior *as a group*, and this is why they prevailed. The authors are convinced that some human groups are so well designed at the group level that they had to have evolved by group selection; nothing else could explain such excellent design. Another sociobiologist to invoke group selection is Kevin MacDonald. In a series of works (MacDonald, 1994, 1998a, 1998b), he has argued that the Jews have been one of the world's most successful ethnic groups because they have followed what he calls a "group evolutionary strategy." Individual Jews have made sacrifices in favor of the group, and the group has prospered as a result.

Few sociobiologists have found arguments like these convincing, nor have I. The mistake these authors are making is a failure to draw a very simple distinction between behavior *that evolves because it benefits the group* and behavior *that has the consequence of benefitting the group.* They provide no evidence to show that the former is occurring; in their examples, the latter is in fact occurring, but only because the groups in question are aggregations of individuals. The group benefits simply because the individuals within it benefit. Sober and Wilson and MacDonald reify the group in that they see it as having a distinct existence from its constituent members.

Most sociobiologists, then, reject the notion of group selection and see selection occurring at the level of genes or individual organisms. Indeed, it is not hard to see why selection should be occurring at this level. Genuine altruism cannot constitute what John Maynard Smith (1974, 1982) has called an *evolutionarily stable strategy.* A population of genuine altruists could not remain stable because it could always be invaded and displaced by selfish strategists. Organisms that sacrifice their genes for the good of others that do not share them will find that their genes for genuine altruism will quickly disappear from the gene pool for the simple reason that the altruists will be out-reproduced by organisms that are reproductively selfish (Low, 2000). And not only is the concept of group selection logically dubious, but there is no real empirical evidence to support it. As Bobbi Low (2000:160) has remarked, "If group good at the expense of individual fitness were relatively powerful, we should expect genetic sacrifice to be common. In fact, it is so rare as to be undetectable in populations of any organism."

Darwinian Psychology versus Darwinian Social Science

Sociobiologists stress the *adaptive* character of many features of human behavior, i.e., that behavior evolves because it is useful in promoting the reproductive interests of each individual. Many sociobiologists take the view that *adaptations pertain only to the Environment of Evolutionary Adaptedness,* or *EEA.* This ancestral environment is the one in which modern humans evolved over the past 100,000 to 200,000 years, during which time they lived exclusively in small hunter-gatherer groups. The argument is that our neurobiology evolved to adapt humans to the ancestral environment, but in the last 10,000 years there has been enormous social evolution and today people live in extremely complex, state-level societies, many of them highly industrialized and urbanized. As a consequence, there is no reason to assume that their behavior will necessarily be adaptive under these conditions. Those sociobiologists holding this view have taken to calling themselves *Darwinian psychologists* or *evolutionary psychologists,* even though many of them are not affiliated with the discipline of psychology (Symons, 1989, 1990, 1992; Daly and Wilson, 1984, 1986; Barkow, 1989; Tooby and Cosmides, 1990).

To a large extent the Darwinian psychologists are reacting against another group that has been called *Darwinian anthropologists* or *Darwinian social scientists* (e.g., R. Alexander, 1990; Turke, 1990a, 1990b), which in fact probably includes the majority of social scientists working today under the broad label of sociobiology. The Darwinian social scientists assume that people in modern environments are, just like their distant ancestors, striving to maximize their inclusive fitness and thus that most behavior is adaptive even under these conditions. This contrasts with the claim of the Darwinian psychologists that it is a waste of time to try to ascertain whether people in modern environments are trying to maximize their inclusive fitness. Because these environments are very different from the ancestral environment, there is little reason to assume that behavior that evolved in the EEA would continue to be adaptive. Moreover, what do the Darwinian social scientists do if they discover that people in modern environments are not acting to maximize their reproductive success? Do they thereby reach the negative conclusion that sociobiology cannot be applied to behavior in such environments? They should not, since it can still be argued that people are behaving in accordance with evolved psychological mechanisms—ancient adaptations—that drive their behavior. For example, men in modern industrial societies still appear to seek sexual variety, but they do not wish to impregnate the women with whom they are having extramarital affairs, for this would lead to unwanted complications in their lives. Therefore, they are not seeking to maximize their reproductive success but rather are behaving in accordance with a psychological mechanism—"mate with attractive women you haven't mated with before"— that would have promoted reproductive success under ancestral conditions. Donald Symons (1989, 1990, 1992), one of the leading proponents of Darwinian psychology, claims that what we should be trying to study is the nature of *evolved psychological mechanisms,* not behavior. As he puts it (1989:137; emphasis added), "In the study of adaptation, the key issue is not whether or not a given phenotypic feature influences reproductive success, but rather *whether differential reproductive success historically influenced the form of the phenotypic feature."*

Important replies to the argument of the Darwinian psychologists have been made by Richard Alexander (1990) and Paul Turke (1990a, 1990b). Alexander agrees that it is important to study adaptive design but argues that it cannot be studied except by direct reference to behavior: "Underlying adaptive design cannot be studied directly. One studies behavioral and other outcomes, judges their reproductive significance . . . and then infers the underlying physiological and morphological designs. Information about psychological and physiological mechanisms can be gained only by observing ultimate expressions of the phenotype" (R. Alexander, 1990:247). Turke makes a similar point and also notes that, in fact, much human behavior in environments other than the ancestral environment has been shown to be reproductively adaptive. Indeed, "notwithstanding the *potentially* disruptive effect of environmental novelty, because long-term directional and stabilizing selection are widely evident in all forms of life, it generally is reasonable to at least consider hypotheses that hold that the mechanisms underlying behavior, as well as the behavior itself, will develop in a manner that leads to adaptive outcomes" (Turke, 1990a:316). Turke goes on to argue that it is important to determine when behavior in modern environments is or is not adaptive, because this throws important light on the nature of underlying psychobiological mechanisms.

My own position on this unresolved debate is that the Darwinian psychologists are suggesting a position that is too narrow and restrictive. We certainly need to be sensitive to the fact that a good deal of behavior in modern social environments may be non-adaptive or even maladaptive and only explicable in terms of adaptations that arose in the ancestral environment. Nonetheless, Turke makes a convincing point when he argues that much modern behavior is adaptive and that the study of modern adaptiveness versus nonadaptiveness is important in yielding an understanding of underlying psychobiological mechanisms (cf. Janicki and Krebs, 1998). Charles Crawford (1998) argues that most environments since the ancestral environment probably have not differed that much from it in terms of the production of adaptive behavior. As Crawford notes, in what I think is an especially telling point, since the social changes over the past 10,000 years have been the result of human action, it is reasonable to assume that these changes have reflected human limitations and predilections and thus have been adaptive products. Most sociobiologists follow in the tradition of Darwinian social science, and in later chapters we shall examine many of the research findings they have produced that demonstrate the adaptiveness of much modern behavior.

SOCIOBIOLOGY AND THE PROBLEM OF PREFERENCES

In chapter 6 I argued that because rational choice theory appears unable to deal with preferences we will have to turn to other theoretical approaches for help in this regard. It was suggested that the most promising approach for the identification of basic human preferences is sociobiology. As Eric Alden Smith and Bruce Winterhalder (1992a:49–50) have pointed out, considerable evidence "suggests strongly that some significant portion of the preferences and beliefs exhibited by humans in diverse times and places have been shaped directly or indirectly by natural selection." Larry Arnhart (1998) has identified twenty basic "categories of desire" that he believes are a fundamental part of the human biogram:

1. *A complete life:* Humans generally desire life, and a complete or long life, and can only be fully happy if they live out their full life span.
2. *Parental care:* Humans generally desire to care for their children, and children desire the care of adults. Despite the burdens of child care, parents are normally highly motivated to provide it.
3. *Sexual identity:* Sex is the most important dimension of personal identity, and humans strongly desire to categorize themselves as male or female. Women tend to be more nurturant than men, and men are more inclined than women to attain dominance and seek high-status positions.
4. *Sexual mating:* Humans strongly desire sexual coupling, and every society displays intense interest in sexuality. Men generally prefer to mate with young, attractive women, whereas women seek to mate with men who have high status and economic resources.
5. *Familial bonding:* Humans generally desire to live within families, the core of which is a mother with her children. All societies provide some arrangement for marriage, and kin relations are among the most important relations in every society, if not the most important.

6. *Friendship:* Humans generally seek social relationships based on mutual affection and shared interests, and humans can have enduring friendships with only a few people.

7. *Social ranking:* Humans generally seek social recognition through ranking in comparison with others, and they attain status by way of gaining prestige, honor, and fame.

8. *Justice as reciprocity:* Humans have a natural sense that justice requires returning benefit for benefit and injury for injury. Humans are inclined to feel the emotions of gratitude, love, and benevolence in response to the benefits conferred on them by others.

9. *Political rule:* Humans are political animals by nature; they have a natural tendency to struggle for power and control.

10. *War:* Humans generally desire to engage in war when such a course of action will advance their interests.

11. *Health:* Humans generally desire to live lives that provide adequately for their bodily needs. Much of social life is devoted to satisfying the desires that are fundamental to a healthy life.

12. *Beauty:* Humans generally desire beauty in the human body, and esteem the bodily signs of health and vigor. They adorn their bodies for pleasing display, and men generally prefer women whose bodies show signs of youth and nubility.

13. *Wealth:* Humans generally desire the economic goods necessary for a healthy and flourishing life.

14. *Speech:* Humans generally desire to communicate about themselves and their world, and children are naturally adapted to learn the language of their group or society.

15. *Practical habituation:* Humans are creatures of habit, and it is through this that they seek to manage their appetites and passions.

16. *Practical reasoning:* Humans seek to deliberate in a rational manner about what a good life is and to organize their actions to conform to their notion of a good life.

17. *Practical arts:* Humans generally desire craftsmanship.

18. *Aesthetic pleasure:* Humans desire and receive pleasure from their own artistic creations and the natural environments in which they live. Humans take pleasure in such activities as singing, dancing, playing musical instruments, painting, and decorating objects. They also take pleasure in the natural landscapes that resemble the environments in which they first evolved.

19. *Religious understanding:* Humans generally desire to understand the world by means of postulating the actions of supernatural powers.

20. *Intellectual understanding:* Humans generally desire to understand the world through the use of the intellect in ways quite apart from religious understanding.

Arnhart claims that these twenty categories of desire "are universally found in all human societies, that they have evolved by natural selection over four million years of human evolutionary history to become components of the species-specific nature of human beings, that they are based in the physiological mechanisms of the brain, and that they direct and limit the social variability of human beings as adapted to diverse ecological circumstances" (1998:36). As we can see, this list of categories overlaps significantly with the list of human universals discussed earlier. Although Arnhart probably considers his list exhaustive, I can think of at least two important categories of desire that he omits. Everywhere humans display a desire to minimize toil and to carry out burdensome activities by minimizing their expenditure of time and energy, a basic principle that has been called the Law of Least Effort (Zipf, 1965). This seems to be an extremely important limiting factor in all human societies, and I would add it as a twenty-first category of desire. In addition, people have an extremely strong desire for group identity, especially as it is expressed in terms of cultural, ethnic, or national affiliations (van den Berghe, 1981a; Reynolds, Falger, and Vine, 1986). This can be added as a twenty-second category of desire. Many of these categories of desire will be explored at length in the chapters to come.

THE ANTISOCIOBIOLOGICAL REACTION

As soon as sociobiology proper got started with the publication of E.O. Wilson's book in 1975 it immediately engendered a storm of controversy. It was attacked as pushing a reactionary philosophy and as being just a new form of social Darwinism. At the annual meetings of the American Association for the Advancement of Science in Washington in 1978, E.O. Wilson was the target of some of the antisociobiological crowd. As he was speaking, someone ran up to him and dumped a pitcher of water on his head, and at the same time several people stood up in the audience denouncing sociobiology, saying that it should not be taught in universities (Pines, 1978). This last point has been uttered many times by others.

Some of the best-known critiques of sociobiology have been made by the Sociobiology Study Group of Science for the People (1976), Marshall Sahlins (1976a), Lewontin, Rose, and Kamin (1984), and Marvin Harris (1979). The Sociobiology Study Group of Science for the People is a group of academics, many of them political radicals, that includes such prominent scholars as the paleontologist Stephen Jay Gould and the geneticist Richard Lewontin, both Marxists in political outlook. This critique focused mostly on E.O. Wilson, the "founder" of sociobiology and its leading representative at that time. The critique's basic claim, repeated over and over, was that sociobiology is just another in a long line of biological determinisms whose main aim is to justify the status quo and legitimize present and past social arrangements. Wilson was accused of basically engaging in political advocacy shrouded in science. The critics charged that sociobiologists' claims for social behavior bear a remarkable similarity to modern market-industrial-entrepreneurial society, with its dog-eat-dog competition and search for profits, power, and status; that no evidence is offered by sociobiologists, beyond the arbitrary postulation of genes, for their claims for the biological basis of behavior; that there is no evidence whatsoever for a genetic basis for social behavior; that sociobiology grossly overemphasizes the role of adaptation in human behavior; and that sociobiology is really a deeply conservative political ideology. They also argued against sociobiological claims for a biological basis to warfare, holding that warfare in band and tribal societies is seldom lethal to more than a few individuals. Warfare in such societies, they said, generally takes the form of minor skirmishes, and the wounding of one individual may be sufficient to call a halt to the "war." As we shall see, all of these claims are false, most of them badly so.

Marshall Sahlins's (1976a) critique, published only a short time later, consisted of two main parts. First, he tried to demolish kin selection theory. He argued that the ethnographic record shows that human kinship systems are actually organized in ways that run completely counter to the predictions of kin selection theory. Kinship, he said, is organized culturally—by social definitions of who is or is not close kin—rather than by actual genetic relatedness. Culture can make a genetically distant relative a close kinsman and vice versa. Second, Sahlins claimed that sociobiology is an intellectual product that has been deeply shaped by the capitalist society of which it is a part. Sociobiologists take the competitive, highly acquisitive nature of modern capitalist society, which is a distinctive and unique type of society, and project it onto all of human society and all of human nature. Thus, sociobiology suffers from a serious ideological bias. Evolutionary biology has degenerated into ethnocentrism. Sociobiologists apply "the model of capitalist society to the animal kingdom," then reapply "this bourgeoisified animal kingdom to the interpretation of human society" (Sahlins, 1976a:101). Sahlins quoted from a letter from Marx to Engels: "It is remarkable how Darwin recognizes among beasts and plants his English society with its division of labor, competition, opening up of new markets, 'inventions,' and the Malthusian 'struggle for existence.'" However, what Sahlins failed to recognize is that *Marx did not conclude from this that Darwin was therefore wrong.* Marx actually had great admiration for Darwin and generally accepted his theory of evolution by natural selection. He thought Darwin was right despite the fact that his ideas may have been stimulated by the nature of the society in which he lived.

Sahlins's critique, as we shall see, misses the mark widely. The theory of kin selection is not nearly as easily demolished as he imagines, and his notion that sociobiology has simply projected the character of capitalist society onto nature and then reprojected this assumed nature back onto society is exceedingly simplistic and rings hollow. What then of the critique by Lewontin, Rose, and Kamin (1984)? Their critique has much the same strident political tone as the Science for the People critique. Sociobiology is charged with being a biological determinism bent to the service of an ideology that attempts to legitimize inequality. Remarkably, the authors claim that there is no evidence for the actions of genes on behavior! It would seem that these authors would like nothing more than to ban sociobiology from universities, and if they could get away with it they probably would. One of the most obvious things about this critique is that *it is Lewontin, Rose, and Kamin themselves who are pushing a political ideology, not the sociobiologists.* There is very little evidence that sociobiologists are motivated by anything except the desire to attain scientific truth, but the evidence is overwhelming that Lewontin, Rose, and Kamin are politically motivated. They are simply beside themselves with fury over what they see as any form of biological determinism. As Vincent Falger (1984:131) has noted, "the radical critics, who make great fuss of undesirable political use of sociobiology, themselves are the main and not least dangerous ideological abusers of sociobiology."

Marvin Harris's critique of sociobiology is greatly overblown and, I shall argue, quite unnecessary, but it at least has the merit of being a scientific critique largely devoid of political motivation or invective. Harris's objections to sociobiology can be more or less summed up in the following way. First, Harris does not deny that there is such a thing as human nature; it exists and social scientists should try to describe it. However, he claims that even if sociobiological claims about human nature are correct, this would at most allow the sociobiologists to provide an understanding of the similarities between societies and could shed no light on their many important differences. This is exactly what I thought myself a quarter-century ago when I first encountered sociobiology, but the work of many sociobiologists since that time has convinced me that this notion is wrongheaded. As noted earlier, much of what is in the human biogram consists of facultative traits that cause people to respond in different adaptive ways to different environments. Second, Harris believes that the sociobiologists are committed to expanding the size and scope of human nature, whereas cultural materialists attempt to reduce the content of human nature to the smallest possible inventory of items. Harris claims that, in fact, human nature consists of only a few basic traits. These traits, which Harris calls biopsychological constants, are that people need to eat and prefer nutritious and high-protein diets with adequate calories, prefer to carry out tasks by minimizing their expenditure of time and energy, are highly sexed and generally prefer heterosexual sex, and need love and affection and will strive to increase the amount of those things that others will give them. Harris analyzes thirteen characteristics of human nature identified by Wilson (1977) and attempts to show that these traits are not under any genetic control. Harris (1979:134) comments that the

> attempt by sociobiologists to add what are at best dubious and hypothetical genes to the human behavioral repertoire leads to the misrepresentation of human nature based on an erroneous construal of the course of human evolution. . . . Even if the dubious hypothetical genetic predispositions of sociobiological human nature actually do exist, knowledge of their existence can lead only to an understanding of the outer "envelope" (to use a metaphor proposed by Wilson . . .) within which cultural evolution has thus far been constrained. It could not lead to an understanding of the differences and similarities within sociocultural evolution.

Harris agrees that humans have a nature, but, apart from the biopsychological constants just mentioned, this nature is basically limited to their extraordinary capacity for culture and learning made possible by their large brains and their linguistic abilities. As I will argue in the next chapter, the evidence is rapidly mounting against the notion that the human brain is just some sort of general, all-purpose mechanism which makes humans solely dependent on learning for adaptation, and that it is in fact a complex composite of special-purpose mechanisms.

In his book *Sociobiology: Sense or Nonsense?* (1985) Michael Ruse, a philosopher of biology, has summarized many of the criticisms and defended sociobiology against most of them. Ruse argues that the political charges are highly unfair and wrongheaded. For all the talk of differences, Ruse says, it is noteworthy that the sociobiologists are really emphasizing the unity of mankind with their search for universal human nature. Ruse also denies that sociobiology is tainted with the ideology of Western capitalism. The critics are reading things into sociobiology that are not there, and are, sad to say, hysterical and paranoid. Sociobiology does not require anyone to endorse any aspect of Western ideology. Many sociobiologists are women who are active feminists. No one is saying that because evolution has worked in a particular way that it is therefore good. No sociobiologist is trying to say that some groups are inferior to others, or that men are superior to women. Regarding gender, sociobiologists would simply say that the sexes differ, not that one is better than the other. And sociobiologists do not say that people have to stay in the roles for which they were selected in biological evolution. Moreover, sociobiology does not paint a picture of humans as nothing but selfish individuals. It also stresses reciprocal altruism, cooperation, and people's conceptions of fairness. Human nature makes people cooperative just as it makes them competitive.[3]

Sociologists have probably been more antisociobiological than any other social scientists. I have long observed very strong sentiment against it among sociologists everywhere. In the Sanderson and Ellis (1992) study, sociobiology was shown to have a pitiful representation among sociologists, with only about 2.5 percent of sociologists identifying with it in any way. In the same study the national sample of sociologists was asked twelve questions dealing with the degree to which they thought biological factors were important determinants of human behavior. The twelve questions dealt with the following dimensions of human behavior: sexual orientation, delinquency and minor crime, serious crime, alcoholism, academic achievement, lifetime earnings, race differences in academic achievement, attitudes toward racial and ethnic minorities, marital stability, sex differences in occupational interests, sex differences in aggressive crimes, and sex differences in child nurturance. The results showed very little support for biological factors. The sociologists were most apt to see sexual orientation, alcoholism, and academic achievement as having biological determinants, but they only saw biology playing a minor role (about 27 percent of variance explained). Across all twelve dimensions the respondents saw biological factors contributing only about 14 percent of the total variance, thus giving social and cultural factors an overwhelming 86 percent of the explained variance. In a more recent study of sociological theorists, Jane Lord and I (Lord and Sanderson, 1999) discovered extremely weak support for sociobiology. We found that only about 1 percent of theorists identified with it as a primary perspective, and that only another 1 percent claimed it as a secondary perspective.

Considerable evidence suggests that psychologists and anthropologists are a good deal more sympathetic to sociobiology. Leonard Lieberman (1989) has surveyed cultural anthropologists' degree of support for certain key sociobiological ideas. He asked them whether they thought that certain key notions were useful for research. Here is what he found:

- kin selection: 35 percent agree, 43 percent disagree
- reciprocal altruism: 29 percent agree, 52 percent disagree
- genetic basis of altruism: 18 percent agree, 58 percent disagree

- male-female reproductive strategy: 44 percent agree, 30 percent disagree
- gene-culture coevolution: 46 percent agree, 26 percent disagree
- average: 34 percent agree, 42 percent disagree.

These cultural anthropologists were almost as supportive of sociobiology as negative toward it; sociologists would probably show nowhere near this kind of support if they were asked these same questions.

As for psychologists, they are much more prominently represented than sociologists as authors of books and articles written from a sociobiological perspective. As noted earlier, sociobiologically oriented psychologists call what they do *evolutionary psychology.* Evolutionary psychologists founded the major scientific society for sociobiology in North America, the Human Behavior and Evolution Society (HBES), and they are currently its most numerous representatives and leading figures. Two textbooks in evolutionary psychology have already appeared (Buss, 1999; Gaulin and McBurney, 2000), as has a handbook (Crawford and Krebs, 1998). Why are anthropologists and psychologists more supportive of evolutionarily oriented social science? Part of the answer may be that they are much better trained in human biology than sociologists. But perhaps the real question is why sociologists are so hostile. The answer, I think, has little to do with science and mostly to do with politics and ideology. Most people who go into sociology want to change the world, and that is their motivation for becoming sociologists. Such people are ideologically convinced in advance that human behavior has little to do with biology. They believe this, and they dearly want to believe it, because they (incorrectly) see the acknowledgment of biological factors as indicating that behavior is resistant to fundamental change. So sociologists dislike sociobiology because they are severely threatened by it politically, and it must be said that sociology has become an increasingly politicized discipline over the past two or three decades.[4]

The importance of ideology in the rejection of biological arguments has been demonstrated decisively by Carl Degler in his *In Search of Human Nature: The Decline and Revival of Darwinism in American Social Thought* (1991). Degler shows that in the late nineteenth and early twentieth centuries Darwinism was highly regarded by social scientists, and biology was considered a major underpinning of human behavior. By the 1920s the tide had begun to turn away from Darwinism and biology, and by the 1930s a cultural determinist or environmentalist position had triumphed and biology was pushed aside. And, Degler says, the reasons for this triumph were ideological: Social scientists wanted a more just and egalitarian society, and arguments for biological causation were perceived as inimical to this. It was not empirical research that was the basis for the triumph, because the data were highly equivocal.

Critics of sociobiology often assert that it is dangerous because it can be misused. It is impossible to deny this, but any social theory can be misused, and many have been. No social theory has been more misused and abused than Marxism (cf. Courtois et al., 1999), which is the preferred stance of many critics of sociobiology. And Skinnerian behaviorism, one of the best-known versions of the SSSM, has enormous potential for mischief, as the novel and film *A Clockwork Orange* showed. In a similar vein, Kevin MacDonald (1998b) has argued, in a most compelling fashion, that the real political danger comes from radical environmentalist rather than sociobiological theories of society. In his words (1998b:40):

> A theory that there is no human nature would imply that humans could easily be programmed to accept all manner of exploitation, including slavery. From a radical environmentalist perspective, it should not matter how societies are constructed, since people should be able to learn to accept any type of social structure. Women could easily be programmed to accept rape, and ethnic groups could be programmed to accept their own domination by other ethnic groups. The view that radical environmentalism is not socially pernicious also ignores the fact that the communist government of the Soviet Union murdered millions of its citizens and later engaged in officially sponsored anti-Semitism while committed to an ideology of radical environmentalism.

We should not refuse to construct social theories just because there is the possibility they will be misused. Actually, I would claim that, if the sociobiologists are right, then failure to acknowledge what they are saying is a sure way to guarantee that we will never be able to change society in ways that we want. We can only change society properly if we recognize the kinds of biological constraints on human behavior that likely exist. If we do not recognize them and they are important, then we will surely fail in our change efforts. It will not do any good to put our heads in the sand and deny the importance of biology just because we are afraid of the possible consequences. To change something one must have a good understanding of what that something is like and what would be involved in trying to change it.

There is another threat perceived by sociologists, though, that we need to recognize. Most sociologists believe that their claim to importance is to show that social and cultural forces shape everything. They seem to feel that without this they have nothing to distinguish themselves and make themselves important. We might call this sociologists' "Durkheimian mandate": Social facts can only be explained in terms of other social facts. Stressing the importance of biology, they think, undermines this, and robs their discipline of its unique importance. Thus sociologists feel threatened disciplinarily (Udry, 1995). As Pierre van den Berghe (1990:180) has noted, "Antireductionism is a territorial display of sociologists, especially against their nearest intellectual rivals, the psychologists." However, sociologists are going to have to change their stripes on this matter or be at serious disciplinary risk in the near future (Udry, 1995; Ellis, 1996). The evidence in favor of sociobiological arguments is growing by leaps and bounds, and most of it is unknown to sociologists because they do not bother to read the books and journals containing this information. If sociologists continue to deny the importance of biology, within twenty years or so, by which time the evidence for biology will have become much more massive, they are going to look increasingly foolish both within the academy and to the larger educated public. They will risk becoming seriously marginalized, if not destroyed, as a discipline.

My grand conclusion is that sociobiology has a great deal to teach us. It is an extremely provocative approach that has produced some extraordinarily important results. But it has limits, too. Sociobiological approaches work best in the areas of sex, gender, kinship, and family life, for reasons that are obvious. It can contribute to other areas of human behavior, but it can go only so far. It can contribute little, for example, to the study of macrodynamics and long-term historical change, except by way of showing how biology constrains the kinds of changes that are likely or unlikely to occur (see Sanderson, 1999:403–28). Social and cultural factors, themselves built up over the generations and millennia as the result of biological influences, also matter greatly and must be given their due as frameworks constraining human action. Sociobiologists, though, have never denied this. Any good social scientist should take a *biosocial* perspective, one that shows the complex interaction of biology and society in human behavior. The main problem with sociobiology is simply that it is an incomplete approach. Although it is an excellent foundation on which to build a general theory of human society, by itself it is not enough. Much more is happening in social life than the efforts of individuals to maximize their inclusive fitness. Sociobiology needs to be combined in a very selective way with those other social theories that have worked best. The achievement of that objective is my next aim in this book.

NOTES

1.   Some of the most important general works in sociobiology are Barash (1977), Daly and Wilson (1978), Dawkins (1976), R. Alexander (1979), Symons (1979), Lopreato (1984, 1989), Trivers (1985), Ruse (1985), Barkow (1989), Barkow, Cosmides, and Tooby (1992), Badcock (1991), Maxwell (1991), Tooby and Cosmides (1989a, 1990), Nielsen (1994), Crippen (1994), Crawford and Krebs (1998), Lopreato and Crippen (1999), Buss (1999), Low (2000), Cronk, Chagnon, and Irons (2000), and Gaulin and McBurney (2000). A collection by Betzig (1997) reprints many classic articles. Ullica Segerstråle (2000) has written an excellent history of sociobiology and the debates and controversies that have centered on it. Her long work is packed with juicy tidbits of inside information often obtained in interviews with the principals. The authors of some of these works prefer the label *evolutionary psychology* rather than sociobiology, a distinction that will be explained later in this chapter. The works by Crawford and Krebs, Buss, and Gaulin and McBurney, for example, are intended as handbooks or textbooks in evolutionary psychology, which is regarded by these authors as a paradigm within the discipline of psychology. It should be noted that some evolutionary psychologists are not affiliated with the discipline of psychology; such scholars are most likely professional anthropologists. Cronk, Chagnon, and Irons (2000), cited above, prefer the name human behavioral ecology, but it is very similar to sociobiology.

2.   A more complete understanding of sex differences in reproductive and mating strategies requires an understanding of the neo-Darwinian concepts of sexual selection and parental investment. These concepts are discussed in later chapters as they become more directly pertinent.

3.   Concerning the alleged politics of sociobiology, Pierre van den Berghe (1981; quoted in Segerstråle, 1992:201) has said the following: "Actually, a review of the politics of leading sociobiologists would lend more credence to the contention that sociobiology is a Communist conspiracy: J.B.S. Haldane, who is generally credited for having first hit on the notion of kin selection—a theoretical cornerstone of sociobiology—was a leading member of the British Communist Party; so was John Maynard Smith. E.O. Wilson and most other leading sociobiologists are left-of-center liberals or social democrats. 'Racist' Trivers is even married to a Jamaican and is heavily involved in radical black politics." Van den Berghe himself, the leading sociobiologist among sociologists, has long been a foe of racism and social inequality, and I suspect that if

the members of the Human Behavior and Evolution Society and the European Sociobiological Society, the two leading associations of sociobiologists in the Western world, were polled, most of them would be shown to be left-of-center politically, some of them strongly so. In reading the works of sociobiologists for a quarter of a century my impression has always been that their writings are remarkably free of any political content whatsoever, suggesting that their overwhelming aim is scientific understanding, not political action of any kind.

In a closely related vein, Ullica Segerstråle (1992) tells the following story. In May of 1976 the Sociobiology Study Group of Science for the People held a meeting at which they tried to persuade Noam Chomsky, a well-known political radical, to write a statement strongly denouncing sociobiology. The group's members discovered, however, much to their chagrin and embarrassment, that *Chomsky was actually in favor of the view that there is such a thing as a constant human nature.* Moreover, Chomsky thought that the postulation of human nature would actually be helpful to the radical cause in fighting for a better society. As Segerstråle points out, under such circumstances it can hardly be surprising that Chomsky was unwilling to write a critique of sociobiology. Peter Singer (1999), a philosopher with Marxist sympathies, takes the same position as Chomsky—that only by understanding human nature can leftists hope to build the kind of society they desire.

4. As noted earlier, this is what has motivated the critiques of Science for the People, Lewontin, Rose, and Kamin, and to some extent Sahlins. The prominent paleontologist Stephen Jay Gould, who has written many widely read books on Darwinism and evolutionary theory in general, has also been a major ideological opponent of sociobiology (see Alcock, 1998, and Segerstråle, 2000). Gould is a prominent member of Science for the People and was actively involved in writing their ideologically driven critique of sociobiology in 1976. Obviously one does not have to be a sociologist to be ideologically opposed to sociobiology. Segerstråle's (2000) history of sociobiology discusses the ideological opposition to it at great length, although she takes the stance, which I strongly question, that even the ideological opponents of sociobiology were motivated to criticize it more on the basis of their view of good science than their political views.

PART IV

Toward Theoretical Synthesis

9

Darwinian Conflict Theory: A Unified Evolutionary Theory of Human Society

We have now reviewed and assessed the strengths and weaknesses of all of the major theoretical strategies in contemporary sociology and even included some from sociology's sister discipline of anthropology. What remains to be done is to show how the most important and valid features of the best strategies can be brought together in a new theoretical synthesis. I call the resulting synthesis *Darwinian conflict theory.* Darwinian conflict theory brings together many of the elements of sociobiology, Marxian and Weberian conflict theory, cultural materialism, and rational choice theory. It acknowledges that much of human society is "socially constructed," but insists that the constructions that result are not arbitrary and capricious products of some sort of autonomous "culture." Social constructions are constrained by the material conditions—biological, ecological, economic, etc.—of human existence. Darwinian conflict theory also recognizes that many of the features of human social life exist because they perform "functions," but claims that these functions pertain to individuals and their needs and goals rather than some reified abstraction called "society."

Darwinian conflict theory is intended as a comprehensive theoretical strategy orienting the formulation of more specific theories of human society. It is, in a very important sense, a kind of marriage of Marx and Darwin, or, more accurately, a marriage of Darwinian biological materialism to the broader economic and ecological materialism and conflict theory that owes its ancestry to Marx and that has been continued by such leading anthropologists as Marvin Harris. Its most important feature is showing that the basic principles of sociobiology are highly compatible with, or at least can be made highly compatible with, some traditional modes of social theorizing that ignore or downplay the biological side of humans. Sociobiology, it is argued, is the ultimate form of materialist and conflict social theory, and other materialist and conflict theories must be grounded in it. As Sebastiano Timpanaro (1975:34) has said:

> By materialism we understand above all acknowledgement of the priority of nature over "mind," or if you like, of the physical level over the biological level, and of the biological level over the socio-economic and cultural level; both in the sense of chronological priority

(the very long time which supervened before life appeared on earth, and between the origin of life and the origin of man), and in the sense of the conditioning which nature *still* exercises on man and will continue to exercise at least for the foreseeable future.

By incorporating sociobiology and using it as its foundation, Darwinian conflict theory is able to provide the "first principles" that are lacking in other social theories. Marvin Harris, for example, is able to identify certain fundamental human preferences but is unable to tell us why humans should have those preferences rather than others. Similarly, Randall Collins tells us that humans are highly conflict-prone organisms but cannot tell us why—in fact, apparently does not even think to ask why. By incorporating sociobiological principles into sociological theory we are able to bring the understanding of human behavior down to its most basic level, beyond which it is not necessary (or even possible) to go. One of the reasons that sociology has failed to progress as much as it can and to fulfill the hope that was once held out for it is because it has not yet had its badly needed Darwinian revolution. Darwinian conflict theory is the outcome of taking that need seriously. Most of the parts of Darwinian conflict theory are already highly familiar to sociological theorists. Darwinian conflict theory's novelty lies not in its specific parts, but in the combining or arranging of the parts.

Darwinian conflict theory is a multitiered or multilayered theoretical strategy. It starts with the deep wellsprings of human action and then moves upward to deal with such things as the principles of group relations and the systemic relations among the parts of societies. The more we get to these higher-level principles the more we must construct specific propositions covered only in the most abstract and general way by the theoretical strategy as a whole. For example, such phenomena as the geopolitical actions of states, social revolutions, and long-term economic cycles are understandable in terms of Darwinian conflict theory's deepest principles, but only in general. Applying these principles to such phenomena is vital, but more specific lines of thinking are also needed.

It is not hard to see how sociobiology is related to at least one of the theoretical strategies forming part of the synthesis, viz., rational choice theory. Both sociobiology and rational choice theory are methodologically individualist approaches that assume a rational actor seeking his or her interests, and sociobiology simply takes rational choice principles further by grounding them in evolutionary principles (Hirschleifer, 1977; Richerson and Boyd, 1992; Nielsen, 1994). However, eyebrows will undoubtedly be raised with respect to the attempt to synthesize sociobiology with Marxian conflict theory and cultural materialism. These are theoretical traditions that seem, on the surface at least, utterly unsynthesizable. After all, Marxists are usually extremely critical of sociobiological arguments, on both theoretical and political grounds, and Harris and the cultural materialists have also been sharp critics of sociobiology. But there is much more of a connection than may initially seem apparent. Jerome Barkow (1989:310) has said, "Like Marxism, a sociobiological view of society yields conflict theory," and Laura Betzig (1986) has noted that Marxism and Darwinism have much in common. As for the old man himself, Marx read *The Origin of Species* in 1860 and in early 1861 said to Engels in a letter that "Darwin's book is very important and serves me as a natural-scientific basis for the class struggle in history" (quoted in Taylor, 1989:409). Indeed, Wilhelm Liebknecht, an important German socialist leader who visited Marx frequently, indicated that "when Darwin drew the consequences of his investigations and presented them to the public, we spoke for months of nothing else but Darwin and the revolutionizing power of his scientific conquests" (quoted in Feuer, 1978:109). Both Marx and Engels were very unhappy with Darwin's reliance on Malthus for his concept of the struggle for existence, but nonetheless the "class struggle came to be regarded as the form which the struggle for existence took in class societies; *the materialistic conception of history was derived as a limiting case of the biological struggle as it obtained for the conditions of the human species*" (Feuer, 1978:110; emphasis added). It is most unfortunate that the extraordinary implications of this last idea have never been properly developed. It is one of the main tasks of Darwinian conflict theory to draw out these implications and state them formally.

As for cultural materialism and sociobiology, it will probably be much more than just a single eyebrow that Harris will raise regarding the validity or even coherence of Darwinian conflict theory. But a close connection is clearly there. Once one looks beyond the surface level, the cultural and biological materialisms are not only highly compatible with each other, but in fact require each other. Harris's entire critique of sociobiology is not only misguided; it is totally unnecessary. In fact, the principles of cultural materialism make sense only *in light of* sociobiological principles. I am hardly the only one to see things this way. Pierre van den Berghe, the leading advocate of sociobiology within the discipline of sociology, has for many years argued that Harris's rejection of sociobiology is entirely gratuitous. "In its materialism," he claims (1991:278), "sociobiology shares much in common with classical Marxism as well as with a prominent school of cultural ecology in anthropology represented by Marvin Harris." Richard Alexander agrees with van den Berghe on the gratuitousness of Harris's rejection of sociobiology, and he has argued more forcefully than anyone that sociobiology and cultural materialism are complementary rather than competing approaches (1987:26–27):

> [L]et us suppose that someone argued that humans are interested in sex because of the pleasure associated with it and not because of procreation. Sexual intercourse in humans may (unlike nearly all or all other organisms) have acquired significance beyond fertilization of eggs per se (e.g., in long-term pair bonding) but this cannot detract from the facts that (1) historically it has been the only way babies were created, (2) the creation of babies is the only reason for our continued existence, and (3) those of us alive today carry in preponderance the genes of those who produced and raised the most babies.
>
> Happiness and its anticipation are thus proximate mechanisms that lead us to perform and repeat acts that in the environments of history, at least, would have led to greater reproductive success. This is a central hypothesis in evolutionary biology. Paralleling it in importance is the hypothesis that control of resources is the most appropriate route to reproductive success. . . . Similarly, I presume that status is typically a vehicle toward resource control and an outcome of it. If these ideas are correct, then humans should always experience pleasure when they gain in status or increase their control of resources (unless they do so at large expense to close relatives or spouses), and they should experience some converse feeling when they lose status or resource control (except, sometimes, when they transfer it to relatives or spouses).

Harris's analysis takes economic or "productive" ends as ultimate rather than as means to the end of reproductive success. Such analyses are like those which take pleasure and happiness as ultimate ends. They cannot explain why the proximate mechanisms of pleasure and happiness (Harris's "bio-psychological benefits") operate as they do, or even why they exist. . . . Harris implies that reproductive success, representing "remote and hypothetical interests," is somehow an *alternative* explanation to more proximate "bio-psychological benefits" as "the most certain and powerful interests served by infrastructure." He sees the "struggle to maintain and enhance differential politico-economic power and wealth" as *opposed* to "the struggle to achieve reproductive success." In the sense of comprehensive explanation, however, the relationship between such proximate and ultimate factors is not adversarial. Rather, neither can be explained without the other. . . . I cannot imagine how cultural materialist explanations of human behavior and institutions can ever make real or complete sense except in light of a continuous history of natural selection of genetic alternatives.

Alexander concludes this argument by claiming that "the cost-benefit analyses of cultural materialism are necessarily subsumed under those which take into account the history of human strategies of reproductive success" (1987:29). This is my view exactly.

In fact, even Harris himself almost seems to dimly recognize the compatibility of cultural materialism and sociobiology. He already has one foot hovering above the sociobiological camp and needs only a little shove to get it planted squarely there (thus giving him one foot solidly in each camp). Harris (1985) has made good use of optimal foraging theory in constructing some of his theories of food preferences and avoidances; in his edited collection *Food and Evolution* (Harris and Ross, 1987b) he has published two articles by anthropologists whose starting point is sociobiology, and he devotes himself as well to important discussions of food and human biology. Optimal foraging theory (discussed in chapter 14 of the present book) derives from evolutionary ecology, which is directly linked to the broader sociobiological paradigm. And Harris has spoken many times of the crucial causal role of the modes of production and *reproduction* in social life without fully realizing the implications of what he is saying. Indeed, reproduction has a crucial impact on social life, but in a more fundamental biological way than Harris has been willing to acknowledge. Moreover, consider the following statement made by Harris (1979:139):

True, sociobiological models based on reproductive success and inclusive fitness can yield predictions about sociocultural differences that enjoy a degree of empirical validity. . . . But the reason for this predictability is that most of the factors which might promote reproductive success do so through the intermediation of bio-psychological benefits that enhance the economic, political, and sexual power and well-being of individuals and groups of individuals.

Yes, exactly, but once again this is perfect grist for Alexander's mill. The proximate and ultimate causes are inextricably intertwined. Consider also Harris's so-called biopsychological constants. Harris proposes only four such constants and claims that these are sufficient to give us a picture of basic human nature. That is an argument that cannot possibly succeed, but here let us focus instead on the content of the constants (Harris, 1979:63):

1. People need to eat and will generally opt for diets that offer more rather than fewer calories and proteins and other nutrients.
2. People cannot be totally inactive, but when confronted with a given task, they prefer to carry it out by expending less rather than more energy.
3. People are highly sexed and generally find reinforcing pleasure from sexual intercourse—more often from heterosexual intercourse.
4. People need love and affection in order to feel secure and happy, and other things being equal, they will act to increase the love and affection which others give them.

These proposed biopsychological constants are not only consistent with sociobiology, but are predicted by them and *only make sense in terms of sociobiological principles.* Consider in particular the third constant. Why should people be so highly sexed, and why should most be oriented toward heterosexual sex than toward any other? The answer can only be, because heterosexual sex, and lots of it, works to promote one's inclusive fitness. The general point is that these biopsychological constants need to be grounded in something deeper, and that is sociobiological theory. Harris's failure to engage in such grounding, as well as his failure to expand the list of biopsychological constants appropriately, is entirely gratuitous and unnecessarily restrictive.

Let us now turn to the basic principles of Darwinian conflict theory.

THE BASIC PRINCIPLES OF DARWINIAN CONFLICT THEORY

I. Principles Concerning the Deep Wellsprings of Human Action

1. Like all other species, humans are organisms that have been built by millions of years of biological evolution, both in their anatomy/physiology and their behavioral predispositions. This means that theories of social life must take into consideration the basic features of human nature that are the products of human evolution.
2. The resources that humans struggle for, which allow them to survive and prosper, are in short supply. This means that humans are caught up in a struggle for survival and reproduction with their fellow humans. This struggle is inevitable and unceasing.
3. In the struggle for survival and reproduction, humans give overwhelming priority to their own selfish interests and to those of their kin, especially their close kin.
4. Human social life is the complex product of this ceaseless struggle for survival and reproduction.
5. Humans have evolved strong behavioral predispositions that facilitate their success in the struggle for survival and reproduction. The most important of these predispositions are:
    *   Humans are highly sexed and are oriented mostly toward heterosexual sex. This predisposition has evolved because it is necessary for the promotion of humans' reproductive interests, i.e., their inclusive fitness. Males compete for females and for sex, and females compete for males as resource providers. Humans do these things in order to promote their reproductive success.

- Humans are strongly predisposed to perform effective parental behavior, and the female desire to nurture is stronger than the male desire. Effective parental behavior has evolved because it promotes reproductive success in a species like humans. The family as a social institution rests on a natural foundation.
- Humans are naturally competitive and highly predisposed toward status competition. Status competition is ultimately oriented toward the securing of resources, which promotes reproductive success. Because of sexual selection, the predisposition toward status competition is greater in males than in females.
- Because of the natural competition for resources, humans are economic animals. They are strongly predisposed toward achieving economic satisfaction and well-being, an achievement that promotes reproductive success.
- In their pursuit of resources and closely related activities, humans, like other species, have evolved to maximize efficiency. Other things being equal, they prefer to carry out activities by minimizing the amount of time and energy they devote to these activities. A Law of Least Effort governs human behavior, especially those forms of behavior that individuals find burdensome or at least not rewarding in and of themselves. The Law of Least Effort places a major limit on the behavior of humans everywhere; much behavior can only be explained satisfactorily by taking it into account.

6. None of the tendencies identified above are rigid. Rather, they are behavioral *predispositions* that move along certain lines rather than others but that interact in various ways with the total physical and sociocultural environment. The behavioral predispositions tend to win out in the long run, but they can be diminished or even negated by certain environmental arrangements. At the same time, other environments can amplify these tendencies, pushing them to increasingly higher levels.

7. From the above it follows that humans' most important interests and concerns are reproductive, economic, and political. Political life is primarily a struggle to acquire and defend economic resources, and economic life is primarily a matter of using resources to promote reproductive success. However, at the experiential level, individuals have no conscious recognition that their behaviors are driven by these motives. People often experience economic and political behaviors as valuable in themselves and are often highly motivated to continue and elaborate such behaviors in their own right.

8. Many, probably most, of the features of human social life are the adaptive consequences of people struggling to satisfy their interests. The following provisos concerning the notion of adaptation are in effect.
- Adaptation must be sharply distinguished from its corollary, adaptedness. Adaptation is the process whereby individuals originate (or inherit or borrow) social forms that are devoted to serving their interests and fulfilling their needs and wants (it refers to the origin or persistence of a social form). Adaptedness, on the other hand, involves the extent to which a social form actually benefits the individuals who originated (inherited, borrowed) it. Adaptedness, in other words, refers to the consequences of a social form that originally arose as an adaptation.

- Although adaptations frequently lead to adaptedness, there are numerous instances in which this is not the case. Although adaptations must logically lead to adaptedness (or at least the perception of adaptedness) in the short run (otherwise they could not exist as adaptations), in the longer run this adaptedness may disappear and even lapse into maladaptedness. Individuals create and re-create society through intentional actions, but the consequences of such actions are often very different from what the intenders intended.
- The extent to which adaptations lead to adaptedness varies greatly from one set of individuals and from one time period to another. The more complex a society, the more this rule of thumb applies. What is adaptive for some individuals and at some times may be maladaptive for other individuals and at other times.
- Adaptation is a process pertaining to individuals and not to units larger than the individual. Social groups and societies in and of themselves cannot be adaptational units—i.e., cannot be the units on which selection operates—because they cannot and do not exist apart from concrete flesh-and-blood individuals and because groups cannot have a critical trait of individuals, viz., consciousness and a brain. Although social groups may be said to have needs and wants, these needs and wants are ultimately only the needs and wants of their constituent members. Any social form that is said to be adaptive for any group or society as a whole is so only because it is adaptive for all (or nearly all) of that group's or society's constituent members. Any so-called adaptation at the level of a group or society is but a statistical aggregate of individual adaptations.
- Adaptation is not necessarily an optimizing process. Individuals often satisfice rather than optimize, i.e., they remain content with a satisfactory rather than an optimal way of meeting their needs and wants.

II. Principles Concerning Group Relations

1. Individuals pursuing their interests are the core of social life. The pursuit of interests leads to both highly cooperative and highly conflictive social arrangements.
2. Many cooperative forms of behavior exist at the level of social groups or entire societies. Cooperative social relations exist because they are the relations that will best promote each individual's selfish interests, not because they promote the well-being of the group or society as a whole. The selection of cooperative social forms occurs at the level of the individual, not the group or society.
3. Cooperative forms of interaction are found most extensively among individuals who share reproductive interests in common, i.e., among kin and especially close kin. This is the basis for the family as a fundamental social institution.
4. Outside of kinship and family life, cooperative relations are most likely to be found among individuals who depend heavily on each other for the satisfaction of their basic interests.
5. When competitive or conflictive behavior will more satisfactorily promote individual interests, cooperative relations will decline in favor of competitive or conflictive relations.

6. People are unequally endowed to compete in the social struggle (i.e., some are bigger, more intelligent, more aggressive or ambitious, more clever, more deceitful, etc.), and as a result social domination and subordination often appear as basic features of social life.

7. Members of dominant groups benefit disproportionately from their social position, and frequently they are able to make use of subordinate individuals to advance their interests. Their use of these individuals frequently takes the form of economic exploitation or social exclusion.

8. Because they benefit from their situation, members of dominant groups are highly motivated to structure society so that their superior social position can be preserved or enhanced.

9. Social life is therefore disproportionately influenced by the interests and actions of the members of dominant groups.

10. The primary forms of social domination and subordination in human social life relate to gender, ethnicity, social class, and politics, although other forms of domination and subordination occur as well. These forms of domination and subordination are most basic because they stem directly from the deep wellsprings of human action.

III. Principles Concerning Systemic Relations within Societies

1. Human societies consist of four basic subunits:
   - Individuals themselves as biological organisms, which we may call the *biostructure.*
   - The basic natural phenomena and social forms that are essential to human biological reproduction and economic production, i.e., the ecological, demographic, technological, and economic structures essential for survival and well-being; this we may call the *ecostructure.*
   - The institutionalized patterns of behavior shared by individuals, especially the patterns of marriage, kinship, and family life; the egalitarian or inegalitarian structuring of the society along the lines of class, ethnicity, race, or gender; a society's mode of political life; and its mode or modes of socializing and educating the next generation; these patterns may be identified as the *structure.*
   - The primary forms of mental life and feeling shared by the members of the society, i.e., its beliefs, values, preferences, and norms as these are expressed in such things as religion, literature, myth, legend, philosophy, art, music, and science; these we may refer to as the *superstructure.*

2. These four components of societies are related such that the flow of causation is primarily from the biostructure to the ecostructure, then from the ecostructure to the structure, and finally from the structure to the superstructure; the flow may sometimes occur in the reverse manner, or in some other manner, but these causal dynamics occur much less frequently.

3. According to the logic of III.2, it is clear that the forces within the biostructure and the ecostructure are the principal causal forces in human social life; the

biostructure structures social life both indirectly, i.e., through its action on the ecostructure (which then acts on the structure and superstructure), and through its direct effect on some of the elements of the structure and super-structure. It follows, then, that the ideas and feelings within the superstructure have the least causal impact on the patterns of social life.

4. The components of societies are related as they are because such causal dynamics flow from the deep wellsprings of human action. The biostructure and the ecostructure have a logical causal priority because they concern vital human needs and interests relating to production and reproduction.

5. Once structures and superstructures have been built by biostructures and ecostructures, they may come to acquire a certain autonomy. New needs and new interests may arise therefrom, and these new needs and interests, along with reproductive, economic, and political interests, may form part of the human preference and value structure characteristic of the members of a society. Thus do new social constraints on—more accurately, new contingencies for—individual action arise.

IV. Modes of Darwinian Conflict Explanation

1. As is obvious from III, Darwinian conflict theory's mode of explanation is materialist; this materialist mode of explanation may take any or all of three forms: biomaterialist, ecomaterialist, or polimaterialist.

2. *Biomaterialist* explanations explain a social form by direct reference to a basic feature of the human biogram. That is to say, an explanation is biomaterialist if it links a social form to the human biogram without reference to any necessary mediation of the causal relationship by some other social form. *Example:* Polygyny is a widespread feature of human societies because it springs from an innate desire of males for sexual variety and from the tendency of females to be attracted to resource-rich males.

3. *Ecomaterialist* explanations explain a social form by linking it directly to the influence of ecological, technological, demographic, or economic forces, and thus only indirectly to a feature of the human biogram. *Example:* Hunter-gatherer societies frequently display intensive sharing and cooperation because these are behaviors that promote individuals' interests within the configuration of hunter-gatherer technoeconomic systems and natural environments.

4. *Polimaterialist* explanations explain a social form by linking it directly to the political interests or situations of the participants. Political interests or situations ordinarily spring from the participants' economic interests, which in turn are ultimately derived from the character of the human biogram. *Examples:* Democratic forms of government emerged earliest in those Western societies with the largest and most politically organized working classes. Third World revolutions occur most frequently in societies where the state is highly vulnerable to a revolutionary coalition.

5. Darwinian conflict theorists formulating materialist explanations are obligated to specify whether their explanations are biomaterialist, ecomaterialist, or polimaterialist.

V. Principles Concerning Social Order and Change

1. Societies exhibit both the persistence and the transformation of their basic structure, and neither may be regarded as more fundamental than the other.
2. Order and change are, in fact, not truly distinct phenomena, but in actuality simply different temporal dimensions of the same reality.
3. It follows from the above that order and change must be explained in essentially the same way. The basic theoretical principles of Darwinian conflict theory therefore apply equally to order and change.
4. The process of socialization cannot explain the persistence of sociocultural arrangements any more than it can explain how these arrangements are transformed. Both order and change must be explained as results of the adaptation of individuals to their circumstances. Persistence involves the adaptation of new generations of individuals to the same circumstances, whereas change is a matter of new generations working out new adaptations to new circumstances.

VI. Principles Concerning the Relationship between Micro and Macro

1. Societies are aggregate expressions of the myriad interactions of individuals pursuing their interests. Macrolevel phenomena are ultimately to be explained in terms of microlevel factors.
2. Societies, however, are "more than" the individuals who created them. In other words, the macro, though stemming from the micro, is "more than" the micro. This means that the macro, though ultimately to be explained in terms of the micro, cannot be fully explained in terms of the micro. Features unique to macro structures must always form part of the theoretical analysis of such structures.
3. Since societies are more than the individuals who created them, they are an important part of the context within which individuals pursue their interests. Societies "act back on" their individual creators. Although the macro comes from the micro, it "acts back on" the micro and partially reconstitutes it.
4. Human social life in all of its complexities is an ongoing process of individuals creating and re-creating social forms designed to serve their interests. Sociocultural systems are constructed and continually reconstructed by the actions of individuals.

VII. The Scope and Sufficiency of the Principles of Darwinian Conflict Theory

1. All of the foregoing principles constitute a broad and highly abstract theoretical strategy. This strategy is deemed to be useful for orienting the sociological analysis of substantive social phenomena. A very large number of much more specific theories can be deduced from Darwinian conflict theory when it is used to confront the substantive world, and it is these theories that do the actual explaining of what we want explained.
2. In and of themselves, the principles of Darwinian conflict theory are incapable of identifying all of the dimensions of all of the variables necessary to the construction of any specific theory. This can only be done on a case-by-case

basis in the actual process of theory formulation and theory testing. In other words, the principles of Darwinian conflict theory are very broad-grained ideas that provide the basis for the formulation of more fine-grained ideas.

Since the proof of the pudding is in the eating, the burden is now squarely placed on me to present the evidence that supports Darwinian conflict theory. The following chapters develop this evidence with respect to most of the major areas of sociological concern. These are reproductive behavior; human sexuality; sex and gender; marriage, kinship, and family patterns; economic behavior and economic systems; social hierarchies; and politics and war. Before getting to the evidence, however, a brief digression regarding the concept of culture is necessary.

DARWINIAN CONFLICT THEORY AND THE CONCEPT OF CULTURE

The Nature of Culture

From the perspective of Darwinian conflict theory, traditional social-scientific conceptions of the relationship between human biology and human culture are highly problematic. These conceptions regard biology and culture as two separate realms that may interact to some extent but that are nonetheless ontologically distinct. Culture is not something that is imbued with biology, but is rather a distinct realm of existence that, however it originates—and it must be said that most sociologists and anthropologists talk about culture as if it simply magically dropped on strings from the sky!—works its charms on human behavior. But from the perspective of Darwinian conflict theory, culture *is itself already in part biological.*[1] This means that it is senseless to talk about the impact of culture on behavior since the two are inextricably intertwined (or, more accurately, the decision modules in the brain that direct behavior are inextricably intertwined with culture). For Darwinian conflict theory, what culture *is* is just as important as what culture *does.*

Let us look at some traditional conceptualizations of culture. As Marvin Harris (1980, 1997) has pointed out, since the middle of the twentieth century culture has tended to be defined by both anthropologists and sociologists as something exclusively mental or ideational. It is a "blueprint for action" that consists primarily of beliefs, values, norms, and role expectations. Surprisingly, the biologist Richard Dawkins (1976:206), who helped to found sociobiology, has perpetuated this notion of culture with his concept of *meme,* which is an idea that propagates itself "by leaping from brain to brain." Equally surprisingly, Lee Cronk (1999), an evolutionarily oriented anthropologist, endorses Dawkins's meme concept and himself insists that culture be defined in a strictly ideational or mentalist way. This narrow conceptualization excludes both behavior and technology as being part of culture. Harris prefers a broader conception of culture that includes both behavior and material technology, as do I. He defines culture as "the learned, socially acquired traditions of thought and behavior found in human societies" (1997:88). Although this broader definition is an improvement on narrow idealist definitions, it is still problematic in the sense that Harris conceptualizes culture as a "thing apart" from humans' biological nature, a reified entity with a life of its own. The evolutionary psychologists John Tooby and Leda Cosmides (1989a, 1992) provide a much more rigorous conceptualization of culture by distinguishing two major forms of it, which they call *transmitted* and *evoked* culture. By transmitted culture they mean roughly what most sociologists and anthropologists who rely on broad definitions of culture mean, minus, of course, the nonbiological emphasis. But before culture can be transmitted it must first be created by the members of a particular group or society. Tooby and Cosmides regard evoked culture as the within-group similarities and between-group differences that result from the way in which functionally organized, domain-specific psychological mechanisms—mechanisms in the brain—are triggered by the local circumstances in which people find themselves. Tooby and Cosmides (1992:116) exemplify evoked culture in the following way:

> For example, when members of a group face new and challenging circumstances (drought, war, migration, abundance), this may activate a common set of functionally organized domain-specific mechanisms, evoking a new set of attitudes and goals. The newly evoked psychological states will make certain new ideas appealing, causing them to spread by transmission, and certain old ideas unappealing, causing them to be discarded. In contrast, the Standard Model "do what your parents did" concept of culture is not a principle that can explain much about why cultural elements change, where new ones come from, why they spread, or why certain complex patterns (e.g., pastoralist commonalities) recur in widely separated cultures.

Tooby and Cosmides's reconceptualization of culture gives whole new meaning to the concept of learning. They note that traditional concepts of learning, just like traditional concepts of culture, have little meaning. As they point out, "most social scientists believe they are invoking a powerful explanatory principle when they claim that a behavior is 'learned' or 'cultural.'" However, "as hypotheses to account for mental or behavioral phenomena, they are remarkably devoid of meaning. At this point in the study of human behavior, *learning and culture are phenomena to be explained, and not explanations in themselves*" (1989a:46; emphasis added).

This crucial but generally overlooked point has been cleverly made by George Homans (1984) by means of his concept of "culture vultures." Culture vultures are social scientists who explain a pattern of social behavior as being the way it is "because of the culture." Most sociologists and anthropologists are culture vultures, in Homans's view. What these social scientists fail to realize is that to explain a behavior pattern as being what it is "because of the culture" explains nothing. What has to be explained is why the culture is the way it is, i.e., how it came to be formed. Take the following example. The Chinese have traditionally had a strong aversion to drinking milk and eating milk products. As Marvin Harris (1985) has said, they regard drinking a tall glass of milk the same way Westerners would regard drinking a tall glass of cow saliva. But throughout much of Europe (especially northern Europe) and the United States and Canada milk is considered an excellent food and is consumed in large quantities. Now if we ask the question, Why does little Chang Wu never drink milk and in fact abhor it?, and answer the question by saying that he was conditioned by his culture to feel that way, our explanation is probably quite correct. But what have we really explained? Nothing, for the real question is: Why did the Chinese come to adopt this dietary habit? The traditional concept of transmitted culture is closely linked to the concept of socialization. Most sociologists and anthropologists hold that people are the way they are because they have been socialized into a particular culture or subculture. But does the concept of socialization explain much of anything? Yes, at the proximate level, but remaining at this level is neither very interesting nor very enlightening. Socialization is a given, something that obviously goes on constantly in all cultures. Older generations obviously have a vested interest in transmitting their cultural patterns to younger generations. This can be taken for granted. But socialization is only the mechanism through which culture gets transported from one generation to the next. It has nothing to do with why a culture became the way it is.

There is an even more serious problem. In modern societies like our own (but even in many preindustrial societies to some extent) there is often considerable slippage between generations. Each new generation may have many different thoughts and actions compared to the previous one. Western societies, for example, are much less sexist today than they were two or three generations ago. Western culture has changed, which can only mean that people do not automatically absorb their culture from the senior generation and are always to some extent resistant to socialization efforts. Humans are not Parsonian "cultural dopes." Cultures are constantly changing, and we cannot explain that crucial fact by claiming that "culture comes from culture" or by invoking the concept of socialization.

The Psychological Foundations of Culture: Domain-General or Domain-Specific?

Adherents of the SSSM have long claimed that the most important way—indeed, in some formulations, the only way—human biology contributes to culture is through the evolution of the "capacity for culture" (Spuhler, 1959; Montagu, 1964; Harris, 1979; Sahlins, 1976a, 1976b). The evolution of the large human brain has endowed humans with the ability to solve problems through superior learning ability, and this has caused culture to become the primary mode of human adaptation, one that has replaced the old biological mode of adaptation. For example, Marvin Harris notes that during the five-million-year period during which we humans have been evolving from our apelike ancestors "natural selection favored a behavioral genotype in which the programming acquired through learning progressively dominated the programming acquired through genetic change. Every discussion of human nature must begin and end with this aspect of the human biogram, for its importance overrides every other conceivable species-specific trait of *Homo sapiens*" (1979:134). Moreover, this capacity for culture is regarded as a highly generalized and flexible trait that allows humans almost infinite plasticity in their mode of cultural adaptation. For many adherents of the SSSM, when it comes to culture almost anything is possible.

The SSSM implies that the human brain is a *domain-general* learning mechanism, or at least consists of a relatively small number of domain-general mechanisms. However, evolutionary psychologists such as Tooby and Cosmides (1989a, 1992) provide a compelling argument to the effect that the brain could not have evolved as a domain-general mechanism (or cluster of mechanisms) because such mechanisms would be too clumsy to have had much adaptive import. In some respects they may have actually been maladaptive (Boyer, 1995). "Many adaptive problems that humans routinely solve," Tooby and Cosmides say, "are simply not solvable by any known general problem-solving strategy, as demonstrated by formal solvability analyses on language acquisition" (1992:111). They argue that the brain evolved as a very complex network of *domain-specific* mechanisms, and that it is these mechanisms that interact with the total human environment to produce the shared patterns of thought and action that we call culture. They say that (1992:111)

> domain-general, content-independent mechanisms are inefficient, handicapped, or inert compared to systems that also include specialized techniques for solving particular families of adaptive problems. A specialized mechanism can make use of the enduring relationships present in the problem-domain or in the related features of the world by reflecting these content-specific relationships in its problem-solving structure. Such mechanisms will be far more efficient than general-purpose mechanisms, which must expend time, energy, and risk learning these relationships through [an inefficient process of trial and error].

Echoing Tooby and Cosmides, Randy Thornhill and Craig Palmer (2000) indicate three reasons why the human brain must consist of a large number of highly specialized, domain-specific mechanisms. First, the adaptive problems confronted by our ancestors in the EEA were very specific. Specialized adaptations are much better than general adaptations in solving specific adaptive problems. This is essentially the main point made by Tooby and Cosmides. Second, because a great deal of successful behavior is dependent on highly variable environmental conditions, humans must show a great deal of behavioral flexibility, and this flexibility actually requires highly specialized rather than general brain mechanisms (the opposite of what most social scientists have thought). Thornhill and Palmer (2000:18) quote Donald Symons (1987) on this point: "Extreme behavioral plasticity implies extreme mental complexity and stability; that is, an elaborate human nature. Behavioral plasticity for its own sake would be worse than useless, random variation suicide. During the course of evolutionary history the more plastic hominid behavior became the more complex the neural machinery must have become to channel this plasticity into adaptive action." Finally, special-purpose mental designs are implied by our knowledge of how nonpsychological adaptations are designed. The human body is nothing at all like a general-purpose system, but rather is an extremely complex system consisting of many highly specialized organs that do very specific things.[2]

Many sociologists and anthropologists continue to genuflect before the altar of their Great God, Culture. But they are worshipping a deity that does not deserve such respect and that to a large extent has created more problems than it has solved. As Steklis and Walter (1991:161) note, "although the culture concept can have limited utility insofar as it is employed as a general analytical abstraction that may be used to summarize a complex set of behavior patterns in a society, it is far too vague a term to be of use in specification of the exact relationships between the variables that govern the expression of behavior." For the most part the concept has outlived its usefulness and must eventually be jettisoned. Unfortunately, we do not yet have a suitable substitute.

In view of this fact, for the time being we must continue to use the concept, but sparingly and in full recognition of its limitations.

NOTES

1. This point has been made by Pierre van den Berghe and a number of others. Essentially the same argument has been made by the behavior geneticist David Rowe (1994) for the individual rather than an entire culture. Rowe points out that most sociologists have conceptualized the environment as something entirely separate from individuals and their biological makeup, when in fact what is called "environment" is itself already partly imbued with individual biology. To some extent the environments of individuals are created by them. Nature and nurture thus cannot be neatly separated, as the SSSM assumes.

2. There are evolutionary psychologists/sociobiologists who do argue for the existence of domain-general mechanisms (e.g., Turke, 1990a, 1990b; MacDonald, 1989, 1991; MacDonald and Geary, 2000). However, domain-general is a relative term, and the kinds of domain-general mechanisms these social scientists are arguing for are much more functionally specific than anything conceived by the SSSM. Moreover, they are weaker than domain-specific mechanisms (MacDonald and Geary, 2000). Undoubtedly the most important domain-general brain mechanism is intelligence, whose general adaptive capacity is really beyond question. MacDonald and Geary (2000) argue that intelligence is an especially adaptive trait when people are confronted with novel or unpredictable environments or situations. Flinn (1997) argues that the brain has evolved some domain-general mechanisms that function to integrate domain-specific mechanisms.

PART V

Darwinian Conflict Theory: The Weight of the Evidence

10

Reproductive Behavior

The natural man has only two primal passions, to get and to beget.

—*Sir William Osler*

For the woman, the man is a means: the end is always the child.

—*Friedrich Nietzsche*

Literature is mostly about having sex and not much about having children. Life is the other way around.

—*David Lodge*

This chapter is devoted to showing how biomaterialist, ecomaterialist, and even polimaterialist theories are all necessary to make sense out of some important dimensions of human reproductive behavior. Human reproductive strategies are highly facultative, and thus are the product of complex interactions between biological predispositions and a range of environmental conditions.

SOCIAL STATUS AND REPRODUCTIVE SUCCESS

Lee Ellis (1995) has conducted an exhaustive review of research (hundreds of studies) on the relationship between dominance and reproductive success in a wide range of animal species. Reproductive success for males is measured among animals in terms of number of copulations, number of copulations with estrous females, or number of offspring sired. Usually it is the first of these.

Ellis's main findings may be summarized as follows: Ignoring both sex and species, about 75 percent of studies using primary indicators of reproductive success report a positive relationship between dominance and reproductive success, and about 80 percent of the studies report a positive relationship when secondary indicators of reproductive

161

success are used. For males only, the findings are stronger. For nonprimate males, 89 percent of studies using primary indicators and 96 percent of studies using secondary indicators report a positive relationship. For nonprimate females, the corresponding numbers are 74 percent and 88 percent. For primate males, the numbers are 69 percent and 96 percent, and for primate females the numbers are 63 percent and 69 percent.

Geary (1998) summarizes research which shows that in one group of wild savannah baboons a single male sired 81 percent of the offspring born during a four-year span. In the years preceeding and following his reign, he fathered only 20 percent of the offspring. Research on three groups of wild long-tailed macaques shows that the dominant male fathered between 52 and 92 percent of the offspring, but the low-ranking males collectively sired only between 2 and 9 percent.

Ellis goes on to elaborate a theory as to why some studies found no relationship between dominance and reproductive success. He argues that most of the variance in the relationship results from differences in resource availability. When resources are extremely plentiful, or when they are very difficult to monopolize, there should be little relationship between dominance and reproductive success. It is when resources become scarce, or when they are highly concentrated or clumped, that dominance has an important relationship to reproductive success. Under these conditions, the dominant males tend to exert more control over resources and can use this control to attract mates.

There is abundant evidence that social status and reproductive success are closely linked in humans as well. Most human societies are polygynous, and it is most often the dominant males who have the most wives. This is an extremely common pattern in all types of societies all over the world and throughout history. As Pérusse (1993) observes, the close link between social status and reproductive success has been observed for such widely diverse societies as the Yomut Turkmen, rural Trinidadians, the Ifalukese of the Western Pacific, sixteenth-century Portuguese, the Kipsigis of East Africa, nineteenth-century Englishmen, and Swedish and German peasants. Indeed, Bobbi Low (2000) points out that there are at least 100 carefully studied societies in which high male status and reproductive success are closely associated. There is every reason to think that this is a true human universal or at least a near universal. (See Pérusse, 1993, and Low, 2000, for lists of studies.)

Laura Betzig (1986) notes that men compete for women in all societies, that women are the chief source of conflict between men in many societies, and that it is the dominant males who gain access to more women. The famous Shinbone of the Yanomamö had 43 children. Shinbone's father had 14 children, 143 grandchildren, 335 great-grandchildren, and 401 great-great-grandchildren. According to Betzig, "the evidence is overwhelming that rich and powerful men do enjoy the greatest degree of polygyny cross culturally" (1986:34). Betzig closely examined 18 highly stratified societies that she calls "despotic societies." In all of these societies rulers were highly polygynous, many having large harems of nubile women. In Dahomey there was a close parallel between the social hierarchy and the reproductive hierarchy. In ancient Israel, men of royal status had many wives and concubines. King Solomon was reported to have had 700 wives and 300 concubines. Among the Zande of Africa the king had at least 500 wives, and even chiefs had anywhere from 30 to 100 wives. Among the Inca of Peru, there was a direct correlation between rank in the political hierarchy and the number of wives a man had. "Principal persons" got 50 women, leaders of vassal nations were allowed 30, heads of provinces of a hundred thousand people received 20, leaders of a thousand people got 15 women, administrators of five hundred people got 12 women, and so on down to the "poor Indian," who took anyone who might be left. It is in these highly stratified preindustrial societies that polygyny is greatest. Using a sample of 99 preindustrial societies, Betzig found a correlation of .719 (Pearson r) between the degree of despotism and the degree of polygyny. The more power men have, the greater the number of wives they can command, and thus the greater their reproductive success. In societies where the power differentials between men are small, the most dominant men usually have only three or four wives.

It is commonly argued that in modern industrial societies there has been something of a reversal of the relationship between status and reproductive success. Higher-status individuals in modern societies seem to have fewer children, on average, than those of lower status. How can we explain this apparent violation of the general principle that social status leads to reproductive success? Some, such as Vining (1986), suggest that in modern societies people gain increased interest in creature comforts, and that children interfere with these enjoyments. This kind of argument fits Lopreato's Modified Maximization Principle. Daniel Pérusse (1993) distributed questionnaires to 3,000 students at two French-speaking universities in Montréal, Canada, nearly half of which were completed and returned. He found that, although higher-status males in his sample did not have greater reproductive success than lower-status males, the higher-status males did have much more sex, or what Pérusse calls "potential conceptions." More specifically, Pérusse found that measures of occupational prestige and on-the-job power together explained about 60 percent of the variance in the number of potential conceptions. Pérusse concludes that his data support the general biomaterialist argument linking social status and reproductive success, because higher-status men in industrial societies would be having more reproductive success than lower-status men were it not for modern contraception and modern socially imposed monogamy.

Van den Berghe and Whitmeyer (1990) have challenged the notion that the relationship between social status and reproductive success is reversed in industrial societies. They claim that this has not occurred in Japan; that a German census for 1981 showed that the fertility of wives increased with increases in their husbands' income; and that in the United States in both 1960 and 1970 the childlessness of wives decreased as their husbands' income increased. They also refer to data (Simon, 1974) from postdemographic transition Sweden, West Germany, and New Zealand showing that socioeconomic status and fertility are positively related in those countries. They also note that, when they remarry, higher-status men are more likely than lower-status men to wed younger, more fertile women, and thus to produce more offspring by second or third wives. Moreover, a Forbes 400 study (Essock-Vitale, 1984) showed that the U.S. superrich have an average fertility of 3.1 compared to a rate of 2.7 for the American population as a whole.

Van den Berghe and Whitmeyer suggest that three different reproductive strategies can be found in industrial societies. In order to understand their analysis, we first need to understand the distinction between r and K selection in animal species (MacArthur and Wilson, 1967; Pianka, 1970; E. O. Wilson, 1975). r-selected species tend to be small animals that leave many offspring but provide little or no parental care. K-selected species, by contrast, are larger animals that leave fewer offspring but that provide much more parental care. Within the same species organisms may vary along the r-K spectrum depending on environmental conditions, being more r in some environments (typically less predictable environments) and more K in other environments (usually more predictable environments). The r-K distinction shows that there is a tradeoff between mating effort and parental effort. The higher the mating effort, the lower the parental effort, and vice versa. Humans are a highly K-selected species, but they have been shown to behave in more r-like ways under certain conditions.

According to van den Berghe and Whitmeyer, in modern industrial societies the stable working class and the middle and upper-middle classes tend to follow an extreme K strategy. Here people limit themselves to two or three children in whom they invest heavily. There is a quality-quantity tradeoff in favor of quality. Parental investment involves high-intensity care and the investment of economic and educational resources in order to equip offspring for success in a highly competitive environment (cf. Kaplan, 1996). A second strategy is employed by the upper classes, whose members can have both quantity and quality. This is a less extreme K strategy. Finally, the lower classes, especially stigmatized racial or ethnic minorities, adopt a more r strategy. Here fertility is higher and parental investment is lower; quantity is preferred over quality as a strategy of reproductive success.

Whatever may turn out to be the relationship between social status and reproductive success in modern industrial societies, the key arguments of a Darwinian biomaterialist perspective are not overturned. Even if high-status men are not leaving more offspring, they appear to be having more sex with more partners and thus having more "potential offspring." Given such behavior, they would have had more offspring in the ancestral environment.

INFANTICIDE

Sarah Blaffer Hrdy (1979) has shown that infanticide is widespread among animal species. Usually it is adult males who kill infants, but females are sometimes involved. Infanticide by adult males occurs among all higher primates (Old and New World monkeys and apes). Hrdy indicates five reasons for infanticide, four of which suggest that infanticide is an evolved adaptation:

- *Exploitation:* The killers may directly benefit from an infant's death; they might eat it, for example, or use it as a "buffer" in fights with others.
- *Resource competition:* Killing an infant may give the killer or his or her descendants access to more resources.
- *Parental manipulation:* A parent might kill an infant because it is defective in some way, because inferior ecological conditions might make its survival difficult, or be-

cause there are older offspring whose well-being would be harmed if resources are devoted to the new infant.

- *Sexual selection:* Adult males may kill offspring if they are not the killer's descendants and if the killing of these offspring would enhance the killer's opportunities to breed. For example, if a male kills a female's offspring sired by another male this will bring her into estrus again and allow him to mate and breed with her.

Infanticide is also a relatively common form of human behavior. It has been found in all types of societies, including modern industrial societies, as well as throughout history (Daly and Wilson, 1988; Hrdy, 1999). At first glance, infanticide seems utterly to contradict the notion of kin selection. However, as Daly and Wilson (1988) point out, infanticide can be a rational act from the point of view of inclusive fitness maximization if letting a child die helps promote the life or well-being of an older child or children in whom a great deal of time, energy, and resources have already been invested. In other words, parental care should not be indiscriminate. It would make little sense in terms of promoting inclusive fitness to invest in children whose chances of survival are low, and who may take away resources from children with a better chance of survival.

Daly and Wilson point to three basic reasons why parents might not want to invest strongly in a particular child: doubts about paternity; indications that the child is of dubious quality, for example is diseased or deformed; and poor circumstances for rearing, such as food scarcities, lack of social support, or the demands of an older child. Using a sample of 60 preliterate societies (39 of which reported the occurrence of infanticide), Daly and Wilson found extremely strong support for their claim. Out of 112 cases of infanticide, 97 resulted from one of their three basic reasons for expecting infanticide. They found only four instances out of 112 in which infanticide could be said to be damaging to the parent's inclusive fitness. In modern industrial societies, where infanticide still occurs occasionally, the risk to an infant is greatest in the case of a teenage mother, and declines as mothers move into their 20s and 30s. Mothers suffering from difficult economic circumstances are also much more likely to commit infanticide, and infanticide is more common among single than among married mothers.

Daly and Wilson note that the data on infanticide are perfectly consistent with the reality of maternal bonding (cf. Hrdy, 1999). They delineate three stages of bonding: initially the mother assesses the quality of the child and her own circumstances; then she begins to establish an individualized love for the child; finally, there is a gradual deepening of maternal love over the course of years. Thus child-specific parental love is variable, and highly dependent on the extent to which circumstances are favorable. Parental feeling seems to be such that the likelihood of infanticide declines progressively with the age of a child. This reflects the child's growing value to the parent, and we might say that parents have evolved to love children more the older they are because of older children's greater reproductive value. Daly and Wilson give recent data for Canada showing support for the effects of age. They point out that, even though there is often much conflict between parents and teenage children, these children are at very low risk for parental homicide. They are much more likely to be killed by nonrelatives than by relatives. When parents kill older children it is usually the result of such things as depression or insanity.

Kin selection theory predicts that stepchildren should be at greater risk of abuse and homicide, and this is exactly what the data show. In fact, Daly and Wilson show that stepparenthood remains the single most powerful risk factor for child abuse that has yet been identified. They present data showing that children living with substitute parents were about one-hundred times as likely to be the victims of fatal abuse as children living with their natural parents (data are for the United States in 1976). A famous childhood story in Western society is that of Cinderella and her evil stepmother and stepsisters, and Daly and Wilson show that similar stories and cultural themes are found throughout the world.

Daly and Wilson also note that most infanticide is female-selective. This has often been interpreted as the result of male domination (which generates a preference for males), or, by Harris (1974, 1977; Divale and Harris, 1976) and other cultural materialists (Divale, 1972), as a population-regulation mechanism, the idea being that the rate of reproduction is determined by the number of females, rather than the number of males, in a group. However, as Daniel Bates and Susan Lees (1979) have pointed out, there is precious little evidence to support the population-regulation argument, and it is even difficult to imagine how people would be able to track their environment in such a sophisticated way so as to achieve the desired result. An alternative interpretation is that people will normally want to invest more in sons because their reproductive potential is much greater than that of daughters. This leads to the notion that sex-selective infanticide should vary by social class. Mildred Dickemann (1979a) has studied sex-selective infanticide in three highly stratified societies: British India in the nineteenth century, China in the nineteenth century, and medieval and early modern Europe. In all of these societies there was extensive hypergyny (i.e., women's marrying men of higher social status). Because of this, and also because of the practice of polygyny, in the middle and upper classes males had greater reproductive value and so female infanticide was practiced extensively, actually reaching 100 percent in some instances. By contrast, among the lower classes females had greater reproductive value because they were in demand by the men of higher social classes, and thus male infanticide was more common (although it failed to reach the levels of female infanticide among the middle and upper classes). Dickemann's research thus suggests that sex-selective infanticide springs from an evolutionary psychology that is derived from the attempt to maximize inclusive fitness: Parents invest in the sex with greater reproductive potential.

PUBERTAL TIMING AS A FACULTATIVE TRAIT

In a fascinating article, Draper and Harpending (1982) have suggested that in societies in which males generally invest heavily in their offspring, females tend to delay sexual bonding and to be very selective in regard to mate choice. On the other hand, in societies, or segments of societies, in which males provide little parental effort, females may adopt a reproductive strategy that emphasizes an early start to reproduction combined with little or no concern for mates. The authors point out that in the United States, adolescent girls from father-absent homes "show 'precocious' sexual interest in boys, a denigrating attitude toward males and masculinity, and little interest in maintaining sexual ties to one male" (1982:263). These behavior patterns are widespread among lower-class American blacks, but are also found to some extent among lower-class whites.

Draper and Belsky (1990) point to studies showing that girls from divorced homes reach puberty and begin sex earlier than girls from intact homes. These findings, plus those of Draper and Harpending mentioned above, suggest to them that girls from father-absent homes are following a more r-like strategy than other girls. They begin reproduction early and emphasize quantity over quality. Reproductive strategies are facultative traits which allow the organism to assess the environment and respond accordingly, as Belsky, Steinberg, and Draper (1991:653) explain:

> What evolutionary mechanism . . . would underlie an accelerated reproductive schedule in the context of *unfavorable environments* such as poverty or social and familial instability, as we propose? We point again to the maxim that organisms have been selected to reproduce themselves and to attend to important environmental cues in the process. In the absence of indications that delayed maturation and reproduction can have benefits, early sexual activity and high fertility have much to recommend them. This strategy may be associated with higher offspring mortality, but from the point of view of fitness, individuals living in such adverse circumstances who *delay* reproducing may well be selected against (i.e., leave few or no offspring). In such an environment, a man who invests disproportionately in one woman and in children (who may not be his own) will leave relatively few of his own offspring behind. Likewise, a young woman who waits for the right man to help rear her children may lose valuable reproductive opportunities at a time when her health and physical capability are at their peak and when her mother and senior female kin are young enough to be effective surrogates.

Recent studies of the effects of early family environment on reproductive strategies have been carried out by, among others, Kim, Smith, and Palermiti (1997), Ellis et al. (1999), and Ellis and Garber (2000). Kim, Smith, and Palermiti studied 380 secondary school students (197 females and 183 males) in two communities in southern Italy. They found that, for women, earlier menarche was correlated with more family stress throughout childhood, more unhappiness in parental marital relations throughout childhood, more conflict with mothers, more rejection from fathers, less emotional closeness to mothers, and more independence from parents in late childhood. For men, earlier spermarche was correlated with more parental marital conflict in early childhood, less emotional closeness to fathers during childhood, and more aggressiveness and unruliness in late childhood. However, most of the correlations obtained by the authors were relatively low, and it is therefore hard to say how theoretically significant (as opposed to statistically significant) the findings are.

Ellis et al. (1999) used a data set from a longitudinal study of 281 girls in the United States to analyze the effects of a variety of environmental variables on pubertal timing. These variables mainly involved family stressors and the quality of family relationships. The authors found that the single most important factor related to pubertal timing was what they called "father-daughter affectionate-positivity." The more affectionate and positive the relationship between fathers and daughters, the later daughters reached puberty, and father-daughter positivity predicted pubertal timing much better than mother-daughter positivity. However, in contrast to Belsky, Steinberg, and Draper (1991) and other studies, Ellis et al. found that negative relationships within the family were not correlated with pubertal timing.

Ellis and Garber (2000) studied the effects of the presence of stepfathers or mothers' boyfriends on girls' pubertal timing in a sample of eighty-seven American girls. They found a correlation of r = −.37 between a girl's age and the entry of an unrelated father figure into her household. Thus, the younger a girl was when this father figure appeared, the earlier her pubertal timing. More importantly, Ellis and Garber found a strong relationship (r = .67) between the level of dyadic stress (i.e., stress between a mother and her romantic partner) in stepfather/boyfriend families and a girl's maturational timing, which indicates that girls reached puberty earlier when this stress was greater. In the biologically intact families in the sample, there was little relationship between dyadic stress and pubertal timing (r = .15). In contrast to the Ellis et al. (1999) study, this study does provide support for the importance of family stressors.

These studies and similar ones clearly suggest that the timing of sexual maturation (and thus potential reproduction) is influenced by key environmental circumstances, especially those involving the family environment. Reproductive strategies, perhaps more than any other human trait, are highly facultative in nature (cf. Chisholm, 1999:149–202).

FERTILITY DECLINE IN THE MODERN WORLD

A well-known feature of life in less-developed countries is the presence of a large number of children per family. Compared to couples in the developed world, couples in less-developed countries produce a good many more offspring. Yet in recent decades there has been a substantial and, to some at least, a surprising reduction in fertility rates. Between 1960 and 1990, total fertility throughout the world fell from 5.56 to 4.29 children per ever-married woman, a 23 percent reduction. Efforts to explain this reduction, as well as efforts to explain fertility reduction in the countries of the original demographic transition of the nineteenth and twentieth centuries, have varied widely.

One of the most widely endorsed theories holds that people adjust their fertility levels to the economic value of children's labor. A major proponent of this ecomaterialist view is Marvin Harris (1989; Harris and Ross, 1987), who draws on research by Mamdani (1972), Benjamin White (1973, 1982), Nag, White, and Peet (1978), and Nag (1983). Harris notes that in societies or regions where the economy is still based on agriculture very young children typically perform such tasks as gathering firewood, carrying water for cooking and washing, grinding and pounding grains, taking food to adults in the fields, sweeping floors, and running errands. Older children are involved in cooking meals, working full time in the fields, hunting, herding, fishing, and making pots, containers, mats, and nets. Under these conditions, it is rational for people to keep their fertility high to maximize the economic benefits their children provide for them. The shift from high fertility to low fertility results, Harris claims, mainly from the changing economic value of children's labor with industrialization. As children cease to be economic assets—become, in fact, very costly to rear—it is much more rational for couples to limit their numbers. The same type of argument has also been pressed by a number of demographers. John Caldwell (1976), for example, holds that the key issue is the direction of wealth flows between parents and children. High-fertility societies—primitive and traditional societies—are those in which wealth flows are primarily from child to parent, whereas low-fertility societies—industrial societies—are those in which wealth flows go primarily from parent to child. Ester Boserup (1986) regards occupational change as the crucial factor leading to fertility decline in countries with high-fertility regimes. Boserup presents fertility rates for people in four different occupations in twenty-eight less-developed countries. Those working in agriculture had the highest rate, 8.38. The lowest rate was obtained by workers in professional, managerial, technical, and clerical jobs, 6.74. People working in sales and service and in manual work had fertility rates that were in between, 7.39 and 7.63 respectively. Note, however, that the fertility differences between occupational groups presented by Boserup are relatively small, and that the fertility of the lowest group is still nearly seven children, much higher than is found in the industrialized countries. This suggests that something is amiss with the ecomaterialist argument.

Several demographers have challenged the view that in preindustrial societies the net flow of benefits is from child to parent (Turke, 1989; Low, 1991, 1993a; Low and Clarke, 1992; Kaplan, 1994). Low has claimed that "children's labor is never sufficient to result in a net economic gain to parents" (1993a:184), and Turke (1989:76) goes so far as to argue that in all societies "the net flow of services and resources will usually be from older to younger generations." Both Turke and Low and Clarke conclude that traditional demographic arguments have had it backwards: People do not use reproductive resources to acquire economic benefits, but rather use economic resources to acquire reproductive benefits. It is the promotion of inclusive fitness rather than the net economic value of children that governs fertility behavior. Hillard Kaplan (1994) has tested the wealth flows argument by using data from three tribal societies in South America, all of which practiced a mixture of hunting and gathering and horticulture. In all three societies fertility was very high—an average of 8.15 for the societies combined—but children in each society were producing far fewer calories than they were consuming. Kaplan's conclusion is that the flow of benefits was overwhelmingly from parent to child rather than the reverse, even taking into consideration other kinds of work that children performed. "The data from all three groups," he says, "show that even though children were very costly to raise, fertility was high" (1994:763).

A second theory of fertility decline is the biomaterialist argument of Carey and Lopreato (1995). Carey and Lopreato argue that the main determinant of the level of fertility is the level of mortality. According to them, humans have evolved a "two-surviving-children psychology" in which they gear their total fertility to the frequency with which offspring survive to adulthood. Where infant and child mortality are high, fertility will be high in order to replace offspring expected to die before they themselves become reproductive. Likewise, where infant and child mortality are low, and thus where most infants survive to reproductive age, fertility is adjusted downward. If two children born are both likely to survive, why have more? Carey and Lopreato note that Darwin himself

"argued that, despite the tendency of populations to outpace the growth of their resources, a countertendency toward population stability is a characteristic of all species.
The theory of natural selection suggests that, given the real or potential Malthusian
scarcity and the associated struggle for existence, the fertility of individuals displays a vigorous tendency to track mortality—a tendency toward a replacement-level reproductive
strategy" (1995:616). Carey and Lopreato go on to remark that the original demographic
transition itself provides highly suggestive evidence for their interpretation. As mortality
levels dropped, fertility dropped even though people were living longer and had more
years in which to reproduce. The authors argue that the maximization of inclusive fitness
is not a matter of the sheer production of offspring, but rather the production of offspring who are likely to survive and reproduce in the next generation. As they say, "parents who invest their limited resources in fewer rather than more children may also have
the greater genetic success" (1995:625). I am skeptical of Carey and Lopreato's argument
that people have evolved to aim for only two surviving children, but accept their more
general point that fertility should track mortality and that the maximization of inclusive
fitness often means having fewer (but higher quality) children. In fact, demographers
have long thought that fertility levels should logically be related to levels of infant mortality; numerous studies have been carried out to test this argument, but highly disparate
results have been obtained (Matthiessen and McCann, 1978; van de Walle, 1986;
Cantrelle, Ferry, and Mondot, 1978). Moderate to high correlations have been found for
some countries at some times, but for other countries and at other times low correlations
have been reported, and in several instances negative correlations have even been found.
On the basis of these studies it is difficult to know what to conclude, but I shall readdress
this point shortly.

A third major interpretation of fertility decline, a type of polimaterialist argument, emphasizes female empowerment (Dyson and Moore, 1983; Malhotra, Vanneman, and
Kishor, 1995; Handwerker, 1993; Murthi, Guio, and Dreze, 1995; Jejeebhoy, 1995; Penn,
1999). In an early study along these lines, Dyson and Moore (1983) showed that fertility
was notably higher in the northern states of India than in the southern states and related
this difference to kinship patterns affecting the autonomy of women; greater female autonomy was associated with lower fertility. Malhotra, Vanneman, and Kishor (1995), also
studying India, found that where gender discrimination and gender bias in the marriage
system were at lower levels, fertility was also lower; the effect of these gender variables remained substantial even when controls for economic development, social stratification,
and region were introduced. Murthi, Guio, and Dreze (1995), in yet another study of Indian fertility differentials, focused in particular on the role of female education. They
found that female literacy and female labor force participation both exerted negative and
statistically significant effects on total fertility. Because the authors presented some of their
raw data, I was able to reanalyze them and found that the effect of female literacy was
much more important than the effect of female labor force participation. The former correlated at $r = -.864$ with total fertility, whereas the latter correlated much more weakly, at
$r = -.166$. Handwerker (1993), in a study of Antigua in the West Indies, found that female empowerment in the form of increased education and expanded employment opportunities was significantly correlated with lower fertility. Jejeebhoy (1995) examined

fifty-nine studies that explored the relationship between female education and fertility in a large number of countries. Most of these studies showed that greater female education is closely linked with lower fertility. In societies at very low levels of development, small amounts of education do not seem to produce a decline in fertility (or in some cases actually are associated with an increase in fertility), but when greater amounts of education are obtained fertility then starts a continual decline. At higher levels of economic development, even small increments in educational attainment lead to fertility decline. Jejeebhoy stresses, as have others, that education exerts its effect on fertility by way of giving women greater autonomy and empowerment with respect to such things as knowledge, decision-making, physical mobility, feelings and loyalties, and economic behavior.

Sanderson and Dubrow (2000) have performed a series of quantitative analyses designed to provide further empirical testing of each of these theories and to compare their relative explanatory power. They used a sample of 121 nations and data collected largely by the World Bank for the years 1960 and 1990. Gross national product per capita, percentage of the labor force in agriculture, percentage urban, female empowerment, and infant and child mortality were in nearly all cases moderately to strongly correlated with fertility in both 1960 and 1990. The number of physicians in the population was highly correlated with fertility, but it washed out when the infant mortality rate was controlled, so it was dropped from further analyses. Several sets of multiple regression analyses were then carried out. In the first, 1960 fertility levels were regressed on the five independent variables. Collectively, these variables explained approximately 60 percent of the variance in 1960 fertility (adjusted R^2), but infant mortality, female empowerment, and percentage urban were clearly the best predictors of fertility, and in that order. As infant mortality fell, fertility fell, and as females became more empowered and more of the population lived in urban areas fertility fell as well. Percentage of the labor force in agriculture largely washed out when the other independent variables were controlled, and thus was an extremely weak predictor. Gross national product was inversely correlated with fertility, as expected, but it underwent a sharp sign reversal when the other variables were factored out. It therefore cannot be regarded as an important predictive variable one way or the other. This analysis was repeated but substituting child mortality (ages one–four) for infant mortality. Matthiessen and McCann (1978) have suggested that if parents are reducing their fertility in response to lower mortality, then what is really important is the rate of child rather than infant survivorship (cf. van de Walle, 1986:210). However, Sanderson and Dubrow's results showed that child mortality was a much poorer predictor of fertility than was infant mortality. In this analysis female empowerment was the best predictor, and child mortality ranked even below percent urban, which was a relatively good predictor.

The third analysis repeated the first analysis but used 1990 levels of all of the variables. Here again infant mortality was the best predictor with female empowerment second. Gross national product, literacy, and percentage urban were very weak predictors, and percentage of the labor force in agriculture was only marginally better. The five independent variables together explained approximately 80 percent of the variance in fertility, with infant mortality and female empowerment explaining the vast majority of this. The next analysis repeated the third analysis but substituted child mortality for infant mortality. Actually, this analysis used the mortality rate for children aged zero–five (because that was the only measure available in the data set), and thus was a combination of infant and child mortality. These results therefore are not strictly comparable to those in the second analysis. In any event, zero–five mortality was easily the best predictor of 1990 fertility, with female empowerment again the next best. Percentage urban essentially washed out, and the predictive ability of gross national product and percentage of the labor force in agriculture was quite modest. The total variance explained was 80 percent, the vast majority of which was being explained by zero–five mortality and female empowerment.

It could be argued that, if declining infant mortality leads to lower fertility, it can only do so if people are given time to assess its effects over the medium to long run (this is similar to the argument that child mortality should be a stronger determinant of fertility than infant mortality). To test this possibility, Sanderson and Dubrow repeated the third analysis but substituted the 1982 infant mortality rate for the 1990 rate. Here it was found that the predictive ability of infant mortality dropped substantially and that female empowerment became the best predictor. The predictive ability of 1982 infant mortality was not only less than that of female empowerment, but it was only a slightly better predictor than the percentage of the labor force in agriculture. It thus appears that, whatever effect infant mortality has on fertility, this effect is felt quickly rather than after a lag in time.

The final analysis examined changes in fertility between 1960 and 1990 and how they related to changes during the same period of levels of the five independent variables. Together changes in the independent variables explained 55 percent of the variance in fertility change. Infant mortality change was by far the best predictor of fertility change (st. beta coeff. = .551), and change in female empowerment was the only other variable with much predictive ability (st. beta coeff. = −.278).

A second set of analyses was carried out to see if these results could be replicated for the original demographic transition between 1880 and 1940. The sample was a group of twenty-seven countries in North America and Europe (Japan was also included) that are now highly developed or at least have achieved substantial levels of industrialization. Of the two most important predictive variables in the first study, infant mortality and female empowerment, it was only possible to examine the effects of infant mortality. As far as I know, no data exist that would measure female empowerment for these rather distant time periods. However, it is unlikely that there was much female empowerment occurring at these times (especially in 1880 and 1910). Married women were a minuscule proportion of the labor force in all of the now-industrialized societies, and they were much less involved in the educational world than is the case today. Therefore it is probably safe to assume that female empowerment could not have been an important determinant of fertility decline during the original demographic transition, at least on the level that female empowerment has reached today. Sanderson and Dubrow did look, however, at the effects of two other independent variables, percentage of the labor force in agriculture and percentage of the labor force in manufacturing. These were designed to measure the economic value of children's labor. Thus, the analyses for the original demographic transition test the ecomaterialist theory against the biomaterialist theory.

The results for 1880 show that infant mortality was the best predictor of fertility, with percentage of the labor force in agriculture a close second and percentage of the labor force in manufacturing a distant third. However, the results were weak and all three variables together explained very little of the variance in fertility. The reason for such weak results is probably the data themselves. Older data are often more unreliable than more recent data, and in this case several values had to be estimated for some countries. This interpretation is reinforced by the fact that the data for 1910 and 1940 showed much stronger results. Infant mortality was far and away the most important predictor of fertility rates in 1910. For 1910, infant mortality and percentage of the labor force in manufacturing together explained 72 percent of the variance, and infant mortality explained most of this. The results were not as strong for 1940, but they were still good. All three variables explained 22 percent of the variance, and infant mortality was clearly the leading predictive variable.

One of the most striking findings of the Sanderson and Dubrow study was that both infant and child mortality were much more strongly related (zero order) to fertility than has been found in most previous studies. The average correlation between infant mortality and fertility for 1960 and 1990 was a whopping .808, and the correlation between 1960–1990 infant mortality change and 1960–1990 fertility change was .724. For the 1880 to 1940 data the average correlation was .588. The average correlation between child mortality and fertility for 1960 and 1990 was .732. No previous study has achieved average correlations anywhere near these numbers. It is not clear why Sanderson and Dubrow's results were so much stronger; one possibility is the higher level of aggregation of their data compared to previous studies.

Sanderson and Dubrow's results are broadly consistent in one way with those from an earlier study by Lopreato and Yu (1988), who carried out a multiple regression analysis on data from sixty-three contemporary nation-states. Their principal finding was that the number of physicians in the population was the best predictor of fertility, and they regarded their physicians variable as a proxy for the rate of infant and/or child survivorship. They included infant mortality in their regression analysis, but it was not a strong predictor. This is surprising in view of the fact that the infant mortality rate is a direct rather than an indirect indicator of infant survivorship. Sanderson and Dubrow found that both the number of physicians and infant mortality were highly correlated (zero order) with fertility, but, as they expected, the number of physicians washed out when infant mortality was controlled. In this respect their results differ from Lopreato and Yu's. Nevertheless, Lopreato and Yu interpret their findings in the same way as Sanderson and Dubrow: The survival rate of infants, which is determined in large part by the level of health care in a society, is a major determinant of the level of fertility. Also in a similar way to Sanderson and Dubrow's study, Lopreato and Yu found that two female empowerment variables, percentage of women in the labor force and percentage of women who are literate, were good predictors of fertility.

Sanderson and Dubrow's results for the 1960–1990 period thus support both the biomaterialist argument that emphasizes infant mortality decline and the polimaterialist argument that emphasizes female empowerment, but the biomaterialist argument receives stronger support because infant mortality was the best predictor in four of the six analyses, and also because it was clearly best in predicting actual fertility *change*. By contrast, their results show weak support for the ecomaterialist argument that fertility is being adjusted primarily to the economic value of children's labor. Three of the standardized beta coefficients for percentage of the labor force in agriculture were not much above zero, and the other coefficients were weak. In terms of percentage of the population living in urban areas, this was a good predictor for 1960 but not for 1990 or for changes during the 1960 to 1990 period. In fact, the beta coefficient with respect to 1960 to 1990 change carried the wrong sign. Finally, it cannot be a simple increase in material wealth or the standard of living that is determining fertility change. Three of the beta coefficients for gross national product were barely above zero and the other three, though substantially larger, were in the wrong direction. The analyses of the original demographic transition, the 1880 to 1940 period, show even more support for the biomaterialist argument. Here infant mortality was easily the best predictor of fertility in all three analyses, and in 1910 it explained well over half of the variance. However, there was slightly more support here for the role of the changing economic value of children's labor, and so this may have been somewhat more important for the original demographic transition than for the 1960 to 1990 period.

Although Sanderson and Dubrow found that fertility does not decline simply because societies develop economically and become wealthier, the transformation of society from a rural and agricultural base to an urban and industrial base is no doubt an important part of the story (even if not in a way that was measured by any of their independent variables). Hillard Kaplan (1996) suggests that modernization has produced a situation in which people reduce the number of offspring they have but invest much more in each: They trade quantity (an r strategy) for quality (a K strategy) (cf. van den Berghe and Whitmeyer, 1990). He proposes that it is the development of skills-based competitive labor markets that is the crucial factor. Such markets have the effect of increasing the importance of parental investment in offspring well-being. In having fewer children but investing more in each, parents are not necessarily maximizing their fitness in the classic sense, even in the long run. However, at the very least they are maximizing the "cultural fitness" of their offspring (and grandoffspring, etc.). Kaplan's argument is highly consistent with the common observation that in modern societies better-educated and wealthier parents tend to have fewer offspring than couples with less education and lower income. Alan Rogers (1995) has argued that the concept of fitness should be expanded to include not only the total number of offspring produced, but also the economic well-being of each offspring. As he puts it, "In a world with heritable wealth, wealth has value over and above its effect on the number of one's offspring. By continuing to earn, a rich person can increase the wealth of descendants several generations removed. Thus, the marginal effect of wealth on fitness may remain positive even among the very wealthy" (1995:94) (cf. Borgerhoff Mulder, 1998).

What is missing in these arguments is any reference to reduced infant mortality. In order for parents to have only two or three children and invest heavily in each child the rate of infant and child survivorship must be very high, as it is in modern industrial societies. As Wiley and Carlin (1999) have persuasively argued, mother-child attachment will be at its highest in those societies that have both low fertility and low infant mortality, i.e., in postdemographic transition societies. "Exclusive attachment," they say, "may . . . be an outcome of low mortality, as parents are relatively assured that their investment will pay off" (1999:153). Strong mother-child attachment (and perhaps even father-child attachment) would seem to be a prerequisite for intensive parental investment.

The importance of female empowerment in the process of fertility decline would seem to fit well into this picture. It has been argued that female empowerment helps reduce fertility because women often regard having a large number of children as a serious burden since it is they who take on most of the duties of child care in all societies; as women are empowered they will be in a better position to act on their desire to have fewer children (Murthi, Guio, and Dreze, 1995; Jejeebhoy, 1995; Penn, 1999).

Unfortunately, the various arguments sketched above only work if we can show that the causal arrows are actually pointing from lower infant mortality to lower fertility, as well as from enhanced female empowerment to lower fertility. With respect to the infant mortality-fertility relationship, a number of demographers have suggested that the causal arrows could be running in the opposite direction (Chowdhury, Khan, and Chen, 1978; Knodel and van de Walle, 1986). In this argument, high fertility leads to high mortality because more children stress family resources and place greater burdens on mothers, both of which produce a poorer level of infant and child care. When fertility declines (for whatever reason) it generates circumstances favorable for a decline in infant mortality. As women have fewer children they are able to provide a higher standard of care to each and thus increase the rate of infant survivorship. A number of demographers have tried to specify the temporal order between mortality change and fertility change. However, the results are highly inconclusive (e.g., Matthiessen and McCann, 1978; van de Walle, 1986; Chowdhury, Khan, and Chen, 1978; Ben-Porath, 1978; Knodel, 1986). For some countries at some times it has been found that infant mortality declined first, but in other countries at other times it was fertility that declined first.

In new research (Sanderson, 2001), I have tried to disentangle the causal relationships between infant mortality decline, female empowerment, and reduced fertility. To test the causal relationship between infant mortality decline and fertility decline I performed a series of panel regression analyses. First, I regressed 1990 levels of fertility on 1960 levels of all of the independent variables, while simultaneously controlling for 1960 levels of fertility. The results showed strong support for the argument that the direction of causation is from infant mortality to fertility. All of the beta coefficients except those for infant mortality and 1960 fertility were small and statistically nonsignificant. The beta for infant mortality was the largest (.586), and it was substantially larger than that for 1960 fertility (.305). Then I made 1990 levels of infant mortality the dependent variable and regressed it on 1960 levels of the independent variables, while at the same time controlling for 1960 levels of infant mortality. Infant mortality in 1960 was by far the best predictor of infant mortality in 1990 (beta = .832), whereas 1960 levels of fertility did not predict infant mortality in 1990 (more accurately, did not predict changes in infant mortality between 1960 and 1990) (beta = −.103). These two panel analyses, then, show that infant mortality decline is causal to fertility decline rather than the other way around.

I also carried out several panel analyses for the 1880 to 1940 period. Unfortunately, these produced mixed and inconclusive results. Infant mortality decline did appear to be an important cause of fertility decline between 1880 and 1910 but not for the 1910 to 1940 period. However, I was able to eliminate the reverse hypothesis for both periods: that fertility decline was the cause of infant mortality decline.

What about the female empowerment-fertility relationship? Two panel analyses were carried out to test for the direction of causation. In the first, 1990 fertility levels were regressed on 1960 levels of the independent variables (infant mortality excluded), while controlling for 1960 fertility levels. The results showed that female empowerment had no causal influence on fertility decline between 1960 and 1990. The beta for female empowerment in 1960 was −.053, whereas that for fertility in 1960 was .411. In the second analysis, 1990 levels of female empowerment were regressed on 1960 levels of the independent variables (again, infant mortality excluded), while controlling for 1960 levels of female empowerment. This analysis was designed to determine whether the causal relationship was running in the opposite direction, i.e., whether it was fertility decline that was causing an enhancement of female empowerment. The results showed that this was indeed the case. The beta for fertility in 1960 was −.387, whereas that for female empowerment in 1960—which should have been the best predictive variable—was only .185. The results of these last two panel analyses thus suggest that fertility does not decline because women become more empowered, but rather that when fertility does decline this opens up opportunities for female empowerment by making it easier for women to pursue more education and to enter the labor force.

This means that we are left with the biomaterialist argument as the only viable explanation of declining fertility. Female empowerment is a result rather than a cause of fertility decline, and, as noted earlier, the changing economic value of children's labor seems to play no significant role in the process of fertility decline. Such is the value of comparative theory testing using rigorous quantitative data.

ADDITIONAL EVIDENCE

Cronk (1989, 1991, 1999, 2000) discusses a number of cases of female-biased parental investment and shows how these can be explained through a combination of biomaterialist and ecomaterialist theories. Sieff (1990) has contributed an important article along similar lines. Hrdy (1999) provides excellent discussions of a variety of reproductive phenomena, especially differential parental investment in sons or daughters and biased sex ratios. Low (1993a) and Low, Clarke, and Lockridge (1992) illustrate a variety of applications of a biomaterialist perspective to demographic phenomena. Harris and Ross (1987) offer an extensive ecomaterialist analysis of demographic phenomena in the main types of human societies. Sometimes their analyses are complementary with biomaterialist analyses, but, as was seen above, often they conflict with them and must give way to them. Blurton Jones (1986) has carried out a classic study of birth spacing among !Kung women. The women he studied had birth-spacing intervals of approximately four years, and he has shown that this was optimal in terms of producing the most surviving offspring.

11

Human Sexuality

The substance of our lives is women. All other things are irrelevancies, hypocrises, subterfuges. We sit talking of sports and politics, and all the while our hearts are filled with memories of women and the capture of women.

—George Moore

Elyot: It doesn't suit women to be promiscuous. Amanda: It doesn't suit men for women to be promiscuous.

—Noel Coward

The sexual organs are the true seat of the will, of which the opposite pole is the brain.

—Simone de Beauvoir

If you live in rock and roll, as I do, you see the reality of sex, of male lust and women being aroused by male lust. It attracts women. It doesn't repel them.

—Camille Paglia

Gay men may seek sex without emotion; lesbians often end up in emotion without sex.

—Camille Paglia

It is a wise father that knows his own child.   *—William Shakespeare*

Mothers are fonder than fathers of their children because they are more certain they are their own.

—Aristotle

A BIOMATERIALIST UNDERSTANDING OF HUMAN SEXUALITY

Differences in sexual attitudes, emotions, and behavior between men and women are best understood not only in terms of the theory of inclusive fitness, but more specifically in terms of the concept of sexual selection. Sexual selection was identified by Darwin (1871) as a special form of natural selection that acts, not upon an organism's capacity to survive, but upon its ability to find mates and reproduce. Darwin identified two mechanisms of sexual selection, which he called male combat and female choice. Males may compete among each other in various kinds of aggressive ways for access to females, with the winners in these aggressive encounters getting the female(s). This is what happens among deer and elk, for example, whose antlers have evolved as weapons to be used in male combat, or among sea lions and walruses. Or, females may choose males who have particular kinds of characteristics that they favor. Among birds, for example, it is usually the male that is more brightly colored, and this coloration has evolved as a cue for female choice. Among peacocks, elaborate coloration and plumage have evolved because they have been chosen by peahens as desirable qualities in their mates.

Our modern understanding of the operation of sexual selection in animals and humans has been greatly influenced by a seminal article written by Robert Trivers (1972). According to Trivers, the key factor in determining how sexual selection works is parental investment, i.e., which sex invests more time and energy in the rearing of offspring. There is commonly a tradeoff between the relative parental investment of the sexes and the energy that is put into mating. Among highly monogamous species, such as most birds, the parental investment of the sexes is approximately equal. Under these circumstances, differences in testosterone levels between the sexes are minimal or nonexistent, and the male is essentially the same size as the female. There is little male dominance and males put as much energy into parental care as into mating effort. Among polygynous species, however, males contribute little to parental care and put their energies into mating effort. Males are larger than females (sometimes much larger), they have much higher levels of testosterone, and they are highly dominant over females. Among such species, males tend to be aggressive and to compete vigorously among themselves for access to females. They also tend to control the sexual behavior of females by limiting or preventing their access to other males. Most species are of this latter type. Humans fall into this category, although human males do tend to invest more in their offspring than the males of other species. We are a moderately polygynous, moderately sexually dimorphic species.[1]

In humans, sexual selection has been fully at work determining men's and women's sexual choices, emotions, and behaviors. Men have competed amongst one another for mates, and both men and women have evolved clear preferences in regard to the opposite sex. Donald Symons's *The Evolution of Human Sexuality* (1979) brilliantly develops a biomaterialist understanding of human sexuality, especially heterosexuality, and shows how it is rooted in sexual selection. Symons first discusses sexual choice. Men everywhere appear to be much more naturally aroused by visual sexual stimuli. In Western societies the male market for pornography is huge, but the female market is extremely small, in fact virtually nonexistent. *Playgirl,* a magazine that shows pictures of nude men, is almost completely supported by gay men. There is an extremely widespread, probably universal, desire on the part of men to be stimulated by the sight of female genitals. As Symons (1979:176) notes, "cross-cultural evidence suggests that the tendency of human males to be sexually aroused by the sight of females—especially the female genitals—and to make great efforts to see female genitals (and any other part of the female body that is typically concealed), simply has no parallel among human females, and is often intuitively incomprehensible to women." Symons interprets this dimension of male sexuality as an evolutionary adaptation that promotes the male's inclusive fitness. The greater the extent to which men are visually aroused the more they will tend to copulate with women, and thus the greater the likelihood of impregnating women. Since human females do not advertise ovulation, there has evolved a male ability to assess a female's reproductive value through visual cues. However, there is no evolutionary advantage to a female to be visually aroused by the sight of naked males. Indeed, this would work against her inclusive fitness because it would compromise her tendency to be choosy and select only those partners she deems most suitable for herself and her future children.

For males, physical attractiveness plays a major role in sexual attraction, and males tend to use certain criteria that are indicators of high female fecundity: health, complexion, cleanliness, condition of the skin, and indicators of disease or disability (see also Symons, 1995). Physical attractiveness of the sexual partner is much more important to men than to women; women are more concerned with social status because this is a strong indicator of a male's ability to provide resources for a woman's offspring. Males everywhere show an extremely strong desire for young females. As men get older, the age gap between them and their mates increases, and this seems to be true in both modern industrial and preindustrial societies (Kenrick and Keefe, 1992; Kenrick, Trost, and Sheets, 1996). On the island of Poro, for example, the age gap between the youngest husbands and their mates was less than one year, whereas the age gap between the oldest husbands and their mates was nearly twenty-one years. This preference for young females is an evolved strategy that promotes males' inclusive fitness. Younger females are much more likely to become pregnant and to produce strong, healthy offspring. They also have a longer reproductive period ahead of them than do older women, and thus men who mate with younger women can produce more offspring over time. In a study of 774 Hungarian males, Bereczkei and Csanaky (1996) found that males who chose younger mates had significantly more surviving children than those who chose older mates. In the same study, the authors interviewed 1,057 Hungarian women and showed that their preference for men of higher status was also reproductively adaptive. Women who married higher-status men left more surviving offspring than women who married men of the same or lower status.

The preference of men for younger women is also indicated by studies of what biologists call *neoteny*, which is the retention of juvenile characteristics in adults. Everyone has had the experience of perceiving the very young offspring of mammals as "cute," and also of perceiving human infants and children in the same way. The features that make babies and children cute are such things as relatively large eyes, a short distance from mouth to chin, a small nose, and full lips. Women often retain these characteristics to some extent as they mature into adulthood, and there seems to be a strong male attraction to such traits. A recent study (Jones, 1995) examined the faces of ten leading female models whose pictures had been displayed on the covers of *Cosmopolitan* and *Glamour* magazines. Measurements of facial features were taken and fed into a computer. A program designed to estimate the models' ages from these facial features alone estimated them to be approximately seven years old! When the study was repeated using male models, no facial neoteny was found, and the computer predicted the models to be approximately their actual ages.

Devendra Singh and his colleagues (Singh, 1993a, 1993b, 1994; Singh and Young, 1995; Singh and Luis, 1995; Barber, 1995; Furnham, Dias, and McClelland, 1998) have carried out a variety of fascinating studies in which they show that the most important dimension of female sexual attractiveness is a certain type of body shape. Singh found that men in all of his studies preferred a woman with a waist-to-hip ratio (WHR) of about .70. This took precedence over breast size and body weight, and as women's WHRs increased they were regarded as increasingly unattractive. Many of these studies have involved college men, but it has been found that men of all ages make essentially the same judgments, and so far the judgments are invariant across different racial and ethnic groups. Evidence is rapidly accumulating that a low WHR is an excellent indicator of female reproductive status and overall female health. Girls with lower WHRs show earlier pubertal endocrine activity, and married women with higher WHRs have more difficulty getting pregnant and give birth to their first child at a later age. Circulating estrogen functions to lower a woman's WHR, but circulating testosterone raises it. As women age, their WHRs increase, and after menopause women's WHRs approximate those of males. A lower WHR is also associated with a lesser incidence of such diseases as diabetes, high blood pressure, heart attack, stroke, menstrual irregularity, elevated plasma triglycerides, and ovarian and breast cancer. Singh suggests that human males the world over are descended from ancestral males who maximized their inclusive fitness by mating with low-WHR females. As he has put it (1993a:303), "males who sought and were successful in mating with females with gynoidal fat distribution [low WHR] would leave more progeny than males who indiscriminately mated with females. The greater reproductive success of such females would maximize their contribution to the gene pool of future generations. Over time, males would favor females with gynoidal fat distribution and find such females more attractive and desirable."

More research in highly diverse cultures will be needed to see whether the male preference for females with low WHRs is a true human universal, or at least a near universal, as would be expected. Nonetheless, to this point studies have been conducted in at least seven different cultures or ethnic populations, and the results are positive. Studies of male judgments of female attractiveness in the United States, England, Germany, India, Indonesia, Hong Kong, and Guinea-Bissau show that men prefer women with low WHRs (Singh, Frohlich, and Haywood, 1999). Moreover, Singh, Frohlich, and Haywood (1999) have collected evidence on female attractiveness as depicted in sculptures. They examined the WHRs in 286 sculptures from ancient India, Egypt, Greece, and Africa, and found that the average female WHR was significantly lower than the average male WHR. The average WHR for women was about .70, that for men about .90. These authors also found that poetry from the European Middle Ages emphasized small waists, and that Chinese and Indian poetry gives much more emphasis to waist size than to breasts, thighs, and legs.

However, some researchers claim to have produced disconfirming evidence. Wetsman and Marlowe (1999) found that the Hadza, hunter-gatherers located in Tanzania, showed no preference for .70 WHRs over .90 WHRs. The Hadza displayed more concern for weight, preferring heavier women to thinner ones. But it is not entirely clear that this is actually a disconfirming case. At the 1999 annual meetings of the Human Behavior and Evolution Society, Wetsman pointed out that Hadza men do like women with lordosis (protruding buttocks), so if the line drawings that are used to depict WHR were drawn from the side rather than from the front it would be the case that Hadza men really do prefer low WHRs. Tassinary and Hansen (1998) also report what they believe is disconfirming evidence. In a study of 136 American undergraduates, they reported that men actually judged drawings with higher WHRs to be more attractive. However, this study seems to suffer from a fatal flaw. Tassinary and Hansen used different line drawings of female WHRs than those originally used by Singh and since used by all other researchers. In creating these drawings, Tassinary and Hansen tried to represent a low WHR by expanding hip size rather than contracting waist size. As Bronstad and Singh (1999) point out, by manipulating the drawings in this way the authors confounded WHR with both hip size and perceived body weight, and as a result drawings with low WHRs were judged to be as much as twenty pounds heavier and fourteen years older than figures with high WHRs. Since American men judge younger women and thinner women to be more attractive, it is no wonder that they judged the drawings with lower WHRs more negatively. Bronstad and Singh (1999) and Streeter and McBurney (1999) show that when Tassinary and Hansen's drawings are properly corrected men judge WHRs of about .70 to be more attractive.

Although males value physical attractiveness more than females, females do regard this attribute as important. Singh (1995) has shown that American women ranging in age from eighteen to sixty-nine had a clear preference for men with a WHR of about .90, which is approximately the average male WHR. It turns out that, just as a low WHR is a good indicator of female health, a high WHR is a good indicator of male health. Women therefore prefer healthy men, and they do so because healthy men are more likely to live longer and to be better providers for their wives and offspring.

Today in Western societies males have a strong preference for thin women, whereas in the past plumper women were preferred. The change relates to the perception of healthiness. In earlier times plumpness was a sign of good health, but it has now become a sign of poor nutrition and it is thinness that signals good eating habits and thus good health. Moreover, plumpness and thinness are closely associated with status. As Symons (1979:199) remarks, "Plumpness has gone out of fashion in Western societies during the last century, probably as a result of the changing relationship between body fat and status: when food was scarce for many people, plumpness was a sign of wealth, but as circumstances improved for the majority, the rich began to distinguish themselves through thinness."

Symons is quick to point out that none of the above findings suggest that there are no cultural differences in standards of attractiveness. Here, as elsewhere, human

behavior is the product of the complex interaction between biological predispositions and the total physical and social environment. However, is it unlikely that cultural differences in standards of attractiveness will be found that directly undermine
the unconscious goals of both males and females in maximizing their reproductive
success. No one has yet discovered a society where men prefer older, unhealthy
women who have low reproductive value or where women prefer diseased men with
low social status and few resources.

Men everywhere also have a tremendous desire for sexual variety for its own sake.
This is highly adaptive in terms of the male's inclusive fitness. The more sexual partners
a man has, the more females he will impregnate and the larger his number of offspring.
Although studies show that the number of married women who have affairs is not dramatically smaller than the number of men who do, Symons interprets this in terms of
what men and women, respectively, are looking for in an extramarital affair. Men, it
seems, desire mainly sex, whereas women value the extramarital relationship *as a relationship* and use sex as a means of establishing and cementing the relationship. Women
often seek extramarital affairs because of a dissatisfaction with their marriages. At the
risk of oversimplification, women are using sex to get love, but men are using love to
get sex. Whereas philandering can promote a male's inclusive fitness, it can actually reduce a female's. Philandering women can reduce their fitness by alienating their husbands, who throughout history have been the economic supporters of females and their
offspring. Moreover, a woman can have a very limited number of pregnancies in her lifetime, and mating with many different men will not alter this.[2] Men, of course, can impregnate literally hundreds or thousands of women, and thus have evolved a reproductive strategy that helps them do so.

From the standpoint of his inclusive fitness, one of the worst things that can happen
to a male is to be cuckolded by his mate, that is, be led by her to believe that her offspring fathered by another man are really his. As a result, he promotes the other man's
inclusive fitness rather than his own. To combat this outcome (which occurs with considerable frequency), males have evolved techniques of guarding their mates from other
males. Sexual jealousy, often taking an extreme form, is an emotion that has evolved as
an anticuckoldry device (Daly, Wilson, and Weghorst, 1982). The pattern of sexual jealousy among humans everywhere only makes sense in terms of sexual selection. Daly, Wilson, and Weghorst (1982) argue that males have aggressively competed for women
throughout hominid history. Throughout the world's societies there is remarkable consistency in the view that sexual intercourse between a married woman and someone who
is not her husband is a violation; the victim is the husband, who is entitled to compensation. Many societies have punished adulterous women severely. A jealous rage is expected in many societies as the result of this offense against a husband. Adultery by a wife
is perhaps the single most common reason for divorce throughout the world, and the
main cause of male aggression against women. And men seek to control female sexuality
in all societies, often by such means as claustration, footbinding, chastity devices, genital
mutilation, and male chaperonage. As the above implies, men have stronger jealousy
than women; it is less easy for them to forgive a wife than for a wife to forgive her husband. Women in many societies are reconciled to the adulterous affairs of their husbands.

Daly, Wilson, and Weghorst examine the claims of many authors (e.g., Whyte, 1978; Stephens, 1963; Ford and Beach, 1951; Leacock, 1980) that there are a number of societies in which jealousy is not displayed and where both sexes are allowed considerable sexual freedom outside marriage. They challenge these claims. With respect to Stephens, they claim that many of the societies which he claims permit adultery do so only under very restrictive circumstances. They claim that Stephens himself gives numerous examples of male aggression toward adulterous wives in some of the twelve societies that he classifies as "permissive." The authors focus on eleven societies that have been identified by others as unusually permissive; in all of these societies, they say, men restrict the sexual liberty of their wives and use violence or the threat of it in doing so.

Daly, Wilson, and Weghorst conclude that sexual jealousy, especially as displayed by husbands toward wives, is probably a human universal, at least as a human emotion. David Buss (2000) agrees, but goes further in giving equal emphasis to female jealousy of husbands. For Buss, female jealousy is just as much an evolutionary adaptation as male jealousy, because philandering men may impose high costs on their wives or lovers. A philandering man may leave his wife or lover for another woman, and thus the wife or lover loses the resources that man provided for her and her children. In the ancestral environment, women were critically dependent on such male provisioning. There may, however, be differences in the extent to which the emotion of jealousy is openly displayed. The authors point to Greece and the Hidatsa/Crow as contrasting cases in terms of the expression of jealousy. Public displays of male jealousy are considered bad form among the Hidatsa/Crow, but it is the lack of such display that is considered shameful among the Greeks. Nevertheless, "the emotional response is present in both societies. Such evidence of the psychic unity of humankind rebuts that extreme environmentalist position that considers particular cultures to be the wellsprings of human passions. Male jealousy cannot be understood as an arbitrary product of a specific social history. It is instead a predictable product of evolution" (Daly, Wilson, and Weghorst, 1982:24).

There appear to be important, and highly predictable, sex differences in jealousy. Buss, Larsen, Westen, and Semmelroth (1992) have carried out several relevant studies. In one study they found that 60 percent of the males reported more distress over sexual infidelity than over their mates' emotional attachment to a rival. By contrast, 83 percent of the women indicated that they would be more distressed over their mates' emotional attachment to a rival. In another study they measured men's and women's physiological arousal to imagined sexual infidelity compared to imagined emotional infidelity. Men showed much more arousal with respect to sexual infidelity, whereas women showed just the opposite, and this difference was very large. Although these results pertain to American subjects, very similar results have been reported from studies in China, Korea, Japan, Germany, the Netherlands, and Sweden (Buss, 2000). These findings are exactly what one would expect from a biomaterialist perspective, the theory of sexual selection in particular. Men are concerned with gaining and controlling mates and preventing other men from inseminating them. That is what promotes their inclusive fitness. Women, on the other hand, are more bothered by emotional infidelity because to promote their inclusive fitness they seek to find mates who will be loyal providers for them and their offspring. Emotional attachment or bonding is what solidifies such a relationship, and so women are more concerned about anything which threatens that emotional bond.

On average, it is the male who has the stronger sex drive and who shows more persistent interest in sex, although there can be considerable variation in the extent to which this is true. Copulation is, Symons argues, a service that females provide for males in all societies, and it is the males who woo and court females rather than the other way around. As Symons (1979:258) notes, "it is not a coincidence that males generally are the gift givers as well as the prostitute payers." Moreover, "copulation as a female service is easily explained in terms of ultimate causation: since the minimum male parental investment is almost zero, males stand to benefit from copulation with any fertile female (if the risk is low enough), whereas females do not stand to benefit reproductively from copulating with many males no matter what the risk is" (Symons, 1979:261).

Symons provides what he believes is a decisive test of these conclusions by looking at the behavior of homosexual men and women. As he notes, pornography has a strong appeal to gay males, but lesbians show little interest in it. Lesbians also have little interest in extramarital affairs and tend to build long-lasting and faithful monogamous relationships. Gay males, by contrast, have a marked tendency toward promiscuity, even more so than heterosexual males. Symons points out that many gay males have reported having over 500 sexual partners in their lifetimes, and he relates the case of one gay male who had anal intercourse with 48 different partners in a single evening. Bell and Weinberg (1978; reported in McKnight, 1997), using a sample of 685 gay men, found that over 90 percent reported having had more than 25 partners, almost half reported more than 500 partners, and nearly a quarter claimed to have had more than 1,000 partners. Symons interprets such high rates of promiscuity as the result of the lack of need of male homosexuals to compromise with women. In all-male relationships, men can give their desires free rein. Symons claims that the actual amount of extramarital activity heterosexual men have always stems from a compromise with their wives. With homosexual men, this necessity for compromise disappears.

In a massive study of over 10,000 individuals from 37 cultures, the evolutionary psychologist David Buss (1992, 1994) has confirmed many of Symons's findings and added several new wrinkles of his own. The large number of individuals who made up this study were located on six different continents, came from both rural and urban areas, and were widely representative of different socioeconomic levels. Buss found women to be about twice as likely as men to give importance to a partner's economic resources, and women were more desirous of a high-status partner. As Buss notes, "social status is a universal cue to the control of resources. Along with status come better food, more abundant territory, and superior health care" (1994:26). Women shun men, he says, who can be easily dominated by other men or who do not command the respect of the group. Interestingly, women who themselves have high status and considerable economic resources do not relax their desire for high-status and resource-rich men; indeed, empirical evidence suggests that such women still prefer men who have more status and resources than they do (B. Ellis, 1992).

Buss also shows that women generally prefer men who are older than they, on average men who are about three and a half years older. This makes sense in evolutionary terms because older men are more emotionally and economically stable and more likely to be good providers. Other qualities that women seek in men are ambitiousness, which turned out to be much more highly regarded by women than by men; intelligence, because more intelligent men are better providers of resources; and size, strength, and physical prowess, qualities that obviously relate closely to resource-providing abilities. Like Kenrick and Keefe (1992), Buss found that men prefer younger mates, and that they take on younger and younger mates to the extent that they can do so. By and large, the more male dominated the society, the greater was the age gap between men and their wives or lovers.

According to Buss, men not only value sexual fidelity, but rate infidelity as the least desirable characteristic in a wife. His research shows that unfaithfulness is more upsetting to men than any other emotional pain a woman can inflict on her mate. This finding dovetails perfectly with the findings discussed earlier regarding sexual jealousy.

Tooby and Cosmides (1989b:37) summarize the enormous importance of all of these empirical findings for a biomaterialist understanding of human sexual behavior:

> Culture theory as it stands predicts the null hypothesis: that differences between cultures are random with respect to evolutionary hypotheses and therefore that, for example, sex differences should occur as frequently in one direction as the other. The assertion that "culture" explains human variation will be taken seriously when there are reports of women war parties raiding villages to capture men as husbands, or of parents cloistering their sons but not their daughters to protect their sons' "virtue," or when cultural distributions for preferences concerning physical attractiveness, earning power, relative age, and so on, show as many cultures with bias in one direction as in the other.

SEXUAL ATTITUDES AND PRACTICES CROSS-CULTURALLY: THE "SOCIAL CONSTRUCTION" OF SEXUALITY

Western society has historically been what Vern Bullough (1976) calls a *sex-negative* society. Societies of this type are less common cross-culturally than permissive or *sex-positive* societies. Many examples of sex-positive societies have been given by Ford and Beach (1951). In some permissive societies infants and young children are actively stimulated sexually by adults. For example, parents frequently masturbate their children among the Hopi and Siriono. Among the Pukapukans of Polynesia, it is considered acceptable for boys and girls to masturbate openly in public. Children among the Seniang will publicly simulate sexual intercourse without being admonished by adults. Among the Alorese, children acquire knowledge of sexuality very early and by age five they have detailed knowledge of sexual intercourse and reproduction. It is thought by the Lepcha of India that girls will not mature properly unless they have had sexual intercourse. Girls aged eleven or twelve normally engage in intercourse, and older men sometimes engage in sex with girls as young as eight. The Trobriand Islanders of Melanesia are renowned for their sexual permissiveness. Sex life may begin for young boys as early as age ten and for young girls as early as age six.

The preceding societies are all band or tribal societies. What of agrarian civilizations? Outside of Western civilization, with its sex-negative religion of Christianity, sexual permissiveness has been the norm. The Greeks were a fairly permissive culture, and are renowned for their institutionalized form of homosexuality between older men and young boys (Cantarella, 1992; Percy, 1996). Within the framework of their educational system, male tutors would take their young boy pupils as lovers for a period of time. They would engage in both anal and intercrural intercourse (intercrural intercourse involved the tutor's placing his penis between the legs of the boy and ejaculating). Fellatio was strictly taboo. This homosexual relationship was highly idealized and regarded as beneficial to both parties. It was thought to make the boy more masculine and was linked with military courage and valor. In due time, however, the tutor abandoned the relationship, married, and took up a conventional heterosexual life. And although the Greeks looked very favorably on the tutor-pupil sexual relationship—or at least the Greek tutors did so; parents of the boys and other members of Greek society often had a very different attitude—they looked most unfavorably on exclusive homosexual relationships between men.

In its early stages, Roman society looked negatively on Greek tutor-pupil homosexuality, although the Romans did consider it acceptable for a man to have sex with a male slave, and such relations were relatively common (Cantarella, 1992). "Passive homosexuals" on the other hand—men who took the receptive position in anal intercourse— were thought to be highly effeminate and were disdained. In due time, however, the Romans moved increasingly toward the Greek pattern, and by the second century BC Roman men were openly courting free-born boys (Cantarella, 1992). Love relationships between men and free-born boys became common, although they were not connected to the educational system. Even passive homosexuality became increasingly common, and male prostitutes emerged. As for female homosexuality, the Romans looked very negatively upon this, considering it morally depraved (Cantarella, 1992).

Much of Islamic civilization was generally sex-positive, and male homosexuality, as long as it was discriminating and selective, was condoned (Bullough, 1976). India was also a sex-positive civilization, in fact perhaps the most sex-positive of all the historic agrarian civilizations. Hindus thought that women enjoyed sex at least as much as men, and a wide range of sexual practices was considered acceptable. The Chinese were quite open about sex and wrote many manuals about its nature and performance (Bullough, 1976). The Chinese also had a form of man-boy homosexuality that resembled the Greek pattern, even in its linkage with the educational system and its disdain for exclusive homosexual relationships between men. Japan was another agrarian civilization with relative sexual openness and institutionalized man-boy homosexuality (Leupp, 1995).

Institutionalized homosexual relationships have also been common in a number of band and tribal societies. In some North American Indian societies, a man known as a *berdache* dressed as a woman, performed women's roles, and engaged in sexual relations with other men, all with social approval. Other societies have had the local equivalent of a *berdache*. In northern India this person is known as a *hijra*, in Polynesia as a *mahu*, and in Oman as a *xanith* (LeVay, 1996).

Ford and Beach (1951) provide insight into homosexuality in band and tribal societies. Among the Siwans of Africa, men and boys engaged in anal intercourse, and males who preferred not to engage in this practice were thought to be peculiar. The Azande of the Sudan exhibited a pattern of homosexuality very similar to the Greek pattern. Institutionalized homosexuality has been widespread throughout Melanesia (Herdt,

1984). Among the Etoro of New Guinea, all men marry, but there are as many as 260 days per year in which they are forbidden to have heterosexual intercourse. Men and young boys sleep together apart from women and girls in men's houses. The Etoro believe that every male possesses a finite amount of semen and that men acquire semen from other men in the form of a gift. This occurs primarily as a result of young boys fellating older men. Boys also engage in receptive anal intercourse with men. As in the case of the Greeks, the man-boy relationship is thought to contribute to the boy's masculinity (Harris, 1981).

How can we explain these various patterns of sexual behavior, especially the widespread existence of socially approved—indeed, sometimes idealized—homosexuality? On the surface, these patterns would seem to confirm the social constructionist view and strongly challenge a biomaterialist interpretation of human sexuality. But closer scrutiny of these patterns shows that biomaterialist and ecomaterialist interpretations make good sense. First, note that all of the patterns of homosexuality described above are ones engaged in by men who are preferentially heterosexual. They either practiced heterosexuality along with homosexuality, or they experienced a brief period of homosexual relations followed by a much longer period of marriage and heterosexuality. As it turns out, heterosexuality is the most common sexual practice in all societies, just as inclusive fitness theory tells us it must be (see chapter 2). Homosexuality, if it is practiced, is always secondary to regular heterosexual relations, and in most cases there are strict rules regarding what kind of homosexual relations may be practiced and with whom and how often. These patterns of homosexuality appear to represent the type of homosexuality that may be called *situational* or *substitutional,* which means that men are substituting homosexual relations for heterosexual ones in situations where they have no sexual access to women or where that access is severely curtailed. The most familiar form of situational homosexuality in modern Western societies is that practiced by men in prisons.

Richard Posner (1992) has argued that the Greek form of homosexuality was a type of situational homosexuality that arose because of the particular way in which access to females was limited in this society. Women of the citizen class were secluded, and marriage was late. Male citizens disdained the use of prostitutes, so this sexual outlet was closed off to them. These men thus turned to their boy pupils as a substitute. Other widely found forms of man-boy homosexuality may have developed for similar reasons. Gilbert Herdt (1984) suggests that the scarcity of females among Melanesian groups like the Etoro may have been due to such factors as widespread polygyny, or, for unclear reasons, many fewer females being born. The Etoro also had systematic rules restricting the amount of heterosexuality men were permitted to engage in, and these rules may have been prompted by population pressure.

Two more features of situational homosexuality help to confirm a biomaterialist interpretation of human sexuality. First, it is obvious that all of the patterns of homosexuality we have been describing are ones engaged in only by men. In fact, there is much less female situational homosexuality throughout the world than male situational homosexuality. (Actually, I am not aware of any well-known instance of female situational homosexuality.) The reason, I think, is that the male sex drive is much stronger than the female's, and thus is much more vigorous in seeking an outlet. Second, situational homosexuality seems to be most commonly man-boy homosexuality, and often the very societies that look favorably on man-boy sexual relations strongly disapprove of homosexual relations between adult men. Why are boys a very common target of men all over the world? The answer seems to be that boys most closely resemble males' ideal sexual target, the adolescent or adult female. Take two twelve–year-old, prepubescent children, one boy and one girl, cut their hair the same length, and turn them facing away. In some cases it will be difficult to tell which is the boy and which the girl.

PREFERENTIAL HOMOSEXUALITY AND ITS CAUSES

There is also much more homosexual *behavior* throughout the world than there are *homosexuals*. What this means is that most homosexual behavior is engaged in by preferentially heterosexual males. The other form of homosexuality is *preferential* homosexuality, which involves persons who are totally, or almost totally, commited to homosexual relationships and are unable to change or to find heterosexual relations gratifying. It is currently estimated that about 2 to 4 percent of the populations of Western industrial societies are preferentially homosexual, a figure that may hold for many other societies as well. This type of homosexuality must be explained very differently, but a biomaterialist interpretation will still hold. We have already examined and criticized social constructionist theories of sexuality. Such theories work no better for preferential than for situational homosexuality.

A great deal of research has been done on the biological roots of homosexuality. In an early article, Lee Ellis and Ashley Ames (1987) reviewed much of this research and offered the following theory:

1. Human sexual orientation is determined in essentially the same way as in all other mammals.
2. Sexual orientation in all mammals is primarily determined by the degree to which the nervous system is exposed to testosterone and other sex hormones during the period in which neurological organization is taking place in the developing fetus.
3. For humans, sexual orientation appears to be primarily determined approximately between the middle of the second and the end of the fifth month of gestation.
4. Homosexuality develops when, during the critical developmental period, the fetus's brain receives an excess of the hormone(s) of the opposite sex. Male homosexuals thus have fetally "feminized" brains, whereas lesbians have fetally "masculinized" brains. [A more accurate way of putting this would be to say that male homosexuals have brains that have not been both "defeminized" and "masculinized." Since all fetuses start out female, the brain starts out feminine.]

On the basis of their theory, Ellis and Ames make the following predictions:

1. *Homosexuality should be primarily a male phenomenon.* This is because all mammals are fundamentally female, and it is only by inserting the Y chromosome into the mammalian genome that masculinity develops. This leads to more sex-

ual inversions in genetic males than in genetic females. The cross-cultural literature supports this notion, as does the cross-species literature.

2. *Homosexuals should have higher frequencies of other sexual inversions than heterosexuals.* In other words, male homosexuals are more likely to be "effeminate" and to have "feminine" interests than male heterosexuals, and lesbians are more likely to have "masculine" characteristics and interests than female heterosexuals. Of course, some male homosexuals do not display feminine characteristics, and some lesbians do not display masculine characteristics. It is not either/or, but a matter of degree. It should also be noted that a high percentage of adult homosexuals exhibited gender-atypical behavior as children, e.g., boys wanting to play with girls and dolls rather than other boys and guns and trucks.

3. *Homosexuality should have a significant degree of heritability.* The evidence does show support for this. There is a higher rate of homosexuality in identical twins than in fraternal twins (see below).

4. *Attempts to alter sexual orientation after birth should be minimally effective or ineffective.* What this means is that homosexuality should be as difficult to change as heterosexuality would be, and the data show this quite strongly. The greatest success seems to be with bisexuals, which is not at all surprising, but even this is quite limited. Successful "treatment" seems to be all but impossible for people who have not had any pleasurable heterosexual experiences before entering a "treatment" program.

Since Ellis and Ames surveyed the research literature, a great deal of additional research has been done, and the data offer very strong support for a biomaterialist interpretation of preferential homosexuality. Fred Whitam (1983; Whitam and Mathy, 1986) studied the childhood experiences of 375 homosexual men in Guatemala, Brazil, the Philippines, Thailand, Peru, and the United States. On the basis of his research, he concluded the following (cited in Burr, 1996):

1. Homosexuality is universal.
2. The percentage of homosexuals in all cultures is approximately the same (about 5 percent) and remains stable over time.
3. The emergence of homosexuality is not affected by social norms regarding it. Homosexuality is just as likely to appear in societies that are homophobic as in those that are much more tolerant of homosexuality.
4. Given a large enough population, homosexual subcultures will be found in all societies.
5. There are striking resemblances in behavioral interests and occupational choices between homosexuals in different societies.
6. In all societies homosexuals run the gamut from highly feminine to highly masculine.

Clearly these findings suggest that preferential homosexuality is innately given rather than some sort of social construction or personal choice.

Widely publicized research by Simon LeVay (1991, 1996), formerly a neuroscientist at the Salk Institute in San Diego, leads to the same conclusion. LeVay examined a small portion of the hypothalamus, known as INAH3, in the brains of homosexual men who had died from AIDS. He found that this region of the brain in the homosexual men was only about one-third to one-half the size of the region in the brains of heterosexual men. He also confirmed an earlier researcher's finding that INAH3 in heterosexual females was about the same size as INAH3 in homosexual men.

Evidence that a behavior pattern widely found among humans is also prominently represented among nonhuman animals is usually taken to be good evidence for the role of biology. In the case of homosexuality, we do find it among many other animal species (studies reviewed in LeVay, 1996). In 1963 a Yale genetic researcher discovered a strain of fruit flies in which the males were "courting" other males. He was eventually able to track down the mutant gene responsible for this behavior, and concluded that it was X-ray induced. A group of researchers at Brigham Young University studied six male rats that refused to mount females. When their brains were examined, a portion of the hypothalamus was found to be only about half the size of the hypothalamus of other male rats, almost exactly what LeVay found for humans. At a sheep experimental station in Idaho, it was found that some rams refused to mount ewes but would mount and anally penetrate other rams. When the brains of these rams were studied, they were shown to differ significantly from the brains of the heterosexual rams. So-called lesbian pairing has been observed in some seagulls.

Research establishes that preferential homosexuality has a clear genetic component (studies reviewed in LeVay, 1996). A study by Bailey and Pillard of male identical twins found that when one twin was gay, 52 percent of the time the other twin was also gay. The number was only 22 percent for fraternal twins. A study by Fred Whitam obtained corresponding numbers of 65 percent and 29 percent, and research by Bailey and colleages of female twins obtained numbers of 48 percent and 16 percent. Dean Hamer (Hamer and Copeland, 1994) has tried to identify a "gay gene." He and his research team have found a region of the X chromosome known as Xq28 that they believe holds a gay gene. This gene is passed only through women. (In order to understand the genetic foundations of behavior we have to realize the complexity and subtlety of genetics. Consider the observation that, in identical twins, if one twin is left-handed, then the other twin has only a 12 percent chance of being left-handed. In gays, if one twin is gay then the other has about a 50 percent chance of being gay. Does this mean that 12 percent of handedness is genetic, 88 percent being due to something environmental, and that 50 percent of homosexuality is genetic, the other 50 percent environmental? Of course not. Handedness surely is entirely genetic, and sexual orientation may be as well. People may have the same gene, but the gene for some reason expresses itself in one person but not in the other.)

If there is a so-called gay gene, how might it work? Actually, there is probably a whole set of gay genes, each of which regulates in a specific way one aspect of neurological development. There is more than one genetic way to become gay. Multiple genes can be strongly suspected, and this is probably what explains some important differences among gays, e.g., that some gay men are effeminate but others are not.[3]

SEXUAL VIOLENCE

Perhaps the most popular theory of rape, or forced sexual copulation, is the feminist theory. This theory holds that rape is only incidentally about sex and is mainly a violent act of power in which men exert or reinforce their domination over women (Ellis, 1990). Randy and Nancy Thornhill (1983, 1992) explode this theory in terms of an analysis of rape laws. As they point out, these laws are made overwhelmingly by men, and for the purpose of protecting men's interests. Rape works against men's interests because a man's own wife, mother, sisters, and daughters can be raped. Men thus stand to lose more from rape than they might benefit. Moreover, the Thornhills review data which show that the greater the prevalence of polygyny in a society, the more severely rape is punished. In an analysis of twenty-nine preindustrial societies, they show that none of the monogamous societies punished rape with death, whereas 22 percent of the mildly polygynous and 83 percent of the highly polygynous societies did so. Rape is undoubtedly much more common the more polygynous the society because as polygyny occurs more frequently women are increasingly removed from circulation, thus becoming unavailable as sexual partners and wives for those men who are unsuccessful in the competition for mates. These men must often resort to rape as their only possibility of mating, and thus rape is punished more severely as a deterrent in these societies. Highly polygynous societies are also apt to be among the most male dominated of societies, and as a result there is a close correlation between male domination and the severity of punishment for rape. This is just the opposite of what the feminist theory is saying—that male domination and toleration for (or actual encouragement of) rape are closely related.

The Thornhills (cf. Shields and Shields, 1983) propose that rape is a reproductive strategy employed by those men who have lost out in the sexual competition for females, for whatever reason. Rapists differ from nonrapists mainly in the fact that they have been unable to climb the social ladder and acquire resources that would attract mates. The Thornhills support their argument with the following lines of evidence:

1. *Rapists focus on women who are near their peak fertility.* The Thornhills review a number of studies showing that the vast majority of rape victims are between the ages of sixteen and thirty-four. After the mid-thirties, the number of rape victims drops off very sharply and continues to decline with advancing age. This is exactly the pattern that should be found if rape is an alternative reproductive strategy, i.e., a matter of sex rather than power.

2. *The rapists themselves are overwhelmingly young men, mostly men between the ages of twenty and thirty.* The tendency of men to rape drops off very sharply after the age of thirty and continues to drop throughout a man's lifetime. What this means is that men are most likely to rape at the age at which the competition for mates is most severe.

3. *Males with the greatest difficulty climbing the social ladder are overrepresented among rapists.* The Thornhills review data which show that rapists come overwhelmingly from lower socioeconomic backgrounds and are poorly educated.

4. As noted above, *punishment for rape is more severe in societies with widespread polygyny, which probably reflects the greater occurrence of rape in such societies.* The greater frequency of rape logically follows from the increased sexual competition produced by widespread polygyny. Also, rape appears to be more common in societies with brideprice than in those without it (brideprice increases economic barriers to mating). Furthermore, a study of the Gusii of Kenya shows that in 1936 and 1937 the brideprice became exorbitant, and during this same period there was a serious outbreak of rape. As the brideprice soared again in the 1950s, rape increased once more.

One additional line of evidence suggesting that rape is primarily about sex has to do with the much greater occurrence of rape during war. As Symons (1979) and others have noted, men desire low-cost sex, and the probability of rapists being caught and punished during war is virtually zero.

Randy Thornhill and Craig Palmer (2000) have elaborated on the earlier work of the Thornhills. They continue the argument that rape is a conditional strategy used by men who have lost out in the competition for mates. Men are most likely to rape when they have limited resources, are socially disenfranchised, have limited sexual access or few or no rewarding romantic relationships, are of low phenotypic or genetic quality, or are presented with rape opportunities in which the benefits are high and the costs low. The authors disagree over the question of whether rape is an evolutionary adaptation. Thornhill views it as such, but Palmer considers it a by-product of an adaptation, viz., male sexual assertiveness.

Thornhill and Palmer pay special attention to the extreme psychological pain that women often suffer as the result of being raped. This pain, they suggest, stems from the high reproductive costs that rape imposes on women: Rape reduces the ability of a woman to decide when she will reproduce and, most significantly, to select the man who will father her children; it prevents a woman from using sex as a means of gaining material benefits from men for the use of herself and her offspring; and, if she is already pair-bonded, rape often has a negative effect on her relationship with her mate inasmuch as he may be suspicious of her story that she was raped (or, alternatively, fear that the rapist has impregnated her) and thus leave her or withdraw resources from her. Their overall argument predicts that women of reproductive age should be more traumatized by rape than prereproductive and postreproductive women, and that married women should experience more psychological pain from rape than unmarried women. Reproductive women should experience more pain from rape because it interferes with their reproductive choices, and married women should find rape more anguishing because it may harm their relationships with their mates. And, indeed, the data offer strong support for these predictions.

Thornhill and Palmer also point to cross-species and cross-cultural evidence of the prevalence of rape to support their argument that rape is a conditional sexual strategy (the very same evidence hammers another nail into the coffin of the feminist or standard social science explanation that rape is only about power). Throughout the animal world we find that males are more sexually assertive and more eager to copulate, especially in polygynous species, and actual rape appears to be widespread among nonhuman species. As Thornhill and Palmer (2000:144) note, "There is no longer any question that physical force, harrassment, and intimidation are used widely by males across animal species, including in the great apes, to obtain mates." Rape also appears to be a cross-cultural universal in spite of arguments to the contrary. A number of "rape-free" cultures have been proposed, but more careful scrutiny of the cases mentioned shows that at least some rape occurs in all of them.[4]

NOTES

1. Alexander et al. (1979) present data on the degree of sexual dimorphism and degree of polygyny in 58 species of animals. Male northern fur seals weigh six times as much as females, and they have an average harem size of 40 and a maximum harem size of 153. At the other end of the spectrum, male and female harp seals are the same size and they are monogamous. Among primates, gorilla males weigh almost twice as much as females, and they have a mean harem size of 5.4 and a maximum harem size of 9. A similar pattern is found among hamadryas baboons. Gibbons are monogamous, and males and females are about the same size. I analyzed some of Alexander et al.'s data, and found strong correlations between sexual dimorphism and polygyny. For all 58 species of animals (pinnipeds, ungulates, and nonhuman primates), length dimorphism correlated (Pearson r) .702 with mean harem size and .591 with maximum harem size; weight dimorphism correlated .807 with mean harem size and .756 with maximum harem size. For primates alone, length dimorphism correlated .589 with mean harem size and .578 with maximum harem size; weight dimorphism correlated .570 with mean harem size and .608 with maximum harem size.

2. More recently, it has been argued that women may actually realize inclusive fitness benefits from infidelity, or at least may have done so under ancestral conditions (Buss, 2000:158–69). By having an affair with another man, a woman may provide herself with "mate insurance": If her husband or lover abandons her, she then has another mate ready to take his place. Or a woman may have an affair with a man whom she judges to be genetically superior to her current husband or lover (Gangestad and Thornhill, 1997). If this man impregnates her, she thus ends up with offspring who have better genes. Another possibility is that in having affairs women may be employing a strategy of "trading up" (Fisher, 1992): A woman may perceive that her current mate's value has declined, or that her own mate value has increased, and thus she believes she can do better in the mating market. These arguments, however, are still somewhat on the speculative side and not enough empirical evidence for them has accumulated. They still need more, and more rigorous, testing.

3. The view taken here is obviously that preferential homosexuality is not an adaptation but rather the result of a biological mistake. However, some scholars have argued that homosexuality is an evolutionary adaptation. Some years ago E.O. Wilson (1978) presented what he called the "nest helper" theory. Homosexual men would sacrifice their own reproduction in order to provide special assistance to their siblings' children. In my view, this theory is highly unconvincing because Wilson fails to provide a compelling argument as to why such a phenomenon would evolve. Nor is there any evidence to show that gay men actually are more attentive to their siblings' offspring than heterosexual men are to their nephews and nieces. A more plausible adaptational theory has been presented by Jim McKnight (1997). He views male homosexuality as a balanced polymorphism akin to sickle-cell anemia. Homosexuality, he says, is adaptive in its heterozygous state but maladaptive when homozygous. His logic runs like this: Men with one gay gene (who

will be preferential heterosexuals) will have a certain kind of charm that makes them alluring to females, and thus they will have more mating and reproductive success than men without a gay gene. But men with two gay genes, who will be preferential homosexuals, will be rejected by women and will not desire them anyway, and thus will engage in little or no reproduction. It must be admitted that this theory is intriguing, but McKnight presents no evidence at all to support his argument except to say that men who are especially charming and sensitive to women's needs will be alluring to them. This may well be true, but we have no knowledge at the moment to suggest that such men carry any type of gay gene. At this point McKnight's argument is pure speculation. McKnight believes an argument such as his is the only way of explaining why homosexual genes continue to be maintained in human populations. However, this is not as difficult as McKnight thinks. Hamer and Copeland's argument that there is a gay gene that is passed through women will work. Since the gene is passed through women who are not gay, and since many of the men who acquire this gene are not gay, there is no difficulty seeing how the gene can persist in populations.

There are also possible biological but nongenetic routes to homosexuality. Ray Blanchard (1999; Blanchard et al., 1998) has shown that a disproportionate number of gay men have a large number of older brothers. Blanchard suggests that this is because of the action of a particular kind of prenatal antigen that builds up in women with the birth of each son (but not with each daughter). A man with many older brothers is thus at greater risk for homosexuality. However, even if Blanchard is right, this will account for only about one gay man in seven.

4.   Thornhill and Palmer (2000:128–40) take up and critique nine specific assertions of the feminist or SSSM theory of rape and convincingly refute each. In my opinion, they completely demolish this theory and, moreover, persuasively show that it has been driven almost entirely by ideology rather than by evidence. An especially interesting question raised by the authors is, if rape is simply about domination, why don't men use much less costly nonsexual forms of aggression to dominate women? Why resort to an act that is usually severely punished and therefore very risky?

12

Sex and Gender

In the theory of gender I began from zero. There is no masculine power or privilege I did not covet. But slowly, step by step, decade by decade, I was forced to acknowledge that even a woman of abnormal will cannot escape her hormonal identity.

—*Camille Paglia*

It would be futile to attempt to fit women into a masculine pattern of attitudes, skills and abilities and disastrous to force them to suppress their specifically female characteristics and abilities by keeping up the pretense that there are no differences between the sexes.

—*Arianna Stassinopoulos*

THE GENERAL PATTERN

All societies have a sexual division of labor, meaning that they all make sex relevant to assigning individuals to tasks within the society. All societies have certain tasks and roles that they consider "masculine," others that they consider "feminine." These tasks will be carried out exclusively or at least predominantly by just one sex. All societies also have sexual inequality, which means that in every society men and women are unequally placed with respect to who has power or authority, who occupies the most valued roles or positions, and who has more control over whom. Societies differ in just how much sexual inequality they have, but there is no society that is completely egalitarian with respect to sex.

In terms of the most basic features of the sexual division of labor, research has shown that, across the world and throughout history, men seem to be assigned tasks that (Parker and Parker, 1979):

- involve greater strength and stamina;
- are more dangerous or risky;
- are not easily interruptible;

- require high levels of skill and training;
- and require long periods of time away from home base.

Women, then, tend to be assigned tasks that are the opposites of these, i.e., that involve little strength, are not dangerous or risky, etc. Why should there be this worldwide pattern? For the most part, it is explainable in terms of women's responsibilities for infant and child care, especially the nursing of infants (J. Brown, 1975; Lancaster, 1991). Heavy infant and child care responsibilities prevent women from being concentrated in roles that require long periods of time away from home. It makes much more sense to leave women at home in charge of infants and children than to disrupt the lives of these offspring by moving them here and there. Moreover, infant and child care responsibilities make it more suitable for women to concentrate in roles that are easily interruptible because infants and children are the source of frequent interruptions. Roles that are easily interruptible are usually ones that involve lower levels of skill and training. Roles that are dangerous are much better suited for men because of the need to keep infants and children away from danger as much as possible. In short, the sexual assignment of work roles seems to be carried out in such a way as to promote the well-being of infants and children and thus the inclusive fitness of their parents.

In terms of sexual inequality, we find a widespread, indeed a universal, pattern in which

- the instititutional sectors of human societies are sexually asymmetrical;
- males monopolize political leadership;
- males monopolize warfare;
- and males monopolize a society's high-status positions.

William Divale and Marvin Harris (1976) have identified a strong male bias to the institutional sectors of band and tribal societies. Marriage and kinship patterns, for example, are markedly biased in favor of males. Patrilineality, the tracing of descent ties through males, is much more common than matrilineality, the tracing of descent ties through females. Patrilocality and virilocality, marital residence practices centered on men, are much more common than matrilocality and uxorilocality, residence practices centered on women. Marriage practices are also highly male biased inasmuch as polygyny is much more common than monogamy and polyandry. The contrast between polygyny and polyandry is particularly stark. About 85 percent of the world's societies permit polygyny, but less than 1 percent of the world's societies practice polyandry (Murdock, 1967). Sexual asymmetry is especially characteristic of the ideological sectors of band and tribal societies. Beliefs in the inferiority of females are widespread, and in many societies women are regarded as sources of evil and pollution. Legendary heroes outnumber legendary heroines, and in the realm of religion male gods outnumber female gods. Sexual asymmetry is also apparent in the widespread preference for male rather than female children. Sexually asymmetrical institutions are by no means restricted to band and tribal societies, for societies at more advanced evolutionary stages often reveal new forms of male-biased institutions. Agrarian societies have in many ways the most male-biased social arrangements of any of the major types of human societies, and industrial societies, although considerably less male biased than agrarian societies, still have noticeable male biases to many of their institutional sectors.

Political leadership and warfare are features of human societies that are almost totally under male control (Goldberg, 1993). In every known society, past and present, political leadership has been predominantly or even exclusively in the hands of men (Low, 1992). In hunter-gatherer societies there are headmen but no headwomen, and in small-scale horticultural societies there are political leaders known as "big men," but there are no "big women." Among the legendary Iroquois, influential females known as matrons had the right to veto the appointment of men to political office, but these offices were open only to men. In more advanced horticultural societies powerful leaders known as chiefs are invariably men. In agrarian societies, kings greatly outnumber queens, and emperors empresses. Martin King Whyte (1978) examined political leadership in ninety-three of the societies in the Standard Cross-Cultural Sample (Murdock and White, 1969), a highly representative sample (N = 186) of the full range of preindustrial societies (henceforth abbreviated as SCCS). In sixty-five of these societies political leadership was exclusively in the hands of men. In most of the others women had some involvement in political leadership, but still took a considerable backseat to men. In only two societies were women said to be holding positions that gave them political power equivalent to men, but men were still found in these positions in greater numbers than women.[1] In modern industrial societies the executive and legislative branches of government are strongly male dominated, and all modern nation-states are overwhelmingly led by men. Vincent Falger (1992:171) reports that on

> June 14, 1992, at the end of the United Nations Conference on Environment and Development (UNCED) in Rio de Janeiro, pictures were taken of the largest collection of heads of state and government ever together in world history. Of the 99 persons shown, only two were women. This is a representative image of the role and position of women in international politics. A like photograph of 65 leaders, assembled in Jakarta on September 1, 1992, at the occasion of the opening of the tenth summit conference of the movement of non-aligned countries, depicts only one woman. The number of female foreign secretaries, ministers of defence, finance, international trade or economic affairs, to mention five other highly "international" top positions in politics, is to be counted on the fingers of two hands. Descending the ladder of political and official positions with a highly international profile, the number of women does rise, but proportionally they are still virtually absent. Tens of years of democratisation and emancipation have hardly, if at all, changed the long history of nearly complete male domination in top political positions, whether elected or not.

Tatu Vanhanen (1992) has reported on the female composition of the national parliaments of 122 contemporary nation-states. In the 1980s, women constituted only 9.9 percent of the members of these parliaments.

As for warfare, this is even more completely dominated by men. In no society have women been the principal warriors, and in most societies women have no involvement in war at all. Some societies even go so far as to prohibit women from gazing at or handling the weapons of war (Divale and Harris, 1976). In examining seventy societies from the SCCS, Whyte (1978) found that in 89 percent only men engaged in any fighting. In the rest, women may have provided aid but men did most of the fighting.

In all known societies, men also monopolize their society's high-status occupational roles, whatever those roles turn out to be (Goldberg, 1993). Moreover, as these roles change in status level, their sexual composition changes. As roles lose status over time, they are increasingly abandoned by men and increasingly pursued by women. In American society in the 1950s, for example, bank tellers were predominantly male, but today they are overwhelmingly female.

EXPLAINING THE GENERAL PATTERN

These gender patterns only make sense from a biomaterialist point of view. An early proponent of a biomaterialist theory of gender universals was Pierre van den Berghe (1973). Van den Berghe made extensive use of studies of primate societies, on the basis of which he speculatively reconstructed hominid evolution. His basic argument was that humans have inherited from their hominid ancestors a basic "biogram" that predisposes men to hunt, to make war, and to protect the group, and women to nurture children. One of the most vigorous advocates of a biomaterialist understanding of gender is Steven Goldberg (1993), who is primarily concerned with explaining why men everywhere monopolize the political leadership and high-status positions of their societies. Goldberg concentrates on hormone differences between the sexes, pointing out that adult males have testosterone levels about ten times as high as those of adult females. Testosterone is known to be closely linked to aggression and to dominance and competitive behaviors. Women are at a natural disadvantage in the competition for positions of leadership and high status. Goldberg is particularly insistent on the true universality of greater male attainment of leadership roles and high-status positions. Not a single society known from sociological, anthropological, or historical research, he says, constitutes an exception to this generalization. As he points out, it would take only one exception to falsify his theory, but no exception has ever been found. A number have been proposed, but when Goldberg subjects these to more careful scrutiny they all collapse.

Most sociologists reject these ideas, and the standard sociological interpretation of gender roles is that they are social and cultural constructions that are transmitted intergenerationally via the socialization process. But van den Berghe and Goldberg would respond that little boys are taught to be aggressive and little girls are taught to be nurturant because little boys *really are* naturally more aggressive and little girls *really are* naturally more nurturant in the first place. Socialization patterns, they would insist, simply represent social conformation to a basic biological reality that is easily recognized by people in all societies. As we will see, this logic is extremely well supported by empirical evidence.

Goldberg's work is important and it rings true, but it is severely limited by a failure to place its argument within a more general evolutionary framework. Van den Berghe (1997:3) comments to the effect that Goldberg "fails to see that male behavior is incomprehensible except conjointly with female behavior, and that sexual dimorphism in size, behavior, physiology, and indeed, everything, is only understandable within the evolutionary paradigm of sexual selection, parental investment, and fitness maximization." Another way of putting this is to say that Goldberg remains at the level of proximate causes and fails to link them to their ultimate causes. As van den Berghe would put it, men have higher levels of testosterone because of the action of sexual selection throughout hominid history. As we saw in chapter 11, at the heart of sexual selection in humans is male control over female sexuality in order to maximize the male's reproductive success. This is the starting point for understanding the origins of male domination (Smuts, 1995; Buss, 1996; Hrdy, 1997).

Sexual selection should have produced systematic differences between the sexes that are highly adaptive from the standpoint of maximizing each sex's reproductive success, and this appears to be exactly what it has done. Differences between the sexes in levels of aggression have been reported for most mammals (Parker and Parker, 1979). Male mammals are usually shown to be considerably more aggressive than female mammals, and among humans' closest relatives, nonhuman primates, males are usually reported to be more likely to engage in rough-and-tumble play and dominance behaviors; these differences begin very early in life and continue throughout the organisms' lifetimes, as they do in humans. Studies of many mammalian species show that testosterone is strongly implicated in aggressive behavior. In rhesus monkeys, for instance, aggressive and dominance behavior is more common in animals with higher levels of testosterone, and such animals are less likely to display "maternal" forms of behavior. Injecting female monkeys with testosterone increases their levels of aggression and dominance, and such females display sexual behavior typical of males, such as mounting other females. Studies of human development show the same basic patterns (Parker and Parker, 1979; Money and Ehrhardt, 1972). Females with above normal levels of the male sex hormone androgen develop differently from other females. In addition to being more aggressive, they exert more energy, more commonly select males rather than females as companions, are less interested in playing with dolls, are more likely to be described as tomboys, and have more interest in occupational careers. Kingsley Browne (1995) points out that aggressiveness is one of the most persistently observed differences between the sexes. In fact, it appears to be universal (cf. Geary, 1998). A search for societies in which women are as aggressive as, or more aggressive than, men has proved fruitless. The greater aggressiveness of men is strongly confirmed by data on homicides. Daly and Wilson (1988) have compiled data on homicide rates in industrial societies and in many other types of societies throughout the world. They compare the rate at which men kill men with the rate at which women kill women. There is an overwhelming predominance of men killing men. In several societies 100 percent of the homicides involved men killing other men, and in no society did the rate drop below 85 percent. On average, 96.4 percent of the homicides involved men only.

Men also tend to show much more competitive behavior in societies throughout the world. Many studies have shown that girls and women behave much more cooperatively in a wide variety of societies. As Browne (1995:1026) has said, "In our ancestral environment, women enhanced their reproductive success by cooperating with sisters and co-wives, situations in which they gained no reproductive advantage through open conflict or changes in coalitions. Men, on the other hand, enhanced their reproductive success by cooperating with male relatives and nonrelatives at times, and competing with them at times. Dominance assertion in male groups is more likely to lead to enhanced reproductive success than it is in female groups." What is true of aggressiveness and competitiveness is also true of risk-taking behavior: Men are much more likely to engage in it than are women. In industrial societies men are much more frequently involved in car accidents and in such risky leisure-time activities as car racing, sky diving, hang gliding, and gambling (Browne, 1995). The greater risk-taking behavior of men is abundantly apparent from preindustrial societies. Two of the most risky behaviors in these societies have been big-game hunting and warfare, and men have virtually totally monopolized these activities.

Where women have a huge edge over men is in activities that involve nurturance and empathy, especially maternal behavior. Browne (1995) refers to numerous studies which show that women are more empathetic than men and are in general more "people oriented." Women are more concerned with interpersonal relations and their maintenance. Geary (1998) summarizes studies reporting that children, especially very small children, spend far more time in proximity or contact with their mothers than with their fathers. In one of these studies (Whiting and Whiting, 1975), children in Kenya, India, Mexico, the Philippines, Japan, and the United States were in proximity or contact with their mothers approximately seven-and-a-half times as much as with their fathers. Whiting and Edwards (1988) found a similar pattern in follow-up studies of children in Africa, South Asia, South and Central America, and North America. Among the !Kung San, who perhaps come closer to gender equality than any society in the world, fathers provide less than 7 percent of the care of children under two years of age (Geary, 1998). Among the Aka Pygmies, fathers hold their infants an average of 57 minutes a day whereas mothers hold them an average of 490 minutes a day (Geary, 1998). Liesen (1995) reports on a cross-cultural analysis of parental behavior in 80 preindustrial societies (Katz and Konner, 1981). It was found that in 59 percent of these societies fathers rarely or never spent time with their infants. Even in the societies in which fathers were most likely to spend time with their children, fathers contributed only 6 percent of direct parental care, and only 14 percent of their time was spent interacting with their children. In Western societies when fathers interact with children it tends to be in terms of playing physical games with them, not providing parental care (Liesen, 1995). Evidence also indicates that girls spend much more time play parenting than boys (Geary, 1998). Interestingly, "the finding that early play parenting substantially improves the survival rate of firstborn offspring in many species of primate suggests that this form of play has evolved by means of natural . . . selection" (Geary, 1998:236).

Alice Rossi (1977, 1984) has summarized evidence showing that compared to males females show greater sensitivity to touch, sound, and odor; have greater fine motor coordination and finger dexterity; pick up nuances of voice and music more readily; are more sensitive to context; and are more attracted to human faces. These traits are precisely ones that would contribute heavily to the successful rearing of a small infant. Rossi notes that, because of long infant and child dependency, prolonged infant care through intense attachment of the mother and the infant is critical to human survival, and that in hunter-gatherer societies there is extremely close contact between mother and infant and infants are nursed for as long as five years. Under such conditions, it is almost inconceivable that the female of the species would not have been selected for strong nurturant tendencies.

A great deal of evidence has also accumulated that strongly suggests there are innate differences between men and women in cognitive skills. It has long been known that in all industrial societies men score higher on tests of mathematical and spatial ability, whereas women score higher on tests of verbal skills. Many studies have shown that males tend to score higher (often much higher) on tests involving route finding, maze running, and the mental rotation of objects, whereas females score higher on tests involving remembering the locations of objects. These differences have been found in a variety of human societies and in numerous other mammal species (Kimura, 1987, 1992; Gaulin and FitzGerald, 1986, 1989; Gaulin and Hoffman, 1988; Silverman and Eals, 1992; James and Kimura, 1997; McBurney, Gaulin, Devineni, and Adams, 1997; Moffat, Hampson, and Hatzipantelis, 1998; Dabbs, Chang, Strong, and Milun, 1998). According to Doreen Kimura (1999:62), "The evidence is now quite clear that the male advantage on imaginal rotation tasks found in Western cultures is practically universal." As she notes, this advantage has been found among African peoples and among East Indians and other Asians. In a fascinating article, Gaulin and FitzGerald (1986) theorize that these differences are shaped by sexual selection, not only in humans but in many species of mammals as well. They argue that, since males are commonly polygynous, they evolved strong spatial abilities in order to navigate over large territories in search of mates. They tested this claim by looking at two different species of voles, one polygynous (meadow voles) and the other monogamous (pine voles). In the polygynous meadow voles, males ranged much farther from home than females, whereas in the monogamous pine voles there were no such sex differences; and in the polygynous voles, males significantly outperformed females in a maze-running task, whereas in the monogamous voles the sexes' maze-running abilities were the same. In a second study, Gaulin and FitzGerald (1989) found that male polygynous meadow voles expanded their navigational ranges only when the breeding season arrived and only after they had reached the status of full reproductive adults. Female meadow voles' navigational ranges remained the same under these different conditions. By contrast with the male meadow voles, male monogamous prairie voles did not expand their ranges during the breeding season or after they reached full reproductive status. Studies of other mammals have provided additional support for Gaulin and FitzGerald's argument concerning the role of sexual selection (Sherry, Jacobs, and Gaulin, 1992; Gaulin, 1995).

In a third study, Gaulin (1992) tested the alternative hypothesis that the observed sex differences in spatial ability are the result of differences in spatial experience rather than differences in brain organization. Gaulin removed prairie vole offspring of both sexes from their wild parents and reared them under laboratory conditions in which they were severely deprived of spatial experience (their ability to move about was curtailed by putting them in small cages). Their maze performance when they reached adulthood was then compared to that of their wild parents. No significant difference was found between the maze-running abilities of the spatially deprived voles and that of their spatially experienced parents. Thus, spatial experience had no effect on spatial ability.

In attempting to generalize his findings on voles to humans, Gaulin (1992) notes that, while detailed systematic study is lacking, there is nonetheless considerable evidence to suggest that in preindustrial human societies males usually have larger navigational ranges, and most preindustrial societies are polygynous. Ethnographers have often remarked that males range much wider than females. This is known to be the case for such societies as the Yanomamö, the Ifaluk, Trinidad, the Kipsigis, and the Aka Pygmies. The best data are available for the Aka Pygmies (Hewlett, van de Koppel, and Cavalli-Sforza, 1986; cited in Gaulin, 1992). It was found that in this society males not only had larger navigational ranges than females, but there was a positive correlation between the size of males' exploration ranges and the size of their mating ranges.

A different interpretation of the causes of sex differences in spatial ability has been offered by Silverman and Eals (1992), who link the differences to the demands of hunting and gathering in the ancestral environment. Tracking and killing animals over large distances would have favored precisely the kinds of spatial abilities at which men excel, they claim, whereas the demands of gathering would have selected for the ability to remember the locations of clumps of plants, the ability at which females outperform males. It is not yet clear which of these scenarios is the more accurate, or, indeed, whether a choice must be made. It could well be that both kinds of demands have operated on humans, thus overdetermining male spatial abilities. (In a personal communication, Gaulin reports that he intends to test these two models directly against each other by using another species, chimpanzees. Unlike voles and humans, male and female chimpanzees do not differ in foraging patterns, but they are sexually dimorphic and males mate with many females. Thus, they would appear to constitute an ideal test.)

There is also hormonal evidence suggesting an innate foundation to sex differences in cognitive skills. As Gaulin and Hoffman (1988:137) note, "sex differences in spatial ability become much more pronounced at adolescence and then decrease in middle age, thus paralleling the pubertal peak and subsequent decline in sex hormones." Research has shown that women receive lower spatial test scores when they are ovulating, which is when their estrogen levels are at their peak, and higher scores when they are menstruating, which is when estrogen levels are normally at their lowest level (Kimura, 1999; Gaulin, Silverman, Phillips, and Reiber, 1997). Moreover, various kinds of hormonal disorders are often associated with anomalies in cognitive skills. For example, males suffering from the disease known as kwashiorkor often have elevated estrogen levels, and such males have been found to be below normal in spatial ability (Gaulin and Hoffman, 1988). Idiopathic hypogonadotrophic hypogonadism (IHH) is a hormone disturbance in which males have small genitals and abnormally low testosterone levels. Such males score lower on spatial abilities than normal males, and often even lower than males who develop a testosterone deficiency later in life (Kimura, 1999). Another hormone anomaly is congenital adrenal hyperplasia (CAH), which occurs in both males and females. This is a condition in which the adrenal glands produce too much androstenedione, a testosterone-like hormone. Girls with this condition have been found to score higher on spatial tests of rotation, visualization, and disembedding abilities, tasks on which males normally score much higher than females (Kimura, 1999).

The typical sociological claim that the various patterns discussed above have been produced by differential socialization of the sexes is implausible in the extreme given the extraordinarily widespread or even universal nature of the patterns. As Kingsley Browne (1995:1050) has argued, "Cross-cultural uniformity is difficult to explain without reference to some underlying component of the human psyche. If this uniformity occurred through independent invention in each culture or group of cultures, the question is why did culture after culture come to the same independent conclusion? The most likely answer would be that there is something about our nature that leads us to come consistently to the same answer." Browne's point is extremely difficult to refute. If socialization is the cause of greater male domination of political leadership and monopolization of high-status positions, greater male aggressiveness, competitiveness, and risk-taking, and the cause as well of the nurturant and empathetic orientations of females, and if the socialization process is itself essentially uncaused or arbitrary, then what we should find in the full range of the world's societies is essentially this: About a third should be led by men, another third by women, and the remaining third by both men and women; about a third of the world's societies should make women the primary child care providers, another third should give men this role, and the final third should assign this responsibility to both men and women equally; and so forth and so on. But this is not even remotely what we find.

Moreover, differential socialization cannot be the cause of these differences if in fact there really is very little differential socialization of the sexes taking place. David Geary (1998) points out that studies carried out in Western societies indicate that parents actually treat boys and girls in very similar ways with respect to such broad areas of socialization as encouragement of achievement, warmth and nurturance, encouragement of dependency, restrictiveness, disciplinary strictness, encouragement of sex-typed activities, and clarity of communication. The most comprehensive assessment of these studies is that of Lytton and Romney (1991), who examined 172 studies involving 27,836 subjects. The one exception seems to be that fathers discourage boys from playing with dolls and other girls' toys. However, it is likely that this difference is simply a parental reaction to differences in boys' and girls' behavior, or to parental concern about sexual orientation, since the doll play of boys is highly correlated with a later gay orientation. Geary also points to a review of evidence (a summary of 81 studies by Barkley, Ullman, Otto, and Brecht, 1977) showing that it is very unlikely that these differences between the sexes result from children selectively imitating the same-sex parent. Girls tend to imitate feminine behavior whether it is displayed by a woman or a man, and boys tend to imitate masculine behavior regardless of the sex of the person displaying it.

Finally, the biomaterialist argument being presented here is also strongly supported by one of those infrequent natural experiments, in this case involving the Israeli kibbutzim (Tiger and Shepher, 1975; Spiro, 1979). These communal settlements were established early in the twentieth century by Eastern European Jews with a Marxist ideological outlook. An attempt was made to abolish the "bourgeois family" and traditional gender roles. In the first generation women and men shared fully in domestic and agricultural tasks and by and large enjoyed a condition of gender equality. When children were born they were reared in a communal nursery by professional nurses rather than by their natural parents, and children merely visited occasionally in their parents' apartment. However, by the third generation this pattern had clearly unraveled. Women were increasingly concentrated in traditional gender roles, such as domestic work, laundering, and cooking, and men took over agricultural and industrial work. Women also disappeared from political leadership, this being taken over by men. Parents became increasingly dissatisfied with the limited contact they were permitted with their children. Mothers in particular demanded greater opportunities to be with their children and to participate in rearing them. Gradually the traditional nuclear family was reestablished, and mothers became the primary child care providers. A reasonable conclusion from all this is that the kibbutz experiment was inconsistent with human biology and as a result social patterns changed to conform more closely to humans' natural biological predispositions.

The biomaterialist understanding of gender should not be seen as somehow opposed to feminism as a political approach. Many sociobiologists are women, and most of these are in fact feminists of one type or another. (To name just a few: Margo Wilson, Laura Betzig, Barbara Smuts, Jane Lancaster, Sarah Blaffer Hrdy, and Monique Borgerhoff Mulder.) Sociobiologists, whether male or female, do not try to use sociobiology as an argument against the push for gender equality. They do not try to justify the gender status quo. Tatu Vanhanen (1992), for example, interprets the overwhelming male monopolization of political leadership in biomaterialist terms, but he nonetheless argues that women in modern societies should work for equality and he prefers it to inequality. In fact, some sociobiologists have tried to show that sociobiology and feminism are highly compatible, and, in fact, are sometimes saying much the same thing (Smuts, 1995; Hrdy, 1997; Buss, 1996; Gowaty, 1992; Buss and Malamuth, 1996; for a dissenting voice see Tang-Martinez, 1997). Both Barbara Smuts (1995) and Sarah Blaffer Hrdy (1997) see male domination (or patriarchy, as they prefer to call it) as rooted in sexual selection, as I have been arguing all along. Smuts, Hrdy, and others recognize that "biology is not destiny," and that we can change the gender status quo if we desire.

Sociobiologists and feminists agree on several basic points: that men tend to control resources and power everywhere; that men frequently control women by way of their control of resources; that the control of women often centers on female sexuality; and that men often think of women as sexual property (Buss, 1996). But feminists and many sociobiologists would argue that there is nothing inevitable about any of these things. Based on her sociobiological analysis of gender relations, Smuts (1995) offers the following proposals for creating greater gender equality in modern societies:

- Male domination is greater where male-male coalitions are strong and female-female coalitions are weak. Therefore, to reduce male domination women should work to build strong alliances with each other.
- Male domination is greater where males control important resources, especially economic resources. Therefore, women should work for greater economic opportunities and legal protection of their property rights.
- Male domination is greater where the inequalities among males are greater. Therefore, women should work for economic and political changes that would reduce inequalities among males.
- Women often contribute to the perpetuation of male domination in various ways. For example, women prefer as mates men who are rich in resources, which promotes inequality among men. Therefore, women can help to dismantle male domination by changing the way they respond to the characteristics of males.

Smuts argues that the characteristics listed above that intensify male domination are elaborations, within specific environments, of the basic male reproductive strategy. They vary considerably from place to place, and thus have a considerable amount of free play.

Of course, most of these changes will be a lot harder to make than to propose. For example, getting women to change their preference for resource-rich males, a preference strongly built into the human biogram, will be very difficult. Nonetheless, the point is made that sociobiology and feminism need not be at odds.

CROSS-CULTURAL VARIATIONS IN THE STATUS OF WOMEN

Despite the overall pattern that we have been discussing, the status of women varies significantly from one society, and one type of society, to another, and it is difficult to explain these differences biomaterialistically. Let us look at the ecomaterialist and polimaterialist alternatives.

Polimaterialist interpretations of gender inequality have been presented by William Divale and Marvin Harris (1976; Harris, 1977) and by Randall Collins (1975, 1985b). Divale and Harris have identified a pervasive male supremacist complex in band and tribal societies and have linked it directly to the practice of warfare. They say that, whenever warfare occurs in band and tribal societies (which it does very frequently), a distinct survival advantage is given to those societies that can rear the most fierce and aggressive warriors. "Given warfare," they say (1976:526), "males rather than females are trained to be fierce and aggressive because in hand combat with muscle-powered weapons the average height and weight advantage of males is decisive for individual and group survival." To make males as fierce and aggressive as possible, male qualities are greatly exaggerated and female qualities denigrated. Women will be part of the reward for military bravery (through such practices as polygyny), and they will be reared to be passive and to accept the authority of males. Collins has developed a similar theory to explain male domination in any society, but especially in agrarian societies. Collins notes that men in many societies have often gone to great lengths to monopolize the weapons of war. Where these weapons are little developed and there is little or no military threat, men will have little incentive to organize themselves into military groups, and the relations between men and women will tend to be egalitarian. But where military weapons are well developed and there is constant fighting, men will be highly organized into cohesive military groups. This will drive a wedge between men and women and produce marked female subordination.

Martin King Whyte (1978) and I have independently tested the basic logic of this polimaterialist argument. Whyte created a large number of gender status variables for half of the SCCS and selected ten of these for cross-tabulational analyses with a variety of independent variables. Only three of the gender status variables turned out to be reliably and consistently correlated with the independent variables: the level of female domestic authority, the existence of female solidarity groups, and the degree of male control of female sexuality. The extent of warfare was correlated with these variables, *but in the wrong direction*. Warfare correlated .44 (gamma) with domestic authority, .36 with female solidarity groups, and .14 with control of female sexuality. These findings not only fail to support the militarism hypothesis, but actually show that warfare is associated with a *higher* rather than a lower gender status.

My own analysis of the SCCS data also strongly contradicts the militarism hypothesis. Overall warfare frequency correlated only −.049 (Pearson r) with female domestic authority, .104 with female solidarity groups, and −.096 with control of female sexuality. When internal and external warfare were separated, the correlations were essentially the same. No matter which study's results are more reliable, Whyte's or mine, both disconfirm the militarism theory of male domination. Because Harris's version of the theory pertains to band and tribal societies, and because Collins is thinking mainly of large-scale agrarian societies, additional correlations were computed separately for three different types of societies. In the case of foraging societies, overall warfare frequency correlated −.324 with female domestic authority, which is consistent with the militarism hypothesis. However, it correlated .243 (.494 in the case of external warfare) with female solidarity groups, and .248 (.517 in the case of internal warfare) with control of female sexuality, correlations that run in the opposite direction from that predicted. For horticultural societies, female domestic authority and control of female sexuality were uncorrelated with warfare, but female solidarity groups correlated .454 with overall warfare frequency, a correlation that once again runs in the wrong direction. Finally, for intensive agricultural societies, there was a correlation running in the wrong direction between overall warfare frequency and control of female sexuality (r = .382, .549 for external warfare), and warfare did not correlate with the other two gender status variables. On the whole, these results require us to reject the militarism hypothesis.

Important ecomaterialist theories of societal variations in gender inequality have been formulated by Friedrich Engels (1970[1884]), Karen Sacks (1975, 1979), Kay Martin and Barbara Voorhies (1975), and Rae Lesser Blumberg (1984) (cf. Chafetz, 1984). Engels's theory, developed in the late nineteenth century, was, unsurprisingly, Marxian in nature. Engels thought that societies prior to the rise of private property, social stratification, and the state were ones in which the sexes were essentially equal. With the emergence of stratification and the state, men gained control over property and used this control to subordinate women. Thus was patriarchy born. There are at least two major problems with this theory. First, little known to Engels, classless and stateless societies are all male dominated, some of them highly so; and second, Engels never tells us why it should be men, rather than women or both men and women, who tended to control private property once it had arisen. Despite the problems with this theory, however, a modified version, one holding that the status of women has at least *declined* throughout social evolution, might be workable.

Karen Sacks (1975, 1979) has developed a modern version of Engels's argument. She argues that the evolutionary decline in the status of women has been most closely associated with the increasing levels of exploitation typical of societies at more advanced stages of societal development. Because men did not have to rear children, they could be more intensively exploited than women, and thus were selected by ruling classes for economic tasks outside the home. As a result, women came to be shunted off into the household where they concentrated on domestic work and child rearing. This set the stage for a dramatic decline in women's status; they came to be defined as dependent wards of men and less than full adults. Like Engels, Sacks is probably correct in seeing at least a decline in women's status with social evolution, but it is not clear that this necessarily has anything to do with the aims and goals of ruling classes. With the rise of stratification and the state, the demands of agricultural work would have become greater with or without the actions of a ruling class, and thus it would have fallen largely into the hands of men.

Martin and Voorhies (1975) argue that gender roles are adaptive results of underlying economic, technological, and economic arrangements. The gender division of labor will reflect the suitability of each sex to particular tasks within the framework of a society's overall mode of production. For example, men are better suited to hunting in hunter-gatherer societies because they are not the primary child care providers, and women are better suited to gathering because it is more compatible with child care. In agrarian societies, men will take control of economic production because of its time, energy, and strength requirements, and because women are vitally needed for reproductive and household roles. Once the sexual division of labor is set, the extent to which men control production will determine their degree of power and dominance over women.

Rae Lesser Blumberg (1984) has proposed a similar argument, holding that the most important factor determining the status of women in the world's societies is *women's level of economic power*. Economic power is a major resource that can be used by women to advance their interests, and thus the more economic power women have the higher their status with respect to men. What factors determine women's level of economic power? Blumberg proposes three: the strategic indispensability of women's labor, the organization of the kinship system, and the nature and extent of the stratification system. Women's labor is indispensable if they make an important contribution to total household subsistence needs, if they perform tasks that require considerable technical expertise, if they are relatively free from male supervision, and if they are organized into cohesive work groups. In terms of the kinship system, matrilocal and matrilineal societies lead to more economic power for women because of women's greater involvement in property ownership and management. As for the stratification system, Blumberg argues that the more intensive and elaborated it is, the lower women's level of economic power. Blumberg stresses that economic power not only increases women's status—the positive regard and respect for them on the part of men—but also gives them more autonomy, or a greater ability to manage their lives free from male control. Or, to use Blumberg's term, economic power gives women more "life options"—more ability to control sexuality, reproduction, household affairs, marriage, divorce, and overall mobility.

An examination of the evidence shows strong support for these ecomaterialist arguments. It is hunter-gatherer societies that for the most part give women the highest status and greatest degree of autonomy, and these societies are ones in which women make a major contribution to subsistence. Women are the principal gatherers, often contributing more than half of the total food that everyone will eat, and they are able to capitalize on this resource control. In fact, the status of women among hunter-gatherers appears to vary in accordance with how much they contribute to subsistence (Friedl, 1975). For example, among the !Kung San the gathering contribution of women is a major contribution to the diet (perhaps as much as 60 to 80 percent of the total food intake), and the !Kung come about as close to a gender egalitarian society as there is. Women are able to express their views on all topics and are generally not subjected to the kinds of sexual stereotypes, taboos, and restrictions that are common in many other societies. Women seem to enjoy a considerable amount of autonomy and, apparently, have high self-esteem. The Eskimo, whose diet consists mostly of food provided by men through hunting, are, by contrast, a highly male-dominated society (Friedl, 1975). Women are treated as sex objects and commonly subjected to male violence.

Horticultural societies, like hunter-gatherer societies, are ones in which women still make an important contribution to subsistence. In most horticultural societies women are the principal cultivators (Martin and Voorhies, 1975). Men usually prepare the garden sites for planting, but then the women commonly take over from that point. For this reason, Ester Boserup (1965, 1970) has called horticultural societies "female farming" societies. It is difficult to generalize about horticultural societies because they exhibit a wide range of female status. However, it is probably fair to say that most horticultural societies are much more male dominated than hunter-gatherer societies. At one extreme are the Yanomamö (Chagnon, 1983), who are one of the most male-dominated societies in the world. Among these people, men control virtually every sphere of social life. Men hunt and control horticultural production. In addition to their complete domination of politics and warfare, men also dominate religious life. Part of their religious ritual involves men blowing a hallucinogenic drug up each others' noses, and women are completely excluded from this activity. Yanomamö men are extremely noteworthy for their aggressiveness and the violence they direct toward women, which includes frequent gang rape. Near the other extreme are the Iroquois, who in recent centuries inhabited parts of western New York state and adjacent parts of Canada (J. Brown, 1975). Although official positions of political leadership were in the hands of men, women had veto power over the men who were appointed to these positions. The Iroquois were a matrilocal and matrilineal society, and thus land was in the hands of women. As a result, women had considerable influence over the affairs of their domestic groups. Women were also significantly involved in religious ritual. Iroquois men spent a great deal of time away from home engaged in warfare and hunting, and women had considerable autonomy.

As Blumberg has suggested, among horticulturalists the status of women is significantly affected by kinship patterns. In patrilineal societies, land is owned and inherited through males in their roles as fathers, and women become economic producers in kin groups that are controlled by their husbands. In these societies women ordinarily have very low status. A husband will acquire rights in a woman as a childbearer, and the woman's offspring belong to the father and his patrilineage. Among matrilineal horticulturalists, women are the focus of the kinship system, with men tracing their genealogical links through their mothers and sisters. Land is owned matrilineally, and women's economic production contributes to their own kinship group rather than to that of their husbands. Because of these things, women fare better in matrilineal than in patrilineal societies.

Among all the major types of human societies, it is in agrarian societies that the status of women reaches its depths. In the transition from horticultural to agrarian societies, major changes took place in technology and economic life (Martin and Voorhies, 1975). With the shift to much more land- and labor-intensive forms of agrarian cultivation, the role of women as economic producers was greatly reduced, and economic production came to be dominated by men. As men took control of production, women became "domesticated"—assigned to the household and the activities connected with it. There emerged what Martin and Voorhies have called the "inside-outside dichotomy," which involved the division of social life into two distinct realms. The "outside" sphere included those activities that occurred outside the home, such as economics, politics, religious life, and education. The outside sphere was a male sphere. The "inside" sphere was, by contrast, a female sphere, and involved activities that occurred within the home, mainly cooking, cleaning, laundering, and the nursing and rearing of children. With the emergence of the inside-outside distinction, men and women came to live in dramatically different worlds, and elaborate sexist ideologies emphasizing the natural inferiority of women spread widely. It is not an exaggeration to say that the rise of the inside-outside dichotomy was associated with the descent of woman to the nadir of her socially assigned inferiority.

In many agrarian societies women have been veiled and secluded and much of their movement and many of their activities have been sharply restricted (Martin and Voorhies, 1975; Mandelbaum, 1988). They have been forbidden to own property, to engage in politics, to pursue education, or to initiate divorce. Many agrarian societies have made women legal minors and dependent wards of men. Agrarian societies are well known for their tight controls over female sexuality. Many have demanded premarital virginity on the part of girls, and premarital and extramarital sex have been severely punished. Agrarian societies have also frequently embraced the forms of genital mutilation known as clitoridectomy and infibulation, practices which indicate that women in these societies are extreme forms of sexual property. By contrast, agrarian societies have permitted and even encouraged nonmarital sexual activity for males. While all societies appear to have a sexual double standard favoring men, this standard is more elaborately developed in agrarian societies than in any other.

There has been a great deal of debate concerning whether the rise of capitalism and industrialism has improved or worsened the status of women (J. Thomas, 1988). Many social scientists, Marxists in particular, have portrayed capitalism as having a negative impact on the overall status and life situation of women (J. Thomas, 1988; Tilly and Scott, 1978). My view, however, is that the evidence strongly supports the notion that women's situation has for the most part improved since the advent of capitalism. Women have, for example, essentially achieved political and legal equality with men and are no longer regarded simply as legal minors and dependent wards of men. Compared to women in nearly all agrarian societies, as well as to women in many horticultural societies, women under capitalism have realized a dramatic improvement in their status and in their capacity to control their own lives free from male control. This improvement may have begun as early as the eighteenth century (Shorter, 1976). After this time women frequently became employed in cottage industries and small-scale factory work, and this employment increased their power and autonomy and improved their status. As Edward Shorter notes, as a result of their new work roles, women gained control over an extremely valuable resource, money, and "the weekly wage packet turned into a weapon in the struggle for domestic power" (1976:520). For the most part the changes in women's status occurred among peasants and workers rather than the middle and upper classes, and for these latter groups the situation was different. However, most women during this time belonged to the peasant and working classes.

These changes in women's status with the shift from agrarian to industrial societies cry out for ecomaterialist explanation. Before the Second World War many single women were in the labor force, but very few married women were. But after the war, there was a veritable flood of married women, including those with small children, into the labor force. In 1948 only about one married woman in nine was in the U.S. labor force (U.S. Department of Commerce, 1975), but by 1980 the percentage had increased to 45 percent and by 1995 it had risen to nearly 64 percent (U.S. Bureau of the Census, 1996). Marvin Harris (1981) has linked the rise of feminism and the women's movement since the 1960s to this rapid entry of women into the labor force. Harris claims that women's labor was increasingly sought by capitalists to fill the rapidly growing number of service and information jobs in the economy. Women also sought employment in order to improve or at least help maintain their families' standards of living. The increased participation of women in the labor force eventually encouraged in them a feminist consciousness. The movement of married women with children outside the home made them increasingly aware of an entire realm of existence previously little known to them. Moreover, as women came to see how much less they were being paid than men, they came to perceive themselves as victims of economic discrimination, which helped to facilitate a broader consciousness regarding their overall social situation. Thus, the most important twentieth-century changes in women's status can be linked directly to major economic changes that occurred after mid-century.

Analyses of SCCS data by Martin King Whyte (1978) and myself provide quantitative reinforcement for these qualitative analyses. Using female domestic authority as the dependent variable, Whyte found that it correlated –.55 (gamma) with the presence of the plow, –.55 with the presence of weaving (a measure of economic differentiation), –.51 with the presence of irrigation, .42 with the importance of hunting and gathering, and –.40 with both the presence of animal herding and the degree of community stratification. Whyte found that female solidarity groups correlated –.65 with the plow, .51 with hunting and gathering, –.40 with the degree of societal complexity, –.39 with weaving, and –.37 with irrigation. Significant associations were also found for male control of female sexuality, which correlated –.65 with the plow, –.65 with weaving, –.55 with community stratification, –.51 with private property, –.49 with irrigation, and –.48 with the cultivation of grains. These data show that as societies adopt more intensive modes of subsistence, become more economically differentiated, and come to be focused on private property and social stratification, the status of women falls substantially. This offers support for a modified version of Engels's theory. Blumberg's ecomaterialist interpretation of gender posits that as women gain more economic power their status rises. Perhaps the best operationalization of women's level of economic power is the extent to which they contribute to subsistence. Surprisingly, Whyte found women's contribution to subsistence to be unrelated to his gender status variables. It correlated .00 (gamma) with female domestic authority, –.01 with female solidarity groups, and .13 with control of female sexuality.

I have attempted to supplement Whyte's analyses with additional analyses of the SCCS of my own. I found an additional number of significant correlations between the three main gender status variables and ecomaterialist independent variables. Female domestic authority correlated –.41 (gamma) with class stratification and –.44 with subsistence type (an ordinal variable ranging from foraging to intensive agriculture using the plow). Forty-seven percent of egalitarian societies gave women high domestic authority, but women had high domestic authority in only 7 percent of the most elaborately stratified societies. And women had high domestic authority in 45 percent of foraging societies but in only 6 percent of intensive agricultural societies with the plow. Female domestic authority also correlated −.44 with patrilocal or virilocal residence. Most importantly, I found that female domestic authority correlated most strongly of all with women's contribution to agriculture (.46). Sixty percent of societies where women contributed 10 percent or less to agricultural production gave women low domestic authority, and in only 7 percent of these societies did women possess high domestic authority. Only 11 percent of societies in which women contributed between 50 and 60 percent of agricultural output scored low on female domestic authority, but women had high domestic authority in 50 percent of these societies. These findings show that women's contribution to subsistence is an important determinant of their status, but it appears to be their contribution to agriculture rather than their overall contribution to subsistence that is important.

The pattern of relationships is much the same when the measure of gender status is female solidarity groups. This measure correlated −.34 with social stratification, −.42 with political role differentiation (a measure of societal complexity), −.52 with patrilineality, −.54 with subsistence type, and .57 with women's contribution to agriculture. A full 55 percent of foraging societies score high on the female solidarity scale as opposed to only 6 percent of intensive agricultural societies with the plow. In the case of the latter type of society, 61 percent score low on the female solidarity scale compared to only 20 percent of foraging societies. As was the case for female domestic authority, the strongest predictor was women's role in agricultural production. Among societies where women do 10 percent of agricultural production or less, 47 percent score low on the female solidarity scale and only 12 percent score high. But where women do 50 to 60 percent of the agricultural production, 63 percent of the societies score high and none at all score low. Correlations were somewhat weaker when control of female sexuality was the measure of gender status. These correlations were .38 for the importance of gathering, −.42 for subsistence type, .51 for women's contribution to foraging, and −.63 for presence of the plow.

I have attempted to refine these analyses by putting the strongest independent variables into multiple regression equations with each of the measures of gender status. The best predictive model for female domestic authority included women's contribution to agriculture, subsistence type, patrilocal or virilocal residence, and class stratification, with R being .457 and 16 percent of the variance explained. Most of this explanation was generated by two variables, women's contribution to agriculture and class stratification. The results were stronger when female solidarity was used as the dependent variable. Here two variables combined achieved an R of .633 and explained 34 percent of the variance. These variables were women's contribution to agriculture and political role differentiation, with the latter contributing slightly more than the former. The regression analysis for control of female sexuality produced weaker findings. The best model achieved an R of .330 and explained only 7 percent of the variance. The variables included in this model were use of the plow, patrilocal or virilocal residence, and the contribution of women to foraging. Use of the plow was the strongest predictor.[2]

In sum, these analyses show that the most important determinants of variations in the status of women are precisely those factors stressed by ecomaterialist theories. As stressed in Blumberg's theory, women's economic contribution, or at least her contribution to agriculture, looms large. Social stratification and societal complexity are also important, giving at least some credence to Engels's theory. The measures of gender status we have had to work with are not ideal measures by any means, and there is undoubtedly measurement error in the SCCS data. Thus it is likely that these results understate the causal role of ecostructural factors.

ADDITIONAL EVIDENCE

An important study of how both biological predispositions and socialization contribute to gender differences has been carried out by the sociologist J. Richard Udry (2000). Udry studied a sample of women from the Child Health and Development Study, which took blood samples from pregnant women in the San Francisco Bay Area between 1960 and 1969. Samples were collected for every trimester and then frozen for thirty years. In 1990 and 1991 Udry and his research team interviewed many of the white daughters born to these women between 1960 and 1963; the daughters were at that time between twenty-seven and thirty years old. The respondents completed a variety of questionnaires and checklists designed to determine their degrees of femininity or masculinity and their sex role socialization experiences. Udry then looked at the relationship between these sex role orientations and the levels of various sex hormones in the mothers' blood samples when their daughters were *in utero*. Udry found that prenatal levels of sex hormone binding globulin (SHBG) had a strong effect on the daughters' levels of femininity or masculinity when they were adults. SHBG binds testosterone and transports it in the blood, and the higher the SHBG level the lower the level of testosterone. Women who had low prenatal SHBG levels (and thus high prenatal levels of testosterone) were significantly more masculine in their orientations and behavior than women with high SHBG levels (and thus low prenatal levels of testosterone). However, this was true only for SHBG levels during the second trimester of pregnancy; SHBG levels during the first and third trimesters were unrelated to masculinity-femininity. This is an extremely important finding, because it is only during the second trimester that fetal neurological organization is taking place; this is the time when the brain is being "sexed."

Udry found that socialization also played a role in determining levels of masculinity and feminity, but that socialization experiences interacted in an important way with prenatal hormone levels. Women who had low prenatal exposure to androgens were fairly responsive to their parents' socialization efforts; feminizing socialization efforts made them even more feminine, and, presumably, masculinizing socialization efforts could turn their behavior in a more masculine direction. By contrast, women who had high prenatal androgen levels, and thus who tended to be more masculine right from the start when they were young girls, were almost completely resistant to their parents' efforts to encourage feminine behavior. As Udry (2000:450–51) puts it, "the more the parents worked to improve below average femininity, the less successful they were; the more they tried, the less feminine the daughters were in adulthood." Respondent answers indicate that if a daughter has natural tendencies to be feminine, encouragement will enhance femininity; but if she has below average femininity in childhood, encouraging her to be more feminine will have no effect."

It is important to remember that Udry was only studying prenatal hormone levels and masculine vs. feminine orientations and behavior in females. There is obviously much less variation in these variables within the female sex than between females and males. What, then, are the implications for male-female differences in sex role orientations? Udry's answer is that it would be predicted that the much higher levels of prenatal androgens in males—levels about ten times as high as those of females—would not only strongly masculinize their later gendered behavior but would also make them highly invulnerable to the effects of socialization experiences designed to make them more feminine. Males, *simply because they are males*, seem to be highly resistant to feminizing socialization efforts.

Udry pulls his findings together and gives us the following biosocial interpretation of gendered behavior the world over (2000:454):

[B]iology sets limits to the macro-constuction of gender and also sets individual limits to the effects of gender socialization. . . . if the statement, "Gender is a socially constructed device invented by males to exploit females," is treated as a premise, an integrated macro model can explain why it is a male rather than a female invention. Differential female exposure to androgens can explain the differential response of females to their disadvantage. [The fetally most androgenized females should be the most "feminist" in their outlooks and interests.]

Broadening the theory I have sketched here leads toward explanation of the cross-cultural similarities of gender structure while leaving intact the sociological explanation of cross-cultural variation in terms of technology and ecological variation. We can theorize about the escape of exceptional women from even the most stultifying and restrictive boundaries of women's roles while not giving up an inch of constructionist territory in explaining the structure from which they escaped.

A biosocial macro theory is simple: Humans form their social structures around gender because males and females have different biologically influenced behavioral predispositions. Gendered social structure is a universal accommodation to this biological fact. Societies demonstrate wide latitude in this accommodation—they can accentuate gender, minimize it, or leave it alone. If they ignore it, it doesn't go away. If they depart too far from the underlying sex dimorphism of biological predispositions, they will generate social malaise and social pressures to drift back toward closer alignment with biology [as is clearly indicated in the famous case of the kibbutzim].

Udry believes that his findings have important implications for social change efforts in the direction of greater gender equality. Most critically, they indicate that efforts to resocialize males to be more feminine will have very limited success. Instead, efforts should concentrate on making females more masculine in their life orientations, occupational interests, and so on. This seems to fit extremely well with changes in gender roles over the past forty or fifty years. Men have changed little, whereas women have changed considerably. Women have become much more like men than men have become like women. (Whether this is a good thing or not depends on one's moral and political values, as Udry himself points out, and is a question that is beyond the scope of this book.) I would only add that, while *gender equality* may be possible, a completely *degendered* society is not. As Udry remarks (2000:454), "A social engineering program to degender society would require a Maoist approach: continuous renewal of revolutionary resolve and a tolerance for conflict." But not only would few people wish to live in such a society; it is likely that such extreme efforts would never, in fact, realize their aim.[3]

NOTES

1.   Bobbi Low (2000) remarks that, even with these qualifications, Whyte still exaggerates the political power of women in some societies. Low examined nine societies identified by Whyte as ones in which women have "significant power." She found that in most of these, that was not actually the case. In three of the societies the only evidence was a conversation or rumor. Whyte regards women among the Saramacca as having power equal to that of men, but it is clear upon closer observation that their power was limited to women's affairs. They had only informal influence over men. This seems to be the case in several of the nine societies, and possibly even in all of them.

2.   Despite the relatively weak results from the regression analysis involving male control of female sexuality, this is clearly an important dimension of female status and it is clearly related to levels of social evolution. In the *Ethnographic Atlas* (Murdock, 1967), a data bank of 1,267 preindustrial societies, in terms of class stratification, 56 percent of societies with complex stratification demand premarital virginity on the part of girls, but only 18 percent of egalitarian societies demand premarital virginity; and 49 percent of egalitarian societies freely permit premarital sex for girls, but only 9 percent of societies with complex stratification freely permit it. In terms of stage of political evolution, 73 percent of large states demand premarital virginity for girls, but only 21 percent of bands and tribes do so.

We know why men want to control female sexuality, but why should they be able to control it much more in societies at higher stages of social evolution? The answer is probably that women are competing more among themselves for men, especially high-status men, who prefer virgin brides and are in a position to demand them. In societies that are more highly stratified, women want men with resources and will be more likely to give in to male wishes under the circumstances. It is a cost-benefit matter. It is notable that in Islamic cultures senior women put intense pressure on girls to remain virgins. As Barbara Smuts has noted (1995:17), "over the course of evolution, male sociopolitical arrangements increased the variance in male wealth and power and perpetuated family differentials across generations. As a result of increasingly unequal relationships among men, women became increasingly vulnerable to the will and whims of the few most powerful men, and women's control over their own sexuality was greatly reduced."

3.   Udry's finding that socialization affects gender role behavior perhaps qualifies but does not contradict the findings of Geary (1998) and Lytton and Romney (1991) that there is little differential sex role socialization currently taking place in Western societies. Udry is focusing only on the degree of masculinity or femininity, whereas Geary and Lytton and Romney's focus is considerably broader. They are looking at such things as encouragement or discouragement of achievement, strictness of parental discipline, restrictiveness, and clarity of communication. Differential sex role socialization does occur, but only in certain areas. Moreover, Udry perhaps overstates the importance of sex role socialization for masculinity or femininity because he, like virtually all sociologists, is still caught in the trap of thinking of socialization as something entirely separate from biology. The fact that mothers encourage femininity in their daughters and fathers masculinity in their sons is clearly closely tied to the fact that mothers are themselves already more feminine and fathers are themselves already more masculine. The encouragement of femininity in girls is the norm because mothers recognize that the female sex *really is more feminine,* fathers that the male sex *really is more masculine.* Socialization is itself a biologically driven phenomenon to a very large extent, and the encouragement of femininity in girls and masculinity in boys is a human universal.

13

Marriage, Family, and Kinship

The family is based on the supremacy of the men, the express purpose being to produce children of undisputed paternity. Such paternity is demanded because these children are later to come into their father's property as his natural heirs.

—Friedrich Engels

Happy marriages are well known to be rare; just because it lies in the nature of marriage that its chief end is not the present but the coming generation.

—Arthur Schopenhauer

INCEST AVOIDANCE AND THE INCEST TABOO

Let us begin with what is perhaps the most fundamental fact pertaining to the family: incest avoidance. Incest avoidance, a cultural universal or near universal, involves the renunciation of sexual relations among individuals who are related by one-half of their genes, that is, parents and offspring and brothers and sisters. Incest does occur to some extent in many societies, most commonly between fathers and daughters; brother-sister incest is much less common, and mother-son incest is virtually unheard of (Fox, 1967; Shepher, 1983). In the early centuries of the first millennium AD, urban Greek settlers in Roman Egypt permitted—actually, encouraged—brother-sister marriage, and on the order of one in six marriages within this population took place between siblings (Hopkins, 1980; Shaw, 1992). There is also evidence of nuclear family incest (both brother-sister and father-daughter, and possibly even mother-son) in Zoroastrian Iran, although less is known about it than about brother-sister marriage in Roman Egypt, and no quantitative data on the frequency of nuclear family marriage are available (Scheidel, 1996). Moreover, some societies have followed a practice known as *royal incest,* which involves institutionalized incestuous marriage within ruling classes. The ancient Egyptians, Hawaiians, and Incas, several African kingdoms, as well as a number of other state-level societies, have practiced royal incest (van den Berghe and Mesher, 1980). However,

215

these instances of royal incest do not constitute genuine exceptions to the generalization that incest avoidance is a human universal. No one has yet discovered a society in which all or even a majority of the population mated incestuously.

Most sociologists explain incest avoidance by means of one or another type of functionalist argument, such as the so-called family disruption theory (K. Davis, 1949), an argument that goes back to the nineteenth century. This theory holds that the incest taboo was a cultural invention necessary for the stability of the family, and for at least two reasons. If the members of nuclear families mated with each other the result would be sexual rivalry, which would introduce dangerous tensions and conflicts of interest into the family. Moreover, if children were born from these unions there would emerge a serious confusion of family statuses and roles. As Kingsley Davis comments (1949:403):

> If sexual relations between parent and child were permitted, sexual rivalry between mother and daughter and between father and son would almost surely arise, and this rivalry would be incompatible with the sentiments necessary between the two. Should children be born the confusion of statuses would be phenomenal. The incestuous child of a father-daughter union, for example, would be a brother of his own mother, i.e., the son of his own sister; a stepson of his own grandmother; possibly a brother of his own uncle; and certainly a grandson of his own father. This confusion of generations would be contrary to the authoritarian relations so essential to the fulfillment of parental duties.[1]

Davis also notes that the absence of an incest taboo would lead to "an extreme concentration of each family within itself." This would inhibit relations between families, since they would no longer be dependent on one another for mates, and thus weaken the cohesion of the wider society.

The role confusion element of Davis's argument does have a superficial plausibility, at least if one thinks like a typical sociologist, but there seems to be very little evidence available to test it. What evidence there is—the instances of incestuous marriage mentioned above—is not accompanied by additional evidence showing that role confusion resulted, at least as far as I know. It is likely that in these instances people were able to work out special arrangements so that role confusion did not occur or was at least minimized. Long ago Durkheim (1964[1898]) argued that, in a society in which it was typical for a man's sister to become his wife, the parties could be socially conditioned to perceive no role incompatibility or conflict. (I would agree so long as the discussion is confined to *roles*. Whether the parties would feel comfortable with each other *at a psychological level* is another matter, as we will see below.) As for the sexual rivalry element of the theory, although nuclear family incest could certainly produce strong sexual jealousy, this argument rests (as does the role confusion argument) on the Freudian assumption that there are strong sexual attractions within the family (as Davis has put it, "Only the most stringent of taboos can restrain the parent from the thought and the deed"). However, this is extremely dubious. Contrary to Freud, one of the most striking things about the nuclear family is the overwhelming absence of sexual attraction between its members.

A biomaterialist theory of incest avoidance was developed over a century ago by Edward Westermarck (1891), the so-called familiarity breeds indifference theory. Westermarck's argument was that a sexual indifference or aversion emerged between individuals who were close childhood associates. He held that such indifference did not depend on the individuals being genetically related. Genetically unrelated persons who were close childhood associates would develop this indifference, whereas brothers and sisters reared apart would not develop feelings of sexual disinterest. Westermarck was a Darwinian. He theorized that the emergence of sexual disinterest among childhood associates was an adaptation that had evolved because it eliminated the negative effects of close inbreeding. Although Westermarck's theory has been much maligned, it was revived in the 1960s and 1970s in connection with the discovery of some highly provocative data. Joseph Shepher (1971) examined 2,769 marriages undertaken between members of several Israeli kibbutzim. Incredibly, he found that only 13 of these marriages were undertaken between children who had grown up in the same communal nursery. This overwhelming preference of young kibbutzniks to marry outside of their own childhood groups occurred despite the absence of any norm against marrying nursery mates; indeed, kibbutzniks were generally encouraged to marry their nursery mates. When Shepher asked these kibbutz youth about their failure to marry childhood associates, they often said such things as "we feel like siblings" or "we have no attraction to each other."

Research by Arthur Wolf (1970, 1995) on Taiwanese marriage practices is also highly consistent with Westermarck's theory. In the early twentieth century two contrasting marriage patterns were found in Taiwan, which Wolf called "major marriages" and "minor marriages," the latter known locally as *sim-pua* marriage. In a major marriage, the bride and groom were individuals who did not know each other in childhood. Often they did not even meet until the day of the wedding. In the *sim-pua* marriages, the bride was a woman who had been adopted into her future husband's household as an infant or young child and brought up in close association with this boy. Wolf predicted that persons who married in *sim-pua* fashion would show much higher levels of marital dissatisfaction than persons who were involved in major marriages, and this is precisely what he found. He determined that 24 percent of the *sim-pua* marriages ended in divorce or separation compared to only 1 percent of the major marriages. Moreover, 33 percent of the women in *sim-pua* marriages had committed adultery compared to only 11 percent of the women in the major marriages. Wolf also found that *sim-pua* marriages produced fewer offspring than did major marriages, which he interpreted to mean that intercourse was considerably less frequent in the *sim-pua* marriages. In his most recent research, Wolf (1995) has tried to determine whether the age at which children associated with each other contributed to the strength of their sexual indifference or aversion. His data show that the first three years are crucial. Taiwanese couples who associated with each other from birth to age three exhibited much higher rates of adultery and divorce and lower rates of fertility than couples whose association began in later years. Wolf also examined Shepher's thirteen kibbutz couples who married despite coming from the same communal nursery. In all but two cases, these couples did not associate with each other until age four or older, and in only one case was there association beginning at birth. Wolf concludes that there is a "critical period" for the acquisition of incest aversions among childhood associates, and that this period ranges from birth until the age of three.

Results similar to Wolf's have been obtained for Lebanese marriage practices (McCabe, 1983). Some Lebanese groups have practiced what is known as patrilateral parallel-cousin marriage, which involves the marriage of cousins who belong to the same descent group and who grew up together. In most societies this practice has been regarded as incestuous; it is found almost exclusively in Arab societies in the Middle East and North Africa. Mc-Cabe found that patrilateral parallel-cousin marriages had the same consequences that Wolf discovered in the Taiwanese *sim-pua* marriages. Compared to all other marriages, parallel-cousin marriages were more than four times as likely to end in divorce and produced about 23 percent fewer children.

Some years ago I undertook a survey of college students in several of my own classes, asking them a simple question: "Have you ever received, from a parent or a parent surrogate, any instruction whatsoever in regard to the necessity of avoiding incest?" I told the students that even if this instruction was extremely slight, they were to count it as a yes. My results confirmed exactly what I predicted: that the vast majority of the students had never been given any such instruction. (Between 90 and 100 percent of the students reported no instruction whatsoever.) I myself had never been given such instruction, even though I had been given considerable instruction on many other aspects of sexual behavior. I reasoned that my experiences were probably typical, and this is what I found. What this means is that the incest taboo can hardly be simply a cultural norm if it is seldom taught, and if the vast majority of people avoid incest even though they are never taught to do so, then the behavior must be springing from natural tendencies.

A biomaterialist interpretation is also strongly suggested by evidence of patterns of inbreeding avoidance among other animals (Bischof, 1975). Incest avoidance is widespread (though not universal) among primates and other mammals, and also common in birds. Chimpanzees for example, avoid close inbreeding by virtue of the fact that females from one community transfer to another community after sexual maturity and mate only with that community's males. Another very strong line of evidence supporting the biomaterialist interpretation is the results of studies of inbreeding depression. Inbreeding depression consists of the genetic defects and premature deaths that occur in the offspring of closely related individuals. In a study by Seemanova (1971), 42 percent of the children born from incestuous matings suffered either severe disability or early mortality, but the rate of disability or mortality in children of nonincestuous matings was only 7 percent. Seemanova's study also shows that the probability of the production of genetically defective offspring increases in direct proportion to the mating couple's degree of genetic relatedness. Other studies of inbreeding depression (reviewed in M. Ember, 1983; Shepher, 1983; Scheidel, 1996; and Durham, 1991) show similar results. The logical conclusion seems to be that incestous mating is fitness reducing and has been strongly selected against in the evolutionary process.

Finally, there have been many cases of incest in which the partners were siblings who had been separated in infancy or early childhood and then were reunited in adulthood. S. Kirson Weinberg (1955) studied incest in six pairs of siblings who met as adults after having been separated in infancy. These individuals had a cognitive awareness of an incest taboo, but they felt no sexual indifference or aversion to each other because they considered each other strangers (Erickson, 1989). Similarly, there are works of fiction that deal with incest in which the partners are relatives who had been separated early in life and reunited much later. A well-known example is Herman Melville's *Pierre, or the Ambiguities.* In this work, the main characters, Pierre and Isabel, are separated siblings reunited in adulthood and the relationship is charged with sexual passion from the very start. This passion triumphs despite Pierre's knowledge of an incest taboo and his resulting internal conflicts (Cory and Masters, 1963; Erickson, 1989).

Despite the large amount of evidence supporting Westermarck's theory,[2] it is probably not the whole answer. Melvin Ember (1983) and William Durham (1991) point out that much evidence shows that people in many preindustrial societies seem to have a good understanding of the relationship between incestuous matings, even of cousins, and inbreeding depression. This conscious recognition that incestuous marriage often produces genetically defective offspring has probably served both to reinforce the natural tendencies toward incest avoidance among childhood associates and to extend incest prohibitions to apply to related individuals who were not childhood associates.

There are three lines of evidence that on the surface seem to refute a biomaterialist interpretation of incest avoidance: royal incest, brother-sister marriage in Roman Egypt and Zoroastrian Iran, and the occurrence of incest in modern societies. On closer inspection, however, the biomaterialist interpretation can withstand this evidence. Royal incest, as the name implies, is limited to the royal families or aristocratic classes of highly stratified societies. This incestuous practice is often explained as a mechanism for keeping wealth and power concentrated within a select circle of ruling kinspeople. This may be one of the conscious motives of the participants, but there is a biomaterialist side to the story that should not be overlooked. Since women all over the world strongly prefer to marry at or above their own social class level and never below it (because women seek men with status and resources), women in royal families actually have very few marital options (van den Berghe and Mesher, 1980; van den Berghe, 1983). They may be forced to marry a brother if they are to marry at all or avoid marrying down. As van den Berghe (1983:100) notes, "What is a poor princess to do? She has almost no way to go but down, unless she is lucky enough to find a king for a husband. Her brother happens to be the nearest kin, and perhaps the only one worthy of her if she was born in the monarchy at the apex of an imperial system (as was the case for both Inca Peru and ancient Egypt)." But royal incest might also be a fitness-maximizing strategy for a king or queen, as van den Berghe (1983:100) explains:

> For the king, incest is a low-risk, moderate-gain strategy. If the king succeeds in producing a fit incestuous heir with an $r = .75$, that person will in turn become highly polygynous and produce many grandchildren with an $r = .375$. If the incestuous strategy is successfully repeated over several generations, the king comes close to cloning himself. For commoners who are monogamous or small-scale polygynists, the risk of inbreeding depression militates against the incestuous strategy. For a large-scale polygynist, however, the risk is low [because many more offspring are being produced]. Should the strategy fail, the king's fitness loss is minimal (being largely limited to his sister's wasted effort), and he still has the option of producing an outbred heir with any of his many other wives.
>
> For the queen, the incestuous strategy is far riskier, since failure seriously reduces her reproductive success, but she also stands to gain much more than the king. In short, for her,

incest is a high-risk, high-stakes strategy. If she succeeds, she hits the fitness jackpot by putting on the throne a son with an $r = .75$ who will in turn be highly successful reproductively through large-scale polygyny.

As for the urban Greek settlers in Roman Egypt, Brent Shaw (1992) has shown that they were a conquering elite that despised the larger Egyptian society. In order to maintain their ethnic identity, marriages with native Egyptians were prohibited, which led to a severe limitation of the supply of marriage partners. In consequence, some of the Greek settlers were forced to marry a sibling unless they were willing to remain unmarried. The logic of this situation is therefore similar to that of royal incest. Too little is known at present about incestuous marriage in Zoroastrian Iran to be able to account for it, but it is likely that incestuous marriage was an alternative to no marriage at all.

Incest occurs to some extent in modern industrial societies, although exactly how frequently is unclear. In all likelihood no more than 1 or 2 percent of the population is involved. Why does it occur? In an extension of Westermarck, Mark Erickson (1989) has argued that incest avoidance results from the failure of what he calls *familial bonding*. Under normal conditions parents and children and brothers and sisters develop strong bonds with one another, and this familial bonding inhibits another form of bonding that Erickson calls *sexual bonding*, or the emergence of sexual desire. But when familial bonding fails to develop, the door is left open to sexual bonding. In his psychiatric practice, Erickson has treated many victims of incest and found that both the victims and the perpetrators typically came from families characterized by an extreme absence of nurturance. If Erickson is right, his argument is a major theoretical achievement in that it allows us to explain at one and the same time both the avoidance of incest by the vast majority of the population and the fact that at least some incest probably occurs in every society.

KIN SELECTION IN HUMAN SOCIETIES

One of the most important features of kinship in human societies is its extraordinary pervasiveness. Not only are family and kinship ties universal, but they are fundamental in every known society. The old expression that "blood is thicker than water" is extremely apt. In all societies relations between kin are given priority over relations with nonkin. This is especially so in preindustrial societies, which anthropologists have documented in great detail. Kinship is so important in these societies that at one time anthropologists virtually equated social structure with the web of kinship (Murdock, 1949), and it is well known that in studying a preindustrial society, especially a preliterate one, anthropologists spend an inordinate amount of time establishing genealogies.

Sociologists have claimed for many decades that family and kinship have "shrunk" in modern industrial societies—that they are not as important in these societies as they are in preindustrial societies. In the 1940s Talcott Parsons (1943) put forth his famous thesis of the "isolated nuclear family" as the most fundamental feature of the American family system. According to Parsons, the nuclear family neither lived with nor pooled its money with the extended kin group of either husband or wife. The nuclear family was economically independent, and many nuclear families were substantially isolated from their extended kin. However, no sooner was this thesis stated than it was challenged. Edward Shorter (1975) looked at working-class families in a section of London and found what he called a "stunning intensity of kin contacts." Sussman and Burchinal (1962) summarized the results of several studies. They found that the disintegration of extended kin networks in urban areas was not a common occurrence; that the leisure-time pursuits of urban working-class couples was dominated by extended family activities; that urban dwellers ranked visiting with kin ahead of visiting with friends, neighbors, and co-workers; and that the urban middle classes expressed nearly a universal desire to interact with extended kin. Winch and Kitson (1977) conducted a more recent study and found that the great majority of the individuals they studied were significantly involved in larger kin networks. They posited the existence of two somewhat different types of American family structure: isolated nuclear families, or nuclear families lacking extended kin in their own local community; and embedded nuclear families, which were nuclear families highly involved in a network of extended kin. They found that only about 13 percent of all nuclear families were isolated nuclear families, but that approximately 75 percent were embedded nuclear families. Based on these studies, it would appear that kin selection is still a fundamental feature of life in modern industrial societies.

It also appears that kin selection reared its head in the Israeli kibbutzim shortly after efforts were made to abolish the traditional family. The desire to abolish the family was based on the kibbutzniks' fervent conviction that the modern "bourgeois" family was a decadent institution that was the source of the domination of women by men and children by parents. As noted earlier, children were removed from their parents and placed in communal nurseries, where they were reared by professional nurses. This system worked for awhile, but in time it broke down as parents, particularly mothers, requested more time with their children. Not only was the nuclear family reestablished, but the extended family was as well (Tiger and Shepher, 1975; van den Berghe, 1979).

CROSS-CULTURAL PATTERNS OF RESIDENCE AND DESCENT

Three basic types of kinship groups are found in the world's societies. The *nuclear family*, which consists of two parents and their offspring maintaining a common household, is the basic family pattern in all modern industrial societies and in many hunter-gatherer societies. *Extended families* are networks of nuclear families that reside together and carry out a variety of joint activities. Extended families are the dominant type of kinship unit in most preindustrial societies. In a great many preindustrial societies, horticultural societies in particular, large-scale extended families known as *corporate descent groups* are dominant. These groups are called corporate because they have a status as a single body that acts in behalf of its members. The corporateness of these groups is signified by some of their most important characteristics: they have a name, collectively own land or other property, forbid marriage within the group, perform common religious and other ritual observances, and are bound by obligations of mutual aid and hospitality (Stephens, 1963).

Since all societies have family units, all must organize households and thus determine where newly married couples will live after marriage. Five basic forms of *postmarital residence* stand out. *Patrilocality* involves the movement of a wife to the extended household of her husband's father (this is called *virilocality* if the wife moves in with her husband but the society is not organized into extended family households). *Matrilocality* involves the movement of a husband into the household of his wife's mother (this is called *uxorilocality* if the husband moves in with his wife but there are no extended family households). It is, in essence, the direct opposite of patrilocality. *Avunculocality* is a variant of patrilocality in which a wife accompanies her husband to the household of his mother's brother. This kind of residence is found almost exclusively in matrilineal societies (see below), and is actually somewhat more common in those societies than matrilocality (38 percent of matrilineal societies are avunculocal compared to 30 percent that are matrilocal). *Ambilocality* gives people a choice of living either with the wife's group or the husband's. *Natolocality* (Fox, 1967) is a rare practice, occurring most often in matrilineal societies, in which husbands and wives remain in the extended households of their birth. Here the marriage tie is weak or brittle, and married couples ordinarily spend little time together. Finally, *neolocality* involves the establishment of a new household, and is found where the nuclear family rather than the extended family is the basic kinship unit. Of the societies in the *Ethnographic Atlas* (Murdock, 1967), a large data bank of 1,267 preindustrial societies, 68.4 percent are patrilocal or virilocal, 13.1 percent are matrilocal or uxorilocal, 7.4 percent are ambilocal, 4.6 percent are neolocal, 4.4 percent are avunculocal, and 0.9 percent are natolocal. Clearly, patrilocality or virilocality are the overwhelming preference.

Distinct from a society's household structure but closely related to it nonetheless is its *descent pattern*. Descent is a matter of how genealogical ties are established, regardless of who lives together. Descent groups are networks of kinspeople who have certain obligations and rights with respect to each other, such as the passing of inheritance or the socialization of children. *Unilineal* descent is the most common pattern in the world's societies. This involves the establishment of descent groups that trace connections through either the father's line or the mother's line, but not both. In *patrilineal* descent a network of kin traces their relationships through a father's line. The most important genealogical relationships are those between father and son and brother and brother. Patrilineal societies are nearly always patrilocal, so the males of a patrilineage remain together, where they carry out various economic activities and exercise authority over the other affairs of their kin group. Since marriage is generally prohibited within the group, a major problem for a patrilineage is to acquire women from other patrilineages so it can obtain children (Fox, 1967). Women are imported from other patrilineages, and the patrilineage exports its own women to some of these groups. Like patrilocality, patrilineality is by far the most common practice in the world's societies, with approximately half of the societies in the *Ethnographic Atlas* being patrilineal.

Matrilineal descent involves the tracing of genealogical connections through one's mother's descent line. It is much less common than patrilineal descent, accounting for only about 9 percent of the world's societies. In a matrilineal society, every person belongs to a descent group organized through his or her mother, and father and all of his relatives belong to other groups. Because of universal male political dominance, matrilineal descent groups run into a special problem not encountered in patrilineality. Although females are the focus of descent, it is the males of the group who exercise authority. This leads to what has been called the *avunculate,* which is the tie between a boy and his mother's brother. In matrilineal systems, there are what Malinowski (1929) identified as two types of fatherhood, which he called biological and sociological fatherhood. In these systems it is the boy's maternal uncle who serves as his sociological father, and this relationship generally overrides the relationship between the boy and his biological father. The core of a matrilineal group is thus a network of matrilineally related men.

In matrilineal societies that are matrilocal, the women of a matrilineal group remain together and the men disperse. One possible source of conflict in this system is the "intrusion of the husband" (Fox, 1967). The maternal uncle may find that his authority over his nephew is being undermined by the boy's biological father, who remains in close daily contact with him. In matrilineal societies that are avunculocal, the men of a matrilineage stay together and the women go to live with their husbands. At puberty or marriage the children born of these unions will leave their natal households and go to live with their own mother's brothers. In the handful of matrilineal societies that are natolocal, the main (and virtually the only) role of the husband is to impregnate his wife on behalf of her matrilineal kin.

A few societies have combined patrilineal and matrilineal descent by having both types of groups, a practice known as *double descent.* In such societies everyone belongs to a patrilineal and a matrilineal group, and each kind of group is given different work to do so that the groups do not interfere with each other. If one group arranges marriages, the other will not; or a person might inherit movable property from one group but fixed property from the other (Fox, 1967). Some societies have corporate descent groups but do not restrict them by sex, thus possessing what have often been called *cognatic descent groups* (Fox, 1967). This system is radically different from a unilineal system in that the descent groups are not mutually exclusive. Indeed, cognatic descent groups extensively overlap and thus cannot ever be residential groups or vengeance groups. For cognatic descent to work, there has to be some type of restriction on their composition. Fox notes that a person may have rights to several different groups, but he or she has to decide at some point which rights to exercise. The key to cognatic descent seems to be flexibility, and as a result it is sometimes called *ambilineal* descent because of the element of choice involved.

All of the groups we have been discussing are based on *ancestor focus* (Fox, 1967), which means that people trace their genealogical relations by beginning with some distant ancestor. In modern industrial societies, however, and in many preindustrial societies, there are no such groups. Instead, the descent system rests on *ego focus* (Fox, 1967), which means that small-scale groups are formed by tracing descent from a given living individual to his or her nearest living relatives. Groups called *kindreds* are formed, and these are usually bilateral, i.e., they involve tracing descent through both "sides" of one's family. Bilateral kindreds are the basic kind of nonnuclear family groups found in modern industrial societies.

Descent and residence patterns are closely related. Ninety-six percent of patrilineal societies in the *Ethnographic Atlas* are patrilocal or virilocal, compared to only 16 percent of matrilineal societies. Sixty-seven percent of patrilocal/virilocal societies are patrilineal. Matrilineal societies are associated with a variety of residence systems, but matrilocality/uxorilocality and avunculocality are by far the most common. Thirty percent of matrilineal societies are matrilocal or uxorilocal, and 38 percent are avunculocal. Ninety-seven percent of avunculocal societies are matrilineal. Ambilocality goes with bilateral descent, as does neolocality. Seventy-one percent of ambilocal societies are bilateral, as are 59 percent of neolocal societies.

What are some of the correlates of descent patterns? In terms of subsistence patterns, 64 percent of hunter-gatherer societies in the *Ethnographic Atlas* are bilateral, compared to 24 percent of societies with a mixture of foraging and horticulture, 13 percent of intensive agriculturalists, and only 5 percent of horticulturalists and pastoralists. Beyond the hunter-gatherer level, patrilineality is clearly the norm. Sixty-five percent of horticulturalists are patrilineal, as are 68 percent of intensive agriculturalists and 82 percent of pastoralists. Matrilineal societies are most likely to have horticulture (33 percent) or to combine horticulture with hunting and gathering (32 percent).

There is a connection between the nuclear family and bilateral descent. Forty-two percent of societies with the nuclear family as the modal type have bilateral descent, but only 27 percent of societies with small extended families, 14 percent of societies with large extended families, and 5 percent of societies with the stem family have bilateral descent. Bilateral descent is most common in hunter-gatherer and modern industrial societies, being universal in the latter.

How can these various types of residence and descent patterns be explained? A number of anthropologists have argued for an ecomaterialist interpretation (Keesing, 1975; M. Harris, 1979; Goody, 1976). For the most part, residence patterns seem to logically precede descent patterns. People must first organize themselves into adaptive household arrangements because it is through these arrangements that they carry out essential economic activities. Descent patterns emerge as means of conceptualizing and validating what is going on at the ground level. However, as we shall see below, there may be instances in which certain kinds of residential arrangements emerge from descent patterns.

If, then, patrilineality springs from patrilocality and matrilineality springs from matrilocality, what accounts for the far greater prevalence of patrilocality and patrilineality? One common ecomaterialist explanation relates these to population pressure, limited land and resources, and the presence of concentrated forms of wealth (M. Harris, 1975; Martin and Voorhies, 1975). The argument seems to be that keeping fathers, sons, and brothers physically together so they can pursue their common interests in land and people is a highly adaptive arrangement. This may well be so, but from the perspective of Darwinian conflict theory what is adaptive at the economic level is also likely to be adaptive genetically. John Hartung (1976, 1982) argues that, since (*ceteris paribus*) the reproductive possibilities of men are usually much greater than the reproductive possibilities of women, it makes sense for people to pass along wealth in the male line and thus organize themselves into patrilocal households and patrilineal kin groups. He notes that "it can be seen that sons represent a higher-risk, higher-profit-potential investment than do daughters (since males have potentially higher reproductive variance). Accordingly, if wealth is viewed as an arbitrarily bestowable reproductive advantage, it follows that this wealth will most benefit the benefactor if it is given to male descendants" (1976:608). Hartung shows that polygynous marriage is associated with a strong male bias in inheritance. He examined 411 societies from the *Ethnographic Atlas* for which data on both marriage type and inheritance pattern were available. Among monogamous societies, 58 percent passed wealth primarily or only to men. On the other hand, among societies with limited polygyny, 80 percent had a strong or exclusive male inheritance bias, and fully 97 percent of societies with general polygyny had a strong or exclusive male bias. These patterns are exactly what should be found if patrilineality is driven by the greater reproductive potential of males. Cowlishaw and Mace (1996) have extended Hartung's analysis by looking at actual changes over time in both marriage practices and inheritance rules. They note that "marriage patterns and inheritance rules are evolving together in a way that is adaptive. Where general polygyny evolves, strongly male-biased inheritance almost always evolves. In contrast, the evolution of monogamy is strongly associated with an absence of sex-biased inheritance. Transitions to limited polygyny are equally associated with both inheritance systems" (1996:93).

If patrilocality and patrilineality are so common because of the greater reproductive potential of males, then why do matrilocality and matrilineality occur at all? There have been two different explanations proposed, one ecomaterialist and the other biomaterialist. The ecomaterialist explanation has been offered by Carol Ember and Melvin Ember (1971; cf. C. Ember, 1974). They relate matrilocality to the long-term absence of men from their home villages, usually as a result of external war. When people fight internal wars, or wars close to home, men are around most or all of the time and patrilocality is the norm. External wars, however, or those fought at long distances from home, often keep men away from their villages for long periods of time, and as a result women must often take control of economic production. If all these things occur, according to the Embers, it makes sense to keep the women together and disperse the men. Marvin Harris (1975, 1979) has given this argument a somewhat different twist. The issue, he says, is one of "who's minding the store." He argues that any situation that requires men to be gone from home for long periods puts pressure on a society to become matrilocal. If societies with long-term male absence were patrilocal and patrilineal, women (or at least married women) would be left in charge of the affairs of their husbands' groups, obviously an undesirable situation from the husbands' point of view. Under such circumstances, Harris argues, it would make more sense to keep women together and build matrilocal and matrilineal institutions. Under these circumstances, while men were away, women would be left in charge of their own groups, which would make much more sense than leaving them in charge of the groups into which they had married.

Ember and Ember provide data that are supportive of their theory, but I conducted my own independent test as well. I located nineteen societies in the SCCS with frequent external war and a female contribution to agriculture of 60 percent or greater. Of these societies, 37 percent are matrilocal or uxorilocal compared to 20 percent of the total SCCS societies that are matrilocal or uxorilocal. This is moderately supportive of Ember and Ember. Moreover, another 11 percent were avunculocal, which suggests that they were matrilocal or uxorilocal sometime in the past. This gives a possible total of 48 percent of the societies that are, or may have been in the past, matrilocal or uxorilocal. Still, given that 47 percent of the societies were patrilocal or virilocal, the support for Ember and Ember is modest at best. What then of Harris's version of the male absence hypothesis? Using the SCCS and cross-tabulating absences of married males against postmarital residence, I found that 24 percent of the societies in which males are not absent have matrilocal or uxorilocal residence, compared to 23 percent of societies in which males are frequently absent. Moreover, 60 percent of societies with men frequently absent have patrilocal or virilocal residence. These results are not at all supportive of Harris.

Additional correlational analyses show that matrilocal or uxorilocal residence is not closely related to any independent variables. It correlates only $-.005$ (Pearson r) with absences of married males and only $-.081$ with external warfare. It correlates more strongly with class stratification $(-.221)$ and internal warfare $(.202)$ than with the predictors argued for by Ember and Ember. Social stratification and subsistence type are two of the best predictors of residence. Sixty-one percent of matrilocal/uxorilocal societies are egalitarian compared to only 33 percent of patrilocal/virilocal societies. Forty-two percent of patrilocal/virilocal societies have dual or complex stratification, compared to only 16 percent of matrilocal/uxorilocal societies. In terms of subsistence, 67 percent of matrilocal/uxorilocal societies are foragers or simple horticulturalists, compared to only 37 percent of patrilocal/virilocal societies; and 47 percent of patrilocal/virilocal societies are intensive agriculturalists compared to only 24 percent of matrilocal/uxorilocal societies. Still, the overall correlations are low, and we appear to be a long way from a good understanding of why societies adopt female-centered rather than male-centered residence patterns.

A biomaterialist explanation of matrilineality has been offered by Richard Alexander (1974) and Jeffrey Kurland (1979) (cf. Gaulin and Schlegel, 1980). They argue that there are many societies in which, for a variety of reasons, males have little confidence of paternity. Under such circumstances, men will tend to invest in their sisters' offspring, to whom they know they are related, usually by one-fourth of their genes, rather than in their wives' offspring, to whom they may not be related at all. This is an ingenious argument, and it does seem to be the case that matrilineal societies are often ones in which men have low paternity certainty (Hartung, 1985). However, as Kurland himself realizes, it is not possible thus far to tell whether or not low paternity certainty is the actual causal variable. It could be that low paternity certainty is just an incidental effect of the unique features of matrilineal societies. (For an extension and modification of the paternity uncertainty argument, see Hartung, 1985.)

The jury is still out on which of these theories works better, but even if we can come to some sort of resolution of that issue there is still the problem of explaining why matrilineal societies are more likely to be avunculocal than matrilocal. It can be suggested that avunculocal societies were originally matrilocal and that that is how they became matrilineal. Then changes occurred which made matrilocality less adaptive and avunculocality more adaptive. As Robin Fox (1967) has noted, matrilocal residence works well when societies are small in scale and egalitarian or only mildly stratified. Although men are dispersed from their matrilineal households, they are not very far away and can still manage their groups' affairs. However, with evolutionary changes in the scale of society and the increasing development of wealth and social stratification, dispersed men live farther away from each other and have more difficulty managing their matrilineages' affairs. The solution to this new problem may be a shift in the residence pattern from matrilocal to avunculocal because this would bring the matrilineally related men back together in the same household. Evidence to support this argument comes from the *Ethnographic Atlas*. Seventy-two percent of matrilocal or uxorilocal societies, but only 24 percent of avunculocal societies, are egalitarian. At the other end of the spectrum, 56 percent of avunculocal societies are stratified compared to only 15 percent of matrilocal or uxorilocal societies. (See M. Ember, 1974, for an alternative interpretation of avunculocality.)

Neolocal residence is the most common pattern in societies in which the nuclear family rather than the extended family is the basic familial unit, i.e., in all industrial and many hunter-gatherer societies. As for cognatic or ambilineal descent (and the ambilocal residence that usually accompanies it), this is often found in island societies in which people and land have to be constantly readjusted to each other. Needed flexibility in people-land arrangements may be well served by flexibility in household and descent organization, which is what cognatic descent provides. Double descent is found in only a small number of societies and may be the result of societies' shifting from matrilocal and matrilineal institutions to patrilocal and patrilineal ones, or vice versa (Fox, 1967). Double descent may be a transitional stage through which some societies pass as they undergo other changes.

MARRIAGE IN COMPARATIVE PERSPECTIVE

Love has been in perpetual strife with monogamy.

—Ellen Key

The three basic forms of marriage in the world's societies are *monogamy, polygyny,* and *polyandry.* Monogamy, the marriage of one man to one woman, is the legally mandated marriage form in all modern industrial societies, and is the institutionally accepted form in a number of other societies. In agrarian societies monogamy has been virtually the only type of marriage found among nonelite classes. Although agrarian elite males have often preferred polygyny and frequently had large harems of nubile women under their control, many agrarian societies have been prescriptively monogamous. The ancient Greeks and Romans, for example, imposed monogamy on everyone, although concubinage was allowed and practiced by many elite men. With the emergence of Christianity, medieval Christian Europe became monogamous. (Actually, because the Germanic tribes that overran the Roman Empire were polygynous, polygyny was still practiced in the early Middle Ages, usually being limited to men of wealth and power. Four Merovingian kings, for example, took multiple wives. Christianity, of course, opposed polygyny, and by about the twelfth century it had won and polygyny was essentially eliminated; see Wemple, 1981, and Brundage, 1987). Only some 15 percent of the societies in the *Ethnographic Atlas* are prescriptively monogamous.

The preferred form of marriage throughout the world has clearly been polygyny, the marriage of one man to two or more women. About 85 percent of the societies in the *Ethnographic Atlas* have adopted this as the ideal or at least allow it. There is a great deal of variation among societies in terms of what proportion of the male population is polygynously married at any given time. Douglas White (1988) has provided data in this regard for the societies of the SCCS. In 58 percent of these societies, fewer than 20 percent of the male population is polygynously married. In another 32 percent of the societies, between 20 and 49 percent of males are polygynously married, and in about 9 percent of the societies half or more of the male population is involved in polygynous marriages. There are some strong regional variations as well. In African societies, an average of 31 percent of the men are polygynously married, and virtually all African societies permit polygyny. This region is far and away the most polygynous. At the other extreme, European and Asian societies have typically been ones in which only 3 or 4 percent of men are polygynists.

In many polygynous societies only a small segment of the male population is able to marry polygynously, either because of the simple fact that there are only so many women to go around, or because only a few men have the resources needed to support more than one wife. The polygynists in these societies are almost invariably men of high social rank. Laura Betzig (1986) has documented the extremely close relationship between a man's political status and the number of wives he has (see chapter 10). Betzig is speaking only of highly stratified societies (what she calls "despotic" societies), but the pattern holds for more egalitarian societies as well. In these societies, it is usually the headmen or the big men who have multiple wives. Polygyny has occurred most often in horticultural societies. It is still found today in parts of the Middle East and throughout Africa, and in these regions occurs much more frequently in the more traditional sectors of society that have been least influenced by the forces of modernization (Ware, 1979; Armstrong et al., 1993).

The explanation most commonly offered for polygyny is that it enhances wealth and is therefore desired for economic reasons (Boserup, 1970; Grossbard, 1976, 1980, 1984; Becker, 1991; White, 1988; cf. White and Burton, 1988). Polygyny is most common in horticultural societies that give women a major role in cultivation of the soil, and in such societies women become important economic assets. The more wives a man has, the more he can enhance the wealth under his control. Likewise, it can be argued that polygyny is generally absent from the nonelite sectors of agrarian societies because in these societies women take little role in cultivation and thus are not economic assets. In fact, the conditions of agrarian societies seem to make wives expensive, and few men can afford to have more than one wife (some cannot afford even one). Betzig is highly critical of the economic argument. As she remarks, "that inability to reproduce and adultery on the part of the wife are significant causes of conjugal dissolution, and that wives frequently are cloistered against the possibility of infidelity, perhaps even to the detriment of their ability to carry on economic activity, remain unaccounted for in the theory that the economic value of women motivates polygyny" (1986:84). Betzig also points out that the economic theory cannot explain why wealthy men take prepubescent girls as wives.

A number of studies have shown a correlation between women's contribution to subsistence and the degree of polygyny (Heath, 1958; Goody, 1976; White, Burton, and Dow, 1981; cf. Betzig, 1986). To explore the matter myself using the SCCS, I examined the relationship between a five–point scale of marriage type (monogamy prescribed, monogamy preferred but some polygyny, polygyny preferred by leaders, polygyny preferred by men of wealth and rank, and polygyny preferred and attained by most men) and a variety of variables thought to be possible predictors of marriage type. The only variable that was more than very weakly correlated with marriage type was the contribution of women to agriculture (r = .385). Where women did 70 percent or more of the agricultural work, 65 percent of SCCS societies were ones in which most men are polygynously married. But where women did only 10 percent of the agricultural work or less, only 13 percent of the societies were ones in which most men marry polygynously. It seems clear that men are more motivated to marry polygynously in societies where women's economic value is high. However, this can only be part of the story, and a modest part at that. The vast majority of societies permit polygyny, and most of those strongly encourage it. Polygyny exists and is often common even in societies where women do very little agricultural work. The pervasiveness of polygyny pushes us in the biomaterialist direction.

The biomaterialist explanation (van den Berghe, 1979; Symons, 1979; Hartung, 1982) holds that the widespread preference for polygyny is a natural result of the differences between male and female reproductive strategies. Men have a natural desire for sexual variety because this promotes their inclusive fitness. As Donald Symons (1979) has pointed out, this male desire for multiple sexual partners is extremely widespread and is probably a true cultural universal (cf. Betzig, 1992a, 1992b). However, it does not seem necessary to construe the biomaterialist and ecomaterialist explanations as mutually exclusive (van den Berghe, 1979). The enhancement of wealth obviously helps promote a man's inclusive fitness, since greater wealth helps him provide better for his offspring. Thus, a man's desire to increase his wealth may be located in the same part of the biogram that governs his desire for sexual variety. A reasonable conclusion would be that men in all societies desire sexual variety and will take advantage of opportunities for it whenever possible. These opportunities are enhanced or limited by underlying ecostructural conditions, especially the extent to which women are available and whether they are expensive or inexpensive as wives. It is surely no accident that it is mostly the high-status men in many polygynous societies who have multiple wives. They have both the means to acquire them and the personality traits (i.e., competitiveness, aggressiveness, dominance orientation) that incline them toward the pursuit of females. High-status males mate more often and leave more offspring, a pattern that is commonly found among other mammals. Polygyny is rooted in humankind's primate and mammalian heritage.

What then of polyandry, the marriage of one woman to two or more men? This marriage practice is rare, being found in less than 1 percent of the world's societies (Murdock, 1967). Biomaterialistically it seems to make little sense, because, other things being equal, it would seem to decrease rather than increase a man's inclusive fitness. It is certainly inconsistent with the male desire for sexual variety and the logic of the male reproductive strategy. Various interpretations of polyandry have been given. Drawing on the work of Melvyn Goldstein (1976; Beall and Goldstein, 1981; cf. Crook and Crook, 1988), William Durham (1991) has offered an explanation that is both eco- and biomaterialist. A peasant population in Tibet originally studied by Goldstein most commonly practiced polyandry, and it was fraternal (a woman married several brothers). However, other forms of marriage also existed. Some marriages were monogamous, others polygynous. And in some cases a group of brothers married to one woman took on a second wife, resulting in what has been called *polygynandry.* According to Goldstein and Durham, polyandry among these people was motivated by extreme land scarcity. The Tibetans lived at a very high altitude and their land was extremely dry, making agricultural productivity very low. Had men inherited land individually, no one would have had enough to make a decent living. Thus, a group of brothers would inherit collective rights to the same plot of land and would bring in a woman to serve as their wife. In addition, the brothers could combine to work the land, creating a more favorable labor situation. The existence of both monogamous and polygynous marriages alongside polyandry seemed to result from the specifics of family composition. If a man had no brothers he would inherit land and take on a wife all by himself. If a man in a monogamous marriage deemed his wife to be infertile, he could take on another, thus creating a polygynous marriage. Or, if a family had daughters but no sons, they could arrange for a polygynous marriage between their daughters and a man who had no brothers. Polygynandry could result when polyandrous brothers married a second woman because they deemed the first infertile.

Durham has stressed that polyandry in Tibet is both economically and reproductively adaptive, even though earlier studies have suggested otherwise. One study (Beall and Goldstein, 1981) concluded that polyandry, though economically adaptive, was reproductively maladaptive, at least for men. Men marrying polyandrously left fewer offspring than men marrying monogamously. However, a serious defect of this study was that it looked at reproductive success in only one generation. Another study (Crook and Crook, 1988) looked at reproductive success over two generations. The investigators found that polyandry was highly reproductively advantageous for women. For men the results were more ambiguous. Brothers with equal sexual access to a wife did not necessarily show lower fitness compared to brothers who married monogamously. However, there was usually differential access to a wife in polyandrous marriages, and this tended to depress the inclusive fitness of polyandrous junior brothers compared to brothers marrying monogamously. Durham has looked at the reproductive results over three or more generations. He has performed computer simulations which show that polyandry was indeed reproductively disadvantageous after only one or two generations; however, after three or more generations fraternal polyandry led to higher levels of reproductive success than would have occurred had family plots been split up and marriage been monogamous. Durham's explanation is thus a true Darwinian conflict explanation in that it is simultaneously biomaterialist and ecomaterialist.[3]

As for monogamy, it is easy to understand why virtually all agrarian peasants adopted it. It was simply too costly for them to have more than one wife, and many could not afford any wife at all. However, this will not explain the imposition of monogamy on elites among the ancient Greeks and Romans and the elite members of other agrarian societies, nor will it explain why monogamy has become the rule of law in all modern industrial societies. Richard Alexander (1987; Alexander et al., 1979) has proposed a biomaterialist explanation that relies on the idea of *reproductive opportunity leveling.* Male competition for wives produces conflict, and societies that recruit large pools of young men for purposes of fighting wars with other societies will need to keep this male-male conflict to a minimum. This can be done, Alexander says, by legally prohibiting polygyny, thus giving all males equal access to wives. Alexander refers to this as *socially imposed monogamy* and claims that it is the product of the large nation-state. The data are reasonably consistent with Alexander's theory. In the SCCS, 46 percent of larger states have socially imposed monogamy, compared to 26 percent of smaller states, 10 percent of chiefdoms, and 11 percent of bands and tribes. In the full *Ethnographic Atlas,* 46 percent of larger states have monogamy and another 39 percent have only occasional polygyny. Monogamy clearly is much more common at the most advanced stages of political evolution.

The only systematic empirical test of Alexander's theory has been undertaken by Michael Price (1999) in a paper that is as yet unpublished. Price actually tests a somewhat expanded version of Alexander's theory. He argues that monogamous societies have been much more successful than polygynous societies because of the greater cooperation promoted by the former, and monogamy has spread from the Western world to other parts of the world because it has led to greater success. Price tests this argument by using five measures of societal success: population size, use of the death penalty, the level of democratization, the level of corruption, and the level of economic development. Price classifies eighty-four contemporary nation-states as monogamous and seventy-two as polygynous. His results are quite consistent with the overall theory. The mean population size of the monogamous societies was 52.15 million, whereas the mean size of the polygynous societies was only 19.93 million. As for the death penalty, monogamous societies were nearly seven times as likely to have abolished it as polygynous societies, which Price interprets as evidence of greater cooperation and less conflict in monogamous societies. In terms of the mode of government, Price found that 64 percent of monogamous societies but only 25 percent of polygynous societies had liberal democracies. Only 11 percent of monogamous societies but 45 percent of polygynous societies had highly authoritarian modes of government. Price also found that monogamous societies were much less corrupt. Specifically, monogamous societies were more than eight times as likely as polygynous societies to be ranked in the least corrupt third of contemporary societies (42 percent vs. 5 percent). Finally, the monogamous societies had a per capita gross domestic product in 1996 of $9,710 whereas the polygynous societies had a per capita GDP of only $2,235. Price also notes that monogamous societies have much greater military strength, which supports Alexander's original point.

Betzig (1986, 1992a) adds her own twist to Alexander's theory. She notes that reproductive inequality (polygyny) goes with economic and political inequality, whereas reproductive equality (monogamy) goes with economic and political equality. Powerful men may give up polygyny and impose monogamy on everyone in order to enlist the cooperation of the masses, or at least large segments of society. Betzig claims that it was not until the industrialization of the past two centuries that monogamy became the general rule. (She denies that the Romans were really monogamous; while this is true legally, she says, in actuality they had de facto polygyny; see Betzig, 1992a, 1992b.) But, as we have seen, monogamy was overwhelmingly the general rule in Europe for many centuries prior to the onset of industrialization. This part of Betzig's theory clearly will not work. However, she may be onto something with her notion that monogamy goes with greater economic and political equality. Think of Betzig's (1986) work on despotism and polygyny discussed in chapter 10; these clearly go together. I have difficulty getting out of my mind Karl Witt-fogel's (1957) famous concept of Oriental despotism, for it does appear that the most despotic states have appeared in this part of the world. By contrast, early forms of democracy (nowhere near our modern systems of parliamentary democracy, but forms of democracy nonetheless) emerged in the West, more specifically in ancient Greece and Rome. Not only were these societies monogamous (at least legally), but the whole monogamous tradition of modern Western civilization is rooted in Greek and Roman monogamy.

One alternative to the reproductive opportunity leveling theory is the ecomaterialist theory of Richard Posner (1992). Posner argues that monogamy has been socially imposed in societies where companionate marriage is the norm. Companionate marriage involves, ideally at least, an intimate and lifelong relationship between a man and a woman, and a crucial element of this form of marriage is sexual exclusivity and fidelity. Polygyny, virtually by definition, is radically incompatible with companionate marriage. Companionate marriage emerged in Western industrial societies in the eighteenth and nineteenth centuries and in Japan in the twentieth. However, as we have just seen, monogamy was introduced into the Western tradition by the ancient Greeks and Romans and by Christianity long before this. Monogamy was already well established before companionate marriage evolved and was obviously a major part of Christianity's whole conception of human sexuality. Although I would predict that companionate marriage would have led to the extinction of polygyny had polygyny still existed at the beginning of the eighteenth century, that prediction can never be tested, and thus a decisive evaluation of Posner's theory cannot be made. However, some empirical evidence is available to shed light on the matter. Japan, a non-Christian society with a tradition of polygyny and concubinage, abolished these practices in the late nineteenth century (Murstein, 1974), which was the time at which it was beginning to modernize and develop companionate marriage. Moreover, polygyny is still permitted throughout much of the less-developed world today, especially in Africa and the Islamic world, even though certain restrictions have been placed on it (Welch and Glick, 1981; Nasir, 1994; Pitshandenge, 1994). Who still practices polygyny in these regions, and who has given it up for monogamy? The general answer is that polygyny is concentrated mainly in the most traditional sectors of these societies. Poorly educated women from rural areas and with low socioeconomic status are much more likely to be in a polygynous marriage (Ware, 1979; Armstrong et al., 1993). That it is the best-educated women who shun polygyny is strong support for Posner's theory, because it is among these women that the ideal of companionate marriage has most thoroughly taken hold.

Nevertheless, it is doubtful that the incompatibility of polygyny with companionate marriage can explain monogamy in most societies throughout history or monogamy in band and tribal societies, since none of these societies have had companionate marriage. Kevin MacDonald (1990, 1995) holds that there may be several different mechanisms that have produced socially imposed monogamy, including the influence of Christianity on the adoption of monogamy throughout the history of Europe during the past two millennia. Socially imposed monogamy in Western Europe, he claims, "originated as a result of conflict in which ecclestiastical authorities attempted to combat the power of the aristocracy" (MacDonald, 1995:8). Socially imposed monogamy may also arise, MacDonald asserts, by way of political activity on the part of lower-status or middle-status males, whose goal is the leveling of reproductive opportunities, or by way of political activity on the part of females or their relatives. Women may support monogamy because of their perception that their status is lowered by polygyny, and, indeed, this is what we see throughout the contemporary Third World where polygyny is still legal.

At this point it seems a bit difficult to avoid MacDonald's somewhat eclectic conclusion, unsatisfying though it is. However, a reconnection with the biomaterialist argument can be made. Alexander has also proposed another type of monogamy that he calls *ecologically imposed monogamy* (Alexander et al., 1979; Flinn and Low, 1986). In this case monogamy is not imposed politically by a powerful nation-state but arises because of the lack of resources available to men to support more than one wife. As Flinn and Low (1986) suggest, this type of monogamy might also be called *resource-limited monogamy*. It is clear that this is a major reason why peasants in agrarian societies almost always marry monogamously, but it could apply to many band and tribal societies as well. Alexander suggests that ecologically imposed monogamy should be found in extreme or marginal habitats, such as the Arctic or deserts, and that it should be found in association with high rates of abortion or infanticide, wide spacing of offspring, long periods of nursing of infants, and extended postpartum taboos on sexual intercourse. There are 186 prescriptively monogamous societies in the 1,267 societies of the *Ethnographic Atlas*. A valuable project for future research would be to analyze these societies in detail, looking for evidence of either socially imposed or ecologically imposed monogamy. Until such a time-consuming project is undertaken, however—and to my knowledge no one has ever done this in any sort of systematic way—we must pronounce our understanding of monogamy limited and inconclusive.

Before closing our discussion of monogamy, however, we should take note of the most recent theory of this puzzling phenomenon, that of Kanazawa and Still (1999). They test empirically two theories of monogamy. The first, which they call the *male compromise theory*, is a distillation of the ideas of Alexander, Betzig, and MacDonald discussed above. The basic idea is that reproductive egalitarianism will prevail where societies are highly democratic: Political equality promotes reproductive equality. I am not sure that this theory is exactly what Alexander and MacDonald had in mind, but it is reasonably close, and let us not quibble unnecessarily. The authors do not agree with the male compromise theory, favoring instead what they call the *female choice theory*. This theory assumes that it is females rather than males who determine who mates with whom, and therefore whether monogamy or polygyny prevails in a society depends on what women want. Kanazawa and Still argue that women will choose polygyny when the resource inequalities among men are great, because it is better to be, say, the tenth wife of a wealthy man than the only wife of a man of modest means. But when resource inequality among men is relatively low, then women will choose monogamy because there is no advantage to be gained from polygyny. In addition to testing this theory, Kanazawa and Still test a deduction from it, which they call the *female power hypothesis:* the greater the level of women's power in societies with extreme resource inequality among men, the greater the extent of polygyny.

The first part of Kanazawa and Still's analysis involved performing computer simulations. These showed that there is a strong positive relationship between economic inequality and the degree of polygyny in a society. They performed their actual empirical tests by compiling data from 127 contemporary countries. The male compromise theory was not supported, but the female choice theory was. Moreover, they also found that as women's power increased in societies with sharp resource inequality among men, the level of polygyny increased. On the other hand, in societies where there was greater resource equality among men, the level of women's power was associated with an actual decline in the level of polygyny.

Kanazawa and Still's study is extremely interesting, and they could be right, but I am skeptical for several reasons. They say that marriage practices emerge from the bottom up rather than being imposed by political leaders, but in all modern industrial societies monogamy is the law and law is made by political leaders. If it is simply a matter of what individuals choose, then why is it enshrined in law? Why not let those women who want to be monogamous be monogamous, and those women who want to be polygynous be polygynous? Why forbid by law more than one woman at a time from marrying Donald Trump, Bill Gates, or Michael Jordan? Explaining why monogamy is enshrined in law in so many countries (and why it was enshrined in law in such ancient societies as Greece and Rome) is one of the main things we have to explain. There appears to be more going on than the strategic choices made by millions of individuals.

Kanazawa and Still's claim that polygyny benefits women and hurts men is dubious, or at least a considerable overstatement. It is true that polygyny hurts those men who lose out in the competition for mates, but it clearly benefits those who win, and there are many societies with a lot of polygynous men. And clearly women in many societies see polygyny as harmful rather than beneficial. As Bobbi Low (2000:74) has commented, "Women often suffer costs in polygynous systems: in a number of societies, second and subsequent polygynous wives have lower fertility than monogamous wives, or than first wives in polygynous households. Children are likely to survive less well in polygynous households, and a major cause of divorce in polygynous societies is conflict among co-wives." This problem is closely related to another, which is that Kanazawa and Still focus on female choice to the exclusion of male choice. Male choice has to be at least as important as, and possibly even more important than, female choice. Otherwise, what sense are we to make out of all the evidence reviewed earlier that men desire young women, attractive women, women with low waist-to-hip ratios, many different women, etc.? I also wonder whether or not Kanazawa and Still's data are adequate to the task of testing these theories. A better test would come from cross-cultural data—the *Ethnographic Atlas* or the SCCS. I looked at the relationship between resource inequality and polygyny in the SCCS and it was in the opposite direction from what their theory predicts. Inequality actually *reduced* the frequency of polygyny (r = −.132), although the relationship was weak.

My conclusion, as stated earlier, is that polygyny springs largely from the male desire for sexual variety, and that men will choose polygyny when it is possible, i.e., when they have the resources to support more than one wife and when they are not prevented by law from doing so. Thus, to explain monogamy I believe we are led back to Alexander's notions of socially imposed and ecologically imposed monogamy. I am ambivalent about these ideas, for which there is thus far only limited empirical support, but they are more plausible and better empirically supported than anything else I have seen, and I will stick with them until something better comes along.

BRIDEWEALTH AND DOWRY

In many societies, when a woman marries her kin group receives one or another form of wealth from the kin group of her husband. This transfer of wealth is known as *bridewealth* or *brideprice*. Bridewealth is most characteristic of patrilineal societies, being much less frequently found in societies having other forms of descent. It is also much more common in polygynous than in monogamous societies. Of the societies in the *Ethnographic Atlas* with general polygyny, 91 percent have bridewealth; this compares to 53 percent of societies with limited polygyny and only 38 percent of monogamous societies that have bridewealth (Hartung, 1982). Bridewealth is highly correlated with polygyny because bridewealth expresses the tremendous sexual and reproductive (and to some extent economic) value of women in these societies. Where women have such value, men are willing to pay out sums of valuables to obtain them. The actual size of bridewealth payments in a particular society is determined by marketlike conditions, and often there is intense bargaining among men over the size of bridewealth (Borgerhoff Mulder, 1988). As Monique Borgerhoff Mulder (1988:65–66) notes, "where the groom enters into a marriage that, for some material or social reason, is advantageous to him and his family a high bridewealth is paid, and where the bride enters a marriage that benefits herself or her family a low bridewealth is demanded." Borgerhoff Mulder goes on to note that for the Kipsigis, a tribal society in Kenya, men were willing to pay more bridewealth for women considered to have high reproductive value, such as early maturing or plump brides. Lower bridewealth was paid for women deemed to have lower reproductive value, such as women who had already given birth to the child of another man.

Much less common than bridewealth is *dowry*. Here a woman, with the help of her parents and perhaps other kin, accumulates property that she takes with her into a marriage. Dowry is in essence a type of early inheritance that a woman uses in order to contract a favorable marriage (van den Berghe, 1979; Goody, 1976). This practice is almost exclusively restricted to complex agrarian societies that are highly stratified. In the *Ethnographic Atlas*, 86 percent of societies with dowry are agrarian societies. And whereas bridewealth correlates highly with polygyny, dowry correlates strongly with monogamy; 74 percent of the *Ethnographic Atlas* societies that have dowry are monogamous.

Important research on bridewealth and dowry has been conducted by Jack Goody (1976) and by Alice Schlegel and Rohn Eloul (1988). Goody's investigations have shown that bridewealth was widespread throughout Africa, whereas dowry was much more common in Europe and Asia. In explaining these observations, Goody relied heavily on the fact that the African societies practiced horticulture, were less stratified, and had lower population densities and more available land. The Eurasian societies, on the other hand, had plow agriculture, social stratification, high population densities, and land was relatively scarce. In Goody's view, these contrasting characteristics of the two regions have made bridewealth adaptive in the one region but dowry more adaptive in the other. Bridewealth is paid when women have economic value, and thus when kinship groups relinquish them they must be compensated for their loss. Dowry, by contrast, occurs under economic conditions in which women are much more costly, and so husbands or husbands' families must be compensated for the high cost of marrying and supporting them. As Marvin Harris (1979:107) has suggested, "Dowry is unintelligible unless it is seen as an attempt to compensate husbands for the responsibility of supporting women whose productive and reproductive potentials are held in small esteem." Schlegel and Eloul (1988) have come to similar conclusions on the basis of detailed cross-cultural research.

Steven Gaulin and James Boster (1990) offer a biomaterialist alternative to this ecomaterialist explanation of dowry (cf. Dickemann, 1979b). Gaulin and Boster attempt to test a version of the ecomaterialist explanation they attribute to Ester Boserup (1970), which they call the *labor value theory,* and their own biomaterialist argument, which they refer to as the *female competition theory.* Gaulin and Boster show that dowry is most common in stratified societies that have prescriptive monogamy. They reason that where polygyny is found some men can achieve much greater reproductive success than any woman because they can father children by several wives. Under these circumstances it makes sense for parents to invest in the reproductive opportunities of their sons, and thus be willing to pay out bridewealth to attract wives. This way parents can help insure many grandchildren. However, in monogamous societies the levels of reproductive success for men and women will be more nearly the same. In monogamous societies that are highly stratified, wealthy men will naturally be more desired by women and their parents because those men can provide the best for the wife's children (her parents' grandchildren). Under these circumstances, it makes sense for parents to invest in daughters by providing them with dowries because women are competing more severely for husbands than they are in polygynous societies. Gaulin and Boster (1990:997) explain:

> In stratified, monogamous societies, large differences in wealth exist among men that are not diluted by their acquisition of additional wives, as in polygynous societies. Any female who marries such a wealthy male monogamously can expect to have the bulk of his resources for her offspring and thereby enjoy greater reproductive success than females who are not so well mated. Thus, we interpret dowry as a means of female competition for desirable (that is, wealthy) husbands in monogamous societies. Parents (and other kin) should be expected to collaborate in such competition whenever a well-married daughter will gain more or less exclusive access to (although not necessarily control over) her husband's resources.

Gaulin and Boster tested the models against each other by discriminant analysis and found that the female competition model was better supported by the data. However, the labor value model also fit the data fairly well, so it could be that both biostructural and ecostructural factors are operative in determining dowry.

MODES OF CROSS-COUSIN MARRIAGE

In numerous band and tribal societies women are often exchanged in marriage between and among exogamous (outmarrying) descent groups according to specific rules and preferences. By far the most famous analysis of the various forms of marital exchange is that developed by Claude Lévi-Strauss (1969a) in his celebrated book *The Elementary Structures of Kinship.* In many societies the form of marital exchange is what Lévi-Strauss has called *restricted exchange,* more commonly known as *bilateral cross-cousin marriage* (Fox, 1967). This practice involves the mutual exchange of women by descent groups in every generation. For example, if the women of the Wolf Clan marry into the Fox Clan, then the women of the Fox Clan will marry into the Wolf Clan generation after generation. The Wolf Clan may also have a marriage agreement with the Beaver Clan, in which case Wolves and Beavers exchange women as marriage partners generation after generation. Restricted exchange in essence involves an agreement among the men of various descent groups to exchange women reciprocally as marriage partners in each generation. A cross-cousin is the offspring of a person's father's sister or mother's brother (offspring of the father's brother or mother's sister are known as parallel cousins). In restricted exchange the marital exchange process works in such a way that a young boy will marry a girl who is both his father's sister's daughter and his mother's brother's daughter. His future wife is thus a double, or bilateral, cross-cousin, which is why this form of exchange is called bilateral cross-cousin marriage.

The other principal form of marital exchange identified by Lévi-Strauss is what he calls *generalized exchange.* This has two subtypes. *Short-cycle generalized exchange,* also known as *patrilateral cross-cousin marriage* (Fox, 1967), involves the mutual exchange of women between descent groups, except in this case the descent groups skip a generation in the return of women. Thus if the Crocodile Clan gave women to the Alligator Clan in one generation, then the Alligator Clan would not give women back to the Crocodile Clan until the next generation. The reason this form of marital exchange is also called patrilateral cross-cousin marriage is because a young boy is likely to marry his father's sister's daughter. *Long-cycle generalized exchange* (Fox, 1967) is characterized by asymmetrical exchange relations between descent groups. This form of marital exchange involves groups standing in permanent wife-giving or wife-taking relations with other groups. Thus if the Bear Clan gives women to the Skunk clan, it never takes women from that clan. Likewise, the Skunk clan may give wives to the Muskrat Clan, but if it does it will never obtain wives from that clan. This marriage arrangement results in a preference for marriage with a young boy's mother's brother's daughter, and for this reason is also known as *matrilateral cross-cousin marriage.*

Of the 752 societies in the *Ethnographic Atlas* for which data are available, 188 practice cross-cousin marriage. Most of these (154, or 82 percent) practice bilateral cross-cousin marriage, thirty (16 percent) practice matrilateral cross-cousin marriage, and only four (2 percent) practice patrilateral cross-cousin marriage.

Lévi-Strauss's theory of marital exchange is at once structuralist and functionalist. On the one hand, marital exchange is predicated on the dichotomization of the social world into "us" and "them," which derives from the tendency of the human mind to think in terms of binary oppositions. On the other hand, exchange results from the attempt of kinship groups to form alliances with one another in order to prevent or minimize destructive social conflict and thus achieve a higher level of social integration than would otherwise be possible. Lévi-Strauss holds that this is true in all three types of exchange. However, he notes that the matrilateral version of generalized exchange is much more common than the patrilateral variety (in fact, as we just saw, it is about eight times as common). This is the case, he claims, because matrilateral marriage binds more groups together and thus is able to produce a higher level of social cohesion than is possible with the other two types.

Although Lévi-Strauss's theory has been widely endorsed by anthropologists, there are some very good reasons for being highly skeptical of it. Melvin Ember (1983:72–73) questions the theory on logical grounds:

> Although there may very well be advantages to marrying outside the family, we need to ask ourselves whether the incest taboo [Ember does not distinguish between exogamy and the incest taboo] is necessary to promote cooperation within and between communities. Is it not possible, for example, that families could have required some of their members to marry with outside groups if they thought it necessary for survival and could have permitted incestuous marriages when such alliances were not needed? A more serious logical problem is that cooperation theory [Ember's name for alliance theory] does not distinguish between marriage and sex. Why not marry outside the family and make love within it? Thus, while the incest taboo might enhance cooperation between families, the need for cooperation does not adequately account for the existence of the incest taboo in all societies, because other marriage and sex rules might also promote alliances between families.

Moreover, not only is outmarriage inessential to promoting alliances, it does not even appear that it actually promotes such alliances. Gay Elizabeth Kang (1979) extracted a sample of fifty societies from the Human Relations Area Files, the largest compilation of ethnographic data in existence, in order to study the problem. Her overall finding was that there was no relationship between the practice of exogamy and the establishment of intergroup alliances. The extent to which alliances were formed correlated only –.03 (gamma) with lineage exogamy and only .10 with local group exogamy; moreover, alliance formation correlated –.47 with clan exogamy, which is a substantial correlation but in the wrong direction from that predicted! Kang went on to reanalyze the data while controlling for the level of societal complexity and region of the world, but these factors made no difference. In agreeing with Kang's analysis, Ember (1983) notes that marriage alliances between the royal houses of Europe did not prevent warfare between their respective countries, and that in-laws in our own society are not especially noted for their cooperation with each other.

If Lévi-Strauss's theory does not hold up to empirical scrutiny, then what alternatives are available? Ember (1983) adopts the view, once extremely widespread and still fairly common, that exogamy rules are simply the extension of nuclear family incest taboos to larger categories of kin. Some social scientists, such as Pierre van den Berghe (1979, 1980), have argued by contrast that exogamy is something distinct from the incest taboo and that it must be explained differently. Van den Berghe argues that incest avoidance concerns sex, whereas exogamy concerns marriage. He also argues that exogamy rules, although they prohibit the marriage of certain kinds of cousins, commonly encourage people to marry other kinds of cousins. Van den Berghe accepts the Westermarck theory as an explanation for incest avoidance, but (despite disconfirming evidence) Lévi-Strauss's alliance theory as an explanation of exogamy rules. Although for many years I agreed with van den Berghe, I now disagree with him because I have become aware of some crucial evidence: the widespread prohibition in human societies of sexual relations and marriage among *all* first cousins, not just cousins in one's own lineage or clan. Many societies, in fact, go even further and prohibit such relations among all *second* cousins. Of 752 societies in the *Ethnographic Atlas* for which there are data, 469 (62 percent) prohibit marriage between all first cousins. Another 46 percent of these go further and extend the prohibition to all second cousins, and another 42 percent of these may prohibit at least *some* second cousins (the data are ambiguous). Only a minority of societies permit the marriage of cousins (mostly cross-cousins). These data not only provide further evidence against the alliance theory (cf. Pasternak, Ember, and Ember, 1997), but they look strikingly like what one would expect to see if people were being motivated by the desire to avoid certain types of incestuous relations. My conclusion is that exogamy rules are just what many anthropologists have been saying throughout the entire twentieth century—an extension of nuclear family incest regulations.

To explore this idea further, I rated the societies in the *Ethnographic Atlas* on a six-point scale of the degree of restrictiveness or permissiveness of cousin marriage, ranging from societies that prohibit the marriage of all first and second cousins to those that allow the marriage of any cousin. The degree of restrictiveness of cousin marriage turns out to be unrelated to the majority of the independent variables against which it was run. It is not significantly related to class stratification, the intensity of cultivation, the mode of marital residence, the descent mode, the type of marriage payment, or the form of marriage. Stage of political evolution, mode of subsistence, and community size, however, do make some difference. Thirty-four percent of bands and tribes prohibit all first and second cousins and only 5 percent allow all cousins. By contrast, only 7 percent of large states prohibit all first and second cousins and 34 percent allow all cousins. The same pattern is evident for subsistence mode and community size: Hunter-gatherers are more restrictive than intensive agriculturalists, and societies with communities larger than 5,000 inhabitants are more permissive than societies with smaller communities. These results are moderately supportive of the Westermarck hypothesis: It is the smaller-scale societies, those in which people have more frequent contact with each other, that are more likely to prohibit the marriage of cousins, and prohibiting cousin marriage is just incest avoidance carried beyond the nuclear family.

Two questions remain to be answered: Why do societies often allow the marriage of cross-cousins while prohibiting the marriage of parallel cousins, and what accounts for the different varieties of cross-cousin marriage? The answer to the first question is relatively straightforward. Parallel cousins will be members of a person's own descent group, and thus in a large number of cases these will be people that he or she has grown up around and has had a great deal of contact with during early childhood. Prohibiting the marriage of parallel cousins can thus be explained in terms of a Westermarck effect. Cross-cousins, on the other hand, will in many cases be individuals with whom a person has had less contact (or even none at all), and thus they are more likely to be considered eligible mates. Parallel cousin marriage does exist, but only in its patrilateral form. It is very uncommon, being confined mostly to Arab societies in North Africa and the Middle East, and it seems to be associated with an unusually high level of male domination (R. Alexander, 1979).

The second question is much more difficult to answer, and there is no consensus at all on what the answer is. Most attention has been given to why more societies have adopted matrilateral cross-cousin marriage than the patrilateral variety. Lévi-Strauss's answer is probably the best known. As noted earlier, he argues that the matrilateral variety, because it links every descent group with every other in a kind of chain or circle that curves back on itself, is more common because it leads to a higher level of social integration. This argument, which is quintessentially functionalist and Durkheimian, was challenged fairly early on by George Homans and David Schneider (1955). On the basis of cross-cultural research, Homans and Schneider discovered that matrilateral marriage is generally found in societies with patrilineality, whereas patrilateral marriage is more commonly found in societies with matrilineality. Their explanation for this is that in patrilineal societies there is a particular kind of tie between a boy and his mother's brother. His relationship with his father is likely to be stern (perhaps even cold and distant), but his relationship with his mother's brother is more relaxed and easygoing. As a result he will become fond of his mother's brother, and more than likely fond of his mother's brother's daughter as well. Marriage between them is therefore sentimentally appropriate. In matrilineal societies the opposite situation is found. Here the relationship between a boy and his mother's brother is stern and formal, but his relationship with his father's sister is relaxed and easygoing. A boy will become fond of his father's sister, and thus very likely of her daughter too, and thus marriage to this daughter (patrilateral marriage) will be sentimentally appropriate. Why then is matrilateral marriage much more common than patrilateral marriage? Simply because there are many more patrilineal than matrilineal societies.

Marvin Harris (1979) has provided an alternative to both Lévi-Strauss and Homans and Schneider. Harris concedes that bilateral cross-cousin marriage can be explained, as Lévi-Strauss argues, as an effort to generate social integration. However, bilateral marriage, he claims, is characteristic of highly egalitarian societies while matrilateral marriage tends to be found in societies that are at least incipiently stratified. He suggests that matrilateral marriage is intertwined with the stratification systems of these societies. Where matrilateral marriage prevails, he argues, the wife-giving groups are superordinate; they establish and maintain their dominant position primarily by giving wives to subordinate groups, because in return for wives they obtain various forms of wealth and other compensation. Among the Kachin of Burma, for example, a tribal society with a carefully studied system of matrilateral marriage (Leach, 1954), the dominant descent groups give women to subordinate groups and obtain in return cattle and labor services. Thus, for Harris matrilateral marriage is a tool of political economy rather than social integration. His explanation is therefore ecomaterialist rather than structuralist or functionalist.

Unfortunately for Harris, *Ethnographic Atlas* data flatly contradict the argument that bilateral marriage is a more "primitive" form and that the matrilateral version is usually found in stratified societies. Forty percent of matrilateral societies are egalitarian, and another 33 percent have wealth distinctions only. A mere 27 percent have any type of stratification, which is actually less than the figure for bilateral societies (41 percent). Moreover, all of the fourteen societies with both complex stratification and cross-cousin marriage have the bilateral form, and 83 percent of the societies with dual or elite stratification are bilateral.

Richard Alexander (1979) has proposed a biomaterialist interpretation of cross-cousin marriage patterns. He points out that, because there is always less certainty of paternity than of maternity, men will be on average more closely related to their daughters' children than to their sons' children; as a result they are more likely to invest in their grandchildren through their daughters than in their grandchildren through their sons. This leads Alexander (1979:190–91) to suggest

> that men would be expected to prefer matrilateral cross-cousin marriages because they are slightly more closely related to daughter's children, because they are less able to influence the success of a son's children by helping a daughter-in-law, and if they are able to assist grandchildren through a daughter married to a nephew by assisting, guiding, and controlling the nephew (who may also be relatively closely related if confidence of paternity is low). In this system each young male will tend to be guided, controlled, and helped by both his father and his maternal uncle. Females will tend to be helped by their fathers and their husbands. In patrilateral cross-cousin marriages, on the other hand, males would tend to be helped by their fathers alone, females by their maternal uncles. Thus, it would appear that men have more balanced and extensive ways of assisting grandchildren under matrilateral as opposed to patrilateral cross-cousin marriage.

Frankly, although I do not accept Lévi-Strauss's theory, I am not sure what to conclude regarding the other theories. I am slightly inclined to favor Alexander's interpretation, if only because of the rapidly growing success of biomaterialist arguments with respect to so many aspects of kinship and family organization. The track record of these arguments is good and getting steadily better. Moreover, there is still the problem of how to explain why bilateral marriage is far more common than either matrilateral or patrilateral marriage. One possibility is that it is the simplest and easiest method of exchange—that the brain has evolved an "exchange organ" that is biased toward simplicity. Another possibility is that, since a person is (at least much of the time) marrying a double cross-cousin, and since that person is more closely related on average to a double cross-cousin than to a patrilateral or matrilateral cross-cousin, bilateral marriage is the form of marriage that would maximize inclusive fitness. It might be the ideal form of marriage if people are seeking an optimal balance between too much inbreeding and too little. This may be an idea worth pursuing in future research.

THE DEVELOPMENT OF THE MODERN WESTERN FAMILY

Industrialism, Capitalism, and the Family

For many years sociological orthodoxy held that prior to industrialization the extended family was the norm, and that it was industrialization itself that brought the modern nuclear family into existence. Early challenges to this position were made by Sidney Greenfield (1961) and Frank Furstenburg (1966), who argued that the nuclear family was widespread in Western Europe and North America long before the beginnings of industrialization. A more serious indictment came from the work of Peter Laslett and his colleagues (Laslett, 1972a, 1972b, 1977). These researchers found that the small nuclear family was the basic family unit in England, northern France, and the Netherlands as early as the sixteenth century.

These findings led Alderson and Sanderson (1991) to argue that the crucial factor in the rise of the nuclear family in the West was the rise of European capitalism sometime after about AD 1500. Alderson and Sanderson reorganized the data used in twelve studies of family structure in historical Europe and discovered that family structure was closely tied to the level and type of economic development. In North America and the most capitalistically advanced parts of Europe (Belgium, northern France, and England), the small nuclear family had emerged as the norm. In the least developed parts of Europe—Russia, Serbia, Estonia, and Hungary—the nuclear family was much less common and large extended families were more commonly found. And finally, in areas of Europe that were moderately developed—Italy, southern France, Austria, and Germany—there was an intermediate level of development of the nuclear family. The three regions investigated corresponded closely to what Immanuel Wallerstein has called the capitalist core, periphery, and semiperiphery. The relationship between economic structure and family pattern can be visualized more clearly by comparing the ratio of nuclear to extended families within each economic region. The ratio in the core was 5.9:1, in the periphery 1.1:1, and in the semiperiphery 1.6:1.

Alderson and Sanderson provide an ecomaterialist interpretation of these findings. In their view, the critical factor in each economic region was the *mode of labor control.* In the core zones, systems of forced labor had increasingly given way to wage labor, and labor was thus "freer." Why does freer wage labor go together with the nuclear family? According to Alderson and Sanderson (1991:425), "It makes no sense for farm laborers who are working for wages to have large families for the simple reason that, under conditions of landlessness, family members become economic liabilities rather than assets (or at least are more of a liability than an asset). And because of the existence of an extensive capitalist labor market, it is more economically efficient for farmers to hire agricultural workers than to produce them themselves." Conversely, large extended families were much more adaptive in peripheral and semiperipheral regions. For peasants in Eastern Europe, large extended households made sense in the context of the economic system they were caught up in. Eastern Europe had experienced the "second serfdom" at about the same time that Western Europe was beginning to move in the direction of wage labor. Eastern European peasants were producing for overlords as well as for their own subsistence. A strong need for household labor was established, and this could be provided most efficiently by increasing the size of the household, especially when there was little or no capitalist labor market from which labor could be hired. In the semiperiphery a prominent economic activity was sharecropping, and sharecroppers were freer than peasants in the periphery and could hire some of the labor they needed. It is this that seems to account for the "in-between" nature of semiperipheral family patterns.

Even though we have to conclude that the small nuclear family arose with the beginnings of modern capitalism rather than with the Industrial Revolution two or three centuries later, industrialization may still have had an impact elsewhere. In Japan, for example, from the seventeenth to the nineteenth centuries the extended family was widespread despite extensive capitalist development, yet in modern Japan the small nuclear family has clearly become the norm. The nuclear family is really the only type of family well suited to modern, urban-industrial settings, with their patterns of work organization and the tremendous geographical mobility of the population.

From the Premodern to the Modern Family

Sometime between the seventeenth and nineteenth centuries family patterns in the most economically advanced Western societies underwent dramatic changes, many of which have been carefully studied by such historians as Edward Shorter (1975) and Lawrence Stone (1979). They characterize what they call the premodern family in the following terms:

1. There is little evidence that the relationship between husband and wife was one of strong affection and companionship.
2. Romantic love existed, as it does in all societies, but it played little role in the selection of marriage partners. Most marriages were arranged, and economic considerations were the basis for the arrangement. A wife's primary value was economic.
3. The parent-child relationship had little sentimentality. Mothers seldom nursed their own children, usually sending them out to wet nurses, and children were frequently treated in ways that would be considered extreme forms of child abuse and neglect by today's standards. Children were often given the name of a sibling who had died, which suggests no conception of the child as a unique individual with a distinct personality.
4. The premodern family had a striking lack of separateness or privacy from the rest of society. Outsiders interacted frequently with family members, and the social relations between family members and outsiders were often as close as the social relations within the family.

In sum, the premodern family was much more an economic—and, I would add, reproductive—than a sentimental or emotional unit. It was preoccupied with reproduction and the intergenerational transmission of property.

In the seventeenth and eighteenth centuries this mode of family life began to give way to another. The modern family was in the process of being born. Stone (1979) has suggested four fundamental changes that the family underwent in this process of modernization:

1. Increasing ties of affection developed between family members. Romantic love blossomed and gradually became the basis for marriage. Increasingly, young people rejected the interference of their families in their choice of a spouse, and

marriage came to be seen more and more as a relationship of companionship, intimacy, and exclusivity—as companionate marriage. The revolution in sentiment also characterized relations between parents and children. Child neglect and abuse declined markedly and there was a growing concern for the well-being of children, both physically and psychologically.

2. Individuals increasingly began to feel that they had a right to individual freedom and happiness in marriage.

3. Concern for sexual pleasure grew and there was an increasing tendency to separate sex from sin and guilt. The frequency of premarital sex increased, and marital sex was given more erotic significance.

4. There were increasing demands for a private family life. The family became an increasingly privatized social unit in which the boundaries between it and the surrounding society became much more sharply drawn. Shorter (1975) has called this the "rise of domesticity."

These dramatic family changes have been linked by Shorter to the rise of capitalism, in particular to the rising standards of living and the economic individualism produced by it. In premodern times infant and child mortality rates were extremely high, and parents knew that many of their children, perhaps half or more, would not survive past their first few years of life. Under these circumstances, parents would have restricted their emotional investment in children in order to reduce the pain that they would feel at the death of a child. These emotions need to be seen in the context of parenting strategies in different kinds of environments. In biomaterialist terms, low emotional investment in children was part of a more r-selected rather than K-selected strategy of parental care, i.e., one involving having many offspring but investing minimally in each. As Andrea Wiley and Leslie Carlin (1999) have shown, strong emotional attachment to infants and children and intensive parental investment are parental behaviors that are mainly limited to societies with both low mortality and low fertility, i.e., today's post-demographic transition societies. In premodern Europe, with its high rates of both mortality and fertility, strong attachment to any given infant or young child was unlikely.

Whereas changes in parent-child relations can be linked to standards of living, the increasing sentimentality of husband-wife relations is more likely to be associated with the economic and moral individualism so characteristic of capitalism. As Shorter (1975:259) has argued, "capitalism exerted its impact on romantic love through involvement in the market labor force: economic individualism leads to cultural egoism; private gratification becomes more important than fitting into the common weal; the wish to be free produces the illegitimacy explosion."

As for the rise of domesticity—the family's increasing separation from the rest of society—Christopher Lasch (1977) emphasizes the family's becoming what he has called a "haven in a heartless world." Capitalism became increasingly ruthless as it evolved, and individuals who were in the center of the maelstrom felt a need for a refuge from all that. They needed to escape, if only temporarily, from the slings and arrows of business competition. As Lasch has said, in the nineteenth century in particular the family increasingly became a last refuge of love and human decency in a world that had grown more savage and warlike.

A NOTE ON PARENTAL INVESTMENT

In a recent article, Jeremy Freese and Brian Powell (1999) attempt to test the well-known hypothesis of Robert Trivers and Dan Willard (1973) that parental investment in children of a particular sex varies by social status. Parents of high social status will tend to invest more in sons than in daughters, whereas parents of low social status will tend to invest more in daughters than in sons. Although much research on a variety of preindustrial societies shows considerable support for the Trivers-Willard hypothesis (e.g., Dickemann, 1979a; Cronk, 1989; Irons, 2000), Freese and Powell are interested in determining whether it will apply to a modern industrial society, specifically the United States. This is partly because Trivers and Willard themselves suggest that the hypothesis should apply to the contemporary United States, but also because Freese and Powell claim (quite dubiously, as we will see below) that "to expect the Trivers-Willard hypothesis to hold under contemporary conditions is consistent with the prevailing theoretical logic of sociobiology" (1999:1713). Freese and Powell's test of the applicability of the Trivers-Willard hypothesis to the United States makes use of the National Educational Longitudinal Study, which surveyed nearly 25,000 eighth-graders in 1988. They supplemented their analysis of this data set with data from the 1980 High School and Beyond study. Their results show that high-status and low-status parents invested about equally in both sons and daughters. When there was a difference in the nature of parental investment by social status, it usually went in the opposite direction to the proposed one: High-status parents invested more in daughters than in sons (although the degree of differential investment was not large).

Freese and Powell's assertion to the contrary, the contemporary United States is not an appropriate society for testing the Trivers-Willard hypothesis. Even if Trivers and Willard believe that their hypothesis should apply universally, there are very good reasons to doubt this. What needs to be shown are the conditions under which it should be expected to hold and the contrasting conditions under which it should be assumed not to hold.

The Trivers-Willard hypothesis is actually a special case of a more general sociobiological hypothesis: Parents will invest more in those offspring with the greatest potential reproductive success. The classic test of Trivers and Willard was carried out by Mildred Dickemann (1979a) in a study referred to in another context in chapter 10. Dickemann looked at parental investment in three different societies: nineteenth-century British India, China between the seventeenth and nineteenth centuries, and medieval Europe. All three of these societies were highly stratified societies in which there was extreme competition for resources and for mates, and in all of them hypergyny was a common practice. Polygyny was practiced in India and China, and in Europe as well until after about the tenth or eleventh century, when polygyny was outlawed and monogamy was imposed by the Church and by law. Dickemann found much greater investment in daughters among lower-status groups and much greater investment in sons in higher-status groups in all three societies. This was indicated by much higher rates of female infanticide among higher-status groups and by the strong efforts made by lower-status parents to provide dowries for their daughters so they could compete for high-status husbands. In Europe female infanticide occurred less frequently among the middle and upper classes than it did in India or China, but female celibacy was common. Differential investment in sons and daughters by social status was especially great in India and China because of polygyny. In highly stratified, polygynous societies, there can be extreme variance in male wealth and male reproductive success; hence the desire of high-status parents to favor sons and lower-status parents to favor daughters. Because it is generally the higher-status males who are polygynous, investment in sons by higher-status parents is the best route to the maximization of the number of grandoffspring, great-grandoffspring, etc. Within such a system, the sons of lower-status parents have less reproductive potential than daughters, and thus arises the practice of lower-status parents providing dowries for their daughters to help them attract high-status, wealthy males who can contribute heavily to the cultural and economic success of generations of descendants.

Dickemann's research helps us to see why the contemporary United States is not an appropriate society for testing the Trivers-Willard hypothesis. Although it is highly stratified, it has socially imposed monogamy, which greatly reduces the variance in male reproductive success. Moreover, the marriage system contains much less hypergyny than in preindustrial agrarian societies, with class endogamy being the general practice. Under such conditions, it is unreasonable to expect that there should be differential investment in sons and daughters by social status. For both lower-status and higher-status parents, the reproductive success of their sons and daughters will in most cases end up being approximately the same, and thus we should expect more or less equal investment in children of both sexes by parents of a wide range of statuses. Given the rapid entry of women into the full-time labor force in the last fifty years, equal investment in daughters and sons makes even more sense.

As noted earlier in this chapter, the importance of the type of marriage system (polygyny vs. monogamy) to parental investment has been shown for preindustrial societies by John Hartung (1976). Recall that in his analysis of *Ethnographic Atlas* societies, Hartung found that polygyny was very strongly associated with a male bias in inheritance. Of the 411 societies he examined, nearly all that practiced general polygyny had a strong or exclusive male bias. Where more limited polygyny prevailed, 80 percent of the societies had a strong or exclusive male bias, and where monogamy was the marriage practice, only slightly more than half of the societies had a strong or exclusive male bias.

Freese and Powell are much too quick to dismiss a well-known sociobiological hypothesis because of results obtained from a single society at a single point in time. Even if the Trivers-Willard hypothesis applied to contemporary industrial societies, Freese and Powell's failure to find support for it would still not falsify the hypothesis. So long as the hypothesis found widespread support in other societies, and it clearly has, Freese and Powell would only have shown how the hypothesis had to be qualified. Monogamy is imposed by law in all industrial societies, but this fact does not falsify the hypothesis that human males are by nature polygynous, since polygyny is extremely common in preindustrial societies.

ADDITIONAL EVIDENCE

Sarah Blaffer Hrdy's recent *Mother Nature: A History of Mothers, Infants, and Natural Selection* (1999) is a brilliant and almost encyclopedic biosocial analysis of motherhood throughout history and across societies. Hrdy shows in great detail just how maternal behavior is the result of the complex interaction between biostructural and ecostructural factors. Although sensitive to the concerns of many feminists (and a feminist herself), Hrdy bursts the balloon of those who claim that motherhood has to be a social construction since mothers often mistreat and abandon their babies and allow them to die. Although there is no such thing as a "maternal instinct," she asserts, motherhood nonetheless rests on a strong biological foundation. The average human female is primed to bond to her infant and to nurture it, but for such behavior to be elicited the conditions for rearing must be adequate. (See, in particular, pages 308–16).

A major social issue and a major topic of social science discussion in the past two decades has been domestic violence. A biomaterialist perspective has a great deal to contribute here. David Buss (2000) reviews a considerable amount of research showing that sexual jealousy is one of the major causes of wife beating, possibly a cultural universal, in all societies (often it is *the* major cause). With respect to child abuse, Korbin (1987) and Gelles (1987) show that children in poor health and thus with poor future reproductive prospects are much more likely to be mistreated than healthy children. Malnourished, apathetic, anorexic, and unresponsive children, as well as children who are physically handicapped and developmentally delayed, are at substantially greater risk for mistreatment. Children are also more likely to be abused if they tax family resources too much, especially when younger children take away resources from older children in whom a great deal has already been invested. Daly and Wilson (1998) show that stepchildren are at much greater risk for abuse than children living with their biological parents, especially for the more severe forms of abuse (such as lethal or near-lethal assault). The story of Cinderella and her evil stepmother and stepsisters is no myth, Daly and Wilson say, and similar stories can be found all over the world. Moreover, the sexual abuse of young girls is much more frequently committed by stepfathers and foster fathers than by natural fathers. The greater abuse of children by steprelatives is perfectly consistent with inclusive fitness theory, and is in fact predicted by it.

In a fascinating article, Low (1990) shows why polygyny and pathogen stress are highly correlated in human societies. Hrdy and Judge (1993) look at the important issue of primogeniture from both biomaterialist and ecomaterialist perspectives. Jankowiak and Fischer (1992), by means of an analysis of cross-cultural data, debunk the idea that romantic love is an invention of the modern world. It is true that it is only with the modernization of the past two or three centuries that romantic love has evolved as the principal basis for marriage, but romantic love has existed in all societies, and the free choice of marriage partners is surprisingly common. Fifty percent of the societies in the SCCS allow individuals to choose a spouse freely, compared to only 33 percent that permit the individual little or no choice. Freedom of choice is most common in small-scale hunter-gatherer and horticultural societies, with approximately 64 percent of these societies allowing the free choice of mates. By contrast, intensive agricultural societies with the plow are least likely to permit a free choice, with only 25 percent doing so. Freedom of choice of a marriage partner has thus declined throughout preindustrial social evolution, only to reverse direction with industrialization and modernization. Little research has explored the reasons for arranged marriages vs. individual choice, but the logical starting point from a Darwinian conflict perspective, I think, would be the extent to which the arrangers (the parents) can realize their genetic interests by choosing their offspring's mates, and also the degree of power that parents have over children. The extent of inequality in societies is likely a crucial factor in both. In the SCCS, only 15 percent of egalitarian societies deprive a son or daughter of the free choice of a mate, whereas 65 percent of highly stratified societies do so. Where there is no resource inequality among men, as in egalitarian societies, it matters little to her parents whom a girl marries, and thus they are not apt to interfere with her choice of a mate. But in highly stratified societies parents will perceive some men—i.e., men of high status and wealth—as much more valuable marriage partners than other men. It is therefore in the parents' economic and genetic interests to try to arrange a marriage with such men, because by doing so they are maximizing the benefits that flow to their grandchildren. This is where dowry comes into the picture. As noted earlier, it seems to be a strategy used by parents to arrange the best marriage for a daughter in monogamous but highly stratified societies. But even (perhaps especially?) in highly stratified polygynous societies parents can benefit enormously from arranging their daughters' marriages. The same logic should also apply to sons, although perhaps in a slightly different way.

NOTES

1.   I have sometimes called this theory the "I'm my own grandpa" theory, in reference to the catchy little song that contains those words.

2.   Westermarck never was able to specify the proximate mechanism whereby close association in early childhood produced an aversion to mating. This problem has been taken up, for the first time as far as I know, by Schneider and Hendrix (2000). On the basis of animal studies, they suggest that the mechanism is olfactory. Family members occupying the same household become familiar with each other's odors, and these odors trigger something in the brain that leads to sexual disinterest or aversion. Schneider and Hendrix's argument needs much more careful testing before it can be confirmed, but they do cite both animal and human evidence that is consistent with their explanation, and thus they are not simply speculating.

3.   See Eric Alden Smith (1998) for further commentary on this complex issue. Smith notes that "ethnographic evidence . . . indicates that polyandry occurs in a number of widely separated human populations, including some foragers (e.g., Eskimo, Paiute, and Shoshone). The general context is often the same: shortage of long-term mating opportunities for males, as defined by local social and economic constraints on marriage and resource control, coupled with some significant advantage to (generally fraternal) male cooperation."

14

Economic Behavior and Economic Systems

It is not from the benevolence of the butcher, or the baker, that we expect our dinner, but from their regard to their own interest. We address ourselves, not to their humanity but to their self-love, and never talk to them of our necessities but of their advantages.

—Adam Smith

Economic systems involve the production, distribution, and exchange of goods and services that people want and find valuable. This chapter explores many of the most important dimensions of economic activity and shows how Darwinian conflict theory can explain a great deal of this activity.

THE SUBSTANTIVISM-FORMALISM CONTROVERSY

In the 1960s and 1970s a debate raged among economic anthropologists that was known as the *substantivism-formalism debate*. The debate was never really settled, although most anthropologists apparently did come down on the substantivist side (Wilk, 1996). The substantivists (e.g., Polanyi, 1957; Dalton, 1967, 1968, 1969; Sahlins, 1972) aimed their sights at modern economists. Modern Western economic theory, they claimed, is useful for the analysis of modern economic systems, but its assumptions are of no use in analyzing preindustrial and precapitalist economies. Indeed, employment of these assumptions can only distort the understanding of precapitalist economic life. Modern economic theory teaches that individuals everywhere are self-interested and are devoted to "maximizing" or "economizing" under conditions of scarcity. Individuals rationally calculate how to achieve their own individual economic ends. The substantivists held that these motives are absent in precapitalist societies. In these societies individuals base economic decisions not on the rational pursuit of selfish ends, but on such things as kinship group affiliation, religious beliefs, or political or other group loyalties. Economic behavior in these societies is not determined by economic decision-making

249

at all, but rather is "embedded" (a favorite substantivist word) in the other institutions of society. Scott Cook (1969:397) summarized the substantivist position in terms of the following postulates:

1. The motive of economic gain is not natural to humans.
2. The expectation of payment for labor is not natural to humans.
3. It is not natural for humans to want to restrict their labor to the unavoidable minimum.
4. In precapitalist societies people labor not for economic reasons but for reasons of reciprocity, competition, joy of work, and social approval.
5. In precapitalist societies, economic behavior is embedded in social relations, and it is noneconomic motives that determine the distribution of material goods.
6. The social life of humans in precapitalist societies is not based on individual food collection solely for the use of self and family.
7. Individual acts of "truck, barter, and exchange" are very seldom found in pre-capitalist societies.

The formalists responded to these claims by acknowledging that capitalist and precapitalist economic behavior certainly differ in important respects, but they insisted that "economizing" and "maximizing" are universal human motives. In all societies, they claimed, resources are scarce and humans are self-interested actors who deliberate and rationally make decisions regarding how to use these resources for their own individual benefit. The formalists were, in essence, using the basic principles of what later came to be known, at least in sociology, as rational choice theory to study economic behavior in precapitalist societies.

Although I do not cast my lot with the substantivists, there are some respects in which they are correct, at least in a very general sense. For example, the profit motive is clearly not present in all societies (Dowling, 1979), and many societies do not have money. Even those societies that do have a type of money often use it in ways that are very different from its use in modern Western societies. Failure to recognize this has gotten economists into serious trouble. Early in the twentieth century, for example, the economist W.E. Armstrong (1924, 1928) studied the monetary system of the Rossel Islanders, a tribal society located in the southern Pacific. The Rossel Islanders had a kind of money known as shell money, which Armstrong believed was essentially equivalent to Western money. According to George Dalton (1965), Armstrong came to all kinds of erroneous conclusions about Rossel Island shell money because he could only think of it in terms of what Western money was like, i.e., as a medium of commercial exchange, a standard of value, and a standard of payment. In many ways shell money did not have these characteristics.

Yet by and large it is my contention that the formalists are right, at least in terms of what John Dowling (1979) calls their primary or universal assumptions, viz., that people's wants are infinitely expandable and that people everywhere behave rationally and are driven by self-interest. Dowling provides a good deal of evidence to suggest that these assumptions are correct, citing Malinowski to the effect that "whenever the native can evade his obligations without the loss of prestige, or without the prospective loss of gain, he does so, exactly as a civilized business man would do" (quoted in Dowling, 1979:297).

Morris Silver (1995) has scrutinized some of the arguments of Karl Polanyi, the founder of the substantivist approach. He has studied ancient economies in light of Polanyi's assertions about them and has found that these assertions are false. Polanyi's perspective on the ancient economies was that they lacked most of the features of modern capitalism. Polanyi asserted that the ancient world did not contain price-setting markets that worked according to the laws of supply and demand, but Silver finds overwhelming evidence to the contrary. In the ancient Near East there is evidence for the existence of a grain market, with documents showing, for example, sharp variations in barley prices and transactions referring to barley prices in terms of copper or silver. There are many documents that make reference again and again to the fluctuation of prices, suggesting the clear operation of market mechanisms. In Silver's words (1995:105), "The evidence indicates that the ancient economy responded in the usual way to the usual economic forces of supply and demand." There is evidence for private ownership of land and for land markets in ancient Mesopotamia, as well as for the selling and leasing of land throughout Egyptian history. Professional money lenders apparently operated in Mesopotamia, giving interest-bearing loans to merchants for the conduct of business. Sophisticated credit systems also existed. Silver has also uncovered evidence for slave markets and markets for wage laborers, as well as for the extensive use of money as a medium of exchange. Some cities in the ancient world had large spinning and weaving workshops that employed hundreds of people, and their specialization in textiles apparently was rooted in a knowledge of comparative advantage. Most interestingly, Silver shows that the ancient world was familiar with opportunity costs. This familiarity, Silver asserts, "is manifested in a provision of an old Babylonian lease calling for the renter to pay the owner of an ox a sum equal to the value of the services or income forgone" (1995:125).

The substantivists have portrayed peasant economic behavior as guided by nonrational considerations unrelated (or even antagonistic) to a motive of individual gain, but here again the evidence suggests otherwise. Samuel Popkin (1979, 1980) points out that substantivist analyses of peasants focus on peasant economies as "moral economies," i.e., economies driven by norms that are culturally rather than economically determined. Popkin shows that, on the contrary, the norms of peasant life are highly flexible and shift in accordance with individual calculation of personal gain. Peasants, like people everywhere, are self-interested actors. "Ironically," Popkin says, "scattered fields, frequently cited as an example of a conservative, 'safety-first' strategy followed by peasants, constitutes an individual-level strategy for avoiding risk which suggests that village-wide insurance schemes are not very comprehensive. It is a clear example of a conflict between individual and group rationality" (1980:443). Popkin also shows that the extensive use of interest and credit in peasant villages contradicts the moral economic (substantivist) approach. The fact that individual peasants bid for credit indicates that they are concerned with maximizing their resources and contradicts the notion that they are acting in terms of the welfare of the entire village. The existence of social stratification in peasant villages also demonstrates that peasants are acting largely out of concern for their own well-being and that of their families.

To my mind, what really confirms the formalist view is the behavior of hunter-gatherers. Here we have people living in the closest thing possible to the ancestral environment. They behave according to the rational calculation of self-interest? Indeed, the evidence is over-whelming that they do. Sharing and reciprocity, patterns of land tenure, hunting strategies, and many other features of hunter-gatherer life can only be understood from this perspec-tive. In a later section we shall examine hunter-gatherer behavior in terms of the pursuit of individual self-interest. (For an excellent general discussion of how well hunter-gatherer so-cieties conform to the formalist model, see Winterhalder, 1993, who places his discussion within the context of a critique of the substantivism of Marshall Sahlins, 1972.) In addi-tion, the discussion in a later section of economic distribution and exchange in the full range of precapitalist societies will solidify this argument.

FOOD: PREFERENCES AND AVOIDANCES

Innate Tastes

Enough evidence has by now accumulated to sustain the argument that humans have a number of innate tastes and preferences. Newborn babies exhibit a clear liking for sweet substances and a clear dislike of bitter ones (Harris, 1987b; Rozin, 1987). Humans ac-quired their "sweet tooth" in the ancestral environment, or perhaps even inherited it from their primate ancestors, since the highly nutritive fruits that they ate in large quan-tity contained considerable amounts of sugar. The innate desire for sweet substances is also suggested by the fact that sweet foods seem to be universally liked. Some societies have had a nonsugar tradition, but no society has rejected sweet-tasting beverages and foods when they have been introduced from the outside (Mintz, 1985; cited in Harris, 1989). The innate aversion to bitter substances seems to be an evolved adaptation that has protected humans against ingesting poisonous or at least dangerous substances (Harris, 1989).

Perhaps the most important innate human preference is for meat (Rozin, 1987). As Harris (1987b:80) has pointed out, "It cannot be mere coincidence that meat and other animal products . . . play a special role in the foodways of most human populations, par-ticularly as a focus of exchange, redistribution, and social cohesion." In the vast major-ity of societies, a meal is not considered complete without meat. Many societies distin-guish between hunger in general and "meat hunger," often having a special word for the latter (Harris, 1985). In highly stratified societies, it is common for people of high so-cial status and wealth to eat much more meat than people farther down the class struc-ture, and meat is also a major focus of the feasts that are such a prominent part of the lives of preindustrial peoples (Harris, 1985). Throughout the last 10,000 years of prein-dustrial social evolution, meat has declined in the diet in favor of grains and other plant foods, but this is the result of growing population pressure and the increased difficulty of raising animals for food. It is certainly not the result of changing human preferences.

H. Leon Abrams (1987) has shown that all human societies include at least some an-imal proteins and fats in their diets and place a very high value on these substances. Al-though some individuals and groups throughout history have been vegetarian, vegetari-anism has never existed at the level of an entire society. Meat has also played a very important role in the diet throughout hominid evolution, and meat was "the mainstay for paleolithic humankind" (Abrams, 1987:209). The most commonly consumed animals and animal products throughout the world's societies have been, in rank order, chicken (flesh and eggs), cattle (flesh and milk), pigs, goats, fish, and sheep. Fewer societies, but still a sizable number, have consumed ducks, turtles, dogs, and rats (Abrams, 1987). Many societies have also consumed insects in large numbers, as we shall see below.

What explains the universal desire for meat? The answer is that humans have an innate preference for it, or at the very least an innate tendency to learn to prefer animal foods, and they have this desire or tendency because of the special nutritional qualities that meat provides (Harris, 1985). Animal flesh is a much better source of protein than plant foods in that important amino acids can be obtained far more efficiently from meat than from plants. But meat also has other nutritional advantages over plant foods, as Leslie Lieberman explains (1987:231):

> Meat provides . . . essential minerals (e.g., iron and zinc); vitamins that are often difficult to obtain elsewhere (e.g., B_{12}); fat (although meat is relatively low in the essential fat linoleic acid); and some glucose, especially in raw muscle meat and liver. Moreover, meat provides these nutrients in an easily digested form and is nutrient-dense. That is, meat is a concentrated form of macro- and micro-nutrients; and therefore much smaller quantities of meat and other animal foods than of vegetables are needed to fulfill the RDAs for protein, fat, iron, zinc, and other nutrients. For example, to obtain eight grams of protein you could eat as little as one ounce of cooked lean meat or one extra large egg but you would need to eat four slices of enriched bread or four medium-sized potatoes for the same protein intake.

An Ecomaterialist Perspective on Food Preferences and Food Taboos

This biomaterialist perspective on food must be complemented with an ecomaterialist perspective in order to explain very much about human dietary preferences. No one has done more to develop an ecomaterialist perspective on food than Marvin Harris (1974, 1977, 1985). Harris's overall theory is that humans build their diets around the costs and benefits of various types of food sources relevant to the ecological, demographic, technological, and economic conditions within which they live. Harris has tried to provide an explicit and stark alternative to structuralist theories of food; food is not "good to think," Harris says, but rather is "good to eat."

Harris's most famous theories have concerned the Hindu sanctification of the cow and the Jewish-Moslem abomination of the pig (1966, 1974, 1977, 1985). Although the refusal of Hindus to eat the cow has usually been attributed to irrational religious beliefs, Harris argues that the cow is not eaten because it is much more valuable alive than dead. The cow is critical as a traction animal to plow the fields, and it is also valuable as a source of manure for fertilizer. Its manure is also used as a material for making floors—it dries into a hard substance that is easy to keep clean—and plastering walls, and it is used as well as a cooking fuel. Harris points out that Hindu farmers who yielded to temptation during times of famine or drought to slaughter their cattle could never plow again and thus had to relinquish their farms and move into the overcrowded cities to scratch out a living as best they could. Since keeping the cow alive was so important, and since temptation to slaughter it occurred often, it was necessary to provide a mechanism to overcome this temptation. A religious taboo making it a sacrilegious act to kill and consume the cow arose as the best way of achieving this aim.

Harris notes that there was a time—probably sometime before AD 700—in Hindu history when there was no taboo on killing and eating cattle. During this time Brahmin priests were ritual slaughterers and consumers of cattle rather than ritual protectors of them. What caused the transformation? Harris's answer focuses on population pressure and resource scarcity. As population grew over time—and India has had one of the densest populations in the world for several millennia—farms became smaller and smaller and eventually a point was reached whereby animals could no longer be raised for food because they competed directly with humans. All animals except the cow, that is. It could not be eliminated because of its critical role as a traction animal, and so it gradually became the subject of divine interdiction.

The Hindu taboo on cattle is what we might call a "positive taboo," by which I mean that the animal is tabooed as a food source because it is seen in such a favorable way. The majority of food taboos have been "negative taboos," i.e., taboos in which animals are forbidden as food sources because they are perceived to have unfavorable and undesirable qualities. The pig, first tabooed by the ancient Israelities and then later by Islam, is such a taboo. The ancient Israelites' own rationale for tabooing the pig was that it was a dirty animal that carried disease, thus making it unfit for human consumption. The later Muslim taboo on the pig was framed in similar terms. But, as Harris explains, the pig is no more a carrier of disease than many other farm animals, and it is not especially dirty when it is found in the type of environment for which it is best suited. Pigs are best suited to cool, forested environments and do poorly in hot environments with little shade. This is because they cannot sweat. In hot, dry environments, they wallow in mud, garbage, and their own feces and urine in order to keep cool, behavior that is no doubt responsible for the origin of the belief that they are inherently dirty.

Harris explains that the ancestors of the ancient Israelites once raised pigs for food, but during these times the environment they inhabited was suitable for pigs. Eventually, however, with population growth and geographical expansion much woodland was cut down and the environment became less and less adequate for raising pigs. They became increasingly costly because they had to be provided artificial sources of shade and moisture, and thus to raise pigs for food was to forgo something else. As a result, they gradually came to be redefined in negative terms, a definition that was encoded in religion, in order to overcome the temptation to raise and eat them. Harris points out that the pig is highly regarded throughout the world and widely used as a food source (this is confirmed by Abrams, 1987, who shows them to be the third most widely consumed animal worldwide), and thus one must explain why only the Jews and the Muslims have abominated them. The answer, we see, is that the members of these religions lived originally in environments in which the costs of raising pigs exceeded their benefits. Harris's argument is reinforced by evidence that pigs were once widely consumed in Scotland, but with the spread of agriculture and the erosion of forests in the Scottish highlands pig raising had virtually ceased by the seventeenth century and pigs came to be regarded with considerable disdain (Ross, 1987). Eric Ross quotes an English officer who wrote in the 1730s: "I own I never saw any swine among the mountains, and there is good reason for it; those people have no offal wherewith to feed them; and were they to give them other food, one single sow would devour all the provisions of a family" (1987:26–27).

The patterns of milk consumption and milk aversion throughout the world, and the reasons for each, have been closely analyzed by Harris (1985) and William Durham (1991). The biggest milk drinkers in the world are located in northern Europe, especially in the British Isles, Scandinavia, Germany, and the Netherlands. The continent of Africa is divided, with some milk drinkers and some milk avoiders. It is in Asia, especially in East and Southeast Asia, that the majority of the world's milk avoiders are located. It turns out that there is a very high correlation between the degree to which the members of a society drink milk and their physiological capacity to digest it. In order to digest the milk sugar lactose, one needs the enzyme lactase. It is now widely recognized that the original human condition (i.e., 8,000 or more years ago) was one in which infants and children possessed this enzyme but gradually lost it in adolescence or adulthood. When adults who cannot digest lactose drink milk they suffer from severe gastrointestinal distress. This original human condition came to be modified for northern Europeans and some Africans but not for East and Southeast Asians. The former became lactase-sufficient (and thus lactose absorbers) as adolescents and adults, but the latter remained lactase-insufficient (and thus lactose malabsorbers). Durham (1991) has presented the following figures for lactose absorbers by region and type of economy: four hunter-gatherer societies (traditionally lacking dairy animals), 12.6 percent; five nondairying agriculturalists, 15.5 percent; five recently dairying agriculturalists, 11.9 percent; five milk-dependent pastoralists, 91.3 percent; sixteen dairying peoples of North Africa and the Mediterranean, 38.8 percent; twelve northern European societies, 91.5 percent; and thirteen populations of mixed dairying and nondairying ancestry, 62.0 percent. Harris points out that less than 5 percent of Chinese, Japanese, Korean, and other East Asian adults are lactose absorbers.

By and large, those populations with a high percentage of lactase-sufficient individuals have had a long history of dairying and milk drinking. It appears that the genetic evolution of lactase-sufficiency and a culture devoted to dairying and milk drinking have coevolved. How did it happen? With the movement of human agricultural populations into northern Europe sometime after 8,000 years ago, people would have been at risk for bone diseases like osteomalacia and rickets, diseases due to a deficiency of calcium. Northern Europeans would have been at risk for these diseases because their agricultural system did not include green, leafy vegetables (a good source of calcium), and because the rainy climate provided few sunny days (sunlight helps the body manufacture vitamin D_3, which improves calcium absorption). Milk, of course, is an excellent source of calcium, and lactose helps the body absorb calcium; it could thus be of great advantage to those individuals who could continue to drink it throughout life. Selective pressure was therefore placed on lactase-sufficient individuals, whose better health would make them more likely to survive and reproduce. This put pressure on populations to develop dairying, and so dairying, milk consumption, and lactase-sufficiency evolved in tandem. It was a case of gene-culture coevolution.

Why did East and Southeast Asian peoples never develop dairying, milk consumption, and a high percentage of lactose absorbers? Harris argues that they had no real need to do so because their agriculture had long contained green, leafy vegetables, and they also had soybeans, an excellent source of calcium. Moreover, plenty of sunny days allowed the body to make more vitamin D_3 and thus absorb calcium better. As for African populations, many of these were nondairying agriculturalists who were under no evolutionary pressure to drink milk; many other African populations were devoted to an economy of pastoralism in areas where agriculture was difficult or impossible, and it is these populations that came to contain a high percentage of lactose absorbers. It is interesting to note that there are populations with dairying traditions in which a high percentage of individuals are lactose malabsorbers. These are populations that have processed most of their milk into such low-lactose forms as cheese, and consequently they have been under no evolutionary pressure to drink fresh milk (Durham, 1991).

The Acquisition of Food Preferences and Aversions

As Marvin Harris (1985) has pointed out, except for such things as a preference for sweet foods and for meat, human food preferences and aversions are learned. Throughout the world an extremely wide range of animals is eaten, but animals that are highly desired in some cultures are thought of as disgusting in others (Rozin and Fallon, 1987). The Chinese abhor milk, thinking of a glass of milk as Western milk drinkers would regard a glass of cow saliva (Harris, 1985). The Yanomamö of the Amazon rain forest eat all kinds of insects, including large spiders, animals that are abhorrent to the members of modern industrial societies. The Yanomamö's favorite delicacy is fresh monkey brains, and yet they regard peanut butter and hot dogs with disgust because they think of the former as some kind of feces and the latter as an animal penis (Chagnon, 1983). The Yanomamö are also like the Chinese in abhoring milk. Many Eskimo groups eat decayed meat and the contents of animal guts (Rozin and Fallon, 1987). One could go on and on in the same vein.

Yet despite the fact that most food preferences and aversions are learned, they are not learned in a vacuum. There seems to be a brain module that directs the learning of preferences and aversions in an evolutionarily adaptive way. Elizabeth Cashdan (1994) proposes that the mode of learning of food tastes and distastes has evolved by natural selection, and she goes on to claim that there is a critical or sensitive period for learning food tastes. This critical period, she argues, is largely confined to the first two years of life. Cashdan carried out a study of American children in which she found that children younger than two were highly receptive to novel foods. However, after the age of two their receptivity to novel foods dropped sharply and continued to drop between the ages of three and four. Cashdan's findings are consistent with data obtained by Rozin, Hammer, Oster, Horowitz, and Marmora (1986), who found that children are much less willing to eat "disgust" food substances once they reach their second birthday. What appears to be happening is that children will eat almost anything offered them by their parents until the age of two and come to regard such foods as "normal" or "proper" foods. Foods encountered after this age, especially animal foods, are regarded with distaste and often outright disgust (Pinker, 1997). Cashdan shows that for her sample of American children there is a very close relationship between receptivity to novel foods and the likelihood of poisonings. Almost 40 percent of all poisonings happen to children who are two years old or younger, and the likelihood of poisoning drops in almost exactly the same fashion as the emergence of disgust reactions. This leads Cashdan to conclude that "sensitive period learning probably evolved as an adaptation to the high costs associated with eating toxic and unwholesome foods" (1994:287). Why is it that disgust reactions occur almost entirely with respect to animal rather than plant foods? Rozin and Fallon (1987) have summarized a variety of interpretations, but I find none of these convincing. This remains a puzzle for further research.

PREINDUSTRIAL MODES OF SUBSISTENCE TECHNOLOGY

For some 99 percent of human existence, people lived in small-scale societies dependent entirely on the the hunting of wild animals and the gathering of wild plant foods. A few of these societies have survived into the modern world and most of what we know about the hunting and gathering way of life is based on studies of these contemporary societies. In hunter-gatherer societies, it is usually men who do the hunting, especially the hunting of big game, and gathering is primarily an activity engaged in by women. Technology is extremely rudimentary, with men hunting with spears, spear throwers, and the bow and arrow. Women usually employ some kind of digging stick if they are taking roots or tubers out of the ground. Otherwise, no gathering technology is really needed. In most environments hunter-gatherers must be nomadic, moving camp frequently in order to have an adequate supply of game and plant foods. They must also remain at extremely low levels of population density in order not to deplete their resources beyond their natural recovery points. Usually hunter-gatherer bands do not exceed fifty members, often being much smaller. In more bountiful environments, such as those of the Indian tribes living along the northwest coast of North America, resources may be sufficient to provide for permanent settlements of hundreds of people.

Beginning around 10,000 years ago in the Middle East and somewhat later in other parts of the world, there was a major technological revolution known as the Neolithic Revolution. This revolution ushered in the first societies that made use of some type of agriculture. The earliest agriculture is best known as horticulture, which means the cultivation of garden sites using hand tools. Horticultural societies are still found today in such parts of the world as Africa, Southeast Asia, New Guinea, and South America. The most common form of horticulture is what is known as slash-and-burn cultivation. Here men cut down the forest and burn off the accumulated debris. The wood ashes that result are spread around the garden plot and make a passable fertilizer. The garden will be cultivated for a few years and then abandoned—allowed to remain fallow—in favor of a new garden, although eventually the first garden site will be cultivated again. In most cases the primary cultivators will be women; they are more likely than men to tend the crops and harvest them. Unlike most hunter-gatherers, horticulturalists occupy permanent settlements, living in villages that may number in the hundreds. Gerhard Lenski (1966, 1970) has drawn a distinction between simple and advanced horticulturalists, and he distinguishes between them on the basis of the technology they use for tending the soil. Simple horticulturalists cultivate using only wooden digging sticks, whereas advanced horticulturalists use metal hoes. I have modified Lenski's distinction by focusing on the length of the fallow period rather than the cultivating tool (Sanderson, 1995a). For me, simple horticulturalists are those that have long fallow periods. They might cultivate a garden for, say, one to three years, and then allow it to remain fallow for another twenty to thirty years. What I call intensive horticulturalists, on the other hand, tend to cultivate a garden plot for a longer time and then allow it to remain fallow for a shorter period. They might, for example, cultivate for five years and then fallow for only five to ten years. In some cases, such as aboriginal Hawaii and other parts of Polynesia, the cultivation of land may become continuous, with no fallow period at all. Some horticulturalists have acquired domesticated animals, such as pigs and chickens, but many have not. The latter still depend on hunting for their supply of meat.

Another type of society dependent on agriculture is what sociologists call an agrarian society and anthropologists an intensive agricultural society, which emerged in human history about 4,000 years ago. Agrarian societies practice a more technologically sophisticated form of agriculture in which large plots of land (fields) are completely cleared of shrubs and trees and cultivated with the use of the plow and traction animals. Land is cultivated permanently or semipermanently (i.e., with the use of crop rotation) and is extensively fertilized with animal manure and other products. In drier parts of the world extensive irrigation systems have had to be constructed in order to provide crops with sufficient water. Because the agrarian mode of subsistence is physically demanding and requires extensive labor inputs, it is men who do the bulk of the agricultural work. For this reason, Ester Boserup (1965, 1970) has called horticultural societies "female-farming" societies and agrarian societies "male-farming" societies. The latter emerged sometime between 4,000 and 5,000 years ago and have dominated world history until the last century or two. Lenski (1966, 1970) has distinguished between simple and advanced agrarian societies. Advanced agrarian societies have acquired iron tools and weapons, whereas simple agrarian societies have tools and weapons made of other metals, normally bronze. There are actually a number of societies, or parts of societies, that use a very intensive mode of agriculture but do not use the plow. These societies can for all practical purposes be classified along with agrarian societies because they cultivate the land permanently, and, like agrarian societies, are extremely productive economically. In some parts of China and Southeast Asia, for example, one finds intensive agricultural societies without the plow.

Pastoral societies are a highly specialized type of society found in very dry regions of the world where agriculture is difficult or impossible. Pastoralists live off animal herds and either practice no agriculture or do so only minimally. They live off the products— meat to some extent, but mostly blood and milk and milk products—supplied by their animals, which are normally goats, sheep, cattle, camels, or even reindeer. Like hunter-gatherers, pastoralists are nomadic, moving in conjunction with the needs and demands of their animals. Pastoralists today are mostly found in the Middle East, North and East Africa, and parts of Siberia.

Leaving out pastoral societies, the modes of subsistence technology we have been discussing can be arranged in an evolutionary sequence in terms of the level of intensity of the mode of subsistence, i.e., how much subsistence demands in terms of the use of labor, time, resources, and technology. This evolutionary typology corresponds closely to the actual historical emergence of these types of societies over the past 10,000 years. What has been responsible for the shift from one subsistence type to another? The answer is ecomaterialist, specifically demographic. In a classic work, Ester Boserup (1965) proposed that in agricultural societies (as in all societies) people are following a kind of Law of Least Effort. They are attempting to minimize inputs of time and energy and wish to use the agricultural practices that will make this possible. They only shift to a more intensive mode of agricultural production when population pressure has built up and there is a need for greater economic production to feed more mouths and to try to maintain an acceptable standard of living. Mark Cohen (1977, 1985) has extended the logic of Boserup's argument to the transition from hunting and gathering to horticulture. He argues that knowledge of agriculture probably existed among hunter-gatherers for tens of thousands of years but was not used because the hunter-gatherer mode of subsistence provided an acceptable standard of living with low labor inputs. By around 10,000 years ago, Cohen argues, a prehistoric "food crisis" had begun to emerge and it was at that point that hunter-gatherers began to incorporate agriculture into their subsistence practices. As population continued to grow, agriculture gradually replaced hunting and gathering.

Archaeological and historical data have shown a close correlation between population density and the mode of subsistence. But ethnographic data also show the same thing. Using the SCCS, I cross-tabulated subsistence type with population density and found an extremely strong relationship. Eighty-one percent of foraging societies have population densities of less than one person per square mile, whereas 62 percent of intensive agriculturalists with the plow have population densities of more than one-hundred persons per square mile. The Pearson r for this relationship is .726. Subsistence type was also closely related to stage of political evolution (r = .670) and community size (r = .587). When these three independent variables were entered into a multiple regression analysis with subsistence type as the dependent variable, the three variables together explained 65 percent of the total variance. Population density explained the most, but stage of political evolution was a fairly close second.

In additional analyses, various subsistence variables were put into regression equations with the same three independent variables along with social stratification. Population density and social stratification explained 59 percent of the variance in the importance of hunting and gathering, with population density explaining a clear majority of this. Population density turned out to be clearly the best predictor of the degree of subsistence contributed by hunting, the degree of subsistence contributed by gathering, the degree of subsistence contributed by agriculture, and the length of the fallow period. However, regarding the use of the plow, stage of political evolution was by far the best predictor, with population density a distant second. Only 9 percent of bands and tribes use the plow, but 67 percent of small states and 100 percent of large states use the plow. It is not completely clear why we should get this result for the use of the plow when population density is clearly the main determinant of subsistence practices as a whole. Lenski (1966, 1970) has argued that the plow was adopted because of its superiority as an instrument of cultivation. This is undoubtedly true, but it could be that the desire to use the plow to increase production has a political context: The plow was adopted when the aim was to generate more surplus for elites to skim off, not to feed more mouths. Thus, at least one aspect of subsistence may have a polimaterialist dimension.

Frederic Pryor (1985) has provided an ecomaterialist alternative to this polimaterialist argument. On the basis of cross-cultural research, he shows that there are several conditions that must be present before the plow is adopted. These are the availability of animals that can be domesticated for purposes of traction, land that is suitable for plowing, short or nonexistent fallowing periods, and the cultivation of "plow-positive" crops such as wheat, barley, rye, and wet rice. Wheat, barley, and rye are crops that require extensive preparation of the land and enough land to produce a sufficient number of calories to feed a family. Wet rice requires that the land can be prepared for cultivation in a short period of time. In these instances the plow contributes heavily to labor productivity. In the absence of further research it is not clear whether the polimaterialist argument, Pryor's ecomaterialist argument, or some combination of the two is the right explanation. In all likelihood it is a combination of the two.[1]

HUNTER-GATHERER SOCIETIES

Hunter-Gatherers or Gatherer-Hunters?

It was during the 1960s that hunter-gatherer societies first became a central object of anthropological research. At this time Richard Lee (1968), one of the leaders in the study of hunter-gatherers, estimated that hunter-gatherers derived approximately two-thirds of their subsistence from gathered rather than hunted foods. This idea was widely accepted, but it turned out to be wrong. Lee was perhaps overgeneralizing from his study of the !Kung, who did in fact draw about two-thirds of their subsistence from gathered foods. Carol Ember (1978) took a closer look at the subsistence patterns of 181 hunter-gatherer societies drawn from the *Ethnographic Atlas* and found that gathered foods provided more than half of the calories people were consuming in only 23 percent of the societies. Moreover, she found that gathering was the most important foraging activity in only 30 percent of the societies, but that hunting (including fishing) was the most important activity in 63 percent. Data presented by Kelly (1995) on 123 hunter-gatherer societies show enormous variation among societies in the proportion of food contributed by hunting or gathering. Among some Eskimo groups, all of the diet is provided by hunting or fishing, and in many others the figure is 90 percent or more. At the other extreme are groups like the Walpiri, !Kung, G/wi, Siriono, Chenchu, and Penan, where anywhere from 70 to 85 percent of the diet comes from gathered foods. This wide variation can be explained ecomaterialistically. I reanalyzed Kelly's data and found that the critical factor was mean annual temperature. Percentage of the diet contributed by gathered foods correlated .638 (Pearson r) with temperature, whereas percentage contributed by fishing correlated −.470 and percentage contributed by hunting correlated −.151. This means that gathered foods form a larger part of the diet in warm or hot regions whereas meat constitutes a bigger part of the diet in cold regions.

Hunter-Gatherers as Optimal Foragers

In the 1970s an approach to the study of how hunter-gatherers spend their time foraging was developed under the name of *optimal foraging theory* (e.g., Winterhalder and

Smith, 1981; E.A. Smith, 1983; Hawkes, Hill, and O'Connell, 1982; Hawkes and O'Connell, 1985; Winterhalder, 1987; Kaplan and Hill, 1992; Kelly, 1995). Based on Darwinian assumptions, optimal foraging theory was originally applied to the study of nonhuman animals but in due time came to have human applications. The theory assumes that natural selection has designed humans to forage in such a way that they receive the greatest possible benefit for individual survival and reproductive success. It assumes that foragers are trying to maximize their rate of energy return for any given unit of foraging time.

Optimal foraging theory contains two separate models, known respectively as the *diet-breadth* (or *prey choice*) model and the *patch-choice* model (E.A. Smith, 1983; Winterhalder, 1987; Kelly, 1995). The diet-breadth model can be summarized in the following way:

1. A forager encounters prey types in a random fashion, i.e., prey types are distributed throughout a foraging area in approximately the same relative proportions.
2. Total foraging time is divided into two separate categories, *search time* and *handling time*. Search time is the amount of time it takes to locate a plant or animal, whereas handling time is the amount of time it takes to harvest, capture, and consume the plant or animal once it has been encountered. This process of time allocation involves opportunity costs in the sense that time spent handling any item means that the same unit of time is unavailable for searching for other items.
3. Foragers rank food items along a single continuum of utility, which is the net energy or food value they obtain from any item relative to the amount of time they spend handling it.
4. Foragers achieve an optimal diet by continuing to collect food items in an order of descending rank until such time as the expected return in net energy is maximized for every unit of foraging time. If a newly encountered food item yields a lower rate of return than the rate that a forager is currently experiencing, it will be ignored.

Kaplan and Hill (1992:170–71) summarize the diet-breadth model as follows:

> First, all resources are ranked in descending order of their profitability. The prey type that yields the highest return upon encounter . . . should always be pursued. Other lower-ranked resources should be included sequentially in the set to be pursued until the next most profitable resource yields a lower rate of return upon encounter than could be obtained by continuing to search for and pursue the more profitable items. None of the resources that are ranked lower in profitability should be pursued when encountered.

An extremely important implication of the diet-breadth model is that decisions to include a food item in the diet are made not in terms of that item's own availability, but rather on the availability of a higher-ranked item. For example, Hadza hunters focus on large game and generally ignore small game even though the latter are much more abundant. Several anthropologists carried out an experiment in which they asked the Hadza to concentrate only on hunting small game. When the hunters did this, their average return per unit of time for small game was significantly lower than the average return for large game, so in ignoring small game Hadza hunters are foraging optimally (Kelly, 1995).

The patch-choice model (sometimes called the *marginal value theorem*) involves decisions concerning whether or not foragers should leave one foraging patch for another. This model assumes that foraging in any patch gradually depletes the resource level of that patch, which in turn leads to a decline in that patch's net return rate. Thus, "the optimal solution is to leave each patch when the marginal capture rate (i.e., the instantaneous capture rate at the end of a foraging period within that patch) is equal to the overall mean capture rate (averaged over the entire set of patches utilized, including travel time between patches)" (E.A. Smith, 1983:631). The patch-choice model leads to several predictions:

1. Foragers should abandon a patch when its resources have been depleted to a point such that foraging in other patches will produce higher returns per unit of time.
2. As the overall productivity of a set of patches—a habitat or environment—increases, foragers should spend less time in any given patch.
3. Any patch not yet being used by foragers should not be included in the total set of foraged patches unless it is capable of producing a marginal return rate that is at least equal to the average return rate for the entire set of patches.

Numerous studies have been carried out attempting to test the diet-breadth model (summarized in E.A. Smith, 1983, and Kaplan and Hill, 1992). These include Winterhalder (1977, 1981) on the Cree, O'Connell and Hawkes (1981) on the Alyawara of Australia, Hawkes, Hill, and O'Connell (1982) on the Aché of Paraguay, Keegan (1986) on the Machiguenga of Peru, E.A. Smith (1991) on the Inuit of the Arctic, and Hames and Vickers (1982) on the Yanomamö and two other Amazonian groups. For the most part, the data collected from these diverse societies fit the diet-breadth model reasonably well. An especially illuminating study is that of Hawkes, Hill, and O'Connell (1982) on the Aché. The authors followed a group of Aché foragers on several foraging trips lasting a total of sixty-one days, noting what plants and animals they collected and how much time they spent obtaining and processing them. They found that the Aché conformed closely to optimal foraging theory and reconstructed the Aché optimal diet as shown in Table 14.1. This table shows the rank order of plants and animals in the diet in terms of the ratio of calorie returns to each hour of time spent handling the resource. These results should be interpreted in the following way: If the Aché took only collared peccaries and deer, they would receive an average rate of return of 148 calories per forager per hour. However, if they took paca and coati as well, their average rate of return for all four resources would increase to 405 calories per hour. Likewise, if they also took the third-ranked resources, armadillo and snake, their average rate of return would improve to 546 calories per hour. The Aché are best off if they take all sixteen resources, because this gives them an average return of 872 calories per hour. They will stop collecting a resource only when it reduces the average rate of return for all resources combined. Hawkes, Hill, and O'Connell note that high-ranked resources never drop out of the Aché diet, whereas low-ranked resources move in and out according to the extent to which they or other low-ranked resources are encountered.

Table 14.1 The Rank Order of Plants and Animals in the Aché Diet

Resource	Calories/Hour	Rank	Average Calories/Hour After Resource Added
Collared peccary	65,000	1	
Deer	27,300	1	148
Paca	6,964	2	
Coati	6,964	2	405
Armadillo	5,909	3	
Snake	5,882	3	546
Oranges	5,071	4	625
Bird	4,769	5	632
Honey	3,266	6	660
White-lipped peccary	2,746	7	783
Palm larvae	2,367	8	799
Fish	2,120	9	821
Palm heart	1,526	10	829
Monkey	1,215	11	
Palm fiber	1,200	11	871
Palm fruit	946	12	872

Source: Hawkes, Hill, and O'Connell (1982: table 3, and p. 390).

There have been no attempts to test the patch-choice model rigorously (E.A. Smith, 1983; Kaplan and Hill, 1992), but some studies do present data that are consonant with this model (summarized in E.A. Smith, 1983). These include Winterhalder (1977) on the Cree, O'Connell and Hawkes (1981) on the Alyawara, Hames (1980) on the Yanomamö, and E.A. Smith (1980) on the Inuit.

One of the great merits of optimal foraging theory is that it shows that the food preferences of foragers are not determined by cultural definitions of what is good to eat (or "good to think"). Rather, preferences themselves derive from a cost-benefit calculus of foraging efficiency. Foods are preferred if they can be collected efficiently relative to other foods. However, one problem with optimal foraging theory is that it is too rigid in its assumption that net energy per unit of foraging time is the only consideration foragers are using. It is clear that they have a preference for animal proteins and fats over plant foods and that such a preference enters into their foraging decisions. As Kaplan and Hill (1992:189) point out,

Aché foragers bias diets away from energy maximization in favor of foods containing high proportions of lipids and protein. During the dry season, Yaminahua foragers of Peru exploited three major food types (wild bananas, caiman, and several species of fish), but would have maximized energy return rates if they only exploited bananas and caiman (Hill and Kaplan, 1989; Hill, 1988). Including fish in their diet decreased overall return rate. Similarly, among the Hiwi foragers of Venezuela, men pass by roots that yield 8500 cal/hr on encounter in favor of hunting, which yields an average of 3070 cal/hr (Hill, 1988). Virtually all South American horticulturalists obtain much higher caloric return rates from farming than they do from hunting or fishing (Beckerman, 1989; Hames, 1988), yet most spend considerably more time hunting and fishing than farming (Hames, 1988). In even more extreme cases net energetic return rates from hunting may be negative, and yet horticulturalists still chose to hunt rather than farm exclusively (e.g., Dwyer, 1974; Johnson and Behrens, 1982). This bias in favor of exploiting resources of relatively low energetic profitability but high in protein-lipid content is found in many other human groups and among nonhuman primates (e.g., McGrew, 1979; Terborgh, 1983).

Some nutritional requirements are absolute and inflexible; other nutrient requirements apparently can be met partially or completely by substituting sufficient quantities of an alternative nutrient. This introduces complexities that have yet to receive substantial theoretical or empirical treatment in foraging research.

This strong preference for animal proteins and fats is consistent with what was said earlier about human food preferences. It does not overturn optimal foraging theory, however, but only serves to qualify it. It seems clear that human foragers are not trying to maximize net energy alone, but maximize certain kinds of energy as well.

Mobility, Land Tenure, and Group Size and Density

Although hunter-gatherers tend to be nomadic, there is considerable variation in how far or how often they move, and some hunter-gatherers actually occupy permanent settlements. The key to the degree of movement appears to be the balance of the costs and benefits of moving or remaining in the same place (Kelly, 1995). As Robert Kelly (1995:160) has put it, "The cost of moving (which is related to the terrain to be crossed but includes the nature of housing), the distance to the next camp (which can be affected by nonfood variables such as water and firewood), the difference between the mean and variance of the current and anticipated return rates, storage, and the time frame over which foraging rates are averaged and decisions are made, all enter into decisions to move." Kelly suggests that hunter-gatherers who are sedentary are likely to be occupying environments characterized by local abundance within a larger context of regional scarcity. The patch-choice model applies here. For hunter-gatherers in this type of environment to move would not be rational because they would be lowering their overall return rate from foraging.

Hunter-gatherers have often been thought of as having little or no concept of ownership or territoriality, which is often the case, but once again considerable variation exists. And, as in the case of group mobility, territorial defense or the lack of it depends on the relative balance of costs and benefits. Dyson-Hudson and Smith (1978; summarized in Kelly, 1995) have developed what they call an *economic defensibility* model of boundary maintenance. The basic assumption of the model is that boundaries will be established to defend resources when the benefits of doing so outweigh the costs. Dyson-Hudson and Smith envision four possible scenarios:

1. *High resource density, low resource predictability.* Here groups will be highly mobile, will share information about the state of resources, and territoriality will be low (because of constantly shifting territories).
2. *High resource density, high resource predictability.* Here territoriality is prominent because the benefits of defending dense resources outweigh the costs.

3. *Low resource density, low resource predictability.* Here groups are highly dispersed and highly mobile. Territoriality is absent because the costs of defending resources outweigh the benefits.

4. *Low resource density, high resource predictability.* Here groups tend to remain in areas of predictable resources, and any territoriality that develops is a "passive territoriality."

To the above should be added the factors of competition and size of the foraging territory (Kelly, 1995). As competition increases, *ceteris paribus,* territoriality will increase. And groups with large foraging territories will, again *ceteris paribus,* often have little or no territoriality because the costs of patroling and defending the territory are too great. However, in the latter situation it may also be costly to allow unregulated visitors into the territory, and so some regulation of territorial access may be necessary (e.g., allowing visitors to use resources so long as there is a reasonable expectation of future reciprocation).

Most hunter-gatherers live in small bands that average around 25 members (Kelly, 1995). This may be an ideal size for several reasons. For one thing a group of this size will contain about five to seven families, which may be the maximum allowable in order to maintain an informal and nonhierarchical decision-making process (G. Johnson, 1982; Kelly, 1995). In addition, a group of 25 will provide about seven or eight full-time foragers. This can be very advantageous, for as Robert Kelly (1995:213) has said, "In most environments, a group containing this number of foragers probably minimizes daily variance in return rates while also minimizing the rate of local resource depletion." In addition to living in small groups, hunter-gatherers virtually always live in very thinly populated groups. Kelly (1995) provides data on population densities for 206 hunter-gatherer societies from all over the world. These vary from a low of 0.001 persons per square mile for the Yellowknife of Canada to a high of 5.23 persons per square mile for the Chumash of California. The average for all of the groups listed by Kelly is 0.31 persons per square mile. Variations in population density are closely related to the density of food resources, as would be expected.

MODES OF ECONOMIC DISTRIBUTION AND EXCHANGE

Reciprocal Altruism and Cooperation

Many sociologists and other social scientists object to biomaterialist arguments because they see them as portraying humans in a very negative light, concentrating as they often do on human selfishness, dominance and status orders, the tendency toward aggression, and so on. However, a biomaterialist perspective recognizes that there is also a much more positive side to humans. They cooperate with each other extensively and frequently behave altruistically. It can even be said that cooperation and helping are just as fundamental a part of human nature and human society as selfishness and competition. Indeed, the famous nineteenth-century Russian prince Petr Kropotkin (1902) argued that it was cooperation that was fundamental to social life (cf. Ridley, 1996). Evolution, he argued, designed people to engage in mutual aid and benefit just as much as it designed them to be competitive. Kropotkin argued that life had to be much more than a competitive struggle because cooperation was such a prominent feature of human society and of many animal societies. Matt Ridley (1996) argues that Kropotkin was about half right, and this seems a fair assessment. However, what we need to see is how cooperation and helping have evolved as *self-interested strategies*. For something to evolve by natural selection, it has to favor the survival and reproductive interests of the organisms behaving in that way.

As we saw in the chapter on sociobiology, in 1971 the biologist Robert Trivers introduced the concept of *reciprocal altruism* in order to understand cooperative and altruistic behavior that occurs between unrelated individuals rather than kin (Trivers, 1971). Reciprocal altruism requires individuals to respond in kind—do for others what was done for them—if the behavior is to continue. Reciprocal altruism is based on the principle "You scratch my back and I'll scratch yours." It involves an organism's assisting another organism with the expectation that, in time, the favor will be repaid. This kind of cooperative behavior could evolve by natural selection, Trivers argued, because it served the selfish interests of the organisms displaying it. Both would be better off in the long run with the behavior than without it. For reciprocal altruism to work, organisms must interact frequently and be able to recognize each other. Fleeting relationships will not allow its development.

In his book *Social Evolution* (1985), Trivers provides a number of examples of reciprocal altruism in different animal species. Vampire bats feed on blood and cannot live for more than about two days without a meal. These bats try to feed at night on the blood of such animals as horses and cattle, but sometimes they are unable to get a meal. Bats missing a meal are usually able to get other bats with very full stomachs to regurgitate blood. However, once this happens, the bat that regurgitated blood expects to be fed at some future time by the other bat when it misses a meal. This kind of pattern does tend to hold up, and bats who are not reciprocated will not reciprocate themselves in the future. Dolphins and whales are legendary for their reciprocal altruism, and they even go so far as to extend their helping behavior to members of other species. They commonly give physical support to the sick, the injured, and the very young. They engage in three forms of help, which Trivers refers to as standing by, assisting, and supporting. Standing by occurs when an animal stays by another animal in distress without directly assisting it. Assisting involves such behaviors as approaching an injured conspecific and swimming between it and its attacker, biting the attacker, or pushing the injured individual away from its attacker. Supporting amounts to maintaining a distressed animal at the water's surface. Dolphins and whales commonly travel together in large groups, with species intermixed. Trivers believes that it is predation that has probably selected for this pattern, especially predation from sharks. The altruistic behavior is adaptive under these conditions.

Moving phylogenetically closer to humans, we find that food sharing and cooperative hunting are common forms of behavior in chimpanzees. Frans de Waal (1996), a leading world expert on chimpanzee behavior, has shown that chimpanzees do not share plant foods but do engage in extensive sharing of meat. When they hunt for small monkeys or other prey, they show themselves to be very good cooperative hunters. They often work in pairs, trios, or sometimes even larger teams when they hunt arboreal monkeys. When a monkey is captured there is usually much celebration, with individuals gatherering into clusters and begging and handing meat to one another. De Waal's analysis of food sharing suggests that it is closely regulated by the principle of reciprocal altruism. He found that the number of transfers of food in one direction correlated with the number moving in the opposite direction. If chimpanzee A shared a lot with chimpanzee B, then B generally shared a lot with A; but if A shared little with C, then C also tended to share little with A. Unsurprisingly, the most extensive and highly developed systems of reciprocal altruism are found in humans. Much of human social life is based on this form of behavior. It is especially prominent in band and tribal societies, with the outstanding example being the sharing of meat among hunter-gatherers. We shall examine this form of reciprocal altruism shortly.

In recent years we have gained considerable insight into how reciprocal altruism may have evolved among highly social species, humans in particular. In game theory there is a famous game known as the Prisoner's Dilemma, which seems to underlie many of the behaviors of ordinary social life. In the Prisoner's Dilemma two people play a game in which neither player knows what the other is doing. If both players cooperate, each gets three points. If one refuses to cooperate (defects) and the other cooperates, the defector gets five points and the cooperator zero (this is known as the sucker's payoff). If both defect, they each get one point. When people play this game, the rational thing for each player to do is to defect in order to avoid the sucker's payoff (no points), and that is what players usually do. However, something else happens when the players play the game more than once and no one knows when the game will end. Robert Axelrod (1984) held a computerized tournament in which he asked a number of game theorists to submit strategies for winning the Prisoner's Dilemma. A variety of strategies was submitted, some of them quite complicated, but the strategy that won was the simplest of all: Tit-for-Tat. In this strategy a player cooperates on the first move and then on each subsequent move does whatever his or her opponent did. Axelrod went on to conduct a second round of the tournament in which many more entries were submitted and in which the participants knew the results of the first round. Tit-for-Tat won again. What do these results mean? According to Axelrod (1984:20), they show that "under suitable conditions, cooperation can indeed emerge in a world of egoists without central authority."

It is important to realize that Tit-for-Tat did better as the tournaments wore on. It often fell behind nastier strategies early on, but gradually got better. Axelrod says that what accounts for its success is that it is nice, retaliatory, forgiving, and clear. Trivers (1985) says there are three features critical to its success: never be the first to defect, retaliate only after your partner has defected, and be forgiving after just one act of retaliation. The success of Tit-for-Tat has immense implications for evolutionary biology. John Maynard Smith (1974, 1978, 1982) has argued that natural selection should have designed species to behave, at least much of the time, according to the logic of Tit-for-Tat. As Axelrod has put it (1984:49),

> imagine that there are many animals of a single species which interact with each other quite often. Suppose the interactions take the form of a Prisoner's Dilemma. When two animals

meet, they can cooperate with each other, not cooperate with each other, or one animal could exploit the other. Suppose further that each animal can recognize individuals it has already interacted with and can remember salient aspects of their interaction, such as whether the other has usually cooperated. A round of the tournament can then be regarded as a simulation of a single generation of such animals, with each decision rule being employed by large numbers of individuals.

Thus the assumption is that various forms of reciprocal altruism have evolved in various species, especially in humans, because reciprocal altruism is the strategy that has done the best job of maximizing benefits for each organism. Or at least reciprocal altruism has done the best for each individual under the kinds of conditions specified in the Prisoner's Dilemma game. Under different conditions, as we shall see, reciprocal altruism is likely to give way to very different strategies.

The big question now is, What does all of this have to do with economic behavior and the formation of different types of economic systems? Economic systems consist of networks of individuals who carry out activities in regard to the production, distribution, and exchange of valued goods and services. Reciprocal altruism underlies much of that kind of economic behavior we call exchange. Over two hundred years ago the famous political economist Adam Smith argued that humans have an innate tendency to "truck, barter, and exchange." This argument has been considered axiomatic by most Western economists, but many sociologists and anthropologists have strongly challenged it, arguing instead that economic behavior is socially constructed and culturally determined. They have considered Smith's argument tantamount to claiming that human nature is essentially "capitalistic." My view is that humans do indeed have a natural tendency to exchange, and to do so in a self-interested manner. However, this does not necessarily make all humans natural capitalists any more than it makes them all natural altruists. Humans are just as naturally one as the other, and the direction in which their behavior moves is determined by the interaction between their natural tendency to exchange and the range of environmental conditions they confront. Leda Cosmides and John Tooby (1992) have argued that the human brain is equipped with a highly specialized set of algorithms for social exchange that provides the biological basis for our economic and social institutions. However, this same set of algorithms leads to very different results in different circumstances. As Cosmides and Tooby (1992:206) put it, "Wherever human beings live, their cultural forms and social life are infused with social exchange relations. . . . Such relations appear in an enormous range of different guises, both simple and highly elaborated, implicit and explicit, deferred and simultaneous, practical and symbolic. The magnitude, variety, and complexity of our social exchange relations are among the most distinctive features of human social life, and differentiate us strongly from all other animal species."

Economic Reciprocity in Human Societies

Reciprocal altruism is found in all human societies and economies, but in many respects it is the essence of economic life in most hunter-gatherer societies. Hunter-gatherers are extremely noteworthy for their extensive food sharing, especially of meat. When a man brings an animal back to camp, he will divide it into portions and give these away, expecting only that he will likely be repaid in some way at some future time. A hunter may give to others repeatedly without any repayment taking place because he knows the chances are excellent that reciprocation will eventually occur. Where reciprocity is of crucial importance, powerful norms of sharing and individual humility develop. As Richard Lee has commented regarding the !Kung San (1978:888), "The most serious accusations that one !Kung can level against another are the charge of stinginess and the charge of arrogance. To be stingy or 'far-hearted' is to hoard one's goods jealously and secretively, guarding them 'like a hyena.' The corrective for this in the !Kung view is to make the hoarder give 'till it hurts,' that is, to make him give generously and without stint until everyone can see that he is truly cleaned out. In order to ensure compliance with this cardinal rule, the !Kung browbeat each other constantly to be more generous and not to set themselves apart by hoarding a little nest-egg."

What explains this enormous emphasis on cooperation and sharing, especially the sharing of meat? Probably the most common answer to that question is that it is a strategy of *variance reduction* (Wiessner, 1982; Cashdan, 1985; Winterhalder, 1986a, 1986b; cf. Kelly, 1995:168–72). The argument goes something like this: Hunter-gatherers normally live in very small groups, and those found in the modern era are usually located in less desirable environments. While resources might not be scarce in any absolute sense, they often vary markedly from region to region and from time to time: This is particularly the case for animal resources. Because of this, and because hunters differ in their skills and levels of motivation, the success of individual hunters varies markedly as well. What to do? A rational response would be to place a great deal of emphasis on sharing because that will work to the advantage of each individual over the long run, and quite often in the short run as well. If Morg kills a big animal now and only he and his immediate family eat it, he and his family will suffer, perhaps even starve, when Morg brings home nothing day after day and no one shares game with them. But if Morg generously shares his kill with others, then those others will likely reciprocate by sharing their kills with him and his family in the future. Thus Morg's generous behavior helps to guarantee security for him and his family. Bruce Winterhalder (1986a, 1986b; discussed in Kelly, 1995) has shown that sharing is most likely to occur in hunter-gatherer societies when there is, in fact, a great deal of variation in the returns of foragers on any given day. However, "a limit is reached at about seven to eight foragers, after which there is no significant reduction in net-return-rate variance. Thus, the limits to sharing are realized at fairly small group sizes. This case accounts for why meat is shared more than plant food, since hunting is usually a riskier venture than plant collection, and, in the case of large game, produces more food than is immediately needed. It also explains why large game is shared more than small game, since the latter is less risky" (Kelly, 1995:170).

The main alternative to the variance reduction argument is that developed by Nicholas Blurton Jones (1984, 1987) and is known as *tolerated theft*. Blurton Jones argues that there is little difference between giving away a piece of food and allowing it to be taken by someone else. He reasons that among hunter-gatherers a common situation will occur in which one hunter will have killed a large animal while others have killed nothing. Since the successful hunter cannot eat the entire animal on the spot, nor would he benefit from trying to do so, it does not pay him to defend the kill against the unsuccessful hunters who happen upon it. By contrast, it would pay the unsuccessful hunters to fight for the remainder of the kill, and thus the most rational thing for the successful hunter to do if he wishes to avoid serious conflict is to allow others to take the rest of the kill. As Blurton Jones notes, this situation will occur again and again, but with a different hunter likely to make the kill, and thus over time individuals will be repeatedly allowing others to take over the rest of their kills. As Blurton Jones puts it (1984:2), "In effect, each individual's 'donations' are sooner or later 'reciprocated.' Individuals who attempt not to reciprocate will suffer the losses of injuries in fights with more motivated opponents. Thus, if we suppose these individuals to meet often, we have exactly the conditions that Trivers (1971) proposed as necessary for the evolution of reciprocal altruism."

Which of these models, variance reduction or tolerated theft, should be preferred? Blurton Jones (1987) claims that his model is the simpler of the two and that, moreover, tolerated theft actually leads to variance reduction. Robert Kelly (1995) suggests that both tolerated theft and variance reduction may explain food sharing. Either model is fully consistent with a Darwinian conflict perspective. To make matters more complicated, a third alternative, also consistent with Darwinian conflict theory, has been proposed by Kristen Hawkes (1993). Hawkes argues that the empirical evidence is against the variance reduction model. This model assumes that one must give in order to receive, and Hawkes claims that among three well-known hunter-gatherer societies, the !Kung, the Hadza, and the Aché, this is just not so. In these societies most of the meat is supplied by only a small number of men, and some men never supply any meat. Hawkes seems to accept the basic logic of the tolerated theft model; it may simply be too costly to try to prevent people from claiming the remains of kills. However, there is still the question of why only a few men hunt if they get back no meat in return. Her answer is that these men enjoy the "social attention" they receive from others. The most successful hunters will get more sex from more women, and as a result increase their reproductive success. It does seem to be the case that among the Aché men must exchange meat for sex. However, Hawkes presents no data showing a general connection between hunting success and reproductive success (Jeske, 1993). In the end, then, it is difficult to know how to choose among these three models of sharing. More research is clearly needed.[2]

When should sharing give way to hoarding? One major circumstance would appear to be a seasonal glut (Blurton Jones, 1987). Hunter-gatherer societies that experience a season of highly abundant resources combined with a season of scarcity, such as a cold and snowy winter, will be highly motivated to store large amounts of food. Indeed, Alain Testart (1982) has drawn an important distinction between hunter-gatherers who store and those who do not, and it seems that sharing is much less common among storers than among nonstorers. Sharing also declines as societies make the transition from hunting and gathering to agriculture, as we shall see shortly.

Three Types of Reciprocity

Marshall Sahlins (1965, 1972) has formulated a celebrated distinction between three types of reciprocity, which he calls *generalized, balanced,* and *negative* reciprocity. Generalized reciprocity is the most altruistic, and involves sharing, generosity, or pure gift. One of the hallmarks of generalized reciprocity is the vagueness of reciprocation. Individuals to whom things have been given incur a debt and are obligated to repay it, but there is no specification of the time, quantity, or quality of the reciprocation. The nature and timing of the reciprocation are highly indefinite. Under this type of reciprocity, it is considered inappropriate that there should be any overt calculation or discussion of the nature of the debt. The sharing of meat in hunter-gatherer societies is guided by generalized reciprocity. Balanced reciprocity is different in that overt calculation and discussion are not only permissible but expected. It is a more direct form of exchange in which the parties come to a clear understanding of the nature of the debt and the time and mode of its repayment. It is less "personal" and "more economic," and includes such things as gift exchange, trade, and buying and selling. Sahlins says that the real test of balanced reciprocity is its intolerance of one-way flows. Finally, negative reciprocity is the unsociable extreme, an attempt to get something for nothing. It is the most impersonal form of exchange and the "most economic," involving as it does such economic transactions as haggling, gambling, and theft. In its most extreme form it amounts to exploitation. The participants understand that their interests are opposed and that each will try to benefit at the expense of the other. In this sense, negative reciprocity is not really a form of reciprocity at all.

One of the most interesting aspects of Sahlins's analysis is the connection he draws between the form of reciprocity and the social circumstances under which each most frequently occurs. Generalized reciprocity is largely limited to the household or to the lineage, and thus occurs primarily among kin. Within the larger village or within the tribe itself, generalized reciprocity normally gives way to balanced reciprocity. Negative reciprocity occurs largely outside the tribal sector and thus is mainly limited to interactions among strangers or at least among individuals with whom one is barely acquainted. The remarkable thing about this formulation is that it fits the expectations of inclusive fitness theory almost perfectly, and yet Sahlins was one of the earliest and most dismissive critics of that approach. As Richard Alexander (1975:91) has noted:

> Sahlins' model concentrates generalized reciprocity in the household and implies its extension across the lineage sector of the village. He is in fact speaking largely of nepotism. Evolutionary biologists have dealt with such behavior under the rubrics of kin selection and inclusive fitness. They have come to expect that selection will mold organisms to assist their closer kin over their more distant kin, and kin over nonkin even when reciprocity in kind is unlikely, and at least to concentrate such one-way beneficence on genetic relatives, perhaps dispensing it to no one else. Sahlins is telling the evolutionists that their expectations are fulfilled to an astonishing degree in primitive human societies in which kinship is "the organizing principle or idiom of most groups and social relations."

And it is the same with respect to balanced reciprocity. As Alexander remarks, it is completely unsurprising that Sahlins concentrates this form of reciprocity in the tribal sector and sees it as seldom extending beyond the limits of the tribe. Nor can it be the least bit surprising that negative reciprocity is concentrated outside the tribal sector. "The more overt or blatant the cheating, the less likely one is to conduct it among relatives or groups of friendly persons, and the more likely he is to receive admiration or appreciation for success involving strangers or, better yet, mutual enemies" (Alexander, 1975:93).

In the book in which he formulated his major critique of sociobiology, Sahlins (1976a) has responded to Alexander's charges by claiming that kinship is culturally constructed rather than biologically determined. Societies' definitions of who counts as a near or distant kinsman, he claims, have little to do with genealogical relationships. This response, though, is thoroughly unconvincing. Is Sahlins denying that most of the members of a household or lineage are genetically related? It would be absurd to do so. And is he denying that people are most altruistic toward their own offspring? That would be equally absurd (Alexander, 1979).

In thinking about generalized, balanced, and negative reciprocity ranging along a continuum from the most cooperative to the most competitive or conflictive forms of economic behavior, what now remains to be done is to show how these behavioral categories relate to the evolution of economic systems. Under what conditions will economic behavior be highly cooperative, and under what conditions will this kind of behavior break down and be replaced by much more competitive and exploitative behavior? People behave most cooperatively among kin, friends, and acquaintances, and they behave most competitively or exploitatively among strangers. The expectation is therefore that throughout social evolution cooperation will gradually be replaced by competition and exploitation. This is because one of the most important features of social evolution is an increase in the scale and complexity of social life. In more large-scale and complex societies most people cease to have either direct or sustained contact with most other people. Moreover, the economic evolution of human societies is closely tied up with technological advance and increases in economic productivity. In more evolutionarily advanced societies there are many more economic goods over which competitive or exploitative behavior can arise. When there is more to be had, and when relationships become more impersonal and remote, people are much less likely to cooperate than to compete. It is a simple matter of people following their economic self-interest. As we will see in the sections ahead, these expectations about economic evolution correspond closely to the actual record revealed by human history and prehistory.

From Reciprocity to Redistribution

As we have seen, in hunter-gatherer societies reciprocal altruism, often in the form of generalized reciprocity, is a fundamental form of economic behavior. This kind of economic behavior generally continues in the transition to horticultural societies, but a new form of behavior known as *redistribution* emerges. Redistribution is a process whereby goods, mostly in the form of food, are sent from individual households to a central source and then eventually returned to those households in some way. Redistribution differs from reciprocity in that it is a more formal process involving the movement of goods into the hands of some agent (person or group) who reallocates them. Moseley and Wallerstein (1978) have distinguished two different forms of redistribution, which they call *pure* and *partial* redistribution. In pure redistribution the redistributive agent reallocates all goods and keeps no extra portion (or at most only a small extra portion) for himself. In partial redistribution the redistributive process is less complete; the redistributive agent, which in this case is likely to be an organized group rather than a single individual, keeps a portion of goods (sometimes a very large portion) for itself.

Pure redistributive economies are most frequently found among simple horticulturalists and vary from place to place and time to time. Perhaps the best-known type of redistributive economy is that which is characteristic of Melanesian village societies. Many of these societies contain very ambitious men known as "big men," individuals who seek recognition through their roles as economic organizers and political leaders (Harris, 1974, 1977). They spend a great deal of time cultivating their gardens and, if they have them, trying to increase the size of their pig herds. A major objective of an actual or potential big man is to accumulate enough goods to hold a feast, at which time the various foodstuffs will be redistributed to other members of the village and perhaps to kin from other villages. One of the interesting things about the big man system is that, although any given village may have only one publicly acknowledged big man, there are apt to be several other ambitious individuals who are competing to attain this position of economic leadership. They too will be working harder in order to accumulate foodstuffs and hold their own feasts. The Kaoka-speakers, who are Melanesian simple horticulturalists, have this type of redistributive economy (Hogbin, 1964; Harris, 1974). When a candidate for bigmanship has made his gardens flourish and has a sufficient number of pigs, he tells people that he wishes to build a larger dwelling, an indication that he intends to compete for the leadership of his village. Once the new dwelling has been constructed the Kaoka-speakers celebrate the end of the job through an elaborate feast that they call the "feast-to-remove-the-splinters." In one such feast, the aspiring big man and his closest relatives contributed 250 pounds of dried fish, 3,000 yam cakes, 11 bowls of yam pudding, and 8 pigs. Other villagers contributed additional foodstuffs, which increased the final total to some 300 pounds of fish, nearly 5,000 yam cakes, 19 bowls of pudding, and 13 pigs. It was then the feast organizer's task to redistribute this food to everyone associated with the feast (Harris, 1974).

Marvin Harris (1974, 1977) stresses that a big man, despite seeking recognition, is still a pure redistributor. Big men are expected to redistribute so that everyone gets something and the leader himself gets no more than anyone else. In the transition to more intensive or advanced horticultural societies, however, the redistributive agents become partial rather than pure redistributors: They redistribute to everyone but keep a portion, often a large portion, of what they accumulate for themselves. Advanced horticultural societies are usually in a position to produce an *economic surplus*, or a quantity of goods above and beyond what is necessary for daily subsistence. Much of this surplus remains in the hands of those who cause it to come into existence. In a classic article, Marshall Sahlins (1963) has highlighted the differences between pure and partial redistribution by comparing the redistributive systems of Melanesian and Polynesian societies. Melanesian societies have tended to have simple horticulture and big-man systems, whereas Polynesian societies have been more frequently characterized by intensive horticulture and partial redistribution. Melanesian big men may have a great deal of prestige, but they hold little or no real power over the rest of the society. By contrast, in many Polynesian societies big men had at some point been transformed into chiefs, political and economic leaders who hold a great deal of power and economic leverage over most of the population. Chiefs are able to produce an economic surplus by compelling the people to work harder and relinquish a portion of their harvests. A "public treasury" or great storehouse is thus created, from which chiefs support themselves and their families. They also use it for providing lavish entertainment for visiting dignitaries, initiating major public projects such as irrigation works, building temples, sponsoring military campaigns, and supporting a vast range of administrative officials. Portions of this storehouse are redistributed to the people as the need arises, either during times of poor harvests or on special ceremonial occasions that require elaborate feasts.

Quite a gulf can separate pure from partial redistributive systems. The latter are redistributive in the sense that they involve a counterflow of goods from the chiefs to the people. However, this counterflow is always less, and often much less, than the flow of goods from the people to the chiefs. While clearly similar in principle to pure redistributive systems, partial redistributive systems constitute a notable evolutionary departure from pure redistribution.

From Redistribution to Expropriation

In agrarian societies, partial redistribution has been replaced by what is often known as *surplus expropriation*. This involves powerful landlords' compelling a large peasantry to work hard enough to produce a large economic surplus and then relinquish it. The surplus may be handed over in various ways, but this normally occurs in the form of rent, taxation, and labor services. Sometimes a fine line can exist between partial redistribution and surplus expropriation, but analytically the distinction is easy to make. Landlords have acquired much more economic power than chiefs, and as a result have been able to place greater economic burdens upon peasant producers than chiefs are capable of placing on their followers. The flow of goods and services between peasants and lords is by and large a one-way flow, there being little counterflow from lords to peasants.

This type of economic relationship has prevailed in virtually all agrarian societies. In medieval Europe, for example, peasants had to pay rent to their landlords, either in the form of cash or a percentage of the crop. They also had to pay various kinds of taxes for, say, having the right to grind their grain in the lord's mill or to fish in the lord's fishpond. Peasants also owed their landlords labor services, being required to spend so many days each week working on the lord's demesne (home farm). In ancient Rome a vast system of surplus expropriation resting primarily on slave rather than peasant labor existed; there were many huge Roman estates worked by large slave gangs. Slavery has also been found in many other agrarian societies, usually in conjunction with serfdom. Where slavery rather than serfdom has been the principal labor mode, the system of surplus expropriation has been more direct and obvious, and the primary producers more brutalized and dehumanized.

Many scholars have used the term *exploitation* to characterize the relationship between landlords and those who worked the land. This seems entirely appropriate. I would say that exploitation exists when one party is compelled to give to another party more than it receives in return. The notion of exploitation implies that one party is benefitting at the expense of another and that the disadvantaged party does not have the means to leave the relationship and enter another that would be less punitive. When exploitation exists there is always an element of compulsion and unequal power. What then of the primary producers in advanced horticultural societies? Were they being exploited as well? Probably, and if so, then we can mark the beginnings of true economic exploitation at the emergence of these types of societies. But the level of exploitation surely was much lower. There were definite limits on the abilities of horticultural chiefs to extract surplus production from the people. Indeed, in precontact Hawaii many a chief was killed who "ate the powers of government too much" (Sahlins, 1963). That is a fate that almost never befell an agrarian landlord.

A major reason for the shift from reciprocity to redistribution to expropriation throughout the course of social evolution has involved who owned the means of production on which people have depended for a living. There is a clear evolutionary pattern in resource ownership away from more communal modes and toward increasingly privatized modes. In hunter-gatherer societies, especially those with low resource density and high resource unpredictability, there is little territoriality and little concept of ownership (Kelly, 1995). Under these conditions, which characterize the majority of contemporary hunter-gatherer societies, hunter-gatherers tend to share land to about the same extent that they share food (Kelly, 1995). In small-scale horticultural societies there is seldom any sort of privatized ownership, but a concept of ownership does exist. Land is usually owned and controlled by lineages or clans, and people only have the right to use the land that belongs to their kinship group. However, within these groups a strikingly egalitarian pattern of use prevails. In terms of the dichotomy communal versus private, land is communally owned in this type of society. The shift to a more privatized form of landownership generally occurs with the shift to more intensive or advanced horticultural societies. Here, as might be suspected, land is often said to be formally owned by powerful chiefs who have the right to make use of it as they see fit, including dispossessing commoners or requiring them to increase their rate of productivity and relinquish a portion of their harvests. It is well known that in some advanced horticultural societies the claim to formal ownership of land by a chief is to some extent a fiction. For example, among the Kpelle of West Africa the ownership rights of chiefs are quite limited (Gibbs, 1965). Here every man in a lineage was entitled to the use of that lineage's land, and a chief was more like a steward than a true owner. In other advanced horticultural societies, such as precontact Hawaii, formal ownership of land by a chief, especially the paramount chief, was actually closer to reality than to fiction. Chiefly ownership marks a significant movement in the direction of private ownership, but because it often retains many of the characteristics of lineage ownership it is not a true mode of private ownership. True private ownership is reached with the emergence of what I have called *seigneurial ownership* (Sanderson, 1995a). This involves ownership of the land by a powerful class of landlords or by a centralized state that has usurped some of the rights and powers of the landlord class. Seigneurial ownership has been most characteristic of large-scale agrarian societies.

The evolution of property rights throughout the past 10,000 years of human history and prehistory has involved a steady movement in the direction of private ownership rights, and by and large the more privatized the system of ownership has become, the more unequal has become the system of economic distribution. What, then, has been driving changing modes of property ownership? A major part of the answer, I think, is population pressure, which has been in fact one of the great driving forces of all of social evolution (Sanderson, 1995b, 1999). Population pressure has increased resource scarcity, especially of land, and this has increased the fight over land with its consequent unbalanced outcomes. Once again we see human nature coming to the fore. When it is advantageous for them to do so, people share food and land, but they readily abandon the sharing of food and land when *that* is to their advantage. They begin adopting those modes of property ownership and resource distribution that are most suitable for them and their kin under the evolving conditions. The evolution of economic ownership and distribution has run in the same basic way all over the globe throughout history and prehistory, and that suggests the existence of the very kind of organism that Darwinian conflict theory has described.

STRATEGIES OF ECONOMIC GROWTH IN WORLD HISTORY

In two recent books the economic historian Graeme Donald Snooks (1996, 1997) has proposed that the members of human societies have relied on one or another of four strategies of economic growth or wealth expansion. These are strategies quite apart from those of redistribution and surplus expropriation just discussed. Snooks calls these strategies, which he refers to as *dynamic strategies,* the *family multiplication strategy,* the *conquest strategy,* the *commerce strategy,* and the *technological strategy.* He argues that the members of a society (or their economic and political elites) select the strategy that works best under the circumstances in which that society finds itself. Any particular dynamic strategy eventually exhausts itself, at which point the society shifts to the next-best strategy.

The dynamic strategy most likely to be found in small-scale preindustrial societies is the family multiplication strategy. Here families hive off from other families and occupy new land. This strategy has also been used by more complex societies in the settling of frontier regions, such as in colonial America. The most common dynamic strategy in the world of large-scale agrarian civilizations has been the conquest strategy. Here the political leaders of a society, usually in close collaboration with its economic leaders, engage in a pattern of constant war against other societies. War becomes a large-scale business, and wealth is created in the form of the spoils of war: "additional agricultural land; additional labour in the form of slaves and soldiers; additional fixed capital in the form of captured military equipment, irrigation systems, buildings, transport facilities, etc.; treasure; and additional tax revenue" (1996:276). This strategy was preferred to all others because it was usually the most cost-efficient and produced the greatest return on investment. In order to achieve this return, ancient civilizations had to emphasize one form of technological advance, that involving military technology. The advance of military technology in the ancient world occurred, Snooks says, because war was not a game but a business, and in fact a very big business.

By far the greatest example of the conquest strategy is the Roman Republic and Empire. The dynamic strategists were the senators, who had launched this strategy by about the middle of the fifth century BC. Later the senators were replaced by the emperor as the primary strategist, a change necessitated by the need for greater centralization of the whole process of conquest. According to Snooks, by AD 138 the Romans had essentially exhausted their conquest strategy, but since there were no real alternatives to it the empire started on a process of long and slow decline. As another example of the conquest strategy Snooks discusses the Aztecs, whose budding empire in the fifteenth and sixteenth centuries was centered on the capital city of Tenochtitlán. Unlike Rome, the Aztecs did not make use of a large slave labor force, and there was no permanent army. But as in Rome, war became a serious business, and merchants, who relied on the commerce strategy, were greatly distrusted; however, since their wealth was useful to the state they were tolerated. The Aztec conquest strategy was cut short by the Spanish conquerors early in the sixteenth century before it had a chance to spread and ultimately to exhaust itself. Snooks speculates that had this not happened the Aztecs would soon have embarked on the conquest of much of North and South America.

A few agrarian societies have been fortunate enough to be able to use the commerce strategy rather than the conquest strategy. This strategy involves the creation of wealth by producing and trading goods over as large an area as possible. It depends on favorable geographical and other circumstances that give a society the necessary access to markets and trade routes. Since commerce societies could not coexist peaceably with conquest societies, the former had to be beyond the reach of the latter. Snooks's leading examples of the commerce strategy are ancient Mesopotamia, Minoan society, the Phoenicians, classical Athens, the Italian city-states of Venice and Genoa at the time of the Renaissance, and Europe between the sixteenth and eighteenth centuries. The greatest commerce society in all of premodern human history was ancient Greece. The Greeks were not only geographically suited for the commerce strategy, but, since they were divided into a number of small and independent states that were equally matched militarily, the conquest strategy could not be successfully employed. The Greeks employed their commerce strategy between approximately 800 and 550 BC. An integral part of this process was the founding of many Greek colonies in both near and distant regions. These colonies were important to the Greeks because "they were the means by which Greek city-states attempted to gain a monopoly over trade in a particular part of the Mediterranean" (Snooks, 1997:213). By around 550 to 500 BC the Greek commerce strategy had exhausted itself and Greece was forced to turn to the conquest strategy. However, it had no particular advantage in the use of this strategy and as a result subsided into insignificance as a world-class society. Venice in the time between approximately AD 1000 and 1500 was also a major commerce society. It followed a path similar to Greece's. It was ideally geographically situated for commerce, and it followed this strategy for several centuries. Soon, however, the strategy had run its course and, like Greece two millennia earlier, it turned to conquest. But since it had, also like Greece, no particular advantage in the use of this strategy, the conquest strategy failed, and early in the sixteenth century Venice opted for a policy of neutrality and diplomacy.

According to Snooks, the history of Europe, England in particular, over the past millennium reveals a sequence of dynamic strategies. Between about AD 1000 and 1450 England used a conquest strategy. Once this strategy had been played out, England adopted a commerce strategy. This latter strategy had itself been played out by the middle of the eighteenth century, and as a result England embarked upon what Snooks calls the technological strategy, or what I think might be more appropriately called the *capitalist* strategy. This involved the substitution of inanimate for animate energy and was marked by, of course, the Industrial Revolution (1997:293–94):

> As far as Britain's dynamic strategists were concerned, the essence of the Industrial Revolution was that it devised cheaper ways (both technically and institutionally) of producing old products, such as cotton textiles, and new products such as consumer durables, and cheaper ways of transporting those products to markets at home (by canals and railways) and abroad (by steam-driven steel ships). . . . By providing ways of achieving favoured access to resources and markets other than the exhausted traditional ways of force, diplomacy, and physical proximity, the British Industrial Revolution imparted a new impetus to commercial expansion. But this time commercial expansion was the outcome of the technological rather than the commerce strategy.

Despite its short history, the United States has also undergone a sequence of dynamic strategies. In colonial America the strategy followed was that of dependent commerce, a version of the commerce strategy in which the colonies were a junior partner to England. This strategy came to an end late in the eighteenth century, and the United States then embarked, according to Snooks, on a strategy of family multiplication by expanding into the Western frontier. Once this strategy had been exhausted by around 1890, the United States took up the technological strategy. Snooks argues that the key to understanding U.S. society is that it was the world's first "megastate" and the first society to create a "megamarket." Prior to the Civil War the United States was really made up of two subsocieties that were committed to different dynamic strategies. The North wanted to expand industrial capitalism into the Western frontier in order to create a megamarket, but the "longrun material success of Southern strategists depended more on their economic relationship with Britain than with the rest of America" (1997:379). The Civil War was really fought over this clash of strategies, and Snooks contends that had the South won the war the United States would have been divided into a number of nation-states rather than becoming one megastate. Thus, the outcome of the Civil War was essential to the preservation of the North's technological strategy, for this strategy could not have been sustained without a megastate and a megamarket.

The technological strategy has been relatively little employed in world history compared to the three other strategies. Why should this be so? Snooks's answer is that it was generally too expensive in comparison to other strategies. Snooks is highly critical of the conventional assumption made by historians that the agrarian civilizations of the ancient world gave little emphasis to technological advance because they were essentially uninterested in economic growth. They were keenly interested in such growth, he says, but had more cost-effective ways of achieving it.

By way of criticism, I have some difficulty understanding just what Snooks means by the family multiplication strategy. His discussion of it in his first book seems to make it clear that this was a strategy suitable to very small-scale societies. Yet in his second book we read that this was the major strategy of American society in the century between 1790 and 1890, and we also learn of the enormous amount of wealth that the use of this strategy created. But surely family multiplication cannot be much of a wealth-creating strategy on its own, let alone of the level of wealth that Snooks is referring to. Perhaps I misunderstand the family multiplication strategy, but it would appear to me that it could not create much wealth unless it were combined with one of the other strategies. For example, the expansion of the railroads was a major aspect of the expansion into the Western frontier of the United States, but this was driven by Snooks's technological strategy (or what I prefer to call the capitalist strategy) rather than by simple family multiplication.

Questions can also be raised concerning Snooks's specific employment of his four economic strategies. To take just one of the more prominent examples, consider Snooks's claim that Europe between AD 1000 and 1500 relied heavily on the technological strategy. To support his claim he is able to cite numerous examples of technological development during this time, but is it not just as logical, if not more logical, to regard European societies at this time as employing the commerce strategy? William McNeill (1982) has argued that the world as a whole experienced a tremendous leap forward in the level of commerce after AD 1000, and certainly Europe, in particular the Italian city-states of Venice and Genoa, was a huge part of this commercial thrust. In fact, why separate the technology and commerce strategies in this case? Could it not be persuasively argued that Europe was using technological advance to promote a commerce strategy, just as the ancient civilizations promoted the development of military technology to support their conquest strategies? And what about the period since the Industrial Revolution? Once again Snooks refers to this period as one characterized by the use of the technological strategy, but could we not argue that it was really the commerce strategy—better labeled the capitalist strategy, since it was world production as well as world trade that was involved—that was dominant and being served by technological advance?

Snooks also gets himself into trouble by seldom if ever looking at world history as a sociologist would. I agree with his rational choice and methodologically individualist grounding assumptions, but one cannot simply stop there. His work seems to contain *only* individuals, there being little if any recognition of the importance of social classes and economic inequalities as strongly implicated in world historical development. A glaring example of this absence involves Snook's analysis of Roman conquest. As he puts it, "Conquest was a business pursued to achieve the materialistic ends of *all Roman citizens*" (1996:293; emphasis added). *All Roman citizens?* Does Snooks really believe that the needs and concerns of all Roman citizens, rather than those of Roman elites, were being considered by the Roman polity in its mapping out of its objectives? Indeed he does, for he says at the beginning of the book that "the dynamics of human society arises from the decision-making not just of small elites but of all members of society both male and female throughout the world" (1996:xiv). Although elites may capture a disproportionate share of the economic surplus, he says, they merely express the general desires of humanity. If we shift our focus from the ancient world to modern times, we run into a similar problem. The modern world, many would say, is quintessentially a capitalist world, but capitalists are strangely absent from Snooks's view of this world. There are just individuals pursuing their economic objectives, all of which are the same.

In my view, one of the most compelling features of Snooks's work is its resolute materialism. Snooks calls the theoretical model that underlies his work *materialist man* or *dynamic materialism*. This model holds that humans have an innate desire to increase their wealth and power. Indeed, he claims that they have an insatiable desire to accumulate material possessions. Snooks also appears, at least on the surface, to be grounding his economic materialism in a deeper Darwinian materialism. Snooks's humans look like Darwinian organisms in the sense that they have been built for a struggle for survival and a maximization of material advantage. Unfortunately, Snooks takes his argument too far and ends up producing a distortion of Darwin. Snooks attacks sociobiology and claims that its adherents have badly misunderstood Darwin. Humans only struggle for wealth and power, he claims, and this has nothing to do with the struggle for reproductive success. Indeed, Snooks claims that the latter struggle does not even exist (at least in the case of humans), and he contends that Darwin himself emphasized only an economic struggle, a struggle for material resources, not a reproductive struggle.

However, it is not the sociobiologists who have misunderstood Darwin; the misunderstanding lies entirely with Snooks. Not only did Darwin emphasize reproductive success, but his theory depended intimately upon it and makes no sense without it. Life is a struggle for both survival and reproductive success, and evolution cannot occur if organisms do not mate and leave copies of their genes in future generations. This is the only way an adaptive trait can spread throughout a population. What Snooks fails to see is that his general theory, materialist man, is not only compatible with sociobiology, but makes sense only in terms of it. Why do people strive for wealth, status, and power? Because these are the resources they need in the struggle, not only to survive and prosper, but to attract mates and perpetuate their genes.

THE TRANSITION FROM FEUDALISM TO CAPITALISM

The Transition in Europe

I take capitalism to be an economic system devoted to the sale of goods in a market in which the objective is to realize the maximum profit. This kind of economic activity has existed for thousands of years, but it has been only in the past few centuries that it has come to be the dominant form of economic action.[3] Immanuel Wallerstein (1974a, 1974b) dates the emergence of modern capitalism in Europe from the sixteenth century, but it is clear that important things were developing even earlier. Maurice Dobb (1963) sees merchant capitalism as beginning in the fourteenth and fifteenth centuries with the disintegration of the old feudal system and the rise of the towns, the latter being associated with the increased importance of the bourgeoisie, or merchant class. The primary source of merchant wealth was trade rather than production; the latter would not become the primary source of merchant wealth until after the middle of the eighteenth century. However, industrial production did exist and grew in importance in the centuries prior to the Industrial Revolution of the eighteenth century. Capitalism was also applied to agriculture in that estates came to be run with hired workers along the lines of capitalist farms (Wallerstein, 1974a).

Some students of European capitalism prefer a very early date for its emergence. Jere Cohen (1980) notes that in Renaissance Italy there was a form of capitalism that satisfied most of Weber's (1981[1927]) criteria for modern rational capitalism. Capitalism was born in Renaissance Italy, Cohen says, and then later copied by northern Europe. Fernand Braudel (1984) also sees European capitalism as beginning in Italy, and of the Italian city-states it was Venice that was the greatest capitalist city of them all. Venice had not only financial and banking institutions, but also factories and wage labor; it was overwhelmingly specialized for trade and its merchants and bankers stood at the very top of the social hierarchy. It was also the Italians who invented double-entry bookkeeping, marine insurance, and commercial law (J. Cohen, 1980). However, for Wallerstein the capitalistic developments of late medieval Europe differed in a crucial respect from what began to develop after the sixteenth century. He stresses that these early capitalist endeavors focused much more on trade in luxury goods or preciosities than staples or basic goods, whereas beginning in the sixteenth century a world-economy began to form on the basis of the production and trade of staples.

As we saw in chapter 4, Wallerstein has stressed that capitalism was never simply a phenomenon limited to the nation-state, but rather from the sixteenth century on existed within the framework of a larger world-economy. At the end of this world-economy's first stage (about 1640), the capitalist core was concentrated in northwest Europe, mostly in the Netherlands, England, and northern France. Agriculture had come to be highly organized along capitalist lines, and industry and trade were of growing importance. Wage labor had largely replaced forced labor (serfdom). In the early seventeenth century all three core societies established mercantilist trading companies that allowed them to gain a monopoly on trade with their newly created colonies. For example, the Dutch East India Company, which formed in 1602, had a navy of between 40 and 60 ships and an army of almost 12,000 men. In the middle third of the seventeenth century it controlled the routes of the Far East and brought into Europe each year on the order of 10 to 12 million florins worth of goods. The periphery was located in Eastern Europe, mainly Poland, and in Iberian America (i.e., the Spanish and Portuguese colonies in the New World). Eastern Europe concentrated on grain farming for export to Western Europe using what Wallerstein has called "coerced-cash-crop labor." Hispanic America concentrated on gold and silver mining using several unique forms of forced labor, and Portuguese America engaged in both mining and plantation agriculture (sugar cane production) using slaves imported from Africa. In the second phase of the capitalist world-economy, which Wallerstein dates from 1640 to 1763, the world-economy expanded to include Sweden, Prussia, and the United States North as part of the semiperiphery and the Caribbean and United States South as part of the periphery. The core remained much the same, although there was great rivalry between the major core powers for control of the system. At this time the world-economy probably included no more than 20 to 25 percent of the world, but in capitalism's third phase, 1763 to 1917, the system expanded to include most of the globe. At the beginning of this phase the British Industrial Revolution got under way and a highly industrialized form of capitalism developed in the nineteenth and twentieth centuries in Western Europe and North America. That is a story much too detailed to tell in the limited space available here, but it is in any event a story that is very well known.

The Transition in Japan

Striking historical parallels seem to have existed between Europe and Japan from late medieval times through to the development of industrial capitalism in the nineteenth and twentieth centuries. Medieval Japan had a form of feudalism that closely resembled European feudalism, and Japan also underwent a transition from feudalism to capitalism that was very similar to the European transition to modern capitalism (Duus, 1969; Reischauer, 1956; Jacobs, 1958; J.W. Hall, 1970; T.C. Smith, 1959; P. Anderson, 1974b; Halliday, 1975). One of the first scholars to recognize the major economic developments in Tokugawa Japan (the period from 1600 to 1868) was Daniel Spencer (1958). Spencer has described a series of interrelated processes involving large-scale urbanization, commercialization of agriculture, increasing flight of peasants into the towns and cities, the worsening economic condition of the nobility, growth in the wealth and economic importance of the merchant class, increased monetization of the economy, and the beginnings of the factory system. More recently, Kozo Yamamura (1980) has shown that between 1550 and 1650 there was an agricultural and commercial revolution in Japan. The main cause of the major increases in agricultural productivity, according to Yamamura, was a change in property rights involving peasants' acquiring more control over their land. This was essentially a shift toward more capitalistic land tenure. With these changing property rights there arose a class of independent farmers similar to the yeoman farmers of early modern Europe. Yamamura holds that greater control over their land gave peasants increased incentives to make it productive. The commercial revolution involved a variety of state-supported measures to promote commerce, such as decrees to protect merchants, decrees designed to eliminate various restrictions on the operation of markets, active development of transportation networks and facilities, and standardization of measurements.

Sheldon (1958) has traced the rising economic importance of the merchant class throughout the Tokugawa period, but, like Yamamura, notes that important economic developments were taking place in the century before Tokugawa. Sheldon sees the Genroku period (1688 to 1703) as the critical one in the merchants' economic evolution, because by this time there was a thriving money economy and the merchant class had grown strong enough so that the nobility was forced to regard it as a serious economic competitor. John Whitney Hall (1970) sees the growth of mercantile activities during the Tokugawa epoch in similar terms, pointing out that it was during this time that a bourgeoisie first rose to a position of national prominence.

An important part of Japanese economic development during the Tokugawa era, the seventeenth century in particular, was urbanization at a level so extensive that Hall

(1970) regards it as very likely without historical precedent (cf. Goldsmith, 1987). For example, Edo (modern Tokyo) was not much more than a small village at the end of the sixteenth century, but by the early eighteenth century it had reached half a million in population and by the end of that century it contained well over a million persons (Spencer, 1958). The extent to which capitalism was emerging in Tokugawa Japan can also be seen by examining one of the most important aspects of capitalist development: proletarianization of the labor force. During the Tokugawa period Japan was becoming a more impersonal, money-dominated society with an increasing part of its labor force being compensated in the form of wages; by the end of the period, wage labor had become the major form of compensation, at least with respect to urban workers (Leupp, 1992). Wage labor even became increasingly important in agricultural work (T.C. Smith, 1959).

By the end of the Tokugawa Shogunate in 1868, Japan had become an essentially capitalist society in economic terms despite retaining largely feudal social and political arrangements. The merchant class had grown enormously in economic importance. Japan had undergone tremendous commercialization, both in agriculture and in industry, and had become one of the most urbanized societies in the world. It has even been claimed that by the end of the eighteenth century nearly 95 percent of Japan's wealth was in the hands of the merchants, a clear indication of the extent of the economic changes (Spencer, 1958). It was the merchant class that was in economic if not political control of late Tokugawa Japan.

Explaining the Transition

My explanation of the rise of capitalism in Europe and Japan is largely ecomaterialist but to some extent polimaterialist. There were several basic characteristics shared by Europe and Japan that I argue operated as important preconditions facilitating their transition to capitalism. However, these preconditions occurred only within the context of a particular historical juncture that marked the culmination of a great historical trend. It was the interaction of these factors—the preconditions on the one hand and a major historical trend on the other—that made the transition possible in these two regions of the world.

What did Europe and Japan have in common that gave them a decided advantage in the capitalist transition? I see five factors as critical. First there was *size*. Japan and two of the three leading capitalist countries of early modern Europe—England and the Netherlands—were small, and as such contrasted markedly with such Asian societies as China and India, which were large bureaucratic empires. This is important because maintaining a large state is more costly than administering a small one (cf. Braudel, 1984, in the case of early modern France); a large state drains resources that could be used more directly for economic development. Large Asian societies like China and India were simply so large that obstacles were put in the way of economic development. In Asia, Japan's much smaller size gave it a clear advantage. Of additional importance was *geography*. Japan, England, and the Netherlands were all located on large bodies of water, and this allowed them to give more emphasis to maritime than to overland trade. Maritime trade is far superior in terms of trade efficiency in that it allows a much greater quantity of goods to be moved, and to be moved more rapidly and at lower cost (Hugill, 1993; Braudel, 1982). A third factor was *climate*. Europe and Japan both had temperate climates, which is significant when we recognize that most of the world colonized by Europe had tropical or subtropical climates. These colonized regions were best suited to the kinds of economic activities—production of raw materials for export—that European states wanted to use its colonies for. Two extremely successful British settler colonies, the northern United States and Australia, had climates poorly suited to peripheral economic activities and as a result were given much more freedom to develop under their own impetus. Climatologically, Japan was like these settler colonies. It may have escaped peripheralization by Europe at least partly because of its climate or its distant northerly location, and escaping peripheralization has proven to be extremely important to a society's economic success. Fourth, there was *demography*. Both Europe and Japan experienced dramatic population growth during their feudal and early capitalist periods. Population grew substantially throughout the first half of the Tokugawa era (Jannetta, 1987), and continued to grow, albeit more slowly, during the second half of this era (Hanley and Yamamura, 1972). The total population of Europe in AD 1000 was approximately thirty million. By 1340 that had increased by some two-and-a-half times to seventy-four million. Population declined between 1350 and 1450, but after about 1450 Europe began to undergo a long trend of increasing population, and between that time and the eve of the Industrial Revolution the total European population more than doubled (Livi-Bacci, 1992). Marvin Harris (1977) and others have seen the buildup of population pressure as contributing to the declining efficiency of European feudalism and the shift toward capitalism, but I see the significance of population growth somewhat differently. Population growth led to growing urbanization, and this provided a larger pool of workers and stimulated expansion in the size of economic markets. Urbanization also promoted economic differentiation and specialization and more efficient utilization of various resources (Boserup, 1981).

The fifth factor, *political structure,* was quite likely the most important precondition of all. Europe and Japan had the only true feudal regimes in world history (Anderson, 1974b). Moreover, the feudal systems of Europe and Japan arose at about the same time in world history and persisted for remarkably similar lengths of time, about seven centuries. The feudal regimes of these two regions were extremely important because of the freedom they gave to their merchant classes to pursue their economic objectives relatively unhindered. It is widely agreed that large bureaucratic empires smother mercantile activity because they see it as a threat to the way in which they extract surplus. The high levels of political decentralization in Europe and Japan meant that mercantile activities could not be constrained as tightly as they were in large bureaucratic states. Perry Anderson (1974a, 1974b) has called attention to the unusual level of economic freedom enjoyed by the towns of Europe and Japan, and Norman Jacobs (1958) has stressed the remarkable freedom and independence of Japanese merchants compared to merchants in China. Mercantile activity had an importance in Europe and Japan that exceeded by a considerable amount the significance it had in Asia.

Yet as significant as these five preconditions were, they could not have produced capitalism when and where they did without another important condition, and that was *the long-term expansion of world trade and the growth of world commercialization over several millennia* (Sanderson, 1995b, 1999:107–13). Between about 3000 BC and the beginnings of the modern capitalist era, there was a dramatic increase on a world scale in the size and density of trade networks and in the level of urbanization. Cities grew larger and there were many more large cities as time went on. Prior to about 2,200 years ago, trade networks did not transcend local or regional levels, but after this time a worldwide network of trade stretching from the Mediterranean to China was established (Curtin, 1984). After approximately AD 1000 trade networks became even more extensive and a greater quantity of goods passed through them (McNeill, 1982; Wilkinson, 1992). This long process of expanding world commercialization was critical for the development of modern capitalism because capitalism could not emerge suddenly, even if "suddenly" is operationally defined to mean a few hundred years. Because agrarian elites were usually hostile to capitalist activity, it could only emerge slowly and therefore required a long period of incubation before it could reach a "critical mass" essential to a tipping of the balance of economic power in its favor.

My explanation of the rise of modern capitalism is thus that it resulted from the interaction between the five preconditions and the level of world commercialization that had been reached by about AD 1000 to 1250. Once a critical threshold of commercialization had been achieved, a capitalist "takeoff" in those two regions of the world most hospitable to capitalist activity was possible. The long-run expansion of world commercialization is in all likelihood the truly critical factor in all this because, as Fernand Braudel (1984:96) has said, "There could be no world economy until there was a dense enough urban network with trade of sufficient volume and regularity to breathe life into a central or core zone." Braudel is speaking of Europe, but his argument applies to Japan as well. Japan carried on a very substantial trade with East Asia during the second millennium AD, and it has been considered a major maritime power in this part of the world between the thirteenth and fifteenth centuries (J.W. Hall, 1970; Braudel, 1982). Of the preconditions that interacted with this expanding level of world commercialization, I regard the most important as the economic freedom allowed to merchants by decentralized political relations. Merchants in Europe and Japan could not have accomplished what they did when they did if they had been smothered by a centralized agrarian state.

ADDITIONAL EVIDENCE

In terms of food preferences, Harris (1985) and Abrams (1987) provide long lists of societies that eat insects and the various types of insects they eat. A surprising number of societies eat insects, and these are not just preliterate societies, but in some cases true civilizations. On the basis of optimal foraging theory, Harris argues, quite persuasively in my view, that societies that eat insects tend to lack large vertebrate species suitable for eating and thus will remain highly meat deficient if they do not turn to insects. Insect eating is most common in tropical forests that contain large swarming insects. Dogs and cats are eaten in some societies, but are not in most because, as carnivores, they have to be fed meat. They are therefore very inefficient sources of animal protein, and tend to be eaten only when other sources are highly restricted. Harris (1985) has some interesting things to say about cannibalism, especially warfare cannibalism. Eric Ross (1980) has developed an interesting ecomaterialist theory of the shift from pork to beef as the most highly esteemed meat in American society in the nineteenth century. He gives emphasis to changes in ecological, technological, and economic forces. Why is hot and spicy food so popular in so many regions of the world? Rozin (1987) suggests that one possibility is that spices like chili peppers cause the brain to secrete opiates that, at a sufficient level, bring pleasure. Billing and Sherman (1998) show that spices are used more frequently in regions with hotter climates. They argue that this is because in such climates food spoils more rapidly and spices have important antimicrobial properties. The hotter the region, the more likely people will use those spices with the greatest antimicrobial properties. Billing and Sherman conclude in good biomaterialist fashion that people spice their food becauses it enhances their health, longevity, and reproductive success.

There has been a major revival in the last several decades of the study of slavery in the New World, and much of the new literature is devoted to showing the economic foundations of slavery. The really pioneering work was undertaken by Fogel and Engerman in their book *Time on the Cross* (1974). These economic historians carried out detailed quantitative analyses of slavery in the American South showing how it was a highly efficient capitalist system through and through. Their book provides the answer to antimaterialist analyses such as those of Genovese (1965, 1968, 1969, 1974). Tomich (1990) shows the relationship between slavery and the capitalist world-economy in Martinique in the middle of the nineteenth century. Blackburn (1997) deals with the relationship between slavery and capitalism in a much broader geographical and historical sense. See also Fogel (1989), Tomich (1991) and McMichael (1991). In a fascinating article, Halliburton (1975) has shown that a number of slaveholders in the U.S. South were black, demonstrating the priority of economics over race in the formation and maintenance of slavery.

NOTES

1. For a much more detailed treatment of subsistence modes and their determinants, see Sanderson (1995a:chapter 4, 1999).

2. The Meriam, who are located between Australia and New Guinea, hunt turtles and a few men do most of the hunting, so here we have a fourth ethnographic instance of a few men bringing home most of the meat (E.A. Smith, 1999; Smith and Bliege Bird, 2000). It is possible that this pattern represents a form of "costly signaling," a term used by Zahavi and Zahavi (1997) with respect to their so-called Handicap Principle. (See chapter 15 for discussion of this concept.)

3. A much more detailed treatment can be found in Sanderson (1994, 1999:134–80).

15

Social Hierarchies

Equality may perhaps be a right, but no power on earth can ever turn it into a fact.

—Honoré de Balzac

However energetically society in general may strive to make all the citizens equal and alike, the personal pride of each individual will always make him try to escape the common level, and he will form some inequality somewhere to his own profit.

—Alexis de Tocqueville

THE BIOLOGICAL FOUNDATIONS OF SOCIAL HIERARCHIES

Social hierarchies are universal to the human condition, despite their enormous variation in type and degree from one society to the next. In this regard I have found it useful, although I seem to be the only sociologist who does, to distinguish between two different types of hierarchical arrangements, social *inequality* and social *stratification*. By social inequality I mean the existence of a hierarchy in which some individuals have greater prestige and social influence than others but without there being differences in wealth that have become crystallized into social classes (although small wealth differences may exist between individuals). Normally where only inequality prevails the superior status of some individuals is achieved rather than hereditary. Hierarchies of this nature are most commonly associated with hunter-gatherer and small-scale horticultural societies. Inequality comes to be converted into stratification when differences in wealth or privilege become significant enough so that distinct social strata or classes form and where one's social class position has a strongly hereditary character. Stratified societies are built around what Morton Fried (1967:186) has called *differential access to resources,* which means that "members of the same sex and equivalent age status do not have equal access to the basic resources that sustain life." Whereas social inequality is typical of

287

hunter-gatherer and simple horticultural societies, stratification is much more characteristic of large-scale horticultural societies with more intensive systems of economic
production, of agrarian societies, and of modern industrial societies.

The argument here will be that social hierarchies must be explained thrice over, i.e.,
bio-, eco-, and polimaterialistically. A strong tendency toward hierarchy is a fundamental
feature of the human biogram, but this tendency is greatly affected by a range of features
of the natural and sociocultural environment. Social hierarchies are biologically rooted but
socially elaborated. Most sociologists disagree with this view, holding that humans do not
have the kind of biogram that I have indicated, and thus that hierarchies are purely cultural arrangements. The evidence, much of which I shall present below, goes strongly
against this latter view, as a number of sociologists and anthropologists have recognized.
As Somit and Peterson (1997:56-57) argue, "it is highly improbable that social learning
can even begin to account for the regularity and similarity of dominance structures and
dominance-related behaviors among peoples separated by vast distances of time, space, and
cultural development." These authors point out that virtually "all languages abound in
honorifics and in pronouns that recognize and reinforce status distinctions" (1997:56).

James Woodburn (1982) notes that there are human societies, most commonly
hunter-gatherer societies, that have been able to achieve and maintain remarkable levels
of social and economic equality. However, as he also notes (1982:432), this equality
never goes unchallenged and "people are well aware of the possibility that individuals or
groups within their own egalitarian societies may try to acquire more wealth, to assert
more power or to claim more status than other people, and are vigilant to prevent or to
limit this." Elizabeth Cashdan (1980) makes the same point. With respect to the !Kung
San, one of the least hierarchical societies on earth, inequality is "always struggling to
get out." The lack of stratification, she says, is not a natural condition at all, but arises
from the high levels of spatial and temporal variation in the food supply available to the
!Kung. Economic equality must be constantly enforced and policed, because natural
human tendencies strongly work against it (cf. Boehm, 1999). As she points out, related
Bushman groups in environments without such variation, such as the //Gana, relax their
attitude toward the necessity of strict equality and are, in fact, more hierarchical. Timothy Earle (1997) indicates that not all individuals are interested in rank and dominance, but in all human populations there will be people who do strive for these things.
Joseph Lopreato (1984) has argued that humans appear to have an innate desire for
creature comforts and that this desire has been progressively intensified throughout social evolution. Jerome Barkow (1989:179) says that "we hunger for prestige, and much
of our behaviour is dominated by this goal." Barkow argues that humans really compete
for prestige more than for resources. This is debatable, but there seems to be little doubt
that the desire for prestige is a fundamental human drive. Barkow asks what a billion-
aire needs another billion for. His answer? Why to achieve greater prestige than fellow
billionaires who have only a single billion!

Moreover, we know why an innate tendency to strive for status and wealth should be
an integral part of the human biogram. The competition for resources and high social
rank is fundamental to mating and the promotion of one's inclusive fitness. In the earlier discussion of reproductive behavior, it was shown that social rank and reproductive

success are closely linked in many mammalian species and in most human societies. Individuals desire not only to acquire resources and social status, but to pass these things along to their offspring whenever possible. As John Hartung (1976:607) has put it, "It follows from the laws of natural selection that postreproductive adults can enhance their own reproductive success over time, or fitness, by endowing their offspring with whatever transferable wealth they have accumulated. . . . Accordingly, an individual will maximize the fitness-enhancing potential of his wealth if he transfers it to descendants who have inherited the highest concentration of his genes."[1]

Despite the link between status, wealth, and reproductive success, it should not be assumed that the competition for status and wealth is devoted only to reproduction, either consciously or unconsciously. Throughout social evolution this competition has become, to a very substantial extent, autonomous from reproductive concerns. As Penny Anthon Green (1994:197) has pointed out, "genetic competition is, strictly speaking, a contest for resources—the means to reproductive success. But humans pursue these means largely as ends, and it is pleasurable to compete successfully. Consequently, high rank and its associated privileges are often pursued for their own sake—for the sheer pleasure of success." Durkheim stressed that human wants are insatiable. The more people have, the more they want, and thus the competition for status and rank is a self-enhancing process. Once allowed a certain breathing room, a certain freedom from constraints, it can elaborate itself seemingly endlessly. As Randolph Nesse (1994; cited in Somit and Peterson, 1997) has suggested, it is often possible for humans to get enough of the basic necessities of life (food, water, shelter, etc.), but they seem to have great difficulty getting enough status. Michael Hammond (1998) argues that in the ancestral environment status striving and resource acquisition would have been capped at relatively low levels, but once humans began to settle down and strive more energetically for status and resources they became caught up in a situation in which "more is not enough." It became necessary, in a psychological sense, for people to run faster and faster (i.e., strive harder and harder for status and resources) just to stay in the same place.

I contend that the evidence for all of these claims is extremely strong. All four of Alice Rossi's four criteria for suspecting a biological basis for a behavioral pattern are met. Social hierarchies are universally found in human societies (even though in some societies they are only minimally developed), they are widely found in the animal world (especially in our closest relatives, the nonhuman primates), dominance and status-oriented behavior is found in young children prior to major socialization influences, and such behavior is closely associated with one or more physiological attributes (in this case, neurochemicals). Pierre van den Berghe (1978:40-41) notes the virtual universality of hierarchy among primates and points out that

> we [humans] are like some other primates and unlike others. Most of the lower primates, like lemurs, and some of the higher ones, like gibbons . . . , show very little dominance behavior. However, the predominantly terrestrial primates, like baboons and macaques, form, like ourselves, strongly hierarchical societies with sharp status differences between various age and sex groups, and even among adult males, and among adult females.
>
> Those monkey societies are hierarchically organized for defense against predators. As the band forages in open country . . . the subordinate males act as sentinels on the periphery,

the females and the young are in the middle, and the oligarchy of dominant males stays on the alert at or near the center prepared to jump into the fray, to cover the retreat, and to bear the brunt of the fighting if the need arises.

Returning to the human situation, a variety of ethological studies of young children, and in some cases even of infants, suggest that dominance- and rank-oriented behavior are found before major socialization influences have had much chance to take effect. A number of studies have reported dominance orders among infants (e.g., Bakeman and Brownlee, 1982; Missakian, 1980; Strayer and Trudel, 1984). One such study (Russon and Waite, 1991) focused on eleven- to sixteen-month-old infants in a day care group and was able to identify high-, middle-, and low-ranking subgroups. Dominance was also related to imitative behavior, with high-ranking infants being imitated more than low-ranking infants. Omark and Edelman (1975) studied kindergartners through third graders in a middle-class private school and queried children in regard to their perceptions of other children. Specifically, the children were asked their perceptions concerning which children were the toughest, smartest, and nicest. From the first grade on, children were in greatest agreement in terms of which children were the toughest. Omark and Edelman (1975:104) comment that relations concerning toughness "seem to be among the first comparisons between self and others that are remembered. These results suggest that toughness is an important dimension in children's early social structures, and may have a significant effect on the way that they first learn to conceptualize the world." Weisfeld, Omark, and Cronin (1980) followed two cohorts of boys between the first and ninth grades, assessing them for toughness, dominance, leadership, and popularity. In both cohorts toughness was highly correlated with the other traits, dominance in particular, and this correlation remained stable over time. The authors concluded that dominance in boys is a highly stable trait that is based mainly on physical characteristics, and that it leads to the acquisition of resources (including females) and opportunities to exercise leadership. They were struck by the consistency between these findings and the findings of ethological studies of other mammals. They assert (1980:214):

> What does seem to be of prime importance in the present study is that males of our species negotiate a critical, or sensitive, period from about 4+ . . . to 7 years of age. During this period they (1) become combative with their peers, (2) become more muscular, (3) acquire the cognitive capacity for transitive reasoning necessary for comprehending rank orders, and (4) begin to experience pride or shame when they succeed or fail.

Barbara Hold (1980) has attempted to determine the extent to which these findings stand up cross-culturally. Hold looked for similarities in the behavior of German and Japanese kindergartners and G/wi San children of comparable age. She found that the children in all three cultures sorted themselves into dominance hierarchies; some G/wi children, just like German and Japanese children, sought the limelight. In all three cultures a select few children were the center of attention and these children were very frequently imitated by lower-ranking children. High-ranking children were much more likely to initiate activities than were lower-ranking children. Two important differences between G/wi children on the one hand and German and Japanese children on the other were that G/wi children did not try to dominate or manipulate other children, and that the G/wi rank order seemed to be less rigid than the German and Japanese rank orders. These differences probably result from the fact that among the G/wi egalitarianism is stressed and strongly policed because of the particular exigencies of the G/wi economic situation.

Daniel Freedman (1979) has shown that height is an extremely widespread, probably universal, indicator of social status (cf. Brown and Yü, 1993; see L. Ellis, 1994a, 1994b, for a review of studies on body size and status among animals and height and status among humans). In a study carried out by a university marketing professor, 140 job recruiters were asked to choose hypothetically between two applicants for a sales position. The only difference between the applicants was that one was 6'1" tall and the other 5'5." It was found that 72 percent chose the taller applicant, 27 percent had no clear preference, and a mere 1 percent chose the shorter applicant. Freedman points out that being short poses a difficulty for men because it appears to be an automatic sign of subordinate status. In American elections for the presidency, the taller man has won the election nearly every time. Throughout Africa it is the taller tribes who are dominant over the shorter tribes. In Nigeria the tall Fulani have long ruled neighboring groups despite being a numerical minority. The very tall Masai have been the most feared warriors of East Africa, and in Rwanda and Burundi the tall Tutsis have long dominated and looked down upon the short Hutus. In Russia and England height and social status have long been highly correlated, "with a full head separating the Oxford working class and the Oxford dons" (Freedman, 1979:90). It is noteworthy that in many horticultural societies the term for a man of high social rank is often a word that means "big man" (Brown and Yü, 1993). There is a widespread, possibly universal, tendency for smaller individuals to be intimidated by bigger individuals. Pierre van den Berghe (1974) points out that throughout the world submission is expressed by individuals' bowing or crouching. In many highly stratified preindustrial societies, commoners threw themselves prostrate on the ground when powerful rulers visited their villages.

Sociologists are apt to claim (and some have claimed—cf. L. Ellis, 1994a) that the causal relationship between height and status is the reverse of what is being claimed here, i.e., that it is greater status that causes people to be taller because, among other things, people of higher social status enjoy better nutrition. In many highly stratified societies, higher-status persons do generally enjoy better nutrition, but this can explain at best only a small portion of the height-status relationship. Lee Ellis (1994b) reviews studies showing that about 90 percent of the variance in human height is due to genetic factors rather than social environment. This can be illustrated by the fact that blacks in the United States are slightly taller than whites despite their lower social status. Moreover, in egalitarian band and tribal societies height and social status are related just as they are in highly stratified agrarian and industrial societies. Since band and tribal societies usually do not have inequalities in nutritional intake, social status differences cannot be causing differences in height.

It appears that the relationship between social status and height in individuals is closely paralleled by a relationship between social status and the physical elevation at which people live. In their study of a medium-sized Midwestern city, Hoiberg and

Cloyd (1971) found an average correlation of .76 (Pearson r) between social status and elevation. They explained this relationship in terms of "the symbolic cultural definition given to the entire concept of height. Such a symbolic meaning can be crudely displayed through the popularity and meaning of such sayings as 'top drawer,' 'high man on the totem pole,' 'top dog,' etc." (1971:71). I do not object to such an interpretation so long as it is not taken to mean that such a symbolic definition is floating free from biological realities. It is likely that every society has the linguistic equivalent of "top dog" because the mental association between height (or elevation) and social status is part of the wiring of the human brain. Hoiberg and Cloyd studied only one community in one society, but I would predict that physical elevation and social status are positively associated in every society, or at least in the vast majority. (I suspect there are studies on this, but I have not yet encountered any.)

If the tendency toward status striving and hierarchy is rooted in the human biogram, as I am claiming it is, then there must be biochemical indicators of such. Can we identify hormones or other chemicals that are responsible for status striving? The answer is a clear yes. Testosterone has long been linked to aggressive, competitive, and dominance-oriented behavior (see Mazur and Booth, 1998, for a review of the evidence), but the neurotransmitter serotonin would appear to be a much better candidate. Research linking serotonin levels to dominance behavior in vervet monkeys (McGuire, 1982; McGuire, Raleigh, and Johnson, 1983) quickly led to research of the same nature on humans by Douglas Madsen (1985, 1986, 1994) and others. In an early study, Madsen (1985) found substantial correlations between men's blood serotonin levels and certain personality characteristics. Men who were highly driven and who had aggressive, competitive, and hard-charging personalities had substantially higher levels of serotonin in their blood than individuals low on these personality characteristics. In a second study, this time experimental, Madsen (1986) divided his subjects into groups with high, average, and low levels of blood serotonin. His major finding was that the high serotonin group showed a very different physiological response to a competitive situation than the average and low serotonin groups. The cortisol levels of the high serotonin group soared in response to the onset of actual competition, whereas no such effect was observed in the other two groups. This led Madsen (1986:268) to say that "the high serotonin individuals are indeed a special lot. A behavior pattern which had been tied to WBS [whole blood serotonin] only through questionnaire data has now been given striking physiological representation. The dynamics of the best understood of the plasma hormones here presented, cortisol and epinephrine, reflect for the high WBS group precisely the kind of internal response that one would expect from aggressive competitors in the context of rivalry." In a third study, Madsen (1994) looked at the relationship between serotonin levels, social rank, and aggressiveness in a game-playing situation. The serotonin levels of individuals who played the game in a nonaggressive way declined as their perceived social rank rose. However, the serotonin levels of individuals who played the game aggressively rose as their perceived social rank rose. Thus, for the nonaggressive individuals serotonin levels are negatively correlated with social rank, whereas for the aggressive individuals serotonin levels are positively correlated with rank. Madsen (1994:156) comments that the "aggressive themselves are a fascinating group. Seemingly classic Machiavellians, they provide a close fit with the politician of popular imagination: ambitious, self-centered, and when it comes to moral questions, a little fast and loose. If the aggressive-manipulative style enhances the likelihood of real-world political success (which is, of course, unproven), then the dominant figures in our major social arenas may in fact show the elevated blood serotonin predicted by the animal model."

Serotonin levels are also known to play a major role in another form of human behavior, viz., depression. Individuals suffering from major depression are frequently seen to have low serotonin levels, and many of the major antidepressant drugs now available are designed to increase these levels. Interestingly, a psychiatrist who had been treating some of his depressed patients with Prozac soon after it became available noticed that the drug not only lifted their depression but also brought about actual personality changes (Kramer, 1993). The most pronounced change was to turn very reticent individuals, some of whom were painfully shy, into much more confident individuals. Confidence is undoubtedly related to the extent to which individuals will strive for success, and thus to eventual social rank. This is further evidence of an important link between serotonin and status seeking. Moreover, research by Michael McGuire and colleagues (reported in Madsen, 1986) has shown that nondominant vervet monkeys treated with fluoxetine (the chemical name for Prozac) moved into the dominant position in their respective groups.[2]

THE SOCIAL AND CULTURAL ELABORATION OF HIERARCHIES

The question now concerns how this human tendency toward hierarchy gets translated into actual systems of inequality and stratification. Jerome Barkow (1992) presents an argument that dovetails beautifully with the theory and massive evidence presented by Gerhard Lenski in his well-known book *Power and Privilege* (1966). Barkow claims that there are three human psychological traits that make it possible for humans to generate stratification under the appropriate conditions. These are the pursuit of high social rank, nepotism, and the capacity for social exchange. Barkow explains how these work together (1992:634; cf. P.A. Green, 1995:68-69, 74-75):

> Individuals seek high relative standing. They engage in social exchange with others in order to achieve and maintain such standing and to transmit it to their children and other close kin. These tendencies are presumably universal. In some societies, however, there is some surplus production. High relative standing automatically would tend to involve some control over that surplus. The social exchanges through which individuals maintain their high status now have a strong economic component. Enter nepotism. Those who achieve high standing and control over resources seek to transmit these advantages to their offspring and to other close kin. Social exchange facilitates that transmission, too, as reciprocal altruism merges with kin altruism so that members of the elite aid one another's children. . . . Among themselves, the higher ranking favor exchanges that eventually cement themselves and their families (despite rivalries) into coherent, self-interested elites or upper classes. These elites favor their own close kin while striving to reduce or eliminate competition from the progeny of the lower strata, producing barriers to social mobility. Thus, whenever a society achieves a relationship among its population density, environment, and technology such

that surplus production of food and other goods reliably results, the psychology of our species makes it very likely that social inequality and, eventually, social stratification will soon follow. . . .

Note that until fairly large-scale societies existed, with accumulated surpluses of resources, the extent to which parents could ensure the future standing of offspring and other close kin was strictly limited. . . . But once we have an increase in societal scale and technology such that there is a possibility of control over some resource, or a surplus of production, then the tendency toward nepotism means that parents will strive to transmit that control or surplus to their offspring (and grandparents to grandchildren).

Systems of inequality and stratification thus represent the social elaboration of a basic innate tendency toward rank and dominance. Stratification emerges and becomes increasingly complex and elaborate when societies grow larger in scale, become more technologically advanced, and begin producing large economic surpluses, and these conditions themselves emerge as responses to population pressure, changing patterns of land tenure, and changing forms of political organization. Stratification is inherent in the human condition, but it is only a latent rather than an actual possibility until the necessary conditions develop. Let us trace out the changing patterns of inequality and stratification throughout the long process of social evolution. (Much of the evidence reviewed below comes from Lenski, 1966.)

With some important exceptions, hunter-gatherer societies are unstratified because in these societies it is uncommon for any individual to have the capacity to deprive others of access to the resources of nature that sustain life and well-being. Usually there are no wealth differences, and social strata or classes seldom exist. Inequalities of prestige or social influence do exist, however, and are typically based on such factors as age and sex. The possession of certain personal traits is also generally a basis for the acquisition of prestige. Men who show special courage, who are thought of as especially wise, or who are particularly skilled hunters are usually highly esteemed. Despite the absence of wealth differences or class distinctions among most hunter-gatherers, it is clear that a tendency toward stratification is present and will emerge when the right conditions are there. One of these conditions is the existence of an economy or environment productive enough to allow for the accumulation and storage of foodstuffs. Alain Testart (1982) has shown that there are some very important differences between hunter-gatherers who store food and those who do not. Storing hunter-gatherers are usually sedentary and have high population densities, and a more individualized or privatized pattern of ownership has often emerged among societies of this type. Using a representative sample of forty hunter-gatherer societies, Testart found that 80 percent of the food-storers were stratified compared to only 7 percent of the nonstoring societies. The classic examples of stratified hunter-gatherers are many of the Indian tribes inhabiting the northwest coast region of North America. This region of the world is characterized by exceptionally rich environments that have permitted high-density, complex societies to be supported. Many of these societies developed elaborate stratification systems characterized by ruling chiefs who were obsessed with social rank and the pursuit of prestige.

It appears that a number of prehistoric hunter-gatherer societies (about 12,000 to 10,000 years ago) had become stratified or at least were characterized by marked distinctions of status or rank. Paul Mellars (1985) has uncovered evidence of complex hunter-gatherer societies with apparently high levels of population density in late Upper Paleolithic southwestern France. Mellars suggests that these societies had begun to exploit a much wider range of food resources than in earlier times, probably as a result of the economic stress produced by population pressure. The archaeological sites show evidence of specialized craftsmen and grave goods that suggest the existence of significant social ranking. Like the Northwest Coast tribes, these were densely populated societies living in regions of abundant resources that had adopted the practice of food storing. In general, I think that prehistoric hunter-gatherers were more likely to be stratified, and some of them highly stratified, than contemporary hunter-gatherers. The latter have generally been found in environments poor in resources compared to most of the environments that prehistoric hunter-gatherers would have occupied (Dickemann, 1975), and thus hunter-gatherers in today's world have generally been unable to be productive enough to allow the emergence of true stratification.

Simple horticultural societies, like hunter-gatherers, are usually characterized by social inequality in the absence of stratification. However, prestige differences in simple horticultural societies are often much more pronounced than they are among hunter-gatherers. Simple horticultural societies are often good examples of what Fried (1967:109) has termed a *rank society*, or one "in which positions of valued status are somehow limited so that not all those of sufficient talent to occupy such statuses actually achieve them" (1967:109). In many simple horticultural societies, a few hard-working and ambitious individuals are able to produce enough from their gardens and animal herds to hold large feasts, and individuals who repeatedly demonstrate their ability to hold successful feasts come to be held in considerable respect and accorded a great deal of prestige. As discussed in the last chapter, in many of these societies, especially those in Melanesia, such persons acquire the status of "big men" (Harris, 1977). Big men typically have many rivals who want to oust them from their positions of high rank. Big men accumulate wealth, but their status is gained by generously distributing it rather than keeping it for themselves. Among the Siuai of Bougainville in the Solomon Islands, for example, the most successful feast givers have praise heaped upon them and are usually deferred to. As Douglas Oliver (1955:401) comments, among the Siuai, big men "are usually spared menial jobs; others fetch water for them, and climb palms to get coconuts and areca nuts for their refreshment. Boisterous talk usually becomes quieter when a leader approaches, and boys leave off rough-housing. In fact, one of the sternest lessons impressed upon a child is to stay away from a leader, or else remain quiet in his presence." Moreover, "few people would assume enough familiarity with him to place a friendly hand on his shoulder—a common gesture among equals."

It is with the shift to more intensive or advanced horticultural societies that we most commonly see the emergence of stratification. Intensive horticultural societies frequently exhibit hereditary strata or classes, the true mark of stratification. Many of these societies contain three main social strata consisting of chiefs, subchiefs, and commoners. The differences among these strata involve differential access to the basic resources of nature, which for Fried (1967) is what separates systems of stratification from systems of mere inequality. The strata are distinguished by differences of social rank, power, dress and ornamentation, consumption patterns, involvement in economic production, availability of leisure time, and general styles of life. Stratification systems of this sort have been found among many advanced horticultural societies in sub-Saharan Africa as well as among a number of the precontact societies of Polynesia, Hawaii in particular (Sahlins, 1958). Hawaii before the arrival of the Europeans was divided into three main strata consisting of high-ranking chiefs and their families, stewards who managed local or regional domains of a chiefdom, and a very large class of commoners. The highest ranking or paramount chief was thought to be divine and a series of elaborate taboos existed concerning contact with him. No one could let his shadow fall on the paramount's house or possessions, wear his robe, or enter his house ahead of him, and commoners were even prohibited from touching anything used by the chief. When in his presence others were required to lie prostrate on the ground. A paramount chief exercised strong control over the use of land and could evict commoners from land for any number of reasons. Persons of high status could call upon lower-status persons for the performance of various labor services, and commoners could be killed for failing to comply with a demand for their labor. High chiefs and their families took no part in the production of daily subsistence and consequently have often been considered a kind of primitive "leisure class."

Although they are often highly stratified, advanced horticultural societies have been permeated nonetheless by what Lenski has called a "redistributive ethic." Chiefs or kings were expected to be generous and their popularity could sharply decline if they were not. As Lenski (1966:165) has noted with respect to some African advanced horticultural societies, "On great public occasions [the king] is expected to slaughter many of his cattle and provide beer and porridge for all who gather at his village. He lends cattle, supports destitute widows and orphans, sends food to sick people and newly confined mothers, and in time of famine distributes corn from his own granaries or, if this is insufficient, purchases supplies from neighboring groups." But with the transition to agrarian societies, with their much more intensive systems of economic production, the limitations formerly placed on the stratification system were lifted. The redistributive ethic essentially disappeared and there emerged a much more extreme form of stratification in which most of the population was thrown into a condition of poverty and social degradation. The gap in power, privilege, and prestige between the dominant and the subordinate classes was immense.

Agrarian stratified orders were complex and often contained numerous strata. At the top was an elite that consisted of the political ruler and his family along with a landowning class. Below this was often a retainer class, which consisted of functionaries who directly served the elite and performed a wide variety of administrative tasks; a merchant class; a class of religious functionaries or priests; a class of artisans or craftsmen; and, at the very bottom, a class of expendables, or people who relied largely on illegitimate or illegal means of support, such as thievery or prostitution. Despite this complexity, however, in nearly all agrarian societies the landowners and the peasantry constituted the most important social classes in the sense that it was their relationship that made the wheels of their economy and society turn.

The ruler in agrarian societies officially stood at the political head of society. What Lenski calls the governing class was normally composed of the principal owners of land.

However, both the ruler and the governing class tended to be both major landowners and major holders of political power, and these two segments of the politico-economic elite were usually closely linked. This elite constituted only a tiny fraction of the population—perhaps no more than 1 or 2 percent—but it may have controlled anywhere from half to two-thirds of the total wealth. Agrarian societies generated huge economic surpluses, the bulk of which usually ended up in the hands of the politico-economic elite. Elites often developed an elaborate status culture and set of manners that were designed to distinguish them sharply from subordinate groups. In the Chinese gentry, for example, the "emphasis was on the idle, highly-cultivated man; status markings, such as wearing long fingernails to indicate remoteness from manual work, were used. The content of Chinese high culture thus developed great subtlety of tastes. Out of this situation came the high aesthetic standards of Chinese arts, cuisine, architecture, and furnishings" (Annett and Collins, 1975:178). And consider also the behavior of members of elites in early modern Europe (Annett and Collins, 1975:179):

> Courts became places of considerable enforced leisure. Large numbers of ladies and gentlemen were obliged to spend a great deal of time waiting upon the king, and developed means of whiling away the hours. Conversation became an art form with elaborate emphasis on politeness and topics of respectable entertainment. It is at this time that verbal taboos began to develop, especially taboos on the vulgar language of the people. Particularly at the court of Louis XIV in the seventeenth century, great emphasis was placed on elaborate mutual bowings and curtseying, flowery greeting and farewell rituals, and polite inquiries after one's health. The correct style of conversation kept politics and other business for the backstage, while entertaining conversation came to consist of *bon mots* and flowery compliments, clever discussions of personalities and love affairs. At Versailles, the mastery of trivial details of etiquette and an elaborate secret language of hints and catch-words could make or break careers.

In most agrarian societies the largest social class by far was the peasantry. Peasants' economic situation was for the most part a miserable one, although just how exploited they were varied greatly from one place and time to another. Peasants everywhere were subjected to taxation, which varied from as little as 10 percent to as much as 70 percent of the crop. Peasants were also normally subjected to forced labor, being required to provide a certain number of days of labor either for their landlord or for the state. In medieval Europe, for example, peasants were required to work on their lord's demesne, or home farm, several days every week. In addition to their severe economic deprivation, peasants occupied a very low social status in all agrarian societies, a huge gulf separating them from the elite. Peasants were regarded as extreme social inferiors, often being considered less than fully human.

It is clear that the system of inequality or stratification is very closely related to a society's stage of technological development. Hunter-gatherer and simple horticultural societies are seldom stratified, intensive horticultural societies are much more likely to exhibit stratification, and agrarian societies are by far the most highly stratified of all preindustrial societies. However, with the transition from agrarian to industrial societies within the last two hundred years there has occurred what Lenski (1966) calls a "historic reversal" in the relationship between stratification and technological development.

Industrial societies appear to be less stratified than their agrarian predecessors. The main line of evidence that Lenski uses to support his claim has to do with the proportion of total wealth claimed by the dominant class in agrarian and industrial societies. He estimates that in agrarian societies perhaps as much as 50 percent of the total wealth was claimed by the dominant class, whereas in industrial societies this proportion has been reduced to about 25 percent. Also, in modern industrial societies there has been a diffusion of wealth throughout the population and the creation of large middle and working classes that enjoy an extremely high standard of living in comparison to the largest social class in agrarian societies, the peasantry.

Nevertheless, industrial societies, especially industrial capitalist societies, are still very highly stratified. One way of assessing the degree of stratification in industrial capitalist societies is by looking at income inequality, especially the proportions of total national income claimed by the top and bottom income quintiles. Kevin Phillips (1990) has reported the following figures for several major capitalist societies in the late 1970s and early 1980s: United States, 12:1; France, 9:1; Canada, 9:1; Britain, 8:1; West Germany, 5:1; Sweden, 5:1; Netherlands, 5:1; and Japan, 4:1. These figures suggest not only that industrial capitalist societies are highly stratified, but that they differ significantly among themselves.

Industrial capitalist societies have a class structure that looks more or less like the following (Rossides, 1976). There is an upper class, called by Marxists a bourgeoisie or capitalist class, whose members possess great wealth and power. This class probably constitutes no more than about 1 or 2 percent of the population. Its members occupy the top positions in corporations, banks, insurance companies, etc., and enjoy extremely high prestige. There is an upper-middle class, constituting perhaps 10 percent of the population, whose members are primarily successful business managers, members of the learned professions, and high-level civil and military officials. The members of this class generally earn very high incomes and are able to accumulate substantial wealth. They enjoy very high prestige. Below this class is a lower-middle class that comprises perhaps 30 percent of the population and includes mainly small businessmen, lower-level professionals, and sales and clerical workers. The members of this class receive moderate incomes and enjoy moderate prestige. The largest social class in industrial capitalist societies is the working class, which may constitute anywhere from 40 to 60 percent of the population. Its members are skilled, semiskilled, and unskilled manual and service workers. The incomes received by the members of this class are relatively low in comparison to those of higher classes. There is usually a lower class in industrial capitalist societies, although its size varies markedly from one society to another. It may consist of as much as 20 percent of the population in Britain and the United States, but its proportions are much smaller in most other industrial capitalist societies (on the order of, say, 5 percent). The members of this class are people whose lives are very economically marginal. They are chronically unemployed or underemployed, frequently suffer from acute economic distress, and have extremely low social prestige.

State socialist societies emerged earlier in this century as an alternative to industrial capitalism. One of their explicit aims was to eliminate the capitalist class struggle and create a "classless" society. What happened, however, was the creation of a new kind of class society rather than a society without classes. This failure to create a classless society despite revolutionary changes in who owned the means of production is, I would argue, strong support for the claim that the tendency toward social hierarchy is an innate and fundamental part of what it means to be human.

The class structure of the old Soviet Union, the leading exemplar of state socialist society, can be delineated approximately as follows (Parkin, 1971):

- the white-collar intelligentsia
- skilled manual workers
- lower-level white-collar workers
- unskilled workers
- peasants

Frank Parkin (1971) has regarded the main class division as that between the intelligentsia and everyone else, and it is clear that the intelligentsia as a whole has been a highly privileged class. This class, comprising roughly 20 percent of the population, has generally consisted of university-educated managerial and administrative workers in the Soviet state and state corporations. Its members have enjoyed more privilege and prestige than the members of other social classes. They have received higher incomes (which have included bonuses and special wage supplements), access to the best housing, opportunities to travel abroad, and the use of official cars and other forms of state property. They have also been highly successful in guaranteeing places for their children in the best schools and universities. However, the real elite in Soviet society has been a tiny segment of the intelligentsia known as the *nomenklatura,* the closest thing in the old Soviet Union to a capitalist *haute bourgeoisie.* It has been by far the most privileged of the privileged class.

It is true that the Soviet Union and other highly industrialized state socialist societies created a more egalitarian income distribution than what has been found within industrial capitalist societies (Lane, 1971; Slama, 1978, cited in Kornai, 1992), and it is true that the state socialist societies for a time created levels of upward social mobility exceeding those of capitalism (Parkin, 1971; Giddens, 1980; Yanowitch, 1977). It is also true that the Soviet bureaucratic elite has been different in nature and composition from a capitalist bourgeoisie (Lane, 1971). These differences between state socialism and capitalism indicate that the nature of the economic structure is surely an important determinant of the stratification system. However, the fact that state socialism has continued to have a privileged elite with an abiding interest in passing along its advantages to its offspring seems to confirm the biomaterialist conception of stratification discussed earlier.

It is also extremely interesting to see what is happening now in Russia since the collapse of the Soviet Union in 1991. With increasing privatization, far greater economic inequalities have emerged. The careers of many members of the old *nomenklatura* have been ruined, whereas other members of this elite have been able to benefit enormously from the new privatization. They have often become co-owners of new private companies and are rapidly forming a private entrepreneurial class. Some members of this class have become extremely rich. They live in extremely expensive apartments in Moscow, for example, and have been exceptionally ostentatious with their new wealth (Zaslavsky, 1995). Once the lid was lifted, things began to change very rapidly. In postsocialist society the primal urge toward hierarchy seems to be taking full advantage of the new possibilities.

THEORETICAL AND EMPIRICAL REPRISE

The evidence, then, shows that humans invariably take advantage of whatever opportunities exist in order to display dominance, rank, and status-oriented behaviors and to accumulate wealth. To me, this strongly suggests an innate tendency toward hierarchy that interacts in complex ways with several crucially important conditions such that social hierarchies become progressively more elaborate and extreme as societies evolve in other respects. As mentioned earlier, the most important of these conditions appear to be changes in population density, changing forms of land tenure, technological advance, increasing economic productivity, and changing forms of political organization. However, exactly how these variables are related to the progressive growth of stratification is a matter of some uncertainty.

One of the best-known attempts to explain hierarchies in social evolutionary terms is Lenski's (1966) ecomaterialist theory. Lenski starts with precisely the same assumption I have been arguing for. Humans will share with each other to the extent that this sharing is necessary or beneficial to themselves, but when conditions change such that sharing is no longer needed, or such that they can do better by not sharing, then people will tend to hoard and to compete, to struggle against one another rather than to cooperate. We recognize such sharing, of course, as reciprocal altruism. Lenski argues that the most important condition undermining cooperation and sharing is technological advancement. As societies improve their subsistence technologies, their economies become more productive. Economic surpluses emerge, and these surpluses grow larger the more technology advances. Wealth now exists and expands and accumulates. As the pie gets bigger, people compete with each other more and more vigorously for larger and larger shares, and thus stratification intensifies.

I call Lenski's theory a *surplus theory* because it makes struggles over the economic surplus the key to stratification. However, this theory makes what seems to me an unwarranted assumption: When technology makes surpluses possible, people will start producing them. That seems to me to violate the all-important Law of Least Effort that is a fundamental grounding assumption of Darwinian conflict theory. Since, other things equal, people try to expend as little time and energy making a living as possible, what would lead them to produce an economic surplus? One possibility is economic. Horticulturalists may want a safeguard against drought and famine, and thus may produce enough food to store away in time of need (Harris, 1975). Hunter-gatherers living in bountiful environments may store food for similar reasons. But most importantly, I think the major human motive lying behind surplus economic production is political compulsion. At some point, some people get themselves into a position by means of which they can compel other people to work for them and produce substantial quantities of storable food. And I think that what gets people into this position is some sort of shift in land tenure, some sort of movement toward private landownership. Some people get control of a lot of land, others get control of much less (or none), and those who control the most can begin to control decisions about how the land is used, including in particular how hard people can be forced to work and how much surplus they are expected to produce. Once this happens, a threshold has been crossed, the threshold marked by Fried's "differential access to resources."

I call this alternative ecomaterialist theory a *scarcity theory* to distinguish it from Lenski's surplus theory (Sanderson, 1995a). It has been put together from suggestions made by Michael Harner (1970), Morton Fried (1967), Richard Wilkinson (1973), and Rae Lesser Blumberg (1978). In terms of a linear chain of causation, the scarcity theory says that population growth and resultant population pressure lead to increased land scarcity, that increased land scarcity leads to increased competition and struggle for the control of land, and that at some point land begins to be controlled in an unequal fashion. Differential access to resources has emerged. Some people can now compel others to begin producing economic surpluses and to relinquish them. Technological advance is also a part of this process, being dictated to a large extent by population pressure. All of these variables change together as parts of a package. Technological advance allows for increased economic productivity, and thus bigger and bigger surpluses can be extracted from the primary producers. Underlying the whole chain is the insatiability of human wants: As people get more, they want more, and so stratification feeds on itself over time and becomes both self-perpetuating and self-enhancing. As the lid gets lifted, the possibilities become greater and greater. People can never have enough wealth or enough status once they start to pursue them vigorously.

In order to shed more light on these two interpretations of the evolution of stratification, I have attempted to supplement Lenski's qualitative analyses with quantitative analyses of data from the *Ethnographic Atlas* and the SCCS. From the *Atlas* I selected the variable "class stratification" (categories = egalitarian, wealth distinctions only, elite, dual, complex) as the dependent variable and ran it against three independent variables: subsistence type, stage of political evolution, and mean size of local communities. Subsistence type was correlated at r = .409 with class stratification, but it mostly washed out when the other variables were controlled. Stage of political evolution correlated with class stratification at r = .657 and community size correlated at r =.650. When all of these variables were entered into a multiple regression analysis, they collectively explained 51 percent of the variance, with community size and political stage contributing about equally and subsistence type contributing very little. A second regression analysis was run in which several more specific subsistence variables were substituted for subsistence type: percent dependence on gathering, percent dependence on hunting, percent dependence on agriculture, and percent dependence on animal husbandry. These subsistence variables, along with community size and political stage, explained 59 percent of the total variance in class stratification, and political stage was by far the most important predictor.

The SCCS contains an additional stratification variable, "social stratification" (categories = egalitarian, hereditary slavery, two social classes, two social classes + caste and slavery, three social classes or castes), that seems to be slightly more sensitive than "class stratification." This variable was entered into a multiple regression analysis with four independent variables: subsistence type, community size, political stage, and population density. All of these variables were moderately to strongly correlated with social stratification, but only political stage remained strong when the effects of the other variables were removed (zero-order r = .770, partial r = .597). Community size, political stage, and subsistence type collectively explained 62 percent of the variance in social stratification, and political stage explained most of this.

These analyses strongly suggest that the emergence and evolution of social stratification is a political process. The fact that subsistence technology is correlated with stratification but largely washes out when the other variables, especially political stage, are controlled suggests that a higher level of subsistence technology is only an *enabler* of stratification. It permits the development of the conditions necessary to stratification (an economic surplus, and all that), but by itself it is not a cause of stratification. For stratification to emerge and become elaborated, power differentials are necessary to turn possibility into reality. This makes sense, but can we make political stage an independent variable to stratification? Theoretically (i.e., from the perspective of Darwinian conflict theory), I have been thinking of political stage as a dependent variable and stratification as an independent variable. Perhaps politics and stratification are related such that each ratchets the other up throughout social evolution. The variables could be codetermining each other.

Are these findings compatible or incompatible with my scarcity interpretation of the emergence and evolution of social stratification? They appear to be compatible. For one thing, that interpretation views stratification as a political process. Population pressure sets everything in motion, but it is only significant if it leads to changes in land tenure and the economic and political power that flow from those changes. This is what the data suggest, for in the SCCS population density is correlated with stratification (r = .526) but largely washes out when other independent variables are controlled (partial r = .052). Like the level of subsistence technology, population pressure appears to be only an enabler of stratification rather than a true cause of it.

The scarcity theory is actually very similar to an argument put forth by Richard Lee (1990), a Marxian anthropologist, except that Lee would certainly reject the biomaterialist side of the argument. Lee has nominated population growth as the variable setting the evolution of stratification in motion. At some point this leads to "(a) an increase in population density, which leads to (b) a relative decrease in per capita resource availability, and therefore a decreased ease of subsistence, which leads to (c) an increase in societal scale and levels of production to meet increased demands, which in turn leads to (d) an increase in internal/external tensions." In the following passage Lee tries to show how the leveling devices of hunter-gatherer societies get eliminated and replaced by increasingly severe forms of stratification (1990:244-45):

> But leveling devices are not simply aspects of value orientation. They also operate on the material plane to prevent both accumulation and destitution. The underlying principles can be modeled as follows: visualize two horizontal parallel lines. The upper line is a ceiling of

accumulation of goods above which an individual cannot rise, and the lower line is a floor of destitution below which one cannot sink. In the communal mode the ceiling and the floor are closely connected; one cannot exist without the other. No one can have too much, and if there is any food in the camp, everybody in the camp is going to get some of it. The obligation to share food and the taboo against hoarding are no less strong and no less ubiquitous in the primitive world than the far more famous taboo against incest. But unlike the incest taboo, which persists to the present, the hoarding taboo became a casualty of social evolution. One of the key developments of social evolution is the lifting of the ceiling of accumulation. Animal domestication represents such a shift. Instead of shooting the animal and eating the meat, one brings the beast into the settlement and it sits there as property. Once the ceiling is raised, the possibility of wealth differences emerges. Someone could have no goats while another person had one; and if no goats and one goat is possible, then so is one goat and ten goats, or one goat and a hundred.

So far we have spoken of raising the ceiling, but at a crucial point in the evolution of societies we observe the lowering of the floor. I don't know exactly how that happens. In the communal mode if someone gets a little uppity, (s)he is leveled out. By the same token, those falling through the cracks are supported by the group. But when the floor is lowered, poverty for some becomes possible. The community safety net for some disappears. One of the elements of social evolution that is of great interest is how the cracks get wider. Do people fall through those cracks by neglect, or are they preyed upon? Does society devour itself by the rich preying on the poor? (In ancient Greece, as some people got wealthier, they first took the land of their neighbors, then they enslaved them.) The ceiling and the floor are dialectically connected.

In the modern world, both floor and ceiling have disappeared. There are billionaires in one area and mass poverty and starvation in others.

The only thing wrong with this argument, in my view, is that it begs the most important question of all: Why should the earliest forms of stratification ever have begun in the first place? Lee is certainly not assuming an organism with a hierarchical tendency of any sort, and that is where he goes wrong. He simply does not see the extent to which status competition is just below the surface (and not always that) of the least hierarchical societies. Lee's human organisms have no real tendencies at all. But then whence that curiously nasty tendency for societies to become progressively more unequal with general social evolution? Doesn't the existence of such a striking trend all over the world throughout both history and prehistory strongly suggest that there is a particular kind of organism there? I cannot see how any other conclusion is possible. If humans have no natural tendency toward rank and hierarchy, then why have those behaviors always emerged and intensified whenever conditions permitted? Social evolution has always run in the same direction all over the world. If we have no innate tendency toward hierarchy, then why didn't some societies refuse it when conditions offered it? Why didn't at least some human societies "just say no" to hierarchy?

A final question. Given the evolutionary trend toward greater stratification, why was there a reversal of this trend in the transition from agrarian to modern industrial societies? Lenski himself points to a number of factors but singles out the rise of democratic ideologies as the most important. With the rise of democratic ideologies, the many could combine against the few to help restructure society in their favor. Lenski is right; that is a big part of the picture. However, I would add that a certain logic of the capitalist economic system was at work as well. Despite Marx's predictions, capitalism did not collapse because of a massive crisis of underconsumption resulting from the increasing impoverishment of the working class. Capitalist industrialization created large and increasingly powerful working classes, and it was these classes that pressed hard for democratization because their economic interests were at stake (Rueschemeyer, Stephens, and Stephens, 1992). Systems of stratification are very sensitive to the underlying economies on which they rest, and they change as these economies change. Capitalism has led to a mass society, something that was unthinkable in agrarian societies, with their large oppressed and often dispossessed peasantries. It is the rise of mass consumer capitalism that is also behind the enormous decline in status and deference cultures within the last century, and the emergence of a widespread egalitarian ideology, especially in the United States.[3] Annett and Collins (1975:13) show that the

> general trend has been the decline of the old pretensions, the evaporation of the old collective conscience and its supporting deference rituals. Changes in styles of clothing, manners, conversation, and entertainment have been apparent since at least the 1940s. . . . the disappearance of the old formal party with its obliging host and array of servants, along with the high theatricality of evening dress; the bowing, hat-tipping, and polite titles of address giving way to a pervasive nicknaming familiarity; the neglect of old rituals of standing when women and superiors entered a room, and of the elaborate handshakings and introductions; the gossipy sociability that replaced the stiff aloofness and clearly marked ritual barriers of the traditional gentry style and the urbane posturing of fashionable society.

Annett and Collins go on to identify a number of conditions associated with the rise of mass consumer capitalism that have caused this status and deference culture to disintegrate. These include the disappearance of servants with the emergence of mass-produced household appliances; increases in the financial resources of the working and middle classes that have allowed them to maintain a style of dress closer to that of the upper classes and, in general, to emulate upper-class culture; and the rise of television and, with it, the emergence of an entertainment culture for a mass audience.

ADDITIONAL EVIDENCE

Amotz Zahavi (1975), in collaboration with Avishag Zahavi (Zahavi and Zahavi, 1997) has introduced a new theoretical concept into neo-Darwinism, the Handicap Principle, which is to some extent a modification of sexual selection theory (G. Miller, 2000). Through the use of this principle the Zahavis hope to be able to explain a variety of features of animal anatomy and behavior. The idea was initially fiercely resisted by most evolutionary biologists when it was first introduced in the mid-1970s, but it is starting to win considerable acceptance. I am not sure how much it can explain—how wide-ranging its explanatory powers are—but it does appear to be the basis for a number of important insights.

The Zahavis use the Handicap Principle to explain such things as the elaborate plumage of peacocks. They reject the traditional explanation given by Sir Ronald Fisher many years ago, and widely accepted even today, that this is due to a runaway process of sexual selection. For them, the peacock's plumage is an *honest signal,* or one that, because of the burden—the handicap—it imposes on its bearer, genuinely signifies that he is of high quality and thus desirable as a mate. It takes a great deal of energy to grow a beautiful, long tail, and only healthy peacocks can do so. Moreover, peacocks hold their tails upright to show them off, and this takes strength, another sign of high quality. The Handicap Principle can also be put to use in understanding the relationship between predator and prey. When a gazelle stots to, say, a lion—jumps on all four legs simultaneously—it is showing the lion that it is too fast for the lion to catch it, thus giving the lion an honest signal of the gazelle's ability to escape. The Zahavis also suggest that animals may seek prestige by providing resources to others, thus signaling that they are of high quality. This applies to humans, as well, they think; people can, for example, show they are of high quality by wasting money in lavish displays. If they can waste money, they must have more than they need.

The Handicap Principle would seem to be almost tailor-made to explain such phenomena as big-man feasting and the famous potlatch practiced by many tribes that lived along the northwest coast of North America (Boone, 1998). The potlatch was an elaborate giveaway feast in which chiefs would invite neighboring chiefs to their villages to give property away. During their potlatches, Northwest Coast chiefs would attempt to shame rival chiefs by giving away large quantities of wealth and by ranting and raving about their own greatness. The more wealth they gave away, the higher their status and the greater the shame that was brought down on their rivals. The greatest act that a chief could perform was pouring oil on his house and burning it to the ground. In terms of the Handicap Principle, the chief who gave away his property and burned down his house was engaged in a form of *costly signaling* or a *costly display:* He was sending a message to other chiefs that he was so rich that these things didn't matter. He could easily recover from such losses.

Among group-living birds known as babblers, individual birds compete to stand sentinel for others and to feed others. The Zahavis make particular note of the fact that higher-ranking birds attempt to feed lower-ranking ones and vigorously resist being fed by them. The act of giving seems to be an honest or costly signal telling other birds that the givers are of high quality. "By investing for the good of the group," they say, "the dominant male shows off both his superiority and his willingness to give to his subordinates. This makes these subordinates less likely to leave and thus helps the dominant bird remain at the head of a large, strong group" (1997:142). There is a striking parallel between this behavior and the behavior of big men in horticultural societies. As we have seen, in these societies the only avenue to big man status is through generous giving to others. Even in advanced horticultural societies, chiefs are still expected to be generous and usually make a special point to be, often referring to themselves as "great providers" (Harris, 1977). In modern industrial societies philanthropic giving by the rich is a well-known fact, and such societies have been notorious for what Veblen (1934[1912]) has called "conspicuous waste" as a status-seeking mechanism. I am also struck by the fact that, as discussed in chapter 14, in a number of hunter-gatherer societies only a few men hunt and most of the meat the band eats is provided by these men, a practice that seems to involve prestige seeking. This is the case for the !Kung, the Hadza, the Aché and the Meriam (Hawkes, 1993; Smith and Bliege Bird, 2000). The Handicap Principle, whatever its other uses, may thus turn out to provide special insight into the biology of prestige seeking in human societies. Research along these lines might be handsomely repaid (cf. Boone, 1998).

NOTES

1.   There seems to be an important sex difference in status striving and resource acquisition. Although women certainly engage in these behaviors, they appear to be stronger in men. Why should this be? As already indicated, men need status and resources in order to attract mates, or at least the most desirable mates. However, except among elites in highly stratified societies and where dowry exists, women do not particularly need either status or resources in order to attract mates. This may explain why men's status striving and resource acquisition efforts are usually more prominent than women's. The question might then arise as to why most women have an innate tendency to strive for these things at all. The answer is that status and resources do translate into greater reproductive success. Sarah Blaffer Hrdy (1999) has shown that Flo, the famous female chimpanzee studied by Jane Goodall, was able to use her high status to gain resources for her offspring and to protect them from attacks by other mothers. As Hrdy (1999:111) comments, "generalized striving for local clout was genetically programmed into the psyches of female primates during a distant past when status and motherhood were totally convergent." Hrdy argues that, although the evidence is less clear, social status and reproductive success also appear to be closely linked in human females. In the ancestral environment "where there was no birth control, and where no female was ever celibate, there was no possibility that female rank and maternal reproductive success could be *other* than correlated" (1999:112).

2.   Although admitting that prestige-seeking men like big men in horticultural societies may have a genetically predisposed desire for approval and recognition that is stronger than that of others, Marvin Harris (1989) denies that human biology contributes much to the formation of social hierarchies. Harris is critical of Thorstein Veblen's (1934[1912]) argument that humans have an innate desire to feel superior and thus an innate desire to emulate the behavior of leisure classes and other high-status individuals or groups. Harris (1989:367) argues that "Veblen's universal drive to emulate the leisure class presupposes that a leisure class exists universally, which is factually untrue. The !Kung, Semai, and Mehinacu get along quite well without manifesting any marked propensity to show themselves superior. Instead of boasting about how great they are, they belittle themselves and their accomplishments precisely in order to reassure each other that they are all equal." But why should the !Kung, Semai, and Mehinacu need such reassurance if they have no natural desire to feel superior? If there is no such tendency toward status-seeking behavior, why do people spend so much time trying to make sure it doesn't arise? It is of course true that humans have nothing as specific as an innate desire to emulate a leisure class, but Harris takes Veblen too literally. Instead of a specific desire to emulate leisure classes, what people have is a more generalized desire to emulate high-status individuals, whatever they may be like in any actual society. But the most serious problem with Harris's argument is that he completely begs the question as to how leisure classes could ever come into existence in the first place. What Harris fails to see is that the formation of particular patterns of social stratification is always the result of the interaction between biological predispositions and a wide range of environmental circumstances. He is still stuck in the antiquated way of thinking promoted by the SSSM, viz., that bi-

ology and culture are opposing rather than cooperating and interacting forces. Correlatively, he is also a relentless "culture vulture": If something varies from one society to another, it can only be "because of the culture."

3. It is this very ideology, in my judgment, an ideology that began to take shape in the 1930s, that has been responsible for the rise of the SSSM and thus the fervently antibiological stance of most modern social science. As egalitarianism has grown, the SSSM has become more deeply entrenched and opposition to biological explanations of human behavior increasingly rigid and hostile. For an insightful discussion of this point, see Degler (1991).

16

Politics and War

POLITICS AND THE STRUGGLE FOR POWER

Politics is the struggle for power or control or, at the very least, for leadership. It is the struggle for dominance, and thus derives from the same basic part of the biogram as the struggle for status. Indeed, the two are inextricably intertwined. Lionel Tiger and Robin Fox (1971) describe political systems as "breeding systems" inasmuch as the struggle for dominance is, ultimately, the struggle for reproductive success. They go on to identify five basic principles of primate politics:

1. The males dominate the political system, and the older males dominate the younger males.
2. Females often have great influence in promoting the dominance of particular males, and their long-term relationships to these males are critical for the stability of the system.
3. The dominant males keep order among and protect the females and juveniles.
4. Cooperation among males is a critical feature of primate politics inasmuch as coalitions of bonded males act as units in the dominance system.
5. The whole structure is held together by the attractiveness of the dominants and the attention that is constantly paid to them by subordinates.

Tiger and Fox hold that all human political systems—aristocracies, oligarchies, plutocracies, tyrannies, despotisms, democracies, etc.—work according to these same basic processes despite their obvious differences.

In their book *Darwinism, Dominance, and Democracy* (1997), Albert Somit and Steven Peterson argue that humans have been built by biological evolution to favor authoritarian political systems. They note that throughout human history authoritarian political regimes of one type or another have been overwhelmingly the rule, and democracy has been rare. From the beginnings of human history some 5,000 years ago until the middle of the nineteenth century, they argue, only ancient Athens and Rome had governments that could be described as at all democratic. They produce a "short list" of contemporary democracies, and are able to come up with only 28 countries (they limit themselves to what they call "macro-nations," or large states), or about 20 percent of the world's 148 macro-nations. They also point out that the ratio of democratic to nondemocratic nations has remained about the same for the past 75 years.

Somit and Peterson offer a great deal of evidence to support their major claim. First, of course, is simply the overwhelming presence of authoritarian states of one type or another throughout human history. Second, they suggest that the masses are easily indoctrinated into political beliefs that favor ruling elites and that they have a striking willingness to obey. In addition to all this, they make much of the fact that the greatest philosophers throughout human history have rarely endorsed democratic modes of government. As they put it (1997:88):

> Our great philosophers . . . have been unanimous in their hostility to democracy. The point warrants repetition: from Athenian days to the present, no major Western philosopher has endorsed the proposition that public policy should be decided either by direct popular vote or by representatives chosen on the basis of anything approximating universal suffrage. Pericles, to be sure, eulogized Athenian democracy, but Plato's and Aristotle's assessment of rule by the majority ranged from the disparaging to the acutely hostile. Nor did their fellow Greek philosophers disagree.
>
> Neither did the Roman or medieval political theorists who followed. In fact, after the fall of Athens, "for more than 2,000 years nearly all leading minds . . . rejected [the idea of] popular government." . . . Not until the English Levellers . . ., circa 1640, will we find an attempt to justify government resting on the will of the many.
>
> There were, to be sure, prominent advocates of representative government—beginning, say, with Marsiglio of Padua and William of Occam in the fourteenth century, continuing with Nicolas of Cusa and his fellow Conciliarists, and then, in England continuing with John Locke and John Stuart Mill. With the exception of Mill, though, representative government was understood by its advocates as a system in which the representatives would be chosen not by a numerical majority but, in Marsiglio's classic phrase, by the "prevailing part [of society], both their number and quality in the community being taken into account." And Mill himself, rightly regarded as the preeminent advocate of representative government, was at best ambivalent about the merits of universal suffrage.
>
> What about Jean-Jacques Rousseau? The most one can say here, given the contradictory nature of much of his work, is that while he may have favored representative government, he did not believe in popular democracy, certainly not as we understand the term.

Somit and Peterson do not mention non-Western philosophers, but the situation is undoubtedly the same there, if not actually worse.

In regard to their point that the masses have a striking tendency to submit to authority, Somit and Peterson cite the famous research of Stanley Milgram (1974) showing the remarkable extent to which people will obey a person of authority even when it means causing serious pain to another individual. Milgram set up a series of experiments in which subjects were told that they were participating in a study of memory. Students were asked to sit in front of a contrived machine, which they were told was to be used for the administration of punishment in the form of electric shocks to a person, a "learner," sitting out of view. They were instructed that if the learner remembered an item correctly they were to do nothing. But if he remembered incorrectly, they were to administer an electric shock. With each incorrect response, a more severe shock was to be administered. What Milgram found, in results that have been extremely well publicized, was that his subjects were disturbingly willing to administer shocks when the experimenter, a scientist with authority, told them they must. Many of the subjects found this emotionally wrenching, but the vast majority obeyed the experimenter, even when they thought the shocks were becoming extremely painful (actually reaching a dangerous level) and the "victim" that they could not see groaned and screamed in apparent agony. It is interesting that Milgram, in the days before sociobiology and evolutionary psychology emerged on the scene, interpreted his findings in evolutionary terms. He comments that (1974:123–25)

> men are not solitary but function within hierarchical structures. In birds, amphibians, and mammals we find dominance structures . . . and in human beings, structures of authority. . . . The formation of hierarchically organized groupings lends enormous advantage to those so organized in coping with dangers of the physical environment, threats posed by competing species, and potential disruption from within. The advantage of a disciplined militia over a tumultuous crowd lies precisely in the organized, coordinated capacity of the military unit brought into play against individuals acting without direction or structure.
>
> An evolutionary bias is implied in this viewpoint; behavior, like any other of man's characteristics, has throughout successive generations been shaped by the requirements of survival. Behaviors that did not enhance the chances of survival were successively bred out of the organism because they led to the eventual extinction of the groups that displayed them. A tribe in which some of the members were warriors, while others took care of children and still others were hunters, had an enormous advantage over one in which no division of labor occurred.
>
> A potential for obedience is the prerequisite of such social organization, and because organization has enormous survival value for any species, such a capacity was bred into the organism through the extended operation of evolutionary processes. I do not intend this as the end point of my argument, but only the beginning, for we will have gotten nowhere if all we can say is that men obey because they have an instinct for it.
>
> Indeed, the idea of a simple instinct for obedience is not what is now proposed. Rather, we are born with a *potential* for obedience, which then interacts with the influence of society to produce the obedient man.

Somit and Peterson limit themselves to state-organized societies, but our knowledge of the main lines of political evolution also offers strong support for their argument (as well as for Milgram's), as we will see in the next section. The simplest societies certainly are not associated with authoritarian forms of political order, but the overwhelming tendency in social evolution is for authoritarian systems to develop once the conditions necessary for their existence have emerged. Once again it seems to be a matter of basic biological tendencies interacting with external conditions.

The existence of power elites in modern democratic societies is also strong confirmation of Somit and Peterson's major claim. Such social scientists as C. Wright Mills (1956), G. William Domhoff (1970, 1978, 1983, 1990), and Michael Useem (1984) have shown the extraordinary degree to which the most important decisions in modern American society are made by a very small number of very powerful people. Marxists (e.g., Miliband, 1977; Szymanski, 1978) have shown that the capitalist class, a tiny segment of the population, exerts an enormous influence over decision-making with respect to the economy. Indeed, C. Wright Mills argued in his famous book *The Power Elite* (1956) that the notion that the United States is a true democracy was actually so mythical that it was a fairy tale. This is not to say that the power elite theorists are right in everything they say, but simply that the reality of power elites is virtually undeniable.

Somit and Peterson argue that modern democracy became the major form of government in some societies in the modern world because of a variety of conditions. They list such things as a more egalitarian distribution of wealth, advanced education, urbanization, and a predisposing civic culture. Most of these are reasonable enough, although I would stress the first because it is the one most compatible with Rueschemeyer, Stephens, and Stephens's (1992) argument that it is the rise of a large and well-organized working class that is the key to democracy (more on which below). But they go on to add that democracy has only become stable and long-lasting because of humans' extraordinary indoctrinability. Since humans are naturally predisposed toward authoritarianism, they have had to be indoctrinated against their nature to accept democracy. It is in this way that democracy has moved from the status of "ugly duckling" to that of "irresistible swan."

Somit and Peterson suggest that democracy may be only a fleeting phase that is destined to disappear in the near future—that authoritarian government is apt to be a persistent phenomenon rather than an archaic stage of political evolution. In this I fear they may be correct. Indeed, many of the leaders of democratic nations seem to have the same fear. Repeatedly it is pointed out that democracy is fragile and requires the constant vigilance of the masses to maintain. We hear frequently of the need for democratic societies to have a well-educated citizenry because only by the presence of such a citizenry can democracy be preserved.

Although Somit and Peterson's major claim concerning the human inclination toward authoritarian politics rings true, at least in my view, there are some features of their analysis that are discomforting. In my view they underestimate considerably the human inclination to disobey. It is true that humans do have a remarkable tendency to obey, but they also have virtually as strong a capacity to resist. Somit and Peterson say (1997:70), "For six millennia or more, rulers have commanded—and almost always their subjects have obeyed. Major collective acts of rebellion have been so relatively infrequent that almost any reasonably well educated person is familiar with most of them." Moreover (1997:70), "From the origin of organized political society, and over sixty some centuries of authoritarian and tyrannical rule by native and alien governors alike, the nearly (but fortunately not completely) invariable human response has been to obey. Taken in broad historical perspective, disobedience is a rarely encountered political phenomenon." I think the evidence will show that major acts of rebellion have been much more common than this—that disobedience is frequently rather than rarely encountered (Scott, 1990). Humans compete for dominance and power, but the losers resent being dominated and frequently challenge the winners (Boehm, 1999). That is what dominance orders are all about. As we have noted at least once before, in precontact Hawaii paramount chiefs who "ate the powers of government too much" were frequently overthrown and killed. In state-level societies people were seldom successful when they rebelled, but they rebelled frequently nonetheless. Peasant revolts and slave rebellions have been commonplace in history, and attempted revolutions have occurred everywhere in the modern world. Indeed, how do we understand the rise of democracy in the modern world, especially in the sense of universal suffrage, but as an effort on the part of the masses to overthrow authoritarian rule? The members of modern states have not accepted democracy simply because of indoctrination. The evidence is clear that they wanted it and struggled hard for it. Again, the very nature of a dominance order is that there is always some resistance from below to that which is imposed from above. In this sense, Somit and Peterson's conception of the human penchant toward authoritarianism is incomplete because it is inaccurate (or at least highly exaggerated) in its conception of what the subordinates are doing.

THE EVOLUTION OF CHIEFDOMS AND STATES

Years ago an extremely useful typology of political systems was proposed by the anthropologist Elman Service (1962, 1971), who distinguished between bands, tribes, chiefdoms, and states. Bands and tribes are political systems found among small-scale and highly undifferentiated societies, usually hunter-gatherers, simple horticulturalists, and some pastoralists. Bands are most characteristic of hunter-gatherer societies. They contain leaders, but these leaders lack any power or authority to coerce the actions of others. They maintain their positions only by the consent of the group and should they antagonize others they can be swiftly removed from their positions. Tribes are most common among simple horticulturalists and pastoralists. Like bands, they have leaders who lack formal power or authority. Tribes have sometimes been called *segmentary societies* because political leadership does not extend beyond the village level and each village is a segment of a larger cultural entity and essentially a replica of every other village. Intervillage linkages exist but are generally limited to kin ties and ceremonial relations.

Tribes become chiefdoms when a political structure unifying the separate villages develops and the villages lose their political autonomy. As the name suggests, chiefdoms are political systems under the control of one or more chiefs. A common situation is for there to be a paramount chief who rules the chiefdom but also delegates various powers and functions to a number of subchiefs who maintain control over regions or villages within the chiefdom. Chiefs and subchiefs possess genuine power and authority to coerce the actions of others in a variety of ways. Chiefdoms are normally highly stratified societies, although a wide range of chiefdoms exists in terms of their size and scale (Carneiro, 1981; Earle, 1987). At one end of the continuum, chiefdoms may contain as few as a thousand persons and be only minimally stratified. At the other end, there are chiefdoms with tens of thousands of persons—occasionally even 100,000 or more— that are highly stratified in the sense of exhibiting an extreme gap between top and bottom. Although some scholars have seen the chiefdom as an evolutionary dead end or as an alternative to the state (discussed below) (Webb, 1973; Sanders and Webster, 1978), others see it as a stage of political evolution necessary for state formation (Carneiro,

1981, 1991; Earle, 1987). I regard the latter view as much more plausible, because it is extremely difficult to see how polities could evolve from autonomous villages all the way to the complexity of the state in one big step. This view is also supported by archaeological evidence showing that chiefdoms have in fact preceded states in many regions of the world (Earle, 1978).

What then of the state? Carneiro (1970:733) defines the state as "an autonomous political unit, encompassing many communities within its territory and having a centralized government with the power to draft men for war or work, levy and collect taxes, and decree and enforce laws." The difficulty with this definition is that it could apply just as well to complex chiefdoms. What else is needed to transform a chiefdom into a state? The answer is, a monopoly over the means of violence. To say that states exercise a monopoly over the means of violence is to say that they have acquired a level of military force sufficient to prevent (in the vast majority of cases at least) being overthrown by a revolt from below. States, or at least the societies under their control, have a number of additional features worth mentioning (Sanders and Webster, 1978; R. Cohen, 1978). These include dense populations based on agriculture, unequal access to subsistence resources, complex economic specialization, a hereditary class structure, urbanism and monumental architecture, a complex system of trade and markets, and a complex set of judicial procedures. The formation of the state in prehistory represents a remarkable process of parallel evolution. States first formed in Mesopotamia and Egypt around 5,100 years ago, but they developed independently in China sometime around 4,100 to 3,800 years ago, in the Indus Valley in India around 4,600 years ago, in Europe perhaps as early as 4,000 years ago and no later than 2,700 years ago, in Mesoamerica sometime after 2,200 years ago, and in Peru after AD 1 (Sanderson, 1999).

A variety of explanations of the rise of the state have been developed. Some theories have proposed the emergence of trade and economic exchange as the crucial factors (Rathje, 1971, 1972; Wright and Johnson, 1975; Blanton, Kowalewski, Feinman, and Appel, 1981; Feinman, 1991). Marxian theories (Engels, 1970[1884]; Fried, 1967, 1978) hold that the state emerged as the result of the formation of a dominant economic class that needed protection from the subordinate classes it was exploiting. Demographic theories have emphasized population pressure (Kirch, 1984; M. Cohen, 1981; Johnson and Earle, 1987). Perhaps the best-known theory of the origin of the state is Robert Carneiro's (1970, 1981, 1987) circumscription theory. This theory, which is a combined eco- and polimaterialist theory, makes use of three primary variables: population pressure, warfare, and what Carneiro calls environmental circumscription. Population pressure sets everything in motion. When population builds up in a region, warfare frequently results. However, if land is relatively plentiful, people have the option of moving away into previously unoccupied land. When land is not sufficiently abundant, or is not well suited to cultivation, this option is not available. Enter environmental circumscription. Circumscribed environments are regions that contain fertile land but in which there are obstacles to movement beyond the region, the obstacles consisting of such things as large bodies of water, mountain ranges, or inhospitable deserts. When population pressure builds up in such regions, warfare intensifies and escalates as societies attempt to take over the land of others. Bands and tribes evolve into chiefdoms, chiefdoms evolve into states, and states sometimes evolve into multistate empires. Carneiro claims empirical support for his theory by noting that all of the major regions of the world in which states first originated were highly circumscribed.

In order to shed light on the process of political evolution I conducted several empirical analyses using data from the the *Ethnographic Atlas* and the SCCS. With respect to the *Atlas,* three variables turned out to be highly correlated with a society's stage of political evolution. Community size correlated .672 (Pearson r), class stratification .657, and subsistence type .525. In terms of the strongest correlate, community size, 76 percent of societies with communities of fewer than one-hundred persons were organized as bands or tribes, 22 percent as chiefdoms, and only 2 percent as states. In societies with communities of 5,000 or more, 3 percent were organized as bands or tribes, 25 percent as chiefdoms, and 72 percent as states. A similar pattern was found with respect to class stratification. Here 67 percent of egalitarian societies were organized as bands or tribes and less than 1 percent as states. No societies with complex stratification were organized as bands or tribes, 28 percent were organized into chiefdoms, and 72 percent were organized into states. Political stage and these three variables were entered into a multiple regression analysis, and together the independent variables explained 56 percent of the variance in political stage. Class stratification was the best predictor, followed very closely by community size. Subsistence type was a much poorer predictor than either of these. A similar multiple regression analysis was conducted for the SCCS. Here the independent variables were social stratification (a slightly better measure than class stratification), community size, population density, and subsistence type. All of the independent variables were moderately to strongly correlated with political stage, but community size and population density washed out completely when the other variables were partialed out. Subsistence type and social stratification together explained 65 percent of the variance, with stratification explaining a clear majority of this.

The results as a whole are to a large extent a mirror image of the results obtained with respect to the determinants of stratification discussed in the last chapter. Political stage and social stratification are clearly very strongly correlated with each other, almost inextricably intertwined. It is difficult to say which is the dependent variable and which the independent variable. It may be best to conclude that these variables are co-determinants—they ratchet each other up in the evolutionary process. Clearly they determine each other more—usually much more—than either is determined by anything else. The findings might also be seen as casting a certain amount of doubt on Carneiro's circumscription theory of political evolution. For Carneiro, population density is the variable that sets political evolution in motion, but our results show that population density, though highly correlated with political stage, washes out when the other variables are considered. Political evolution seems to be much more a matter of the struggle for wealth than for anything else, a process not recognized by Carneiro; he completely ignores patterns of economic ownership and social stratification (Webb, 1975; Schacht, 1988). This puts Marxian-oriented ecomaterialist theories back into the picture as identifying a crucial part of the process of political evolution (cf. Earle, 1991). None of this necessarily means that Carneiro's theory is altogether wrong, but it can be at best only a part of the story.[1]

THE EMERGENCE OF PARLIAMENTARY DEMOCRACY

Although an early form of democracy developed in ancient Athens (Bollen and Paxton, 1997), fully democratic societies—those with mass suffrage and constitutions granting civil liberties—did not develop until the nineteenth and twentieth centuries in the Western world. A number of cross-national, quantitative studies have been carried out showing a close link between democracy and economic development (e.g., Lipset, 1959; Cutright, 1963; Bollen, 1979, 1983). It has been primarily highly industrialized societies that have generated democracies. Unfortunately, it has been difficult to conclude from these studies exactly why economic development and democracy should be closely associated. What is it about development that leads to democracy?

In perhaps the most detailed cross-national, quantitative study of democracy ever carried out, one based on 172 countries, Tatu Vanhanen (1997) has attempted to identify the key determinants of democracy. Vanhanen argues that democracy emerges when the large mass of the population acquires resources that it can use to force autocratic states to open themselves up to mass suffrage and political rights. He stresses that these crucial resources are not limited to economic ones. Vanhanen identifies six types of resources and thus six major variables that should contribute to democratization: size of the nonagricultural population (NAP), size of the urban population (UP), the degree to which farms are independently owned by families (FF) , the literacy rate (LR), the number of students in institutions of higher education (STU), and the decentralization of nonagricultural economic resources (DD). He combines these six variables into a comprehensive supervariable that he calls the Index of Power Resources (IPR), which he then correlates with an Index of Democracy that is based on the extent of both electoral participation and political party competition. The average correlation of the IPR for three different years (1991, 1992, and 1993) was .786, which translates into 62 percent of the variance being explained.

One problem with Vanhanen's analysis is that he stops with simple correlations, failing to control for any other variables. Moreover, he makes the assumption that all of the six subvariables within his IPR are of equal significance in producing democracy. I find this extremely implausible, but we do not have to leave it at that. Since Vanhanen reports all of his data, we can decompose his IPR into its six dimensions and put all of them into a multiple regression analysis. I did this while at the same time adding two more independent variables, gross national product per capita (GNP) and degree of unionization of the labor force (ULF). Using Vanhanen's Index of Democracy for 1993 as the dependent variable, I found that it was correlated moderately to strongly with all eight independent variables. However, the zero-order correlations for NAP, UP, FF, STU, and GNP all but disappeared when the other seven independent variables were controlled. The best predictors of the level of democracy were DD, LR, and ULF. These three variables alone explained 66 percent of the variance (slightly more than Vanhanen explained with his entire IPR), and DD was clearly the strongest of these. Obviously, then, Vanhanen's subvariables are very unequal in their ability to explain democratization.

Vanhanen's Index of Democracy combines measures of electoral participation and party competition. He argues that this index will reflect the extent to which a government grants political and civil rights. This may be true to some extent, but I employed measures of political and civil rights as additional dependent variables. Vanhanen's IPR was correlated .703 with political rights, thus explaining 49 percent of the variance. This was considerably improved by putting the eight independent variables used earlier into a multiple regression analysis. In this instance, just two variables, DD and LR, explained 72 percent of the variance, and DD explained the great bulk of this. Both of these analyses were repeated with a measure of civil rights as the dependent variable. IPR correlated .687 with civil rights, explaining 47 percent of the variance. In my multiple regression analysis, DD and LR explained 64 percent of the civil rights variable and, again, DD explained most of this.

As a final analysis, I created a new measure of democracy, which I call "superdemocracy" (SD), by combining Vanhanen's Index of Democracy with the measures of political and civil rights. DD and LR were able to explain a huge 85 percent of the variance in SD, with DD explaining about 59 percent and LR about 26 percent. When various world regions were considered separately, DD was far and away the most important predictor of SD in Europe/North America, Asia, and Africa, and marginally the best predictor in Latin America. DD was also quite clearly the best predictor among both the poorer and the richer halves of the world's countries.

My regression analyses extend Vanhanen's important research by showing that it is the decentralization of nonagricultural economic resources that is by far the best predictor of democracy. This dimension of Vanhanen's IPR is far more important than his other five dimensions, and four of his dimensions turn out to be relatively unimportant. However, which way are the causal arrows pointing? Conceptually and theoretically I prefer the argument that it is the decentralization of economic resources that leads to greater democracy, but this cannot be demonstrated on the basis of the analyses carried out thus far. It is possible that as societies democratize they give people the opportunity to decentralize economic resources. Lenski (1966), for example, has argued that the key to greater economic equality in modern industrial capitalist societies has been democratization. And Rueschemeyer, Stephens, and Stephens (1992:297) say that "the greater weight of the subordinate classes in the political process should in turn express itself in state policies which redistribute resources from the privileged to the underprivileged. This is what, in fact, has happened."

To make a reasonable assessment of the direction of causation I selected two different points in time (1920 and 1970) and performed two panel analyses. Because Vanhanen did not include data on DD for any dates earlier than 1990, I had to use IPR as a rough proxy for DD on the assumption that the most important part of IPR is, in fact, DD. In the first analysis, I regressed the 1970 Index of Democracy on 1920 levels of IPR, while controlling for the 1920 Index of Democracy. The results showed that 1920 IPR predicted 1920 to 1970 changes in the Index of Democracy better than the 1920 Index of Democracy did (respective betas = .401 and .337), an excellent result. In the second analysis, 1970 levels of IPR were regressed on the 1920 Index of Democracy, while simultaneously controlling for 1920 levels of IPR. Here the 1920 Index of Democracy was a weak predictor (beta = .162), whereas 1920 IPR was a very strong predictor (beta = .673). The conclusion to be drawn is that IPR is exerting a much greater causal effect on the Index of Democracy than the Index of Democracy is exerting on

IPR. If IPR is a reasonably satisfactory proxy for DD, then changes in DD cause changes in the level of democratization.

Dietrich Rueschemeyer, Evelyne Huber Stephens, and John D. Stephens (1992) are highly criticial of quantitative studies of democracy primarily because they believe that they do not allow us to establish a clear causal order among the variables. They have carried out the most comprehensive qualitative study of democracy known to me. On the basis of detailed comparative and historical study, they show that democracy developed earliest and most extensively in the most industrialized societies. They argue that this is because those societies developed large and well-organized working classes that engaged in political struggle in order to get the vote. Democracy was inhibited in less-industrialized or nonindustrialized societies not only because the working class was small and weak, but also because the landed nobility was the dominant social class and it fiercely resisted democracy because of its incompatibility with its need for a submissive peasantry. In Europe, democracy developed first in Switzerland, France, Norway, and Denmark and then shortly thereafter in Britain, the Netherlands, Belgium, and Sweden. These were the most industrialized European societies with the largest working classes. Italy, Germany, Austria, and Spain made a fairly early transition to democracy, but in each case democracy broke down after a short time. These cases fit Rueschemeyer, Stephens, and Stephens's argument because they were less-industrialized countries with weaker working classes and powerful landed nobilities. With later industrialization these countries returned to democracy, although in the case of Spain quite late. Democracy also developed early in the British settler colonies—the United States, Canada, Australia, and New Zealand—and long before they experienced substantial industrialization. However, despite their limited industrialization, Rueschemeyer, Stephens, and Stephens point out that these societies began as societies of free farmers; there was no peasantry or landed nobility, and thus no class obstacle to democracy.

How compatible are the results of Rueschemeyer, Stephens, and Stephens with my reanalyses and extensions of Vanhanen? At a general level they seem highly compatible, since Vanhanen's DD seems to be the kind of thing that Ruschemeyer, Stephens, and Stephens are referring to when they talk about the growing size and power of the working class. But under more careful scrutiny the results seem to be at variance with the conclusions of Ruschemeyer, Stephens, and Stephens. These authors claim that democracies developed earliest in those capitalist societies that had moved farthest along the path of industrialization. Presumably, this can be measured best by two of Vanhanen's variables, NAP and UP. Although these variables were substantially correlated with the level of democracy, the correlations washed out when the other independent variables were controlled. Moreover, Vanhanen's IPR and DD were much better predictors of democracy than ULF (degree of unionization of the labor force). In terms of Rueschemeyer, Stephens, and Stephens's theoretical logic, this last variable should be a major predictor of the level of democratization; that it was not casts doubt on their causal chain. The crux of the difference between their variables and Vanhanen's DD seems to be that DD is more Marxian in nature inasmuch as DD involves ownership of the means of production (Rueschemeyer, Stephens, and Stephens stress that their analysis is not a Marxian one). My conclusion, therefore, is that the critical factor in the democratization of Western and other societies has been shifts in the ownership of capital resources in a more decentralized and egalitarian direction. Rueschemeyer, Stephens, and Stephens are correct to point out that industrialization preceded democracy, but they have not identified exactly what it is about industrialization that produces higher levels of democratization.

Does the emergence of democracy in the modern world contradict the argument of Somit and Peterson (1997) that political authoritarianism is part of human nature? In my view, no. As argued earlier, humans are both naturally authoritarian and naturally resist authoritarian behavior directed toward themselves. Throughout human history the conditions necessary to sustain democracy rarely existed, but in the modern world these conditions have emerged. Nonetheless, I would still argue that democracy is a rather fragile phenomenon that takes a great deal of effort to maintain. There is no necessary evolutionary trend toward greater democracy, and future governments may see a return to less democratic politics. It is not at all out of the question that democracy could be a fleeting form of government that will emerge only under very special circumstances.

WAR IN HUMAN SOCIETIES

The relation of the sexes . . . is the cause of war and the end of peace.

—*Arthur Schopenhauer*

He butchered three of them with an ax and decapitated them. In other words, instead of using a gun to kill them he took a hatchet to chop their heads off. He struggled face to face with one of them, and throwing down his ax managed to break his neck and devour his flesh in front of his comrades. . . . I awarded him the Medal of the Republic.

—*General Mustafa T'las*

Man's greatest good fortune is to chase and defeat his enemy, seize his total possessions, leave his married women weeping and wailing, ride his gelding, [and] use the bodies of his women as a nightshirt and support.

—*Ghengis Khan*

War is regarded as nothing but the continuation of politics by other means.

—*Carl von Clausewitz*

A warlike spirit, which alone can create and civilize a state, is absolutely essential to national defense and to national perpetuity. . . . The more warlike the spirit of the people, the less need for a large standing army. . . . Every male brought into existence should be taught from infancy that the military service of the Republic carries with it honor and distinction, and his very life should be permeated with the ideal that even death itself may become a boon when a man dies that a nation may live and fulfill its destiny.

—*General Douglas MacArthur*

How common is war in human societies past and present? The answer seems to be that humans are a highly war-prone species. Clark McCauley (1990) asserts that peaceful societies have been rare, a judgment strongly seconded by Lawrence Keeley (1996). Keeley summarizes findings from three cross-cultural studies of warfare using ethnographic data. In a study of 50 societies by Otterbein (1989), 90 percent of the societies were without question engaged in warfare, with the remaining societies at least occasionally engaged in some violent conflict. In another study of 90 societies (Ross, 1983), only 13 percent seldom or never engaged in warfare. However, 6 of these societies were ethnic or tribal minorities that had been pacified by modern nation-states, and 3 were living in geographical isolation, thus making the practice of war difficult or impossible. In the third study, which examined 157 North American Indian societies (Jorgensen, 1980), only 4.5 percent were reported to be truly peaceful, and all of these were small bands living in very dry and highly isolated environments. Shaw and Wong (1989) show that data on some 90 hunter-gatherer societies indicate that only 3 can be classified as relatively peaceful (the Eskimos of the Yukon, the Siriono of Bolivia, and the Semai of Malaysia). Peaceful hunter-gatherer bands, they point out, are those that are highly isolated or so nomadic that territorial conflict tends not to be possible. But even the most peaceful hunter-gatherer societies are not entirely free from war. Keeley argues that the war proneness of humans is also strikingly revealed by the archaeological record (cf. Ferguson, 1997, for a contrary view). He claims that

- evidence from Czechoslovakian cemeteries dating between 35,000 and 24,000 years ago suggests a high level of violent conflict;
- human skeletons found in Egyptian Nubia between 12,000 and 14,000 years ago suggest common and brutal warfare;
- violent death is suggested by the remains of hunter-gatherer societies in western Europe between 5,000 and 10,000 years ago;
- many villages of early agricultural tribes and simple chiefdoms in Neolithic Europe were fortified with ditches and palisades and, at least in Britain, several of these enclosures reveal clear evidence of having been attacked and burned;
- several areas of the prehistoric United States, especially those where archaeological study has been extensive, reveal violent deaths and in some periods these were extremely common.

What then of the frequency of warfare? Otterbein's study of 50 societies found that 66 percent of prestate societies were engaged in war every year, as were 40 percent of state-level societies. In Ross's study of 90 societies it was found that 62 percent of tribes and chiefdoms engaged in war yearly, as did 77 percent of state-level societies. Shaw and Wong summarize evidence collected by Montagu (1976) showing that there have been on the order of 14,500 wars over the past 5,600 years of world history, as well as evidence from Burke (1975) indicating that in the last 3,400 years of history there have been a mere 268 years of peace. Pitirim Sorokin (1937:352) has shown that throughout the history of Greece and Rome and over the past several hundred years of European history, "Almost every generation (25 to 30 years) in the past, with very few exceptions, has been a witness of, or an actor in, war phenomena." Shaw and Wong note that war proneness is also a relative constant in modern history. The proper conclusion seems to be that almost all societies have been warlike and most of these have engaged in war on a very frequent basis.

EXPLAINING WAR: BANDS AND TRIBES

Perhaps the most famous theory of warfare in bands and tribes is the ecomaterialist theory of Marvin Harris (Divale and Harris, 1976; Harris, 1984) in which war is seen basically as a population-regulating mechanism. Population pressure and resource scarcity, especially scarcity in the availability of animal protein, are regarded as the proximate causes of warfare. Warfare leads in turn to a male supremacist complex since societies that go to war frequently need to rear large numbers of fierce and combat-ready warriors, and the best way to do this is to exaggerate the characteristics of masculinity and denigrate the characteristics of femininity. The male supremacist complex helps provide a justification for female infanticide, which, in addition to male deaths from combat, helps to regulate population growth. Warfare also helps to balance out numbers of people against the supply of animal protein by creating "no-man's lands," or areas where people do not live that can be protected zones for animals. For Harris, band and tribal warfare is adaptive in the sense of producing a better standard of living than would otherwise be possible.

Harris's theory has been highly controversial ever since it was introduced. It has been strongly challenged by Napoleon Chagnon (1983; Chagnon, Flinn, and Melancon, 1979). Since Chagnon views protein scarcity as the crux of Harris's theory, he has tried to show that the Yanomamö, an Amazonian horticultural tribe studied extensively by Chagnon and used by Harris to illustrate his theory, are eating plenty of animal protein. In fact, Chagnon shows that the Yanomamö and several other Amazonian groups consume more animal protein per capita per day than the USSR, the United Kingdom, Germany, Portugal, and Japan, and nearly as much as Australia and New Zealand, the world leaders in the consumption of animal protein. Chagnon himself favors a biomaterialist interpretation of band and tribal warfare, arguing that the Yanomamö fight over women and that they have a natural tendency toward violence that, in the absence of a state, cannot be suppressed. But more on that later.

Brian Ferguson (1989b) has challenged the relevance of Chagnon's calculation of how much animal protein the Yanomamö and other Amazonian groups are eating. He notes that Harris's protein hypothesis does not predict an actual deficiency of animal protein in the diet, but, rather, implies that war will stop the decline in dietary animal protein before it has a chance to reach unhealthy levels. For Ferguson, then, it is no surprise that Amazonian groups seem to be eating enough meat. However, Ferguson challenges Harris's theory on other grounds. He notes that it has commonly been observed that the threat of war leads people to establish larger villages than would normally be the case, and that large villages lead to a greater depletion of local game than do smaller villages (Ferguson, 1989a). Thus, war cannot be seen as producing a better fit between population and natural resources. Ferguson insists that war is not adaptive. "War may produce a fit between population and resources," he says, "but it is a bad fit. Life is worse for war" (1989a:258). Ferguson (1989b) admits that the decreasing availability of game does lead to increasing interpersonal conflict within villages, but he denies that this leads to actual warfare between villages. This conflict, he believes, is simply not sufficient to start wars. The logical outcome of interpersonal conflict, he claims, is movement, not war.

By way of further test of Harris's theory, Keeley (1996) found no correlation between population density and the frequency of warfare for eighty-seven societies. Surprised by this result, I undertook my own test of the relationship for the band and tribal societies in the SCCS. The correlation was not only low, but was running in the wrong direction ($r = -.119$). A true test of Harris's theory requires a measure of actual population *pressure* rather than simple population density. I created such a variable by combining population density with the intensity of production. The results were almost exactly the same ($r = -.109$). These results call Harris's theory seriously into question inasmuch as the theory emphasizes resource scarcity as the result of population pressure as the major cause of war in band and tribal societies.

Ferguson (1984, 1990a) has proposed an ecomaterialist theory of warfare that is broader than Harris's, broad enough in fact to explain war beyond the level of bands and tribes. Ferguson agrees with the Harris school that war arises from material causes and comments that nonmaterial goals and aims will ordinarily not lead to war unless these aims are accompanied by material objectives. Ferguson's basic theory is that wars will occur when the decision makers believe that the material benefits of war will outweigh the material costs. Ferguson specifies six material interests decision makers can have and thus six strategic objectives of war (1990a:30):

1. to increase access to fixed resources by eliminating competitors;
2. to capture movable goods;
3. to impose an exploitative relationship on one or more previously independent groups;
4. to conquer and incorporate one or more other groups;
5. to enhance the power and status of those who make decisions about whether or not to make war;
6. to defend against attacks by other groups.

This seems to me a very sensible theory of human warfare in general, some parts of which apply in particular to bands and tribes. Harris has emphasized the first strategic objective of war among bands and tribes, whereas Ferguson emphasizes this but also the second, third, and sixth objectives. Ferguson (1990b, 1995a) claims that the most fundamental cause of warfare among the Yanomamö and other Amazonian groups, both historically and at present, is Western contact (cf. Ferguson and Whitehead, 1992). Historically, native populations have often been drawn into colonial rivalries between European powers and engaged in war as a result. Europeans have often introduced epidemic diseases that have created severe population imbalances and led to warfare designed to capture women and children in order to redress these imbalances. Most significantly, however, Ferguson emphasizes conflict over the allocation and control of Western manufactured goods, especially steel axes. Ferguson points to studies which show that steel axes are far superior to stone axes in terms of efficiency, being able to reduce work time and energy expended by a factor of anywhere from three to nine. Among the Yanomamö, forest can be cleared seven to ten times faster using steel axes. Many native Amazonian peoples long ago acquired great dependence on steel axes and maintain such dependence to this very day. They have also become dependent on such manufactured goods as shotguns, machetes, knives, fishhooks, pots, manioc griddles, matches, tobacco, kerosene, beads, and clothing. Throughout Amazonia, and in all historical periods, Ferguson claims, native groups have gone to war to gain access to these and other highly desired goods. As he (1990b:245) puts it,

> we know for certain that many Native peoples have gone to war in order to obtain Western manufactures, especially steel tools. Throughout virtually all regions and time periods, Native peoples have been willing to kill and risk death to get these precious means of production. That leads to a question: what happens when something this valuable enters Native systems of exchange? The answer, I believe, is that this entry both creates conflicting vital interests and transforms relations of cooperation at all levels of social organization. Furthermore, these conflicting interests, fully embedded in the totality of social relations, shape political alignments and general social hostilities, up to and including war.

Ferguson is not implying that there was no war in Amazonia prior to European intrusion, for most certainly there was. But he does see the introduction of Western goods as greatly intensifying war and keeping it alive.

A third major type of explanation of band and tribal warfare is biomaterialist, one subtype of which is the classical sociobiological theory: Men compete among themselves for access to women, and when the scarcity of women becomes severe enough intervillage warfare is the result (Chagnon, 1988; Low, 1993b; van der Dennen, 1995:317–31). This scarcity can result from such factors as female infanticide, unbalanced sex ratios that develop for other reasons (Fisher, 1958[1930]; Chagnon, Flinn, and Melancon, 1979), or the practice of polygyny. However, Donald Symons (1979) points out that women are always scarce to at least some extent in all societies, and that men therefore are always in competition for them. The men who will be most reproductively successful will in most cases be the most successful warriors, and men will therefore be strongly motivated to form coalitional bands and go to war (cf. Tooby and Cosmides, 1988). As Bobbi Low (1993b:33) has pointed out, "The benefits of warfare to men in preindustrial societies thus include increased direct access to reproductive females, and increased material resources useful for the lineage and in contracting marriages."

Focusing in particular on the Yanomamö case, Chagnon (1988) argues that this group fights primarily over women and that blood revenge is a major motive for war once it has started. Chagnon says that most fights begin over such things as infidelity and suspicions of infidelity, seductive attempts directed at other men's wives, stealing women from visiting groups, and sexual jealousy. Many of the fights that arise over sexual matters culminate in both intra- and intervillage killings. "Aggressive groups," he says, "coerce nubile females from less aggressive groups whenever the opportunity arises. Many appear to calculate the costs and benefits of forcibly appropriating or coercing females from groups that are perceived to be weak" (1988:986). The Yanomamö themselves explain their own warfare in terms of competition for women. In an amusing anecdote, Chagnon (1983) conveyed to a Yanomamö village he was living with Harris's protein scarcity explanation of their warfare. Upon hearing this, they laughed and said that they liked meat but they liked women a whole lot more! An important status among Yanomamö men is that of *unokai,* or one who has killed another man, and Chagnon shows that *unokais* have more wives and greater reproductive success than non-*unokais*. In a study of 380 Yanomamö men (137 *unokais* and 243 non-*unokais*), Chagnon (1988) has shown that the *unokais* had an average of 1.63 wives per man, whereas the non-*unokais* averaged only 0.63 wives per man. The gap was particularly wide among men aged 20 to 24. In this age group, 5 *unokais* had a total of 4 wives, but 78 non-*unokais* had a total of only 10 wives. Obviously the key to mates and reproductive success among Yanomamö men is to gain status by killing other men.

There is a great deal of evidence from other bands and tribes that conflict over women is a major cause of war. As Laura Betzig (1986:26) has pointed out:

> Disputes over women "stand apart" among modern Turks, invariably calling for violence . . . ; elopements may lead to physical fighting among the Mohla in the Western Punjab. . . . adultery is regarded as the most serious crime among the Semang . . . ; and over 90% of Tiwi disputes were matters in which women were somehow involved. . . . Among Kapauku, Pospisil noted that most wars start because of violations of a husband's exclusive sexual rights . . . ; Linton found Marquesan killings followed two motives: sexual jealousy and revenge. . . . Among the Saramacca of the upper Suriname River Basin, quarrels over women were more frequent than any other kinds of disputes . . . ; and among Trumai, "the chief source of conflict in the village was sex."

I have tried to test this sociobiological hypothesis empirically in a rough sort of way. Using the SCCS, correlational analyses were run between overall warfare frequency and twelve independent variables. The only variables that were substantially correlated with warfare were frequency of homicide ($r = .417$) and frequency of socially organized homicide ($r = .548$). When only bands and tribes were included in the analysis, the respective correlations were .507 and .520. This suggests to me support for the sociobiological argument. Warfare is most closely related to male violence outside the context of war, and it is likely that this violence is occurring mostly over women, as Chagnon and others have suggested. Harris and Ferguson stress resource scarcity as the primary cause of band and tribal warfare, but it would appear to be women that are the most crucial resource.

A biological foundation for human warfare is also strongly suggested by a human-chimpanzee comparison. Chimps and humans share about 98.5 percent of their DNA, and chimps are actually more closely related to humans than they are to gorillas. Chimps are humans' closest relative, and they shared a common ancestor that is believed to have lived between about five and seven million years ago. In the last two decades or so it has become evident that chimpanzees are animals who frequently engage in lethal violence. Patterns of chimpanzee violence and their similarities to human violence have been carefully studied by the biological anthropologist Richard Wrangham (Manson and Wrangham, 1991; Wrangham and Peterson, 1996). Evidence has accumulated to show that the males of chimpanzee communities commonly patrol their community's borders and raid neighboring communities. Often this raiding appears to have as its main objective the killing of the other community's adult males. Small groups of males will seek out lone males, attack them, and kill them mercilessly, often mutilating the body. There is a stunning similarity between intergroup violence among chimpanzees and human warfare between bands and villages, and it is striking that chimps and humans are the only primates who engage in this particular type of behavior. Wrangham notes that about 30 percent of adult male chimpanzees die as the result of violence, a figure that closely approximates the situation in many human bands and tribes. About 30 percent of Yanomamö men die from violence, as do 20 percent of men among the Huli, 25 percent of Mae Enga men, and 29 percent of men among the Dugum Dani, all groups from highland New Guinea. Among the Murngin of Australia in aboriginal times, about 28 percent of men died from violence.

Wrangham refers to human and chimpanzee males as *demonic males* and argues that chimps and humans are the only species with such males. He argues that human and chimpanzee males have inherited their strong aggressive tendencies from their common ancestor. And these demonic males have not evolved in isolation from females; females have collaborated in the evolution of demonic males because they have preferred such males as mates. Demonic males are the most successful reproducers, and thus females who mate with them are likely to have sons who will be good reproducers. Females can maximize their reproductive success by mating with demonic males. Wrangham says that the "individual men and women who make up our species are extraordinarily ready to admire, to love, and to reward male demonism in many of its manifestations; and that admiration, love, and rewarding perpetuates the continuation, for generation after generation, of the demonic male within us" (Wrangham and Peterson, 1996:241).

Shaw and Wong (1989) offer yet another type of biomaterialist explanation of war. They root band and tribal warfare in ethnocentrism, which is itself driven by xenophobia, or fear of and hostility to strangers. In state-level societies warfare is driven by nationalism and ethnic mobilization, which are modern expressions of ethnocentrism. A large literature has now accumulated (e.g., van den Berghe, 1981a; Reynolds, Falger, and Vine, 1986) which provides strong evidence that ethnocentrism is an evolutionary adaptation. In the ancestral environment strong attachment to one's group and willingness to fight in defense of it would have been highly adaptive. On the whole and in the long run, individuals who behaved in such a fashion would have more often lived to fight another day, and to acquire mates and leave offspring, compared to individuals with weaker group attachments. Darwin himself saw ethnicity and ethnocentrism as evolutionary adaptations. He said that a "tribe including many members who, from possessing in a high degree the spirit of patriotism, fidelity, obedience, courage, and sympathy, were always ready to aid each other and to sacrifice themselves for the common good would be victorious over other tribes." Darwin even made the connection between ethnocentrism and warfare explicit: In-group amity and out-group enmity go together as two sides of the very same coin. In support of Shaw and Wong, it must be recognized that in preindustrial societies, band and tribal societies in particular, in-group attachments are usually intense and out-groups are not only regarded as inferior, but are often vilified as the very essence of evil (Reynolds, Falger, and Vine, 1986). Under such circumstances, it is no wonder that war among bands and tribes is so common.

Shaw and Wong's position fits very well with Wrangham's analysis of chimp-human similarities. Chimpanzees seem to show the same xenophobia that is so characteristic of humans in societies that approximate the ancestral environment. The extreme forms of in-group amity and out-group enmity that we observe in so many human societies dovetail with the neo-Hobbesian position on war (Keeley, 1996), or at least with one fundamental aspect of the neo-Hobbesian position: The condition of war is normal in the absence of a state. Of course, war is also common in the presence of a state, but it is a very different type of war (to be discussed in a moment). The basic point is that it is extremely difficult to stop war in prestate societies once it gets going, and it gets going with remarkable ease. Napoleon Chagnon (1988:990) puts the matter poignantly:

> It is difficult for us to imagine the terror that might characterize our own social lives in the absence of laws prohibiting individuals from seeking lethal retribution when a close kinsman dies at the hands of another human. . . . A particularly acute insight into the power of law to thwart killing for revenge was provided to me by a young Yanomamö man in 1987. He had been taught Spanish by missionaries and sent to the territorial capital for training in practical nursing. There he discovered the police and laws. He excitedly told me that he had visited the town's largest *pata* (the territorial governor) and urged him to make law and police available to his people so that they would not have to engage any longer in their wars of revenge and have to live in constant fear. Many of his close kinsmen had died violently and had, in turn, exacted lethal revenge; he worried about being a potential target of retaliations and made it known to all that he would have nothing to do with raiding.

My grand conclusions on all these theories are approximately as follows: Harris's ecomaterialist theory does not work very well because it is too narrow; Ferguson's broader ecomaterialist theory is extremely useful because it gives us a comprehensive picture of the kinds of material motivations that are capable of producing war. However, Ferguson overemphasizes Western contact and neglects a crucial resource—women. Human ethnocentrism and xenophobia are also likely to be powerful factors in the initiation and perpetuation of war. We must take seriously the neo-Hobbesian position that humans in a state of nature tend to be quite violent and that war results easily when there is no formal authority to prevent it. Humans are remarkably war prone and seem to have an extremely low threshold for initiating it. It can easily be caused by a wide range of ecological, demographic, economic, sexual, and political factors acting in concert with humans' low threshold for aggression.

EXPLAINING WAR: CHIEFDOMS AND STATES

Although it might be thought that conflict over women is much less likely to be a cause of war in chiefdoms and states than in bands and tribes, I found that frequency of homicide correlated .442 (Pearson r) and frequency of socially organized homicide correlated a whopping .808 with overall warfare frequency for the societies of the SCCS that are organized into chiefdoms. However, the situation was completely different for states. For the state-level societies of the SCCS, frequency of homicide correlated $-.053$ and frequency of socially organized homicide correlated $-.153$ with overall warfare frequency. This means that conflict over women, although it still seems to be a major cause of war in chiefdoms, no longer contributes to war in societies organized into states. This suggests additional support for the neo-Hobbesian position on war in that states do suppress interpersonal conflict among males over women.

Considerable evidence has accumulated to show that the nature and causes of war have changed substantially throughout humankind's evolutionary history (Ferguson, 1990a). Broch and Galtung (1966) have shown that what they call "economic war" and "political war"—presumably war fought for land or other economic valuables, as well as to conquer and incorporate other societies—are closely intertwined with the overall evolution of society. They created an index of social evolution for 652 widely different societies. At the lowest level of the index, no society was characterized by economic or political war; at an intermediate level of social evolution, 39 percent of the societies had economic and political war; and at the highest level of social evolution, economic and political war were found in 95 percent of the societies. Using a sample of 125 societies from the Human Relations Area Files, and adding to it 7 industrial societies, Leavitt (1977) found that 10 measures of societal complexity (level of agricultural technology, military energy source, military artillery systems, level of transportation technology, level of communication technology, degree of social stratification, presence or absence of metallurgy, presence or absence of weaving, level of political differentiation, and settlement size) were positively correlated at $R = .598$ with external warfare (war fought between societies), and that these 10 variables explained 36 percent of the variance in external warfare. For the frequency of civil war, the corresponding numbers were $R = .632$ and 40 percent of the variance explained, and for the frequency of riots R was a huge .866 with 75 percent of the variance explained. Simple feuding, however, was negatively related to most of the measures of societal complexity.

While several of the motives for war that prevail among bands and tribes appear to continue in the transition to chiefdoms, a new motive, that of political conquest, comes onto the scene. Chiefdoms are hierarchical societies under the formal authority of a chief, and they are capable of establishing much larger fighting forces than anything imagined in bands and tribes. Carneiro (1990) notes that whereas small-scale tribal societies are usually capable of putting together warrior bands of a few dozen at most, chiefdoms can put together fighting forces in the hundreds or thousands. Carneiro has studied chiefdom-level warfare in the Cauca Valley of Colombia and in Fiji. He notes that warfare among chiefdoms in these regions was nearly constant. Fiji was seldom without war, and in the Cauca Valley "warfare was universal, acute, and unending" (1990:193). As to the causes of warfare among these chiefdoms, Carneiro has this to say (1990:193–94):

> The sorts of grievances that provoked warfare between autonomous villages continued to provoke it at the chiefdom level. But in addition, such things as offenses against the dignity

of persons of rank, especially the paramount chief, began to play a role. Thus, Williams . . . cites "pride and jealousy of the chiefs" as a common cause of war among the Fijians. And of course, the very existence of multi-village chiefdoms is *prima facie* evidence that the seizure of land and the subjection of peoples had already been acting as causes—or at least consequences—of war. Thus for Fiji, Williams . . . noted that "the fact of there being so many independent governments, each of which seeks aggrandizement at the expense of the rest," was a common motive for hostilities.

In the Cauca Valley, a chief's desire to expand his domain and gain control of natural resources such as gold mines and salt deposits are cited by Trimborn . . . as leading causes of war. Territorial conquest was a particular incentive for Guaca and Popayan, two chiefdoms of the valley which, when the Spaniards arrived in the early 1500s, were actively expanding their territory and apparently well on their way to becoming states.

Patrick Kirch (1984) sounds the same theme with respect to warfare among ancient Polynesian chiefdoms. Warfare was primarily centered on a struggle for power between chiefs and a desire for domination over resources and people. Once the shackles of band and tribal society are released, we see the innate human desire for power and control begin to assert itself in much more vigorous form. States carry the process still further.

In states, as in chiefdoms, economic and political factors are also at the forefront of war. Historically, many state-level societies have been organized as large political empires. Empires are extremely predatory forms of political life, and in fact depend on this for much of their sustenance. The major way wealth is created is through expropriation of an economic surplus from the peasantry, and the best way to enlarge wealth is through incorporating more peasants by conquering neighboring societies. Along with peasants, many other important resources are captured as well—land, slaves, tribute, booty, etc. Political conquest is a major key to wealth. William Eckhardt (1992) has collected data on population size, empires, civilizations, battles, and wars for the last 5,000 years of world history. I analyzed some of his data and found that all of these dimensions of state-level societies are extremely highly intercorrelated, as shown below:

- empires and wars: .931
- civilizations and wars: .924
- population and wars: .964
- empires and battles: .933
- civilizations and battles: .949
- population and battles: .953
- empires and civilizations: .910
- empires and population: .961
- population and civilizations: .960

These results suggest that war virtually defines the essence of the agrarian civilizations and empires that dominated world history. Chiefdoms, especially larger ones, are organized for political and military conquest and the incorporation of conquered and subjugated societies, but states, especially large-scale imperial states, carry out these goals on a scale and to a degree unimagined in most chiefdoms. Speaking of ancient Rome, Graeme Donald Snooks (1997:140) has said that the "defining characteristic of Roman warfare was its continuous nature. Rome was a society committed to war and conquest as a business." What was true of Rome has in general been true of all imperial states throughout world history, except perhaps on a less grand scale.

EXPLAINING WAR: MODERN SOCIETIES

Mesquida and Wiener (1996) have tried to show that even in modern societies war may stem from male competition over females and other resources. They examined eighty-eight modern nation-states, the majority of which were less-developed countries, and looked at the proportion of the male population that was in the age group fifteen–twenty-nine. They then took the ratio of fifteen–twenty-nine-year-old males to males thirty years and older, and correlated this ratio with the level of war. The two variables were correlated at $r = .69$, a very high correlation that explained 47 percent of the variance in war. But what is the causal relationship between these variables? Mesquida and Wiener reasoned that, since men in the age category fifteen–twenty-nine are at their peak level of aggressiveness and competitiveness, a greater proportion of fifteen–twenty-nine-year-olds in the population means more competition for resources, females included, and as a result the level of social conflict escalates. At some point war is initiated by governments as a means of enhancing resources in order to reduce internal social conflict. However, there is another interpretation of Mesquida and Wiener's finding that seems just as plausible, if not more plausible: Modern states are more likely to go to war when they have more fifteen–twenty-nine-year-olds in the population simply because this allows them to muster a larger fighting force and thus to have a greater likelihood of success.[2]

As in agrarian states, war in modern societies is rooted largely in economics and politics, but very few modern societies are conquest societies (e. g., the old Soviet Union to some extent; occasionally others have tried to be, e. g., Nazi Germany). Marxists stress that war is motivated by the economic competition of capitalists in different nation-states (for instance, they explain the two world wars, as well as colonial wars, in this manner). Weberians emphasize that one of the main defining features of the state is its organization for war. In this view, the state does not simply fight wars for the benefit of its capitalists, but has its own interests and motives in going to war. It is, in essence, a war-making machine, and it fights for political glory. The Marxists and the Weberians are both partially right, but I think the evidence will show that the economic motives of modern war generally outstrip the political motives.

To understand war in the modern world it cannot be forgotten that for the past 500 years there has been a capitalist world-system and an international system of states that in the twentieth century became truly global (Wallerstein, 1974a, 1974b, 1979, 1980, 1989). This system has been driven by the imperative of capitalist accumulation and war must be understood within this context. States within these intertwined systems engage in war with one another because they wish to become upwardly mobile both economically and politically, because they wish to avoid downward mobility, or out of pure self-defense against the aggression of other states. As Rasler and Thompson (1994:1) have put it, "The most significant wars, which also tend to be among the most deadly ones, take place within the context of ascent and decline among the world system's most powerful state actors. It is movement toward and away from the apex of the world system's status hierarchy, and the associated costs and benefits associated with leading positions, that cause so much trouble." For example, when the Netherlands (the United Provinces) achieved hegemony within the capitalist world-economy during the middle of the seventeenth century its economic efficiency was so great that its main rivals, Britain and France, were relatively unsuccessful in competing with it on purely economic grounds. Because of this they resorted repeatedly to war to try to undermine The Netherlands' economic position and promote their own (Israel, 1989). When Britain finally became hegemonic within the world-system in the nineteenth century, it could only secure that hegemony by maintaining a powerful military apparatus, especially a strong navy. The hegemony of the United States after World War II was guaranteed by the world's pre-eminent military apparatus and the United States became, as Britain was before it, a "world policeman." However, we need to be clear that modern war, even major war, is not only about gaining or defending economic advantage. Geopolitical considerations are also of considerable importance (Skocpol, 1979; Collins, 1986b). The behavior of the old Soviet Union in the international states system, for example, was determined as much by geopolitical as by economic factors, especially its conquest of Eastern Europe in the aftermath of World War II.

The political scientist Joshua Goldstein (1988) has studied cyclical trends in the largest wars of the past 500 years, looking in particular at the relationship between Kondratieff waves and the outbreak of major wars. Kondratieff waves are periods of economic upturn and downturn that last approximately 40 to 60 years. A period of upturn lasts about 20 to 25 years, reaches a crest, and then is followed by a downturn of another 20 to 25 years. Then a new period of upturn begins. Goldstein has shown that in 9 out of the past 10 Kondratieff waves, a major war broke out during the second half of the upturn phase. Goldstein argues that this is because it is during this period of economic prosperity that states have the revenues they need to launch a large-scale war. Goldstein's finding dovetails neatly with my reinterpretation of Mesquida and Wiener's finding that states are more likely to fight wars when they have a high proportion of 15–29-year-old males in the population. In order to fight wars states need resources, especially financial resources, and when they have these resources they are apt to fight wars.

Let us not forget that most wars in modern societies are not major wars; most are on a relatively small scale. Although economic and geopolitical factors may enter in here, often it is ethnic hostility or the desire for political autonomy that are the motivating factors (Low, 1993b). Consider, for example, wars between Hindu India and what became Pakistan, between Nigeria and Biafra, between Tutsis and Hutus in Rwanda and Burundi, and so on. Surveys of wars around the world since 1945 generally show that most of these are between ethnic groups rather than large nation-states (Low, 1993b). What are in essence tribal conflicts of interest are extremely important in most of these wars. So the biological nature of humans—in this instance ethnocentrism and xenophobia—continues to rear its ugly head even in the modern world.

The biological nature of humans is also involved in modern warfare in a more general sense. As Bobbi Low (1993b:40) has remarked, "It is almost certainly true that past correlations between warriors' behavior and reproductive success no longer hold; . . . Nonetheless, several aspects of men's behavior in wars, and of the organization of fighting forces, suggest that *proximate* correlates of reproductive success due to risky and aggressive behavior still exist in modern wars, and successful leaders organize field units in ways that play on the past kinship structure of warring groups."

NOTES

1. For a much more detailed discussion of political evolution and theories about it, see Sanderson (1999:53–95).

2. I am grateful to Frank Salter for this suggestion.

Epilogue

Darwinian conflict theory has a direct bearing on six basic dichotomies in sociological theory: *materialism-idealism, individualism-holism, structure-agency, scientific-nonscientific, micro-macro,* and *historical-ahistorical.* It should be obvious that Darwinian conflict theory is a materialist approach, in fact as rigorously materialist as an approach can get. It is also committed to a thoroughly scientific attitude and is the very antithesis of those recent tendencies, such as postmodernism, which demean and diminish science. Darwinian conflict theory concedes that science is not the only way of knowing, but it is a way of knowing that has been immensely more successful than all the other paths to knowledge. Darwinian conflict theory is also historical in the sense that it holds that one must analyze social behavior in its historical (especially evolutionary) context in order to make sense of it. Static or synchronic analyses will tell us much less than we want to know.

How does Darwinian conflict theory deal with the crucial structure-agency problem? Basically, it claims that this problem is much more easily solved than has been previously recognized. Darwinian conflict theory views structure and agency as reciprocally implicated in each other, as inextricably intertwined. Humans create structures but only within the constraints within which they operate. Once created, new structures act as constraints on further acts of human agency (it is perhaps more accurate to say that structures provide the *contingencies* within which people act as agents). Structures certainly do not determine behavior directly. Although Darwinian conflict theory has a clear concept of agency, its concept is certainly very different from the concept of agency held by such approaches as symbolic interactionism and ethnomethodology. From the point of view of these highly voluntaristic approaches, agents have an enormous amount of freedom to act in accord with personal wishes and desires. Anthony Giddens's (1984) notion of agency is similarly voluntaristic despite his claim that he has bridged the structure-agency divide. By contrast, Darwinian conflict theory's agent is much more constrained, especially by internal biological forces, but he or she is an agent nonetheless. Society is the creation of individuals acting in accordance with preferences and aims.

331

Darwinian conflict theory is an individualist approach, yet it is not a strict form of methodological individualism. It recognizes that the social level reacts back on the individual level once the social level is formed, and thus society, though a creation of individuals, always reconstitutes those individuals to some extent. Darwinian conflict theory also aims to bridge the micro and the macro by showing that this problem, like the structure-agency problem, is not the conundrum that many sociological theorists have thought it to be. In many ways this problem is not really a problem at all. The macro is the creation of the micro, but then acts back on it and the two levels mutually interpenetrate. Far too much time has been wasted by sociological theorists on this problem. Both micro-macro and structure-agency are essentially false dichotomies that have garnered far more attention than they deserve.

What remains to be done regarding the Darwinian conflict paradigm? I cannot say how close it is to being in a reasonably finished state, but it is clear that it will need considerable tinkering and polishing, and much empirical work remains to be done to extend its range of empirical application. I hope to be able to do as much as I can in all of these ways in the years to come. As indicated in the preface, a coherent Darwinian conflict account of ethnicity remains to be developed, as does such an account of religion, another human universal. And we still have a great deal to learn about all of the substantive issues discussed in this book. In some areas our understanding is good, whereas in others it is feeble at best.

The reader is entitled to know why I appear to be so confident that Darwinian conflict theory as a new sociological paradigm is going to last and grow. After all, sociology is today an extreme cacophony of voices, and paradigms come and go, rise and fall, ebb and flow. Why should Darwinian conflict theory be any different? The answer lies in its ultimate foundations: It is based on the most successful theoretical concept ever developed in the entire history of human thought, Darwinian natural selection. This concept has been of immense importance in biology as a whole, unifying various of its subfields and providing the basis for enormous theoretical and empirical advances; it has been of great service to anthropology as well, especially biological anthropology. It is the greatest theory that ever was in terms of parsimony, scope, empirical success, and productivity. As Lopreato and Crippen (1999) suggest, perhaps the most important reason sociology has failed to develop is because it has not yet had its Darwinian revolution. But with the Darwinian revolution that I see coming soon, even within such a stubborn and resistant discipline as sociology, sociology at last has a realistic chance of becoming a genuine cumulative science and fulfilling the expectations that such founders of the discipline as Comte and Durkheim had for it so many years ago. I agree with Randall Collins (1975) that we have been making intellectual progress in sociology in recent decades, but in order to continue this progress, and to give it a proper theoretical and conceptual foundation, the embracement of Darwinian thinking is absolutely essential.[1]

NOTE

1. The reader might wonder whether my advocacy of a rigorous materialist approach to explaining the social world implies a materialist *ontology.* Is reality itself basically material? My an-

swer is an unequivocal yes. Before everything else there is the material world, and ideas them-selves, at bottom, are simply matter in motion (i.e., chemical messages in the brain). If in sociol-ogy the micro-macro and structure-agency dichotomies are false dichotomies, then the mind-brain dichotomy must rank as perhaps the greatest false dichotomy in the entire history of scholarship. We are rapidly learning that the mind *is* the brain. It can be no other. I have no space, and no real inclination, to pursue this fascinating subject any further here, but for those who are interested, the following works can be recommended: Crook (1980), Damasio (1994), Church-land (1995), Calvin (1997), Pinker (1997).

References

Abell, Peter. 1990. "Denzin on rational choice theory." *Rationality and Society* 2:495–99.

Abrams, H. Leon, Jr. 1987. "The preference for animal protein and fat: A cross-cultural survey." In Marvin Harris and Eric B. Ross (eds.), *Food and Evolution: Toward a Theory of Human Food Habits*. Philadelphia: Temple University Press.

Akers, Ronald L. 1997. *Criminological Theories*. 2nd ed. Los Angeles: Roxbury.

Alcock, John. 1998. "Unpunctuated equilibrium in the *Natural History* essays of Stephen Jay Gould." *Evolution and Human Behavior* 19:321–36.

Alderson, Arthur S., and Stephen K. Sanderson. 1991. "Historic European household structures and the capitalist world-economy." *Journal of Family History* 16:419–32.

Alexander, Jeffrey C. 1983. *Theoretical Logic in Sociology*. Vol. 3: *The Classical Attempt at Theoretical Synthesis: Max Weber*. Berkeley: University of California Press.

_____. 1984. *Theoretical Logic in Sociology*. Vol. 4: *The Modern Reconstruction of Classical Thought: Talcott Parsons*. Berkeley: University of California Press.

_____ (ed). 1985 *Neofunctionalism*. Beverly Hills, CA: Sage.

_____. 1987. *Twenty Lectures: Sociological Theory since World War II*. New York: Columbia University Press.

_____. 1988. "The new theoretical movement." In Neil J. Smelser (ed.), *Handbook of Sociology*. Newbury Park, CA: Sage.

Alexander, Jeffrey C., and Paul Colomy. 1990. "Neofunctionalism today: Reconstructing a theoretical tradition." In George Ritzer (ed.), *Frontiers of Social Theory*. New York: Columbia University Press.

Alexander, Richard D. 1974. "The evolution of social behavior." *Annual Review of Ecology and Systematics* 5:325–83.

_____. 1975. "The search for a general theory of behavior." *Behavioral Science* 20:77–100.

_____. 1979. *Darwinism and Human Affairs*. Seattle: University of Washington Press.

_____. 1987. *The Biology of Moral Systems*. New York: Aldine de Gruyter.

_____. 1990. "Epigenetic rules and Darwinian algorithms: The adaptive study of learning and development." *Ethology and Sociobiology* 11:241–303.

Alexander, Richard D., John L. Hoogland, Richard D. Howard, Katharine M. Noonan, and Paul W. Sherman. 1979. "Sexual dimorphisms and breeding systems in pinnipeds, ungulates, primates, and humans." In Napoleon A. Chagnon and William Irons (eds.), *Evolutionary Biology and Human Social Behavior*. North Scituate, MA: Duxbury Press.

334

Althusser, Louis. 1969. *For Marx*. London: Penguin.

_____. 1971. *Lenin and Philosophy and Other Essays*. New York: Monthly Review Press.

Althusser, Louis, and Étienne Balibar. 1970. *Reading Capital*. London: New Left Books.

Anderson, Perry. 1974a. *Passages from Antiquity to Feudalism*. London: New Left Books.

_____. 1974b. *Lineages of the Absolutist State*. London: New Left Books.

Annett, Joan, and Randall Collins. 1975. "A short history of deference and demeanor." In Randall Collins, *Conflict Sociology: Toward an Explanatory Science*. New York: Academic Press.

Antonio, Robert J., and Ronald M. Glassman (eds.). 1985. *A Weber-Marx Dialogue*. Lawrence: University Press of Kansas.

Applebaum, R. 1979. "Born again functionalist? A reconsideration of Althusser's structuralism." *Insurgent Sociologist* 9(1):18–33.

Armstrong, Alice, et al. 1993. "Uncovering reality: Excavating women's rights in African family law." *International Journal of Law and the Family* 7:314–69.

Armstrong, W.E. 1924. "Rossel Island money: A unique monetary system." *Economic Journal* 34:423–29.

_____. 1928. *Rossel Island*. Cambridge, UK: Cambridge University Press.

Arnhart, Larry. 1998. *Darwinian Natural Right: The Biological Ethics of Human Nature*. Albany: State University of New York Press.

Attewell, Paul. 1974. "Ethnomethodology since Garfinkel." *Theory and Society* 1:179–210.

Axelrod, Robert. 1984. *The Evolution of Cooperation*. New York: Basic Books.

Badcock, C.R. 1975. *Lévi-Strauss: Structuralism and Sociological Theory*. New York: Holmes & Meier.

_____. 1991. *Evolution and Individual Behavior: An Introduction to Human Sociobiology*. Oxford: Blackwell.

Bakeman, Roger, and John R. Brownlee. 1982. "Social rules governing object conflicts in toddlers and preschoolers." In Kenneth H. Rubin and Hildy S. Ross (eds.), *Peer Relationships and Social Skills in Childhood*. New York: Springer-Verlag.

Balch, Stephen H. 1986. "'The neutered civil servant': Eunuchs, celibates, abductees, and the maintenance of organizational loyalty." In Elliott White and Joseph Losco (eds.), *Biology and Bureaucracy*. Lanham, MD: University Press of America.

Baran, Paul, and Paul Sweezy. 1966. *Monopoly Capital*. New York: Monthly Review Press.

Barash, David P. 1977. *Sociobiology and Behavior*. New York: Elsevier.

Barber, Nigel. 1995. "The evolutionary psychology of physical attractiveness: Sexual selection and human morphology." *Ethology and Sociobiology* 16:395–424.

Barkley, Russell A., Douglas G. Ullman, Lori Otto, and Jan M. Brecht. 1977. "The effects of sex typing and sex appropriateness of modeled behavior on children's imitation." *Child Development* 48:721–25.

Barkow, Jerome H. 1989. *Darwin, Sex, and Status*. Toronto: University of Toronto Press.

_____. 1992. "Beneath new culture is old psychology: Gossip and social stratification." In Jerome H. Barkow, Leda Cosmides, and John Tooby (eds.), *The Adapted Mind: Evolutionary Psychology and the Generation of Culture*. New York: Oxford University Press.

Barkow, Jerome H., Leda Cosmides, and John Tooby (eds.). 1992. *The Adapted Mind: Evolutionary Psychology and the Generation of Culture*. New York: Oxford University Press.

Barnes, Barry. 1976. *Interests and the Growth of Knowledge*. London: Routledge & Kegan Paul.

Barrow, John D. 1991. *Theories of Everything: The Quest for Ultimate Explanation*. New York: Oxford University Press.

Bates, Daniel G., and Susan H. Lees. 1979. "The myth of population regulation." In Napoleon A. Chagnon and William Irons (eds.), *Evolutionary Biology and Human Social Behavior*. North Scituate, MA: Duxbury Press.

Beall, Cynthia M., and Melvyn C. Goldstein 1981. "Tibetan fraternal polyandry: A test of sociobiological theory." *American Anthropologist* 83:5–12.

Becker, Gary S. 1991. *Treatise on the Family*. Enlarged ed. Cambridge, MA: Harvard University Press.

Becker, Howard. 1963. *Outsiders: Studies in the Sociology of Deviance*. New York: Free Press.

———. 1982. *Art Worlds*. Berkeley: University of California Press.

Beckerman, Stephen. 1989. "Hunting and fishing in Amazonia." Paper presented at Wenner-Gren Symposium 109, Nova Friburgo, Brazil.

Bell, Alan P., and Martin S. Weinberg. 1978. *Homosexualities: A Study of Diversity Among Men and Women*. New York: Simon & Schuster.

Belsky, Jay, Laurence Steinberg, and Patricia Draper. 1991. "Childhood experience, interpersonal development, and reproductive strategy: An evolutionary theory of socialization." *Child Development* 62:647–70.

Bendix, Reinhard. 1961. *Max Weber: An Intellectual Portrait*. Berkeley: University of California Press.

———. 1971. "Two sociological traditions." In Reinhard Bendix and Guenther Roth (eds.), *Scholarship and Partisanship: Essays on Max Weber*. Berkeley: University of California Press.

Ben-Porath, Yoram. 1978. "Fertility response to child mortality: Microdata from Israel." In Samuel H. Preston (ed.), *The Effects of Infant and Child Mortality on Fertility*. New York: Academic Press.

Benton, Ted. 1984. *The Rise and Fall of Structural Marxism*. London: Macmillan.

Bereczkei, Tamas, and Andras Csanaky. 1996. "Mate choice, marital success, and reproduction in a modern society." *Ethology and Sociobiology* 17:17–35.

Berg, Ivar. 1971. *Education and Jobs: The Great Training Robbery*. Boston: Beacon Press.

Best, Steven, and Douglas Kellner. 1991. *Postmodern Theory: Critical Interrogations*. New York: Guilford.

Betzig, Laura L. 1986. *Despotism and Differential Reproduction*. New York: Aldine de Gruyter.

———. 1992a. "Roman polygyny." *Ethology and Sociobiology* 13:309–49.

———. 1992b. "Roman monogamy." *Ethology and Sociobiology* 13:351–83.

——— (ed.). 1997. *Human Nature: A Critical Reader*. New York: Oxford University Press.

Betzig, Laura L., Monique Borgerhoff Mulder, and Paul W. Turke (eds.). 1988. *Human Reproductive Behavior: A Darwinian Perspective*. New York: Cambridge University Press.

Billing, Jennifer, and Paul W. Sherman. 1998. "Antimicrobial functions of spices: Why some like it hot." *Quarterly Review of Biology* 73:3–49.

Bischof, Norbert. 1975. "Comparative ethology of incest avoidance." In Robin Fox (ed.), *Biosocial Anthropology*. London: Malaby Press.

Blackburn, Robin. 1997. *The Making of New World Slavery*. London: Verso.

Blanchard, Ray. 1999. "Theory and research on birth order and sexual orientation." Paper presented at the annual meetings of the Human Behavior and Evolution Society, University of Utah, Salt Lake City, June 2–6.

Blanchard, Ray, K.J. Zucker, M. Siegelman, R. Dickey, and P. Klassen. 1998. "The relation of birth order to sexual orientation in men and women." *Journal of Biosocial Science* 30:511–19.

Blanton, Richard E., Stephen A. Kowalewski, Gary Feinman, and Jill Appel. 1981. *Ancient Mesoamerica: A Comparison of Change in Three Regions*. New York: Cambridge University Press.

Blau, Peter M. 1964. *Exchange and Power in Social Life*. New York: John Wiley & Sons.

Blauner, Robert. 1964. *Alienation and Freedom*. Chicago: University of Chicago Press.

Bloor, David. 1976. *Knowledge and Social Imagery.* London: Routledge & Kegan Paul.

_____. 1981. "The strengths of the strong programme." *Philosophy of the Social Sciences* 11:199–213.

Blumberg, Rae Lesser. 1978. *Stratification: Socioeconomic and Sexual Inequality.* Dubuque, IA: Wm. C. Brown.

_____. 1984. "A general theory of gender stratification." In Randall Collins (ed.), *Sociological Theory 1984.* San Francisco: Jossey-Bass.

Blumer, Herbert. 1969. *Symbolic Interactionism: Perspective and Method.* Englewood Cliffs, NJ: Prentice-Hall.

_____. 1990. *Industrialization as an Agent of Social Change.* New York: Aldine de Gruyter.

Blurton Jones, Nicholas G. 1984. "A selfish origin for human food sharing: Tolerated theft." *Ethology and Sociobiology* 5:1–3.

_____. 1986. "Bushman birth spacing: A test for optimal interbirth intervals." *Ethology and Sociobiology* 7:91–105

_____. 1987. "Tolerated theft: Suggestions about the ecology and evolution of sharing, hoarding, and scrounging." *Social Science Information* 26:31–54.

Boehm, Christopher. 1999. *Hierarchy in the Forest: The Evolution of Egalitarian Behavior.* Cambridge, MA: Harvard University Press.

Boli, John, Francisco O. Ramirez, and John W. Meyer. 1985. "Explaining the origins and expansion of mass education." *Comparative Education Review* 29:145–70.

Bollen, Kenneth A. 1979. "Political democracy and the timing of development." *American Sociological Review* 44:572–87.

_____. 1983. "World system position, dependency, and democracy: The cross-national evidence." *American Sociological Review* 48:468–79.

Bollen, Kenneth A., and Pamela M. Paxton. 1997. "Democracy before Athens." In Manus I. Midlarsky (ed.), *Inequality, Democracy, and Economic Development.* Cambridge, UK: Cambridge University Press.

Bonacich, Edna. 1972. "A theory of ethnic antagonism: The split labor market." *American Sociological Review* 37:547–59.

_____. 1979. "The past, present, and future of split labor market theory." In Cora B. Marrett and Cheryl Leggon (eds.), *Research in Race and Ethnic Relations.* Vol. 1. Greenwich, CT: JAI Press.

_____. 1981. "Capitalism and race relations in South Africa: A split labor market analysis." In Maurice Zeitlin (ed.), *Political Power and Social Theory.* Vol. 2. Greenwich, CT: JAI Press.

Boone, James L. 1998. "The evolution of magnanimity: When is it better to give than to receive?" *Human Nature* 9:1–21.

Borgerhoff Mulder, Monique. 1988. "Kipsigis bridewealth payments." In Laura L. Betzig, Monique Borgerhoff Mulder, and Paul W. Turke (eds.), *Human Reproductive Behavior: A Darwinian Perspective.* New York: Cambridge University Press.

_____. 1992. "Reproductive decisions." In Eric Alden Smith and Bruce Winterhalder (eds.), *Evolutionary Ecology and Human Behavior.* New York: Aldine de Gruyter.

_____. 1998. "The demographic transition: Are we any closer to an evolutionary explanation?" *Trends in Ecology and Evolution* 13:266–70.

Boserup, Ester. 1965. *The Conditions of Agricultural Growth.* Chicago: Aldine.

_____. 1970. *Women's Role in Economic Development.* New York: St. Martin's Press.

_____. 1981. *Population and Technological Change.* Chicago: University of Chicago Press.

_____. 1986. "Shifts in the determinants of fertility in the developing world: Environmental, technical, economic, and cultural factors." In David Coleman and Roger Schofield (eds.), *The State of Population Theory.* Oxford: Blackwell.

Boshu, Zhang. 1994. *Marxism and Human Sociobiology.* Albany: State University of New York Press.

Boswell, Terry E. 1986. "A split labor market analysis of discrimination against Chinese immigrants, 1850–1882." *American Sociological Review* 51:352–71.

Bowler, Peter J. 1983. *The Eclipse of Darwinism.* Baltimore: Johns Hopkins University Press.

_____. 1988. *The Non-Darwinian Revolution: Reinterpreting a Historical Myth.* Baltimore: Johns Hopkins University Press.

Bowles, Samuel, and Herbert Gintis. 1976. *Schooling in Capitalist America: Educational Reform and the Contradictions of Economic Life.* New York: Basic Books.

Boyer, Pascal. 1995. "Cultural evolution on cognitive tracks: How intuitive ontology governs cultural acquisition." Paper presented at the annual meetings of the Human Behavior and Evolution Society.

Braudel, Fernand. 1982. *The Wheels of Commerce.* (*Civilization and Capitalism 15th-18th Century,* Vol. 2.) Trans. Sian Reynolds. New York: Harper & Row.

_____. 1984. *The Perspective of the World.* (*Civilization and Capitalism 15th-18th Century,* Vol. 3.) Trans. Sian Reynolds. New York: Harper & Row.

Braverman, Harry. 1974. *Labor and Monopoly Capital: The Degradation of Work in the Twentieth Century.* New York: Monthly Review Press.

Brenner, Robert. 1977. "The origins of capitalist development: A critique of neo-Smithian Marxism." *New Left Review* 104:25–92.

Broch, Tom, and Johan Galtung. 1966. "Belligerence among the primitives." *Journal of Peace Research* 3:33–45.

Bronstad, P.M., and Devendra Singh. 1999. "Why did Tassinary and Hansen fail to replicate the relationship between WHR and female attractiveness"? Paper presented at the annual meetings of the Human Behavior and Evolution Society, University of Utah, Salt Lake City, June 2–6.

Broude, Gwen J., and Sarah J. Greene. 1976. "Cross-cultural codes on twenty sexual attitudes and practices." *Ethnology* 15:409–29.

Brown, Donald E. 1991. *Human Universals.* New York: McGraw-Hill.

Brown, Donald E., and Yü Chia-yun. 1993. "'Big man' in universalistic perspective." Manuscript, Department of Anthropology, University of California at Santa Barbara.

Brown, Judith K. 1975. "Iroquois women: An ethnohistoric note." In Rayna R. Reiter (ed.), *Toward an Anthropology of Women.* New York: Monthly Review Press.

Browne, Kingsley. 1995. "Sex and temperament in modern society: A Darwinian view of the glass ceiling and the gender gap." *Arizona Law Review* 37:970–1106.

Brundage, James A. 1987. *Law, Sex, and Christian Society in Medieval Europe.* Chicago: University of Chicago Press.

Brustein, William. 1996. *The Logic of Evil: The Social Origins of the Nazi Party, 1925–1933.* New Haven, CT: Yale University Press.

Buckle, Leslie, Gordon G. Gallup Jr., and Zachary A. Rodd. 1996. "Marriage as a reproductive contract: Patterns of marriage, divorce, and remarriage." *Ethology and Sociobiology* 17:363–77.

Bullough, Vern L. 1976. *Sexual Variance in Society and History.* Chicago: University of Chicago Press.

Burawoy, Michael. 1981. "The capitalist state in South Africa: Marxist and sociological perspectives on race and class." In Maurice Zeitlin (ed.), *Political Power and Social Theory.* Vol. 2. Greenwich, CT: JAI Press.

Burke, Charles. 1975. *Aggression in Man.* Secaucus, NJ: Lyle Stuart.

Burr, Chandler. 1996. *A Separate Creation: The Search for the Biological Origins of Sexual Orientation.* New York: Hyperion.

Burris, Val. 1979. "The structuralist influence in Marxist theory and research." *Insurgent Sociologist* 9(1):4–17.

_____. 1987. "The neo-Marxist synthesis of Marx and Weber on class." In Norbert Wiley (ed.), *The Marx-Weber Debate*. Beverly Hills, CA: Sage.

Buss, David M. 1989. "Sex differences in human mate preferences: Evolutionary hypotheses tested in 37 cultures." *Behavioral and Brain Sciences* 12:1–49.

_____. 1992. "Mate preference mechanisms: Consequences for partner choice and intrasexual competition." In Jerome H. Barkow, Leda Cosmides, and John Tooby (eds.), *The Adapted Mind: Evolutionary Psychology and the Generation of Culture*. New York: Oxford University Press.

_____. 1994. *The Evolution of Desire: Strategies of Human Mating*. New York: Basic Books.

_____. 1996. "Sexual conflict: Evolutionary insights into feminism and the 'battle of the sexes.'" In David M. Buss and Neil M. Malamuth (eds.), *Sex, Power, Conflict: Evolutionary and Feminist Perspectives*. New York. Oxford University Press.

_____. 1999. *Evolutionary Psychology: The New Science of the Mind*. Boston: Allyn & Bacon.

_____. 2000. *The Dangerous Passion: Why Jealousy is as Necessary as Love and Sex*. New York: Free Press.

Buss, David M., and Neil M. Malamuth (eds.). 1996. *Sex, Power, Conflict: Evolutionary and Feminist Perspectives*. New York: Oxford University Press.

Buss, David M., Randy J. Larsen, Drew Westen, and Jennifer Semmelroth. 1992. "Sex differences in jealousy: Evolution, physiology, and psychology." *Psychological Science* 3:251–55.

Caldwell, John C. 1976. "Toward a restatement of demographic transition theory." *Population and Development Review* 2:321–66.

Calvin, William H. 1997. *How Brains Think*. New York: Basic Books.

Cantarella, Eva. 1992. *Bisexuality in the Ancient World*. Trans. Cormac O'Cuilleanain. New Haven, CT: Yale University Press.

Cantrelle, P., B. Ferry, and J. Mondot. 1978. "Relationships between fertility and mortality in tropical Africa." In Samuel H. Preston (ed.), *The Effects of Infant and Child Mortality on Fertility*. New York: Academic Press.

Carey, Arlen D., and Joseph Lopreato. 1995. "The evolutionary demography of the fertility-mortality quasi-equilibrium." *Population and Development Review* 21:613–30.

Carling, Alan. 1986. "Rational choice Marxism." *New Left Review* 160:24–62.

Carneiro, Robert L. 1970. "A theory of the origin of the state." *Science* 169:733–38.

_____. 1981. "The chiefdom: Precursor of the state." In Grant D. Jones and Robert R. Kautz (ed.), *The Transition to Statehood in the New World*. New York: Cambridge University Press.

_____. 1987. "Further reflections on resource concentration and its role in the rise of the state." In Linda Manzanilla (ed.), *Studies in the Neolithic and Urban Revolutions*. Oxford: British Archaeological Reports. International Series, No. 349.

_____. 1990. "Chiefdom-level warfare as exemplified in Fiji and the Cauca Valley." In Jonathan Haas (ed.), *The Anthropology of War*. New York: Cambridge University Press.

_____. 1991. "The nature of the chiefdom as revealed by evidence from the Cauca Valley of Colombia." In A. Terry Rambo and Kathleen Gillogly (eds.), *Profiles in Cultural Evolution*. Anthropology Papers, Museum of Anthropology, University of Michigan, No. 85.

Carver, Terrell, and Paul Thomas. 1995. *Rational Choice Marxism*. University Park: Pennsylvania State University Press.

Cashdan, Elizabeth A. 1980. "Egalitarianism among hunters and gatherers." *American Anthropologist* 82:116–20.

_____. 1985. "Coping with risk: Reciprocity among the Basarwa of northern Botswana." *Man* 20:454–74.

_____. 1994. "A sensitive period for learning about food." *Human Nature* 5:279–91.

Chafetz, Janet Saltzman. 1984. *Sex and Advantage: A Comparative, Macro-Structural Theory of Sex Stratification*. Totowa, NJ: Rowman and Allanheld.

_____. 1993. "Sociological theory: A case of multiple personality disorder." *Perspectives: The Theory Section Newsletter* 6(1):1–2.

Chagnon, Napoleon A. 1983. *Yanomamö: The Fierce People*. 3rd ed. New York: Holt, Rinehart, and Winston.

_____. 1988. "Life histories, blood revenge, and warfare in a tribal population." *Science* 239:985–92.

Chagnon, Napoleon A., Mark V. Flinn, and Thomas F. Melancon. 1979. "Sex-ratio variation among the Yanomamö Indians." In Napoleon A. Chagnon and William Irons (eds.), *Evolutionary Biology and Human Social Behavior*. North Scituate, MA: Duxbury Press.

Chase-Dunn, Christopher. 1989. *Global Formation: Structures of the World-Economy*. Oxford: Blackwell.

_____. 1998. *Global Formation: Structures of the World-Economy*. Updated ed. Lanham, MD: Rowman & Littlefield.

Chisholm, James S. 1999. *Death, Hope, and Sex: Steps to an Evolutionary Ecology of Mind and Morality*. New York: Cambridge University Press.

Chowdhury, A.K.M. Alauddin, Atiqur Rahman Khan, and Lincoln C. Chen. 1978. "Experience in Pakistan and Bangladesh." In Samuel H. Preston (ed.), *The Effects of Infant and Child Mortality on Fertility*. New York: Academic Press.

Churchland, Paul M. 1995. *The Engine of Reason, the Seat of the Soul*. Cambridge, MA: MIT Press.

Clark, Burton R. 1962. *Educating the Expert Society*. San Francisco: Chandler.

Cohen, G.A. 1978. *Karl Marx's Theory of History: A Defence*. Princeton, NJ: Princeton University Press.

_____. 1984. "Restrictive and inclusive historical materialism." *Irish Philosophical Journal* 1:3–31.

Cohen, Ira J. 1985. "The underemphasis on democracy in Marx and Weber." In Robert J. Antonio and Ronald M. Glassman (eds.), *A Weber-Marx Dialogue*. Lawrence: University Press of Kansas.

Cohen, Jere. 1980. "Rational capitalism in Renaissance Italy." *American Journal of Sociology* 85:1340–55.

Cohen, Jere, Lawrence E. Hazelrigg, and Whitney Pope. 1975. "De-Parsonizing Weber: a critique of Parsons's interpretation of Weber's sociology." *American Sociological Review* 40:229–41.

Cohen, Mark N. 1977. *The Food Crisis in Prehistory*. New Haven: Yale University Press.

_____. 1981. "The ecological basis of New World state formation: General and local model building." In Grant D. Jones and Robert R. Kautz (eds.), *The Transition to Statehood in the New World*. New York: Cambridge University Press.

_____. 1985. "Prehistoric hunter-gatherers: The meaning of social complexity." In T. Douglas Price and James A. Brown (eds.), *Prehistoric Hunter-Gatherers*. New York: Academic Press.

Cohen, Percy. 1968. *Modern Social Theory*. New York: Basic Books.

Cohen, Ronald. 1978. "State origins: A reappraisal." In Henri J.M. Claessen and Peter Skalnik (eds.), *The Early State*. The Hague: Mouton.

Coleman, James S. 1990. *Foundations of Social Theory*. Cambridge, MA: Harvard University Press (Belknap Press).

Collins, H.M. 1981. "Stages in the empirical programme of relativism." *Social Studies of Science* 11:3–10.

Collins, H.M., and Trevor Pinch. 1982. *Frames of Meaning: The Social Construction of Extraordinary Science*. London: Routledge & Kegan Paul.

Collins, Randall. 1974. "Reassessments of sociological history: The empirical validity of the conflict tradition." *Theory and Society* 1:147–78.

_____. 1975. *Conflict Sociology: Toward an Explanatory Science*. New York: Academic Press.

_____. 1977. "Review of Lewis A. Coser (ed.), *The Idea of Social Structure: Papers in Honor of Robert K. Merton* (Harcourt Brace Jovanovich, 1975). *Contemporary Sociology* 6:150–54.

_____. 1979. *The Credential Society: An Historical Sociology of Education and Stratification*. New York: Academic Press.

_____. 1981. "On the microfoundations of macrosociology." *American Journal of Sociology* 86:984–1014.

_____. 1983. "Upheavals in biological theory undermine sociobiology." In Randall Collins (ed.), *Sociological Theory 1983*. San Francisco: Jossey-Bass.

_____. 1985a. "Jeffrey Alexander and the search for multi-dimensional theory." *Theory and Society* 14:877–92.

_____. 1985b. *Sociology of Marriage and the Family: Gender, Love, and Property*. Chicago: Nelson-Hall.

_____. 1986a. *Max Weber: A Skeleton Key*. Beverly Hills, CA: Sage.

_____. 1986b. *Weberian Sociological Theory*. New York: Cambridge University Press.

_____. 1988. *Theoretical Sociology*. San Diego: Harcourt Brace Jovanovich.

_____. 1992. "The confusion of the modes of sociology." In Steven Seidman and David G. Wagner (eds.), *Postmodernism and Social Theory*. Oxford: Blackwell.

_____. 1993. "Maturation of the state-centered theory of revolution and ideology." *Sociological Theory* 11:117–28.

_____. 1994. *Four Sociological Traditions*. New York: Oxford University Press.

_____. 1997. "An Asian route to capitalism: Religious economy and the origins of self-transforming growth in Japan." *American Sociological Review* 62:843–65.

_____. 1998. *The Sociology of Philosophies: A Global Theory of Intellectual Change*. Cambridge, MA: Harvard University Press.

Cook, Scott. 1969. "The 'anti-market' mentality re-examined: A further critique of the substantive approach to economic anthropology." *Southwestern Journal of Anthropology* 25:378–406.

Cornish, Derek B., and Ronald V. Clarke (eds.). 1986. *The Reasoning Criminal: Rational Choice Perspectives on Offending*. New York: Springer-Verlag.

Cory, Donald W., and R.E.L. Masters. 1963. *Violation of Taboo: Incest of the Great Literature of the Past and the Present*. New York: Julian Press.

Coser, Lewis. 1956. *The Functions of Social Conflict*. New York: Free Press.

_____. 1964. "The political functions of eunuchism." *American Sociological Review* 29:880–85.

Cosmides, Leda, and John Tooby. 1989. "Evolutionary psychology and the generation of culture, part II. Case study: A computational theory of social exchange." *Ethology and Sociobiology* 10:51–97.

_____. 1992. "Cognitive adaptations for social exchange." In Jerome H. Barkow, Leda Cosmides, and John Tooby (eds.), *The Adapted Mind: Evolutionary Psychology and the Generation of Culture*. New York: Oxford University Press.

Couch, Carl J. 1990. *Constructing Civilizations*. Greenwich, CT: JAI Press.

Courtois, Stéphane, Nicholas Werth, Jean-Louis Panné, Andrzej Paczkowski, Karel Bartošek, and Jean-Louis Margolin. 1999. *The Black Book of Communism: Crimes, Terror, Repression*. Trans. Jonathan Murphy and Mark Kramer. Cambridge, MA: Harvard University Press.

Cowlishaw, Guy, and Ruth Mace. 1996. "Cross-cultural patterns of marriage and inheritance: A phylogenetic approach." *Ethology and Sociobiology* 17:87–97.

Cox, Oliver C. 1948. *Caste, Class, and Race.* New York: Monthly Review Press.

Crawford, Charles. 1998. "Environments and adaptations: Then and now." In Charles Crawford and Dennis L. Krebs (eds.), *Handbook of Evolutionary Psychology.* Mahwah, NJ: Lawrence Erlbaum.

Crawford, Charles, and Dennis L. Krebs (eds.). 1998. *Handbook of Evolutionary Psychology.* Mahwah, NJ: Lawrence Erlbaum.

Crippen, Timothy. 1994. "Toward a neo-Darwinian sociology: Its nomological principles and some illustrative applications." *Sociological Perspectives* 37:309–35.

Cronk, Lee. 1989. "Low socioeconomic status and female-biased parental investment: The Mukogodo example." *American Anthropologist* 91:414–29.

_____. 1991. "Preferential parental investment in daughters over sons." *Human Nature* 2:387–417.

_____. 1999. *That Complex Whole: Culture and the Evolution of Human Behavior.* Boulder, CO: Westview Press.

_____. 2000. "Female-biased parental investment and growth performance among the Mukogodo." In Lee Cronk, Napoleon Chagnon, and William Irons (eds.), *Adaptation and Human Behavior: An Anthropological Perspective.* New York: Aldine de Gruyter.

Cronk, Lee, Napoleon Chagnon, and William Irons (eds.). 2000. *Adaptation and Human Behavior: An Anthropological Perspective.* New York: Aldine de Gruyter.

Crook, J.H. 1980. *The Evolution of Consciousness.* Oxford: Oxford University Press (Clarendon Press).

Crook, John H., and Stamati J. Crook. 1988. "Tibetan polyandry: Problems of adaptation and fitness." In Laura L. Betzig, Monique Borgerhoff Mulder, and Paul W. Turke (eds.), *Human Reproductive Behavior: A Darwinian Perspective.* New York: Cambridge University Press.

Curtin, Philip D. 1984. *Cross-Cultural Trade in World History.* New York: Cambridge University Press.

Cutright, Phillips. 1963. "National political development: Measurement and analysis." *American Sociological Review* 28:253–64.

Dabbs, James M., Jr., E-Lee Chang, Rebecca A. Strong, and Rhonda Milun. 1998. "Spatial ability, navigation strategy, and geographic knowledge among men and women." *Evolution and Human Behavior* 19:89–98.

Dahrendorf, Ralf. 1958. "Out of utopia: Toward a reorientation of sociological analysis." *American Journal of Sociology* 64:115–27.

_____. 1959. *Class and Class Conflict in Industrial Society.* Palo Alto, CA: Stanford University Press.

Dalton, George. 1965. "Primitive money." *American Anthropologist* 67:44–65.

_____ (ed.). 1967. *Tribal and Peasant Economies.* Austin: University of Texas Press.

_____ (ed.). 1968. *Primitive, Archaic, and Modern Economies: Essays of Karl Polanyi.* Boston: Beacon Press.

_____. 1969. "Theoretical issues in economic anthropology." *Current Anthropology* 10:63–102.

Daly, Martin, and Margo Wilson. 1978. *Sex, Evolution, and Behavior.* North Scituate, MA: Duxbury Press.

_____. 1984. "A sociobiological analysis of human infanticide." In Glenn Hausfater and Sarah Blaffer Hrdy (eds.), *Infanticide.* New York: Aldine de Gruyter.

_____. 1986. "A theoretical challenge to a caricature of Darwinism." *Behavioral and Brain Sciences* 9:189–90.

_____. 1988. *Homicide*. New York: Aldine de Gruyter.

_____. 1998. *The Truth About Cinderella: A Darwinian View of Parental Love*. New Haven, CT: Yale University Press.

Daly, Martin, Margo Wilson, and Suzanne J. Weghorst. 1982. "Male sexual jealousy." *Ethology and Sociobiology* 3:11–27.

Damasio, Antonio R. 1994. *Descartes's Error: Emotion, Reason, and the Human Brain*. New York: Putnam's.

Darwin, Charles. 1871. *The Descent of Man and Selection in Relation to Sex*. London: John Murray.

Davies, R.H. 1979. *Capital, State and White Labour in South Africa, 1900–1960: An Historical Materialist Analysis of Class Formation and Class Relations*. New York: Humanities Press.

Davis, Kingsley. 1949. *Human Society*. New York: Macmillan.

Davis, Kingsley, and Wilbert E. Moore. 1945. "Some principles of stratification." *American Sociological Review* 10:242–49.

Dawkins, Richard. 1976. *The Selfish Gene*. Oxford: Oxford University Press.

Degler, Carl N. 1991. *In Search of Human Nature: The Decline and Revival of Darwinism in American Social Thought*. New York: Oxford University Press.

Denzin, Norman K. 1969. "Symbolic interactionism and ethnomethodology: A proposed synthesis." *American Sociological Review* 34:922–34.

_____. 1986. "Postmodern social theory." *Sociological Theory* 4:194–204.

_____. 1987. *The Alcoholic Self*. Newbury Park, CA: Sage.

_____. 1989. *Interpretive Interactionism*. Newbury Park, CA: Sage.

_____. 1990. "Reading rational choice theory." *Rationality and Society* 2:172–89.

Derrida, Jacques. 1978. *Writing and Difference*. Trans. Alan Bass. Chicago: University of Chicago Press.

Deutsch, David. 1997. *The Fabric of Reality*. New York: Allen Lane (The Penguin Press).

de Waal, Frans. 1996. *Good Natured: The Origins of Right and Wrong in Humans and Other Animals*. Cambridge, MA: Harvard University Press.

Diamond, Stanley. 1974. "The myth of structuralism." In Ino Rossi (ed.), *The Unconscious in Culture: The Structuralism of Claude Lévi-Strauss in Perspective*. New York: E.P. Dutton.

Dickemann, Mildred. 1975. "Demographic consequences of infanticide in man." *Annual Review of Ecology and Systematics* 6:107–37.

_____. 1979a. "Female infanticide, reproductive strategies, and social stratification: A preliminary model." In Napoleon A. Chagnon and William Irons (eds.), *Evolutionary Biology and Human Social Behavior*. North Scituate, MA: Duxbury Press.

_____. 1979b. "The ecology of mating systems in hypergynous dowry societies." *Social Science Information* 18:163–95.

Dickens, David R., and Andrea Fontana (eds.). 1994. *Postmodernism and Social Inquiry*. New York: Guilford.

Divale, William Tulio. 1972. "Systematic population control in the Middle and Upper Paleolithic: Inferences based on contemporary hunter-gatherers." *World Archaeology* 4:22–43.

Divale, William Tulio, and Marvin Harris. 1976. "Population, warfare, and the male supremacist complex." *American Anthropologist* 78:521–38.

Dobb, Maurice. 1963. *Studies in the Development of Capitalism*. Rev. ed. New York: International Publishers.

Domhoff, G. William. 1970. *The Higher Circles*. New York: Random House.

_____. 1978. *The Powers That Be: Processes of Ruling Class Domination*. New York: Random House (Vintage).

_____. 1983. *Who Rules America Now? A View for the '80s.* New York: Simon & Schuster (Touchstone).

_____. 1990. *The Power Elite and the State: How Policy is Made in America.* New York: Aldine de Gruyter.

Dowling, John H. 1979. "The goodfellows vs. the Dalton gang: The assumptions of economic anthropology." *Journal of Anthropological Research* 35:292–307.

Draper, Patricia, and Jay Belsky. 1990. "Personality development in evolutionary perspective." *Journal of Personality* 58:141–61.

Draper, Patricia, and Henry Harpending. 1982. "Father absence and reproductive strategy: An evolutionary perspective." *Journal of Anthropological Research* 38:255–73.

Dumont, Louis. 1980. *Homo Hierarchicus: The Caste System and its Implications.* Trans. Mark Sainsbury, Louis Dumont, and Basi Gulati. Chicago: University of Chicago Press.

Durham, William H. 1991. *Coevolution: Genes, Culture, and Human Diversity.* Stanford, CA: Stanford University Press.

Durkheim, Émile. 1964. *Incest: The Nature and Origin of the Taboo.* Trans. Edward Sagarin. New York: Lyle Stuart (Originally published 1898).

Duus, Peter. 1969. *Feudalism in Japan.* New York: Alfred A. Knopf.

Dwyer, Peter D. 1974. "The price of protein: Five hundred hours of hunting in the New Guinea highlands." *Oceania* 44:278–93.

Dyson, Tim, and Mick Moore. 1983. "On kinship structure, female autonomy, and demographic behavior in India." *Population and Development Review* 9:35–60.

Dyson-Hudson, Rada, and Eric Alden Smith. 1978. "Human territoriality: An ecological reassessment." *American Anthropologist* 80:21–41.

Earle, Timothy. 1978. "Economic and social organization of a complex chiefdom: The Halelea district, Kaua'i, Hawai'i." University of Michigan Museum of Anthropology, Anthropological Papers No. 63.

_____. 1987. "Chiefdoms in archaeological and ethnohistorical perspective." *Annual Review of Anthropology* 16:279–308.

_____. 1989. "The evolution of chiefdoms." *Current Anthropology* 30:84–88.

_____ (ed.). 1991. *Chiefdoms: Power, Economy, and Ideology.* New York: Cambridge University Press.

_____. 1997. *How Chiefs Come to Power: The Political Economy in Prehistory.* Stanford, CA: Stanford University Press.

Earle, Timothy, and Robert W. Preucel. 1987. "Processual archaeology and the radical critique." *Current Anthropology* 28:501–38.

Eckhardt, William. 1992. *Civilizations, Empires, and Wars.* Jefferson, NC: McFarland.

Ekeh, Peter P. 1974. *Social Exchange Theory: The Two Traditions.* Cambridge, MA: Harvard University Press.

Ellis, Bruce J. 1992. "The evolution of sexual attraction: Evaluative mechanisms in women." In Jerome H. Barkow, Leda Cosmides, and John Tooby (eds.), *The Adapted Mind: Evolutionary Psychology and the Generation of Culture.* New York: Oxford University Press.

Ellis, Bruce J., and Judy Garber. 2000. "Psychosocial antecedents of variation in girls' pubertal timing: Maternal depression, stepfather prescence, and marital and family stress." *Child Development* 71:485–501.

Ellis, Bruce J., Steven McFadyen-Ketchum, Kenneth A. Dodge, Gregory S. Pettit, and John E. Bates. 1999. "Quality of early family relationships and individual differences in the timing of pubertal maturation in girls: A longitudinal test of an evolutionary model." *Journal of Personality and Social Psychology* 77:387–401.

Ellis, Lee. 1990. *Theories of Rape*. New York: Hemisphere.

_____. 1994a. "The high and the mighty among man and beast: How universal is the relationship between height (or body size) and social status?" In Lee Ellis (ed.), *Social Stratification and Socioeconomic Inequality*. Vol. 2. Westport, CT: Praeger.

_____. 1994b. "Relationships between height, health, and social status (plus birth weight, mental health, intelligence, brain size, and fertility): A broad theoretical integration." In Lee Ellis (ed.), *Social Stratification and Socioeconomic Inequality*. Vol. 2. Westport, CT: Praeger.

_____. 1995. "Dominance and reproductive success among nonhuman animals: A cross-species comparison." *Ethology and Sociobiology* 16:257–333.

_____. 1996. "A discipline in peril: Sociology's future hinges on curing its biophobia." *American Sociologist* 27:21–41.

Ellis, Lee, and M. Ashley Ames. 1987. "Neurohormonal functioning and sexual orientation: A theory of homosexuality-heterosexuality." *Psychological Bulletin* 101:233–58.

Elster, Jon. 1985. *Making Sense of Marx*. Cambridge, UK: Cambridge University Press.

Ember, Carol R. 1974. "An evaluation of alternative theories of matrilocal versus patrilocal residence." *Behavior Science Research* 9:135–49.

_____. 1978. "Myths about hunter-gatherers." *Ethnology* 17:439–48.

Ember, Melvin. 1974. "The conditions that may favor avunculocal residence." *Behavior Science Research* 9:203–09.

_____. 1983. "On the origin and extension of the incest taboo." In Melvin Ember and Carol R. Ember (eds.), *Marriage, Family, and Kinship*. New Haven, CT: HRAF Press.

Ember, Melvin, and Carol Ember. 1971. "The conditions favoring matrilocal versus patrilocal residence." *American Anthropologist* 73:571–94.

Engels, Friedrich. 1970. *The Origin of the Family, Private Property, and the State*. Ed. Eleanor Burke Leacock. New York: International Publishers (Originally published 1884).

Erickson, Mark. 1989. "Incest avoidance and familial bonding." *Journal of Anthropological Research* 45:267–91.

Essock-Vitale, Susan M. 1984. "The reproductive success of wealthy Americans." *Ethology and Sociobiology* 5:45–49.

Falger, Vincent S.E. 1984. "Sociobiology and political ideology: Comments on the radical point of view." *Journal of Human Evolution* 13:129–35.

_____. 1992. "Sex differences in international politics? An exploratory study of coalitional behaviour in biopolitical perspective." In Johan M.G. van der Dennen (ed.), *The Nature of the Sexes: The Sociobiology of Sex Differences and the "Battle of the Sexes."* Groningen, Netherlands: Origin Press.

Feinman, Gary. 1991. "Demography, surplus, and inequality: Early political formations in highland Mesoamerica." In Timothy Earle (ed.), *Chiefdoms: Power, Economy, and Ideology*. New York: Cambridge University Press.

Ferguson, R. Brian. 1984. "Introduction: Studying war." In R. Brian Ferguson (ed.), *Warfare, Culture, and Environment*. New York: Academic Press.

_____. 1989a. "Ecological consequences of Amazonian warfare." *Ethnology* 28:249–64.

_____. 1989b. "Game wars? Ecology and conflict in Amazonia." *Journal of Anthropological Research* 45:179–206.

_____. 1990a. "Explaining war." In Jonathan Haas (ed.), *The Anthropology of War*. New York: Cambridge University Press.

_____. 1990b. "Blood of the Leviathan: Western contact and warfare in Amazonia." *American Ethnologist* 17:237–57.

_____. 1995a. *Yanomami Warfare: A Political History*. Santa Fe, NM: School of American Research Press.

_____. 1995b. "Infrastructural determinism." In Martin F. Murphy and Maxine L. Margolis (eds.), *Science, Materialism, and the Study of Culture*. Gainesville: University Press of Florida.

_____. 1997. "Review of Lawrence Keeley, *War Before Civilization: The Myth of the Peaceful Savage* (New York: Oxford University Press, 1996)." *American Anthropologist* 99:424–25.

Ferguson, R. Brian, and Neil L. Whitehead. 1992. *War in the Tribal Zone: Expanding States and Indigenous Warfare*. Santa Fe, NM: School of American Research Press.

Feuer, Lewis S. 1978. "Marx and Engels as sociobiologists." *Survey* 23(4):109–36.

Fine, Gary Alan. 1990. "Symbolic interactionism in the post-Blumerian age." In George Ritzer (ed.), *Frontiers of Social Theory*. New York: Columbia University Press.

_____. 1993. "The sad demise, mysterious disappearance, and glorious triumph of symbolic interactionism." *Annual Review of Sociology* 19:61–87.

Fisher, Helen E. 1992. *The Anatomy of Love*. New York: Norton.

Fisher, Ronald A. 1958. *The Genetical Theory of Natural Selection*. Rev. ed. New York: Dover (First edition 1930).

Flinn, Mark V. 1997. "Culture and the evolution of social learning." *Evolution and Human Behavior* 18:23–67.

Flinn, Mark V., and Bobbi S. Low. 1986. "Resource distribution, social competition, and mating patterns in human societies." In Daniel I. Rubenstein and Richard W. Wrangham (eds.), *Ecological Aspects of Social Evolution*. Princeton, NJ: Princeton University Press.

Fogel, Robert William. 1989. *Without Consent or Contract: The Rise and Fall of American Slavery*. New York: Norton.

Fogel, Robert William, and Stanley L. Engerman. 1974. *Time on the Cross: The Economics of American Negro Slavery*. Boston: Little, Brown.

Ford, Clellan S., and Frank A. Beach. 1951. *Patterns of Sexual Behavior*. New York: Harper & Row.

Foucault, Michel. 1973a. *Madness and Civilization: A History of Insanity in the Age of Reason*. Trans. Richard Howard. New York: Random House (Vintage).

_____. 1973b. *The Order of Things: An Archaeology of the Human Sciences*. Trans. from the French. New York: Random House (Vintage).

_____. 1976. *The Archaeology of Knowledge and the Discourse of Language*. Trans. A.M. Sheridan Smith. New York: Harper Colophon.

_____. 1978. *The History of Sexuality*. Vol. 1. Trans. Robert Hurley. New York: Random House (Vintage).

_____. 1979. *Discipline and Punish: The Birth of the Prison*. Trans. Alan Sheridan. New York: Random House (Vintage).

Fox, Robin. 1967. *Kinship and Marriage*. London: Penguin.

Freedman, Daniel G. 1979. *Human Sociobiology*. New York: Free Press.

Freese, Jeremy, and Brian Powell. 1999. "Sociobiology, status, and parental investment in sons and daughters." *American Journal of Sociology* 106: 1704–43.

Fried, Morton H. 1967. *The Evolution of Political Society*. New York: Random House.

_____. 1978. "The state, the chicken, or the egg: Or, what came first?" In Ronald Cohen and Elman R. Service (eds.), *Origins of the State*. Philadelphia: Institute for the Study of Human Issues.

Friedl, Ernestine. 1975. *Women and Men: An Anthropologist's View*. New York: Holt, Rinehart and Winston.

Friedman, Debra, and Michael Hechter. 1988. "The contribution of rational choice theory to macrosociological research." *Sociological Theory* 6:201–18.

_____. 1990. "The comparative advantages of rational choice theory." In George Ritzer (ed.), *Frontiers of Social Theory*. New York: Columbia University Press.

Friedman, Jonathan. 1974. "Marxism, structuralism, and vulgar materialism." *Man* 9:444–69.

Furnham, Adrian, Melanie Dias, and Alastair McClelland. 1998. "The role of body weight, waist-to-hip ratio, and breast size in judgments of female attractiveness." *Sex Roles* 39:311–26.

Furstenburg, Frank F., Jr. 1966. "Industrialization and the American family: A look backward." *American Sociological Review* 31:326–37.

Gallant, Mary J., and Sherryl Kleinman. 1983. "Symbolic interactionism vs. ethnomethodology." *Symbolic Interaction* 6:1–18.

Gangestad, Steven W., and Randy Thornhill. 1997. "The evolutionary psychology of extrapair sex: The role of fluctuating asymmetry." *Evolution and Human Behavior* 18:69–88.

Gans, Herbert J. 1972. "The positive functions of poverty." *American Journal of Sociology* 78:275–89.

Garfinkel, Harold. 1967. *Studies in Ethnomethodology.* Engelwood Cliffs, NJ: Prentice-Hall.

Gaulin, Steven J.C. 1992. "Evolution of sex differences in spatial ability." *Yearbook of Physical Anthropology* 35:125–51.

_____. 1995. "Does evolutionary theory predict sex differences in the brain?" In Michael S. Gazzaniga (ed.), *The Cognitive Neurosciences.* Cambridge, MA: MIT Press.

Gaulin, Steven J.C., and James S. Boster. 1990. "Dowry as female competition." *American Anthropologist* 92:994–1005.

Gaulin, Steven J.C., and R.W. FitzGerald. 1986. "Sex differences in spatial ability: An evolutionary hypothesis and test." *American Naturalist* 127:74–88.

_____. 1989. "Sexual selection for spatial-learning ability." *Animal Behavior* 37:322–31.

Gaulin, Steven J.C., and Carol A. Hoffman. 1988. "Evolution and development of sex differences in spatial ability." In Laura A. Betzig, Monique Borgerhoff Mulder, and Paul W. Turke (eds.), *Human Reproductive Behavior: A Darwinian Perspective.* New York: Cambridge University Press.

Gaulin, Steven J.C., and Donald McBurney. 2000. *Psychology: An Evolutionary Approach.* Upper Saddle River, NJ: Prentice Hall.

Gaulin, Steven J.C., and Alice Schlegel. 1980. "Paternal confidence and paternal investment: A cross-cultural test of a sociobiological hypothesis." *Ethology and Sociobiology* 1:301–9.

Gaulin, Steven J.C., Irwin Silverman, Krista Phillips, and Christine Reiber. 1997. "Activational hormone influences on abilities and attitudes." *Evolution and Cognition* 3:191–99.

Geary, David C. 1998. *Male, Female: The Evolution of Human Sex Differences.* Washington, DC: American Psychological Association.

Gelles, Richard J. 1987. "What to learn from cross-cultural and historical research on child abuse and neglect: An overview." In Richard J. Gelles and Jane B. Lancaster (eds.), *Child Abuse and Neglect: Biosocial Dimensions.* New York: Aldine de Gruyter.

Genovese, Eugene D. 1965. *The Political Economy of Slavery.* New York: Random House (Vintage).

_____. 1968. "Materialism and idealism in the history of Negro slavery in the Americas." *Journal of Social History* 1:371–94.

_____. 1969. *The World the Slaveholders Made.* New York: Random House (Vintage).

_____. 1974. *Roll, Jordan, Roll: The World the Slaves Made.* New York: Random House (Vintage).

Gerth, H.H., and C. Wright Mills (eds.). 1946. *From Max Weber: Essays in Sociology.* New York: Oxford University Press.

Gibbs, J.P. 1975. *Crime, Punishment, and Deterrence.* New York: Elsevier.

Gibbs, James L., Jr. 1965. "The Kpelle of Liberia." In James L. Gibbs, Jr. (ed.), *Peoples of Africa.* New York: Holt, Rinehart, and Winston.

Giddens, Anthony. 1980. *The Class Structure of the Advanced Societies.* 2nd ed. London: Hutchinson.

———. 1981. *A Contemporary Critique of Historical Materialism.* Berkeley: University of California Press.

———. 1982. "From Marx to Nietzsche? Neo-conservatism, Foucault, and problems in contemporary political theory." In Anthony Giddens, *Profiles and Critiques in Social Theory.* Berkeley: University of California Press.

———. 1984. *The Constitution of Society: Outline of the Theory of Structuration.* Berkeley: University of California Press.

———. 1987. *Social Theory and Modern Sociology.* Cambridge, UK: Polity Press.

Gilbert, G. Nigel, and Michael Mulkay. 1985. *Opening Pandora's Box: A Sociological Analysis of Scientists' Discourse.* Cambridge, UK: Cambridge University Press.

Glaser, Barney G., and Anselm L. Strauss. 1965. *Awareness of Dying.* Chicago: Aldine.

Godelier, Maurice. 1975. "Modes of production, kinship, and demographic structures." In Maurice Bloch (ed.), *Marxist Analyses and Social Anthropology.* London: Malaby Press.

———. 1977. *Perspectives in Marxist Anthropology.* Cambridge, UK: Cambridge University Press.

———. 1978. "Infrastructures, societies, and history." *Current Anthropology* 19:763–71.

Goffman, Erving. 1959. *The Presentation of Self in Everyday Life.* New York: Doubleday (Anchor).

Goldberg, Steven. 1993. *Why Men Rule: A Theory of Male Dominance.* Chicago: Open Court.

Goldsmith, Raymond W. 1987. *Premodern Financial Systems.* New York: Cambridge University Press.

Goldstein, Joshua S. 1988. *Long Cycles: Prosperity and War in the Modern Age.* New Haven, CT: Yale University Press.

Goldstein, Melvyn. 1976. "Fraternal polyandry and fertility in a high Himalayan valley in northwest Nepal." *Human Ecology* 4:223–33.

Goldstone, Jack A. 1991. *Revolution and Rebellion in the Early Modern World.* Berkeley: University of California Press.

Goody, Jack. 1976. *Production and Reproduction: A Comparative Study of the Domestic Domain.* Cambridge, UK: Cambridge University Press.

Gowaty, Patricia. 1992. "Evolutionary biology and feminism." *Human Nature* 3:217–49.

Green, Penny Anthon. 1994. "Toward a biocultural theory of class circulation: An application of Joseph Lopreato's sociology." *Revue éuropéenne des sciences sociales* 32:195–214.

———. 1995. "Evolutionary insights into problems of sexism, classism, and racism, including prospects for their elimination." *Race, Gender, and Class* 2(2):65–83.

Greenfield, Sidney M. 1961. "Industrialization and the family in sociological theory." *American Journal of Sociology* 67:312–22.

Gross, Paul R., and Norman Levitt. 1994. *Higher Superstition: The Academic Left and its Quarrels with Science.* Baltimore: Johns Hopkins University Press.

Grossbard, Amyra S. 1976. "An economic analysis of polygyny: The case of Maiduguri." *Current Anthropology* 17:701–7.

———. 1980. "The economics of polygamy." In Julian L. Simon and Julie DaVanzo (eds.), *Research in Population Economics.* Vol. 2. Greenwich, CT: JAI Press.

———. 1984. "A theory of allocation of time in markets for labour and marriage." *Economic Journal* 94:863–82.

Haas, Jonathan (ed.). 1990. *The Anthropology of War.* New York: Cambridge University Press.

Hall, John Whitney. 1970. *Japan: From Prehistory to Modern Times.* New York: Delacorte Press.

Halliburton, R., Jr. 1975. "Free black owners of slaves: A reappraisal of the Woodson thesis." *South Carolina Historical Magazine* 76:129–42.

Halliday, Jon. 1975. *A Political History of Japanese Capitalism*. New York: Monthly Review Press.

Hamer, Dean, and Peter Copeland. 1994. *The Science of Desire: The Search for the Gay Gene and the Biology of Behavior*. New York: Simon & Schuster (Touchstone).

Hames, Raymond B. 1980. "Game depletion and hunting zone rotation among the Ye'kwana and Yanomamö of Amazonas, Venezuela." In Raymond B. Hames (ed.), *Working Papers on South American Indians*. Bennington, VT: Bennington College.

_____. 1988. "The allocation of parental care among the Ye'kwana." In Laura L. Betzig, Monique Borgerhoff Mulder, and Paul W. Turke (eds.), *Human Reproductive Behavior: A Darwinian Perspective*. New York: Cambridge University Press.

Hames, Raymond B., and William T. Vickers. 1982. "Optimal foraging theory as a model to explain variability in Amazonian hunting." *American Ethnologist* 9:358–78.

Hamilton, William D. 1964. "The genetical evolution of social behavior, parts 1 and 2." *Journal of Theoretical Biology* 7:1–51.

Hammond, Michael. 1998. "When more is not enough: Arouser depreciation and the expansion of human needs." Paper presented at the annual meetings of the Human Behavior and Evolution Society, University of California at Davis, July.

Handwerker, W. Penn. 1993. "Empowerment and fertility transition on Antigua, WI: Education, employment, and the moral economy of childbearing." *Human Organization* 52:41–52.

Hanley, Susan B., and Kozo Yamamura. 1972. "Population trends and economic growth in preindustrial Japan." In D.V. Glass and Roger Revelle (eds.), *Population and Social Change*. London: Edward Arnold.

Harding, Sandra. 1986. *The Science Question in Feminism*. Ithaca, NY: Cornell University Press.

Harner, Michael J. 1970. "Population pressure and the social evolution of agriculturalists." *Southwestern Journal of Anthropology* 26:67–86.

Harris, Marvin. 1964. *Patterns of Race in the Americas*. New York: Norton.

_____. 1966. "The cultural ecology of India's sacred cattle." *Current Anthropology* 7:51–66.

_____. 1968. *The Rise of Anthropological Theory*. New York: Crowell.

_____. 1974. *Cows, Pigs, Wars, and Witches: The Riddles of Culture*. New York: Random House.

_____. 1975. *Culture, People, Nature: An Introduction to General Anthropology*. 2nd ed. New York: Crowell.

_____. 1976. "History and significance of the emic/etic distinction." *Annual Review of Anthropology* 5:329–50.

_____. 1977. *Cannibals and Kings: The Origins of Cultures*. New York: Random House.

_____. 1979. *Cultural Materialism: The Struggle for a Science of Culture*. New York: Random House.

_____. 1980. "History and ideological significance of the separation of social and cultural anthropology." In Eric B. Ross (ed.), *Beyond the Myths of Culture: Essays in Cultural Materialism*. New York: Academic Press.

_____. 1981. *America Now: The Anthropology of a Changing Culture*. New York: Simon & Schuster.

_____. 1984. "A cultural materialist theory of band and village warfare: The Yanomamö test." In R. Brian Ferguson (ed.), *Warfare, Culture, and Environment*. New York: Academic Press.

_____. 1985. *Good to Eat: Riddles of Food and Culture*. New York: Simon & Schuster.

_____. 1987a. "Cultural materialism: Alarums and excursions." In Kenneth Moore (ed.), *Waymarks: The Notre Dame Inaugural Lectures in Anthropology.* Notre Dame, IN: University of Notre Dame Press.

_____. 1987b. "Foodways: Historical overview and theoretical prolegomenon." In Marvin Harris and Eric B. Ross (eds.), *Food and Evolution: Toward a Theory of Human Food Habits.* Philadelphia: Temple University Press.

_____. 1989. *Our Kind.* New York: Harper & Row.

_____. 1990. "Emics and etics revisited." In Thomas N. Headland, Kenneth L. Pike, and Marvin Harris (eds.), *Emics and Etics: The Insider/Outsider Debate.* Newbury Park, CA: Sage.

_____. 1991. "Anthropology: Ships that crash in the night." In Richard Jessor (ed.), *Perspectives on Behavioral Science.* Boulder, CO: Westview Press.

_____. 1992. "Distinguished lecture: Anthropology and the theoretical and paradigmatic significance of the collapse of Soviet and East European communism." *American Anthropologist* 94:295–305.

_____. 1994. "Cultural materialism is alive and well and won't go away until something better comes along." In Robert Borofsky (ed.), *Assessing Cultural Anthropology.* New York: McGraw-Hill.

_____. 1995. "Anthropology and postmodernism." In Martin F. Murphy and Maxine L. Margolis (eds.), *Science, Materialism, and the Study of Culture.* Gainesville: University Press of Florida.

_____. 1997. *Culture, People, Nature: An Introduction to General Anthropology.* 7th ed. New York: Longman.

_____. 1999. *Theories of Culture in Postmodern Times.* Walnut Creek, CA: AltaMira Press.

Harris, Marvin, and Eric B. Ross. 1987a. *Death, Sex and Fertility: Population Regulation in Preindustrial and Developing Societies.* New York: Columbia University Press.

_____. (eds.). 1987b. *Food and Evolution: Toward a Theory of Human Food Habits.* Philadelphia: Temple University Press.

Hartung, John. 1976. "On natural selection and the inheritance of wealth." *Current Anthropology* 17:607–22.

_____. 1982. "Polygyny and inheritance of wealth." *Current Anthropology* 23:1–12.

_____. 1985. "Matrilineal inheritance: New theory and analysis." *Behavioral and Brain Sciences* 8:661–88.

Harvey, David. 1989. *The Condition of Postmodernity.* Oxford: Blackwell.

Hawkes, Kristen. 1993. "Why hunter-gatherers work: An ancient version of the problem of public goods." *Current Anthropology* 34:341–61.

Hawkes, Kristen, and James F. O'Connell. 1985. "Optimal foraging models and the case of the !Kung." *American Anthropologist* 87:401–05.

Hawkes, Kristen, Kim Hill, and James F. O'Connell. 1982. "Why hunters gather: Optimal foraging and the Aché of eastern Paraguay." *American Ethnologist* 9:379–98.

Hayden, Brian, Morley Eldridge, Anne Eldridge, and Aubrey Cannon. 1985. "Complex hunter-gatherers in interior British Columbia." In T. Douglas Price and James A. Brown (ed.), *Prehistoric Hunter-Gatherers.* San Diego: Academic Press.

Headland, Thomas N., Kenneth L. Pike, and Marvin Harris (eds.). 1990. *Emics and Etics: The Insider/Outsider Distinction.* Newbury Park, CA: Sage.

Heath, D.B. 1958. "Sexual division of labor and cross-cultural research." *Social Forces* 37:77–79.

Hechter, Michael. 1983a. "Introduction." In Michael Hechter (ed.), *The Microfoundations of Macrosociology.* Philadelphia: Temple University Press.

_____ (ed.). 1983b. *The Microfoundations of Macrosociology.* Philadelphia: Temple University Press.

_____. 1990. "Reading Denzin." *Rationality and Society* 2:500–503.

_____. 1992. "Should values be written out of the social scientist's lexicon?" *Sociological Theory* 10:214–30.

_____. 1994. "The role of values in rational choice theory." *Rationality and Society* 6:318–33.

Hechter, Michael, and Satoshi Kanazawa. 1997. "Sociological rational choice theory." *Annual Review of Sociology* 23:191–214.

Hechter, Michael, Karl-Dieter Opp, and Reinhard Wippler. 1990. *Social Institutions: Their Emergence, Maintenance, and Effects.* New York: Walter de Gruyter.

Henry, Stuart, and Dragan Milovanovic. 1991. "Constitutive criminology: The maturation of critical theory." *Criminology* 29:293–315.

Herdt, Gilbert H. 1984. *Ritualized Homosexuality in Melanesia.* Berkeley: University of California Press.

Heritage, John. 1984. *Garfinkel and Ethnomethodology.* Cambridge, UK: Polity Press.

Hewlett, B.S., J.M.H. van de Koppel, and L.L. Cavalli-Sforza. 1986. "Exploration and mating ranges of Aka Pygmies of the Central African Republic." In L.L. Cavalli-Sforza (ed.), *African Pygmies.* New York: Academic Press.

Hilbert, Richard A. 1990. "Ethnomethodology and the micro-macro order." *American Sociological Review* 55:794–808.

_____. 1992. *The Classical Roots of Ethnomethodology: Durkheim, Weber, and Garfinkel.* Chapel Hill: University of North Carolina Press.

Hill, Kim. 1988. "Macronutrient modifications of optimal foraging theory: An approach using indifference curves applied to some modern foragers." *Human Ecology* 16:157–97.

Hill, Kim, and Hillard Kaplan. 1989. "Population description and dry season subsistence among the newly contacted Yora (Yaminahua) of Manu National Park, Peru." *National Geographic Research* 5:317–34.

Himmelfarb, Gertrude. 1994. *On Looking into the Abyss.* New York: Knopf.

Hindess, Barry, and Paul Q. Hirst. 1975. *Pre-Capitalist Modes of Production.* London: Routledge & Kegan Paul.

Hirshleifer, Jack. 1977. "Economics from a biological viewpoint." *Journal of Law and Economics* 20:1–52.

Hodder, Ian. 1990. "Post-processual archaeology: The current debate." In Robert W. Preucel (ed.), *Between Past and Present: Issues in Contemporary Archaeological Discourse.* Carbondale: Southern Illinois University Press.

_____. 1991. *Reading the Past: Current Approaches to Interpretation in Archaeology.* 2nd ed. Cambridge, UK: Cambridge University Press.

Hogbin, H. Ian. 1964. *A Guadalcanal Society: The Kaoka Speakers.* New York: Holt, Rinehart, and Winston.

Hoiberg, Eric O., and Jerry S. Cloyd. 1971. "Definition and measurement of continuous variation in ecological analysis." *American Sociological Review* 36:65–74.

Hold, Barbara C.L. 1980. "Attention structure and behavior in G/wi San children." *Ethology and Sociobiology* 1:275–90.

Hollinger, Robert. 1994. *Postmodernism and the Social Sciences.* Thousand Oaks, CA: Sage.

Holton, Robert J., and Bryan S. Turner (eds.). 1986. *Talcott Parsons on Economy and Society.* London: Routledge.

Homans, George C. 1958. "Social behavior as exchange." *American Journal of Sociology* 63:597–606.

_____. 1961. *Social Behavior: Its Elementary Forms.* New York: Harcourt, Brace, and World.

_____. 1962. *Sentiments and Activities: Essays in Social Science.* Glencoe, IL: Free Press.

_____. 1964. "Bringing men back in." *American Sociological Review* 29:809–18.

_____. 1983. "Steps to a theory of social behavior: An autobiographical account." *Theory and Society* 12:1–45.

_____. 1984. *Coming to My Senses: The Autobiography of a Sociologist.* New Brunswick, NJ: Transaction.

Homans, George C., and David M. Schneider. 1955. *Marriage, Authority, and Final Causes.* New York: Free Press.

Hopkins, Keith. 1980. "Brother-sister marriage in Roman Egypt." *Comparative Studies in Society and History* 22:303–54.

Horowitz, Irving Louis. 1993. *The Decomposition of Sociology.* New York: Oxford University Press.

Hrdy, Sarah Blaffer. 1979. "Infanticide in animals." *Ethology and Sociobiology* 1:13–40.

_____. 1997. "Raising Darwin's consciousness: Female sexuality and the prehominid origins of patriarchy." *Human Nature* 8:1–49.

_____. 1999. *Mother Nature: A History of Mothers, Infants, and Natural Selection.* New York: Pantheon.

Hrdy, Sarah Blaffer, and Debra S. Judge. 1993. "Darwin and the puzzle of primogeniture: An essay on biases in parental investment after death." *Human Nature* 4:1–45.

Huaco, George A. 1963. "A logical analysis of the Davis-Moore theory of stratification." *American Sociological Review* 28:801–04.

_____. 1986. "Ideology and general theory: The case of sociological functionalism." *Comparative Studies in Society and History* 28:34–54.

Hugill, Peter J. 1993. *World Trade Since 1431.* Baltimore: Johns Hopkins University Press.

Hull, David L. 1988. *Science as a Process: An Evolutionary Account of the Social and Conceptual Development of Science.* Chicago: University of Chicago Press.

Irons, William. 2000. "Why do the Yomut raise more sons than daughters?" In Lee Cronk, Napoleon Chagnon, and William Irons (eds.), *Adaptation and Human Behavior: An Anthropological Perspective.* New York: Aldine de Gruyter.

Israel, Jonathan I. 1989. *Dutch Primacy in World Trade, 1585–1740.* Oxford: Oxford University Press (Clarendon Press).

Jacobs, Norman. 1958. *The Origin of Modern Capitalism and Eastern Asia.* Hong Kong: Hong Kong University Press.

James, Thomas W., and Doreen Kimura. 1997. "Sex differences in remembering the locations of objects in an array: Location-shifts versus location-exchanges." *Evolution and Human Behavior* 18:155–63.

Janicki, Maria, and Dennis L. Krebs. 1998. "Evolutionary approaches to culture." In Charles Crawford and Dennis L. Krebs (eds.), *Handbook of Evolutionary Psychology.* Mahwah, NJ: Lawrence Erlbaum.

Jankowiak, William R., and Edward F. Fischer. 1992. "A cross-cultural perspective on romantic love." *Ethnology* 31:149–55.

Jankowski, Martín Sánchez. 1991. *Islands in the Street: Gangs and American Urban Society.* Berkeley: University of California Press.

Jannetta, Ann Bowman. 1987. *Epidemics and Mortality in Early Modern Japan.* Princeton, NJ: Princeton University Press.

Jefferson, Gail. 1979. "A technique for inviting laughter and its subsequent acceptance declination." In George Psathas (ed.), *Everyday Language: Studies in Ethnomethodology.* New York: Irvington.

Jejeebhoy, Shireen J. 1995. *Women's Education, Autonomy, and Reproductive Behaviour: Experience from Developing Countries.* Oxford: Oxford University Press (Clarendon Press).

Jeske, Robert J. 1993. "Comment on Hawkes, 'Why hunter-gatherers work.'" *Current Anthropology* 34:354–55.

Johnson, Allen W., and Timothy Earle. 1987. *The Evolution of Human Societies: From Foraging Group to Agrarian State.* Stanford, CA: Stanford University Press.

Johnson, Allen W., and Clifford A. Behrens. 1982. "Nutritional criteria in Machiguenga food production decisions: A linear-programming analysis." *Human Ecology* 10:167–90.

Johnson, Gregory A. 1982. "Organizational structure and scalar stress." In Colin Renfrew, Michael J. Rowlands, and Barbara Abbott Segraves (eds.), *Theory and Explanation in Archaeology*. New York: Academic Press.

Johnstone, Frederick A. 1976. *Race, Class, and Gold: A Study of Class Relations and Racial Discrimination in South Africa*. London: Routledge & Kegan Paul.

Jones, Doug. 1995. "Sexual selection, physical attractiveness, and facial neotony: Cross-cultural evidence and implications." *Current Anthropology* 36:723–48.

Jorgensen, Joseph G. 1980. *Western Indians*. San Francisco: Freeman.

Kanazawa, Satoshi. 2001. "De gustibus *est* disputandum." *Social Forces*, forthcoming.

Kanazawa, Satoshi, and Mary C. Still. 1999. "Why monogamy?" *Social Forces* 78:25–50.

_____. 2000. "Why men commit crimes (and why they desist)." *Sociological Theory* 18: 434–47.

Kang, Gay Elizabeth. 1979. "The nature of exogamy in relation to cross-allegiance/alliance of social units." *Behavior Science Research* 4:255–76.

Kaplan, Hillard. 1994. "Evolutionary and wealth flows theories of fertility: Empirical tests and new models." *Population and Development Review* 20:753–91.

_____. 1996. "A theory of fertility and parental investment in traditional and modern human societies." *Yearbook of Physical Anthropology* 39:91–135.

Kaplan, Hillard, and Kim Hill. 1992. "The evolutionary ecology of food acquisition." In Eric Alden Smith and Bruce Winterhalder (eds.), *Evolutionary Ecology and Human Behavior*. New York: Aldine de Gruyter.

Katz, Mary Maxwell, and Melvin J. Konner. 1981. "The role of the father: An anthropological perspective." In Michael E. Lamb (ed.), *The Role of the Father in Child Development*. New York: Wiley.

Keegan, William F. 1986. "The optimal foraging analysis of horticultural production." *American Anthropologist* 88:92–107.

Keeley, Lawrence H. 1996. *War Before Civilization: The Myth of the Peaceful Savage*. New York: Oxford University Press.

Keesing, Roger M. 1975. *Kin Groups and Social Structure*. New York: Holt, Rinehart and Winston.

Keller, Evelyn Fox. 1985. *Science and Gender*. New Haven, CT: Yale University Press.

Kellner, Douglas. 1990. "The postmodern turn: Positions, problems, and prospects." In George Ritzer (ed.), *Frontiers of Social Theory*. New York: Columbia University Press.

Kelly, Raymond C. 1985. *The Nuer Conquest: The Structure and Development of an Expansionist System*. Ann Arbor: University of Michigan Press.

Kelly, Robert L. 1995. *The Foraging Spectrum: Diversity in Hunter-Gatherer Lifeways*. Washington, DC: Smithsonian Institution Press.

Kelm, Matthia. 1997. "Schumpeter's theory of economic evolution: A Darwinian interpretation." *Journal of Evolutionary Economics* 7:97–130.

Kenrick, Douglas T., and Richard C. Keefe. 1992. "Age preferences in mates reflect sex differences in human reproductive strategies." *Behavioral and Brain Sciences* 15:75–133.

Kenrick, Douglas T., Melanie R. Trost, and Virgil L. Sheets. 1996. "Power, harrassment, and trophy mates: The feminist advantages of an evolutionary perspective." In David M. Buss and Neil M. Malamuth (eds.), *Sex, Power, Conflict: Evolutionary and Feminist Perspectives*. New York: Oxford University Press.

Kieve, Ronald A. 1986. "From necessary illusion to rational choice? A critique of neo-Marxist rational-choice theory." *Theory and Society* 15:557–82.

354 *References*

Kim, Kenneth, Peter K. Smith, and Anna-Lisa Palermiti. 1997. "Conflict in childhood and reproductive development." *Evolution and Human Behavior* 18:109–42.

Kimura, Doreen. 1987. "Are men's and women's brains really different?" *Canadian Psychology* 28:133–47.

_____. 1992. "Sex differences in the brain." *Scientific American* 267(3):119–25.

_____. 1999. *Sex and Cognition.* Cambridge, MA: MIT Press.

Kincaid, Harold. 1996. *Philosophical Foundations of the Social Sciences: Analyzing Controversies in Social Research.* New York: Cambridge University Press.

Kirch, Patrick Vinton. 1984. *The Evolution of the Polynesian Chiefdoms.* New York: Cambridge University Press.

Kiser, Edgar. 1987. "The formation of state policy in Western European absolutisms: A comparison of England and France." *Politics and Society* 15:259–96.

Kiser, Edgar, Kriss A. Drass, and William Brustein. 1995. "Ruler autonomy and war in early modern Western Europe." *International Studies Quarterly* 39:109–38.

Kiser, Edgar, and Michael Hechter. 1998. "The debate on historical sociology: Rational choice theory and its critics." *American Journal of Sociology* 104:785–816.

Kiser, Edgar, and Xiaoxi Tong. 1992. "Determinants of the amount and type of corruption in state fiscal bureaucracies." *Comparative Political Studies* 25:300–331.

Knodel, John. 1986. "Demographic transitions in German villages." In Ansley J. Coale and Susan Cotts Watkins (eds.), *The Decline of Fertility in Europe.* Princeton, NJ: Princeton University Press.

Knodel, John, and Etienne van de Walle. 1986. "Lessons from the past: Policy implications of historical fertility studies." In Ansley J. Coale and Susan Cotts Watkins (eds.), *The Decline of Fertility in Europe.* Princeton, NJ: Princeton University Press.

Knorr-Cetina, Karin D., and Michael Mulkay (eds.). 1983. *Science Observed: Perspectives on the Social Study of Science.* Beverly Hills, CA: Sage.

Kolko, Gabriel. 1959. "A critique of Max Weber's philosophy of history." *Ethics* 70:21–36.

Korbin, Jill. 1987. "Child maltreatment in cross-cultural perspective: Vulnerable children and circumstances." In Richard J. Gelles and Jane B. Lancaster (eds.), *Child Abuse and Neglect: Biosocial Dimensions.* New York: Aldine de Gruyter.

Kornai, János. 1992. *The Socialist System: The Political Economy of Communism.* Princeton, NJ: Princeton University Press.

Kramer, Peter D. 1993. *Listening to Prozac.* New York: Penguin.

Kropotkin, Petr. 1902. *Mutual Aid: A Factor of Evolution.* London: William Heinemann.

Kuhn, Thomas S. 1970. *The Structure of Scientific Revolutions.* 2nd ed. Chicago: University of Chicago Press.

Kumar, Krishan. 1978. *Prophecy and Progress: The Sociology of Industrial and Post-Industrial Society.* Harmondsworth, UK: Penguin Books.

Kurland, Jeffrey A. 1979. "Paternity, mother's brother, and human sociality." In Napoleon A. Chagnon and William Irons (eds.), *Evolutionary Biology and Human Social Behavior.* North Scituate, MA: Duxbury Press.

Kurzweil, Edith. 1980. *The Age of Structuralism: Lévi-Strauss to Foucault.* New York: Columbia University Press.

Kuznar, Lawrence A. 1997. *Reclaiming a Scientific Anthropology.* Walnut Creek, CA: AltaMira.

Lakatos, Imre. 1970. "Falsification and the methodology of scientific research programmes." In Imre Lakatos and Alan Musgrave (eds.), *Criticism and the Growth of Knowledge.* Cambridge, UK: Cambridge University Press.

Lancaster, Jane. 1991. "A feminist and evolutionary biologist looks at women." *Yearbook of Physical Anthropology* 34:1–11.

Lane, David. 1971. *The End of Inequality? Stratification Under State Socialism.* London: Penguin Books.

Lasch, Christopher. 1977. *Haven in a Heartless World: The Family Besieged.* New York: Basic Books.

Laslett, Peter (ed.) 1972a. *Household and Family in Past Time.* Cambridge, UK: Cambridge University Press.

———. 1972b. "La famille et le ménage: Approches historiques." *Annales E.S.C.* 27:847–72.

———. 1977. *Family Life and Illicit Love in Earlier Generations.* Cambridge, UK: Cambridge University Press.

Latour, Bruno. 1987. *Science in Action: How to Follow Scientists and Engineers through Society.* Cambridge, MA: Harvard University Press.

Latour, Bruno, and Steve Woolgar. 1979. *Laboratory Life: The Construction of Scientific Facts.* Princeton, NJ: Princeton University Press.

Laudan, Larry. 1977. *Progress and its Problems: Towards a Theory of Scientific Growth.* Berkeley: University of California Press.

———. 1982. "A note on Collins's blend of relativism and empiricism." *Social Studies of Science* 12:131–32.

———. 1996. *Beyond Positivism and Relativism.* Boulder, CO: Westview Press.

Lawler, Edward J., and Shane R. Thye. 1999. "Bringing emotions into social exchange theory." *Annual Review of Sociology* 25:217–44.

Leach, Edmund R. 1954. *Political Systems of Highland Burma.* Boston: Beacon Press.

Leacock, Eleanor. 1980. "Social behavior, biology, and the double standard." In George W. Barlow and James Silberberg (eds.), *Sociobiology: Beyond Nature/Nurture?* Boulder, CO: Westview Press.

Leavitt, Gregory C. 1977. "The frequency of warfare: An evolutionary perspective." *Sociological Inquiry* 47:49–58.

Lee, Richard B. 1968. "What hunters do for a living, or, how to make out on scarce resources." In Richard B. Lee and Irven DeVore (eds.), *Man the Hunter.* Chicago: Aldine.

———. 1978. "Politics, sexual and nonsexual, in an egalitarian society." *Social Science Information* 17:871–95.

———. 1990. "Primitive communism and the origin of social inequality." In Steadman Upham (ed.), *The Evolution of Political Systems.* New York: Cambridge University Press.

———. 1992. "Art, science, or politics? The crisis in hunter-gatherer studies." *American Anthropologist* 94:31–54.

Lenski, Gerhard E. 1966. *Power and Privilege: A Theory of Social Stratification.* New York: McGraw-Hill.

———. 1970. *Human Societies: An Introduction to Macro-Level Sociology.* New York: McGraw-Hill.

Lett, James. 1990. "Emics and etics: Notes on the epistemology of anthropology." In Thomas N. Headland, Kenneth L. Pike, and Marvin Harris (eds.), *Emics and Etics: The Insider/Outsider Debate.* Newbury Park, CA: Sage.

Leupp, Gary P. 1992. *Servants, Shophands, and Laborers in the Cities of Tokugawa Japan.* Princeton, NJ: Princeton University Press.

———. 1995. *Male Colors: The Construction of Homosexuality in Tokugawa Japan.* Berkeley: University of California Press.

LeVay, Simon. 1991. "A difference in the hypothalamic structure between heterosexual and homosexual men." *Science* 253:1034–37.

———. 1996. *Queer Science: The Use and Abuse of Research into Homosexuality.* Cambridge, MA: MIT Press.

Levine, Andrew, Elliott Sober, and Erik Olin Wright. 1987. "Marxism and methodological individualism." *New Left Review* 162:67–84.

Lévi-Strauss, Claude. 1963. *Structural Anthropology.* Trans. Claire Jacobson and Brooke Grundfest Schoepf. New York: Basic Books.

_____. 1966. *The Savage Mind.* Trans. from the French. Chicago: University of Chicago Press.

_____. 1969a. *The Elementary Structures of Kinship.* Rev. ed. Trans. James Harle Bell and John Richard von Sturmer. Boston: Beacon Press.

_____. 1969b. *The Raw and the Cooked.* Trans. John and Doreen Weightman. New York: Harper & Row.

_____. 1973a. *From Honey to Ashes.* Trans. John and Doreen Weightman. New York: Harper & Row.

_____. 1973b. *Tristes Tropiques.* Trans. John and Doreen Weightman. New York: Atheneum.

_____. 1985. *The View from Afar.* Trans. Joachim Neugroschel and Phoebe Hoss. New York: Basic Books.

Lewontin, Richard C., Steven Rose, and Leon J. Kamin. 1984. *Not in Our Genes: Biology, Ideology, and Human Nature.* New York: Pantheon.

Lichtheim, George. 1972. *Europe in the Twentieth Century.* New York: Praeger.

Lieberman, Leonard. 1989. "A discipline divided: Acceptance of human sociobiological concepts in anthropology." *Current Anthropology* 30:676–82.

Lieberman, Leslie Sue. 1987. "Biocultural consequences of animals versus plants as sources of fats, proteins, and other nutrients." In Marvin Harris and Eric B. Ross (eds.), *Food and Evolution: Toward a Theory of Human Food Habits.* Philadelphia: Temple University Press.

Liesen, Laurette T. 1995. "Feminism and the politics of reproductive strategies." *Politics and the Life Sciences* 14:145–97.

Lipset, Seymour Martin. 1959. "Some social requisites of democracy: Economic development and political legitimacy." *American Political Science Review* 53:69–105.

Livi-Bacci, Massimo. 1992. *A Concise History of World Population.* Trans. Carl Ipsen. Oxford: Blackwell.

Lockwood, David. 1956. "Some remarks on the social system." *British Journal of Sociology* 5:134–45.

Lopreato, Joseph. 1984. *Human Nature and Biocultural Evolution.* Winchester, MA: Allen and Unwin.

_____. 1989. "The maximization principle: A cause in search of conditions." In Robert W. Bell and Nancy J. Bell (eds.), *Sociobiology and the Social Sciences.* Lubbock, TX: Texas Tech University Press.

Lopreato, Joseph, and Timothy Crippen. 1999. *Crisis in Sociology: The Need for Darwin.* New Brunswick, NJ: Transaction.

Lopreato, Joseph, and Mei-yu Yu. 1988. "Human fertility and fitness optimization." *Ethology and Sociobiology* 9:269–89.

Lord, Jane T., and Stephen K. Sanderson. 1999. "Current theoretical and political perspectives of Western sociological theorists." *American Sociologist* 30(3):37–61.

Low, Bobbi S. 1990. "Marriage systems and pathogen stress in human societies." *American Zoologist* 30:325–39.

_____. 1991. "Reproductive life in nineteenth-century Sweden: An evolutionary perspective on demographic phenomena." *Ethology and Sociobiology* 12:411–48.

_____. 1992. "Sex, coalitions, and politics in preindustrial societies." *Politics and the Life Sciences* 11:63–80.

_____. 1993a. "Ecological demography: A synthetic focus in evolutionary anthropology." *Evolutionary Anthropology* 1:177–87.

_____. 1993b. "An evolutionary perspective on war." In William Zimmerman and Harold K. Jacobsen (eds.), *Behavior, Culture, and Conflict in World Politics.* Ann Arbor: University of Michigan Press.

_____. 2000. *Why Sex Matters: A Darwinian Look at Human Behavior.* Princeton, NJ: Princeton University Press.

Low, Bobbi S., and Alice L. Clarke. 1992. "Resources and the life course: Patterns through the demographic transition." *Ethology and Sociobiology* 13:463–94.

Low, Bobbi S., Alice L. Clarke, and Kenneth A. Lockridge. 1992. "Towards an ecological demography." *Population and Development Review* 18:1–31.

Lyman, Stanford M. 1984. "Interactionism and the study of race relations at the macro-sociological level: The contribution of Herbert Blumer." *Symbolic Interaction* 7:107–20.

Lyotard, Jean-François. 1985. *The Postmodern Condition.* Minneapolis: University of Minnesota Press.

Lytton, Hugh, and David M. Romney. 1991. "Parents' differential socialization of boys and girls: A meta-analysis." *Psychological Bulletin* 109:267–96.

MacArthur, Robert H., and Edward O. Wilson. 1967. *The Theory of Island Biogeography.* Princeton, NJ: Princeton University Press.

MacDonald, Kevin. 1989. "The plasticity of human social organization and behavior: Contextual variables and proximal mechanisms." *Ethology and Sociobiology* 10:171–94.

_____. 1990. "Mechanisms of sexual egalitarianism in Western Europe." *Ethology and Sociobiology* 11:195–238.

_____. 1991. "A perspective on Darwinian psychology: The importance of domain-general mechanisms, plasticity, and individual differences." *Ethology and Sociobiology* 12:449–80.

_____. 1994. *A People that Shall Dwell Alone: Judaism as a Group Evolutionary Strategy.* Westport, CT: Praeger.

_____. 1995. "The establishment and maintenance of socially imposed monogamy in Western Europe." *Politics and the Life Sciences* 14:3–46.

_____. 1998a. *Separation and its Discontents: Toward an Evolutionary Theory of Anti-Semitism.* Westport, CT: Praeger.

_____. 1998b. *The Culture of Critique: An Evolutionary Analysis of Jewish Involvement in Twentieth-Century Intellectual and Political Movements.* Westport, CT: Praeger.

MacDonald, Kevin, and David C. Geary. 2000. "The evolution of general intelligence: Domain-general cognitive mechanisms and human adaptation." Paper presented at the annual meetings of the Human Behavior and Evolution Society, Amherst, Massachusetts, June 7–11.

MacLeod, Jay. 1995. *Ain't No Makin' It: Aspirations and Attainment in a Low-Income Neighborhood.* Boulder, CO: Westview Press.

McBurney, Donald H., Steven J.C. Gaulin, Trishul Devineni, and Christine Adams. 1997. "Superior spatial memory of women: Stronger evidence for the gathering hypothesis." *Evolution and Human Behavior* 18:165–74.

McCabe, Justine. 1983. "FBD marriage: Further support for the Westermarck hypothesis of the incest taboo?" *American Anthropologist* 85:50–69.

McCauley, Clark. 1990. "Conference overview." In Jonathan Haas (ed.), *The Anthropology of War.* New York: Cambridge University Press.

McGrew, William C. 1979. "Evolutionary implications of sex differences in chimpanzee predation and tool use." In David A. Hamburg and Elizabeth R. McCown (eds.), *The Great Apes.* Menlo Park, CA: Benjamin/Cummings.

McGuire, Michael T. 1982. "Social dominance relationships in male vervet monkeys." *International Political Science Review* 3:11–32.

McGuire, Michael T., M. Raleigh, and C. Johnson. 1983. "Social dominance in adult male vervet monkeys II: Behavior-biochemical relationships." *Social Science Information* 22:311–28.

McKnight, Jim. 1997. *Straight Science? Homosexuality, Evolution, and Adaptation.* London: Routledge.

McMichael, Philip. 1991. "Slavery in capitalism: The rise and demise of the U.S. ante-bellum cotton culture." *Theory and Society* 20:321–49.

McNeill, William H. 1982. *The Pursuit of Power: Technology, Armed Force, and Society Since AD 1000.* Chicago: University of Chicago Press.

Madsen, Douglas. 1985. "A biochemical property relating to power seeking in humans." *American Political Science Review* 79:448–57.

_____. 1986. "Power seekers are different: Further biochemical evidence." *American Political Science Review* 80:261–69.

_____. 1994. "Serotonin and social rank among human males." In Roger D. Masters and Michael T. McGuire (eds.), *The Neurotransmitter Revolution.* Carbondale: Southern Illinois University Press.

Maines, David R. 1988. "Myth, text, and interactionist complicity in the neglect of Blumer's macrosociology." *Symbolic Interaction* 11:43–57.

Malhotra, Anju, Reeve Vanneman, and Sunita Kishor. 1995. "Fertility, dimensions of patriarchy, and development in India." *Population and Development Review* 21:281–305.

Malinowski, Bronislaw. 1927. *Sex and Repression in Savage Society.* London: Kegan Paul.

_____. 1929. *The Sexual Life of Savages in North-western Melanesia; An Ethnographic Account of Courtship, Marriage, and Family Life Among the Natives of Trobriand Islands, British New Guinea.* New York: Harcourt, Brace.

_____. 1944. *A Scientific Theory of Culture.* Chapel Hill: University of North Carolina Press.

Mamdani, Mahmood. 1972. *The Myth of Population Control: Family, Caste, and Class in an Indian Village.* New York: Monthly Review Press.

Mandelbaum, David G. 1988. *Women's Seclusion and Men's Honor: Sex Roles in North India, Bangladesh, and Pakistan.* Tucson: University of Arizona Press.

Manis, Jerome G., and Bernard N. Meltzer. 1994. "Chance in human affairs." *Sociological Theory* 12:45–56.

Mann, Michael. 1986. *The Sources of Social Power. Vol. 1: A History of Power from the Beginning to AD 1760.* Cambridge, UK: Cambridge University Press.

Manson, Joseph H., and Richard W. Wrangham. 1991. "Intergroup aggression in chimpanzees and humans." *Current Anthropology* 32:369–90.

Marcuse, Herbert. 1968. *Negations.* Trans. Jeremy J. Shapiro. Boston: Beacon Press.

Martin, M. Kay, and Barbara Voorhies. 1975. *Female of the Species.* New York: Columbia University Press.

Martindale, Don. 1960. *The Nature and Types of Sociological Theory.* Boston: Houghton Mifflin.

Marx, Karl. 1963. *The Eighteenth Brumaire of Louis Bonaparte.* New York: International Publishers (Originally written 1852).

_____. 1967. *Capital.* Vol. 1. Trans. Samuel Moore and Edward Aveling. Ed. Friedrich Engels. New York: International Publishers (Originally published 1867).

Maryanski, Alexandra, and Jonathan H. Turner. 1991. "The offspring of functionalism: French and British structuralism." *Sociological Theory* 9:106–15.

Mason, Karen Oppenheim, and Anju Malhotra Taj. 1987. "Differences between women's and men's reproductive goals in developing countries." *Population and Development Review* 13:611–38.

Matthiessen, Poul C., and James C. McCann. 1978. "The role of mortality in the European fertility transition: Aggregate-level relations." In Samuel H. Preston (ed.), *The Effects of Infant and Child Mortality on Fertility.* New York: Academic Press.

Maxwell, Mary. 1991. *The Sociobiological Imagination*. Albany: State University of New York Press.

Maxwell, Nicholas. 1974. "The rationality of scientific discovery, part II: An aim oriented theory of scientific discovery." *Philosophy of Science* 41:247–95.

Mayer, Tom. 1994. *Analytical Marxism*. Thousand Oaks, CA: Sage.

Maynard Smith, John. 1974. "The theory of games and the evolution of animal conflict." *Journal of Theoretical Biology* 47:209–21.

———. 1978. "The evolution of behavior." *Scientific American* 239:176–92.

———. 1982. *Evolution and the Theory of Games*. Cambridge, UK: Cambridge University Press.

Mazur, Allan, and Alan Booth. 1998. "Testosterone and dominance in men." *Behavioral and Brain Sciences* 21:353–97.

Meadows, Donella, Dennis L. Meadows, and Jørgen Randers. 1992. *Beyond the Limits: Confronting Global Collapse, Envisioning a Sustainable Future*. Post Mills, VT: Chelsea Green.

Mellars, Paul A. 1985. "The ecological basis of social complexity in the Upper Paleolithic of southwestern France." In T. Douglas Price and James A. Brown (eds.), *Prehistoric Hunter-Gatherers*. New York: Academic Press.

Mencher, Joan P. 1974. "The caste system upside down: Or the not-so-mysterious East." *Current Anthropology* 15:469–94.

———. 1980. "On being an untouchable in India: A materialist perspective." In Eric B. Ross (ed.), *Beyond the Myths of Culture: Essays in Cultural Materialism*. New York: Academic Press.

Merton, Robert K. 1957. *Social Theory and Social Structure*. New York: Free Press.

Mesquida, Christian G., and Neil I. Wiener. 1996. "Human collective aggression: A behavioral ecology perspective." *Ethology and Sociobiology* 17:247–62.

Meyer, John W., David Tyack, Joanne Nagel, and Audri Gordon. 1979. "Public education as nation-building in America: Enrollments and bureaucratization in the American states, 1870–1930." *American Journal of Sociology* 85:591–613.

Milgram, Stanley. 1974. *Obedience to Authority: An Experimental View*. New York: Harper & Row.

Miliband, Ralph. 1977. *Marxism and Politics*. Oxford: Oxford University Press.

Miller, Geoffrey F. 2000. *The Mating Mind: How Sexual Choice Shaped the Evolution of Human Nature*. New York: Doubleday.

Miller, James. 1992. *The Passion of Michel Foucault*. New York: Simon & Schuster.

Miller, Richard W. 1984. *Analyzing Marx: Morality, Power and History*. Princeton, NJ: Princeton University Press.

Mills, C. Wright. 1956. *The Power Elite*. New York: Oxford University Press.

Mintz, Sydney. 1985. *Sweetness and Power*. New York: Viking.

Missakian, Elizabeth A. 1980. "Gender differences in agonistic behavior and dominance relations of Synanon communally reared children." In Donald R. Omark, Fred F. Strayer, and Daniel G. Freedman (eds.), *Dominance Relations: An Ethological View of Human Conflict and Social Interaction*. New York: Garland.

Moffat, Scott D., Elizabeth Hampson, and Maria Hatzipantelis. 1998. "Navigation in a 'virtual' maze: Sex differences and correlation with psychometric measures of spatial ability in humans." *Evolution and Human Behavior* 19:73–87.

Mommsen, Wolfgang J. 1985. "Capitalism and socialism: Max Weber's dialogue with Marx." In Robert J. Antonio and Ronald M. Glassman (eds.), *A Marx-Weber Dialogue*. Lawrence: University Press of Kansas.

Money, John, and Anke A. Ehrhardt. 1972. *Man and Woman, Boy and Girl*. Baltimore: Johns Hopkins University Press.

Montagu, M.F.A. (ed.). 1964. *Culture: Man's Adaptive Dimension.* Chicago: University of Chicago Press.

_____. 1976. *The Nature of Human Aggression.* New York: Oxford University Press.

Moseley, K.P., and Immanuel Wallerstein. 1978. "Precapitalist social structures." *Annual Review of Sociology* 4:259–90.

Mulkay, Michael. 1985. *The Word and the World: Explorations in the Forms of Sociological Analysis.* London: Allen & Unwin.

Murdock, George Peter. 1949. *Social Structure.* New York: Macmillan.

_____. 1967. *Ethnographic Atlas.* Pittsburgh: University of Pittsburgh Press.

Murdock, George P., and Douglas R. White. 1969. "Standard Cross-Cultural Sample." *Ethnology* 8:329–69.

Murphy, Raymond. 1988. *Social Closure: The Theory of Monopolization and Exclusion.* Oxford: Oxford University Press (Clarendon Press).

Murstein, Bernard I. 1974. *Love, Sex, and Marriage Through the Ages.* New York: Springer.

Murthi, Mamta, Anne-Catherine Guio, and Jean Dreze. 1995. "Mortality, fertility, and gender bias in India: A district-level analysis." *Population and Development Review* 21:745–82.

Nag, Moni. 1983. "Modernization affects fertility." *Populi* 10:56–77.

Nag, Moni, Benjamin N.F. White, and R. Creighton Peet. 1978. "An anthropological approach to the study of the economic value of children in Java and Nepal." *Current Anthropology* 19:293–306.

Nasir, Jamal J. 1994. *The Status of Women Under Islamic Law and Under Modern Islamic Legislation.* London: Graham & Trotman.

Ndabezitha, Siyabonga W., and Stephen K. Sanderson. 1988. "Racial antagonism and the origins of apartheid in the South African gold mining industry, 1886–1924: A split labor market analysis." In Cora Bagley Marrett and Cheryl Leggon (eds.), *Research in Race and Ethnic Relations.* Vol. 5. Greenwich, CT: JAI Press.

Nesse, Randolph N. 1994. "An evolutionary perspective on substance abuse." *Ethology and Sociobiology* 15:339–48.

Nielsen, François. 1994. "Sociobiology and Sociology." *Annual Review of Sociology* 20:267–303.

Oakes, Guy. 1981. "The epistemological foundations of cultural materialism." *Dialectical Anthropology* 6:1–21.

O'Connell, James F., and Kristen Hawkes. 1981. "Alyawara plant use and optimal foraging theory." In Eric Alden Smith and Bruce Winterhalder (eds.), *Hunter-Gatherer Foraging Strategies.* Chicago: University of Chicago Press.

O'Meara, Tim. 1997. "Causation and the struggle for a science of culture." *Current Anthropology* 38:399–418.

Oliver, Douglas. 1955. *A Solomon Island Society: Kinship and Leadership Among the Siuai of Bougainville.* Cambridge, MA: Harvard University Press.

Omark, Donald R., and Murray S. Edelman. 1975. "A comparison of status hierarchies in young children: An ethological approach." *Social Science Information* 14:87–107.

Otterbein, Keith F. 1989. *The Evolution of War: A Cross-Cultural Study.* 3rd ed. New Haven, CT: HRAF Press.

Parker, Seymour, and Hilda Parker. 1979. "The myth of male superiority: Rise and demise." *American Anthropologist* 81:289–309.

Parkin, Frank. 1971. *Class Inequality and Political Order: Social Stratification in Capitalist and Communist Societies.* New York: Holt, Rinehart, and Winston.

_____. 1979. *Marxism and Class Theory: A Bourgeois Critique.* New York: Columbia University Press.

_____. 1982. *Max Weber*. London: Tavistock.

Parsons, Talcott. 1937. *The Structure of Social Action*. Glencoe, IL: Free Press.

_____. 1943. "The kinship system of the contemporary United States." *American Anthropologist* 45:22–38.

_____. 1951. *The Social System*. Glencoe, IL: Free Press.

_____. 1966. *Societies: Evolutionary and Comparative Perspectives*. Englewood Cliffs, NJ: Prentice-Hall.

_____. 1971. *The System of Modern Societies*. Englewood Cliffs, NJ: Prentice-Hall.

Pasternak, Burton, Carol R. Ember, and Melvin Ember. 1997. *Sex, Gender, and Kinship: A Cross-Cultural Perspective*. Upper Saddle River, NJ: Prentice Hall.

Patterson, Orlando. 1982. *Slavery and Social Death*. Cambridge, MA: Harvard University Press.

Paul, Luci, Mark A. Foss, and Mary Ann Baenninger. 1996. "Double standards for sexual jealousy: Manipulative morality or a reflection of evolved sex differences?" *Human Nature* 7:291–324.

Penn, Dustin. 1999. "Why do empowered women have fewer offspring?" Paper presented at the annual meetings of the Human Behavior and Evolution Society, University of Utah, Salt Lake City, June 2–6.

Percy, William Armstrong, III. 1996. *Pederasty and Pedagogy in Archaic Greece*. Urbana: University of Illinois Press.

Peribanayagam, Robert S. 1974. "The definition of the situation and an analysis of the ethnomethodological and dramaturgical view." *Sociological Quarterly* 15:521–42.

_____. 1975. "The significance of others in the thought of Alfred Schutz, G.H. Mead, and C.H. Cooley." *Sociological Quarterly* 16:500–21.

Pérusse, Daniel. 1993. "Cultural and reproductive success in industrial societies: Testing the relationship at the proximate and ultimate levels." *Behavioral and Brain Sciences* 16:267–322.

Petras, John W., and Bernard N. Meltzer. 1973. "Theoretical and ideological variations in contemporary interactionism." *Catalyst* 7:1–8.

Pezzin, Liliana E. 1995. "Earnings prospects, matching effects, and the decision to terminate a criminal career." *Journal of Quantitative Criminology* 11:29–50.

Phillips, Kevin. 1990. *The Politics of Rich and Poor*. New York: Random House.

Pianka, Eric R. 1970. "On *r* and *K* selection." *American Naturalist* 104:592–97.

Pickering, Andrew. 1981. "Constraints on controversy: The case of the magnetic monopole." *Social Studies of Science* 11:63–93.

Pinch, Trevor. 1986. *Confronting Nature: The Sociology of Solar Neutrino Detection*. Dordrecht, Netherlands: Reidel.

Pines, Maya. 1978. "Is sociobiology all wet?" *Psychology Today* 11(12):23–24.

Pinker, Steven. 1994. *The Language Instinct: How the Mind Creates Language*. New York: Morrow.

_____. 1997. *How the Mind Works*. New York: Norton.

Pitshandenge, Iman Ngondo. 1994. "Marriage law in sub-Saharan Africa." In Caroline Bledsoe and Gilles Pison (eds.), *Nuptiality in Sub-Saharan Africa*. Oxford: Clarendon Press.

Polanyi, Karl. 1957. "The economy as instituted process." In Karl Polanyi, Conrad M. Arensburg, and Harry W. Pearson (eds.), *Trade and Market in the Early Empires*. Glencoe, IL: Free Press.

Popkin, Samuel L. 1979. *The Rational Peasant*. Berkeley: University of California Press.

_____. 1980. "The rational peasant: The political economy of peasant society." *Theory and Society* 9:411–71.

Posner, Richard A. 1992. *Sex and Reason*. Cambridge, MA: Harvard University Press.

Poulantzas, Nicos. 1974. *Political Power and Social Classes*. London: New Left Books.

_____. 1975. *Classes in Contemporary Capitalism*. London: New Left Books.

Price, Michael. 1999. "The political advantages of monogamy." Manuscript, University of California at Santa Barbara.

Pryor, Frederic L. 1985. "The invention of the plow." *Comparative Studies in Society and History* 27:727–43.

Radcliffe-Brown, A.R. 1948. *A Natural Science of Society*. Glencoe, IL: Free Press.

_____. 1952. *Structure and Function in Primitive Society*. Oxford: Oxford University Press.

Rappaport, Roy. 1967. *Pigs for the Ancestors*. New Haven, CT: Yale University Press.

Rasler, Karen A., and William R. Thompson. 1994. *The Great Powers and the Global Struggle, 1490–1990*. Lexington: University Press of Kentucky.

Rathje, William L. 1971. "The origin and development of lowland Maya Classic civilization." *American Antiquity* 36:275–85.

_____. 1972. "Praise the gods and pass the metates: A hypothesis of the development of lowland rainforest civilizations in Mesoamerica." In Mark P. Leone (ed.), *Contemporary Archaeology*. Carbondale: Southern Illinois University Press.

Reich, Michael. 1977. "The economics of racism." In David M. Gordon (ed.), *Problems in Political Economy*. 2nd ed. Lexington, MA: Heath.

Reischauer, Edwin O. 1956. "Japanese feudalism." In Rushton Coulborn (ed.), *Feudalism in History*. Princeton, NJ: Princeton University Press.

Rex, John. 1961. *Key Problems of Sociological Theory*. London: Routledge & Kegan Paul.

Reynolds, Larry T. 1993. *Interactionism: Exposition and Critique*. 3rd ed. Dix Hills, NY: General Hall.

Reynolds, Vernon, Vincent S.E. Falger, and Ian Vine (eds.). 1986. *The Sociobiology of Ethnocentrism*. Athens: University of Georgia Press.

Rich, Adrienne. 1980. "Compulsory heterosexuality and lesbian experience." *Signs: Journal of Women in Culture and Society* 5:631–60.

Richerson, Peter J., and Robert Boyd. 1992. "Cultural inheritance and evolutionary ecology." In Eric Alden Smith and Bruce Winterhalder (eds.), *Evolutionary Ecology and Human Behavior*. New York: Aldine de Gruyter.

Ridley, Matt. 1996. *The Origins of Virtue: Human Instincts and the Evolution of Cooperation*. New York: Viking.

Ritzer, George. 1997. *Postmodern Social Theory*. New York: McGraw-Hill.

Roach, Jack, and Janet Roach. 1973. "Comment on Gans." *American Journal of Sociology* 78:1499–1507.

Robertson, Roland, and Bryan S. Turner. 1991. *Talcott Parsons: Theorist of Modernity*. Beverly Hills, CA: Sage.

Rock, Paul. 1979. *The Making of Symbolic Interactionism*. Totowa, NJ: Rowman & Littlefield.

Roes, Frans L. 1995. "The size of societies, stratification, and belief in high gods supportive of human morality." *Politics and the Life Sciences* 14:73–77.

Rogers, Alan R. 1995. "For love or money: The evolution of reproductive and material motivations." In R.I.M. Dunbar (ed.), *Human Reproductive Decisions: Biological and Social Perspectives*. New York: St. Martin's Press.

Rosenau, Pauline Marie. 1992a. "Modern and post-modern science: Some contrasts." *Review* 15:49–89.

_____. 1992b. *Post-Modernism and the Social Sciences*. Princeton, NJ: Princeton University Press.

Ross, Eric B. 1980. "Patterns of diet and forces of production: An economic and ecological history of the ascendancy of beef in the United States diet." In Eric B. Ross (ed.), *Beyond the Myths of Culture: Essays in Cultural Materialism*. New York: Academic Press.

_____. 1987. "An overview of trends in dietary variation from hunter-gatherer to modern capitalist societies." In Marvin Harris and Eric B. Ross (eds.), *Food and Evolution: Toward a Theory of Human Food Habits*. Philadelphia: Temple University Press.

Ross, Marc Howard. 1983. "Political decision making and conflict: Additional cross-cultural codes and scales." *Ethnology* 22:169–92.

Rossi, Alice S. 1977. "A biosocial perspective on parenting." *Daedalus* 106:1–31.

_____. 1984. "Gender and parenthood." *American Sociological Review* 49:1–19.

Rossi, Ino (ed.). 1974. *The Unconscious in Culture: The Structuralism of Claude Lévi-Strauss in Perspective*. New York: E.P. Dutton.

Rossides, Daniel. 1976. *The American Class System: An Introduction to Social Stratification*. Boston: Houghton Mifflin.

Rowe, David C. 1994. *The Limits of Family Experience: Genes, Experience, and Behavior*. New York: Guilford Press.

Rozin, Paul. 1987. "Psychobiological perspectives on food preferences and avoidances." In Marvin Harris and Eric B. Ross (eds.), *Food and Evolution: Toward a Theory of Human Food Habits*. Philadelphia: Temple University Press.

Rozin, Paul, and April E. Fallon. 1987. "A perspective on disgust." *Psychological Review* 94:23–41.

Rozin, Paul, Larry Hammer, Harriet Oster, Talia Horowitz, and Veronica Marmora. 1986. "The child's conception of food: Differentiation of categories of rejected substances in the 16 months to 5 year age range." *Appetite* 7:141–51.

Rueschemeyer, Dietrich, Evelyne Huber Stephens, and John D. Stephens. 1992. *Capitalist Development and Democracy*. Chicago: University of Chicago Press.

Rule, James B. 1997. *Theory and Progress in Social Science*. New York: Cambridge University Press.

Ruse, Michael. 1985. *Sociobiology: Sense or Nonsense?* 2nd ed. Dordrecht, Netherlands: Reidel.

Russon, A.E., and B.E. Waite. 1991. "Patterns of dominance and imitation in an infant peer group." *Ethology and Sociobiology* 12:55–73.

Ryave, A. Lincoln, and James N. Schenkein. 1974. "Notes on the art of walking." In Roy Turner (ed.), *Ethnomethodology: Selected Readings*. Harmondsworth, UK: Penguin Books.

Sacks, Karen. 1975. "Engels revisited: Women, the organization of production, and private property." In Rayna R. Reiter (ed.), *Toward an Anthropology of Women*. New York: Monthly Review Press.

_____. 1979. *Sisters and Wives: The Past and Future of Sexual Equality*. Westport, CT: Greenwood Press.

Sahlins, Marshall D. 1958. *Social Stratification in Polynesia*. Seattle: University of Washington Press.

_____. 1963. "Poor man, rich man, big man, chief: Political types in Melanesia and Polynesia." *Comparative Studies in Society and History* 5:285–303.

_____. 1965. "On the sociology of primitive exchange." In Michael Banton (ed.), *The Relevance of Models for Social Anthropology*. London: Tavistock.

_____. 1972. *Stone Age Economics*. Chicago: Aldine.

_____. 1976a. *The Use and Abuse of Biology: An Anthropological Critique of Sociobiology*. Ann Arbor: University of Michigan Press.

_____. 1976b. *Culture and Practical Reason*. Chicago: University of Chicago Press.

Salomon, Albert. 1920. "Max Weber." *Die Gesellschaft* 3:131–53.

Salter, Frank Kemp. 1995. *Emotions in Command: A Naturalistic Study of Institutional Dominance*. Oxford: Oxford University Press.

Sanders, William T., and David Webster. 1978. "Unilinealism, multilinealism, and the evolution of complex societies." In Charles L. Redman et al. (eds.), *Social Archeology: Beyond Subsistence and Dating*. New York: Academic Press.

Sanderson, Stephen K. 1987. "Eclecticism and its alternatives." In John Wilson (ed.), *Current Perspectives in Social Theory*. Vol. 8. Greenwich, CT: JAI Press.

_____. 1988. "The neo-Weberian revolution: A theoretical balance sheet." *Sociological Forum* 3:307–14.

_____. 1990. *Social Evolutionism: A Critical History*. Oxford: Blackwell.

_____. 1994. "The transition from feudalism to capitalism: The theoretical significance of the Japanese case." *Review* 17:15–55.

_____. 1995a. *Macrosociology: An Introduction to Human Societies*. 3rd ed. New York: Harper-Collins.

_____. 1995b. *Social Transformations: A General Theory of Historical Development*. Oxford: Blackwell.

_____. 1998a. "Extending sociobiology's explanatory power: Synthetic materialism—an integrated theory of human society." Paper presented at the annual meetings of the European Sociobiological Society, Russian State University of the Humanities, Moscow, May 31–June 4, and at the annual meetings of the Human Behavior and Evolution Society, University of California-Davis, July 8–12.

_____. 1998b. "Synthetic materialism: An integrated theory of human society." Paper presented at the annual meetings of the American Sociological Association, San Francisco, August 21–25.

_____. 1999. *Social Transformations: A General Theory of Historical Development*. Expan. ed. Lanham, MD: Rowman & Littlefield.

_____. 2001. "An evolutionary interpretation of fertility decline: New evidence." *Population and Environment*, forthcoming.

Sanderson, Stephen K., and Joshua Dubrow. 2000. "Fertility decline in the modern world and in the original demographic transition: Testing three theories with cross-national data." *Population and Environment* 21:511–37.

Sanderson, Stephen K., and Lee Ellis. 1992. "Theoretical and political perspectives of American sociologists in the 1990s." *American Sociologist* 23:26–42.

Schacht, Robert M. 1988. "Circumscription theory: A critical review." *American Behavioral Scientist* 31:438–48.

Scheff, Thomas J. 1992. "Rationality and emotion: Homage to Norbert Elias." In James S. Coleman and Thomas J. Fararo (eds.), *Rational Choice Theory: Advocacy and Critique*. Newbury Park, CA: Sage.

Schegloff, Emanuel A. 1979. "Identification and recognition in telephone conversation openings." In George Psathas (ed.), *Everyday Language: Studies in Ethnomethodology*. New York: Irvington.

Scheidel, Walter. 1996. "Brother-sister and parent-child marriage outside royal families in Ancient Egypt and Iran: A challenge to the sociobiological view of incest avoidance." *Ethology and Sociobiology* 17:319–40.

Schlegel, Alice, and Rohn Eloul. 1988. "Marriage transactions: Labor, property, and status." *American Anthropologist* 90:291–309.

Schluchter, Wolfgang. 1981. *The Rise of Western Rationalism: Max Weber's Developmental History*. Berkeley: University of California Press.

Schneider, Mark A., and Lewellyn Hendrix. 2000. "Olfactory sexual inhibition and the Westermarck effect." *Human Nature* 11:65–91.

Schroeter, Gerd. 1985. "Dialogue, debate, or dissent? The difficulties of assessing Max Weber's relation to Marx." In Robert J. Antonio and Ronald M. Glassman (eds.), *A Weber-Marx Dialogue*. Lawrence: University Press of Kansas.

Schumpeter, Joseph A. 1947. *Capitalism, Socialism, and Democracy.* 2nd ed. New York: Harper & Brothers.

Sciulli, David, and Dean Gerstein. 1985. "Social theory and Talcott Parsons in the 1980s." *Annual Review of Sociology* 11:369–87.

Scott, James C. 1990. *Domination and the Arts of Resistance.* New Haven, CT: Yale University Press.

Seemanova, Eva. 1971. "A study of children of incestuous matings." *Human Heredity* 21:108–28.

Segerstråle, Ullica. 1992. "Reductionism, 'bad science,' and politics: A critique of anti-reductionist reasoning." *Politics and the Life Sciences* 11:199–214.

_____. 2000. *Defenders of the Truth: The Battle for Science in the Sociobiology Debate and Beyond.* Oxford: Oxford University Press.

Seidman, Steven. 1991. "The end of sociological theory: The postmodern hope." *Sociological Theory* 9:131–46.

_____. 1992. "Postmodern social theory as narrative with a moral intent." In Steven Seidman and David G. Wagner (eds.), *Postmodernism and Social Theory.* Oxford: Blackwell.

_____. 1996. *Queer Theory/Sociology.* Oxford: Blackwell.

Seidman, Steven, and David G. Wagner (eds.). 1992. *Postmodernism and Social Theory.* Oxford: Blackwell.

Service, Elman R. 1962. *Primitive Social Organization: An Evolutionary Perspective.* New York: Random House.

_____. 1971. *Primitive Social Organization: An Evolutionary Perspective.* 2nd ed. New York: Random House.

Shankman, Paul. 1969. "Le roti et le bouilli: Lévi-Strauss' theory of cannibalism." *American Anthropologist* 71:54–69.

Shanks, Michael, and Christopher Tilley. 1987a. *Re-Constructing Archaeology.* Cambridge, UK: Cambridge University Press.

_____. 1987b. *Social Theory and Archaeology.* Albuquerque: University of New Mexico Press.

Shannon, Thomas Richard. 1996. *An Introduction to the World-System Perspective.* 2nd ed. Boulder, CO: Westview Press.

Sharrock, Wes, and Bob Anderson. 1986. *The Ethnomethodologists.* Chichester, UK: Ellis Horwood.

Shaw, Brent D. 1992. "Explaining incest: Brother-sister marriage in Graeco-Roman Egypt." *Man* 27:267–99.

Shaw, R. Paul, and Yuwa Wong. 1989. *Genetic Seeds of Warfare: Evolution, Nationalism, and Patriotism.* Boston: Unwin Hyman.

Sheldon, Charles David. 1958. *The Rise of the Merchant Class in Tokugawa Japan, 1600–1868.* (Monographs of the Association for Asian Studies, V.) Locust Valley, NY: J.J. Augustin.

Shepher, Joseph. 1971. *Self-Imposed Incest Avoidance and Exogamy in Second-Generation Kibbutz Adults.* Ann Arbor, MI: Xerox Monograph Series no. 72–871.

_____. 1983. *Incest: A Biosocial View.* New York: Academic Press.

Sherry, David F., Lucia F. Jacobs, and Steven J.C. Gaulin. 1992. "Spatial memory and adaptive specialization of the hippocampus." *Trends in Neuroscience* 15:298–303.

Shields, William M., and Lea M. Shields. 1983. "Forcible rape: An evolutionary perspective." *Ethology and Sociobiology* 4:115–36.

Shorter, Edward. 1975. *The Making of the Modern Family.* New York: Basic Books.

_____. 1976. "Women's work: What difference did capitalism make?" *Theory and Society* 3:513–27.

Sica, Alan. 1983. "Parsons, Jr." *American Journal of Sociology* 89:200–19.

Sieff, Daniela F. 1990. "Explaining biased sex ratios in human populations: A critique of recent studies." *Current Anthropology* 31:25–48.

Silver, Morris. 1995. *Economic Structures of Antiquity.* Westport, CT: Greenwood Press.

Silverman, Irwin, and Marion Eals. 1992. "Sex differences in spatial abilities: Evolutionary theory and data." In Jerome H. Barkow, Leda Cosmides, and John Tooby (eds.), *The Adapted Mind: Evolutionary Psychology and the Generation of Culture.* New York: Oxford University Press.

Simon, Herbert A. 1976. *Administrative Behavior.* 3rd ed. New York: Free Press.

Simon, Julian L. 1974. *The Effects of Income on Fertility.* Chapel Hill: University of North Carolina Press.

Singer, Peter. 1999. *A Darwinian Left: Politics, Evolution, and Cooperation.* New Haven, CT: Yale University Press.

Singh, Devendra. 1993a. "Adaptive significance of female physical attractiveness: Role of waist-to-hip ratio." *Journal of Personality and Social Psychology* 65:293–307.

——. 1993b. "Body shape and women's sexual attractiveness." *Human Nature* 4:297–321.

——. 1994. "Body fat distribution and perception of desirable female body shape by young black men and women." *International Journal of Eating Disorders* 16:289–94.

——. 1995. "Female judgment of male attractiveness and desirability for relationships: Role of waist-to-hip ratio and financial success." *Journal of Personality and Social Psychology* 69:1089–1101.

Singh, Devendra, C. Frohlich, and M. Haywood. 1999. "Waist-to-hip ratio representation in ancient sculptures from four cultures." Paper presented at the annual meetings of the Human Behavior and Evolution Society, University of Utah, Salt Lake City, June 2–6.

Singh, Devendra, and Suwardi Luis. 1995. "Ethnic and gender consensus for the effect of waist-to-hip ratio on judgment of women's attractiveness." *Human Nature* 6:51–65.

Singh, Devendra, and Robert K. Young. 1995. "Body weight, waist-to-hip ratio, breasts, and hips: Role in judgments of female attractiveness and desirability for relationships." *Ethology and Sociobiology* 16:483–507.

Skocpol, Theda. 1979. *States and Social Revolutions.* New York: Cambridge University Press.

——. 1992. *Protecting Soldiers and Mothers: The Political Origins of Social Policy in the United States.* Cambridge, MA: Harvard University Press (Belknap Press).

——. 1994. *Social Revolutions in the Modern World.* New York: Cambridge University Press.

Slama, Jiri. 1978. "A cross-country regression model of social inequality." In Zvi Griliches et al. (eds.), *Income Distribution and Economic Inequality.* Frankfurt am Main: Campus Verlag, Halsted and Eiley.

Smelser, Neil J. 1992. "The rational choice perspective: A theoretical assessment." *Rationality and Society* 4:381–410.

Smith, Anthony D. 1973. *The Concept of Social Change: A Critique of the Functionalist Theory of Social Change.* London: Routledge & Kegan Paul.

Smith, C. 1978. "Tubatulabal." In Robert F. Heizer (ed.), *Handbook of North American Indians. Vol. 11: California.* Washington, DC: Smithsonian Institution Press.

Smith, Eric Alden. 1980. "Evolutionary ecology and the analysis of human foraging behavior: An Inuit example from the east coast of Hudson Bay." Ph.D. dissertation, Cornell University.

——. 1983. "Anthropological applications of optimal foraging theory: A critical review." *Current Anthropology* 24:625–51.

——. 1991. *Inujjuamiut Foraging Strategies: Evolutionary Ecology of an Arctic Hunting Economy.* New York: Aldine de Gruyter.

_____. 1998. "Is Tibetan polyandry adaptive? Methodological and metatheoretical analyses." *Human Nature* 9:225–61.

_____. 1999. "Costly signaling and evolutionary solutions to collective action problems." Paper presented at the annual meetings of the Human Behavior and Evolution Society, University of Utah, Salt Lake City, June 2–6.

Smith, Eric Alden, and Rebecca L. Bliege Bird. 2000. "Turtle hunting and tombstone opening: Public generosity as costly signaling." *Evolution and Human Behavior* 21:245–61.

Smith, Eric Alden, and Bruce Winterhalder. 1992a. "Natural selection and decision making: Some fundamental principles." In Eric Alden Smith and Bruce Winterhalder (eds.), *Evolutionary Ecology and Human Behavior*. New York: Aldine de Gruyter.

Smith, Eric Alden, and Bruce Winterhalder (eds.). 1992b. *Evolutionary Ecology and Human Behavior*. New York: Aldine de Gruyter.

Smith, Thomas C. 1959. *The Agrarian Origins of Modern Japan*. Palo Alto, CA: Stanford University Press.

Smuts, Barbara. 1992. "Male aggression against women." *Human Nature* 3:1–44.

_____. 1995. "The evolutionary origins of patriarchy." *Human Nature* 6:1–32.

Snooks, Graeme Donald. 1996. *The Dynamic Society: Exploring the Sources of Global Change*. London: Routledge.

_____. 1997. *The Ephemeral Civilization: Exploding the Myth of Social Evolution*. London: Routledge.

Sober, Elliott, and David Sloan Wilson. 1998. *Unto Others: The Evolution and Psychology of Unselfish Behavior*. Cambridge, MA: Harvard University Press.

Sociobiology Study Group of Science for the People. 1976. "Sociobiology: Another biological determinism." *BioScience* 26:182–86.

Sokal, Alan, and Jean Bricmont. 1998. *Fashionable Nonsense: Postmodern Intellectuals' Abuse of Science*. New York: Picador.

Somit, Albert, and Steven A. Peterson. 1997. *Darwinism, Dominance, and Democracy: The Biological Bases of Authoritarianism*. Westport, CT: Praeger.

Sorokin, Pitirim. 1937. *Social and Cultural Dynamics*. 4 vols. New York: Bedminster Press.

South, Scott J., and Kim M. Lloyd. 1995. "Spousal alternatives and marital dissolution." *American Sociological Review* 60:21–35.

Spencer, Daniel Lloyd. 1958. "Japan's pre-Perry preparation for economic growth." *American Journal of Economics and Sociology* 17:195–216.

Spiro, Melford. 1979. *Gender and Culture: Kibbutz Women Revisited*. Durham, NC: Duke University Press.

Spuhler, J.N. (ed.). 1959. *The Evolution of Man's Capacity for Culture*. Detroit: Wayne State University Press.

Stark, Rodney. 1994. "Rational choice theories of religion." *The Agora* 2(1):1–5.

_____. 1996. *The Rise of Christianity*. Princeton, NJ: Princeton University Press.

Stark, Rodney, and William Sims Bainbridge. 1987. *A Theory of Religion*. New Brunswick, NJ: Rutgers University Press.

Stein, Arlene, and Ken Plummer. 1994. "'I can't even think straight': 'Queer' theory and the missing sexual revolution in sociology." *Sociological Theory* 12:178–87.

Stein, Edward. 1992. "Conclusion: The essentials of constructionism and the construction of essentialism." In Edward Stein (ed.), *Forms of Desire: Sexual Orientation and the Social Constructionist Controversy*. New York: Routledge.

Steklis, Horst D., and Alex Walter. 1991. "Culture, biology, and human behavior." *Human Nature* 2:137–69.

Stephens, William N. 1963. *The Family in Cross-Cultural Perspective.* New York: Holt, Rinehart, and Winston.

Stone, Lawrence. 1979. *The Family, Sex and Marriage in England, 1500–1800.* Abr. ed. New York: Harper & Row.

Strauss, Anselm L. 1959. *Mirrors and Masks.* Glencoe, IL: Free Press.

———. 1975. *Professions, Work, and Careers.* New Brunswick, NJ: Transaction.

Strayer, F.F., and M. Trudel. 1984. "Developmental changes in the nature and function of social dominance among young children." *Ethology and Sociobiology* 5:279–95.

Streeter, S.A., and Donald H. McBurney. 1999. "Waist-hip ratio and attractiveness: New evidence and a critique of 'a critical test.'" Paper presented at the annual meetings of the Human Behavior and Evolution Society, University of Utah, Salt Lake City, June 2–6.

Stryker, Sheldon. 1980. *Symbolic Interactionism.* Menlo Park, CA: Benjamin/Cummings.

Sussman, Marvin B., and Lee Burchinal. 1962. "Kin family network: Unheralded structure in current conceptualizations of family functioning." *Marriage and Family Living* 24:231–40.

Symons, Donald. 1979. *The Evolution of Human Sexuality.* New York: Oxford University Press.

———. 1987. "If we're all Darwinians, what's the fuss about?" In Charles Crawford et al. (eds.), *Sociobiology and Psychology.* Mahwah, NJ: Lawrence Erlbaum.

———. 1989. "A critique of Darwinian anthropology." *Ethology and Sociobiology* 10:131–44.

———. 1990. "Adaptiveness and adaptation." *Ethology and Sociobiology* 11:427–44.

———. 1992. "On the use and misuse of Darwinism in the study of human behavior." In Jerome H. Barkow, Leda Cosmides, and John Tooby (eds.), *The Adapted Mind: Evolutionary Psychology and the Generation of Culture.* New York: Oxford University Press.

———. 1995. "Beauty is in the adaptations of the beholder: The evolutionary psychology of human female sexual attractiveness." In Paul R. Abramson and Steven D. Pinkerton (eds.), *Sexual Nature, Sexual Culture.* Chicago: University of Chicago Press.

Szymanski, Albert. 1971. "Malinowski, Marx, and functionalism." *Insurgent Sociologist* 1:35–43.

———. 1976. "Racial discrimination and white gain." *American Sociological Review* 41:403–13.

———. 1978. *The Capitalist State and the Politics of Class.* Cambridge, MA: Winthrop.

Tainter, Joseph A. 1988. *The Collapse of Complex Societies.* New York: Cambridge University Press.

Tang-Martinez, Zuleyma. 1997. "The curious courtship of sociobiology and feminism: A case of irreconcilable differences." In Patricia Adair Gowaty (ed.), *Feminism and Evolutionary Biology.* New York: Chapman and Hall.

Tassinary, Louis G., and Kristi A. Hansen. 1998. "A critical test of the waist-to-hip ratio hypothesis of female physical attractiveness." *Psychological Science* 9:150–55.

Taylor, Angus. 1989. "The significance of Darwinian theory for Marx and Engels." *Philosophy of the Social Sciences* 19:409–23.

Terborgh, John W. 1983. *Five New World Primates: A Study in Comparative Ecology.* Princeton, NJ: Princeton University Press.

Testart, Alain. 1982. "The significance of food storage among hunter-gatherers: Residence patterns, population densities, and social inequalities." *Current Anthropology* 23:523–37.

Thibaut, John W., and Harold H. Kelley. 1959. *The Social Psychology of Groups.* New York: Wiley.

Thiessen, Del. 1998. *A Sociobiology Compendium: Aphorisms, Sayings, Asides.* New Brunswick, NJ: Transaction.

Thomas, Janet. 1988. "Women and capitalism: Oppression or emancipation?" *Comparative Studies in Society and History* 30:534–49.

Thomas, L.L., J.Z. Kronenfeld, and D.B. Kronenfeld. 1976. "Asdiwal crumbles: A critique of Lévi-Straussian myth analysis." *American Ethnologist* 3:147–73.

Thompson, E.P. 1963. *The Making of the English Working Class.* New York: Random House (Vintage).

_____. 1978. *The Poverty of Theory and Other Essays.* New York: Monthly Review Press.

Thornhill, Randy, and Craig T. Palmer. 2000. *A Natural History of Rape: Biological Bases of Sexual Coercion.* Cambridge, MA: MIT Press.

Thornhill, Randy, and Nancy Wilmsen Thornhill. 1983. "Human rape: An evolutionary analysis." *Ethology and Sociobiology* 4:137–73.

_____. 1992. "The evolutionary psychology of men's coercive sexuality." *Behavioral and Brain Sciences* 15:363–421.

Tiger, Lionel, and Robin Fox. 1971. *The Imperial Animal.* New York: Holt, Rinehart and Winston.

Tiger, Lionel, and Joseph Shepher. 1975. *Women in the Kibbutz.* New York: Harcourt Brace Jovanovich.

Tilly, Charles. 1978. *From Mobilization to Revolution.* New York: McGraw-Hill.

_____. 1984. *Big Structures, Large Processes, Huge Comparisons.* New York: Russell Sage Foundation.

Tilly, Louise A., and Joan W. Scott. 1978. *Women, Work, and Family.* New York: Holt, Rinehart and Winston.

Timpanaro, Sebastiano. 1975. *On Materialism.* London: New Left Books.

Tomich, Dale W. 1990. *Slavery in the Circuit of Sugar: Martinique and the World Economy, 1830–1848.* Baltimore: Johns Hopkins University Press.

_____. 1991. "World slavery and Caribbean capitalism: The Cuban sugar industry, 1760–1868." *Theory and Society* 20:297–319.

Tooby, John, and Leda Cosmides. 1988. "The evolution of war and its cognitive foundations." Institute for Evolutionary Studies, Technical Report No. 88–1.

_____. 1989a. "Evolutionary psychology and the generation of culture, part I. Theoretical considerations." *Ethology and Sociobiology* 10:29–49.

_____. 1989b. "The innate versus the manifest: How universal does universal have to be?" *Behavioral and Brain Sciences* 12:36–37.

_____. 1990. "The past explains the present: Emotional adaptations and the structure of ancestral environments." *Ethology and Sociobiology* 11:375–424.

_____. 1992. "The psychological foundations of culture." In Jerome H. Barkow, Leda Cosmides, and John Tooby (eds.), *The Adapted Mind: Evolutionary Psychology and the Generation of Culture.* New York: Oxford University Press.

Trivers, Robert L. 1971. "The evolution of reciprocal altruism." *Quarterly Review of Biology* 46:35–57.

_____. 1972. "Parental investment and sexual selection." In Bernard Campbell (ed.), *Sexual Selection and the Descent of Man, 1871–1971.* Chicago: Aldine.

_____. 1985. *Social Evolution.* Menlo Park, CA: Benjamin/Cummings.

Trivers, Robert L., and Dan Willard. 1973. "Natural selection of parental ability to vary the sex ratio of offspring." *Science* 179:90–92.

Trow, Martin. 1966. "The second transformation of American secondary education." In Reinhard Bendix and Seymour Martin Lipset (eds.), *Class, Status, and Power.* 2nd ed. New York: Free Press.

Tumin, Melvin M. 1953. "Some principles of stratification: A critical analysis." *American Sociological Review* 18:387–93.

Turke, Paul W. 1989. "Evolution and the demand for children." *Population and Development Review* 15:61–90.

_____. 1990a. "Which humans behave adaptively, and why does it matter?" *Ethology and Sociobiology* 11:305–39.

_____. 1990b. "Just do it." *Ethology and Sociobiology* 11:445–63.

Turner, Bryan S. 1981. *For Weber: Essays on the Sociology of Fate*. London: Routledge & Kegan Paul.

Turner, Jonathan H. 1996. "American sociology: Can what was never coherently composed be decomposed?" *Sociological Imagination* 33:191–201.

Turner, Jonathan H., and Alexandra Maryanski. 1979. *Functionalism*. Menlo Park, CA: Benjamin/Cummings.

Udry, J. Richard. 1995. "Sociology and biology: What biology do sociologists need to know?" *Social Forces* 73:1267–78.

_____. 2000. "Biological limits of gender construction." *American Sociological Review* 65:443–57.

U.S. Bureau of the Census. 1996. *Statistical Abstract of the United States*. Washington, DC: U.S. Government Printing Office.

U.S. Department of Commerce. 1975. *Historical Statistics of the United States*. Washington, DC: U.S. Government Printing Office.

Useem, Michael. 1984. *The Inner Circle: Large Corporations and the Rise of Business Political Activity in the U.S. and the U.K.* New York: Oxford University Press.

van den Berghe, Pierre L. 1973. *Age and Sex in Human Societies: A Biosocial Perspective*. Belmont, CA: Wadsworth.

_____. 1974. "Bringing beasts back in: Toward a biosocial theory of aggression." *American Sociological Review* 39:777–88.

_____. 1975. *Man in Society: A Biosocial View*. New York: Elsevier.

_____. 1978. *Man in Society: A Biosocial View*. 2nd ed. New York: Elsevier.

_____. 1979. *Human Family Systems: An Evolutionary View*. New York: Elsevier.

_____. 1980. "Incest and exogamy: A sociobiological reconsideration." *Ethology and Sociobiology* 1:151–62.

_____. 1981a. *The Ethnic Phenomenon*. New York: Elsevier.

_____. 1981b. "Sociobiology: Several views." *BioScience* 31:406.

_____. 1983. "Human inbreeding avoidance: Culture in nature." *Behavioral and Brain Sciences* 6:91–123.

_____. 1990. "Why most sociologists don't (and won't) think evolutionarily." *Sociological Forum* 5:173–83.

_____. 1991. "Sociology." In Mary Maxwell (ed.), *The Sociobiological Imagination*. Albany: State University of New York Press.

_____. 1997. "Review of Steven Goldberg, *Why Men Rule: A Theory of Male Dominance* (Chicago: Open Court, 1993)." *European Sociobiological Society Newsletter*, no. 44:2–3.

van den Berghe, Pierre L., and David P. Barash. 1977. "Inclusive fitness and human family structure." *American Anthropologist* 79:809–23.

van den Berghe, Pierre L., and Gene M. Mesher. 1980. "Royal incest and inclusive fitness." *American Ethnologist* 7:300–17.

van den Berghe, Pierre L., and Joseph Whitmeyer. 1990. "Social class and reproductive success." *International Journal of Contemporary Sociology* 27:29–48.

van der Dennen, Johan M.G. 1995. *The Origin of War: The Evolution of a Male-Coalitional Reproductive Strategy*. Groningen, Netherlands: Origin Press.

van de Walle, Francine. 1986. "Infant mortality and the European demographic transition." In Ansley J. Coale and Susan Cotts Watkins (eds.), *The Decline of Fertility in Europe*. Princeton, NJ: Princeton University Press.

Vanhanen, Tatu. 1992. *On the Evolutionary Roots of Politics*. New Delhi, India: Sterling.

_____. 1997. *Prospects of Democracy: A Study of 172 Countries*. London: Routledge.

van Parijs, Phillipe. 1993. *Marxism Recycled*. Cambridge, UK: Cambridge University Press.

Veblen, Thorstein. 1934. *The Theory of the Leisure Class*. New York: The Modern Library (Originally published 1912).

Vining, Daniel. 1986. "Social versus reproductive success: The central theoretical problem of human sociobiology." *Behavioral and Brain Sciences* 9:167–216.

Vogel, Lise. 1983. *Marxism and the Oppression of Women*. New Brunswick, NJ: Rutgers University Press.

Wallace, Walter L. 1990. "Rationality, human nature, and society in Weber's theory." *Theory and Society* 19:199–223.

Wallerstein, Immanuel. 1974a. *The Modern World-System: Capitalist Agriculture and the Origins of the European World-Economy in the Sixteenth Century*. New York: Academic Press.

_____. 1974b. "The rise and future demise of the world capitalist system: Concepts for comparative analysis." *Comparative Studies in Society and History* 16:387–415.

_____. 1979. *The Capitalist World-Economy*. New York: Cambridge University Press.

_____. 1980. *The Modern World-System II: Mercantilism and the Consolidation of the European World-Economy, 1600–1750*. New York: Academic Press.

_____. 1989. *The Modern World-System III: The Second Era of Great Expansion of the Capitalist World-Economy, 1730–1840s*. San Diego: Academic Press.

Ware, Helen. 1979. "Polygyny: Women's views in a transitional society, Nigeria 1975." *Journal of Marriage and the Family* 41:185–95.

Warner, Michael. 1991. "Fear of a queer planet." *Social Text* 9(14):3–18.

Watson, Richard A. 1990. "Ozymandias, king of kings: Postprocessual radical archaeology as critique." *American Antiquity* 55:673–89.

Webb, Malcom C. 1973. "The Petén Maya decline viewed in the perspective of state formation." In T. Patrick Culbert (ed.), *The Classic Maya Collapse*. Albuquerque: University of New Mexico Press.

_____. 1975. "The flag follows trade: An essay on the necessary interaction of military and commercial factors in state formation." In C.C. Lamberg-Karlovsky and Jeremy A. Sabloff (eds.), *Ancient Civilization and Trade*. Albuquerque: University of New Mexico Press.

Weber, Max. 1978. *Economy and Society*. 2 vols. Ed. Guenther Roth and Claus Wittich. Berkeley: University of California Press (Originally published 1923).

_____. 1981. *General Economic History*. Trans. Frank H. Knight, intro. Ira J. Cohen. New Brunswick, NJ: Transaction (Originally published 1927).

Weeks, Jeffrey. 1986. *Sexuality*. London: Routledge.

Weinberg, S. Kirson. 1955. *Incest Behavior*. New York: Citadel.

Weinberg, Steven. 1993. *Dreams of a Final Theory: The Scientist's Search for the Ultimate Laws of Nature*. New York: Random House.

Weinrich, James. 1992. "Reality or social construction?" In Edward Stein (ed.), *Forms of Desire: Sexual Orientation and the Social Constructionist Controversy*. New York: Routledge.

Weisfeld, Glenn E., Donald R. Omark, and Carol L. Cronin. 1980. "A longitudinal and cross-sectional study of dominance in boys." In Donald R. Omark, Fred F. Strayer, and Daniel G. Freedman (eds.), *Dominance Relations: An Ethological View of Human Conflict and Social Interaction*. New York: Garland.

Welch, Charles E., III, and Paul C. Glick. 1981. "The incidence of polygamy in contemporary Africa: A research note." *Journal of Marriage and the Family* 43:191–93.

Weldes, Jutta. 1989. "Marxism and methodological individualism: A critique." *Theory and Society* 18:353–86.

Wemple, Suzanne Fonay. 1981. *Women in Frankish Society: Marriage and the Cloister, 500 to 900*. Philadelphia: University of Pennsylvania Press.

Wenger, Morton G. 1987. "Class closure and the historical/structural limits of the Marx-Weber convergence." In Norbert Wiley (ed.), *The Marx-Weber Debate*. Beverly Hills, CA: Sage.

Westermarck, Edward. 1891. *The History of Human Marriage*. London: Macmillan Press.

Wetsman, Adam, and Frank Marlowe. 1999. "How universal are preferences for female waist-to-hip ratios? Evidence from the Hadza of Tanzania." *Evolution and Human Behavior* 20:219–28.

Whitam, Frederick L. 1983. "Culturally invariable properties of male homosexuality: Tentative conclusions from cross-cultural research." *Archives of Sexual Behavior* 12:207–26.

Whitam, Frederick L., and Robin M. Mathy. 1986. *Male Homosexuality in Four Societies: Brazil, Guatemala, the Philippines, and the United States*. Westport, CT: Praeger.

White, Benjamin. 1973. "Demand for labor and population growth in colonial Java." *Human Ecology* 2:217–36.

———. 1982. "Child labor and population growth in rural Asia." *Development and Change* 13:587–610.

White, Douglas R. 1988. "Rethinking polygyny: Co-wives, codes, and cultural systems." *Current Anthropology* 29:529–72.

White, Douglas R., Michael L. Burton, and M.M. Dow. 1981. "Sexual division of labor in African agriculture: A network autocorrelation analysis." *American Anthropologist* 83:824–49.

White, Douglas R., and Michael L. Burton. 1988. "Causes of polygyny: Ecology, economy, kinship, and warfare." *American Anthropologist* 90:871–87.

Whiting, Beatrice B., and C.P. Edwards. 1988. *Children of Different Worlds: The Formation of Social Behavior*. Cambridge, MA: Harvard University Press.

Whiting, Beatrice B., and John W. M. Whiting. 1975. *Children of Six Cultures: A Psycho-Cultural Analysis*. Cambridge, MA: Harvard University Press.

Whyte, Martin King. 1978. *The Status of Women in Preindustrial Societies*. Princeton, NJ: Princeton University Press.

Wickham-Crowley, Timothy P. 1992. *Guerrillas and Revolution in Latin America*. Princeton, NJ: Princeton University Press.

Wiener, Jonathan M. 1982. "Max Weber's Marxism." *Theory and Society* 11:389–401.

Wiessner, Polly. 1982. "Risk, reciprocity, and social influence on !Kung San economies." In Eleanor Burke Leacock and Richard B. Lee (eds.), *Politics and History in Band Societies*. New York: Cambridge University Press.

Wiley, Andrea S., and Leslie C. Carlin. 1999. "Demographic contexts and the adaptive role of mother-infant attachment." *Human Nature* 10:135–61.

Wiley, Norbert (ed.). 1987. *The Marx-Weber Debate*. Beverly Hills, CA: Sage.

Wilk, Richard R. 1996. *Economies and Cultures: Foundations of Economic Anthropology*. Boulder, CO: Westview Press.

Wilkinson, David. 1992. "Cities, civilizations, and oikumenes: I." *Comparative Civilizations Review* 27:51–87.

Wilkinson, Richard G. 1973. *Poverty and Progress: An Ecological Perspective on Economic Development*. New York: Praeger.

Williams, George C. 1966. *Adaptation and Natural Selection: A Critique of Some Current Evolutionary Thought*. Princeton, NJ: Princeton University Press.

Williams, Terry. 1989. *The Cocaine Kids: The Inside Story of a Teenage Drug Ring*. Reading, MA: Addison-Wesley.

Wilson, David Sloan, and Elliott Sober. 1994. "Reintroducing group selection to the human behavioral sciences." *Behavioral and Brain Sciences* 17:585–654.

Wilson, Edward O. 1975. *Sociobiology: The New Synthesis*. Cambridge, MA: Harvard University Press.

_____. 1977. "Biology and the social sciences." *Daedalus* 106(4):127–40.

_____. 1978. *On Human Nature*. Cambridge, MA: Harvard University Press.

Winch, Robert F., and Gay C. Kitson. 1977. "Types of American families: An unsatisfactory classification." In Robert F. Winch, *Familial Organization*. New York: Free Press.

Winterhalder, Bruce. 1977. "Foraging strategies and adaptations of the Boreal Forest Cree: An evaluation of theory and models from evolutionary ecology." Ph.D. dissertation, Cornell University.

_____. 1981. "Foraging strategies in the boreal environment: An analysis of Cree hunting and gathering." In Bruce Winterhalder and Eric Alden Smith (eds.), *Hunter-Gatherer Foraging Strategies*. Chicago: University of Chicago Press.

_____. 1986a. "Diet choice, risk, and food sharing in a stochastic environment." *Journal of Anthropological Archaeology* 5:369–92.

_____. 1986b. "Optimal foraging: Simulation studies of diet choice in a stochastic environment." *Journal of Ethnobiology* 6:205–23.

_____. 1987. "The analysis of hunter-gatherer diets: Stalking an optimal foraging model." In Marvin Harris and Eric B. Ross (eds.), *Food and Evolution: Toward a Theory of Human Food Habits*. Philadelphia: Temple University Press.

_____. 1993. "Work, resources, and population in foraging societies." *Man* 28:321–40.

Winterhalder, Bruce, and Eric Alden Smith (eds.). 1981. *Hunter-Gatherer Foraging Strategies: Ethnographic and Archaeological Analyses*. Chicago: University of Chicago Press.

Wittfogel, Karl. 1957. *Oriental Despotism*. New Haven, CT: Yale University Press.

Wolf, Arthur P. 1970. "Childhood association and sexual attraction: A further test of the Westermarck hypothesis." *American Anthropologist* 72:503–15.

_____. 1995. *Sexual Attraction and Childhood Association: A Chinese Brief for Edward Westermarck*. Stanford, CA: Stanford University Press.

Woodburn, James. 1982. "Egalitarian societies." *Man* 27:431–51.

Woolgar, Steve. 1988. *Science: The Very Idea*. London: Tavistock.

Wrangham, Richard, and Dale Peterson. 1996. *Demonic Males: Apes and the Origins of Human Violence*. Boston: Houghton Mifflin.

Wright, Erik Olin. 1979. *Class Structure and Income Determination*. New York: Academic Press.

_____. 1985. *Classes*. London: Verso.

_____. 1997. *Class Counts: Comparative Studies in Class Analysis*. New York: Cambridge University Press.

Wright, Erik Olin, Andrew Levine, and Elliott Sober. 1992. *Reconstructing Marxism*. London: Verso.

Wright, Henry T., and Gregory A. Johnson. 1975. "Population, exchange, and early state formation in southwestern Iran." *American Anthropologist* 77:267–89.

Wright, Robert. 1994. *The Moral Animal: Evolutionary Psychology and Everyday Life*. New York: Random House (Vintage).

Wrong, Dennis H. 1959. "The functional theory of stratification: Some neglected considerations." *American Sociological Review* 24:772–82.

_____. 1976. *Skeptical Sociology*. New York: Columbia University Press.

_____. 1997. "Late, late thoughts on the debate over the Davis-Moore theory of inequality." Manuscript, Department of Sociology, New York University.

Wynne-Edwards, V.C. 1962. *Animal Dispersion in Relation to Social Behaviour*. Edinburgh, Scotland: Oliver & Boyd.

Yamamura, Kozo. 1980. "The agricultural and commercial revolution in Japan, 1550–1650." In Paul Uselding (ed.), *Research in Economic History*. Vol. 5. Greenwich, CT: JAI Press.

Yanowitch, Murray. 1977. *Social and Economic Inequality in the Soviet Union*. White Plains, NY: M.E. Sharpe.

Young, Lawrence A. (ed.). 1997. *Rational Choice Theory and Religion*. New York: Routledge.

Zahavi, Amotz. 1975. "Mate selection: A selection for a handicap." *Journal of Theoretical Biology* 53:205–14.

Zahavi, Amotz, and Avishag Zahavi. 1997. *The Handicap Principle: A Missing Piece of Darwin's Puzzle*. New York: Oxford University Press.

Zaslavsky, Victor. 1995. "From redistribution to marketization: Social and attitudinal change in post-Soviet Russia." In Gail W. Lapidus (ed.), *The New Russia: Troubled Transformation*. Boulder, CO: Westview Press.

Zeitlin, Irving. 1973. *Rethinking Sociology: A Critique of Contemporary Theory*. Englewood Cliffs, NJ: Prentice-Hall.

Zimmerman, Don H., and Lawrence Wieder. 1970. "Ethnomethodology and the problem of order: Comment on Denzin." In Jack Douglas (ed.), *Understanding Everyday Life*. Chicago: Aldine.

Zipf, George Kingsley. 1965. *Human Behavior and the Principle of Least Effort*. New York: Hafner.

Index

About the Author

Stephen K. Sanderson is professor and chair of sociology at Indiana University of Pennsylvania, where he specializes in sociological theory, comparative-historical sociology, and evolution and human behavior. He is the author of several dozen journal articles, book chapters, and five books including *Macrosociology: An Introduction to Human Societies* (4th ed., 1999), *Social Evolutionism: A Critical History* (1990), and *Social Transformations: A General Theory of Historical Development* (1995; expanded ed., 1999).